MW01000685

CCNA
Data Center
DCICN 200-150
Official Cert Guide

CHAD HINTZ, CCIE® No. 15729

CESAR OBEDIENTE, CCIE® No. 5620

OZDEN KARAKOK, CCIE® No. 6331

Cisco Press
800 East 96th Street
Indianapolis, IN 46240

CCNA Data Center DCICN 200-150 Official Cert Guide

Chad Hintz, Cesar Obediente, Ozden Karakok

Copyright© 2017 Pearson Education, Inc.

Published by:
Cisco Press
800 East 96th Street
Indianapolis, IN 46240 USA

Printed in the United States of America

Library of Congress Control Number: 2016950552

1   17

ISBN-13: 978-1-58720-596-5

ISBN-10: 1-58720-596-3

Warning and Disclaimer

This book is designed to provide information about the 200-150 DCICN exam for CCNA Data Center certification. Every effort has been made to make this book as complete and as accurate as possible, but no warranty or fitness is implied.

The information is provided on an "as is" basis. The authors, Cisco Press, and Cisco Systems, Inc., shall have neither liability nor responsibility to any person or entity with respect to any loss or damages arising from the information contained in this book or from the use of the discs or programs that may accompany it.

The opinions expressed in this book belong to the author and are not necessarily those of Cisco Systems, Inc.

Trademark Acknowledgments

All terms mentioned in this book that are known to be trademarks or service marks have been appropriately capitalized. Cisco Press or Cisco Systems, Inc., cannot attest to the accuracy of this information. Use of a term in this book should not be regarded as affecting the validity of any trademark or service mark.

Special Sales

For information about buying this title in bulk quantities, or for special sales opportunities (which may include electronic versions; custom cover designs; and content particular to your business, training goals, marketing focus, or branding interests), please contact our corporate sales department at corpsales@pearsoned.com or (800) 382-3419.

For government sales inquiries, please contact governmentsales@pearsoned.com.

For questions about sales outside the United States, please contact intlcs@pearson.com.

Feedback Information

At Cisco Press, our goal is to create in-depth technical books of the highest quality and value. Each book is crafted with care and precision, undergoing rigorous development that involves the unique expertise of members from the professional technical community.

Readers' feedback is a natural continuation of this process. If you have any comments regarding how we could improve the quality of this book, or otherwise alter it to better suit your needs, you can contact us through email at feedback@ciscopress.com. Please make sure to include the book title and ISBN in your message.

We greatly appreciate your assistance.

Editor-in-Chief: Mark Taub

Business Operation Manager, Cisco Press: Ronald Fligge

Managing Editor: Sandra Schroeder

Project Editor: Mandie Frank

Technical Editor: Jason Viera

Designer: Chuti Prasertsith

Indexer: Ken Johnson

Product Line Manager: Brett Bartow

Executive Editor: Mary Beth Ray

Development Editor: Ellie Bru

Copy Editor: Bart Reed

Editorial Assistant: Vanessa Evans

Composition: TnT Design, Inc.

Proofreader: The Wordsmithery LLC

ı|ı.ı|ı.
CISCO

Americas Headquarters
Cisco Systems, Inc.
San Jose, CA

Asia Pacific Headquarters
Cisco Systems (USA) Pte. Ltd.
Singapore

Europe Headquarters
Cisco Systems International BV
Amsterdam, The Netherlands

Cisco has more than 200 offices worldwide. Addresses, phone numbers, and fax numbers are listed on the Cisco Website at www.cisco.com/go/offices.

CCDE, CCENT, Cisco Eos, Cisco HealthPresence, the Cisco logo, Cisco Lumin, Cisco Nexus, Cisco StadiumVision, Cisco TelePresence, Cisco WebEx, DCE, and Welcome to the Human Network are trademarks; Changing the Way We Work, Live, Play, and Learn and Cisco Store are service marks; and Access Registrar, Aironet, AsyncOS, Bringing the Meeting To You, Catalyst, CCDA, CCDP, CCIE, CCIP, CCNA, CCNP, CCSP, CCVP, Cisco, the Cisco Certified Internetwork Expert logo, Cisco IOS, Cisco Press, Cisco Systems, Cisco Systems Capital, the Cisco Systems logo, Cisco Unity, Collaboration Without Limitation, EtherFast, EtherSwitch, Event Center, Fast Step, Follow Me Browsing, FormShare, GigaDrive, HomeLink, Internet Quotient, IOS, iPhone, iQuick Study, IronPort, the IronPort logo, LightStream, Linksys, MediaTone, MeetingPlace, MeetingPlace Chime Sound, MGX, Networkers, Networking Academy, Network Registrar, PCNow, PIX, PowerPanels, ProConnect, ScriptShare, SenderBase, SMARTnet, Spectrum Expert, StackWise, The Fastest Way to Increase Your Internet Quotient, TransPath, WebEx, and the WebEx logo are registered trademarks of Cisco Systems, Inc. and/or its affiliates in the United States and certain other countries.

All other trademarks mentioned in this document or website are the property of their respective owners. The use of the word partner does not imply a partnership relationship between Cisco and any other company. (0812R)

About the Authors

Chad Hintz, CCIE No. 15729, is a Principal Systems Engineer for the Cisco Commercial East Area focusing on designing enterprise solutions for customers around the Cisco data center technologies. He also holds three CCIEs: Routing and Switching, Security, and Storage. He has more than 15+ years of experience in the industry and has held certifications from Novell, VMware, and Cisco. His focus is working with enterprise/commercial customers to address their challenges with comprehensive end-to-end data center architectures. Chad has been with Cisco for 11 years, and working as a solution architect has provided unique experiences in building these types of solutions. Chad is a regular speaker at Cisco Live and industry conferences on data center technologies. Chad lives near Buffalo, New York, with his wife and two wonderful children, and enjoys coaching youth sports in his spare time. You can reach Chad on Twitter: @chadh0517.

Cesar Obediente, CCIE No. 5620, is a Principal Systems Engineer for Cisco Global Enterprise Segment specializing in the Data Center area, where he helps customers design and build their next-generation data centers. He has been with Cisco Systems for over 17 years, where he began his career in the Technical Assistant Center (TAC) and then moved to the Catalyst 6500 Escalation Business Unit Team, supporting multicast in the Cat6K platform. Cesar is a frequent speaker at Cisco Live and Data Center events. He holds a CCIE in routing and switching and holds a degree in computer engineering from the University of South Florida. You can reach Cesar on Twitter: @cobedien.

Ozden Karakok, CCIE No. 6331, is a technical leader from the Data Center Products and Technologies team in the Technical Assistant Center (TAC). She has been with Cisco Systems for 17 years and specializes in storage area and data center networks. Prior to joining Cisco, Ozden spent five years working for a number of Cisco's large customers in various telecommunication roles. She is a Cisco Certified Internetwork Expert in routing and switching, SNA/IP, and storage. A frequent speaker at Cisco and data center events, she serves as a member of the patent committee at Cisco Services. Ozden holds a degree in computer engineering from Istanbul Bogazici University. Currently, she is focused on application centric infrastructure (ACI) and software-defined storage (SDS). You can reach Ozden on Twitter: @okarakok.

About the Technical Reviewers

Jason Viera, CCIE 12534 (DC & RS), is a Technical Director for Carousel Industries, a national technology solutions provider based out of New England. He's focused on core networking, public/private cloud, and "emerging" technologies (RFC 1925 #11). With nearly two decades of industry experience, Jason has held over 15 certifications from the likes of Cisco, Juniper, Microsoft, and VMware. He serves as a trusted advisor to customers across multiple verticals, with an emphasis on addressing their challenges by providing comprehensive end-to-end architectures that meet both their business and technical requirements. Before his tenure at Carousel Industries, Jason served as a Technical Solutions Architect for Cisco Systems and also spent a good amount of time as an Architect in the Fortune 500. When not helping customers or immersed in technology, Jason enjoys relaxing with his amazing wife and four exceptional children in the Ocean State.

Dedications

Chad Hintz: This booked is dedicated to my loving wife and my two children, Tyler and Evan. You are my inspiration, and without your love and support, I would have never been able to complete this project. This book is also dedicated to my late father, Edward Hintz: You inspire me every day to be a better husband, father, and friend. I miss you every day.

Cesar Obediente: I dedicate this book to my loving wife, Jackie, for the support and understanding she has given me throughout my career; to my two daughters, Yvette and Veronica, for the joy they bring to my life; and to my parents—especially my late mom—who taught me the value of life and family.

Ozden Karakok: To my loving husband, Tom, for his endless support, encouragement, and love. Merci beaucoup, Askim.

To Remi and Mira, for being the most incredible miracles of my life and being my number-one source of happiness.

To my wonderful parents, who supported me in every chapter of my life and are an inspiration for life.

To my awesome sisters, Gulden and Cigdem, for their unconditional support and loving me just the way I am.

Acknowledgments

It just so happens that Cisco begins its first Data Center certifications with CCNA Data Center. Cisco requires you to pass two exams to achieve CCNA Data Center certification, with this book discussing the first such exam—the Introducing Cisco Data Center Networking (DCICN) exam.

Eleanor Bru did a phenomenal job of keeping us authors on track for book features, style, and organization. Thank you, Ellie, for your support by being the editor of this book!

The technical editor for this book, Jason Viera, did an excellent job reviewing the manuscript. Jason's great understanding in data center helped us make sure that we covered what was needed and also focused on ease of understanding from a reader's perspective. It is always a pleasure working with you Jason; thank you for the great job!

Mary Beth Ray served as executive editor on the book. No matter the issue, Mary Beth was always there and ready to help figure out the right course of action. It is great to have her steady hand keeping us on track, from the original idea to publication and beyond. Thanks, Mary Beth.

A big thank you to the entire Cisco Press team for all their support in getting this book published.

To the extended teams at Cisco: Thank you for being patient while our minds were in the book. Thank you for believing in and supporting us on this journey. Thank you for the innovative organization and development team at Cisco.

To all extended family and friends: Thank you for your patience and endless support.

Contents at a Glance

Contents

Icons Used in This Book

Command Syntax Conventions

The conventions used to present command syntax in this book are the same conventions used in the IOS Command Reference. The Command Reference describes these conventions as follows:

- **Boldface** indicates commands and keywords that are entered literally as shown. In actual configuration examples and output (not general command syntax), boldface indicates commands that are manually input by the user (such as a **show** command).

- *Italic* indicates arguments for which you supply actual values.

- Vertical bars (|) separate alternative, mutually exclusive elements.

- Square brackets ([ ]) indicate an optional element.

- Braces ({ }) indicate a required choice.

- Braces within brackets ([{ }]) indicate a required choice within an optional element.

Introduction

About the Exam

Congratulations! If you are reading far enough to look at this book's Introduction, you've probably already decided to go for your Cisco CCNA Data Center certification, and that begins with the Introducing Cisco Data Center Networking (DCICN 200-150) exam. Cisco dominates the networking marketplace, and in a few short years after entering the data center server marketplace, they have achieved significant market share and become one of the primary vendors of data center server hardware as well. If you want to succeed as a technical person in the networking industry, and in data centers in particular, you need to know Cisco. Getting your CCNA Data Center certification is a great first step toward building your skills and becoming respected by others in the data center field.

CCNA Data Center and the Other CCNA Certifications

Cisco offers a wide variety of Cisco Certified Network Associate certifications. Cisco first offered CCNA back in 1998, using the name CCNA, with the certification focusing on routing and switching. Since that time, Cisco has added the CCNA certifications for various technology areas, as listed in Figure I-2. Cisco even renamed the original CCNA to CCNA Routing & Switching, so each and every CCNA certification's topic area is part of the name.

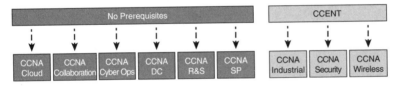

Figure I-2   *Cisco CCNA Certifications: CCENT Prerequisite or Not*

* The CCNA R&S has two different exam paths. One begins with CCENT, whereas the other allows you to get CCNA R&S certified using one exam: the CCNA 200-125 exam. With the single-exam path, CCENT is technically not a prerequisite; however, the single exam includes coverage of the topics in CCENT, so you still need to know CCENT content to achieve CCNA R&S.

Interestingly, Cisco uses the Cisco Certified Entry Networking Technician (CCENT) certification as the minimum prerequisite for some of the CCNA certifications, but not all. As you can see in Figure I-2, CCNA Data Center, and five others, do not require you to first achieve CCENT (or some other more advanced routing and switching certification). Why? All six of these CCNA certifications that have no prerequisites cover the required routing and switching topics within the certification already. For instance, almost all the concepts discussed in this book are included in the scope of the ICND1 100-101 exam.

NOTE   Always check www.cisco.com/go/certifications for current prerequisites. Cisco sometimes changes the prerequisites with the introduction of a new version of an exam or certification.

The Exams That Help You Achieve CCNA Data Center Certification

The Cisco CCNA Data Center certification is the most basic Cisco Data Center certification, and it acts as a prerequisite for the other Cisco Data Center certifications. CCNA Data Center itself has no other prerequisites. To achieve the CCNA Data Center cert, you simply have to pass two exams: Introducing Cisco Data Center Networking (DCICN) and Introducing Cisco Data Center Technologies (DCICT), as shown in Figure I-1.

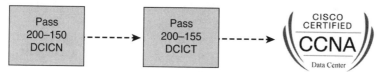

Figure I-1 *Path to Cisco CCNA Data Center Certification*

The DCICN and DCICT differ quite a bit in terms of the topics covered. DCICN focuses on networking technology. In fact, it overlaps quite a bit with the topics in the ICND1 100-101 exam, which leads to the Cisco Certified Entry Network Technician (CCENT) certification. DCICN explains the basics of networking, focusing on Ethernet switching and IP routing. The only data center focus in DCICN happens to be the fact that all the configuration and verification examples use Cisco Nexus switches, which Cisco builds specifically for use in the data center.

The DCICT exam instead focuses on technologies specific to the data center. These technologies include storage networking, Unified Computing (the term used by Cisco for its server products and services), and data networking features unique to the Nexus model series of switches.

Basically, DCICN touches on concepts that you might see in all parts of a corporate network (including the data center), and DCICT then hits the topics specific to data centers.

Types of Questions on the Exams

Cisco certification exams follow the same general format. At the testing center, you sit in a quiet room with a PC. Before the exam timer begins, you have a chance to do a few other tasks on the PC. For instance, you can take a sample quiz just to get accustomed to the PC and the testing engine. Anyone who has user-level skills in getting around a PC should have no problems with the testing environment.

Once the exam starts, the screen shows you question after question. The questions typically fall into one of the following categories:

- Multiple choice, single answer
- Multiple choice, multiple answer
- Testlet
- Drag and drop (DND)
- Simulated lab (sim)
- Simlet

The first three items in the list are all actually multiple-choice questions. The multiple-choice format simply requires that you point and click a circle beside the correct answer(s). Cisco traditionally tells you how many answers you need to choose, and the testing software prevents you from choosing too many answers. The testlet asks you several multiple-choice questions, all based on the same larger scenario.

DND questions require you to move some items around on the graphical user interface (GUI). You left-click and hold, move a button or icon to another area, and release the clicker to place the object somewhere else (usually into a list). Or, you might see a diagram, and you have to click and drag the icons in the figure to the correct place to answer a question. For some questions, to get the question correct, you might need to put a list of five things in the proper order.

The last two types, sim and simlet questions, both use a network simulator. Interestingly, the two types actually allow Cisco to assess two very different skills. First, sim questions generally describe a problem, and your task is to configure one or more routers and switches to fix the problem. The exam then grades the question based on the configuration you changed or added. Basically, these questions begin with a broken configuration, and you have to fix the configuration to answer the question.

Simlet questions also use a network simulator, but instead of you answering the question by changing the configuration, the simlet includes one or more multiple-choice questions that require you to use the simulator to examine the current behavior of a network and interpret the output of any **show** commands that you can remember to answer the question. Whereas sim questions require you to troubleshoot problems related to a configuration, simlets require you to analyze both working and broken networks as well as correlate **show** command output with your knowledge of networking theory and configuration commands.

You can watch and even experiment with these command types using the Cisco Certification Exam Tutorial. To find the Cisco Certification Exam Tutorial, go to www.cisco.com, and search for "exam tutorial."

What's on the DCICN Exam?

Everyone wants to know what is on the test, for any test, ever since the early days of school. Cisco tells the world the topics on each of its exams. For every Cisco certification exam, Cisco wants the public to know the variety of topics as well as to have an idea about the kinds of knowledge and skills required for each topic. To that end, Cisco publishes a set of exam topics for each exam.

While each exam topics lists the specific topics, such as IP addressing, OSPF, and VLANs, the verb in the exam topic is just as important. The verb tells us to what degree the topic must be understood and what skills are required. The topic also implies the kinds of skills required for that topic. For example, one topic might start with "Describe…," another with "Configure…," another with "Verify…," and another might begin with "Troubleshoot…." That last topic has the highest required skill level, because to troubleshoot, you must understand the topic, be able to configure it (to see what is wrong with the configuration), and verify it (to find the root cause of the problem). By listing the topics and skill levels, Cisco helps us all prepare for its exams.

Cisco's posted exam topics, however, are only guidelines. Cisco's disclaimer language mentions that fact. Cisco makes the effort to keep the exam questions within the confines of the stated exam topics, and I know from talking to those involved that every question is analyzed for whether it fits within the stated exam topics.

DCICN 200-150 Exam Topics

You can easily find exam topics for both the DCICN and DCICT exams with a simple search at Cisco.com. Alternatively, you can go to www.cisco.com/go/ccna, which gets you to the page for CCNA Routing and Switching, and then easily navigate to the nearby CCNA Data Center page.

Over time, Cisco has begun making two stylistic improvements to the posted exam topics. In the past, the topics were simply bulleted lists, with some indentation to imply subtopics under a major topic. More and more often today, including for the DCICN and DCICT exam topics, Cisco also numbers the exam topics, making it easier to refer to specific topics. In addition, Cisco lists the weighting for each of the major topic headings. The weighting tells you the percentage of points from your exam that should come from each major topic area. The DCICN contains five major headings, with the weightings shown in Table I-1.

Table I-1   Four Major Topic Areas in the DCICN 200-150 Exam

Number	Exam Topic	Weighting
1.0	Data Center Physical Infrastructure	15%
2.0	Basic Data Center Networking Concepts	23%
3.0	Advanced Data Center Networking Concepts	23%
4.0	Basic Data Center Storage	19%
5.0	Advanced Data Center Storage	20%

Note that while the weighting of each topic area tells you something about the exam, in the authors' opinion, the weighting probably does not change how you study. All five topic areas hold enough weighting so that if you completely ignore one topic, you will likely not pass. Also, networking requires that you put many concepts together, so you need all the pieces before you can understand the whole network. The weightings might tell you where to spend a little more of your time during the last days before taking the exam, but otherwise, plan on studying for all the exam topics.

Tables I-2 through I-6 list the details of the exam topics, with one table for each of the major topic areas listed in Table I-1. Note that these tables also list the book chapters that discuss each of the exam topics.

Table I-2   Exam Topics in the First Major DCICN Exam Topic Area

Number	Exam Topic	Chapter
1.0	Data Center Physical Infrastructure	1
1.1	Describe different types of cabling, uses, and limitations	1
1.2	Describe different types of transceivers, uses, and limitations	1
1.3	Identify physical components of a server and perform basic troubleshooting	1
1.4	Identify physical port roles	1
1.5	Describe power redundancy modes	1

Table I-3   Exam Topics in the Second Major DCICN Exam Topic Area

Number	Exam Topic	Chapter
2.0	Basic Data Center Networking Concepts	2, 3, 5, 6, 8, 10
2.1	Compare and contrast the OSI and the TCP/IP models	2
2.2	Describe Classic Ethernet fundamentals	3
2.2.a	Forward	3
2.2.b	Filter	3
2.2.c	Flood	3
2.2.d	MAC address table	3
2.3	Describe switching concepts and perform basic configuration	10
2.3.a	STP	8
2.3.b	802.1q	6
2.3.c	Port channels	3
2.3.d	Neighbor discovery	3
2.3.d.1	CDP	3
2.3.d.2	LLDP	3
2.3.e	Storm control	3

Table I-4   Exam Topics in the Third Major DCICN Exam Topic Area

Number	Exam Topic	Chapter
3.0	Advanced Data Center Networking Concepts	1, 11, 16, 17, 20, 21
3.1	Basic routing operations	16
3.1.a	Explain and demonstrate IPv4/IPv6 addressing	11
3.1.b	Compare and contrast static and dynamic routing	16

Number	Exam Topic	Chapter
3.1.c	Perform basic configuration of SVI/routed interfaces	17
3.2	Compare and contrast the First-Hop Redundancy Protocols	20
3.2.a	VRRP	20
3.2.b	GLBP	20
3.2.c	HSRP	20
3.3	Compare and contrast common data center network architectures	1
3.3.a	2 Tier	1
3.3.b	3 Tier	1
3.3.c	Spine-leaf	1
3.4	Describe the use of access control lists to perform basic traffic filtering	21
3.5	Describe the basic concepts and components of authentication, authorization, and accounting	21

Table I-5   Exam Topics in the Fourth Major DCICN Exam Topic Area

Number	Exam Topic	Chapter
4.0	Basic Data Center Storage	22
4.1	Differentiate between file- and block-based storage protocols	22
4.2	Describe the roles of FC/FCoE port types	22
4.3	Describe the purpose of a VSAN	22
4.4	Describe the addressing model of block-based storage protocols	22
4.4.a	FC	22
4.4.b	iSCSI	22

Table I-6   Exam Topics in the Fifth Major DCICN Exam Topic Area

Number	Exam Topic	Chapter
5.0	Advanced Data Center Storage	23
5.1	Describe FCoE concepts and operations	23
5.1.a	Encapsulation	23
5.1.b	DCB	23
5.1.c	vFC	23
5.1.d	Topologies	23

Number	Exam Topic	Chapter
5.1.d.1	Single hop	23
5.1.d.2	Multihop	23
5.1.d.3	Dynamic	23
5.2	Describe node port virtualization	23
5.3	Describe zone types and their uses	23
5.4	Verify the communication between the initiator and target	23
5.4.a	FLOGI	23
5.4.b	FCNS	23
5.4.c	Active zoneseset	23

NOTE   Because it is possible that the exam topics may change over time, it may be worth double-checking the exam topics as listed on the Cisco website (go to www.cisco.com/go/certifications and navigate to the CCNA Data Center page). In the unlikely event that Cisco does happen to add exam topics at a later date, note that Appendix B, "DCICN Exam Updates," describes how to go to www.ciscopress.com and download additional information about those newly added topics.

About the Book

This book discusses the content and skills needed to pass the 200-150 DCICN exam.

Book Features and Exam Preparation Methods

This book uses several key methodologies to help you discover the exam topics for which you need more review, to help you fully understand and remember those details, and to help you prove to yourself that you have retained your knowledge of those topics. Therefore, this book does not try to help you pass the exams only by memorization, but by truly learning and understanding the topics.

The book includes many features that provide different ways to study so you can be ready for the exam. If you understand a topic when you read it, but do not study it any further, you probably will not be ready to pass the exam with confidence. The features included in this book give you tools that help you determine what you know, review what you know, better learn what you don't know, and be well prepared for the exam. These tools include the following:

- "Do I Know This Already?" Quizzes: Each chapter begins with a quiz that helps you determine the amount of time you need to spend studying that chapter.
- Foundation Topics: These are the core sections of each chapter. They explain the protocols, concepts, and configurations for the topics in that chapter.

- **Exam Preparation Tasks:** The "Exam Preparation Tasks" section lists a series of study activities that should be done after reading the "Foundation Topics" section. Each chapter includes the activities that make the most sense for studying the topics in that chapter. The activities include the following:

  - **Key Topics Review:** The Key Topic icon appears next to the most important items in the "Foundation Topics" section of the chapter. The "Key Topics Review" activity lists the key topics from the chapter and their page numbers. Although the contents of the entire chapter could be on the exam, you should definitely know the information listed in each key topic. Review these topics carefully.

  - **Definition of Key Terms:** Although certification exams might be unlikely to ask a question such as "Define this term…," the DCICN 200-150 and DCICT 200-155 exams require you to learn and know a lot of terminology. This section lists some of the most important terms from the chapter, asking you to write a short definition and compare your answer to the Glossary.

  - **End of Chapter Review Questions:** Confirm that you understand the content you just covered.

Book Organization, Chapters, and Appendixes

This book contains 23 core chapters (Chapters 1 through 23), with Chapter 24 including some suggestions for how to approach the actual exams. Each core chapter covers a subset of the topics on the DCICN exam. The core chapters are organized into sections. The core chapters cover the following topics.

Part I: Networking Fundamentals

- **Chapter 1, "Introduction to Nexus Data Center Infrastructure and Architecture:"** Introduces the Cisco Nexus product lines and their capabilities and also discusses the evolution of data center network design.

- **Chapter 2, "The TCP/IP and OSI Networking Models:"** Introduces the terminology surrounding two different networking architectures, namely Transmission Control Protocol/Internet Protocol (TCP/IP) and Open Systems Interconnection (OSI).

- **Chapter 3, "Fundamentals of Ethernet LANs:"** Covers the concepts and terms used for the most popular option for the data link layer for local area networks (LANs), namely Ethernet.

- **Chapter 4, "Fundamentals of IPv4 Addressing and Routing:"** IP is the main network layer protocol for TCP/IP. This chapter introduces the basics of IP Version 4 (IPv4), including IPv4 addressing and routing.

Part II: Data Center Nexus Switching & Routing Fundamentals

- **Chapter 5, "Installing and Operating Nexus Switches:"** Explains how to access, examine, and configure Cisco Nexus switches.

- **Chapter 6, "VLAN and Trunking Concepts:"** Explains the concepts surrounding virtual LANs, including VLAN trunking and the VLAN Trunking Protocol (VTP).

- **Chapter 7, "VLAN Trunking and Configuration:"** Explains the configuration surrounding VLANs, including VLAN trunking and VTP.

- **Chapter 8, "Spanning Tree Protocol Concepts:"** Discusses the concepts behind the IEEE Spanning Tree Protocol (STP) and how it makes some switch interfaces block frames to prevent frames from looping continuously around a redundant switched LAN.

- **Chapter 9, "Cisco Nexus Spanning Tree Protocol Implementation:"** Shows how to configure, verify, and troubleshoot STP implementation on Cisco switches.

- **Chapter 10, "Configuring Ethernet Switching:"** Shows how to configure a variety of Nexus switch features, including duplex and speed, port security, securing the command-line interface (CLI), and the switch IP address.

Part III: IPv4/IPv6 Subnetting

- **Chapter 11, "Perspectives on IPv4 Subnetting:"** Walks through the entire concept of subnetting, from starting with a Class A, B, or C network to analyzing requirements, making choices, calculating the resulting subnets, and assigning those on paper—all in preparation to deploy and use those subnets by configuring the devices.

- **Chapter 12, "Analyzing Classful IPv4 Networks:"** IPv4 addresses originally fell into several classes, with unicast IP addresses being in Class A, B, and C. This chapter explores all things related to address classes and the IP network concept created by those classes.

- **Chapter 13, "Analyzing Subnet Masks:"** In most jobs, someone else came before you and chose the subnet mask used in a network. What does that mean? What does that mask do for you? This chapter focuses on how to look at the mask (and IP network) to discover key facts, such as the size of a subnet (number of hosts) and the number of subnets in the network.

- **Chapter 14, "Analyzing Existing Subnets:"** Most troubleshooting of IP connectivity problems starts with an IP address and mask. This chapter takes that paired information and shows you how to find and analyze the subnet in which that IP address resides, including finding the subnet ID, range of addresses in the subnet, and subnet broadcast address.

- **Chapter 15, "Fundamentals of IP Version 6:"** Surveys the big concepts, addressing, and routing created by the new version of IP: IP Version 6 (IPv6). This chapter attempts to show the similarities with IPv4, as well as the key differences—in particular the differences in IPv6 addresses.

Part IV: IPv4 Routing

- **Chapter 16, "IPv4 Routing Concepts:"** Looks at the IPv4 packet-forwarding process. It shows how a pure router forwards packets. This chapter also breaks down the multilayer switches (which include Cisco Nexus switches), including the Layer 3 routing logic in the same device that does Layer 2 Ethernet switching.

- **Chapter 17, "Cisco Nexus IPv4 Routing Configuration:"** Discusses how to implement IPv4 on Nexus switches. This chapter includes the details of configuring IPv4 addresses, static IPv4 routes, and multilayer switching.

- **Chapter 18, "IPv4 Routing Protocol Concepts:"** Examines a variety of protocols available to routers and multilayer switches to dynamically learn routes for the IP subnets in an internetwork. This chapter focuses on the routing protocol theory that applies to any routing device, with discussion of RIP, OSPF, and EIGRP.

- **Chapter 19, "Nexus Routing Protocol Configuration:"** Explains how to implement IPv4 routing protocols on Cisco Nexus switches, specifically for RIP, OSPF, and EIGRP.

- **Chapter 20, "Nexus First-Hop Redundancy Protocols and Configurations:"** Discusses the different types of FHRPs and how to configure them using Cisco Nexus product lines.

- **Chapter 21, "IPv4 Access Control Lists on Cisco Nexus Switches:"** Discusses the basic concept of how an access control list (ACL) can filter packets as well as the implementation of IPv4 ACLs with Nexus switches.

Part V: Data Center Storage Technologies

- **Chapter 22, "Introduction to Storage and Storage Networking:"** Provides an overview of the data center storage-networking technologies. It compares Small Computer System Interface (SCSI), Fibre Channel, network-attached storage (NAS) connectivity for remote server storage, and storage-area network (SAN). It covers Fibre Channel, Internet Small Computer System Interface (iSCSI), and Fibre Channel over Ethernet protocols and operations in detail. The edge/core layer of the SAN design is also included.

- **Chapter 23, "Advanced Storage Area Network (SAN) Technologies and Configurations:"** Provides an overview of how to configure Cisco MDS 9000 Series multilayer switches. It also describes how to verify virtual storage-area networks (VSANs), zoning, the fabric login, fabric domain, VSAN trunking, and setting up an ISL port using the command-line interface. It discusses node port virtualization and storage virtualization concepts. It introduces principles behind IEEE data center bridging standards and various options for multihop FCoE topologies to extend the reach of Unified Fabric beyond the single-hop boundary.

Part VI: Final Preparation

- **Chapter 24, "Final Review:"** Suggests a plan for final preparation once you have finished the core parts of the book, in particular explaining the many study options available in the book.

Part VII: Appendices (In Print)

- **Appendix A, "Answers to the 'Do I Know This Already?' Quizzes:"** Includes the answers to all the questions from Chapters 1 through 23.

- **Appendix B, "DCICN Exam Updates:"** Covers a variety of short topics that either clarify or expand upon topics covered earlier in the book. This appendix is updated from time to time and posted at www.ciscopress.com/title/9781587205965, with the most recent version available at the time of printing included here as Appendix B. (The first page of the appendix includes instructions on how to check to see whether a later version of Appendix B is available online.)

- **Glossary:** Contains definitions for all of the terms listed in the "Definitions of Key Terms" section at the conclusion of Chapters 1 through 23.

Part VII: Appendices (Online)

- **Appendix C, "Memory Tables:"** Holds the key tables and lists from each chapter, with some of the content removed. You can print this appendix and, as a memory exercise, complete the tables and lists. The goal is to help you memorize facts that can be useful on the exams.

- **Appendix D, "Memory Tables Answer Key:"** Contains the answer key for the exercises in Appendix I.

- **Appendix E, "Practice for Chapter 12: Analyzing Classful IPv4 Networks:"** Lists practice problems associated with Chapter 12. In particular, the practice questions ask you to find the classful network number in which an address resides, and all other facts about that network.

- **Appendix F, "Practice for Chapter 13: Analyzing Subnet Masks:"** Lists practice problems associated with Chapter 13. In particular, the practice questions ask you to convert masks between the three formats, and to examine an existing mask, determine the structure of the IP addresses, and calculate the number of hosts per subnet and the number of subnets.

- **Appendix G, "Practice for Chapter 14: Analyzing Existing Subnets:"** Lists practice problems associated with Chapter 14. In particular, the practice questions ask you to take an IP address and mask and find the subnet ID, subnet broadcast address, and range of IP addresses in the subnet.

- **Appendix H, "Practice for Chapter 21: IPv4 Access Control Lists on Cisco Nexus Switches:"** Lists practice problems associated with Chapter 21. In particular, the practice questions give you a chance to practice working with access control list (ACL) wildcard masks.

- **Appendix I, "Numeric Reference Tables:"** Lists several tables of numeric information, including a binary-to-decimal conversion table and a list of powers of 2.

- **Appendix J, "Nexus Lab Guide:"** Gives some advice on options for building hands-on skills with NX-OS, the operating system on Cisco Nexus switches.

- **Appendix K, "Study Planner:"** A spreadsheet with major study milestones, where you can track your progress.

Companion Website

Register this book to get access to the Pearson IT Certification test engine and other study materials, plus additional bonus content. Check this site regularly for new and updated postings written by the authors that provide further insight into the more troublesome topics on the exam. Be sure to check the box that you would like to hear from us to receive updates and exclusive discounts on future editions of this product or related products.

To access this companion website, follow these steps:

1. Go to www.pearsonITcertification.com/register and log in or create a new account.
2. Enter the ISBN: 9781587205965
3. Answer the challenge question as proof of purchase.

4.   Click the "Access Bonus Content" link in the Registered Products section of your account page to be taken to the page where your downloadable content is available.

Please note that many of our companion content files can be very large, especially image and video files. If you are unable to locate the files for this title by following these steps, please visit www.pearsonITcertification.com/contact and select the "Site Problems/Comments" option. Our customer service representatives will assist you.

Pearson IT Certification Practice Test Engine and Questions

The companion website includes the Pearson IT Certification Practice Test engine—software that displays and grades a set of exam-realistic multiple-choice questions. Using the Pearson IT Certification Practice Test engine, you can either study by going through the questions in Study Mode or take a simulated exam that mimics real exam conditions. You can also serve up questions in a Flash Card Mode, which will display just the question and no answers, challenging you to state the answer in your own words before checking the actual answers to verify your work.

The installation process requires two major steps: installing the software and then activating the exam. The website has a recent copy of the Pearson IT Certification Practice Test engine. The practice exam (the database of exam questions) is not on this site.

NOTE   The cardboard sleeve in the back of this book includes a piece of paper. The paper lists the activation code for the practice exam associated with this book. Do not lose the activation code. On the opposite side of the paper from the activation code is a unique, one-time-use coupon code for the purchase of the Premium Edition eBook and Practice Test.

Install the Software

The Pearson IT Certification Practice Test is a Windows-only desktop application. You can run it on a Mac using a Windows virtual machine, but it was built specifically for the PC platform. The minimum system requirements are as follows:

- Windows 10, Windows 8.1, or Windows 7
- Microsoft .NET Framework 4.0 Client
- Pentium-class 1GHz processor (or equivalent)
- 512MB RAM
- 650MB disk space plus 50MB for each downloaded practice exam
- Access to the Internet to register and download exam databases

The software installation process is routine as compared with other software installation processes. If you have already installed the Pearson IT Certification Practice Test software from another Pearson product, there is no need for you to reinstall the software. Simply launch the software on your desktop and proceed to activate the practice exam from this book by using the activation code included in the access code card sleeve in the back of the book.

The following steps outline the installation process:

1. Download the exam practice test engine from the companion site.

2. Respond to Windows prompts, as with any typical software installation process.

The installation process will give you the option to activate your exam with the activation code supplied on the paper in the cardboard sleeve. This process requires that you establish a Pearson website login. You need this login to activate the exam, so please do register when prompted. If you already have a Pearson website login, there is no need to register again. Just use your existing login.

Activate and Download the Practice Exam

Once the exam engine is installed, you should then activate the exam associated with this book (if you did not do so during the installation process), as follows:

1. Start the Pearson IT Certification Practice Test software from the Windows Start menu or from your desktop shortcut icon.

2. To activate and download the exam associated with this book, from the My Products or Tools tab, click the **Activate Exam** button.

3. At the next screen, enter the activation key from the paper inside the cardboard sleeve in the back of the book. Once this is entered, click the **Activate** button.

4. The activation process will download the practice exam. Click **Next** and then click **Finish**.

When the activation process completes, the My Products tab should list your new exam. If you do not see the exam, make sure that you have selected the **My Products** tab on the menu. At this point, the software and practice exam are ready to use. Simply select the exam and click the **Open Exam** button.

To update a particular exam you have already activated and downloaded, display the **Tools** tab and click the **Update Products** button. Updating your exams will ensure that you have the latest changes and updates to the exam data.

If you want to check for updates to the Pearson Cert Practice Test exam engine software, display the **Tools** tab and click the **Update Application** button. You can then ensure that you are running the latest version of the software engine.

Activating Other Exams

The exam software installation process, and the registration process, only has to happen once. Then, for each new exam, only a few steps are required. For instance, if you buy another Pearson IT Certification Cert Guide, extract the activation code from the cardboard sleeve in the back of that book; you do not even need the exam engine at this point. From there, all you have to do is start the exam engine (if not still up and running) and perform steps 2 through 4 from the previous list.

Assessing Exam Readiness

Exam candidates never really know whether they are adequately prepared for the exam until they have completed about 30 percent of the questions. At that point, if you are not prepared, it is too late. The best way to determine your readiness is to work through the "Do I Know This Already?" quizzes at the beginning of each chapter and review the Foundation Topics and Key Topics presented in each chapter. It is best to work your way through the entire book, unless you can complete each subject without having to do any research or look up any answers.

How to View Only DIKTA Questions by Part

Each "Part Review" section asks you to repeat the Do I Know This Already (DIKTA) quiz questions from the chapters in that part. Although you could simply scan the book pages to review these questions, it is slightly better to review these questions from inside the PCPT software, just to get a little more practice in how to read questions from the testing software. But you can just read them in the book as well.

To view these DIKTA (book) questions inside the PCPT software, follow these steps:

Step 1. Start the PCPT software.

Step 2. From the main (home) menu, select the item for this product, with a name like **DCICN 200-150 Official Cert Guide**, and click **Open Exam**.

Step 3. The top of the next window that appears should list some exams; select the box beside **DCICN Book Questions** and deselect the other boxes. This selects the "book" questions (that is, the DIKTA questions from the beginning of each chapter).

Step 4. In this same window, click at the bottom of the screen to deselect all objectives (chapters). Then select the box beside each chapter in the part of the book you are reviewing.

Step 5. Select any other options on the right side of the window.

Step 6. Click **Start** to start reviewing the questions.

How to View Only Part Review Questions by Part

The exam databases you get with this book include a database of questions created solely for study during the part review process. DIKTA questions focus more on facts, with basic application. The part review questions instead focus more on application, and they look more like real exam questions.

To view these questions, follow the same process as you did with DIKTA/book questions, but select the part review database instead of the book database, as follows:

Step 1. Start the PCPT software.

Step 2. From the main (home) menu, select the item for this product, with a name like **DCICN 200-150 Official Cert Guide**, and click **Open Exam**.

Step 3. The top of the next window should list some exams; select the box beside **Part Review Questions** and deselect the other boxes. This selects the questions intended for part-ending review.

Step 4. On this same window, click at the bottom of the screen to deselect all objectives, and then select (check) the box beside the book part you want to review. This tells the PCPT software to give you part review questions from the selected part.

Step 5. Select any other options on the right side of the window.

Step 6. Click **Start** to start reviewing the questions.

Premium Edition eBook and Practice Tests

This book also includes an exclusive offer for 70% off the Premium Edition eBook and Practice Tests edition of this title. Please see the coupon code included with the cardboard sleeve for information on how to purchase the Premium Edition.

For More Information

If you have any comments about the book, submit them via www.ciscopress.com. Just go to the website, select **Contact Us**, and type your message.

Cisco might make changes that affect the CCNA Data Center certification from time to time. You should always check www.cisco.com/go/certification for the latest details.

The *CCNA Data Center DCICN 200-150 Official Cert Guide* helps you attain the CCNA Data Center certification. This is the DCICN exam prep book from the only Cisco-authorized publisher. We at Cisco Press believe that this book certainly can help you achieve CCNA Data Center certification, but the real work is up to you! We trust that your time will be well spent.

Part I of this book introduces you to the most important topics in TCP/IP networking and data center architecture. Chapter 1 introduces data center architecture evolution and the infrastructure used to create these architectures. Chapter 2 introduces the terms, concepts, and protocols for TCP/IP. Chapter 3 focuses on the links between nearby devices (local area networks). Finally, Chapter 4 focuses on the rules of IP routing, which pull the LAN and WAN links together by forwarding data all the way from one user device to another.

Part I

Networking Fundamentals

This chapter covers the following exam topics:

1.0. Data Center Physical Infrastructure

1.1. Describe different types of cabling, uses, and limitations

1.2. Describe different types of transceivers, uses, and limitations

1.3. Identify physical components of a server and perform basic troubleshooting

1.4. Identify physical port roles

1.5. Describe power redundancy modes

CHAPTER 1

Introduction to Nexus Data Center Infrastructure and Architecture

The Cisco Nexus product family offers a broad portfolio of LAN and SAN switching products, ranging from software switches that integrate with multiple types of hypervisors to hardware data center core switches and campus core switches. Cisco Nexus products provide the performance, scalability, and availability to accommodate diverse data center needs, including different types of data center protocols, such as FCoE, FC, iSCSI, and so on.

This chapter focuses on the Cisco Nexus product family. You learn the different specifications of each product, which includes Nexus 9000, Nexus 7000, Nexus 6000, Nexus 5000, Nexus 3000, and Nexus 2000.

"Do I Know This Already?" Quiz

The "Do I Know This Already?" quiz enables you to assess whether you should read this entire chapter thoroughly or jump to the "Exam Preparation Tasks" section. If you are in doubt about your answers to these questions or your own assessment of your knowledge of the topics, read the entire chapter. Table 1-1 lists the major headings in this chapter and their corresponding "Do I Know This Already?" quiz questions. You can find the answers in Appendix A, "Answers to the 'Do I Know This Already?' Quizzes."

Table 1-1 "Do I Know This Already?" Section-to-Question Mapping

Foundation Topics Section	Questions
Describe the Cisco Nexus Product Family	1-13
Evolution of Data Center Architecture	14, 15

CAUTION The goal of self-assessment is to gauge your mastery of the topics in this chapter. If you do not know the answer to a question or are only partially sure of the answer, you should mark that question as wrong for purposes of the self-assessment. Giving yourself credit for an answer you correctly guess skews your self-assessment results and might provide you with a false sense of security.

1. Which of the following Nexus 9000 hardware models can work as a spine in a spine-leaf topology? (Choose three.)

   a. Nexus 9508
   b. Nexus 9516
   c. Nexus 9396PX
   d. Nexus 93128TX
   e. Nexus 9336PQ

2. True or false? The Nexus N9K-X9736PQ can be used in standalone mode when the Nexus 9000 modular switches use NX-OS.

   a. True

   b. False

3. How many strands do the 40F Bi-Di optics use?

   a. 8

   b. 2

   c. 12

   d. 16

4. What is the current bandwidth per slot for the Nexus 7700?

   a. 550 Gbps

   b. 220 Gbps

   c. 1.3 Tbps

   d. 2.6 Tbps

5. True or false? The F3 modules can be interchanged between the Nexus 7000 and Nexus 7700.

   a. True

   b. False

6. How many VDCs can a SUP2 have?

   a. 2+1

   b. 16+1

   c. 8+1

   d. 4+1

7. True or false? By upgrading SUP1 to the latest software and using the correct license, you can use FCoE with F2 cards.

   a. True

   b. False

8. How many unified ports does the Nexus 6004 currently support?

   a. 20

   b. 24

   c. 48

   d. 64

9. True or false? The 40Gbps ports on the Nexus 6000 can be used as 10Gbps ports.

   a. True

   b. False

10. Which of the following statements are correct? (Choose two.)

   a. The Nexus 5548P has 48 fixed ports, and the Nexus 5548UP has 32 fixed ports and 16 unified ports.

   b. The Nexus 5548P has 32 fixed ports, which are Ethernet ports only, and the Nexus 5548UP has 32 fixed unified ports.

   c. The Nexus 5548P has 32 fixed ports and can have 16 unified ports, whereas the Nexus 5548UP has all ports unified.

   d. The Nexus 5548P has 32 fixed ports, which are Ethernet only, and the Nexus 5548UP has 32 fixed FCoE only ports.

11. How many unified ports does the Nexus 5672 have?

   a. 12

   b. 16

   c. 8

   d. 24

12. Which vendors support the B22 FEX?

   a. HP

   b. IBM

   c. Dell

   c. Fujitsu

   e. All the above

13. Which models from the following list of switches support FCoE ? (Choose two.)

   a. Nexus 2232PP

   b. Nexus 2248PQ

   c. Nexus 2232TM

   d. Nexus 2248TP-E

14. Which Cisco Nexus technology enables two switches to look like one, from a Layer 2 perspective, allowing for all links to be active between the switch and host tiers?

   a. Spanning tree

   b. Virtual Port Channel (vPC)

   c. MCLAG

   d. Stacking

15. Which technology term refers to a network that uses layer 3 between scale out architecture in the Data Center?

   a. Spanning tree

   b. Virtual Port Channel (vPC)

   c. VSS

   d. Spine-leaf

Foundation Topics

Evolution of Data Center Architecture

As architectures for compute and applications have evolved over the past 10 years, so too have the network architectures that support them. Originally, most of the traffic data center network architects designed around was client-to-server communication or what we call "north-south." With client-to-server traffic being the most dominant, network engineers/architects primarily built data centers based on the traditional Core/Aggregation/Access layer design, as seen in Figure 1-1, and the Collapsed Core/Aggregation design, as seen in Figure 1-2.

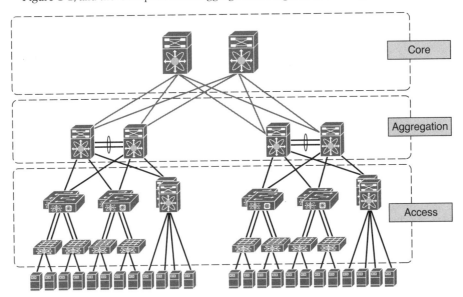

Figure 1-1 *Cisco Three-Tier Network Design*

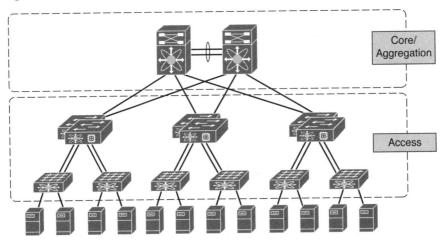

Figure 1-2 *Collapsed Core/Aggregation Network Design*

In the three-tier and Collapsed Core designs, the architecture is set up for allowing optimal traffic flow for clients accessing servers in the data center, and the return traffic and links between the tiers are set for optimal oversubscription ratios to deal with traffic coming in to and out of the data center. As the increase in link speeds and virtualization became more prevalent, network engineers looked for a way to use all links in between any tiers and hide spanning tree from blocking certain links, as shown in Figure 1-3. To do this in the data center, the Nexus product line introduced virtual Port Channel (vPC). vPC enables two switches to look like one, from a Layer 2 perspective, allowing for all links to be active between tiers, as seen in Figure 1-4.

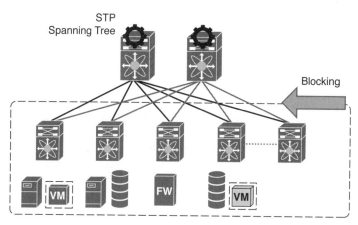

Figure 1-3 *Spanning Tree Between Tiers*

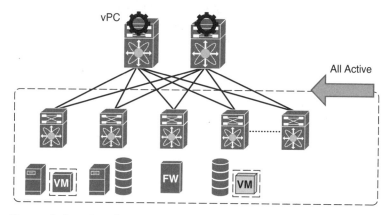

Figure 1-4 *Virtual Port Channel (vPC)*

In the latest trends in the data center, the traffic patterns have shifted to virtualization and new application architectures. This new traffic trend is called "east to west," which means the majority of the traffic and bandwidth being used is actually between nodes within the data center, such as when motioning a virtual machine from one node to another or application clustering.

This topology is a spine-leaf, as seen in Figure 1-5. Spine-leaf has several desirable characteristics that play into the hands of engineers who need to optimize east-west traffic.

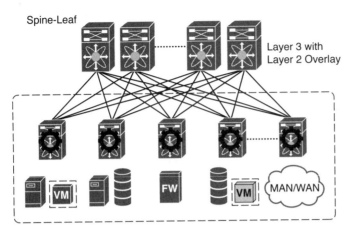

Figure 1-5   *Spine-Leaf Network Topology*

Just to name a few benefits, a spine-leaf design scales horizontally through the addition of spine switches which add availability and bandwidth, which a spanning tree network cannot do. Spine-leaf also uses routing with equal-cost multipathing to allow for all links to be active with higher availability during link failures. With these characteristics, spine-leaf has become the de facto architecture of network engineers and architects for their next wave of data center architectures.

Describe the Cisco Nexus Product Family

The Cisco Nexus product family is a key component of the Cisco unified data center architecture, which is the Unified Fabric. The objective of the Unified Fabric is to build highly available, highly secure network fabrics. Using the Cisco Nexus products, you can build end-to-end data center designs based on three-tier architecture or based on spine-leaf architecture. Cisco Nexus Product line offers high-density 10G, 40G, and 100G ports as well.

Modern data center designs need the following properties:

- Effective use of available bandwidth in designs where multiple links exist between the source and destination and one path is active and the other is blocked by spanning tree, or the design is limiting you to use Active/Standby NIC teaming. This is addressed today using Layer 2 multipathing technologies such as FabricPath and virtual Port Channels (vPC).

- Computing resources must be optimized, which happens by building a computing fabric and dealing with CPU and memory as resources that are utilized when needed. Doing capacity planning for all the workloads and identifying candidates to be virtualized help reduce the number of compute nodes in the data center.

- Using the concept of a service profile and booting from a SAN in the Cisco Unified Computing system will reduce the time to instantiate new servers. This makes it easy to build and tear down test and development environments.

- Power and cooling are key problems in the data center today. Ways to address them include using Unified Fabric (converged SAN and LAN), using Cisco virtual interface cards, and using technologies such as VM-FEX and Adapter-FEX. Rather than using, for example, eight 10G links, you can use two 40G links, and so on. Reducing cabling creates efficient airflow, which in turn reduces cooling requirements.

- The concept of hybrid clouds can benefit your organization. Hybrid clouds extend your existing data center to public clouds as needed, with consistent network and security policies. Cisco is helping customers utilize this concept using CliQr/Cisco CloudCenter.

- Improved reliability during software updates, configuration changes, or adding components to the data center environment, which should happen with minimum disruption.

- Hosts, especially virtual hosts, must move without the need to change the topology or require an address change.

In this chapter you will learn about the Cisco Nexus product family. Figure 1-6 shows the different product types available at the time this chapter was written. These products are explained and discussed in the following sections.

> **NOTE**   Cisco is always innovating and creating new modules/switches. Therefore, while studying for your exam, it is always a good idea to check Cisco.com/go/nexus to verify new modules/switches and their associated features.

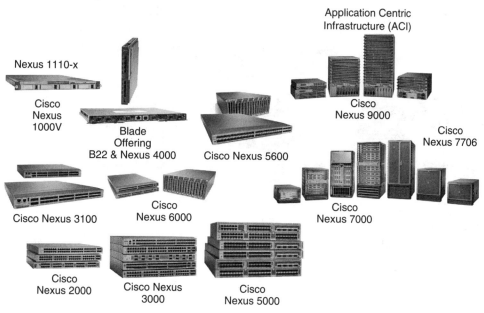

Figure 1-6   *Cisco Nexus Product Family*

Cisco Nexus 9000 Family

The two types of switches in the Nexus 9000 Series are the Nexus 9500 modular switches and the Nexus 9300 fixed configuration switches. They can run in two modes. When they run in ACI mode and in combination with a Cisco Application Policy Infrastructure Controller (APIC), they provide an application-centric infrastructure. In this case, the design follows the spine-leaf architecture shown in Figure 1-7. When they run in NX-OS mode and use the enhanced NX-OS software, they function as a classical Nexus switch. Therefore, the design follows the standard three-tier architecture.

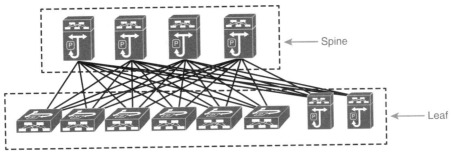

Figure 1-7 *Nexus 9000 Spine-Leaf Architecture*

Cisco Nexus 9500 Family

The Nexus 9500 family consists of three types of modular chassis, as shown in Figure 1-8: the 4-slot Nexus 9504, the 8-slot Nexus 9508, and the 16-slot Nexus 9516.

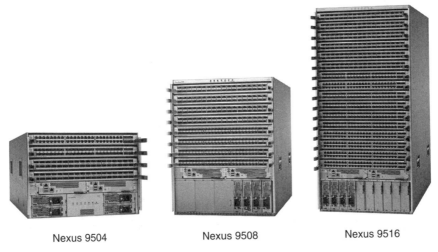

Nexus 9504   Nexus 9508   Nexus 9516

Figure 1-8 *Nexus 9500 Chassis Options*

The Cisco Nexus 9500 Series switches have a modular architecture that consists of the following:

- Switch chassis
- Supervisor engine
- System controllers
- Fabric modules
- Line cards
- Power supplies
- Fan trays
- Optics

Among these parts, supervisors, system controllers, line cards, and power supplies are common components that can be shared among the entire Nexus 9500 product family. Table 1-2 shows the comparison between the different models of the Nexus 9500 switches.

Table 1-2 Nexus 9500 Modular Platform Comparison

	Nexus 9504 4-Slot	Nexus 9508 8-Slot	Nexus 9516 16-Slot
Height	7RU	13 RU	20 RU
Supervisor Slots	2	2	2
Fabric Module Slots	6	6	6
I/O Module Slots	4	8	16
Max BW per Slot (Tbps)	3.84 Tbps	3.84 Tbps	3.84 Tbps
Max BW per System (Tbps)	15 Tbps	30 Tbps	60 Tbps
Max 1/10/40 Ports	192/576/144	384/1152/288	768/2304/576
Air Flow	Front-to-back	Front-to-back	Front-to-back
Power Supplies	4 x 3kW AC PSUs	6 x 3kW PSUs	10 x 3kW PSUs
Fan Trays	3	3	3
Application	EoR or Core	EoR or Core	EoR or Core

Chassis

The Nexus 9500 chassis doesn't have a midplane, as shown in Figure 1-9. Midplanes tend to block airflow, which results in reduced cooling efficiency. Because there is no midplane with a precise alignment mechanism, fabric cards and line cards align together.

Figure 1-9 *Nexus 9500 Chassis*

Supervisor Engine

The Nexus 9500 modular switch supports two redundant half-width supervisor engines, as shown in Figure 1-10. The supervisor engine is responsible for the control plane function. The supervisor modules manage all switch operations. Each supervisor module consists of a Romely 1.8GHz CPU, quad core, and 16GB RAM, upgradable to 48GB RAM and 64GB SSD storage. The supervisor has an external clock source; that is, pulse per second (PPS). There are multiple ports for management, including two USB ports, an RS-232 serial port (RJ-45), and a 10/100/1000MBps network port (RJ-45).

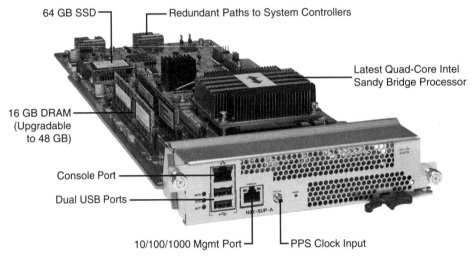

Figure 1-10 *Nexus 9500 Supervisor Engine*

System Controller

A pair of redundant system controllers can be found at the back of the Nexus 9500 chassis, as shown in Figure 1-11. They offload chassis management functions from the supervisor modules. The system controllers are responsible for managing power supplies and fan trays. They host two main control and management paths—the Ethernet Out-of-Band Channel (EOBC) and the Ethernet Protocol Channel (EPC)—between supervisor engines, line cards, and fabric modules. The EOBC provides the intrasystem management communication across modules, and the EPC channel handles the intrasystem data plane protocol communication.

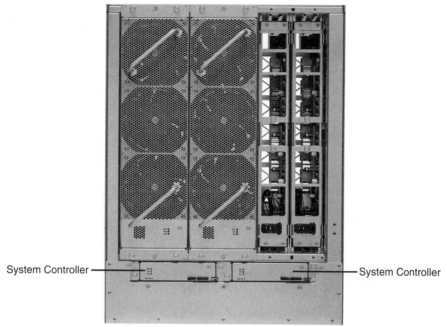

System Controller —   — System Controller

Figure 1-11   *Nexus 9500 System Controllers*

Fabric Modules

The platform supports up to six fabric modules. The packet lookup and forwarding functions involve both the line cards and the fabric modules; both contain multiple network
forwarding engines (NFEs). The NFE is a Broadcom trident two ASIC (T2), and the T2 uses
24 40GE ports to guarantee the line rate. All fabric modules are active; each fabric module
consists of multiple NFEs, as shown in Figure 1-12. The Nexus 9504 has one NFE per fabric
module, the Nexus 9508 has two, and the Nexus 9516 has four.

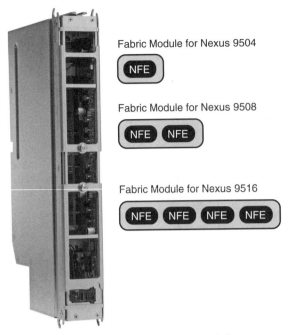

Figure 1-12   *Nexus 9500 Fabric Module*

When you use the 1/10G + four 40GE line cards, you need a minimum of three fabric modules to achieve line-rate speeds. When you use the 36-port 40GE line cards, you will need six fabric modules to achieve line-rate speeds.

> **NOTE**   The fabric modules are behind the fan trays, so to install them you must remove the fan trays.

Line Cards

It is important to understand that there are multiple types of Nexus 9500 line cards. There are cards that can be used in standalone mode when used with enhanced NX-OS, in a classical design. There are line cards that can be used in application-centric infrastructure mode (ACI) only. There are also line cards that can be used in both modes: standalone mode using NX-OS and ACI mode.

All line cards have multiple NFEs for packet lookup and forwarding. In addition, the ACI-ready leaf line cards contain an additional ASIC called an application leaf engine (ALE). ALE performs the ACI leaf function when the Nexus 9500 is used as a leaf node when deployed in ACI mode.

The ACI-only line cards contain an additional ASIC called an application spine engine (ASE); the ASE performs ACI spine functions when the Nexus 9500 is used as a spine in ACI mode. Figure 1-13 shows the high-level positioning of the different cards available for the Nexus 9500 Series network switches.

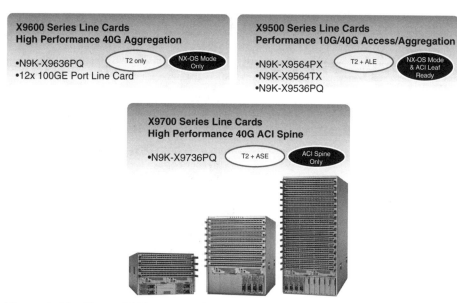

Figure 1-13 *Nexus 9500 Line Cards Positioning*

Nexus 9500 line cards are also equipped with dual-core CPUs, which are used to speed up some control functions, such as programming the hardware table resources, collecting and sending line card counters, statistics, and offloading BFD protocol handling from the supervisors. Table 1-3 shows the different types of cards available for the Nexus 9500 Series switches and their specification.

Table 1-3   Nexus 9500 Modular Platform Line Card Comparison

Line Card Part Number	Specification
N9K-X9636PQ 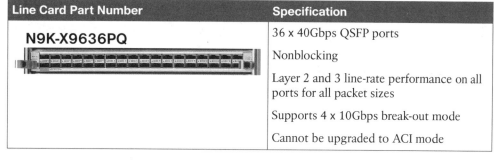	36 x 40Gbps QSFP ports
	Nonblocking
	Layer 2 and 3 line-rate performance on all ports for all packet sizes
	Supports 4 x 10Gbps break-out mode
	Cannot be upgraded to ACI mode

Line Card Part Number	Specification
N9K-X9564PX	48-port 1 and 10 Gigabit Ethernet SFP+ with 4-port 40 Gigabit Ethernet QSFP+ line card
	Designed for use with Cisco Nexus 2000 Series fabric extenders and for mixed 10 and 40 Gigabit Ethernet aggregation
	Supports both direct-attach 10 Gigabit Ethernet copper cabling and optical transceivers
	Supports 100 Megabit Ethernet, 1 Gigabit Ethernet, and 10GBASE-T copper cabling connectivity for server access
	Layer 2 and 3 line-rate performance on all ports for all packet sizes
	Cisco Enhanced NX-OS and Application Centric Infrastructure (ACI) mode
N9K-X9564TX	48-port 1 and 10GBASE-T plus 4-port 40 Gigabit Ethernet QSFP+ line card
	Supports 100 Megabit Ethernet, 1 Gigabit Ethernet, and 10GBASE-T copper cabling connectivity for server access
	Layer 2 and 3 line-rate performance on all ports for all packet sizes
	Cisco Enhanced NX-OS and Application Centric Infrastructure (ACI) mode
N9K-X9736PQ	36-port 40 Gigabit Ethernet QSFP+ line card
	Nonblocking
	Designed for use in a spine switch role when used in ACI mode
	Works only in ACI mode

Power Supplies

The Nexus 9500 platform supports up to 10 power supplies; they are accessible from the front and are hot swappable. Two 3000W AC power supplies can operate a fully loaded chassis; they support N+1 and N+N (grid redundancy). The 3000W AC power supply shown in Figure 1-14 is 80 Plus platinum rated and provides more than 90% efficiency.

Figure 1-14 *Nexus 9500 AC Power Supply*

NOTE The additional four power supply slots are not needed with existing line cards shown in Table 1-3; however, they offer head room for future port densities, bandwidth, and optics.

Fan Trays

The Nexus 9500 consists of three fan trays; each tray consists of three fans. Dynamic speed is driven by temperature sensors and front-to-back air flow with N+1 redundancy per tray. Fan trays are installed after the fabric module installation, as shown in Figure 1-15.

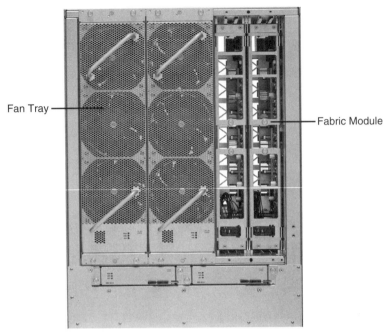

Fan Tray

Fabric Module

Figure 1-15   *Nexus 9500 Fan Tray*

> **NOTE**   To service the fabric modules, the fan tray must be removed first. If one of the fan trays is removed, the other two fan trays will speed up to compensate for the loss of cooling.

Cisco QSFP Bi-Di Technology for 40 Gbps Migration

As data center designs evolve from 1G to 10G at the access layer, access to aggregation and spine-leaf design at the spine layer will move to 40G. The 40G adoption is slow today because of multiple barriers; the first is the cost barrier of the 40G port itself. Second, when you migrate from 10G to 40G, you must replace the cabling. 10G operates on what is referred to as two strands of fiber; however, 40G operates on eight strands of fiber. Bi-Di optics are standard based, and they enable customers to take the current 10G cabling plant and use it for 40G connectivity without replacing the cabling. Figure 1-16 shows the difference between the QSFP SR and the QSFP Bi-Di.

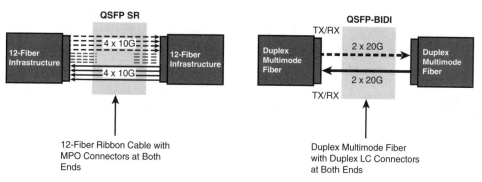

Figure 1-16   *Cisco Bi-Di Optics*

Cisco Nexus 9300 Family

The previous section discussed the Nexus 9500 Series modular switches. This section discusses details of the Cisco Nexus 9300 fixed configuration switches. There are currently four chassis-based models in the Nexus 9300 platform. Table 1-4 summarizes the different specifications of each chassis. The Nexus 9300 is designed for top-of-rack (ToR) and mid-of-row (MoR) deployments.

Table 1-4   Nexus 9500 Fixed-Platform Comparison

	Nexus 9396PX 48-Port 1/10GE	Nexus 9396TX 48-Port 1/10GE	Nexus 93128TX 96-Port 1/10GE	Nexus 9336PQ 36-Port 40GE
Height	2 RU	2RU	2RU	RU
I/O Module Slots	1 GEM (12 QSFP)	1 GEM (12 QSFP)	1 GEM (8 QSFP)	Fixed
Max BW/ System	480 Gbps (nonblocking)	480 Gbps (nonblocking)	3:1 (oversubscription)	1.44 Tbps (nonblocking)
Max 1/10/40/ Ports	48/48/12	48/48/12	96/96/8	0/0/36
Air Flow	Front-to-back Back-to-front	Front-to-back Back-to-front	Front-to-back Back-to-front	Front-to-back
Power Supply Configurations	(1+1) x 650W AC	(1+1) x 650W AC	(1+1) x 650W/1200W AC	(1+1) x 1200W AC
Application	ToR	ToR	ToR	EoR
Software Mode	NX-OS or ACI mode (leaf)	NX-OS or ACI mode (leaf)	NX-OS or ACI mode (leaf)	ACI mode only (spine)

The 40Gbps ports for Cisco Nexus 9396PX, 9396TX, and 93128TX are provided on an uplink module that can be serviced and replaced by the user. The uplink module is the same for all switches. If used with the Cisco Nexus 93128TX, eight out of the 12 x 40Gbps QSFP+ ports will be available.

As shown in Table 1-4, the Nexus 9396PX, 9396TX, and 93128TX can operate in NX-OS mode and in ACI mode (acting as a leaf node). The Nexus 9336PQ can operate in ACI mode only and act as a spine node.

Figure 1-17 shows the different models available today from the Nexus 9300 switches.

Nexus 9336PQ   Nexus 9396PQ   Nexus 93128TX

Nexus 9396TX

Figure 1-17   *Cisco Nexus 9300 Switches*

Cisco Nexus 7000 and Nexus 7700 Product Family

The Nexus 7000 Series switches form the core data center networking fabric. There are multiple chassis options from the Nexus 7000 and Nexus 7700 product family, as shown in Table 1-5. The Nexus 7000 and the Nexus 7700 switches offer a comprehensive set of features for the data center network. The modular design of the Nexus 7000 and Nexus 7700 enables them to offer different types of network interfaces—1G, 10G, 40G, and 100G—in a high-density, scalable way with a switching capacity beyond 15 Tbps for the Nexus 7000 Series and 83 Tbps for the Nexus 7700 Series. The Nexus 7000 hardware architecture offers redundant supervisor engines, redundant power supplies, and redundant fabric cards for high availability. It is very reliable by supporting in-service software upgrades (ISSUs) with zero packet loss. It is easy to manage using the command line or through data center network manager; you can utilize NX-OS APIs to manage it.

Table 1-5   Nexus 7000 and Nexus 7700 Modular Platform Comparison

	7004	7009	7010	7018	7706	7710	7718
Supervisor Redundancy	Yes	Yes	Yes	Yes	Yes	Yes	Yes
I/O Module Slots	2	7	8	16	4	8	16
Bandwidth per Slot	440 Gbps	550 Gbps	550 Gbps	550 Gbps	1.3 Tbps	1.3 Tbps	1.3 Tbps
Switching Capacity (Tbps)	1.92	7.7	8.8	17.6	21	42	83
1GE Port Density	96	336	384	768	192	384	768
10GE Port Density	96	336	384	768	192	384	768
40GE Port Density	24	84	96	192	96	192	384
100GE Port Density	4	14	16	32	48	96	192
Rack Space (RU)	7	14	21	25	9	14	26
Airflow	Side-rear	Side-side	Front-back	Side-side	Front-back	Front-back	Front-back

The Nexus 7000 and Nexus 7700 product family is modular in design with great focus on the redundancy of all the critical components; this has been applied across the physical, environmental, power, and system software aspects of the chassis.

- **Supervisor module redundancy:** The chassis can have up to two supervisor modules operating in active and standby modes. State and configuration are in sync between the two supervisors, which provide seamless and stateful switchover in the event of a supervisor module failure.

NOTE   There are dedicated slots for the supervisor engines in all Nexus chassis; the supervisor modules are not interchangeable between the Nexus 7000 and Nexus 7700 chassis.

- **Switch fabric redundancy:** The fabric modules support load sharing. You can have multiple fabric modules; the Nexus 7000 supports up to five fabric modules, and Nexus 7700 supports up to six fabric modules. With the current shipping fabric cards and current I/O modules, the switches support N+1 redundancy.

NOTE   The fabric modules between the Nexus 7000 and Nexus 7700 are not interchangeable.

- **Cooling subsystem:** The system has redundant fan trays. There are multiple fans on the fan trays, and any failure of one of the fans will not result in loss of service.
- **Power subsystem availability features:** The system will support the following power redundancy options:
  - Combined mode, where the total power available is the sum of the outputs of all the power supplies installed. (This is not redundant.)
  - PSU redundancy, where the total power available is the sum of all power supplies minus 1, otherwise commonly called N+1 redundancy.
  - Grid redundancy, where the total power available is the sum of the power from only one input on each PSU. Each PSU has two supply inputs, allowing it to be connected to separate isolated A/C supplies. In the event of an A/C supply failure, 50% of power is secure.
  - Full redundancy, which is the combination of PSU redundancy and grid redundancy. In most cases, this will be the same as grid mode but will assure customers that they are protected for either a PSU or a grid failure, but not both at the same time.
  - PSU redundancy is the default.
- **Modular software upgrades:** The NX-OS software is designed with a modular architecture, which helps to address specific issues and minimize the system overall impact. Each service running is an individual memory-protected process, including multiple instances of a particular service that provide effective fault isolation between services and that make each service individually monitored and managed. Most of the services allow stateful restart, enabling a service that's experiencing a failure to be restarted and resume operation without affecting other services.

- **Cisco NX-OS in-service software upgrade (ISSU):** With the NX-OS modular architecture, you can support ISSU, which enables you to do a complete system upgrade without disrupting the data plane and achieve zero packet loss.

- **Cable management:** The integrated cable management system is designed to support the cabling requirements of a fully configured system to either or both sides of the switch, allowing maximum flexibility.

- **System-level LEDs:** A series of LEDs at the top of the chassis provides a clear summary of the status of the major system components. The LEDs alert operators to the need to conduct further investigation. These LEDs report the power supply, fan, fabric, supervisor, and I/O module status.

- **Cable management:** The cable management cover and optional front module doors provide protection from accidental interference with both the cabling and modules that are installed in the system. The transparent front door allows observation of cabling and module indicator and status lights.

Nexus 7000 and Nexus 7700 have multiple models with different specifications. Figure 1-18 shows these switching models, and Table 1-5 shows their specifications.

Figure 1-18   *Cisco Nexus 7000 and Nexus 7700 Product Families*

NOTE   When you go through Table 1-5, you might wonder how the switching capacity was calculated. For example, the Nexus 7010 has eight line cards slots, so the calculation is

(550 Gbps/slot) x (8 payload slots) = 4400 Gbps, (4400 Gbps) x (2 for full duplex operation) = 8800 Gbps = 8.8 Tbps system bandwidth

For the Nexus 7700 Series, we'll use the Nexus 7718 as an example. Although the bandwidth/slot shown in the table gives us 1.3 Tbps, the Nexus 7700 is capable of more than double its capacity, and that can be achieved by upgrading the fabric cards for the chassis. Therefore, if the bandwidth/slot is 2.6 Tbps, the calculation is

(2.6 Tbps/slot) x (16 payload slots) = 41.6 Tbps, (4400Gbps) x (2 for full duplex operation) = 83.2 Tbps system bandwidth

In some bandwidth calculations for the chassis, the supervisor slots are taken into consideration because each supervisor slot has a single channel of connectivity to each fabric card, so that makes a total of five crossbar channels.

So, for example, the Cisco Nexus 7010 bandwidth is being calculated like so:

(550 Gbps/slot) x (9 payload slots) = 4950 Gbps, (4950 Gbps) x (2 for full duplex operation) = 9900 Gbps = 9.9 Tbps system bandwidth

Using this type of calculation, a 9-slot chassis will have 8.8 Tbps, and the 18-slot chassis will have 18.7 Tbps.

Cisco Nexus 7004 Series Switch Chassis

The Cisco Nexus 7004 switch chassis shown in Figure 1-19 has two supervisor module slots and two I/O modules; the complete specification for the Nexus 7004 is shown in Table 1-5. It is worth mentioning that the Nexus 7004 doesn't have any fabric modules; the local I/O module fabrics are connected back-to-back to form a two-stage crossbar that interconnects the I/O modules and the supervisor engines. It has one fan tray and four 3kW power supplies.

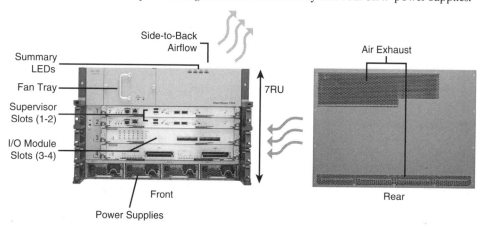

Figure 1-19 *Cisco Nexus 7004 Switch*

Cisco Nexus 7009 Series Switch Chassis

The Cisco Nexus 7009 switch chassis shown in Figure 1-20 has two supervisor module slots and seven I/O module slots; the complete specification for the Nexus 7009 is shown in Table 1-5. The Nexus 7009 switch has a single fan tray. The fan redundancy is two parts: individual fans in the fan tray and fan tray controllers. The fan controllers are fully redundant, reducing the probability of a total fan tray failure. The fans in the fan trays are individually wired to isolate any failure and are fully redundant so that other fans in the tray can take over when one or more fans fail. So, there is redundancy within the cooling system due to the number of fans. If an individual fan fails, other fans automatically run at higher speeds, and the system will continue to function, giving you time to get a spare and replace the fan tray.

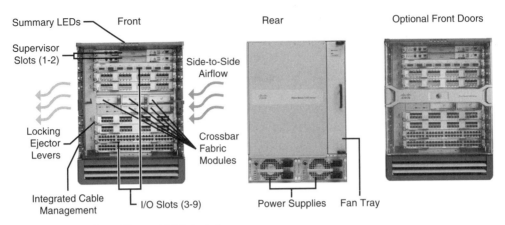

Figure 1-20   *Cisco Nexus 7009 Switch*

Although the Nexus 7009 has side-to-side airflow, there is a solution for hot aisle–cold aisle design with the 9-slot chassis.

Cisco Nexus 7010 Series Switch Chassis

The Cisco Nexus 7010 switch chassis shown in Figure 1-21 has two supervisor engine slots and eight I/O modules slots; the complete specification is shown in Table 1-5. There are multiple fans on the 7010 system fan trays. The fans on the trays are N+1 redundant. Any single fan failure will not result in degradation in service; the box does not overheat, and the fan tray will need replacing to restore N+1.

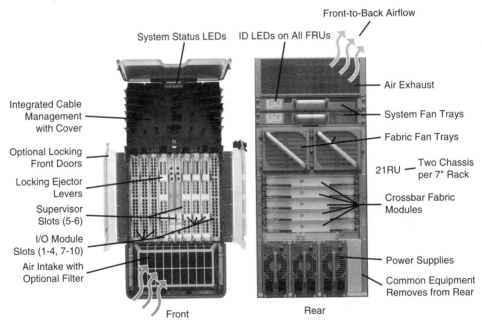

Figure 1-21   *Cisco Nexus 7010 Switch*

There are two system fan trays in the 7010. If either of the fan trays fails, the system will keep running without overheating as long as the operating environment is within specifications, until the fan tray is replaced. Fan tray replacement restores N+1 redundancy.

There are two fabric fan modules in the 7010; both are required for normal operation. If either fabric fan fails, the remaining fabric fan will continue to cool the fabric modules until the fan is replaced, restoring the N+1 redundancy. The system should not be operated with either the system fan tray or the fabric fan components removed, apart from the hot swap period of up to 3 minutes.

Cisco Nexus 7018 Series Switch Chassis

The Cisco Nexus 7018 switch chassis shown in Figure 1-22 has two supervisor engine slots and 16 I/O module slots; the complete specification is shown in Table 1-5. For the 7018 system, there are two system fan trays—one for the upper half and one for the lower half of the system. Both fan trays must be installed at all times (apart from maintenance). Each fan tray contains 12 fans that are in three rows of four. Each row cools three module slots (I/O and supervisor). The failure of a single fan will result in the other fans increasing speed to compensate, and they will continue to cool the system. The fan tray should be replaced to restore the N+1 fan resilience. Integrated into the system fan tray are the fabric fans. The fabric fans are at the rear of the system fan tray. The two fans are in series so that the air passes through both to leave the switch and cool the fabric modules. Failure of a single fabric fan will not result in a failure; the remaining fan will cool the fabric modules.

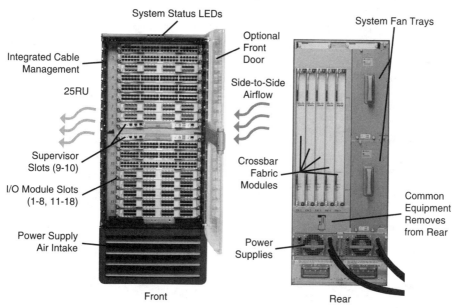

Figure 1-22   *Cisco Nexus 7018 Switch*

> **NOTE**   Although both system fan trays are identical, the fabric fans operate only when installed in the upper fan tray position. Fan trays are fully interchangeable, but when inserted in the lower position the fabric fans are inoperative.

Cisco Nexus 7706 Series Switch Chassis

The Cisco Nexus 7706 switch chassis shown in Figure 1-23 has two supervisor module slots and four I/O module slots; the complete specification is shown in Table 1-5. There are 192 10G ports, 96 40G ports, 48 100G ports, true front-to-back airflow, redundant fans, and redundant fabric cards.

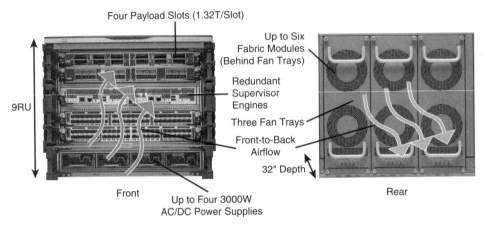

Figure 1-23   *Cisco Nexus 7706 Switch*

Cisco Nexus 7710 Series Switch Chassis

The Cisco Nexus 7710 switch chassis shown in Figure 1-24 has two supervisor engine slots and eight I/O module slots; the complete specification is shown in Table 1-5. There are 384 1-G ports, 192 40-G ports, 96 100-G ports, true front-to-back airflow, redundant fans, and redundant fabric cards.

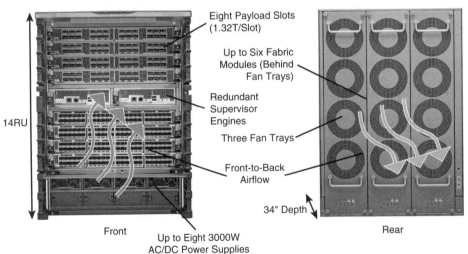

Figure 1-24   *Cisco Nexus 7710 Switch*

Cisco Nexus 7718 Series Switch Chassis

The Cisco Nexus 7718 switch chassis shown in Figure 1-25 has two supervisor engine slots and 16 I/O module slots; the complete specification is shown in Table 1-5. There are 768 10G ports, 384 40G ports, 192 100G ports, true front-to-back airflow, redundant fans, and redundant fabric cards.

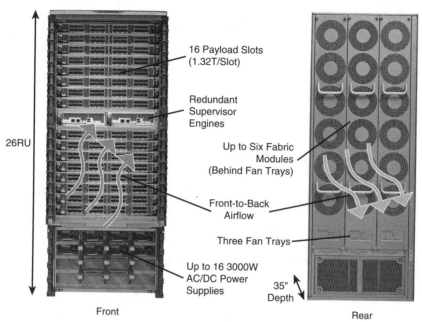

Figure 1-25   *Cisco Nexus 7718 Switch*

Cisco Nexus 7000 and Nexus 7700 Supervisor Module

Nexus 7000 and Nexus 7700 Series switches have two slots that are available for supervisor modules. Redundancy is achieved by having both supervisor slots populated. Table 1-6 describes different options and specifications of the supervisor modules.

Table 1-6   Nexus 7000 and Nexus 7700 Supervisor Modules Comparison

	Nexus 7700 Supervisor 2E	Nexus 7000 Supervisor 2E	Nexus 7000 Supervisor 2	Nexus 7000 Supervisor 1
CPU	Dual Quad-Core Xeon	Dual Quad-Core Xeon	Quad-Core Xeon	Dual-Core Xeon
Speed (GHz)	2.13	2.13	2.13	1.66
Memory (GB)	32	32	12	8
Flash memory	USB	USB	USB	Compact Flash
Fiber Channel over Ethernet (FCoE) on F2 module	Yes	Yes	Yes	No

	Nexus 7700 Supervisor 2E	Nexus 7000 Supervisor 2E	Nexus 7000 Supervisor 2	Nexus 7000 Supervisor 1
CPU Share	Yes	Yes	Yes	No
Virtual Device Contexts (VDC)	8+1 admin VDC	8+1 admin VDC	4+1 admin VDC	4
Cisco Fabric Extender (FEX) Support	64 FEX/3072 ports	64 FEX/3072 ports	32 FEX/1536 ports	32 FEX/1536 ports
Connectivity Management Processor (CMP)	Not supported	Not supported	Not supported	Supported

Cisco Nexus 7000 Series Supervisor 1 Module

The Cisco Nexus 7000 supervisor 1 module shown in Figure 1-26 is the first-generation supervisor module for the Nexus 7000. As shown in Table 1-6, the operating system runs on a dedicated dual-core Xeon processor; dual supervisor engines run in active-standby mode with stateful switch over (SSO) and configuration synchronization between both supervisors. There are dual redundant Ethernet out-of-band channels (EOBC) to each I/O and fabric modules to provide resiliency for the communication between control and line card processors. An embedded packet analyzer reduces the need for a dedicated packet analyzer to provide faster resolution for control plane problems. The USB ports allow access to USB flash memory devices to software image loading and recovery.

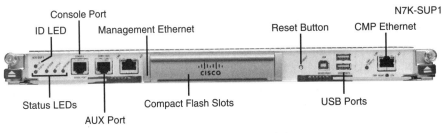

Figure 1-26 *Cisco Nexus 7000 Supervisor 1 Module*

The Connectivity Management Processor (CMP) provides an independent remote system management and monitoring capability. It removes the need for separate terminal server devices for OOB management, and it offers complete visibility during the entire boot process. It has the capability to initiate a complete system restart and shutdown. Administrators must authenticate to get access to the system through CMP, and it also allows access to supervisor logs and full console control on the supervisor engine.

The Cisco Nexus 7000 supervisor 1 module incorporates highly advanced analysis and debugging capabilities. The Power-on Self Test (POST) and Cisco Generic Online Diagnostics (GOLD) provide proactive health monitoring both at startup and during system operation. This is useful in detecting hardware faults. If a fault is detected, corrective action can be taken to mitigate the fault and reduce the risk of a network outage.

Cisco Nexus 7000 Series Supervisor 2 Module

The Cisco Nexus 7000 supervisor 2 module shown in Figure 1-27 is the next-generation supervisor module. As shown in Table 1-6, it has a quad-core CPU and 12G of memory compared to the supervisor 1 module, which has single-core CPU and 8G of memory. The supervisor 2E module is the enhanced version of the supervisor 2 module with two quad-core CPUs and 32G of memory.

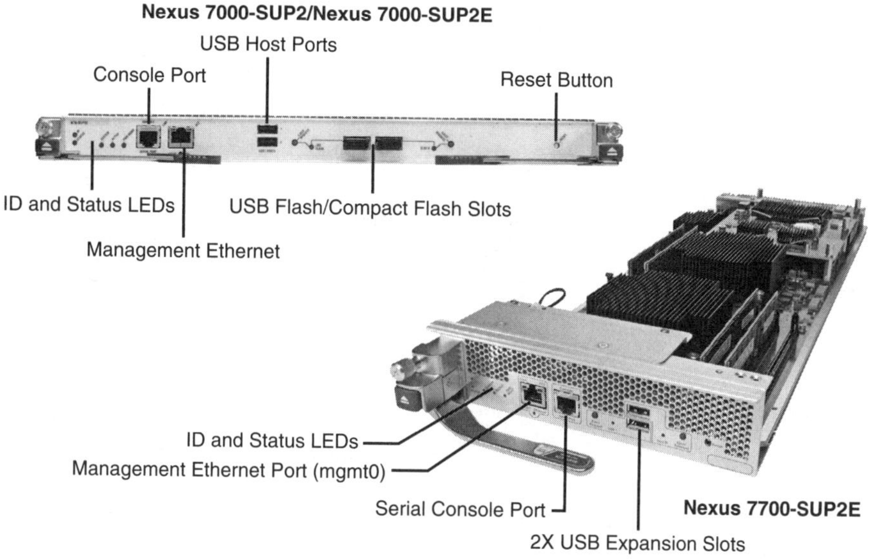

Figure 1-27 *Cisco Nexus 7000 Supervisor 2 Module*

The supervisor 2 module and supervisor 2E module have more powerful CPUs, larger memory, and next-generation ASICs that together will result in improved performance, such as enhanced user experience, faster boot and switchover times, and a higher control plane scale, such as higher VDC and FEX.

Both the supervisor 2 module and supervisor 2E module support FCoE; when you are choosing the proper line card, they support CPU shares, which will enable you to carve out CPU for higher priority VDCs. Sup2E supports 8+1 VDCs. Sup2 scale is the same as Sup1; it will support 4+1 VDCs.

NOTE You cannot mix Sup1 and Sup2 in the same chassis. Note that this will be a disruptive migration requiring removal of supervisor 1. Sup2 and Sup2E can be mixed for migration only. This will be a nondisruptive migration.

Cisco Nexus 7000 and Nexus 7700 Fabric Modules

The Nexus 7000 and Nexus 7700 fabric modules provide interconnection between line cards and provide fabric channels to the supervisor modules. The Nexus 7000 has five fabric modules, and the Nexus 7700 has six; adding fabric modules increases the available bandwidth per I/O slot because all fabric modules are connected to all slots. Figure 1-28 shows the different fabric modules for the Nexus 7000 and Nexus 7700 products.

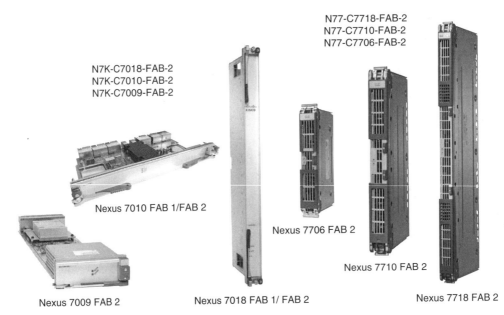

N7K-C7018-FAB-2
N7K-C7010-FAB-2
N7K-C7009-FAB-2

N77-C7718-FAB-2
N77-C7710-FAB-2
N77-C7706-FAB-2

Nexus 7010 FAB 1/FAB 2

Nexus 7706 FAB 2

Nexus 7710 FAB 2

Nexus 7009 FAB 2

Nexus 7018 FAB 1/ FAB 2

Nexus 7718 FAB 2

Figure 1-28   *Cisco Nexus 7000 Fabric Module*

In the case of Nexus 7000, when using Fabric Module 1, which is 46 Gbps, you can deliver a maximum of 230 Gbps per slot using five fabric modules. When using Fabric Module 2, which is 110 Gbps, you can deliver a maximum of 550 Gbps per slot. In Nexus 7700, by using Fabric Module 2, which is 220 Gbps per slot, you can deliver a maximum of 1.32 Tbps per slot.

All fabric modules support load sharing, and the architecture supports lossless fabric failover. In case of a failure or removal of one of the fabric modules, the remaining fabric modules will load balance the remaining bandwidth to all the remaining line cards.

Nexus 7000 supports virtual output queuing (VOQ) and credit-based arbitration to the crossbar to increase performance. VOQ and credit-based arbitration allow fair sharing of resources when a speed mismatch exists to avoid head-of-line (HOL) blocking.

The Nexus 7000 implements a three-stage crossbar switch. Fabric stage 1 and fabric stage 3 are implemented on the line card module, and stage 2 is implemented on the fabric module. Figure 1-29 shows how these stages are connected to each other. There are four connections from each fabric module to the line cards, and each one of these connections is 55 Gbps. When populating the chassis with six fabric modules, the total number of connections from the fabric cards to each line card is 24. It provides an aggregate bandwidth of 1.32 Tbps per slot.

There are two connections from each fabric module to the supervisor module. These connections are also 55 Gbps. When all the fabric modules are installed, there are 12 connections from the switch fabric to the supervisor module, providing an aggregate bandwidth of 275 Gbps.

NOTE   Cisco Nexus 7000 fabric 1 modules provide two 23Gbps traces to each fabric module, providing 230 Gbps of switching capacity per I/O slot for a fully loaded chassis. Each supervisor module has a single 23Gbps trace to each fabric module.

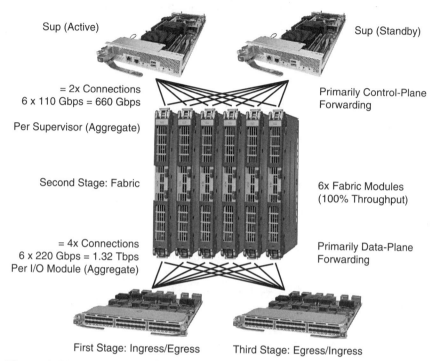

Nexus 7700 Is Using FAB-2 ASICS and Offering 1.32 Tbps

Sup (Active)

Sup (Standby)

= 2x Connections
6 x 110 Gbps = 660 Gbps

Primarily Control-Plane
Forwarding

Per Supervisor (Aggregate)

Second Stage: Fabric

6x Fabric Modules
(100% Throughput)

= 4x Connections
6 x 220 Gbps = 1.32 Tbps
Per I/O Module (Aggregate)

Primarily Data-Plane
Forwarding

First Stage: Ingress/Egress   Third Stage: Egress/Ingress

Figure 1-29 *Cisco Nexus 7700 Crossbar Fabric*

Cisco Nexus 7000 and Nexus 7700 Licensing

Different types of licenses are required for the Nexus 7000 and the Nexus 7700. Table 1-7 describes each license and the features it enables.

Table 1-7 Nexus 7000 and Nexus 7700 Software Licensing Features

Feature License	Features
Enterprise Services Package	Open Shortest Path First (OSPF) protocol.
LAN_ENTERPRISE_SERVICES_PKG	Border Gateway Protocol (BGP).
	Intermediate System-to-Intermediate System (IS-IS) Protocol (Layer 3 only).
	Protocol Independent Multicast (PIM), which includes sparse mode, bidirectional mode, and source-specific mode (SSM).
	Multicast Source Discovery Protocol (MSDP).
	Policy-based routing.
	Generic routing encapsulation (GRE) tunnel.
	Enhanced Interior Gateway Routing Protocol (EIGRP).

Feature License	Features
Advanced Services Package LAN_ADVANCED_SERVICES_PKG	Virtual device contexts (VDCs).
VDC licenses VDC_PKG	Increments four VDC licenses that enable the Cisco Nexus 7000 Series Supervisor 2 Enhanced module to support eight VDCs.
Transport Services Package LAN_TRANSPORT_SERVICES_PKG	Overlay Transport Virtualization (OTV). Locator/ID Separation Protocol (LISP).
Scalable Services Package SCALABLE_SERVICES_PKG	A single license per system enables all XL-capable I/O modules to operate in XL mode. The license increases the performance of the following features: ■ IPv4 routes ■ IPv6 routes ■ ACL entries
Enhanced Layer 2 Package ENHANCED_LAYER2_PKG	FabricPath support on the F Series module.
MPLS Services Package MPLS_PKG	Multiprotocol Label Switching (MPLS). Layer 3 virtual private network (VPN). Layer 2 Ethernet over MPLS (EoMPLS). Layer 2 Virtual Private LAN Services (VPLS).
Storage Enterprise Package STORAGE_ENT	Inter-VSAN routing (IVR) over Fibre Channel and FCoE IVR Network Address Translation (NAT) over Fibre Channel. VSAN-based access control. Fabric binding for open systems.
FCoE Services Package (FCOE_PKG)	Fibre Channel over Ethernet (FCoE). **Note:** You do not need the Advanced Services Package to enable the storage VDC required for FCoE.
FCoE F1-Series	Fibre Channel over Ethernet (FCoE) for Cisco Nexus 7000 48-port 10G SFP+ (F2). FCoE for Cisco Nexus 7700 Enhanced F2e Series 48 Port 10G (SFP+).

It is worth mentioning that Nexus switches have a grace period, which is the amount of time the features in a license package can continue functioning without a license. Enabling a licensed feature that does not have a license key starts a counter on the grace period. You then have 120 days to install the appropriate license keys, disable the use of that feature, or disable the grace period feature. If at the end of the 120-day grace period the device does not have a valid license key for the feature, the Cisco NX-OS software automatically disables the feature and removes the configuration from the device. There is also an evaluation license, which is a temporary license. Evaluation licenses are time bound (valid for a specified number of days) and are tied to a host ID (device serial number).

NOTE   To manage the Nexus 7000, two types of licenses are needed: the DCNM LAN and DCNM SAN, each of which is a separate license.

To get the license file, you must obtain the serial number for your device by entering the **show license host-id** command. The host ID is also referred to as the device serial number, as shown in Example 1-1.

Example 1-1   *NX-OS Command to Obtain the Host ID*

```
switch# show license host-id
License hostid: VDH=FOX064317SQ
```

TIP   Use the entire ID that appears after the equal sign (=). In this example, the host ID is FOX064317SQ.

After executing the copy licenses command from the default VDC, save your license file to one of four locations—the bootflash: directory, the slot0: device, the usb1: device, or the usb2: device.

Perform the installation by using the **install license** command on the active supervisor module from the device console, as shown in Example 1-2.

Example 1-2   *Command Used to Install the License File*

```
switch# install license bootflash:license_file.lic
Installing license ..done
```

You can check what licenses are already installed by issuing the command shown in Example 1-3.

Example 1-3   *Command Used to Obtain Installed Licenses*

```
switch# show license usage
Feature                          Ins    Lic      Status Expiry Date Comments
                                                               Count
LAN_ENTERPRISE_SERVICES_PKG      Yes     -      In use Never          -
```

Cisco Nexus 7000 and Nexus 7700 Line Cards

Nexus 7000 and Nexus 7700 support various types of I/O modules. There are two types of I/O modules: the M-I/O modules and the F-I/O modules. Each has different performance metrics and features. Table 1-8 shows the comparison between M-Series modules.

Table 1-8   Nexus 7000 and Nexus 7700 M-Series Modules Comparison

	N7KM148GS -11L	N7KM148GT -11L	N7KM108X2 -12L	N7KM132XP -12L	N7KM224XP -23L	N7KM206FQ -23L	N7KM202CF -22L
Line Card Family	M1	M1	M1	M1	M2	M2	M2
Ports (Number and Type)	48, 1GE	48, 10/100/1000GE	8, 10GE	32, 10GE	24, 10GE	6, 40GE	2, 40/100GE
Interface Type	SFP	RJ-45	X2	SFP+	SFP+	QSFP+	CFP
Fabric Bandwidth (Gbps)	46	46	80	80	240	240	240
Performance (Mpps)	60	60	120	60	120	120	120
NetFlow	Full/sampled	Full/sampled	Full/sampled	Full/sampled	Full/sampled	Full/sampled	Full/sampled
FEX Support	No	No	Yes	Yes	Yes	Yes	Yes
Virtual PC (vPC) Support	Yes	Yes	Yes	Yes	Yes	Yes	Yes
QinQ	Yes	Yes	Yes	Yes	Yes	Yes	Yes
MPLS Support	Yes	Yes	Yes	Yes	Yes	Yes	Yes
Overlay Transport Virtualization (OTV)	Yes	Yes	Yes	Yes	Yes	Yes	Yes
Locator/ID Separation Protocol (LISP)	No	No	No	Yes	No	No	No
FCoE, FabricPath Support	No	No	No	No	No	No	No
IEEE 1588 PTP	No	No	No	No	Yes	Yes	Yes
PONG	No	No	No	No	Yes	Yes	Yes

NOTE   From the table, you see that the M1 32-port I/O module is the only card that supports LISP.

Table 1-9 shows the comparison between F-Series modules.

Table 1-9   Nexus 7000 and Nexus 7700 F-Series Modules Comparison

	N7KF248XP-25	N7KF248XP-25	N7KF248XT-25E	N7KF312FQ-25	N77-F248XP-23E	N77-F348XP-23	N77-F324FQ-25	N77-F312CK-26
Line Card Family	F2	F2e	F2e	F3	F2e	F3	F3	F3
Chassis Supported	Cisco Nexus 7000	Cisco Nexus 7000	Cisco Nexus 7000	Cisco Nexus 7000	Cisco Nexus 7700	Cisco Nexus 7700	Cisco Nexus 7700	Cisco Nexus 7700
Ports (Number and Type)	48 ports, 1 and 10GE	48 ports, 1 and 10GE	48 ports, 1 and 10GE	11-port 40GE	11-port 40GE	48-port 1 and 10GE	24-port 40GE	11-port 100GE
Interface Type	SFP, SFP+	SFP, SFP+	RJ-45	QSFP+, Bi-Di	SFP, SFP+	SFP, SFP+	QSFP+, Bi-Di	Cisco CPAK
Fabric Bandwidth (Gbps)	480	480	480	480	480	480	960	1200
Performance (Mpps)	720	720	720	720	720	720	1440	1800
NetFlow	Sampled	Sampled	Sampled	Sampled	Sampled	Sampled	Sampled	Sampled
FEX Support	Yes	Yes	Yes	Yes	Yes	Yes	Yes	Yes
vPC Support	Yes	Yes	Yes	Yes	Yes	Yes	Yes	Yes
FabricPath Support	Yes	Yes	Yes	Yes	Yes	Yes	Yes	Yes
Layer 3 Interface	Yes	Yes	Yes	Yes	Yes	Yes	Yes	Yes
FCoE, FabricPath Support	Yes	Yes	Yes	Yes	Yes	Yes	Yes	Yes
OTV, LISP, MPLS	No	No	No	Yes	No	Yes	Yes	Yes
M-Series Interoperability in Same VDC	No	Yes	Yes	Yes	N/A	N/A	N/A	N/A

Key Topic

Cisco Nexus 7000 and Nexus 7700 Series Power Supply Options

The Nexus 7000 and Nexus 7700 use power supplies with +90% power supply efficiency, reducing power wasted as heat and reducing associated data center cooling requirements. The switches offer different types of redundancy modes. They offer visibility into the actual power consumption of the total system, as well as modules enabling accurate power consumption monitoring, for the right sizing of power supplies, UPSs, and environmental cooling. Variable-speed fans adjust dynamically to lower power consumption and optimize system cooling for true load.

- **Power redundancy:** Multiple system-level options for maximum data center availability.
- **Fully hot-swappable:** Continuous system operations; no downtime in replacing power supplies.
- **Internal fault monitoring:** Detects component defect and shuts down unit.
- **Temperature measurement:** Prevents damage due to overheating (every ASIC on the board has a temperature sensor).
- **Real-time power draw:** Shows real-time power consumption.
- **Variable fan speed:** Automatically adjusts to changing thermal characteristics; lower fan speeds use lower power.

Cisco Nexus 7000 and Nexus 7700 Series 3.0kW AC Power Supply Module

The 3.0kW AC power supply shown in Figure 1-30 is designed only for the Nexus 7004 chassis and is used across all the Nexus 7700 Series chassis. It is a single 20-ampere (A) AC input power supply. When connecting to high line nominal voltage (220 VAC) it will produce a power output of 3000W; connecting to low line nominal voltage (110 VAC) will produce a power output of 1400W.

Figure 1-30   *Cisco Nexus 7000 3.0kW AC Power Supply*

NOTE   Although the Nexus 7700 chassis and the Nexus 7004 use a common power supply architecture, different PIDs are used on each platform. Therefore, if you interchange the power supplies, the system will log an error complaining about the wrong power supply in the system; although technically this might work, it is not officially supported by Cisco.

Cisco Nexus 7000 and Nexus 7700 Series 3.0kW DC Power Supply Module

The 3.0kW DC power supply shown in Figure 1-31 is designed only for the Nexus 7004 chassis and is used across all the Nexus 7700 Series chassis. The Nexus 3.0kW DC power supply has two isolated input stages, each delivering up to 1500W of output power. Each stage uses a –48V DC connection. The unit will deliver 1551W when only one input is active and 3051W when two inputs are active.

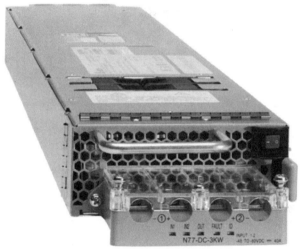

Figure 1-31   *Cisco Nexus 7000 3.0kW DC Power Supply*

Cisco Nexus 7000 Series 6.0kW and 7.5kW AC Power Supply Modules

The 6.0kW and 7.5kW power supplies shown in Figure 1-32 are common across Nexus 7009, 7010, and 7018. They allow mixed-mode AC and DC operation, enabling migration without disruption and providing support for dual environments with unreliable AC power, with battery backup capability.

6kW Dual 20A AC (110/220V)

7.5kW Dual 30A AC (Fixed Cables)

Figure 1-32 *Cisco Nexus 7000 6.0kW and 7.5kW Power Supplies*

Table 1-10 shows the specifications of both power supplies with different numbers of inputs and input types.

Table 1-10   Nexus 7000 and Nexus 7700 6.0kW and 7.5kW Power Supply Specifications

Power Supply Type	Number of Inputs	Input Power	Output
6.0kW	Single input	220V	3000W
		110V	1200W
	Dual input	220V	6000W
		110V	2400W
	Dual input	110 and 220V	4200W
7.5kW	Single input	220V	3750W
	Dual input	220V	7500W

Cisco Nexus 7000 Series 6.0kW DC Power Supply Module

The 6kW DC power supply shown in Figure 1-33 is common to the 7009, 7010, and 7018 systems. The 6kW has four isolated input stages, each delivering up to 1500W of power (6000W total on full load) with peak efficiency of 91% (high for a DC power supply). The power supply can be used in combination with AC units or as an all DC setup. It supports the same operational characteristics as the AC units:

- Redundancy modes (N+1 and N+N)
- Real-time power—actual power levels
- Single input mode (3000W)
- Online insertion and removal
- Integrated lock and On/Off switch (for easy removal)

Figure 1-33 *Cisco Nexus 7000 6.0kW DC Power Supply*

Multiple power redundancy modes can be configured by the user:

- Combined mode, where the total power available is the sum of the outputs of all the power supplies installed. (This is not redundant.)
- PSU redundancy, where the total power available is the sum of all power supplies minus one, otherwise commonly called N+1 redundancy.
- Grid redundancy, where the total power available is the sum of the power from only one input on each PSU. Each PSU has two supply inputs, allowing them to be connected to separate isolated A/C supplies. In the event of an A/C supply failure, 50% of power is secure.
- Full redundancy, which is the combination of PSU redundancy and grid redundancy. You can lose one power supply or one grid; in most cases this will be the same as grid redundancy.

Full redundancy provides the highest level of redundancy, so it is recommended. However, it is always better to choose the mode of power supply operation based on the requirements and needs.

An example of each mode is shown in Figure 1-34.

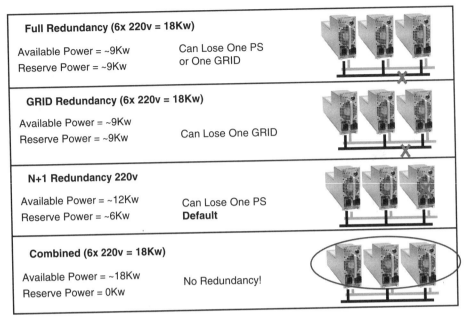

Figure 1-34 *Nexus 6.0kW Power Redundancy Modes*

To help with planning for the power requirements, Cisco has made a power calculator that can be used as a starting point. It is worth mentioning that the power calculator cannot be taken as a final power recommendation.

The power calculator can be found at http://www.cisco.com/go/powercalculator.

Cisco Nexus 6000 Product Family

The Cisco Nexus 6000 product family is a high-performance, high-density, low-latency 1G/10G/40G/FCoE Ethernet port. When using the unified module on the Nexus 6004, you can get native FC as well. Multiple models are available: Nexus 6001T, Nexus 6001P, Nexus 6004EF, and Nexus 6004X. Table 1-11 describes the difference between the Nexus 6000 models.

Table 1-11   Nexus 6000 Product Specification

	Nexus 6001P/Nexus 6001T	Nexus 6004EF/Nexus 6004X
Switch Fabric Throughput	1.28 Tbps	7.68 Tbps
Port-to-Port Latency	~1.0 microseconds for Nexus 6001P ~3.3 microseconds for Nexus 6001T	~ 1.0 microseconds
Layer 3 Capability	Integrated line-rate	Integrated line-rate

	Nexus 6001P/Nexus 6001T	Nexus 6004EF/Nexus 6004X
Switch Footprint	1RU	4RU
10 Gigabit Ethernet Port Density	64	384
40 Gigabit Ethernet Port Density	4 True 40 G	96 True 40 G
Unified Ports	—	48
1 Gigabit Ethernet FEX Port Scalability	1152	2304
10 Gigabit Ethernet FEX Port Scalability	1152	2304
Packet Buffer	25MB per 3 x 40G (or 12 x 10G)	25MB per 3 x 40G (or 12 x 10G)

NOTE   At the time this chapter was written, the Nexus 6004X was renamed Nexus 5696Q.

Cisco Nexus 6001P and Nexus 6001T Switches and Features

The Nexus 6001P is a fixed configuration 1RU Ethernet switch. It provides 48 1G/10G SFP+ ports and four 40G Ethernet QSFP+ ports. Port-to-port latency is around 1 microsecond. It provides integrated Layer 2 and Layer 3 at wire speed.

It offers two choices of airflow: front-to-back (port side exhaust) and back-to-front (port side intake). Each 40GE port can be split into four 10GE ports; this can be done by using a QSFP+ break-out cable (Twinax or Fiber).

The Nexus 6001T is a fixed configuration 1RU Ethernet switch. It provides 48 1G/10G BASE-T ports and four 40G Ethernet QSFP+ ports; port-to-port latency is around 3.3 microseconds. It provides integrated Layer 2 and Layer 3 at wire speed. It offers two choices of air flow: front-to-back (port side exhaust) and back-to-front (port side intake). Each 40GE port can be split into four 10GE ports. The split can be done by using a QSFP+ break-out cable (Twinax or Fiber). Nexus 6001T supports FCOE on the RJ-45 ports for up to 30M when CAT 6, 6a, or 7 cables are used. Both switches are shown in Figure 1-35.

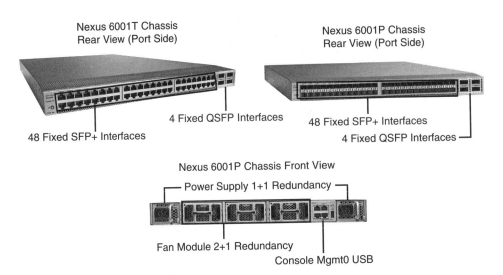

Nexus 6001T Chassis
Rear View (Port Side)

Nexus 6001P Chassis
Rear View (Port Side)

4 Fixed QSFP Interfaces

48 Fixed SFP+ Interfaces

48 Fixed SFP+ Interfaces

4 Fixed QSFP Interfaces

Nexus 6001P Chassis Front View

Power Supply 1+1 Redundancy

Fan Module 2+1 Redundancy

Console Mgmt0 USB

Figure 1-35 *Cisco Nexus 6001 Switches*

Cisco Nexus 6004 Switch's Features

The Nexus 6004 is shown in Figure 1-36. Currently, there are two models: the Nexus 6004EF and the Nexus 6004X. The main difference is that the Nexus 6004X supports Virtual Extensible LAN (VXLAN). The Nexus 6004 is a 4RU 10G/40G Ethernet switch; it offers eight line card expansion module (LEM) slots. There are two choices of LEMs: 11-port 10G/40G QSFP and 20-port unified ports offering either 1G/10G SFP+ or 2/4/8 G FC. The Nexus 6004 offers integrated Layer 2 and Layer 3 at wire rate. Port-to-port latency is approximately 1 microsecond for any packet size. It offers up to 96 40G QSFP ports and up to 384 10G SFP+ ports.

- Up to 8 Expansion Modules
- Any Module On Any Slot

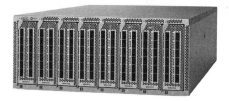

- 12p 40G QSFP+
- Flexibility to Use 40G or 4X10G Mode
- Support for QSA Adapter, BiDi Optics

Redundant 3+3 or 1+1 AC Power Supplies
Airflow: F2B and B2F Options

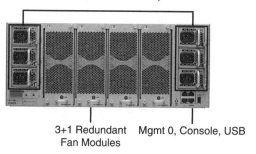

3+1 Redundant   Mgmt 0, Console, USB
Fan Modules

- 20p 10G SFP+ Unified Ports
- Support for Ethernet, FCoE, FC
- FC Support 2/4/8G FC

Figure 1-36 *Nexus 6004 Switch*

NOTE The Nexus 6004 can support 1G ports using a QSA converter (QSFP to SFP adapter) on a QSFP interface. This converts each QSFP+ port to one SFP+ port. The SFP+ can support both 10G and 1GE transceivers.

Cisco Nexus 6000 Switches Licensing Options

Different types of licenses are required for the Nexus 6000. Table 1-12 describes each license and the features it enables. It is worth mentioning that Nexus switches have a grace period, which is the amount of time the features in a license package can continue functioning without a license, enabling a licensed feature that does not have a license key to start a counter on the grace period. You then have 120 days to install the appropriate license keys, disable the use of that feature, or disable the grace period feature. If at the end of the 120-day grace period the device does not have a valid license key for the feature, the Cisco NX-OS software automatically disables the feature and removes the configuration from the device.

Table 1-12   Nexus 6000 Licensing Options

Feature License	Product ID	Features
FabricPath Services Package ENHANCED_LAYER2_PKG	N6001-EL1-SSK9 N6004-EL1-SSK9	FabricPath
FCoE NPV Package FCOE_NPV_PKG	N6K-FNPV-SSK9	FCoE NPV
Layer 3 Base Services Package LAN_BASE_SERVICES_PKG	N6K-BAS1K9	Unlimited static routes and maximum of 256 dynamic routes Static routes RIPv2 OSPFv2 and OSPFv3 EIGRP HSRP 2 VRRP 3 IGMP v2/v3 PIMv2 (sparse mode) Routed ACL uRPF MSDP
Layer 3 Enterprise Services Package LAN_ENTERPRISE_ SERVICES_PKG	N6001-LAN1K9 N6004-LAN1K9	N6001-LAN1K9/N6004-LAN1K9 includes the following features in addition to the ones under the N6KBAS1K9 license: BGP VRF Lite PBR PIMv2 (all modes) L3 IS-IS 6

Feature License	Product ID	Features
Storage Protocols Services Package FC_FEATURES_PKG ENTERPRISE_PKG VM-FEX Package	N6001-16P-SSK9 N6004-4Q-SSK9 N6004-12Q-SSK9 N6K-16P-SSK97 N6K-20P-SSK98 N6001-64P-SSK9 N6004-96Q-SSK9 N6K-VMFEXK9	Native Fibre Channel FCoE FC NPV FC Port Security Fabric Binding Fibre Channel Security Protocol (FCSP) authentication VM-FEX

There is also an evaluation license, which is a temporary license. Evaluation licenses are time bound (valid for a specified number of days) and are tied to a host ID (device serial number).

NOTE   To manage the Nexus 6000, two types of licenses are needed: the DCNM LAN and DCNM SAN. Each of them is a separate license.

Cisco Nexus 5500 and Nexus 5600 Product Family

The Cisco Nexus 5000 product family is a Layer 2 and Layer 3 1G/10G Ethernet with unified ports; it includes Cisco Nexus 5500 and Cisco Nexus 5600 platforms. Table 1-13 shows the comparison between different models.

Table 1-13   Nexus 5500 and Nexus 5600 Product Specification

	Cisco Nexus 5548P	Cisco Nexus 5548UP	Cisco Nexus 5596UP	Cisco Nexus 5596T	Cisco Nexus 5672UP	Cisco Nexus 56128P
Rack Unit (RU)	1	1	2	2	1	2
Switching Capacity	960 Gbps	960 Gbps	1.92 Tbps	1.92 Tbps	1.44 Tbps	2.56 Tbps
Expansion Slots	1	1	3	3	None	2
Fixed, Built-in Ports	32	32	48	48	48	48
1/10GE, 10Gbps FCoE Port Density	Up to 48	Up to 48	Up to 96	Up to 96	Up to 72	Up to 128
1/10G BASE-T	None	None	None	Up to 68	None	None

	Cisco Nexus 5548P	Cisco Nexus 5548UP	Cisco Nexus 5596UP	Cisco Nexus 5596T	Cisco Nexus 5672UP	Cisco Nexus 56128P
40GE Uplinks	Up to 4 (through Expansion module)	Up to 4 (through expansion module)	Up to 4 (through expansion module)	Up to 4 (through expansion module)	6	Up to 8 (through expansion module)
Fibre Channel Port Density (8/4/2/1 Gbps)	Up to 16 (through expansion module)	Up to 48	Up to 96	Up to 64	16	Up to 48 (through expansion modules only)
160Gbps Layer 3 Routing Engine	Daughter card	Daughter card	Expansion module	Expansion module	Native line rate L3	Native line rate L3
Fabric Extender Support	Yes, up to 24	Yes, up to 24	Yes, up to 24	Yes, up to 24	Yes, up to 24 (L2, L3)	Yes, up to 24 (L2, L3)
Hot Swappable Power Supplies and Fan Trays	Yes	Yes	Yes	Yes	Yes	Yes
Air Flow	Front-back (port side exhaust)	Front-back (port side exhaust) and back-front (port side inlet)	Front-back (port side exhaust) and back-front (port side inlet)	Front-back (port side exhaust) and back-front (port side inlet)	Front-back (port side exhaust) and back-front (port side inlet)	Front-back (port side exhaust) and back-front (port side inlet)
VXLAN	N	N	N	N	Y	Y

> **NOTE** The Nexus 5010 and 5020 switches are considered end-of-sale products, so they are not covered in this book. Refer to www.cisco.com for more information.

Cisco Nexus 5548P and 5548UP Switches' Features

The Nexus 5548P and the Nexus 5548UP are 1/10Gbps switches with one expansion module. The Nexus 5548P has all the 32 ports as 1/10Gbps Ethernet only. The Nexus 5548UP has the 32 ports as unified ports, meaning that the ports can run 1/10 Gbps or they can run 8/4/2/1 Gbps native FC or a mix between both. Figure 1-37 shows the layout for them.

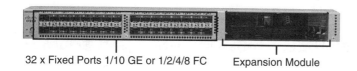

32 x Fixed Ports 1/10 GE or 1/2/4/8 FC   Expansion Module

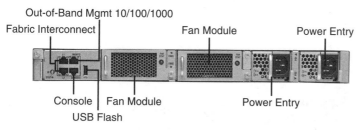

Figure 1-37   *Nexus 5548P and Nexus 5548UP Switches*

Cisco Nexus 5596UP and 5596T Switches' Features

The Nexus 5596T shown in Figure 1-38 is a 2RU 1/10Gbps Ethernet, native Fibre Channel, and FCoE switch. It has 32 fixed ports of 10G BASE-T and 16 fixed ports of SFP+. The switch has three expansion modules; the switch supports unified ports on all SFP+ ports; the 10G BASE-T ports support FCoE up to 30m with Category 6a and Category 7 cables.

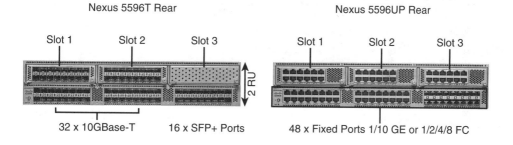

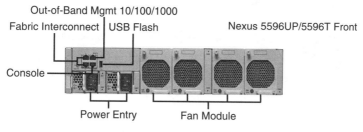

Figure 1-38   *Nexus 5596UP and Nexus 5596T Switches*

Cisco Nexus 5500 Products' Expansion Modules

You can have additional Ethernet and FCoE ports or native Fibre Channel ports with the Nexus 5500 products by adding expansion modules. The Nexus 5548P/5548UP has one expansion module, and the Nexus 5596UP/5596T has three.

The Cisco N55-M16P module shown in Figure 1-39 has 16 ports, 1/10Gbps Ethernet, and FCoE using SFP+ interfaces.

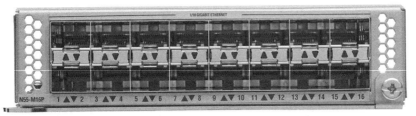

Figure 1-39   *Cisco N55-M16P Expansion Module*

The Cisco N55-M8P8FP module shown in Figure 1-40 is a 16-port module. It has eight ports, 1/10Gbps Ethernet, and FCoE using SFP+ interfaces, and eight 8/4/2/1Gbps Native Fibre Channel ports using SFP+ and SFP interfaces.

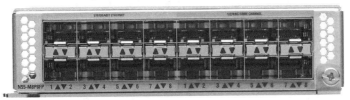

Figure 1-40   *Cisco N55-M8P8FP Expansion Module*

The Cisco N55-M16UP shown in Figure 1-41 is a 16 unified ports module. It has 16 ports, 1/10Gbps Ethernet, and FCoE using SFP+ interfaces, or up to 16 8/4/2/1-Gbps Native Fibre Channel ports using SFP+ and SFP interfaces.

Figure 1-41   *Cisco N55-M16UP Expansion Module*

The Cisco N55-M4Q shown in Figure 1-42 is a 4-port 40Gbps Ethernet module. Each QSFP 40GE port can only work in 4x10G mode and supports DCB and FCoE.

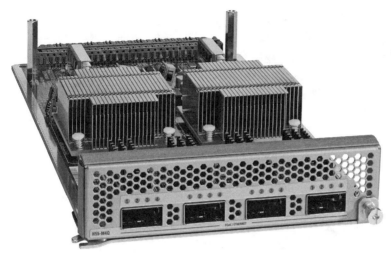

Four Ports QSFP+ GEM

Figure 1-42   *Cisco N55-M4Q Expansion Module*

The Cisco N55-M12T, shown in Figure 1-43, is an 11-port 10Gbps BASE-T module; it supports FCoE up to 30m on category 6a and category 7 cables. This module is supported only in the Nexus 5596T.

12 x 10GBase-T Ports GEM Module

Figure 1-43   *Cisco N55-M12T Expansion Module*

The Cisco 5500 Layer 3 daughter card shown in Figure 1-44 is used to enable Layer 3 on the Nexus 5548P and 5548UP, which can be ordered with the system, or it is field upgradable as a spare. This daughter card provides 160 Gbps of Layer 3 forwarding (240 million packets per second, or mpps), which is shared among all 48 ports.

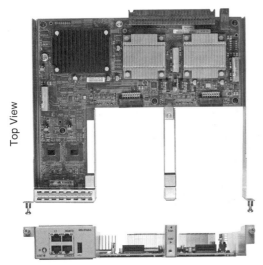

Figure 1-44 *Cisco Nexus 5548P and 5548UP Layer 3 Daughter Card*

To install the Layer 3 module, you must replace the Layer 2 I/O module, power off the switch, and follow the steps as shown in Figure 1-45. There is no need to remove the switch from the rack.

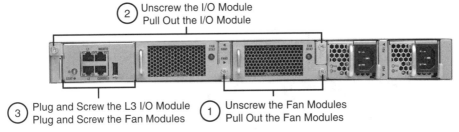

Figure 1-45 *Cisco Nexus 5548P and 5548UP Layer 3 Daughter Card Upgrade Procedure*

To enable Layer 3 on the Nexus 5596P and 5596UP, you must have a Layer 3 expansion module, which can be ordered with the system or as a spare. This daughter card provides 160Gbps of Layer 3 forwarding (240 million packets per second, [mpps]), which is shared among all 48 ports. Figure 1-46 shows the Layer 3 expansion module; currently, you can have only one Layer 3 expansion module per Nexus 5596P and 5596UP.

Enabling Layer 3 affects the scalability limits for the Nexus 5500. For example, the maximum FEXs per Cisco Nexus 5500 Series switches is 24 with Layer 2 only. Enabling Layer 3 makes the supported number per Nexus 5500 to be 16. Verify the scalability limits based on the NX-OS you will be using before creating a design.

Figure 1-46   *Cisco Nexus 5596UP Layer 3 Daughter Card Upgrade Procedure*

Cisco Nexus 5600 Product Family

The Nexus 5600 is the new generation of the Nexus 5000 switches. The Nexus 5600 has two models: Nexus 5672UP and Nexus 56128P. Both models bring integrated L2 and L3, 1-microsecond port-to-port latency with all frame sizes, true 40Gbps flow, 40Gbps FCoE, cut-through switching for 10/40Gbps, and 25MB buffer per port ASIC. Table 1-14 shows the summary of the features.

Table 1-14   Nexus 5600 Product Switches Feature

	Nexus 5600-72UP	Nexus 5600-128P
Switch Fabric Throughput	1.44 Tbps	2.56 Tbps
Port-to-Port Latency	~ 1.0 microsecond	~ 1.0 microsecond
Layer 3 Capability	Integrated line rate	Integrated line rate
Switch Footprint	1RU	2RU
10 Gigabit Ethernet Port Density	72	128
40 Gigabit Ethernet Port Density	6	8
	True 40G	True 40G
Unified Ports	Yes	Yes
1 Gigabit Ethernet FEX Port Scalability	1152	1152
10 Gigabit Ethernet FEX Port Scalability	1152	1152
Packet Buffer	25 MB per 3 x 40G (or 12 x 10G)	25 MB per 3 x 40 G (or 12 x 10 G)

Cisco Nexus 5672UP Switch Features

The Nexus 5672UP shown in Figure 1-47 has 48 fixed 1/10Gbps SFP+ ports, of which 16 ports are unified, meaning that the ports can run 8/4/2Gbps Fibre Channel as well as 10 Gigabit Ethernet and FCoE connectivity options. True 40Gbps ports use QSFP+ for Ethernet/FCOE. The switch has two redundant power supplies and three fan modules. The switch supports both port-side exhaust and port-side intake.

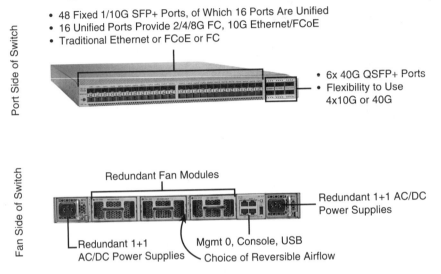

Figure 1-47   *Cisco Nexus 5672UP*

Cisco Nexus 56128P Switch Features

The Cisco Nexus 56128P shown in Figure 1-48 is a 2RU switch. It has 48 fixed 1/10Gbps Ethernet SFP+ ports and four 40Gbps QSFP+ ports. The 48 fixed SFP+ ports and four 40Gbps QSFP+ ports support FCOE as well. The Cisco Nexus 56128P has two expansion modules that support 24 unified ports.

The 24 unified ports provide 8/4/2Gbps Fibre Channel as well as 10 Gigabit Ethernet and FCoE connectivity options, plus two 40Gbps ports. It has four N+N redundant, hot-swappable power supplies; four N+1 redundant, hot-swappable independent fans; and a management and console interface on the fan side of the switch.

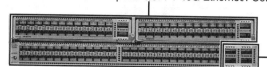

- 48 Fixed 10G SFP+ Ports
- Two Expansion Slots
- Expansion module provides 24 ports 10G Ethernet/FCoE
  or 2/4/8G FC and 2 ports QSFP+ 40G Ethernet/FCoE.

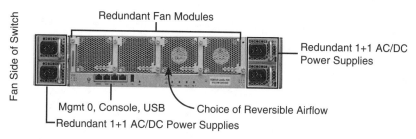

Port Side of Switch

Base Chassis
- 4x 40G QSFP+ Ports
- Flexibility to Use 4x10
  or 40G
- Up to 4 x 40G Ports and
  96x 10G Ports

Fan Side of Switch

Redundant Fan Modules

Redundant 1+1 AC/DC
Power Supplies

Mgmt 0, Console, USB — Choice of Reversible Airflow

Redundant 1+1 AC/DC Power Supplies

Figure 1-48   *Cisco Nexus 56128P*

Cisco Nexus 5600 Expansion Modules

Expansion modules enable the Cisco Nexus 5600 switches to support unified ports with native Fibre Channel connectivity. The Nexus 56128P currently supports one expansion module—the N56-M24UP2Q expansion module, as shown in Figure 1-49. That module provides 24 ports, 10G Ethernet/FCoE or 2/4/8G Fibre Channel, and two 40 Gigabit QSFP+ Ethernet/FCoE ports.

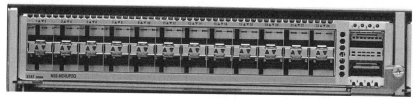

Figure 1-49   *Cisco Nexus 56128P Unified Port Expansion Module*

Cisco Nexus 5500 and Nexus 5600 Licensing Options

Different types of licenses are required for the Nexus 5500 and Nexus 5600. Table 1-15 describes each license and the features it enables. Nexus switches have a grace period, which is the amount of time the features in a license package can continue functioning without a license. Enabling a licensed feature that does not have a license key starts a counter on the grace period. You then have 120 days to install the appropriate license keys, disable the use of that feature, or disable the grace period feature. If at the end of the 120-day grace period the device does not have a valid license key for the feature, the Cisco NX-OS software automatically disables the feature and removes the configuration from the device. There is also an evaluation license, which is a temporary license. Evaluation licenses are time bound (valid for a specified number of days) and are tied to a host ID (device serial number).

Table 1-15   Nexus 5500 Product Licensing

Feature License	Product ID	Features
FabricPath Services Package	N5548-EL1-SSK9	FabricPath
ENHANCED_LAYER2_PKG	N5596-EL1-SSK9 N5671-EL1-SSK9 N56128-EL1-SSK9	
FCoE NPV Package FCOE_NPV_PKG	N5548-FNPV-SSK9 N5596-FNPV-SSK9 N56-FNPV-SSK9	FCoE NPV
Layer 3 Base Services Package LAN_BASE_SERVICES_PKG 15	N55-BAS1K9 N56-BAS1K9	Unlimited static routes and maximum of 256 dynamic routes: ■ Static routes ■ RIPv2 ■ OSPFv2 and OSPFv3 ■ EIGRP ■ HSRP ■ VRRP ■ IGMP v2/v3 ■ PIMv2 (sparse mode) ■ Routed ACL ■ NAT ■ MSDP ■ Static routes ■ RIPv2 ■ OSPFv2 and OSPFv3
Layer 3 Enterprise Services Package LAN_ENTERPRISE_SERVICES_PKG 1819	N55-LAN1K9 N56-LAN1K9	N55-LAN1K9 includes the following features in addition to the ones under N55-BAS1K9 license: BGP ■ VRF Lite ■ PBR ■ PIMv2 (all modes) L3 IS-IS
Storage Protocols Services Package	N55-8P-SSK9	Native Fibre Channel

Feature License	Product ID	Features
FC_FEATURES_PKG	N55-48P-SSK9	■ FCoE
ENTERPRISE_PKG	N56-16p-SSK9	■ NPV
	N5671-72P-SSK9	■ FC Port Security
	N56128-128P-SSK9	■ Fabric Binding
	N55-8P-SSK9	Fibre Channel Security Protocol (FC-SP) authentication
VM-FEX Package	N55-VMFEXK9	VM-FEX

NOTE   To manage the Nexus 5500 and Nexus 5600, two types of licenses are needed: the DCNM LAN and DCNM SAN. Each is a separate license.

Cisco Nexus 3000 Product Family

The Nexus 3000 switches are part of the Cisco Unified Fabric architecture; they offer high performance and high density at ultra low latency. The Nexus 3000 switches are 1RU server access switches. This product family consists of multiple switch models: the Nexus 3000 Series, Nexus 3100 Series, and Nexus 3500 switches.

The Nexus 3000 Series consists of five models: Nexus 3064X, Nexus 3064-32T, Nexus 3064T, Nexus 3016Q, and 3048; they are shown in Figure 1-50. All of them offer wire rate Layer 2 and Layer 3 on all ports, and ultra low latency. These are compact 1RU 1/10/40Gbps Ethernet switches. Table 1-16 provides a comparison and specifications of these different models.

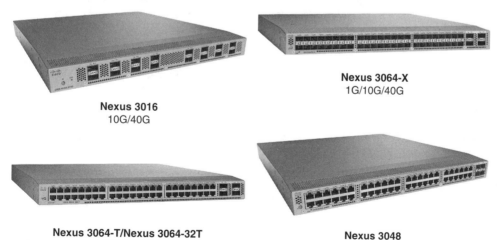

Nexus 3016
10G/40G

Nexus 3064-X
1G/10G/40G

Nexus 3064-T/Nexus 3064-32T
1G/10GT/40G

Nexus 3048
10M/100M/1G

Figure 1-50   *Cisco Nexus 3000 Switches*

Table 1-16 Nexus 3000 Product Model Comparison

	Cisco Nexus 3064X	Cisco Nexus 3064-32T	Cisco Nexus 3064-32T	Cisco Nexus 3016Q	Cisco Nexus 3048
VXLAN Capability	No	No	No	No	No
Openflow Support	Yes	Yes	Yes	Yes	Yes
Cisco OnePK Support	Yes	Yes	Yes	Yes	Yes
Rack Unit (RU)	1	1	1	1	1
Switching Capacity	1.28 Tbps	960 Gbps	1.28 Tbps	1.28 Tbps	176 Gbps
Interface Type	48 SFP+ and 4 QSFP+	32 RJ-45 and 4 QSFP+	48 RJ-45 and 4 QSFP+	16 QSFP+	48 RJ-45 and 4 SFP+
Maximum 1GE Ports	48	32 enabled (48 maximum)	48	0	Up to 48
Maximum 10GE Ports	Up to 64 (48 fixed; 16 using 4 QSFP-to-SFP+ cables)	32 10G BASE-T and 16 using 4 QSFP-to-SFP+ cables are enabled; additional 16 ports with a license	Up to 64 (48 fixed; 16 using 4 QSFP-to-SFP+ cables)	Up to 64 (using 16 QSFP-to-SFP+ cables)	4
Maximum 40GE Ports	Up to 4	4	4	Up to 16	0
Switch Latency	Submicrosecond	3 to 4 Microseconds	3 to 4 Microseconds	Submicrosecond	2.7 to 7.2 Microseconds
Line-Rate Traffic Throughput (Both Layer 2 and 3) on All Ports	Yes	Yes	Yes	Yes	Yes
Redundant and Hot-Swappable Power Supply and Fans	Yes	Yes	Yes	Yes	Yes
Air Flow	Front-back and back-front	Front-back and back-front	Front-back and back-front	Front-back and back-front	Front-back and back-front

The Nexus 3100 switches have four models: Nexus 3132Q, Nexus 3164Q, Nexus 3172PQ, and Nexus 3172TQ. Shown in Figure 1-51, all of them offer wire rate Layer 2 and Layer 3 on all ports and ultra low latency. These are compact 1RU 1/10/40Gbps Ethernet switches.

Table 1-17 provides a comparison and the specifications of the different models.

Nexus 3132Q

Nexus 3172PQ

Nexus 3172TQ

Nexus 3164Q

Figure 1-51 *Cisco Nexus 3100 Switches*

Table 1-17 Nexus 3100 Product Model Comparison

	Cisco Nexus 3132Q	Cisco Nexus 3164Q	Cisco Nexus 3172PQ	Cisco Nexus 3172TQ
Virtual Extensible LAN (VXLAN) Capable	Yes	Yes	Yes	Yes
Openflow Support	Yes	Yes	Yes	Yes
OnePK Support	Yes	Yes	Yes	Yes
Rack Unit (RU)	1	2	1	1
Switching Capacity	1280 Gbps	5120 Gbps	720 Gbps	720 Gbps
Interface Type	32 QSFP+	64 QSFP+	48 SFP+ and 6 QSFP+	48 RJ-45 and 6 Quad Small Form-Factor Pluggable Plus (QSFP+)
Maximum 1 Gigabit Ethernet (GE) Ports	4	None	48	48
Maximum 10GE Ports	104	256 (coming shortly with software release)	72	72

	Cisco Nexus 3132Q	Cisco Nexus 3164Q	Cisco Nexus 3172PQ	Cisco Nexus 3172TQ
Maximum 40GE Ports	32	64	6	6
Line-Rate Traffic Throughput (Both Layer 2 and 3) on All Ports	Yes	Yes	Yes	Yes
Redundant and Hot-Swappable Power Supply and Fans	Yes	Yes	Yes	Yes
Air Flow	Port-side intake or port-side exhaust	Port-side intake	Port-side intake or port-side exhaust	Port-side intake or port-side exhaust

The Nexus 3500 switches have two models: Nexus 3524 and Nexus 3548. They are shown in Figure 1-52. Both offer wire rate Layer 2 and Layer 3 on all ports and ultra low latency. These are compact 1RU 1/10Gbps Ethernet switches. Table 1-18 gives a comparison and specifications of the different models.

Nexus 3524

Nexus 3548

Figure 1-52 *Cisco Nexus 3500 Switches*

Table 1-18   Nexus 3500 Product Model Comparison

	Cisco Nexus 3524	Cisco Nexus 3548
Algo Boost-Capable (NAT, Active Buffer Monitoring)	Yes	Yes
VXLAN Capable	No	No
Openflow Support	No	No
OnePK Support	No	No
Rack Unit (RU)	1	1
Switching Capacity	480 Gbps	480 Gbps
Interface Type	24 SFP+	48 SFP+
Maximum 1GE ports	24 enabled (48 max)	48
Maximum 10GE ports	24 10G SFP+ ports; additional 24 ports via license	48

	Cisco Nexus 3524	Cisco Nexus 3548
Maximum 40 GE ports	0	0
Switch Latency	Sub–250 nanoseconds	Sub–250 nanoseconds
Line-Rate Traffic Throughput (Both Layer 2 and 3) on All Ports	Yes	Yes
Redundant and Hot-Swappable Power Supply and Fans	Yes	Yes
Air Flow	Front-back and back-front	Front-back and back-front

NOTE The Nexus 3524 and the Nexus 3548 support a forwarding mode called warp mode, which uses a hardware technology called Algo boost. Algo boost provides ultra-low latency—as low as 190 nanoseconds (ns). Both are very well suited for high-performance trading and high-performance computing environments.

Cisco Nexus 3000 Licensing Options

There are different types of licenses for the Nexus 3000. It is worth mentioning that the Nexus 3000 doesn't support the grace period feature. Table 1-19 shows the license options.

Table 1-19 Nexus 3000 Licensing Options

Feature License	Product ID	Features
Layer 3 Base Services Package LAN_BASE_SERVICES_PKG	N3548-BAS1K9	Static routing RIPv2 EIGRP stub OSPFv2 (limited routes) PIMv2 (sparse mode)
Layer 3 Enterprise Services Package LAN_ENTERPRISE_SERVICES_PKG	N3548-LAN1K9	OSPF (unlimited routes) BGP and VRF-lite (IP-VPN) **Note:** Requires Base Services Package.
Cisco Nexus 3500 Algo Boost License ALGO_BOOST_SERVICES_PKG	N3548-ALGK9	Warp Mode Warp SPAN Static NAT

Feature License	Product ID	Features
Layer 3 Base Services Package LAN_BASE_SERVICES_PKG	N3K-BAS1K9	Static routing RIPv2 EIGRP stub OSPFv2 (limited routes) PIMv2 (sparse mode) **Note:** The Cisco Nexus 3164 switch supports a base-level Layer 3 feature set by default and does not require the Layer 3 Base Services Package license.
Layer 3 Enterprise Services Package	N3K-LAN1K9	OSPF (unlimited routes) EIGRP (unlimited routes) BGP VXLAN (Cisco Nexus 3164 only) **Note:** The Layer 3 Base Services Package license is a prerequisite for the Layer 3 Enterprise Services Package license on all Cisco Nexus 3000 Series switches except the Cisco Nexus 3164 switch.

Cisco Nexus 2000 Fabric Extenders Product Family

The Cisco Nexus 2000 Fabric Extenders behave as remote line cards. They appear as an extension to the parent switch to which they connect. The parent switch can be Nexus 5000, Nexus 6000, Nexus 7000, and Nexus 9000 Series switches. Using Nexus 2000 gives you great flexibility when it comes to the type of connectivity and physical topology. This type of architecture provides the flexibility and benefit of both architectures: top-of-rack (ToR) and end-of-row (EoR). It also enables highly scalable servers access design without the dependency on spanning tree. All Nexus 2000 Fabric Extenders connected to the same parent switch are managed from a single point. Figure 1-53 shows both types, ToR and EoR.

As shown in Figure 1-53, Rack-01 is using a dual-redundant Cisco Nexus 2000 Series Fabric Extender, which is placed at the top of the rack. The uplink ports on the Cisco Nexus 2000 Series Fabric Extenders can be connected to a Cisco Nexus 5000, Nexus 6000, Cisco Nexus 7000, or Nexus 9000 Series switch that is installed in the EoR position as the parent switch.

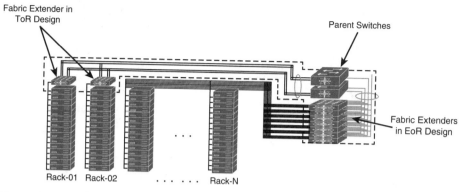

Figure 1-53   *Cisco Nexus 2000 Top-of-Rack and End-of-Row Design*

This is a ToR design from a cabling point of view, but from an operation point of view this design looks like an EoR design, because all these Nexus 2000 Fabric Extenders will be managed from the parent switch. So no configuration or software maintenance tasks need to be done with the FEXs. The cabling between the servers and the Cisco Nexus 2000 Series Fabric Extenders is contained within the rack, thus reducing cabling between racks. Only the cables between the Nexus 2000 and the parent switches will run between the racks, which can be 10 Gbps or 40 Gbps.

Multiple connectivity options can be used to connect the FEX to the parent switch, as shown in Figure 1-54, which is explained shortly.

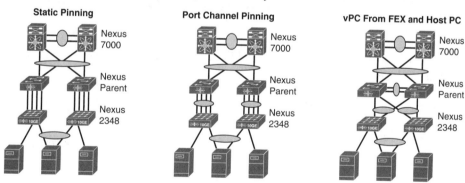

Figure 1-54   *Cisco Nexus 2000 Connectivity Options*

- **Straight-through, using static pinning:** To achieve a deterministic relationship between the host port on the FEX to which the server connects and the fabric interfaces that connect to the parent switch, the host port will be statically pinned to one of the uplinks between the FEX and the parent switch. This method is used when the FEX is connected straight through to the parent switch. The server port will always use the same uplink port.

- You must use the **pinning max-links** command to create pinned fabric interface connections so that the parent switch can determine a distribution of host interfaces. The host interfaces are divided by the number of the max-links and distributed accordingly. The default value is max-links equals 1.

> **NOTE**   The Cisco Nexus 2248PQ Fabric Extender does not support the static pinning fabric interface connection.

- **Straight-through, using dynamic pinning (port channel):** You can use this method to load balance between the down link ports connected to the server and the fabric ports connected to the parent switch. This method bundles multiple uplink interfaces to one logical port channel. The traffic is being distributed using a hashing algorithm. For Layer 2, it uses Source MAC and Destination MAC; for Layer 3, it uses Source MAC, Destination MAC, and Source IP Destination IP.

- **Active-active FEX using vPC:** In this scenario, the FEX is dual homed using vPC to different parent switches.

> **NOTE**   The Cisco Nexus 7000 Series switches currently support only straight-through deployment using dynamic pinning. Static pinning and active-active FEX are currently supported only on the Cisco Nexus 5000 Series switches.

Table 1-20 shows the different models of the 1/10Gbps fabric extenders.

Table 1-20   Nexus 2000 1/10Gbps Model Comparison

	Cisco Nexus 2232PP	Cisco Nexus 2248PQ	Cisco Nexus 2232TM	Cisco Nexus 2232TM-E	Cisco Nexus 2348UPQ
Fabric Extender Host Interfaces	32	48	32	32	48
Fabric Extender Host Interface Types	1/10 Gigabit Ethernet ports SFP/SFP+	1/10 Gigabit Ethernet ports SFP/SFP+	1/10GBASE-T ports: RJ-45 connectors	1/10GBASE-T ports: RJ-45 connectors	48 Fixed 1/10 G SFP+ Unified Capable Ports, 4 x 40G QSFP+(SIF)
Fabric Extender Fabric Interfaces	8	4 QSFP+ (16 x 10GE)	Uplink module: 8 SFP+ (N2KM2800P)	8 SFP+	6 x 40G QSFP+
Fabric Speed	80 Gbps in each direction (160 Gbps full duplex)	160 Gbps in each direction (320 Gbps full duplex)	80 Gbps in each direction (160 Gbps full duplex)	80 Gbps in each direction (160 Gbps full duplex)	240 Gbps in each direction (480 Gbps full duplex)
Oversubscription	4:1	3:1	4:1	4:1	2:1

	Cisco Nexus 2232PP	Cisco Nexus 2248PQ	Cisco Nexus 2232TM	Cisco Nexus 2232TM-E	Cisco Nexus 2348UPQ
Performance	Hardware forwarding at 560 Gbps or 595 mpps	Hardware forwarding at 960 Gbps or 952 mpps	Hardware forwarding at 560 Gbps or 595 mpps	Hardware forwarding at 560 Gbps or 595 mpps	Hardware forwarding at 1200 Gbps or 952 mpps
Cisco Parent Switch	Cisco Nexus 5000, 6000, 7000, and 9000 Series	Cisco Nexus 5000, 6000, 7000, and 9000 Series	Cisco Nexus 5000, 6000, 7000, and 9000 Series	Cisco Nexus 5000, 6000, 7000, and 9000 Series	Cisco Nexus 5000, 6000, 7000, and 9000 Series
FCoE Support	Yes	Yes	No	Yes (supports up to 30 meters)	Yes

Table 1-21 shows the different models of the 100Mbps and 1Gbps fabric extenders.

Key Topic

Table 1-21 Nexus 2000 100Mbps and 1Gbps Model Comparison

	Cisco Nexus 2224TP	Cisco Nexus 2248TP	Cisco Nexus 2248TP-E
Fabric Extender Host Interfaces	24	48	48
Fabric Extender Host Interface Types	100BASET/1000BASE-T ports: RJ-45 connectors	100BASET/1000BASE-T ports: RJ-45 connectors	100BASET/1000BASE-T ports: RJ-45 connectors
Fabric Extender Fabric Interfaces	2	4	4
Fabric Speed	20 Gbps in each direction (40 Gbps full duplex)	40 Gbps in each direction (80 Gbps full duplex)	40 Gbps in each direction (80 Gbps full duplex)
Oversubscription	1.2:1	1.2:1	1.2:1
Performance	Hardware forwarding at 88 Gbps or 65 mpps	Hardware forwarding at 176 Gbps or 131 mpps	Hardware forwarding at 176 Gbps or 131 mpps
Cisco Parent Switch	Cisco Nexus 5000, 6000, 7000, and 9000 Series	Cisco Nexus 5000, 6000, 7000, and 9000 Series	Cisco Nexus 5000, 6000, 7000, and 9000 Series
FCoE Support	No	No	No

As shown in Figure 1-55, the Cisco Nexus B22 Fabric Extender is part of the fabric extenders family. It extends the FEX to third-party blade centers from HP, Fujitsu, Dell, and IBM. There is a separate hardware model for each vendor. They simplify the operational model by making the blade switch management part of the parent switch, and make it appear as a remote line card to the parent switch, similar to the Nexus 2000 fabric extenders.

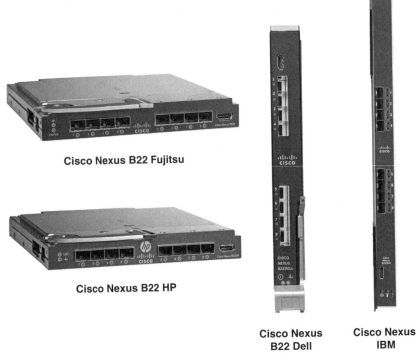

Cisco Nexus B22 Fujitsu

Cisco Nexus B22 HP

Cisco Nexus B22 Dell

Cisco Nexus IBM

Figure 1-55 *Cisco Nexus B22 Fabric Extender*

The B22 topology shown in Figure 1-56 creates a highly scalable server access design with no spanning tree running. This architecture gives the benefit of centralized management through the Nexus parent switch. It is similar to the Nexus 2000 Series management architecture. Similar to the Nexus 2000 Series, the B22 consists of two types of ports, host ports for blade server attachments and uplink ports, which are called fabric ports. The uplink ports are visible and are used for the connectivity to the upstream parent switch, as shown in Figure 1-56.

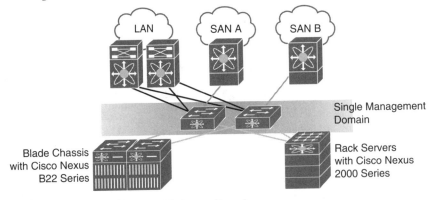

Figure 1-56 *Cisco Nexus B22 Access Topology*

The number of host ports and fabric ports for each model is shown in Table 1-22.

Key Topic

Table 1-22   Nexus B22 Specifications

	Cisco Nexus B22HP	Cisco Nexus B22F	Cisco Nexus B22IBM	Cisco Nexus B22DELL
Supported Blade Chassis	HP BladeSystem c3000 enclosure HP BladeSystem c7000 enclosure	Fujitsu PRIMERGY BX400 enclosure Fujitsu PRIMERGY BX900 enclosure	IBM Flex System	Dell PowerEdge M1000e blade enclosure
Fabric Extender Host Interfaces	16	16	14	16
Fabric Extender Host Interface Type	1/10GBASE-KR internal midplane connections	10GBASE-KR internal midplane connections	10GBASE-KR internal midplane connections	1/10GBASE-KR internal midplane connections
Fabric Extender Fabric Interfaces	8	8	8	8

The Server Evolution

Like so many aspects of the technology industry, the evolution of servers has been rapid. Computers have gone from the size of a room as in early days of mainframes to being able to fit in one's pocket. We create data at a quicker rate than ever; by 2020, over 50 billion devices will be connected to the Internet, compared to none just a few decades ago.

Servers have evolved at quite a pace. Development of the first web server began in 1989 by Tim Berners-Lee; it ran on a NeXT computer at CERN in Switzerland. These days, anyone can turn an old laptop into a web server in a short period of time. It is difficult to talk about the evolution of servers without talking about virtualization. Pioneered primarily by IBM, virtualization's evolution can be traced back to the 1960s. It was the introduction of virtualization in x86 server technology that really brought virtualization to the masses.

These days, over 70% of x86 server workloads are virtualized, according to industry watch group Gartner. It's clear to see why the server industry is evolving toward a more virtualized future. Server virtualization makes a company much more flexible and agile; being able to spin server resources up and down as needed makes for a much more efficient environment. Also, because there is less hardware vendor lock-in, the data center is made a greener place.

As the usage of virtualized servers has increased, so too has the support requirements that go with it. One of those requirements is server input/output (I/O), which is basically how the server communicates with the outside world. Server I/O can become complicated when it comes to virtual servers because of the increased bandwidth, network, and storage requirements. Virtualizing the I/O increases the available bandwidth, which can then be allocated as and when needed, thus ensuring I/O doesn't become a bottleneck that slows the whole system down.

Nowadays, servers can of course cope with the huge storage demands placed on them, thanks to the way storage technology has evolved. These units can fit in tiny spaces as well, without compromising performance or power. However, it's not just the size and power of servers that has evolved over the years. Systems used to keep servers cool, for example, have also had to evolve massively. Obviously, when the servers within a data center need additional power, more cooling is required to keep those systems operational.

In the past, cooling systems for servers relied heavily on fans that move air around, but they weren't particularly efficient. Now, data center cooling techniques have evolved to keep servers cool in other ways, such as raised floors to increase airflow as well as liquid cooling and fresh air cooling from the outside, to name just a few. Today, servers come in all shapes and sizes: web servers, application servers, email servers, database servers, file servers, print servers, and so on. We have seen a rapid progression from where it all began, and it will be very interesting to see where the next few decades take us.

We also need to talk about the challenges IT organizations are facing these days:

- **Increased workload diversity:** The workloads being placed on IT infrastructure are becoming increasingly diverse. Not long ago, virtualization and cloud computing promised to support every business application, from Internet information services to enterprise applications such as database management systems and SAP. But then a new class of applications arose that needed massive scale-out capacity on bare-metal servers, including back-end support for mobile applications. Today, Big Data applications perform in-memory analytics and require local storage and massive memory capacity. In the future, computing on the edge, or fog computing, will be more important for aggregating data and supporting the Internet of Things.

- **Increased speed of operational change:** The tempo at which IT organizations must roll out new applications and services has increased relentlessly. They need to deploy and redeploy IT assets rapidly to support agile, iterative development processes. Manual configuration has become so cumbersome that most organizations agree that zero-touch management is essential. Consistent policy and security are also essential, but unless they can be supported as a transparent, integrated part of IT processes, your clients may balk and seek services from public cloud providers. Also, management must span clusters of local data centers, geographically distributed data centers, and systems at remote and branch locations.

Workloads dictate application architecture, which affects server design, the relationship between servers and storage resources, and network architecture. Support for different types of workloads is creating technology silos within data centers, which creates additional challenges. Cloud computing environments, with disaggregated storage and dense blade server farms, are very different from Big Data environments, with massive amounts of local disk storage and large memory capacities. Then factor in new applications that require massive amounts of scale-out capacity on bare-metal servers, in which applications themselves are programmed to handle individual server failures. Given the different architectural models these disparate systems require, IT staff struggles to deftly configure and deploy application infrastructure and faces a nearly impossible task in maintaining security and standards compliance across all environments.

Cisco Unified Computing System (UCS) is an integrated computing infrastructure with embedded management that automates and accelerates deployment of all your applications, including virtualization and cloud computing, scale-out and bare-metal workloads, in-memory analytics, and edge computing, which supports remote and branch locations and massive amounts of data from the Internet of Things (IoT).

The system has an intelligent infrastructure that is configured through integrated, model-based management. Server identity, personality, and I/O connectivity are abstracted so that the system accomplishes for physical environments what hypervisors accomplish for virtualized ones. Cisco UCS enables you to run any workload on any resource with dynamic provisioning.

A hierarchy of Cisco management tools extends this concept across all the data centers and remote locations. Cisco UCS Central Software uses the same model-based management to support up to 6000 servers regardless of location as if they were in a single Cisco UCS domain. Cisco UCS Director provides comprehensive infrastructure automation and orchestration, managing all the resources in Cisco Integrated Infrastructure solutions, including Cisco UCS, storage, and a higher-level switching infrastructure. Cisco UCS Director automates your workflows, and it enables IT as a Service (ITaaS) offerings by providing a self-service portal through which administrators and clients can order infrastructure instances that are configured on demand. The fundamental, standards-based XML API that is exposed to the outside world has been accepted and incorporated into third-party management tools from a large ecosystem of third-party vendors.

Cisco Unified Computing System

Cisco UCS is the first unified data center platform that combines industry-standard, x86-architecture servers with networking and storage access into a single system. The system's x86-architecture rack and blade servers are powered exclusively by Intel Xeon processors and enhanced with Cisco innovations. These innovations include the capability to abstract and automatically configure the server state, built-in virtual interface cards (VICs), and leading memory capacity. Cisco's enterprise-class servers deliver performance to power mission-critical workloads. Cisco's cloud-scale servers support a lower-performance, bare-metal deployment model in which massive numbers of servers support many instances of a single application.

Cisco UCS is integrated with a standards-based, high-bandwidth, low-latency, virtualization-aware 10Gbps unified fabric, with a new generation of Cisco UCS fabric enabling an update to 40 Gbps. Cisco SingleConnect technology is implemented with an end-to-end system I/O architecture that uses Cisco Unified Fabric and Cisco Fabric Extender Technology (FEX Technology) to connect every Cisco UCS server within a single network and a single network layer. The system is wired once to support the desired bandwidth, and it carries all Internet protocol, storage, management, and virtual machine traffic with security isolation, visibility, and control equivalent to that of physical networks. The network fabric exceeds the bandwidth demands of today's multicore processors and eliminates the cost of separate networks for each type of traffic while increasing workload agility, reliability, and performance. The Cisco UCS I/O architecture is based on open, reliable, and secure standards.

With integrated, model-based management, administrators manipulate a model of a desired system configuration and associate a model's service profile with hardware resources, and the system configures itself to match the model. This automation accelerates provisioning and workload migration with accurate and rapid scalability. The process of establishing and maintaining configuration management databases (CMDBs) can be automated through the system's XML API, facilitating approaches based on Information Technology Infrastructure Library (ITIL) concepts.

With SingleConnect technology, the unified fabric requires fewer components and networks, and Cisco fabric extenders reduce the number of network layers by directly connecting physical and virtual servers to the system's fabric interconnects. This combination eliminates blade server, top-of-rack, and hypervisor-based switches by logically connecting fabric interconnect ports directly to individual servers and virtual machines. Virtual networks are now managed exactly the same way as physical networks, but they have massive scalability.

The combination of unified fabric and Cisco fabric extenders in SingleConnect technology creates a system with one network layer and one point of management and connectivity for the entire system. As a result, Cisco UCS scales more gracefully, in smaller increments, and at lower cost than other systems. With low-cost and low-power-consuming fabric extenders supporting the system's growth, the infrastructure cost per server is dramatically lower than for traditional systems. Because Cisco fabric extenders act as distributed line cards and are implicitly managed by the system's fabric interconnects, the system can grow without the need to add a single management point. Fewer components and management points contribute to easier and more rapid scaling with lower capital and operating costs.

Blade and rack servers are designed for minimal airflow obstruction, reducing the number of watts (W) used by cooling fans. In particular, the system's blade server chassis midplane is 63% open for easy front-to-back cooling. This design supports thermal conditions in which Intel Turbo Boost Technology can apply more processing power to handle workload peaks, helping Cisco UCS establish performance records for functions as basic as CPU performance. Power supplies are sourced to maintain high efficiency even at moderate power utilization levels. The elimination of blade chassis switching, top-of-rack switching, and blade-chassis management modules reduces the number of devices that need to be powered, thus reducing overall power consumption. The elimination of multiple parallel networks for IP, storage, and management traffic reduces the number of network interface cards (NICs) and host bus adapters (HBAs) and corresponding upstream ports that need to be powered and cooled. Large memory capacities help support large virtual machine footprints in 2-socket servers, eliminating the need to use 4-socket servers just to have a larger memory capacity, thereby also eliminating the energy cost. Cisco originally led the industry with Cisco Extended Memory Technology, and today offers one of the largest memory capacities available in a half-width blade server. Intel Xeon processors used in Cisco UCS servers adjust their energy consumption to the workload by scaling down energy use in small increments as workload conditions permit it as well as scaling up the processor clock rate when workload conditions demand and thermal conditions permit it.

Cisco UCS is built using the hierarchy of components illustrated in Figure 1-57 and described in the sections that follow. Each Cisco UCS domain is established with a pair of Cisco UCS fabric interconnects, with a comprehensive set of options for connecting various servers to them either directly or indirectly.

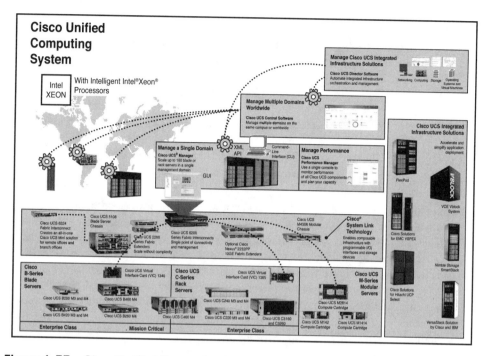

Figure 1-57 *Cisco Unified Computing System Component Hierarchy*

Cisco UCS Manager

Cisco UCS Manager integrates blade and rack servers into a single self-aware, self-integrating, unified system. It quickly and accurately configures computing, network, storage, and storage-access resources to increase compliance and reduce the chance of errors that can cause downtime. It uses a role- and policy-based approach that helps organizations more easily align policies and configurations with workloads, and it automates system configuration through a "create once, deploy many" approach. Cisco UCS Manager acts as a single point of management and monitoring for the entire system. It is embedded software that runs on the system's fabric interconnects, typically in a redundant, high-availability configuration. It can be accessed through an intuitive GUI, command-line interface (CLI), or XML API. Cisco UCS Central Software and Cisco UCS Director access the XML API to provide higher-level management functions. More than 22 high-level management tools integrate with Cisco UCS through the Cisco UCS Manager's XML API.

Cisco SingleConnect Technology

SingleConnect technology provides an exceptionally easy, intelligent, and efficient way to connect and manage computing in the data center. An exclusive Cisco innovation, SingleConnect technology dramatically simplifies the way that data centers connect to rack and blade servers, physical servers and virtual machines, as well as LAN, SAN, and management networks.

- Cisco UCS fabric interconnects provide a single point of connectivity and management for the entire system. Typically deployed as an active-active pair, the system's fabric interconnects integrate all components into a single, highly available management domain controlled by Cisco UCS Manager. The fabric interconnects manage all I/O efficiently and securely at a single point, resulting in deterministic I/O latency regardless of a server or virtual machine's topological location in the system. Cisco UCS 6200 Series Fabric Interconnects support line-rate, lossless 10 Gigabit Ethernet and FCoE connectivity. The Cisco UCS 6200 Series can be used to create Cisco UCS domains containing blade or rack servers. Cisco UCS 6300 Series Fabric Interconnects support line-rate, lossless 40 Gigabit Ethernet and FCoE connectivity. Cisco UCS 6324 Fabric Interconnects can be used to create a self-contained Cisco UCS Mini solution for branch offices and remote locations.

- Cisco fabric extenders are zero-management, low-cost, low-power-consuming devices that distribute the system's connectivity and management planes to rack servers and blade chassis to scale the system without adding complexity or new management points. Cisco fabric extenders eliminate the need for top-of-rack switches and blade-server-resident Ethernet and Fibre Channel switches or management modules, thus dramatically reducing the infrastructure cost per server. Rack servers can be connected directly to Cisco fabric interconnects for outstanding dedicated network bandwidth. Rack servers can be connected through fabric extenders for increased scale. Regardless of connectivity method, all servers are integrated through single-wire management in which all network, storage-access, and management traffic is carried over a single set of cables.

- Cisco UCS virtual interface cards (VICs) extend the network fabric directly to both servers and virtual machines so that a single connectivity mechanism can be used to connect both physical and virtual servers with the same level of visibility and control. Cisco VICs provide complete programmability of the Cisco UCS I/O infrastructure, with the number and type of I/O interfaces configurable on demand with a zero-touch model.

Cisco UCS Chassis and Racks

Cisco UCS blade chassis and racks act as containers for the system components:

- The **Cisco UCS 5108 Blade Server Chassis** features flexible bay configurations for blade servers. It can support up to eight half-width blades, up to four full-width blades, or up to two full-width double-height blades in a compact 6-rack-unit (6RU) form factor. The blade chassis is a highly simplified device, in contrast to traditional blade chassis that host multiple switches and management modules. The chassis adds no points of management to the system because it is logically part of the fabric interconnects. The Cisco UCS 5100 Series Blade Server Chassis hosts up to two fabric extenders, which are low-power-consuming devices that leave the chassis with the power budget and sufficient airflow to support multiple future generations of blade servers and network connectivity options. You can deploy a chassis as a standalone Cisco UCS Mini solution by installing two Cisco UCS 6324 Fabric Interconnects in the slots that would normally be used for the fabric extenders.

- **Cisco UCS R-Series Racks** are standard 19-inch racks optimized to house both Cisco UCS blade chassis and rack servers in the same physical chassis, providing the flexibility to enhance a system using the server form factor most appropriate for the task.

Cisco UCS servers can power every workload, including workloads for agile development environments requiring bare-metal servers, Big Data, and content delivery as well as cloud computing environments delivering virtual machines and bare-metal servers as a service, database management systems, high-frequency trading, high-performance computing, gaming applications, Internet infrastructure applications, mission-critical enterprise applications, mobile application back-end services, and virtualized environments.

■ **Cisco UCS B-Series Blade Servers** provide massive amounts of computing power in a compact form factor, helping increase density in computation-intensive and enterprise application environments. Blade servers are available in three form factors (half-width, full-width, and full-width double-height) with two or four Intel Xeon processors. Cisco UCS M3 and later blade servers can be ordered with built-in modular LAN on motherboard (mLOM) Cisco VICs to increase I/O flexibility and accelerate deployment.

■ **Cisco UCS C-Series Rack Servers** provide a rack-server entry point to Cisco UCS. With world-record-setting performance for 2- and 4-socket servers, Cisco rack servers can integrate into Cisco UCS through a single set of cables. Cisco UCS rack servers provide a wide range of I/O, memory, internal disk, and solid-state disk (SSD) drive capacity, enabling you to easily match servers to workloads.

You can create a variety of Cisco UCS configurations based on Cisco UCS fabric extenders. Figure 1-58 shows how Cisco UCS 6200 Series Fabric Interconnects can connect directly to servers or indirectly through fabric extenders, depending on the server form factor and deployment choices.

Blade server chassis can be connected to the fabric interconnects through a pair of Cisco UCS 2200 Series Fabric Extenders, which can support up to eight 10Gbps unified fabric uplinks per fabric extender. With Cisco UCS 6300 Series Fabric Interconnects, Cisco UCS 2300 Series Fabric Extenders can support up to four 40Gbps unified fabric uplinks per fabric extender.

Rack servers can be connected directly to the fabric interconnects or indirectly through Cisco Nexus 2232PP 10GE Fabric Extenders (for 10 Gigabit Ethernet using Cisco UCS 6200 Series Fabric Interconnects) and through Cisco Nexus 2348UPC 10GE Fabric Extenders (for 40 Gigabit Ethernet using Cisco UCS 6300 Series Fabric Interconnects) to achieve greater scale.

Cisco UCS Mini solutions can be created by using Cisco UCS 6234 Fabric Interconnects in the blade server chassis instead of fabric extenders. This creates a standalone Cisco UCS instance that supports blade servers, rack servers, and external storage systems.

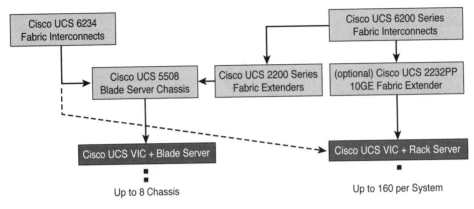

Figure 1-58 *Cisco UCS Component Hierarchy*

The UCS system is typically configured with A and B fabrics that are used in an active-active configuration to help provide high availability, increase resource utilization, and reduce costs. Each Cisco UCS domain is wired for the desired bandwidth, with up to 320 Gbps from each blade chassis and with bandwidth shared between servers. All network features and capabilities are controlled through software settings. As a result, bandwidth is shared between all I/O modalities so that bursts in one class of traffic can temporarily borrow bandwidth from other functions to achieve the best performance. Cisco Unified Fabric is based on open standards, and we will be discussing these open standards in Chapter 23, "Advanced Data Center Storage."

Cisco UCS Servers

Cisco UCS is based on industry-standard, x86-architecture servers with Intel Xeon processors. Although many vendors offer servers with the same processors, Cisco UCS Servers are integrated into a system with a balance of CPU, memory, and I/O resources.

Cisco UCS servers are grouped into four categories:

- **Mission-critical servers:** These servers are optimized for high performance and high reliability, availability, and serviceability (RAS). This category includes 2- and 4-socket servers with up to 6 TB of memory, up to 10 PCIe slots for massive I/O bandwidth and flexibility, and up to 12 internal disk drives, with optional high-performance SSD drive and RAID options. Equipped with the Intel Xeon processor E7 family, these servers are for mission-critical applications, including enterprise databases, enterprise resource planning (ERP) applications, and consolidation and virtualization workloads.

- **Enterprise-class servers:** These servers are optimized for performance and offer a wide variety of processing, memory, I/O, and internal disk capacity options. Powered by the Intel Xeon processor E5 family, these servers support up to 1.5 TB of main memory, up to five PCIe slots for I/O bandwidth and flexibility, and up to 56 internal disk drives with built-in and additional RAID options. These servers are optimized for database and data warehouse workloads, Big Data applications, enterprise application middleware, and collaboration, web, and IT infrastructure functions.

- **Scale-out servers:** These servers are optimized for good performance with excellent value. They offer slightly more limited processor, memory, and I/O expansion capabilities and are suited for scale-out applications, including Big Data, as well as web workloads and IT infrastructure functions, including proxy and caching servers.

Powered by Intel Xeon Processors

Cisco Unified Computing Servers are equipped with three advanced microprocessor families from Intel:

- **Intel Xeon processor E7 family:** The Intel Xeon processor E7 family is designed to meet the mission-critical IT challenge of managing and keeping business-critical data secure. Powerful, reliable servers such as the Cisco UCS C460 M2 High-Performance Rack Server are equipped with the top-of-the-line Intel Xeon processor E7 family to deliver performance that is excellent for the most data-demanding workloads, with improved scalability and increased memory and I/O capacity. These features help businesses quickly adapt to short-term changes in business needs while addressing requirements for long-term business growth. Advanced reliability and security features help maintain data integrity, accelerate encrypted transactions, and increase the availability of mission-critical applications. The powerful and reliable Intel Xeon processor E7 product family delivers flexibility for business-critical solutions.

- **Intel Xeon processor E5 family:** The Intel Xeon processor E5 family is at the core of a flexible and efficient data center that meets diverse business needs and is used in Cisco scale-out and enterprise-class servers. This family of processors is designed to deliver versatility, with the best combination of performance, built-in capabilities, and cost effectiveness. The Intel Xeon processor E5 family delivers exceptional performance to a broad range of data center environments and applications: from virtualization and cloud computing to design automation and real-time financial transactions. With these processors, I/O latency is dramatically reduced with Intel Integrated I/O, which helps eliminate data bottlenecks, simplify operations, and increase agility.

Memory Density

When Cisco first entered the server market, virtualization was gaining widespread use but was forcing IT organizations into making costly compromises. The bottleneck in most environments was not CPU capacity, but memory footprint. This challenge lead organizations to move from 2-socket servers to 4-socket servers simply to gain the increased memory capacity that 4-socket servers offered. Cisco was the first to recognize this limitation and to develop and patent extended memory technology that would allow the state-of-the-art Intel Xeon processors of the time to access twice the amount of memory. Cisco Extended Memory Technology gave IT organizations the choice of using a 2-socket server to achieve greater memory capacity than the capacities that other vendors could achieve or of populating the additional DIMM slots with lower-cost, lower-density memory. Both options helped increase virtual machine density and reduce total cost of ownership (TCO), including by helping customers make more effective use of software licenses by increasing utilization and performance on 2-socket servers. The Cisco UCS C460 M4 is remarkable in its support for 6 TB of memory—enough memory that only a few servers can support an entire ERP system.

Bandwidth

Cisco UCS rack servers are designed to host up to 10 industry-standard PCIe form-factor I/O cards, giving organizations freedom and flexibility to use the I/O configuration that best meets their needs. Cisco UCS blade servers are designed to accommodate up to two mezzanine form-factor I/O cards made by Cisco and third parties to provide access to massive amounts of backplane capacity.

Cisco UCS virtual interface cards, available only in Cisco servers, have dramatically simplified the deployment of servers for specific applications. By making the number and type of I/O devices programmable on demand, organizations can deploy and repurpose server I/O configurations without ever touching the servers.

Cisco UCS VICs provide access to more blade server midplane bandwidth than any other mezzanine card. With access to up to 80 Gbps of bandwidth from a half-width blade server and up to 160 Gbps of bandwidth from a full-width blade server (equipped with two cards), Cisco is poised to keep I/O bottlenecks in abeyance even as future multicore processors demand even more I/O bandwidth.

This massive amount of I/O capacity, combined with the simplified I/O infrastructure of Cisco UCS, allows more total bandwidth per blade server compared to traditional systems. Without the complexity of stacking ports, separate Ethernet and Fibre Channel switching in each chassis, and the physical partitioning of bandwidth between I/O modalities, Cisco UCS delivers up to 320 Gbps of bandwidth for every eight blades compared to only 92 Gbps for a traditional 16-server blade system, an improvement of almost six times (using Cisco UCS 6300 Series Fabric Interconnects).

Servers with Lower Infrastructure Cost

Cisco UCS is designed for lower infrastructure cost per server, a choice that makes scaling fast, easy, and inexpensive in comparison to manually configured approaches. This choice is evident in the design of the Cisco UCS 5108 Blade Server Chassis.

The blade server chassis is designed to be low cost, and therefore it is little more than sheet metal, a passive midplane, sensors, and slots for modular power supplies, fans, and blade servers. The chassis intelligence is contained in the modular Cisco UCS fabric extenders that plug into the rear of the chassis. These devices separate the management plane from the data plane and provide access to the chassis temperature and power sensors and to each server's integrated management controller. Because the fabric extenders are logically part of the Cisco UCS fabric interconnects, the entire blade chassis is part of a single centrally managed but physically distributed system.

The lower infrastructure cost that characterizes Cisco UCS also derives from the use of low-cost, low-power-consuming Cisco fabric extenders to bring all three networks—data, storage access, and management—to each blade server chassis without the need for three pairs of redundant management, Ethernet, and Fibre Channel modules.

Cisco UCS C-Series Rack Servers are similarly integrated into Cisco UCS with lower infrastructure cost per server. Instead of requiring up to five active switching components at the top of every rack (two Ethernet, two Fibre Channel, and one management network switch), Cisco UCS requires only two low-cost, low-power-consuming Cisco Nexus fabric extenders at the top of every other rack. This arrangement dramatically simplifies the network and physical infrastructure needed to support a large server farm. Figure 1-57 demonstrates the simplified infrastructure of Cisco UCS which contributes to 38% lower TCO for a 160-server installation.

Flexibility for Unified or Standalone Operation

Cisco UCS C-Series Rack Servers can be integrated with Cisco UCS or used as standalone servers. This capability offers IT organizations the flexibility to purchase Cisco rack servers today and integrate them as part of a single unified system as their needs dictate.

Integrated Operation with Single-Wire Management

When integrated as part of Cisco UCS, Cisco rack servers gain the same benefits of Cisco unified fabric and unified management as Cisco blade servers. Just as blade servers integrate into the system through a single set of cables that carry network, storage, and management traffic, Cisco rack servers connect through a single set of cables.

Single-wire management is enabled with Cisco rack servers through the Cisco UCS VIC 1225 or 1385, which separates management traffic from production data and storage traffic, passing it to an internal switch that connects to the Cisco Integrated Management Controller (IMC). The internal switch also makes the controller accessible for standalone management through the server's network management ports.

When single-wire management is configured, the unified fabric carries management traffic that is securely separated by connecting the fabric interconnect's management network directly to the controller using the IEEE 802.1BR standard. To prevent any high-traffic condition on the network from impeding management traffic, Cisco UCS gives management traffic the highest priority using the IEEE 802.1Qbb Priority Flow Control standard.

Standalone Operation with Cisco Integrated Management Controller

When operated as standalone servers, Cisco UCS C-Series Rack Servers provide up to three management interfaces that can be accessed by in-band or out-of-band tools and techniques (see in Figure 1-59):

■ Ethernet network access to the Integrated Management Controller.

■ Agent and agentless management with third-party tools through in-band data-plane connections.

■ Front- or back-panel access for video, USB (with the capability to boot from a USB CD/ DVD drive), and serial console access.

The Cisco IMC runs in the system's baseboard management controller (BMC) and can be accessed through the server network management ports for standalone operation. The Cisco controller provides out-of-band management that can be accessed through standard management protocols, CLIs, and web-based interfaces.

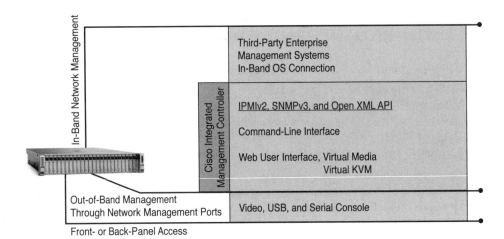

Figure 1-59 *Cisco UCS C-Series Rack Servers Managed Through Physical and Logical Management Interfaces*

Intelligent Platform Management Interface Version 2

Intelligent Platform Management Interface (IPMI) supports out-of-band management through third-party tools, including commercial enterprise management systems and open-source tools such as ipmitool. IPMI allows these tools to manage server power states and monitor operation parameters available through temperature, fan-speed, power-supply voltage, and power sensors.

Simple Network Management Protocol Version 3

Simple Network Management Protocol (SNMP) supports out-of-band management with third-party tools, including network management tools that use SNMP to monitor system status variables and receive SNMP traps in the event that the status falls outside predetermined ranges.

Open XML API

The Integrated Management Controller supports an open XML API that enables third-party software to access all the system's features and capabilities.

Command-Line Interface

The Cisco UCS Integrated Management Controller CLI can be accessed through a Secure Shell (SSH) connection to the controller. Through this interface, administrators can perform server control and administration tasks, and they can write scripts for configuration tasks so that these tasks can be reliably reproduced on a number of servers without errors.

Web User Interface

The web user interface supports out-of-band management through a standard web browser. It includes server management, virtual media, and remote keyboard, video, and mouse (KVM) capabilities:

- Server management includes power management, server reset, component inventory, and event logging.

- Virtual media capabilities enable peripherals such as CD and DVD drives to appear as if they were connected directly to the server, facilitating remote OS and application software installation.

- Remote KVM capabilities gives remote administrators the same level of control, including console video control, as when they are physically connected to the server.

Enterprise Management Tools

Third-party management tools typically use a combination of in-band and out-of-band management techniques, both of which are supported by Cisco UCS C-Series servers:

- In-band management is performed through the server's data network connection. Different tools use different techniques, including interaction with the host operating system, with and without the use of agents. In-band management can interact with OS-based management tools to accomplish tasks such as inventory and performance management, troubleshooting, and OS and interface provisioning.

- Out-of-band management tools such as Altiris Deployment Solution, BMC BladeLogic, CA Spectrum, HP IT Performance Suite, IBM Tivoli, and Microsoft System Center use Integrated Management Controller interfaces available through the network management port. These tools typically interact with servers through IPMI, SNMP, or the open XML API.

Troubleshooting Cisco UCS C-Series Server

Successful troubleshooting can be challenging, so you should have working knowledge of the Cisco UCS C-Series hardware and software components. You should be able to navigate the Cisco Integrated Management Controller (Cisco IMC) quickly and effectively. In addition, you should be familiar with the Cisco UCS C-Series components and features, and understand the impact of any troubleshooting procedures or actions.

Screenshots can be an effective tool for determining the circumstances that led up to a failure or configuration event. They form a historical record of the situation and can streamline and facilitate swift problem resolution by providing a reliable knowledge base.

The ability to re-create failures or misconfigurations can contribute valuable results to a knowledge base. Maintaining a detailed log can assist you with troubleshooting efforts by eliminating a haphazard approach to problem resolution.

Issuing the **show tech-support** command from the Cisco UCS C-Series Cisco IMC CLI can provide useful details about an issue and help you determine the source of the problem.

Troubleshooting Memory

This section describes the steps that are used to identify memory configuration errors and memory failures for Cisco UCS C-Series servers. There are various memory troubleshooting tools. Technical support files and management logs are commonly used.

You must choose the right corrective action to fix the problem because DIMM errors are not always straightforward and not necessarily solved by replacing the DIMMs. Correctable errors do not always indicate a bad DIMM. In other cases, it might be prudent to monitor the errors for a while to see if any more are logged. If the number of errors increases, it might indicate that it is time to replace the DIMM.

The following is the sequence for error reporting, from boot-up to runtime:

1. Hardware completes power sequence.

2. DIMM serial presence detection data is acquired for BIOS and Cisco IMC.

3. BIOS and Cisco IMC configure the correct voltage level for DIMM modules, based on DIMM inventory and user settings in the BIOS setup menu.

4. BIOS enters the MRC stage for memory training and executing MEMBIST.

5. BIOS maps out bad DIMMs and reports DIMM errors by sending SEL events to Cisco IMC.

6. BIOS steps through the rest of the BIOS initialization code and provides effective memory inventory for operating system.

7. Cisco IMC de-asserts DIMM-related sensors and LEDs if the stick bit is cleared and DIMMs pass the MEMBIST test.

8. Cisco IMC asserts DIMM-related sensors and LEDs, based on SEL events.

9. BIOS POST is completed and the system boots from a specified boot device from the boot order.

10. BIOS reports DIMM error-correcting code errors based on machine check architecture, and sends SEL events to Cisco IMC during runtime.

Identifying at which stage a memory error is reported often helps with diagnosing the problem.

Summary

In this chapter, you learned about the Cisco Nexus family of switches. The Nexus product family is designed to meet the stringent requirements of the next-generation data center. Following are some points to remember:

- With the Nexus product family, you can have an infrastructure that can be scaled cost effectively, and that helps you increase energy, budget, and resource efficiency.

- The Nexus product family offers different types of connectivity options that are needed in the data center—from 100 Mbps per port and going up to 100 Gbps per port.

- The Nexus family provides operational continuity to meet your needs for an environment where system availability is assumed and maintenance windows are rare, if not totally extinct.

- Nexus modular switches are the Nexus 7000, Nexus 7700, and the Nexus 9000 switches.

- The Nexus 7000 can scale up to 550 Gbps per slot; the Nexus 7700 can scale up to 1.32 Tbps per slot; and the Nexus 9000 can scale up to 3.84 Tbps per slot.

- Multiple supervisor modules are available for the Nexus 7000 switches and the Nexus 7700 switches: supervisor 1 module, supervisor 2 module, and supervisor 2E module.

- Nexus modular switches go from 1Gbps ports up to 100Gbps ports. If you want 100Mbps ports, you must use Nexus 2000 fabric extenders.

- The Nexus 5600 Series is the latest addition to the Nexus 5000 family of switches. It supports true 40Gbps ports with 40Gbps flows. Some of the key features it supports is VXLAN and true 40Gbps ports.

- The Nexus 6004X is the latest addition to the Nexus 6000 family. It supports unified ports, true 40 Gbps, and is the only switch in the Nexus 6000 family that supports VXLAN.

- Nexus 2000 fabric extenders must have a parent switch connected to them. The Nexus 2000 can be connected to Nexus 7000, Nexus 9000, Nexus 6000, and Nexus 5000 switches. They act as the parent switch for the Nexus 2000.

- Nexus 3000 is part of the unified fabric architecture. It is an ultra-low-latency switch that is well suited to high-performance trading and high-performance computing environments.

Exam Preparation Tasks

Review All Key Topics

Review the most important topics from this chapter, noted with the Key Topic icon in the outer margin of the page. Table 1-23 lists a reference for these key topics and the page numbers on which each is found.

Table 1-23   Key Topics for Chapter 1

Key Topic Element	Description	Page Number
Section	Chassis	13
Section	System Controller	14
Section	Fabric Modules	15
Section	Line Cards	16
Table 1-3	Nexus 9500 Modular Platform Line Card Comparison	17
Section	Cisco QSFP Bi-Di Technology for 40Gbps Migration	20
Table 1-4	Nexus 9500 Fixed-Platform Comparison	21
Table 1-5	Nexus 7000 and Nexus 7700 Modular Platform Comparison	22
Section	Cisco Nexus 7004 Series Switch Chassis	25
Table 1-6	Nexus 7000 and Nexus 7700 Supervisor Modules Comparison	29
Table 1-7	Nexus 7000 and Nexus 7700 Software Licensing Features	33
Table 1-8	Nexus 7000 and Nexus 7700 M-Series Modules Comparison	36
Table 1-9	Nexus 7000 and Nexus 7700 F-Series Modules Comparison	37
List	Redundancy Modes Configurable by Users	38
Note	Nexus 6004 Can Support 1G Ports	45
Table 1-13	Nexus 5500 and Nexus 5600 Product Specification	47
Section	Cisco Nexus 5548P and 5548UP Switches' Features	48
Section	Cisco Nexus 5500 Products' Expansion Modules	50
Table 1-14	Nexus 5600 Product Switches' Feature	53
Section	Cisco Nexus 5600 Expansion Modules	55
Table 1-20	Nexus 2000 1/10Gbps Module Comparison	64
Table 1-21	Nexus 2000 100Mbps/1Gbps Module Comparison	65
Table 1-22	Nexus B22 Specifications	67

Define Key Terms

Define the following key terms from this chapter, and check your answers in the glossary:

port channel (PC), virtual Port Channel (vPC), Fabric Extender (FEX), top-of-rack (ToR), end-of-row (EoR), spine-leaf

This chapter covers the following exam topics:

2.0. Basic data center networking concepts

2.1. Compare and contrast the OSI and the TCP/IP models

CHAPTER 2

The TCP/IP and OSI Networking Models

This chapter begins Part I, "Networking Fundamentals," which focuses on the basics of networking. Because networks require all the devices to follow the rules, this part starts with a discussion of networking models, which gives you a big-picture view of the networking rules.

You can think of a networking model as you think of a set of architectural plans for building a house. A lot of different people work on building your house, such as framers, electricians, bricklayers, painters, and so on. The blueprint helps ensure that all the different pieces of the house work together as a whole. Similarly, the people who make networking products, and the people who use those products to build their own computer networks, follow a particular networking model. That networking model defines rules about how each part of the network should work, as well as how the parts should work together, so that the entire network functions correctly.

The DCICN exam includes detailed coverage of one networking model: Transmission Control Protocol/Internet Protocol (TCP/IP). TCP/IP is the most pervasively used networking model in the history of networking. You can find support for TCP/IP on practically every computer operating system (OS) in existence today, from mobile phones to mainframe computers. Every network built using Cisco products today supports TCP/IP.

The DCICN exam also covers a second networking model, called the Open Systems Interconnection (OSI) reference model. Historically, OSI was the first large effort to create a vendor-neutral networking model. Because of that timing, many of the terms used in networking today come from the OSI model, so this chapter's section on OSI discusses OSI and the related terminology.

> **NOTE** As promised in the Introduction, this note is meant to help those of you who have already read the *ICND1 100-101 Official Cert Guide*. This chapter has the exact same material as the ICND1 book. See the Introduction's section "For Those Studying Routing & Switching."

"Do I Know This Already?" Quiz

Use the "Do I Know This Already?" quiz to help decide whether you might want to skim this chapter, or a major section, moving more quickly to the "Exam Preparation Tasks" section near the end of the chapter. Table 2-1 lists the major headings in this chapter and their corresponding "Do I Know This Already?" quiz questions. For thorough explanations, see Appendix A, "Answers to the 'Do I Know This Already?' Quizzes."

Table 2-1   "Do I Know This Already?" Foundation Topics Section-to-Question Mapping

Foundation Topics Section	Questions
TCP/IP Networking Model	1–6
OSI Networking Model	7–9

1. Which of the following protocols are examples of TCP/IP transport layer protocols? (Choose two answers.)

   a. Ethernet

   b. HTTP

   c. IP

   d. UDP

   e. SMTP

   f. TCP

2. Which of the following protocols are examples of TCP/IP data link layer protocols? (Choose two answers.)

   a. Ethernet

   b. HTTP

   c. IP

   d. UDP

   e. SMTP

   f. TCP

   g. PPP

3. The process of HTTP asking TCP to send some data and making sure that it is received correctly is an example of what?

   a. Same-layer interaction.

   b. Adjacent-layer interaction.

   c. OSI model.

   d. All of these answers are correct.

4. The process of TCP on one computer marking a TCP segment as segment 1, and the receiving computer then acknowledging the receipt of TCP segment 1, is an example of what?

   a. Data encapsulation.

   b. Same-layer interaction.

   c. Adjacent-layer interaction.

   d. OSI model.

   e. All of these answers are correct.

5. The process of a web server adding a TCP header to the contents of a web page, followed by adding an IP header and then adding a data link header and trailer, is an example of what?

   a. Data encapsulation.

   b. Same-layer interaction.

   c. OSI model.

   d. All of these answers are correct.

6. Which of the following terms is used specifically to identify the entity created when encapsulating data inside data link layer headers and trailers?

   a. Data

   b. Chunk

   c. Segment

   d. Frame

   e. Packet

7. Which OSI layer defines the functions of logical network-wide addressing and routing?

   a. Layer 1

   b. Layer 2

   c. Layer 3

   d. Layer 4

   e. Layer 5, 6, or 7

8. Which OSI layer defines the standards for cabling and connectors?

   a. Layer 1

   b. Layer 2

   c. Layer 3

   d. Layer 4

   e. Layer 5, 6, or 7

9. Which of the following are not valid terms for the names of the seven OSI layers? (Choose two answers.)

   a. Application

   b. Data link

   c. Transmission

   d. Presentation

   e. Internet

   f. Session

Foundation Topics

This chapter introduces some of the most basic ideas about computer networking, while also defining the structure of two networking models: TCP/IP and OSI. The chapter begins with a brief introduction of how most people view a network, which hopefully connects with where you are to start your CCNA Data Center journey. The middle of this chapter introduces networking by explaining some of the key features of TCP/IP. The chapter closes with some additional concepts and terminology related to the OSI model.

Perspectives on Networking

So, you are new to networking. Like many people, your perspective about networks might be that of a user of the network, as opposed to the network engineer who builds networks. For some, your view of networking might be based on how you use the Internet, from home, using a high-speed Internet connection such as Fiber or cable TV, as shown in Figure 2-1.

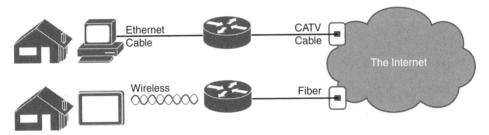

Figure 2-1 *End-User Perspective on High-Speed Internet Connections*

The top part of the figure shows a typical high-speed cable Internet user. The PC connects to a cable modem using an Ethernet cable. The cable modem then connects to a cable TV (CATV) outlet in the wall using a round coaxial cable—the same kind of cable used to connect your TV to the CATV wall outlet. Because cable Internet services provide service continuously, the user can just sit down at the PC and start sending email, browsing websites, making Internet phone calls, and using other tools and applications as well.

The lower part of the figure uses two different technologies. First, the tablet computer uses wireless technology that goes by the name wireless local area network (wireless LAN), or Wi-Fi, instead of using an Ethernet cable. In this example, the router uses a different technology, Fiber, to communicate with the Internet.

Although the technologies included in the DCICN (640-911) exam can be used to build a small home network, the exam focuses more on networking technology used inside a company. The Information Technology (IT) world refers to a network created by one corporation, or enterprise, for the purpose of allowing its employees to communicate, as an *enterprise network*. The smaller networks at home, when used for business purposes, often go by the name small office/home office (SOHO) networks.

Users of enterprise networks have some idea about the enterprise network at their company or school. People realize that they use a network for many tasks. PC users might realize that their PC connects through an Ethernet cable to a matching wall outlet, as shown at the top of Figure 2-2. Those same users might use wireless LANs with their laptop when going to a meeting in the conference room as well. Figure 2-2 shows these two end-user perspectives on an enterprise network.

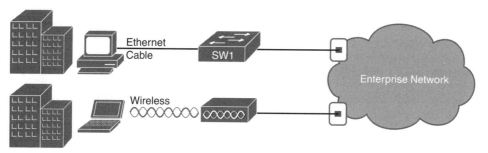

Ethernet Cable

SW1

Wireless

Enterprise Network

Figure 2-2   *Example Representation of an Enterprise Network*

NOTE   In networking diagrams, a cloud represents a part of a network whose details are not important to the purpose of the diagram. In this case, Figure 2-2 ignores the details of how to create an enterprise network.

Some users might not even have a concept of the network at all. Instead, these users just enjoy the functions of the network—the ability to post messages to social media sites, make phone calls, search for information on the Internet, listen to music, and download countless apps to their phones—without caring about how it works or how their favorite device connects to the network.

Regardless of how much you already know about how networks work, this book, and the related certifications, help you learn how networks do their job. That job is simply this: moving data from one device to another. The rest of this chapter, and the rest of this first part of the book, reveals the basics of how to build both SOHO and enterprise networks so that they can deliver data between two devices.

In the building business, much work happens before you nail the first boards together. The process starts with some planning, an understanding of how to build a house, and some architectural blueprints of how to build that specific house. Similarly, the journey toward building any computer network does not begin by installing devices and cables, but instead by looking at the architectural plans for those modern networks: the TCP/IP model.

TCP/IP Networking Model

A *networking model*, sometimes also called either a *networking architecture* or *networking blueprint*, refers to a comprehensive set of documents. Individually, each document describes one small function required for a network; collectively, these documents define everything that should happen for a computer network to work. Some documents define a *protocol*, which is a set of logical rules that devices must follow to communicate. Other documents define some physical requirements for networking. For example, a document could define the voltage and current levels used on a particular cable when transmitting data.

You can think of a networking model as you think of an architectural blueprint for building a house. Sure, you can build a house without the blueprint. However, the blueprint can ensure that the house has the right foundation and structure so that it will not fall down, and it has the correct hidden spaces to accommodate the plumbing, electrical, gas, and so on. Also, the many different people that build the house using the blueprint—such as framers, electricians, bricklayers, painters, and so on—know that if they follow the blueprint, their part of the work should not cause problems for the other workers.

Similarly, you could build your own network—write your own software, build your own networking cards, and so on—to create a network. However, it is much easier to simply buy and use products that already conform to some well-known networking model or blueprint. Because the networking product vendors build their products with some networking model in mind, their products should work well together.

History Leading to TCP/IP

Today, the world of computer networking uses one networking model: TCP/IP (Transmission Control Protocol/Internet Protocol). However, the world has not always been so simple. Once upon a time, networking protocols didn't exist, including TCP/IP. Vendors created the first networking protocols; these protocols supported only that vendor's computers. For example, IBM published its Systems Network Architecture (SNA) networking model in 1974. Other vendors also created their own proprietary networking models. As a result, if your company bought computers from three vendors, network engineers often had to create three different networks based on the networking models created by each company, and then somehow connect those networks, thus making the combined networks much more complex. The left side of Figure 2-3 shows the general idea of what a company's enterprise network might have looked like back in the 1980s, before TCP/IP became common in enterprise internetworks.

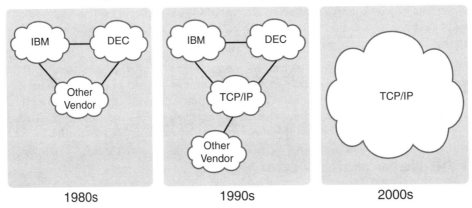

Figure 2-3 *Historical Progression: Proprietary Models to the Open TCP/IP Model*

Although vendor-defined proprietary networking models often worked well, having an open, vendor-neutral networking model would aid competition and reduce complexity. The International Organization for Standardization (ISO) took on the task to create such a model, starting as early as the late 1970s, beginning work on what would become known as the Open Systems Interconnection (OSI) networking model. ISO had a noble goal for the

OSI model: to standardize data networking protocols to allow communication between all computers across the entire planet. ISO worked toward this ambitious and noble goal, with participants from most of the technologically developed nations on Earth participating in the process.

A second, less formal effort to create an open, vendor-neutral, public networking model sprouted forth from a U.S. Department of Defense (DoD) contract. Researchers at various universities volunteered to help further develop the protocols surrounding the original DoD work. These efforts resulted in a competing open networking model called TCP/IP.

During the 1990s, companies began adding OSI, TCP/IP, or both to their enterprise networks. However, by the end of the 1990s, TCP/IP had become the common choice, and OSI fell away. The center part of Figure 2-3 shows the general idea behind enterprise networks in that decade—still with networks built upon multiple networking models, but including TCP/IP.

Here in the twenty-first century, TCP/IP dominates. Proprietary networking models still exist, but they have mostly been discarded in favor of TCP/IP. The OSI model, whose development suffered in part because of a slower formal standardization process as compared with TCP/IP, never succeeded in the marketplace. And TCP/IP, the networking model originally created almost entirely by a bunch of volunteers, has become the most prolific network model ever, as shown on the right side of Figure 2-3.

In this chapter, you will read about some of the basics of TCP/IP. Although you will learn some interesting facts about TCP/IP, the true goal of this chapter is to help you understand what a networking model or networking architecture really is and how it works.

Also in this chapter, you will learn about some of the jargon used with OSI. Will any of you ever work on a computer that is using the full OSI protocols instead of TCP/IP? Probably not. However, you will often use terms relating to OSI. Also, the DCICN exam covers the basics of OSI, so this chapter also covers OSI to prepare you for questions about it on the exam.

Overview of the TCP/IP Networking Model

The TCP/IP model both defines and references a large collection of protocols that allow computers to communicate. To define a protocol, TCP/IP uses documents called Requests for Comments (RFCs). (You can find these RFCs using any online search engine.) The TCP/IP model also avoids repeating work already done by some other standards body or vendor consortium by simply referring to standards or protocols created by those groups. For example, the Institute of Electrical and Electronic Engineers (IEEE) defines Ethernet LANs; the TCP/IP model does not define Ethernet in RFCs, but refers to IEEE Ethernet as an option.

An easy comparison can be made between telephones and computers that use TCP/IP. You go to the store and buy a phone from one of a dozen different vendors. When you get home and plug in the phone to the same cable in which your old phone was connected, the new phone works. The phone vendors know the standards for phones in their country and build their phones to match those standards.

Similarly, when you buy a new computer today, it implements the TCP/IP model to the point that you can usually take the computer out of the box, plug in all the right cables, turn it on, and it connects to the network. You can use a web browser to connect to your favorite website. How? Well, the OS on the computer implements parts of the TCP/IP model. The Ethernet card, or wireless LAN card, built into the computer implements some LAN standards referenced by the TCP/IP model. In short, the vendors that created the hardware and software implemented TCP/IP.

To help people understand a networking model, each model breaks the functions into a small number of categories called *layers*. Each layer includes protocols and standards that relate to that category of functions. TCP/IP actually has two alternative models, as shown in Figure 2-4.

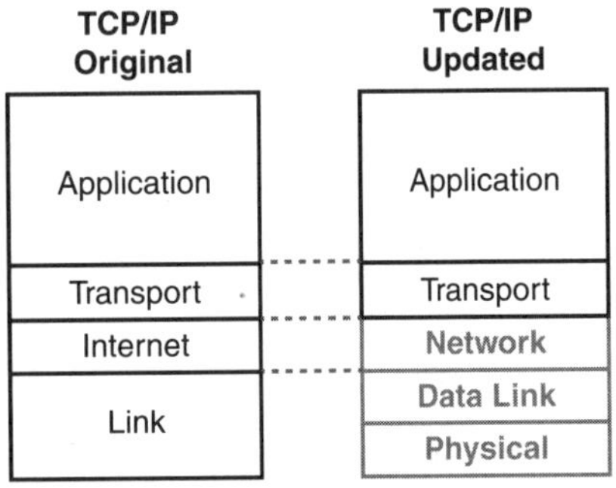

TCP/IP Original	TCP/IP Updated
Application	Application
Transport	Transport
Internet	Network
Link	Data Link
	Physical

Figure 2-4   *Two TCP/IP Networking Models*

The model on the left shows the original TCP/IP model listed in RFC 1122, which breaks TCP/IP into four layers. The top two layers focus more on the applications that need to send and receive data. The bottom layer focuses on how to transmit bits over each individual link, with the internet layer focusing on delivering data over the entire path from the original sending computer to the final destination computer.

The TCP/IP model on the right is a common method used today to refer to the layers formed by expanding the original model's link layer on the left into two separate layers: data link and physical (similar to the lower two layers of the OSI model). Note that the model on the right is used more often today.

NOTE   The original TCP/IP model's link layer has also been referred to as the *network access* and *network interface* layer.

Many of you will have already heard of several TCP/IP protocols, such as the examples listed in Table 2-2. Most of the protocols and standards in this table will be explained in more detail as you work through this book. Following the table, this section takes a closer look at the layers of the TCP/IP model.

Table 2-2 TCP/IP Architectural Model and Example Protocols

TCP/IP Architecture Layer	Example Protocols
Application	HTTP, POP3, SMTP
Transport	TCP, UDP
Internet	IP
Link	Ethernet, Point-to-Point Protocol (PPP), T1

TCP/IP Application Layer

TCP/IP application layer protocols provide services to the application software running on a computer. The application layer does not define the application itself, but it defines services that applications need. For example, application protocol HTTP defines how web browsers can pull the contents of a web page from a web server. In short, the application layer provides an interface between software running on a computer and the network itself.

Arguably, the most popular TCP/IP application today is the web browser. Many major software vendors either have already changed or are changing their application software to support access from a web browser. And thankfully, using a web browser is easy: You start a web browser on your computer and select a website by typing the name of the website, and the web page appears.

HTTP Overview

What really happens to allow that web page to appear on your web browser?

Imagine that Bob opens his browser. His browser has been configured to automatically ask for web server Larry's default web page, or *home page*. The general logic looks like Figure 2-5.

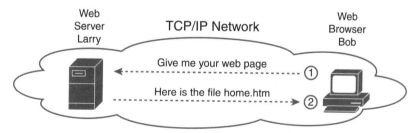

Figure 2-5 *Basic Application Logic to Get a Web Page*

So, what really happened? Bob's initial request actually asks Larry to send his home page back to Bob. Larry's web server software has been configured to know that the default web page is contained in a file called home.htm. Bob receives the file from Larry and displays the contents of the file in Bob's web browser window.

HTTP Protocol Mechanisms

Taking a closer look, this example shows how applications on each endpoint computer—specifically, the web browser application and web server application—use a TCP/IP application layer protocol. To make the request for a web page and return the contents of the web page, the applications use the Hypertext Transfer Protocol (HTTP).

HTTP did not exist until Tim Berners-Lee created the first web browser and web server in the early 1990s. Berners-Lee gave HTTP functions to ask for the contents of web pages, specifically by giving the web browser the ability to request files from the server, and giving the server a way to return the content of those files. The overall logic matches what was shown in Figure 2-5; Figure 2-6 shows the same idea, but with details specific to HTTP.

> **NOTE** The full version of most web addresses—also called Uniform Resource Locators (URLs)—begins with the letters "http," which means that HTTP is used to transfer the web pages.

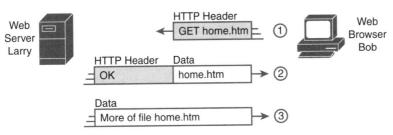

Figure 2-6 *HTTP GET Request, HTTP Reply, and One Data-Only Message*

To get the web page from Larry, at Step 1, Bob sends a message with an HTTP header. Generally, protocols use headers as a place to put information used by that protocol. This HTTP header includes the request to "get" a file. The request typically contains the name of the file (home.htm, in this case), or if no filename is mentioned, the web server assumes that Bob wants the default web page.

Step 2 in Figure 2-6 shows the response from web server Larry. The message begins with an HTTP header, with a return code (200), which means something as simple as "OK" returned in the header. HTTP also defines other return codes so that the server can tell the browser whether the request worked. (Here is another example: If you ever looked for a web page that was not found, and then received an HTTP 404 "not found" error, you received an HTTP return code of 404.) The second message also includes the first part of the requested file.

Step 3 in Figure 2-6 shows another message from web server Larry to web browser Bob, but this time without an HTTP header. HTTP transfers the data by sending multiple messages, each with a part of the file. Rather than wasting space by sending repeated HTTP headers that list the same information, these additional messages simply omit the header.

TCP/IP Transport Layer

Although many TCP/IP application layer protocols exist, the TCP/IP transport layer includes a smaller number of protocols. The two most commonly used transport layer protocols are the *Transmission Control Protocol (TCP)* and the *User Datagram Protocol (UDP)*.

Transport layer protocols provide services to the application layer protocols that reside one layer higher in the TCP/IP model. How does a transport layer protocol provide a service to a higher-layer protocol? This section introduces that general concept by focusing on a single service provided by TCP: error recovery. Later chapters examine the transport layer in more detail, and discuss more functions of the transport layer.

TCP Error Recovery Basics

To appreciate what the transport layer protocols do, you must think about the layer above the transport layer, the application layer. Why? Well, each layer provides a service to the layer above it, like the error-recovery service provided to application layer protocols by TCP.

For example, in Figure 2-5, Bob and Larry used HTTP to transfer the home page from web server Larry to Bob's web browser. But what would have happened if Bob's HTTP GET request had been lost in transit through the TCP/IP network? Or, what would have happened if Larry's response, which included the contents of the home page, had been lost? Well, as you might expect, in either case, the page would not have shown up in Bob's browser.

TCP/IP needs a mechanism to guarantee delivery of data across a network. Because many application layer protocols probably want a way to guarantee delivery of data across a network, the creators of TCP included an error-recovery feature. To recover from errors, TCP uses the concept of acknowledgments. Figure 2-7 outlines the basic idea behind how TCP notices lost data and asks the sender to try again.

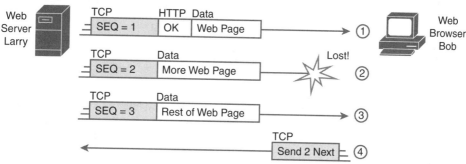

Figure 2-7   *TCP Error-Recovery Services as Provided to HTTP*

Figure 2-7 shows web server Larry sending a web page to web browser Bob, using three separate messages. Note that this figure shows the same HTTP headers as Figure 2-6, but it also shows a TCP header. The TCP header shows a sequence number (SEQ) with each message. In this example, the network has a problem, and the network fails to deliver the TCP message (called a segment) with sequence number 2. When Bob receives messages with sequence numbers 1 and 3, but does not receive a message with sequence number 2, Bob realizes that message 2 was lost. That realization by Bob's TCP logic causes Bob to send a TCP segment back to Larry, asking Larry to send message 2 again.

Same-Layer and Adjacent-Layer Interactions

The example in Figure 2-7 also demonstrates a function called *adjacent-layer interaction*, which refers to the concepts of how adjacent layers in a networking model, on the same computer, work together. In this example, the higher-layer protocol (HTTP) wants error recovery, and the higher layer uses the next lower-layer protocol (TCP) to perform the service of error recovery; the lower layer provides a service to the layer above it.

Figure 2-7 also shows an example of a similar function called *same-layer interaction.* When a particular layer on one computer wants to communicate with the same layer on another computer, the two computers use headers to hold the information that they want to communicate. For example, in Figure 2-7, Larry set the sequence numbers to 1, 2, and 3 so that Bob could notice when some of the data did not arrive. Larry's TCP process created that TCP header with the sequence number; Bob's TCP process received and reacted to the TCP segments. This process through which two computers set and interpret the information in the header used by that layer is called *same-layer interaction*, and it occurs between computers that are communicating over a network.

Table 2-3 summarizes the key points about how adjacent layers work together on a single computer and how one layer on one computer works with the same networking layer on another computer.

Table 2-3   Summary: Same-Layer and Adjacent-Layer Interactions

Concept	Description
Same-layer interaction on different computers	The two computers use a protocol (an agreed-to set of rules) to communicate with the same layer on another computer. The protocol defined by each layer uses a header that is transmitted between the computers to communicate what each computer wants to do. Header information added by a layer of the sending computer is processed by the same layer of the receiving computer.
Adjacent-layer interaction on the same computer	On a single computer, one layer provides a service to a higher layer. The software or hardware that implements the higher layer requests that the next lower layer perform the needed function.

TCP/IP Network Layer

The application layer includes many protocols. The transport layer includes fewer, most notably TCP and UDP. The TCP/IP network layer includes a small number of protocols, but only one major protocol: the *Internet Protocol (IP)*. In fact, the name *TCP/IP* is simply the names of the two most common protocols (TCP and IP) separated by a slash (/).

IP provides several features, the most important of which are addressing and routing. This section begins by comparing IP's addressing and routing with another commonly known system that uses addressing and routing: the postal service. Following that, this section introduces IP addressing and routing. (More details follow in Chapter 4, "Fundamentals of IPv4 Addressing and Routing.")

Internet Protocol and the Postal Service

Imagine that you just wrote two letters: one to a friend on the other side of the country and one to a friend on the other side of town. You address the envelopes and put on the stamps, so both are ready to give to the postal service. Is there much difference in how you treat each letter? Not really. Typically, you would just put them in the same mailbox and expect the postal service to deliver both letters.

The postal service, however, must think about each letter separately, and then make a decision of where to send each letter so that it is delivered. For the letter sent across town, the people in the local post office probably just need to put the letter on another truck.

For the letter that needs to go across the country, the postal service sends the letter to another post office, then another, and so on, until the letter gets delivered across the country. At each post office, the postal service must process the letter and choose where to send it next.

To make it all work, the postal service has regular routes for small trucks, large trucks, planes, boats, and so on, to move letters between postal service sites. The service must be able to receive and forward the letters, and it must make good decisions about where to send each letter next, as shown in Figure 2-8.

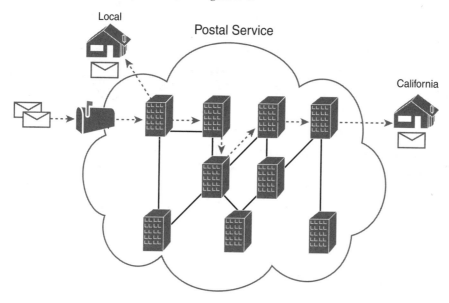

Figure 2-8 *Postal Service Forwarding (Routing) Letters*

Still thinking about the postal service, consider the difference between the person sending the letter and the work that the postal service does. The person sending the letters expects that the postal service will deliver them most of the time. However, the person sending the letters does not need to know the details of exactly what path the letters take. In contrast, the postal service does not create the letters, but they accept the letters from the customer. Then, the postal service must know the details about addresses and postal codes that group addresses into larger groups, and it must have the ability to deliver the letters.

The TCP/IP application and transport layers act like the person sending letters through the postal service. These upper layers work the same way regardless of whether the endpoint host computers are on the same LAN or are separated by the entire Internet. To send a message, these upper layers ask the layer below them, the network layer, to deliver the message.

The lower layers of the TCP/IP model act more like the postal service to deliver those messages to the correct destinations. To do so, these lower layers must understand the underlying physical network because they must choose how to best deliver the data from one host to another.

So, what does this all matter to networking? Well, the network layer of the TCP/IP networking model, primarily defined by the *Internet Protocol (IP)*, works much like the postal service. IP defines that each host computer should have a different IP address, just as the postal service defines addressing that allows unique addresses for each house, apartment, and business. Similarly, IP defines the process of routing so that devices called routers can work like the post office, forwarding packets of data so that they are delivered to the correct destinations. Just as the postal service created the necessary infrastructure to deliver letters—post offices, sorting machines, trucks, planes, and personnel—the network layer defines the details of how a network infrastructure should be created so that the network can deliver data to all computers in the network.

NOTE TCP/IP defines two versions of IP: IP Version 4 (IPv4) and IP Version 6 (IPv6). The world still mostly uses IPv4 (although on the public IPv4 address exhaustion has happened), so this introductory part of the book uses IPv4 for all references to IP.

Internet Protocol Addressing Basics

IP defines addresses for several important reasons. First, each device that uses TCP/IP—each TCP/IP *host*—needs a unique address so that it can be identified in the network. IP also defines how to group addresses together, just like the postal system groups addresses based on postal codes (like ZIP codes in the United States).

To understand the basics, examine Figure 2-9, which shows the familiar web server Larry and web browser Bob; but now, instead of ignoring the network between these two computers, this figure includes part of the network infrastructure.

First, note that Figure 2-9 shows some sample IP addresses. Each IP address has four numbers, separated by periods. In this case, Larry uses IP address 1.1.1.1, and Bob uses 2.2.2.2. This style of number is called a *dotted-decimal notation (DDN)*.

Figure 2-9 also shows three groups of addresses. In this example, all IP addresses that begin with 1 must be on the upper left, as shown in shorthand in the figure as 1._.._. All addresses that begin with 2 must be on the right, as shown in shorthand as 2._.._. Finally, all IP addresses that begin with 3 must be at the bottom of the figure.

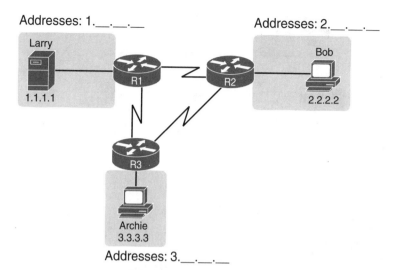

Addresses: 1.__.__.__

Addresses: 2.__.__.__

Addresses: 3.__.__.__

Figure 2-9 *Simple TCP/IP Network: Three Routers with IP Addresses Grouped*

Additionally, Figure 2-9 introduces icons that represent IP routers. Routers are networking devices that connect the parts of the TCP/IP network together for the purpose of routing (forwarding) IP packets to the correct destination. Routers do the equivalent of the work done by each post office site: They receive IP packets on various physical interfaces, make decisions based on the IP address included with the packet, and then physically forward the packet out some other network interface.

IP Routing Basics

The TCP/IP network layer, using the IP protocol, provides a service of forwarding IP packets from one device to another. Any device with an IP address can connect to the TCP/IP network and send packets. This section shows a basic IP routing example for perspective.

NOTE The term *IP host* refers to any device, regardless of size or power, that has an IP address and connects to any TCP/IP network.

Figure 2-10 repeats the familiar case in which web server Larry wants to send part of a web page to Bob, but now with details related to IP. On the lower left, note that server Larry has the familiar application data, HTTP header, and TCP header ready to send. Additionally, the message now also contains an IP header. The IP header includes a source IP address of Larry's IP address (1.1.1.1) and a destination IP address of Bob's IP address (2.2.2.2).

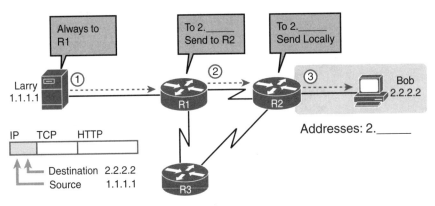

Figure 2-10 *Basic Routing Example*

Step 1, on the left of Figure 2-10, begins with Larry being ready to send an IP packet. Larry's IP process chooses to send the packet to some router—a nearby router on the same LAN—with the expectation that the router will know how to forward the packet. (This logic is much like you and me sending all our letters by putting them in a nearby post office box.) Larry doesn't need to know anything more about the topology or the other routers.

At Step 2, router R1 receives the IP packet, and R1's IP process makes a decision. R1 looks at the destination address (2.2.2.2), compares that address to its known IP routes, and chooses to forward the packet to router R2. This process of forwarding the IP packet is called *IP routing* (or simply *routing*).

At Step 3, router R2 repeats the same kind of logic used by router R1. R2's IP process will compare the packet's destination IP address (2.2.2.2) to R2's known IP routes and make a choice to forward the packet to the right on to Bob.

Practically half the chapters in this book discuss some feature that relates to addressing, IP routing, and how routers perform routing.

TCP/IP Link Layer (Data Link Plus Physical)

The TCP/IP model's original link layer defines the protocols and hardware required to deliver data across some physical network. The term *link* refers to the physical connections, or links, between two devices and the protocols used to control those links.

Just like every layer in any networking model, the TCP/IP link layer provides services to the layer above it in the model. When a host's or router's IP process chooses to send an IP packet to another router or host, that host or router then uses link-layer details to send that packet to the next host/router.

Because each layer provides a service to the layer above it, take a moment to think about the IP logic related to Figure 2-10. In that example, host Larry's IP logic chooses to send the IP packet to a nearby router (R1), with no mention of the underlying Ethernet. The Ethernet network, which implements link-layer protocols, must then be used to deliver that packet from host Larry over to router R1. Figure 2-11 shows four steps of what occurs at the link layer to allow Larry to send the IP packet to R1.

NOTE   Figure 2-11 depicts the Ethernet as a series of lines. Networking diagrams often use this convention for showing Ethernet LANs, in cases where the actual LAN cabling and LAN devices are not important to the discussion, as is the case here. The LAN would have cables and devices such as LAN switches, which are not shown in this figure.

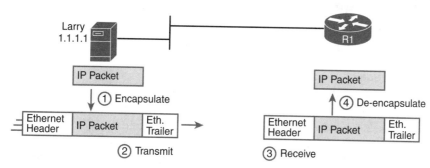

Figure 2-11   *Larry Using Ethernet to Forward an IP Packet to Router R1*

Figure 2-11 shows four steps. The first two occur on Larry, and the last two occur on router R1, as follows:

Step 1.   Larry encapsulates the IP packet between an Ethernet header and Ethernet trailer, creating an Ethernet *frame*.

Step 2.   Larry physically transmits the bits of this Ethernet frame, using electricity flowing over the Ethernet cabling.

Step 3.   Router R1 physically receives the electrical signal over a cable, and re-creates the same bits by interpreting the meaning of the electrical signals.

Step 4.   Router R1 de-encapsulates the IP packet from the Ethernet frame by removing and discarding the Ethernet header and trailer.

By the end of this process, the link-layer processes on Larry and R1 have worked together to deliver the packet from Larry to router R1.

NOTE   Protocols define both headers and trailers for the same general reason, but headers exist at the beginning of the message and trailers exist at the end.

The link layer includes a large number of protocols and standards. For example, the link layer includes all the variations of Ethernet protocols, along with several other LAN standards that were more popular in decades past. The link layer includes wide area network (WAN) standards for different physical media, which differ significantly compared to LAN standards because of the longer distances involved in transmitting the data. This layer also includes the popular WAN standards that add headers and trailers, as shown generally in Figure 2-11—protocols such as the Point-to-Point Protocol (PPP) and Frame Relay.

In short, the TCP/IP link layer includes two distinct functions: functions related to the physical transmission of the data, plus the protocols and rules that control the use of the physical media. The five-layer TCP/IP model simply splits out the link layer into two layers (data link and physical) to match this logic.

TCP/IP Model and Terminology

Before completing this introduction to the TCP/IP model, this section examines a few remaining details of the model and some related terminology.

Comparing the Original and Modern TCP/IP Models

The original TCP/IP model defined a single layer—the link layer—below the internetwork layer. The functions defined in the original link layer can be broken into two major categories: functions related directly to the physical transmission of data and those only indirectly related to the physical transmission of data. For example, in the four steps shown in Figure 2-11, Steps 2 and 3 were specific to sending the data, but Steps 1 and 4—encapsulation and de-encapsulation—were only indirectly related. This division will become clearer as you read about additional details of each protocol and standard.

Today, most documents use a more modern version of the TCP/IP model, as shown in Figure 2-12. Comparing the two, the upper layers are identical, except a name change from "internet" to "network." The lower layers differ in that the single link layer in the original model is split into two layers to match the division of physical transmission details from the other functions. Figure 2-12 shows the two versions of the TCP/IP model again, with emphasis on these distinctions.

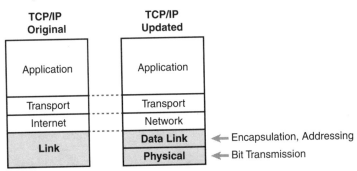

Figure 2-12 *Link Versus Data Link and Physical Layers*

Data Encapsulation Terminology

As you can see from the explanations of how HTTP, TCP, IP, and Ethernet do their jobs, each layer adds its own header (and for data-link protocols, also a trailer) to the data supplied by the higher layer. The term *encapsulation* refers to the process of putting headers (and sometimes trailers) around some data.

Many of the examples in this chapter show the encapsulation process. For example, web server Larry encapsulated the contents of the home page inside an HTTP header in Figure 2-6. The TCP layer encapsulated the HTTP headers and data inside a TCP header in Figure 2-7.

IP encapsulated the TCP headers and the data inside an IP header in Figure 2-10. Finally, the Ethernet link layer encapsulated the IP packets inside both a header and a trailer in Figure 2-11.

The process by which a TCP/IP host sends data can be viewed as a five-step process. The first four steps relate to the encapsulation performed by the four TCP/IP layers, and the last step is the actual physical transmission of the data by the host. In fact, if you use the five-layer TCP/IP model, one step corresponds to the role of each layer. The steps are summarized in the following list:

Step 1.   **Create and encapsulate the application data with any required application layer headers.** For example, the HTTP OK message can be returned in an HTTP header, followed by part of the contents of a web page.

Step 2.   **Encapsulate the data supplied by the application layer inside a transport layer header.** For end-user applications, a TCP or UDP header is typically used.

Step 3.   **Encapsulate the data supplied by the transport layer inside a network layer (IP) header.** IP defines the IP addresses that uniquely identify each computer.

Step 4.   **Encapsulate the data supplied by the network layer inside a data link layer header and trailer.** This layer uses both a header and a trailer.

Step 5.   **Transmit the bits.** The physical layer encodes a signal onto the medium to transmit the frame.

The numbers in Figure 2-13 correspond to the five steps in this list, graphically showing the same concepts. Note that because the application layer often does not need to add a header, the figure does not show a specific application layer header.

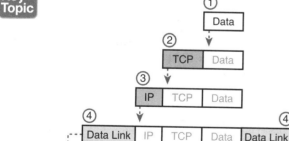
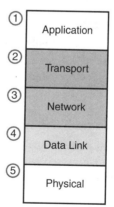

Figure 2-13   *Five Steps of Data Encapsulation: TCP/IP*

Names of TCP/IP Messages

Finally, take particular care to remember the terms *segment, packet,* and *frame* and the meaning of each. Each term refers to the headers (and possibly trailers) defined by a particular layer and the data encapsulated following that header. Each term, however, refers to a different layer: segment for the transport layer, packet for the network layer, and frame for the link layer. Figure 2-14 shows each layer along with the associated term.

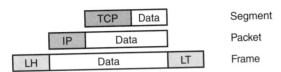

Segment

Packet

Frame

Figure 2-14 *Perspectives on Encapsulation and "Data"**

* The letters LH and LT stand for link header and link trailer, respectively, and refer to the data link layer header and trailer.

Figure 2-14 also shows the encapsulated data as simply "data." When focusing on the work done by a particular layer, the encapsulated data typically is unimportant. For example, an IP packet can indeed have a TCP header after the IP header, an HTTP header after the TCP header, and data for a web page after the HTTP header. However, when discussing IP, you probably just care about the IP header, so everything after the IP header is just called "data." So, when drawing IP packets, everything after the IP header is typically shown simply as "data."

OSI Networking Model

At one point in the history of the OSI model, many people thought that OSI would win the battle of the networking models discussed earlier. If that had occurred, instead of TCP/IP running on every computer in the world, those computers would be running with OSI.

However, OSI did not win that battle. In fact, OSI no longer exists as a networking model that could be used instead of TCP/IP, although some of the original protocols referenced by the OSI model still exist.

So, why is OSI even in this book? Terminology. During those years in which many people thought the OSI model would become commonplace in the world of networking (mostly in the late 1980s and early 1990s), many vendors and protocol documents started using terminology from the OSI model. That terminology remains today. So, although you will never need to work with a computer that uses OSI, to understand modern networking terminology, you need to understand something about OSI.

Comparing OSI and TCP/IP

The OSI model has many similarities to the TCP/IP model from a basic conceptual perspective. It has layers (seven, in fact), and each layer defines a set of typical networking functions. As with TCP/IP, each OSI layer refers to multiple protocols and standards that implement the functions specified by each layer. In other cases, just as for TCP/IP, the OSI committees did not create new protocols or standards, but instead referenced other protocols that were already defined. For example, the IEEE defines Ethernet standards, so the OSI committees did not waste time specifying a new type of Ethernet; it simply referred to the IEEE Ethernet standards.

Today, the OSI model can be used as a standard of comparison to other networking models. Figure 2-15 compares the seven-layer OSI model with both the four-layer and five-layer TCP/IP models.

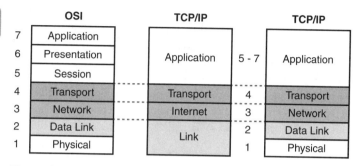

Figure 2-15 *OSI Model Compared to the Two TCP/IP Models*

Next, this section will examine two ways in which we still use OSI terminology today: to describe other protocols and to describe the encapsulation process. Along the way, the text will briefly examine each layer of the OSI model.

Describing Protocols by Referencing the OSI Layers

Even today, networking documents often describe TCP/IP protocols and standards by referencing OSI layers, both by layer number and layer name. For example, a common description of a LAN switch is "Layer 2 switch," with "Layer 2" referring to OSI Layer 2. Because OSI did have a well-defined set of functions associated with each of its seven layers, if you know those functions, you can understand what people mean when they refer to a product or function by its OSI layer.

For another example, TCP/IP's original internet layer, as implemented mainly by IP, equates most directly to the OSI *network* layer. So, most people say that IP is a *network layer protocol*, or a *Layer 3 protocol*, using OSI terminology and numbers for the layer. Of course, if you numbered the TCP/IP model, starting at the bottom, IP would be either Layer 2 or 3, depending on what version of the TCP/IP model you care to use. However, even though IP is a TCP/IP protocol, everyone uses the OSI model layer names and numbers when describing IP or any other protocol for that matter.

The claim that a particular TCP/IP layer is similar to a particular OSI layer is a general comparison, but not a detailed comparison. The comparison is a little like comparing a car to a truck: Both can get you from point A to point B, but they have many specific differences, like the truck having a truck bed in which to carry cargo. Similarly, both the OSI and TCP/IP network layers define logical addressing and routing. However, the addresses have a different size, and the routing logic even works differently. So the comparison of OSI layers to other protocol models is a general comparison of major goals, and not a comparison of the specific methods.

OSI Layers and Their Functions

The exam requires a basic understanding of the functions defined by each OSI layer, as well as remembering the names of the layers. It is also important that, for each device or protocol referenced throughout the book, you understand which layers of the OSI model most closely match the functions defined by that device or protocol.

Today, because most people happen to be much more familiar with TCP/IP functions than with OSI functions, one of the best ways to learn about the function of different OSI layers is to think about the functions in the TCP/IP model and to correlate those with the OSI model. If you use the five-layer TCP/IP model, the bottom four layers of OSI and TCP/IP map closely together. The only difference in these bottom four layers is the name of OSI Layer 3 (network) compared to the original TCP/IP model (internet). The upper three layers of the OSI reference model (application, presentation, and session—Layers 7, 6, and 5, respectively) define functions that all map to the TCP/IP application layer. Table 2-4 defines the functions of the seven layers.

Table 2-4 OSI Reference Model Layer Definitions

Layer	Functional Description
7	**Application layer:** This layer provides an interface between the communications software and any applications that need to communicate outside the computer on which the application resides. It also defines processes for user authentication.
6	**Presentation layer:** This layer's main purpose is to define and negotiate data formats, such as ASCII text, EBCDIC text, binary, BCD, and JPEG. Encryption is also defined by OSI as a presentation layer service.
5	**Session layer:** This layer defines how to start, control, and end conversations (called sessions). This includes the control and management of multiple bidirectional messages so that the application can be notified if only some of a series of messages are completed. This allows the presentation layer to have a seamless view of an incoming stream of data.
4	**Transport layer:** This layer's protocols provide a large number of services; whereas OSI Layers 5 through 7 focus on issues related to the application, Layer 4 focuses on issues related to data delivery to another computer (for example, error recovery and flow control).
3	**Network layer:** This layer defines three main features: logical addressing, routing (forwarding), and path determination. Routing defines how devices (typically routers) forward packets to their final destination. Logical addressing defines how each device can have an address that can be used by the routing process. Path determination refers to the work done by routing protocols to learn all possible routes and choose the best route.
2	**Data link layer:** This layer defines the rules that determine when a device can send data over a particular medium. Data link protocols also define the format of a header and trailer that allows devices attached to the medium to successfully send and receive data.
1	**Physical layer:** This layer typically refers to standards from other organizations. These standards deal with the physical characteristics of the transmission medium, including connectors, pins, use of pins, electrical currents, encoding, light modulation, and the rules for how to activate and deactivate the use of the physical medium.

Table 2-5 provides a sampling of the devices and protocols covered in this book and their comparable OSI layers. Note that many network devices must actually understand the protocols at multiple OSI layers, so the layer listed in Table 2-5 actually refers to the highest layer that the device normally thinks about when performing its core work. For example, routers need to think about Layer 3 concepts, but they must also support features at both Layers 1 and 2.

Table 2-5   OSI Reference Model—Example Devices and Protocols

Layer Name	Protocols and Specifications	Devices
Application, presentation, session (Layers 5–7)	Telnet, HTTP, FTP, SMTP, POP3, VoIP, SNMP	Hosts, firewalls
Transport (Layer 4)	TCP, UDP	Hosts, firewalls
Network (Layer 3)	IP	Router
Data link (Layer 2)	Ethernet (IEEE 802.3), HDLC	LAN switch, wireless access point, cable modem, Fiber
Physical (Layer 1)	RJ-45, Ethernet (IEEE 802.3)	LAN hub, LAN repeater, cables

Besides remembering the basics of the features of each OSI layer (as in Table 2-4) and some sample protocols and devices at each layer (as in Table 2-5), you should also memorize the names of the layers. Although you can simply memorize them, some people like to use a mnemonic phrase to make memorization easier. In the following three phrases, the first letter of each word is the same as the first letter of an OSI layer name, in the order specified in parentheses:

- All People Seem To Need Data Processing (Layers 7 to 1)
- Please Do Not Take Sausage Pizzas Away (Layers 1 to 7)
- Pew! Dead Ninja Turtles Smell Particularly Awful (Layers 1 to 7)

OSI Layering Concepts and Benefits

Although networking models use layers to help humans categorize and understand the many functions in a network, networking models also use layers for many other reasons. For example, consider another postal service analogy. A person writing a letter does not have to think about how the postal service will deliver a letter across the country. The postal worker in the middle of the country does not have to worry about the contents of the letter. Likewise, networking models that divide functions into different layers enable one software package or hardware device to implement functions from one layer and then assume that other software/hardware will perform the functions defined by the other layers.

The following list summarizes the benefits of layered protocol specifications:

- **Less complex:** Compared to not using a layered model, network models break the concepts into smaller parts.
- **Standard interfaces:** The standard interface definitions between each layer allow multiple vendors to create products that fill a particular role, with all the benefits of open competition.

- **Easier to learn:** Humans can more easily discuss and learn about the many details of a protocol specification.

- **Easier to develop:** Reduced complexity allows easier program changes and faster product development.

- **Multivendor interoperability:** Creating products to meet the same networking standards means that computers and networking gear from multiple vendors can work in the same network.

- **Modular engineering:** One vendor can write software that implements higher layers—for example, a web browser—and another vendor can write software that implements the lower layers—for example, Microsoft's built-in TCP/IP software in its OSs.

OSI Encapsulation Terminology

Like TCP/IP, each OSI layer asks for services from the next lower layer. To provide the services, each layer makes use of a header and possibly a trailer. The lower layer encapsulates the higher layer's data behind a header. The final topic of this chapter explains some of the terminology and concepts related to OSI encapsulation.

The TCP/IP model uses terms such as *segment*, *packet*, and *frame* to refer to various layers and their respective encapsulated data (refer to Figure 2-13). OSI uses a more generic term: *protocol data unit (PDU)*.

A PDU represents the bits that include the headers and trailers for that layer, as well as the encapsulated data. For example, an IP packet, as shown in Figure 2-14, using OSI terminology, is a PDU. In fact, an IP packet is a *Layer 3 PDU* (abbreviated L3PDU) because IP is a Layer 3 protocol. So, rather than use the term *segment*, *packet*, or *frame*, OSI simply refers to the "Layer x PDU" (LxPDU), with "x" referring to the number of the layer being discussed.

Figure 2-16 represents the typical encapsulation process, with the top of the figure showing the application data and application layer header and the bottom of the figure showing the L2PDU that is transmitted onto the physical link.

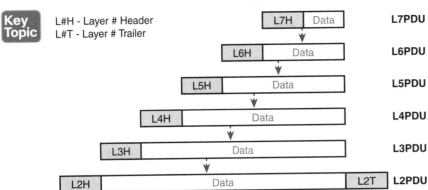

Figure 2-16 *OSI Encapsulation and Protocol Data Units*

Exam Preparation Tasks

Review All Key Topics

Review the most important topics from this chapter, noted with the Key Topic icon in the outer margin of the page. Table 2-6 lists references for these key topics and the page number on which each is found.

Table 2-6 Key Topics for Chapter 2

Key Topic Elements	Description	Page Number
Table 2-3	Provides definitions of same-layer and adjacent-layer interaction	96
Figure 2-10	Shows the general concept of IP routing	100
Figure 2-11	Depicts the data link services provided to IP for the purpose of delivering IP packets from host to host	101
Figure 2-13	Five steps to encapsulate data on the sending host	103
Figure 2-14	Shows the meaning of the terms *segment, packet,* and *frame*	104
Figure 2-15	Compares the OSI and TCP/IP network models	105
List	Lists the benefits of using a layered networking model	107
Figure 2-16	Terminology related to encapsulation	108

Definitions of Key Terms

After your first reading of the chapter, try to define these key terms, but do not be concerned about getting them all correct at that time. Chapter 24, "Final Review" directs you in how to use these terms for late-stage preparation for the exam.

adjacent-layer interaction, de-encapsulation, encapsulation, frame, networking model, packet, protocol data unit (PDU), same-layer interaction, segment

This chapter covers the following exam topics:

2.2. Describe classic Ethernet fundamentals

2.2.a. Forward

2.2.b. Filter

2.2.c. Flood

2.2.d. MAC address table

CHAPTER 3

Fundamentals of Ethernet LANs

Most every enterprise computer network can be separated into two general types of technology: local area networks (LAN) and wide area networks (WAN). LANs typically connect nearby devices: devices in the same room (whether a large data center or a small office), in the same building, or in a campus of buildings. In contrast, WANs connect devices that are typically relatively far apart. Together, LANs and WANs create a complete enterprise computer network, working together to deliver data from one device to another.

Many types of LANs have existed over the years, but today's networks use two general types of LANs: Ethernet LANs and wireless LANs. Ethernet LANs happen to use cables for the links between nodes, and because many types of cables use copper wires, Ethernet LANs are often called *wired LANs*. In comparison, wireless LANs do not use wires or cables; instead, they use radio waves to communicate between nodes.

Data center networks make extensive use of Ethernet LAN technology. For example, most individual servers today have multiple Ethernet connections to Ethernet LAN switches. This chapter begins laying a foundation of Ethernet knowledge that you can apply to all uses of Ethernet LAN technology, with the chapters in Part II, "Data Center Nexus Switching and Routing Fundamentals," and Part III, "IPv4/IPv6 Subnetting," adding many more details.

"Do I Know This Already?" Quiz

Use the "Do I Know This Already?" quiz to help decide whether you might want to skim this chapter, or a major section, moving more quickly to the "Exam Preparation Tasks" section near the end of the chapter. Table 3-1 lists the major headings in this chapter and their corresponding "Do I Know This Already?" quiz questions. For thorough explanations, see Appendix A, "Answers to the 'Do I Know This Already?' Quizzes."

Table 3-1 "Do I Know This Already?" Foundation Topics Section-to-Question Mapping

Foundation Topics Section	Questions
An Overview of LANs	1, 2
Building Physical Ethernet Networks	3, 4
Sending Data in Ethernet Networks	5–8

1. In the LAN for a small office, some user devices connect to the LAN using a cable, while others connect using wireless technology (and no cable). Which of the following is true regarding the use of Ethernet in this LAN?

   a. Only the devices that use cables are using Ethernet.

   b. Only the devices that use wireless are using Ethernet.

   c. Both the devices using cables and those using wireless are using Ethernet.

   d. None of the devices are using Ethernet.

2. Which of the following Ethernet standards defines Gigabit Ethernet over UTP cabling?

   a. 10GBASE-T.

   b. 100BASE-T.

   c. 1000BASE-T.

   d. None of the other answers is correct.

3. Which of the following is true about Ethernet crossover cables for Fast Ethernet?

   a. Pins 1 and 2 are reversed on the other end of the cable.

   b. Pins 1 and 2 on one end of the cable connect to pins 3 and 6 on the other end of the cable.

   c. Pins 1 and 2 on one end of the cable connect to pins 3 and 4 on the other end of the cable.

   d. The cable can be up to 1000 meters long to cross over between buildings.

   e. None of the other answers is correct.

4. Each answer lists two types of devices used in a 100BASE-T network. If these devices were connected with UTP Ethernet cables, which pairs of devices would require a straight-through cable? (Choose three answers.)

   a. PC and router

   b. PC and switch

   c. Hub and switch

   d. Router and hub

   e. Wireless access point (Ethernet port) and switch

5. Which of the following is true about the CSMA/CD algorithm?

   a. The algorithm never allows collisions to occur.

   b. Collisions can happen, but the algorithm defines how the computers should notice a collision and how to recover.

   c. The algorithm works with only two devices on the same Ethernet.

   d. None of the other answers is correct.

6. Which of the following is true about the Ethernet FCS field?

   a. Ethernet uses FCS for error recovery.

   b. It is 2 bytes long.

   c. It resides in the Ethernet trailer, not the Ethernet header.

   d. It is used for encryption.

7. Which of the following are true about the format of Ethernet addresses? (Choose three answers.)

   a. Each manufacturer puts a unique OUI code into the first 2 bytes of the address.

   b. Each manufacturer puts a unique OUI code into the first 3 bytes of the address.

   c. Each manufacturer puts a unique OUI code into the first half of the address.

   d. The part of the address that holds this manufacturer's code is called the MAC.

   e. The part of the address that holds this manufacturer's code is called the OUI.

   f. The part of the address that holds this manufacturer's code has no specific name.

8. Which of the following terms describe Ethernet addresses that can be used to send one frame that is delivered to multiple devices on the LAN? (Choose two answers.)

   a. Burned-in address

   b. Unicast address

   c. Broadcast address

   d. Multicast address

Foundation Topics

An Overview of LANs

The term *Ethernet* refers to a family of LAN standards that together define the physical and data link layers of the world's most popular wired LAN technology. The standards, defined by the Institute of Electrical and Electronics Engineers (IEEE), explain the cabling, the connectors on the ends of the cables, the protocol rules, and everything else required to create an Ethernet LAN.

Typical SOHO LANs

To begin, first think about a small office/home office (SOHO) LAN today, specifically a LAN that uses only Ethernet LAN technology. First, the LAN needs a device called an *Ethernet LAN switch*, which provides many physical ports into which cables can be connected. An Ethernet LAN uses *Ethernet cables*, which is a general reference to any cable that conforms to any one of several Ethernet standards. The LAN uses Ethernet cables to connect different Ethernet devices or nodes to one of the switch's Ethernet ports.

Figure 3-1 shows a drawing of a SOHO Ethernet LAN. The figure shows a single LAN switch, five cables, and five other Ethernet nodes: three PCs, a printer, and one network device called a *router*. (The router connects the LAN to the WAN—in this case, to the Internet.)

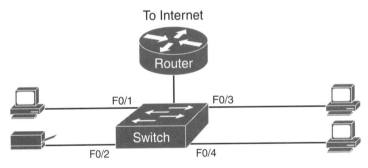

Figure 3-1 *Typical Small Ethernet-Only SOHO LAN*

Although Figure 3-1 shows a simple Ethernet LAN, many SOHO Ethernet LANs today combine the router and switch into a single device. Vendors sell consumer-grade integrated networking devices that work as a router and Ethernet switch, as well as perform other functions. These devices usually have "router" on the packaging, but many models also have four-port or eight-port Ethernet LAN switch ports built in to the device.

Typical SOHO LANs today also support wireless LAN connections. Ethernet defines wired LAN technology only; in other words, Ethernet LANs use cables. However, you can build one LAN that uses both Ethernet LAN technology as well as wireless LAN technology, which is also defined by the IEEE. Wireless LANs, defined by the IEEE using standards that begin with 802.11, use radio waves to send the bits from one node to the next.

Most wireless LANs rely on yet another networking device: a wireless LAN access point (*AP*). The AP acts somewhat like an Ethernet switch, in that all the wireless LAN nodes communicate with the Ethernet switch by sending and receiving data with the wireless AP. Of course, as a wireless device, the AP does not need Ethernet ports for cables, other than for a single Ethernet link to connect the AP to the Ethernet LAN, as shown in Figure 3-2.

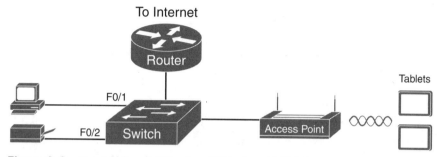

Figure 3-2   *Typical Small Wired and Wireless SOHO LAN*

Note that this drawing shows the router, Ethernet switch, and wireless LAN AP as three separate devices so that you can better understand the different roles. However, most SOHO networks today would use a single device, often labeled as a *wireless router*, that does all these functions.

Typical Enterprise Campus LANs

Companies (enterprises) need to support the devices used by their employees at the enterprise's business sites. Each site used by the enterprise might be only a few floors in an office building, or it might be the entire building, or even a campus with many buildings. Regardless, the term *campus* LAN refers to the LAN created to support the devices used by the people in an enterprise at a particular site.

Campus networks have similar needs compared to a SOHO network, but on a much larger scale. For example, enterprise Ethernet LANs begin with LAN switches installed in a wiring closet behind a locked door on each floor of a building. The electricians install the Ethernet cabling from that wiring closet to cubicles and conference rooms where devices might need to connect to the LAN. At the same time, most enterprises also support wireless LANs in the same space, to allow people to roam around and still work and to support a growing number of devices that do not have an Ethernet LAN interface.

Figure 3-3 shows a conceptual view of a typical enterprise LAN in a three-story building. Each floor has an Ethernet LAN switch and a wireless LAN AP. To allow communication between floors, each per-floor switch connects to one centralized distribution switch. For example, PC3 can send data to PC2, but it would first flow through switch SW3 to the first floor to the distribution switch (SWD) and then back up through switch SW2 on the second floor.

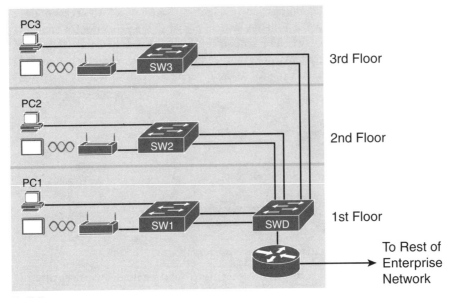

Figure 3-3 *Single-Building Enterprise Wired and Wireless LAN*

The figure also shows the typical way to connect a LAN to a WAN using a router. LAN switches and wireless APs work to create the LAN itself. Routers connect to both the LAN and the WAN. To connect to the LAN, the router simply uses an Ethernet LAN interface and an Ethernet cable, as shown in the lower-right corner of Figure 3-3.

Typical Data Center Ethernet LAN

Data center Ethernet LANs use many of the same Ethernet technologies and concepts used in SOHO and campus LANs. However, the networking needs for data centers differ enough from SOHO and campus LANs for Cisco to offer an entirely different certification track (routing and switching) for core networking functions in the rest of the enterprise, as compared to the data center certification track that begins with the DCICN exam.

Whereas a campus or SOHO LAN connects to end-user devices, a data center LAN connects to servers that users never see with their own eyes. The data center holds a number of servers in a relatively small space, with the servers often sitting in equipment racks. Each server then connects to an Ethernet switch, with the switches connecting together so that the servers can communicate with each other, as well as with end-user devices. Figure 3-4 shows the general idea.

NOTE Figure 3-4 uses a slightly different switch icon than the previous figures. Cisco supplies a large variety of standard icons to use when drawing network diagrams. Figures 3-2 and 3-3 show the typical icon for a generic switch. The icons shown in Figure 3-4 are for any model of Cisco Nexus switch, with the Nexus switch product line being specifically built for data centers.

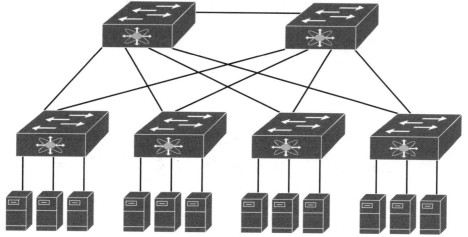

Figure 3-4 *Typical Data Center LAN Design with Four Racks*

No matter whether the Ethernet LAN is a single-room small office, a large data center, or some campus LAN, almost all LANs today use Ethernet as the primary LAN technology.

The rest of this chapter focuses on Ethernet in particular.

The Variety of Ethernet Physical Layer Standards

The term *Ethernet* refers to an entire family of standards. Some standards define the specifics of how to send data over a particular type of cabling and at a particular speed. Other standards define protocols, or rules, that the Ethernet nodes must follow to be a part of an Ethernet LAN. All these Ethernet standards come from the IEEE and include the number 802.3 as the beginning part of the standard name.

Ethernet supports a large variety of options for physical Ethernet links given its long history over the past 40 or so years. Today, Ethernet includes many standards for different kinds of optical and copper cabling, and for speeds from 10 megabits per second (Mbps) up to 100 gigabits per second (Gbps). The standards also differ as far as the types of cabling and the allowed length of the cabling.

The most fundamental cabling choice has to do with the materials used inside the cable for the physical transmission of bits: either copper wires or glass fibers. The use of unshielded twisted-pair (UTP) cabling saves money compared to optical fibers, with Ethernet nodes using the wires inside the cable to send data over electrical circuits. Fiber-optic cabling, the more expensive alternative, allows Ethernet nodes to send light over glass fibers in the center of the cable. Although more expensive, optical cables typically allow longer cabling distances between nodes.

To be ready to choose the products to purchase for a new Ethernet LAN, a network engineer must know the names and features of the different Ethernet standards supported in Ethernet products. The IEEE defines Ethernet physical layer standards using a couple of naming conventions. The formal name begins with 802.3 followed by some suffix letters. The IEEE also uses more meaningful shortcut names that identify the speed, in addition to a clue about whether the cabling is UTP (with a suffix that includes *T*) or fiber (with a suffix that includes *X*).

Table 3-2 lists a few Ethernet physical layer standards. First, the table lists enough names so that you get a sense of the IEEE naming conventions. It also lists the four most common standards that use UTP cabling, because this book's discussion of Ethernet focuses mainly on the UTP options.

Table 3-2   Examples of Types of Ethernet

Speed	Common Name	Informal IEEE Standard Name	Formal IEEE Standard Name	Cable Type, Maximum Length
10 Mbps	Ethernet	10BASE-T	802.3	Copper, 100 m
100 Mbps	Fast Ethernet	100BASE-T	802.3u	Copper, 100 m
1000 Mbps	Gigabit Ethernet	1000BASE-LX	802.3z	Fiber, 5000 m
1000 Mbps	Gigabit Ethernet	1000BASE-T	802.3ab	Copper, 100 m
10 Gbps	10 Gig Ethernet	10GBASE-T	802.3an	Copper, 100 m

NOTE   Fiber-optic cabling contains long, thin strands of fiberglass. The attached Ethernet nodes send light over the glass fiber in the cable, encoding the bits as changes in the light. For copper cabling, certain categories of cables are required; to reach 100m for 10G, please reference this guide: http://www.cisco.com/c/en/us/solutions/data-center-virtualization/10-gigabit-ethernet-technologies/index.html#~copper.

Consistent Behavior over All Links Using the Ethernet Data Link Layer

Although Ethernet includes many physical layer standards, it acts like a single LAN technology because it uses the same data link layer standard over all types of Ethernet physical links. That standard defines a common Ethernet header and trailer. (As a reminder, the header and trailer are bytes of overhead data that Ethernet uses to do its job of sending data over a LAN.) No matter whether the data flows over a UTP cable, or any kind of fiber cable, and no matter the speed, the data-link header and trailer use the same format.

Whereas the physical layer standards focus on sending bits over a cable, the Ethernet data-link protocols focus on sending an *Ethernet frame* from source to destination Ethernet node. From a data-link perspective, nodes build and forward frames. As first defined in Chapter 2, "The TCP/IP and OSI Networking Models," the term *frame* specifically refers to the header and trailer of a data-link protocol, plus the data encapsulated inside that header and trailer. The various Ethernet nodes simply forward the frame, over all the required links, to deliver it to the correct destination.

Figure 3-5 shows an example of the process. In this case, PC1 sends an Ethernet frame to PC3. The frame travels over a UTP link to Ethernet switch SW1, then over fiber links to Ethernet switches SW2 and SW3, and finally over another UTP link to PC3. Note that the bits actually travel at four different speeds in this example: 10 Mbps, 1 Gbps, 10 Gbps, and 100 Mbps, respectively.

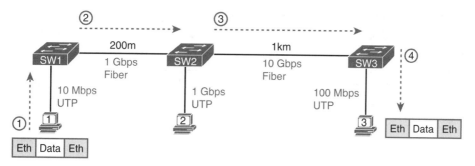

Figure 3-5 *Ethernet LAN Forwards a Data-Link Frame over Many Types of Links*

So, what is an Ethernet LAN? It is a combination of user devices, LAN switches, and different kinds of cabling. Each link can use different types of cables, at different speeds. However, they all work together to deliver Ethernet frames from the one device on the LAN to some other device.

The rest of this chapter takes these concepts a little deeper, first looking at the details of building the physical Ethernet network, followed by some discussion of the rules for forwarding an Ethernet frame from source to destination Ethernet node.

Building Physical Ethernet Networks with UTP

This second of three major sections of this chapter focuses on the individual physical links between any two Ethernet nodes. Before the Ethernet network as a whole can send Ethernet frames between user devices, each node must be ready and able to send data over an individual physical link. This section looks at some of the particulars of how Ethernet sends data over these links.

This section focuses on the three most commonly used Ethernet standards: 10BASE-T (Ethernet), 100BASE-T (Fast Ethernet, or FE), and 1000BASE-T (Gigabit Ethernet, or GE). Specifically, this section looks at the details of sending data in both directions over a UTP cable. It then examines the specific wiring of the UTP cables used for 10Mbps, 100Mbps, and 1000Mbps Ethernet.

Transmitting Data Using Twisted Pairs

Although it is true that Ethernet sends data over UTP cables, the physical means to send the data uses electricity that flows over the wires inside the UTP cable. To better understand how Ethernet sends data using electricity, break the idea down into two parts: how to create an electrical circuit and then how to make that electrical signal communicate 1s and 0s.

First, to create one electrical circuit, Ethernet defines how to use the two wires inside a single twisted pair of wires, as shown Figure 3-6. The figure does not show a UTP cable between two nodes, but instead shows two individual wires that are inside the UTP cable. An electrical circuit requires a complete loop, so the two nodes, using circuitry on their Ethernet ports, connect the wires in one pair to complete a loop, allowing electricity to flow.

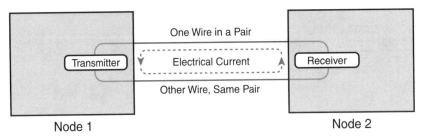

Figure 3-6 *Creating One Electrical Circuit over One Pair to Send in One Direction*

To send data, the two devices follow some rules called an *encoding scheme*. The idea works a lot like when two people talk using the same language: The speaker says some words in a particular language, and the listener, because she speaks the same language, can understand the spoken words. With an encoding scheme, the transmitting node changes the electrical signal over time, while the other node, the receiver, using the same rules, interprets those changes as either 0s or 1s. (For example, 10BASE-T uses an encoding scheme that encodes a binary 0 as a transition from higher voltage to lower voltage during the middle of a 1/10,000,000th-of-a-second interval.)

Note that in an actual UTP cable, the wires will be twisted together and not parallel, as shown in Figure 3-6. The twisting helps solve some important physical transmission issues. When electrical current passes over any wire, it creates electromagnetic interference (EMI) that obstructs the electrical signals in nearby wires, including the wires in the same cable. (EMI between wire pairs in the same cable is called *crosstalk*.) Twisting the wire pairs together helps cancel out most of the EMI, so most networking physical links that use copper wires use twisted pairs.

Breaking Down a UTP Ethernet Link

The term *Ethernet link* refers to any physical cable between two Ethernet nodes. To learn about how a UTP Ethernet link works, it helps to break down the physical link into those basic pieces, as shown in Figure 3-7: the cable itself, the connectors on the ends of the cable, and the matching ports on the devices into which the connectors will be inserted.

First, think about the UTP cable itself. The cable holds some copper wires, grouped as twisted pairs. The 10BASE-T and 100BASE-T standards require two pairs of wires, and the 1000BASE-T standard requires four pairs. Each wire has a color-coded plastic coating, with the wires in a pair having a color scheme. For example, for the blue wire pair, one wire's coating is all blue; the other wire's coating is blue and white striped.

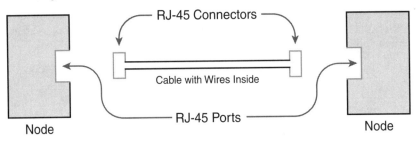

Figure 3-7 *Basic Components of an Ethernet Link*

Many Ethernet UTP cables use an RJ-45 connector on both ends. The RJ-45 connector has eight physical locations into which the eight wires in the cable can be inserted, called *pin positions*, or simply *pins*. These pins create a place where the ends of the copper wires can touch the electronics inside the nodes at the end of the physical link so that electricity can flow.

NOTE If available, find a nearby Ethernet UTP cable and examine the connectors closely. Look for the pin positions and the colors of the wires in the connector.

To complete the physical link, each node needs an RJ-45 *Ethernet port* that matches the RJ-45 connectors on the cable so that the connectors on the ends of the cable can attach to each node. PCs often include this RJ-45 Ethernet port as part of a network interface card (NIC), which can be an expansion card on the PC or can be built in to the system itself. Switches typically have many RJ-45 ports because switches give user devices a place to connect to the Ethernet LAN.

Figure 3-8 shows photos of the cables, connectors, and ports.

NOTE The RJ-45 connector is slightly wider than, but otherwise similar to, the RJ-11 connectors commonly used for telephone cables in homes in North America.

The figure shows a connector on the left and ports on the right. The left shows the eight pin positions in the end of the RJ-45 connector. The upper right shows an Ethernet NIC that is not yet installed in a computer. The lower-right part of the figure shows the side of a Cisco 2960 switch, with multiple RJ-45 ports, allowing multiple devices to easily connect to the Ethernet network.

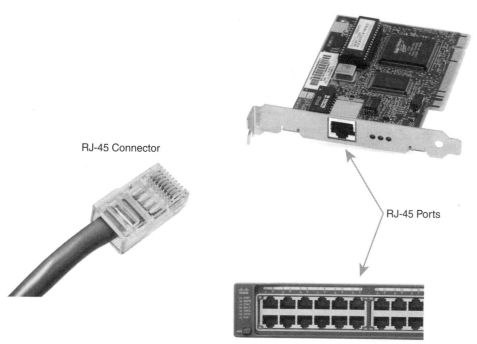

Figure 3-8 *RJ-45 Connectors and Ports (Ethernet NIC © Mark Jansen, LAN Cable © Mikko Pitkänen)*

Finally, while RJ-45 connectors with UTP cabling can be common, Cisco LAN switches often support other types of connectors as well. When you buy one of the many models of Cisco switches, you need to think about the mix and number of each type of physical port you want on the switch.

To give customers flexibility as to the type of Ethernet links, Cisco switches include some physical ports whose port hardware can be changed later, after the switch has been purchased. One type of port is called a *gigabit interface converter* (GBIC), which happened to first arrive on the market around the same time as Gigabit Ethernet, so it was given the same "gigabit" name. More recently, improved and smaller types of removable interfaces, called *small form-factor pluggables* (SFPs), provide the same function of enabling users to swap hardware and change the type of physical link. Figure 3-9 shows a photo of a Cisco switch with an SFP sitting slightly outside the SFP slot.

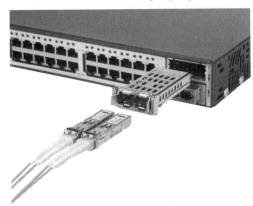

Figure 3-9   *Gigabit Fiber SFP Sitting Just Outside a Switch SFP Port*

UTP Cabling Pinouts for 10BASE-T and 100BASE-T

So far in this section, you have learned about the equivalent of how to drive a truck on a 1000-acre ranch, but you do not know the equivalent of the local traffic rules. If you worked the ranch, you could drive the truck all over the ranch, any place you wanted to go, and the police would not mind. However, as soon as you get on the public roads, the police want you to behave and follow the rules. Similarly, so far this chapter has discussed the general principles of how to send data, but it has not yet detailed some important rules for Ethernet cabling: the rules of the road so that all the devices send data using the right wires inside the cable.

This next topic discusses conventions for 10BASE-T and 100BASE-T together because they use UTP cabling in similar ways (including the use of only two wire pairs). A short comparison of the wiring for 1000BASE-T (Gigabit Ethernet), which uses four pairs, follows.

Straight-Through Cable Pinout

10BASE-T and 100BASE-T use two pairs of wires in a UTP cable, one for each direction, as shown in Figure 3-10. The figure shows four wires, all of which sit inside a single UTP cable that connects a PC and a LAN switch. In this example, the PC on the left transmits using the top pair, and the switch on the right transmits using the bottom pair.

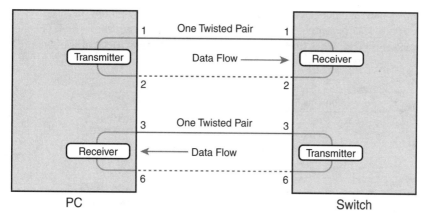

Figure 3-10 *Using One Pair for Each Transmission Direction with 10Mbps and 100Mbps Ethernet*

For correct transmission over the link, the wires in the UTP cable must be connected to the correct pin positions in the RJ-45 connectors. For example, in Figure 3-10, the transmitter on the PC on the left must know the pin positions of the two wires it should use to transmit. Those two wires must be connected to the correct pins in the RJ-45 connector on the switch so that the switch's receiver logic can use the correct wires.

To understand the wiring of the cable—which wires need to be in which pin positions on both ends of the cable—you need to first understand how the NICs and switches work. As a rule, Ethernet NIC transmitters use the pair connected to pins 1 and 2; the NIC receivers use a pair of wires at pin positions 3 and 6. LAN switches, knowing those facts about what Ethernet NICs do, do the opposite: Their receivers use the wire pair at pins 1 and 2, and their transmitters use the wire pair at pins 3 and 6.

To allow a PC NIC to communicate with a switch, the UTP cable must also use a *straight-through cable pinout*. The term *pinout* refers to the wiring of which color wire is placed in each of the eight numbered pin positions in the RJ-45 connector. An Ethernet straight-through cable connects the wire at pin 1 on one end of the cable to pin 1 at the other end of the cable; the wire at pin 2 needs to connect to pin 2 on the other end of the cable; pin 3 on one end connects to pin 3 on the other, and so on, as shown in Figure 3-11. Also, it uses the wires in one wire pair at pins 1 and 2, and another pair at pins 3 and 6.

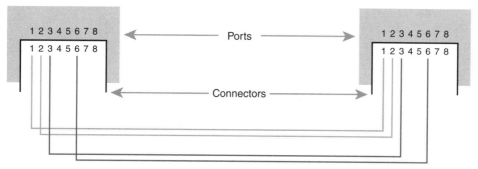

Figure 3-11 *10BASE-T and 100BASE-T Straight-Through Cable Pinout*

Figure 3-12 shows one final perspective on the straight-through cable pinout. In this case, PC Larry connects to a LAN switch. Note that the figure again does not show the UTP cable, but instead shows the wires that sit inside the cable, to emphasize the idea of wire pairs and pins.

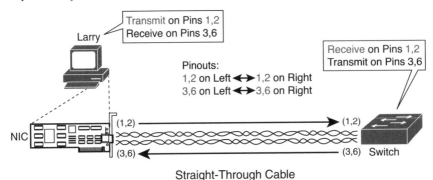

Figure 3-12   *Ethernet Straight-Through Cable Concept*

Crossover Cable Pinout

A straight-through cable works correctly when the nodes use opposite pairs for transmitting data. However, when two like devices connect to an Ethernet link, they both transmit over the same pins. In that case, you then need another type of cabling pinout called a *crossover cable*. The crossover cable pinout crosses the pair at the transmit pins on each device to the receive pins on the opposite device.

Although the previous sentence is true, this concept is much clearer with a figure, such as Figure 3-13. The figure shows what happens on a link between two switches. The two switches both transmit on the pair at pins 3 and 6, and they both receive on the pair at pins 1 and 2. So, the cable must connect a pair at pins 3 and 6 on each side to pins 1 and 2 on the other side, connecting to the other node's receiver logic. The top of the figure shows the literal pinouts, and the bottom half shows a conceptual diagram.

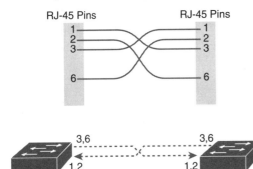

Figure 3-13   *Crossover Ethernet Cable*

Choosing the Right Cable Pinouts

For the exam, be well prepared to choose which type of cable (straight-through or crossover) is needed in each part of the network. The key is to know whether a device acts like a PC NIC, transmitting at pins 1 and 2, or like a switch, transmitting at pins 3 and 6. Then, just apply the following logic:

Crossover cable: If the endpoints transmit on the same pin pair

Straight-through cable: If the endpoints transmit on different pin pairs

Table 3-3 lists the devices mentioned in this book and the pin pairs they use, assuming that they use 10BASE-T and 100BASE-T.

Table 3-3   10BASE-T and 100BASE-T Pin Pairs Used

Transmits on Pins 1,2	Transmits on Pins 3,6
PC NICs	Hubs
Routers	Switches
Wireless AP (Ethernet interface)	—

For example, Figure 3-14 shows a campus LAN in a single building. In this case, several straight-through cables are used to connect PCs to switches. In addition, the cables connecting the switches require crossover cables.

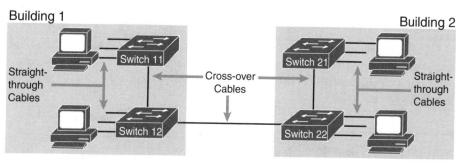

Figure 3-14   *Typical Uses for Straight-Through and Crossover Ethernet Cables*

NOTE If you have some experience with installing LANs, you might be thinking that you have used the wrong cable before (straight-through or crossover), but the cable worked. Cisco switches have a feature called *auto-MDIX* that notices when the wrong cable is used and automatically changes its logic to make the link work. However, for the exams, be ready to identify whether the correct cable is shown in the figures.

UTP Cabling Pinouts for 1000BASE-T

1000BASE-T (Gigabit Ethernet) differs from 10BASE-T and 100BASE-T as far as the cabling and pinouts. First, 1000BASE-T requires four wire pairs. Second, it uses more advanced electronics that allow both ends to transmit and receive simultaneously on each wire pair. However, the wiring pinouts for 1000BASE-T work almost identically to the earlier standards, adding details for the additional two pairs.

The straight-through cable connects each pin with the same numbered pin on the other side, but it does so for all eight pins—pin 1 to pin 1, pin 2 to pin 2, up through pin 8. It keeps one pair at pins 1 and 2 and another at pins 3 and 6, just like in the earlier wiring. It adds a pair at pins 4 and 5 and the final pair at pins 7 and 8 (refer to Figure 3-13).

The Gigabit Ethernet crossover cable crosses the same two-wire pairs as the crossover cable for the other types of Ethernet (the pairs at pins 1,2 and 3,6). It also crosses the two new pairs as well (the pair at pins 4,5 with the pair at pins 7,8).

Sending Data in Ethernet Networks

Although physical layer standards vary quite a bit, other parts of the Ethernet standards work the same way, regardless of the type of physical Ethernet link. Next, this final major section of this chapter looks at several protocols and rules that Ethernet uses regardless of the type of link. In particular, this section examines the details of the Ethernet data link layer protocol, plus how Ethernet nodes, switches, and hubs forward Ethernet frames through an Ethernet LAN.

Ethernet Data-Link Protocols

One of the most significant strengths of the Ethernet family of protocols is that these protocols use the same data-link standard. In fact, the core parts of the data-link standard date back to the original Ethernet standards.

The Ethernet data-link protocol defines the Ethernet frame: an Ethernet header at the front, the encapsulated data in the middle, and an Ethernet trailer at the end. Ethernet actually defines a few alternate formats for the header, with the frame format shown in Figure 3-15 being commonly used today.

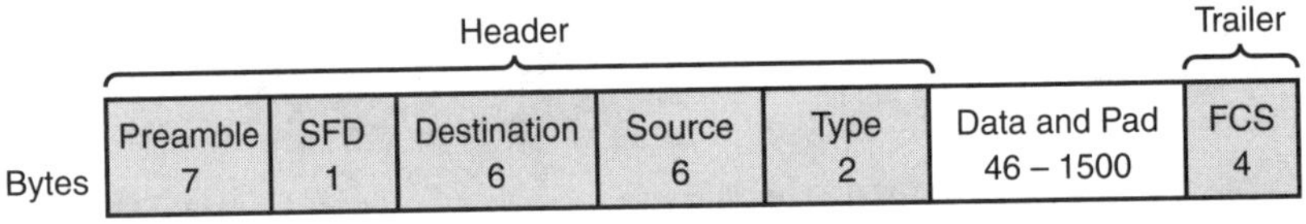

Figure 3-15 *Commonly Used Ethernet Frame Format*

All the fields in the frame matter, but some matter more to the topics discussed in this book. Table 3-4 lists the fields in the header and trailer, and it provides a brief description for reference, with the upcoming pages including more detail about a few of these fields.

Table 3-4 IEEE 802.3 Ethernet Header and Trailer Fields

Field	Field Length in Bytes	Description
Preamble	7	Synchronization.
Start Frame Delimiter (SFD)	1	Signifies that the next byte begins the Destination MAC Address field.

Field	Field Length in Bytes	Description
Destination MAC Address	6	Identifies the intended recipient of this frame.
Source MAC Address	6	Identifies the sender of this frame.
Type	2	Defines the type of protocol listed inside the frame; today, this most likely identifies IP version 4 (IPv4) or IP version 6 (IPv6).
Data and Pad*	46–1500	Holds data from a higher layer, typically an L3PDU (usually an IPv4 or IPv6 packet). The sender adds padding to meet the minimum length requirement for this field (46 bytes).
Frame Check Sequence (FCS)	4	Provides a method for the receiving NIC to determine whether the frame experienced transmission errors.

* The IEEE 802.3 specification limits the data portion of the 802.3 frame to a minimum of 46 bytes and a maximum of 1500 bytes. The term *maximum transmission unit* (MTU) defines the maximum Layer 3 packet that can be sent over a medium. Because the Layer 3 packet rests inside the data portion of an Ethernet frame, 1500 bytes is the largest IP MTU allowed over an Ethernet.

Ethernet Addressing

The source and destination Ethernet address fields play a big role in much of the Ethernet logic included in all the CCNA certifications (including DC). The general idea for each is relatively simple: The sending node puts its own address in the source address field and the intended Ethernet destination device's address in the destination address field. The sender transmits the frame, expecting that the Ethernet LAN, as a whole, will deliver the frame to that correct destination.

Ethernet addresses, also called *Media Access Control (MAC)* addresses, are 6-byte-long (48-bit-long) binary numbers. For convenience, most computers list MAC addresses as 12-digit hexadecimal numbers. Cisco devices typically add some periods to the number for easier readability as well; for example, a Cisco switch might list a MAC address as 0000.0C12.3456.

Most MAC addresses represent a single NIC or other Ethernet port, so these addresses are often called a *unicast* Ethernet address. The term *unicast* is simply a formal way to refer to the fact that the address represents one interface to the Ethernet LAN. (This term also contrasts with two other types of Ethernet addresses, *broadcast* and *multicast*, which are defined later in this section.)

The entire idea of sending data to a destination unicast MAC address works well, but it works only if all the unicast MAC addresses are unique. If two NICs try to use the same MAC address, there could be confusion. (The problem is like the confusion caused to the postal service if you and I both try to use the same mailing address. Would the postal service deliver mail to your house or to mine?) If two PCs on the same Ethernet try to use the same MAC address, to which PC should frames sent to that MAC address be delivered?

Ethernet solves this problem using an administrative process so that, at the time of manufacture, all Ethernet devices are assigned a universally unique MAC address. Before a manufacturer can build Ethernet products, it must ask the IEEE to assign the manufacturer a universally unique 3-byte code, called the *organizationally unique identifier* (OUI). The manufacturer agrees to give all NICs (and other Ethernet products) a MAC address that begins with its assigned 3-byte OUI. The manufacturer also assigns a unique value for the last 3 bytes, a number that manufacturer has never used with that OUI. As a result, the MAC address of every device in the universe is unique.

NOTE The IEEE also calls these universal MAC addresses global MAC addresses.

Figure 3-16 shows the structure of the unicast MAC address, with the OUI.

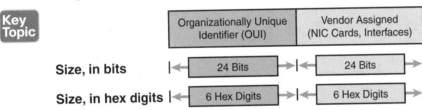

Figure 3-16 *Structure of Unicast Ethernet Addresses*

These addresses go by many names: LAN address, Ethernet address, hardware address, burned-in address, physical address, universal address, and MAC address. For example, the term *burned-in address* (BIA) refers to the idea that a permanent MAC address has been encoded (burned) into the ROM chip on the NIC. As another example, the IEEE uses the term *universal address* to emphasize the fact that the address assigned to a NIC by a manufacturer should be unique among all MAC addresses in the universe.

In addition to unicast addresses, Ethernet also uses group addresses. *Group addresses* identify more than one LAN interface card. A frame sent to a group address might be delivered to a small set of devices on the LAN, or even to all devices on the LAN. In fact, the IEEE defines two general categories of group addresses for Ethernet:

Broadcast address: Frames sent to this address should be delivered to all devices on the Ethernet LAN. It has a value of FFFF.FFFF.FFFF.

Multicast addresses: Frames sent to a multicast Ethernet address will be copied and forwarded to a subset of the devices on the LAN that volunteers to receive frames sent to a specific multicast address.

Table 3-5 summarizes most of the details about MAC addresses.

Table 3-5   LAN MAC Address Terminology and Features

LAN Addressing Term or Feature	Description
MAC	Media Access Control. 802.3 (Ethernet) defines the MAC sublayer of IEEE Ethernet.
Ethernet address, NIC address, LAN address	Other names often used instead of MAC address. These terms describe the 6-byte address of the LAN interface card.
Burned-in address	The 6-byte address assigned by the vendor making the card.
Unicast address	A term for a MAC address that represents a single LAN interface.
Broadcast address	An address that means "all devices that reside on this LAN right now."
Multicast address	On Ethernet, a multicast address implies some subset of all devices currently on the Ethernet LAN.

Identifying Network Layer Protocols with the Ethernet Type Field

Whereas the Ethernet header's address fields play an important and more obvious role in Ethernet LANs, the Ethernet Type field plays a more obscure role. The Ethernet Type field, or EtherType, sits in the Ethernet data link layer header, but its purpose is to directly help the network processing on routers and hosts. Basically, the Type field identifies the type of network layer (Layer 3) packet that sits inside the Ethernet frame.

First, think about what sits inside the data part of the Ethernet frame shown earlier in Figure 3-15. Typically, it holds the network layer packet created by the network layer protocol on some device in the network. Over the years, those protocols have included IBM Systems Network Architecture (SNA), Novell NetWare, Digital Equipment Corporation's DECnet, and Apple Computer's AppleTalk. Today, the most common network layer protocols are both from TCP/IP: IP version 4 (IPv4) and IP version 6 (IPv6).

The original host has a place to insert a value (a hexadecimal number) to identify the type of packet encapsulated inside the Ethernet frame. However, what number should the sender put in the header to identify an IPv4 packet as the type? Or an IPv6 packet? As it turns out, the IEEE manages a list of EtherType values, so that every network layer protocol that needs a unique EtherType value can have a number. The sender just has to know the list. (Anyone can view the list; just go to www.ieee.org and search for "*EtherType*.")

For example, a host can send one Ethernet frame with an IPv4 packet and the next Ethernet frame with an IPv6 packet. Each frame would have a different Ethernet Type field value, using the values reserved by the IEEE, as shown in Figure 3-17.

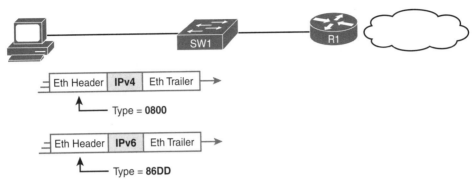

Figure 3-17 *Use of Ethernet Type Field*

Error Detection with FCS

Ethernet also defines a way for nodes to find out whether a frame's bits changed while crossing over an Ethernet link. (Usually, the bits could change because of some kind of electrical interference or a bad NIC.) Ethernet, like most every other data-link protocol covered on the CCNA exams, uses a field in the data-link trailer for the purpose of error detection.

The Ethernet Frame Check Sequence (FCS) field in the Ethernet trailer—the only field in the Ethernet trailer—gives the receiving node a way to compare results with the sender, to discover whether errors occurred in the frame. The sender applies a complex math formula to the frame before sending it, storing the result of the formula in the FCS field. The receiver applies the same math formula to the received frame. The receiver then compares its own results with the sender's results. If the results are the same, the frame did not change; otherwise, an error occurred, and the receiver discards the frame.

Note that *error detection* does not also mean *error recovery*. Ethernet does error detection so that if a frame's content has changed, the Ethernet device can simply discard the frame. Ethernet does not attempt to recover the lost frame. Other protocols, notably TCP, recover the lost data by noticing that it is lost and sending the data again.

Sending Ethernet Frames with Switches and Hubs

Ethernet LANs behave slightly differently depending on whether the LAN has mostly modern devices (in particular, LAN switches instead of some older LAN devices called *LAN hubs*). Basically, the use of more modern switches allows the use of full-duplex logic, which is much faster and simpler than half-duplex logic, which is required when using hubs. The final topic in this chapter looks at these basic differences.

Sending in Modern Ethernet LANs Using Full-Duplex

Modern Ethernet LANs use a variety of Ethernet physical standards, but with standard Ethernet frames that can flow over any of these types of physical links. Each individual link can run at a different speed, but each link allows the attached nodes to send the bits in the frame to the next node. They must work together to deliver the data from the sending Ethernet node to the destination node.

The process is relatively simple, on purpose; the simplicity lets each device send a large number of frames per second. Figure 3-18 shows an example in which PC1 sends an Ethernet frame to PC2.

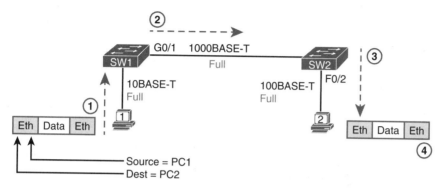

Figure 3-18 *Example of Sending Data in a Modern Ethernet LAN*

The following list details the steps in the figure:

1. PC1 builds and sends the original Ethernet frame, using its own MAC address as the source address and PC2's MAC address as the destination address.

2. Switch SW1 receives and forwards the Ethernet frame out its G0/1 interface (short for Gigabit interface 0/1) to SW2.

3. Switch SW2 receives and forwards the Ethernet frame out its F0/2 interface (short for Fast Ethernet interface 0/2) to PC2.

4. PC2 receives the frame, recognizes the destination MAC address as its own, and processes the frame.

The Ethernet network in Figure 3-18 uses full-duplex on each link, but the concept might be difficult to see. Full-duplex means that the NIC or switch port has no half-duplex restrictions. So, to understand full-duplex, you need to understand half-duplex, as follows:

Half-duplex: Logic in which a port sends data only when it is not also receiving data; in other words, it cannot send and receive at the same time.

Full-duplex: The absence of the half-duplex restriction.

So, with all PCs and LAN switches, and no LAN hubs, all the nodes can use full-duplex. All nodes can send and receive on their port at the same instant in time. For example, in Figure 3-18, PC1 and PC2 could send frames to each other simultaneously, in both directions, without any half-duplex restrictions.

Using Half-Duplex with LAN Hubs

To understand the need for half-duplex logic in some cases, you have to understand a little about an older type of networking device called a LAN hub. When the IEEE first introduced 10BASE-T in 1990, the Ethernet did not yet include LAN switches. Instead of switches, vendors created LAN hubs. The LAN hub provided a number of RJ-45 ports as a place to connect links to PCs, just like a LAN switch, but it used different rules for forwarding data.

LAN hubs forward data using physical layer standards and are therefore considered to be Layer 1 devices. When an electrical signal comes in one hub port, the hub repeats that electrical signal out all other ports (except the incoming port). By doing so, the data reaches all the rest of the nodes connected to the hub, so the data hopefully reaches the correct destination. The hub has no concept of Ethernet frames, of addresses, and so on.

The downside of using LAN hubs is that if two or more devices transmit a signal at the same instant, the electrical signal collides and becomes garbled. The hub repeats all received electrical signals, even if it receives multiple signals at the same time. For example, Figure 3-19 shows the idea, with PCs Archie and Bob sending an electrical signal at the same instant of time (Steps 1A and 1B) and the hub repeating both electrical signals out toward Larry on the left (Step 2).

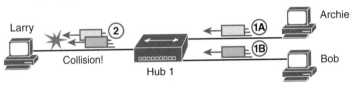

Figure 3-19 *Collision Occurring Because of LAN Hub Behavior*

NOTE For completeness, note that the hub floods each frame out all other ports (except the incoming port). So, Archie's frame goes to both Larry and Bob; Bob's frame goes to Larry and Archie.

If you replace the hub in Figure 3-19 with a LAN switch, the switch prevents the collision on the left. The switch operates as a Layer 2 device, meaning that it looks at the data-link header and trailer. A switch would look at the MAC addresses, and even if the switch needed to forward both frames to Larry on the left, the switch would send one frame and queue the other frame until the first frame was finished.

Now back to the issue created by the hub's logic: collisions. To prevent these collisions, the Ethernet nodes must use half-duplex logic instead of full-duplex logic. A problem only occurs when two or more devices send at the same time; half-duplex logic tells the nodes that if someone else is sending, wait before sending.

For example, back in Figure 3-19, imagine that Archie began sending his frame early enough so that Bob received the first bits of that frame before Bob tried to send his own frame. Bob, at Step 1B, would notice that he was receiving a frame from someone else, and using half-duplex logic, would simply wait to send the frame listed at Step 1B.

Nodes that use half-duplex logic actually use a relatively well-known algorithm called *carrier sense multiple access with collision detection* (CSMA/CD). The algorithm takes care of the obvious cases but also the cases caused by unfortunate timing. For example, two nodes could check for an incoming frame at the exact same instant, both realize that no other node is sending, and both send their frames at the exact same instant, thus causing a collision. CSMA/CD covers these cases as well, as follows:

Step 1.   A device with a frame to send listens until the Ethernet is not busy.

Step 2.   When the Ethernet is not busy, the sender begins sending the frame.

Step 3.   The sender listens while sending to discover whether a collision occurs; collisions might be caused by many reasons, including unfortunate timing. If a collision occurs, all currently sending nodes do the following:

> **A.** They send a jamming signal that tells all nodes that a collision happened.
>
> **B.** They independently choose a random time to wait before trying again, to avoid unfortunate timing.
>
> **C.** The next attempt starts again at Step 1.

Although most modern LANs do not often use hubs, and therefore do not need to use half-duplex, enough old hubs still exist in enterprise networks that you need to be ready to understand duplex issues. Each NIC and switch port has a duplex setting. For all links between PCs and switches, or between switches, full-duplex should be used. However, for any link connected to a LAN hub, the connected LAN switch and NIC port should use half-duplex. Note that the hub itself does not use half-duplex logic, instead just repeating incoming signals out every other port.

Figure 3-20 shows an example, with full-duplex links on the left and a single LAN hub on the right. The hub then requires SW2's F0/2 interface to use half-duplex logic, along with the PCs connected to the hub.

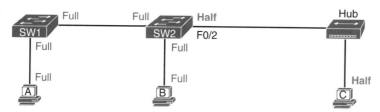

Figure 3-20   *Full- and Half-Duplex in an Ethernet LAN*

Traffic Storm Control in Ethernet Networks

A traffic storm happens when packets flood the LAN, creating excessive traffic and degrading network performance. You can use the traffic storm control feature to prevent disruptions on Layer 2 ports by a broadcast, multicast, or unicast traffic storm on physical interfaces.

Storm control allows you to monitor the levels of the incoming broadcast, multicast, and unicast traffic more than a 1-second interval. During this interval, the traffic level, which is a percentage of the total available bandwidth of the port, is compared with the traffic storm control level that you configured. If the ingress traffic reaches the storm control level that is configured on the port, traffic storm control drops the traffic until the interval ends.

Figure 3-21 shows the broadcast traffic patterns on a Layer 2 interface over a given interval. In this example, traffic storm control occurs between times T1 and T2 and between T4 and T5. During those intervals, the amount of broadcast traffic exceeded the configured threshold.

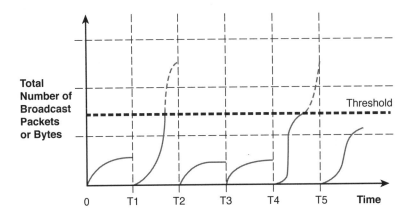

Figure 3-21 *Storm Control Intervals*

Exam Preparation Tasks

Review All Key Topics

Review the most important topics from this chapter, noted with the Key Topic icon in the outer margin of the page. Table 3-6 lists references for these key topics and the page number on which each is found.

Table 3-6   Key Topics for Chapter 3

Key Topic Element	Description	Page Number
Figure 3-3	Drawing of a typical wired and wireless enterprise LAN	116
Figure 3-4	Drawing of a typical data center LAN	117
Table 3-2	Several types of Ethernet LANs and some details about each	118
Figure 3-10	Conceptual drawing of transmitting in one direction, each over two different electrical circuits between two Ethernet nodes	123
Figure 3-11	10Mbps and 100Mbps Ethernet straight-through cable pinouts	123
Figure 3-13	10Mbps and 100Mbps Ethernet crossover cable pinouts	124
Table 3-3	List of devices that transmit on wire pair 1,2 and wire pair 3,6	125
Figure 3-14	Typical uses for straight-through and crossover Ethernet cables	125
Figure 3-16	Format of Ethernet MAC addresses	128
List	Definitions of half-duplex and full-duplex	131
Figure 3-20	Examples of which interfaces use full-duplex and which interfaces use half-duplex	133

Complete the Tables and Lists from Memory

Print a copy of Appendix C, "Memory Tables," or at least the section for this chapter, and complete the tables and lists from memory. Appendix D, "Memory Tables Answer Key," includes completed tables and lists for you to check your work.

Definitions of Key Terms

After your first reading of the chapter, try to define these key terms, but do not be concerned about getting them all correct at that time. Chapter 24, "Final Review," directs you in how to use these terms for late-stage preparation for the exam.

Ethernet, IEEE, wired LAN, Ethernet frame, 10BASE-T, 100BASE-T, 1000BASE-T, Fast Ethernet, Gigabit Ethernet, Ethernet link, RJ-45, Ethernet port, network interface card (NIC), straight-through cable, crossover cable, Ethernet address, MAC address, unicast address, broadcast address, Frame Check Sequence

This chapter covers the following exam topics:

2.0. Basic data center networking concepts

2.1. Compare and contrast the OSI and the TCP/IP models

CHAPTER 4

Fundamentals of IPv4 Addressing and Routing

The TCP/IP network layer (Layer 3) defines how to deliver IP packets over the entire trip, from the original device that creates the packet to the device that needs to receive the packet. That process requires cooperation between several different jobs and concepts on a number of devices.

This chapter begins with an overview of all these cooperating functions, and then it dives into more detail about each area. These areas include IP routing, IP addressing, and IP routing protocols, all of which play a vital role in data center networks.

IP addressing and routing matters quite a bit to data center networking as well. You can think of the end users of the servers as sitting out in the network somewhere—on the other side of the Internet, at another WAN site in the same enterprise, and so on. The data center part of the network must be connected to the rest of the enterprise and to the Internet; otherwise, the servers will not be accessible to the users. IPv4 defines the rules that enable users to connect to the servers and for traffic to flow back out to the users' devices.

> **NOTE** As promised in the Introduction's section "For Those Studying Routing & Switching," this chapter's content mirrors the content in Chapter 4 of the *ICND1 100-101 Official Cert Guide*, with no additional information hidden here.

"Do I Know This Already?" Quiz

Use the "Do I Know This Already?" quiz in Table 4-1 to help decide whether you might want to skim this chapter, or a major section, moving more quickly to the "Exam Preparation Tasks" section near the end of the chapter. For thorough explanations, see Appendix A, "Answers to the 'Do I Know This Already?' Quizzes."

Table 4-1 "Do I Know This Already?" Foundation Topics Section-to-Question Mapping

Foundation Topics Section	Questions
Overview of Network Layer Functions	1, 2
IPv4 Addressing	3–5
IPv4 Routing	6–8
IPv4 Routing Protocols	9
Other Network Layer Features	10

1. Which of the following are functions of OSI Layer 3 protocols? (Choose two answers.)

   a. Logical addressing

   b. Physical addressing

   c. Path selection

   d. Arbitration

   e. Error recovery

2. Imagine that PC1 needs to send some data to PC2, and PC1 and PC2 are separated by several routers. Both PC1 and PC2 sit on different Ethernet LANs. What are the largest entities (in size) that make it from PC1 to PC2? (Choose two answers.)

   a. Frame

   b. Segment

   c. Packet

   d. L5 PDU

   e. L3 PDU

   f. L1 PDU

3. Which of the following is a valid Class C IP address that can be assigned to a host?

   a. 1.1.1.1

   b. 200.1.1.1

   c. 128.128.128.128

   d. 224.1.1.1

4. What is the assignable range of values for the first octet for Class A IP networks?

   a. 0 to 127

   b. 0 to 126

   c. 1 to 127

   d. 1 to 126

   e. 128 to 191

   f. 128 to 192

5. PC1 and PC2 are on two different Ethernet LANs that are separated by an IP router. PC1's IP address is 10.1.1.1, and no subnetting is used. Which of the following addresses could be used for PC2? (Choose two answers.)

   a. 10.1.1.2

   b. 10.2.2.2

   c. 10.200.200.1

   d. 9.1.1.1

   e. 225.1.1.1

   f. 1.1.1.1

6. Imagine a network with two routers that are connected with a point-to-point HDLC serial link. Each router has an Ethernet, with PC1 sharing the Ethernet with Router1 and PC2 sharing the Ethernet with Router2. When PC1 sends data to PC2, which of the following is true?

    a. Router1 strips the Ethernet header and trailer off the frame received from PC1, never to be used again.

    b. Router1 encapsulates the Ethernet frame inside an HDLC header and sends the frame to Router2, which extracts the Ethernet frame for forwarding to PC2.

    c. Router1 strips the Ethernet header and trailer off the frame received from PC1, which is exactly re-created by Router2 before forwarding data to PC2.

    d. Router1 removes the Ethernet, IP, and TCP headers and rebuilds the appropriate headers before forwarding the packet to Router2.

7. Which of the following does a router normally use when making a decision about routing TCP/IP packets?

    a. Destination MAC address

    b. Source MAC address

    c. Destination IP address

    d. Source IP address

    e. Destination MAC and IP address

8. Which of the following are true about a LAN-connected TCP/IP host and its IP routing (forwarding) choices? (Choose two answers.)

    a. The host always sends packets to its default gateway.

    b. The host sends packets to its default gateway if the destination IP address is in a different class of IP network than the host.

    c. The host sends packets to its default gateway if the destination IP address is in a different subnet than the host.

    d. The host sends packets to its default gateway if the destination IP address is in the same subnet as the host.

9. Which of the following are functions of a routing protocol? (Choose two answers.)

    a. Advertising known routes to neighboring routers

    b. Learning routes for subnets directly connected to the router

    c. Learning routes, and putting those routes into the routing table, for routes advertised to the router by its neighboring routers

    d. Forwarding IP packets based on a packet's destination IP address

10. A company implements a TCP/IP network, with PC1 sitting on an Ethernet LAN. Which of the following protocols and features requires PC1 to learn information from some other server device?

    a. ARP

    b. ping

    c. DNS

    d. None of these answers is correct.

Foundation Topics

Overview of Network Layer Functions

While many protocol models have existed over the years, today the TCP/IP model dominates. And at the network layer of TCP/IP, two options exist for the main protocol around which all other network layer functions revolve: IP version 4 (IPv4) and IP version 6 (IPv6). Both IPv4 and IPv6 define the same kinds of network layer functions, but with different details. This chapter introduces these network layer functions for IPv4.

NOTE   All references to IP in this chapter refer to the older and more established IPv4.

IP focuses on the job of routing data, in the form of IP packets, from the source host to the destination host. IP does not concern itself with the physical transmission of data, instead relying on the lower TCP/IP layers to do the physical transmission of the data. IP concerns itself with the logical details, instead of physical details, of delivering data. In particular, the network layer specifies how packets travel end to end over a TCP/IP network, even when the packet crosses many different types of LAN and WAN links.

This first section of the chapter begins a broad discussion of the TCP/IP network layer by looking at IP routing and addressing. The two topics work together, because IP routing relies on the structure and meaning of IP addresses, and IP addressing was designed with IP routing in mind. Following that, this overview section looks at routing protocols, which let routers learn the information they need to know to do routing correctly.

Network Layer Routing (Forwarding) Logic

Routers and end-user computers (called *hosts* in a TCP/IP network) work together to perform IP routing. The host operating system (OS) has TCP/IP software, including the software that implements the network layer. Hosts use that software to choose where to send IP packets, oftentimes to a nearby router. Those routers make choices of where to send the IP packet next. Together, the hosts and routers deliver the IP packet to the correct destination, as seen in the example in Figure 4-1.

The IP packet, created by PC1, goes from the top of the figure all the way to PC2 at the bottom of the figure. The next few pages discuss the network layer routing logic used by each device along the path.

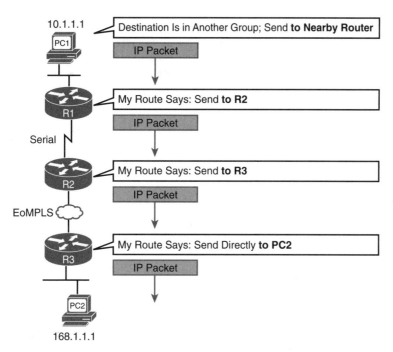

Figure 4-1 *Routing Logic: PC1 Sending an IP Packet to PC2*

NOTE The term *path selection* is sometimes used to refer to the routing process shown in Figure 4-1. At other times, it refers to routing protocols, specifically how routing protocols select the best route among the competing routes to the same destination.

Host Forwarding Logic: Send the Packet to the Default Router

In this example, PC1 does some basic analysis and then chooses to send the IP packet to the router so that the router will forward it. PC1 analyzes the destination address and realizes that PC2's address (168.1.1.1) is not on the same LAN as PC1. So PC1's logic tells it to send the packet to a device whose job it is to know where to route data: a nearby router, on the same LAN, called PC1's default router.

To send the IP packet to the default router, the sender sends a data-link frame across the medium to the nearby router; this frame includes the packet in the data portion of the frame. This frame uses data link layer (Layer 2) addressing in the data-link header to ensure that the nearby router receives the frame.

NOTE The *default router* is also referred to as the *default gateway*.

R1 and R2's Logic: Routing Data Across the Network

All routers use the same general process to route the packet. Each router keeps an *IP routing table*. This table lists IP address *groupings*, called *IP networks* and *IP subnets*. When a router receives a packet, it compares the packet's destination IP address to the entries in the routing table and makes a match. This matching entry also lists directions that tell the router where to forward the packet next.

In Figure 4-1, R1 would have matched the destination address (168.1.1.1) to a routing table entry, which in turn told R1 to send the packet to R2 next. Similarly, R2 would have matched a routing table entry that told R2 to send the packet, over an Ethernet over MPLS (EoMPLS) link, to R3 next.

The routing concept works a little like driving down the freeway when approaching a big interchange. You look up and see signs for nearby towns, telling you which exits to take to go to each town. Similarly, the router looks at the IP routing table (the equivalent of the road signs) and directs each packet over the correct next LAN or WAN link (the equivalent of a road).

R3's Logic: Delivering Data to the End Destination

The final router in the path, R3, uses almost the same logic as R1 and R2, but with one minor difference. R3 needs to forward the packet directly to PC2, not to some other router. On the surface, that difference seems insignificant. In the next section, when you read about how the network layer uses LANs and WANs, the significance of the difference will become obvious.

How Network Layer Routing Uses LANs and WANs

While the network layer routing logic ignores the physical transmission details, the bits still have to be transmitted. To do that work, the network layer logic in a host or router must hand off the packet to the data link layer protocols, which, in turn, ask the physical layer to actually send the data. And as was described in Chapter 3, "Fundamentals of Ethernet LANs," the data link layer adds the appropriate header and trailer to the packet, creating a frame, before sending the frames over each physical network.

The routing process forwards the network layer packet from end to end through the network, while each data link frame only takes a smaller part of the trip. Each successive data link layer frame moves the packet to the next device that thinks about network layer logic. In short, the network layer thinks about the bigger view of the goal, such as "Send this packet to the specified next device…," while the data link layer thinks about the specifics, such as "Encapsulate the packet in a data link frame and transmit it." Figure 4-2 points out the key encapsulation logic on each device, using the same examples as shown in Figure 4-1.

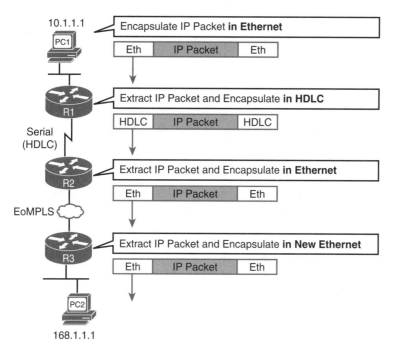

Figure 4-2 *Network Layer and Data Link Layer Encapsulation*

Because the routers build new data link headers and trailers, and because the new headers contain data link addresses, the PCs and routers must have some way to decide what data link addresses to use. An example of how the router determines which data link address to use is the *IP Address Resolution Protocol* (*ARP*). *ARP* dynamically learns the data link address of an IP host connected to a LAN. For example, at the last step, at the bottom of Figure 4-2, router R3 would use ARP once to learn PC2's MAC address before sending any packets to PC2.

Routing as covered so far has two main concepts:

- The process of routing forward Layer 3 packets, also called *Layer 3 protocol data units (L3 PDU)*, based on the destination Layer 3 address in the packet.

- The routing process uses the data link layer to encapsulate the Layer 3 packets into Layer 2 frames for transmission across each successive data link.

IP Addressing and How Addressing Helps IP Routing

IP defines network layer addresses that identify any host or router interface that connects to a TCP/IP network. The idea basically works like a postal address: Any interface that expects to receive IP packets needs an IP address, just like you need a postal address before receiving mail from the postal service.

TCP/IP groups IP addresses together so that IP addresses used on the same physical network are part of the same group. IP calls these address groups an *IP network* or an *IP subnet*. Using that same postal service analogy, each IP network and IP subnet works like a postal code (or in the United States, a ZIP code). All nearby postal addresses are in the same postal code (ZIP code), while all nearby IP addresses must be in the same IP network or IP subnet.

> **NOTE**   IP defines the word *network* to mean a very specific concept. To avoid confusion when writing about IP addressing, this book (and others) often avoids using the term *network* for other uses. In particular, this book uses the term *internetwork* to refer more generally to a network made up of routers, switches, cables, and other equipment.

IP defines specific rules about which IP address should be in the same IP network or IP subnet. Numerically, the addresses in the same group have the same value in the first part of the addresses. For example, Figures 4-1 and 4-2 could have used the following conventions:

- Hosts on the top Ethernet: Addresses start with 10
- Hosts on the R1-R2 serial link: Addresses start with 168.10
- Hosts on the R2-R3 EoMPLS link: Addresses start with 168.11
- Hosts on the bottom Ethernet: Addresses start with 168.1

It's similar to the USPS ZIP code system and how it requires local governments to assign addresses to new buildings. It would be ridiculous to have two houses, next door to each other, whose addresses have different ZIP codes. Similarly, it would be silly to have people who live on opposite sides of the country to have addresses with the same ZIP code.

Similarly, to make routing more efficient, network layer protocols group addresses, both by their location and by the actual address values. A router can list one routing table entry for each IP network or subnet, instead of one entry for every single IP address.

The routing process also makes use of the IPv4 header, as shown in Figure 4-3. The header lists a 32-bit source IP address as well as a 32-bit destination IP address. The header, of course, has other fields, a few of which matter for other discussions in this book. The book will refer back to this figure as needed, but otherwise, be aware of the 20-byte IP header and the existence of the source and destination IP address fields.

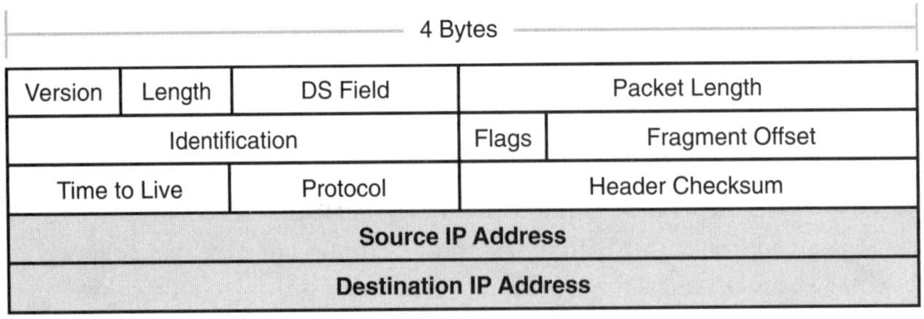

4 Bytes			
Version	Length	DS Field	Packet Length
Identification		Flags	Fragment Offset
Time to Live		Protocol	Header Checksum
Source IP Address			
Destination IP Address			

Figure 4-3   *IPv4 Header, Organized as Four Bytes Wide, for a Total of 20 Bytes*

Routing Protocols

For routing logic to work on both hosts and routers, each needs to know something about the TCP/IP internetwork. Hosts need to know the IP address of their default router so that they can send packets to remote destinations. Routers, however, need to know routes so they know how to forward packets to each and every IP network and IP subnet.

Although a network engineer could configure (type) all the required routes, on every router, most network engineers instead simply enable a routing protocol on all routers. If you enable the same routing protocol on all the routers in a TCP/IP internetwork, with the correct settings, the routers will send routing protocol messages to each other. As a result, all the routers will learn routes for all the IP networks and subnets in the TCP/IP internetwork.

Figure 4-4 shows an example, using the same diagram as in Figures 4-1 and 4-2. In this case, IP network 168.1.0.0, which consists of all addresses that begin with 168.1, sits on the Ethernet at the bottom of the figure. R3, knowing this fact, sends a routing protocol message to R2 (Step 1). R2 learns a route for network 168.1.0.0 as a result, as shown on the left. At Step 2, R2 turns around and sends a routing protocol message to R1 so that R1 now has a route for that same IP network (168.1.0.0).

R1 Routing Table

Subnet	Interface	Next Hop
168.1.0.0	Serial0	R2

R2 Routing Table

Subnet	Interface	Next Hop
168.1.0.0	F0/0	R3

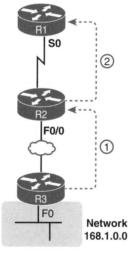

Figure 4-4   *Example of How Routing Protocols Advertise About Networks and Subnets*

This concludes the overview of how the TCP/IP network layer works. The rest of this chapter reexamines the key components in more depth.

IPv4 Addressing

By the time you have finished reading this book, you should be comfortable and confident in your understanding of IP addresses, their formats, the grouping concepts, how to subdivide groups into subnets, how to interpret the documentation for existing networks' IP addressing, and so on. Simply put, you had better know addressing and subnetting!

This section introduces IP addressing and subnetting and also covers the concepts behind the structure of an IP address, including how it relates to IP routing. In Part IV, "IPv4 Routing," you will read more about the concepts and math behind IPv4 addressing and subnetting.

Rules for IP Addresses

If a device wants to communicate using TCP/IP, it needs an IP address. When the device has an IP address and the appropriate software and hardware, it can send and receive IP packets. Any device that has at least one interface with an IP address can send and receive IP packets and is called an *IP host*.

IP addresses consist of a 32-bit number, usually written in *dotted-decimal notation (DDN)*. The "decimal" part of the term comes from the fact that each byte (8 bits) of the 32-bit IP address is shown as its decimal equivalent. The four resulting decimal numbers are written in sequence, with "dots," or decimal points, separating the numbers—hence the name *dotted-decimal*. For example, 168.1.1.1 is an IP address written in dotted-decimal form; the actual binary version is 10101000 00000001 00000001 00000001.

Each DDN has four decimal *octets*, separated by periods. The term *octet* is just a vendor-neutral term for *byte*. Because each octet represents an 8-bit binary number, the range of decimal numbers in each octet is between 0 and 255, inclusive. For example, the IP address of 168.1.1.1 has a first octet of 168, the second octet of 1, and so on.

Finally, note that each network interface uses a unique IP address. Most people tend to think that their computer has an IP address, but actually their computer's network card has an IP address. For example, if your laptop has both an Ethernet network interface card (NIC) and a wireless NIC, with both working at the same time, both will have an IP address. Similarly, routers, which typically have many network interfaces that forward IP packets, have an IP address for each interface.

Rules for Grouping IP Addresses

The original specifications for TCP/IP grouped IP addresses into sets of consecutive addresses called *IP networks*. The addresses in a single IP network have the same numeric value in the first part of all addresses in the network. Figure 4-5 shows a simple internetwork that has three separate IP networks.

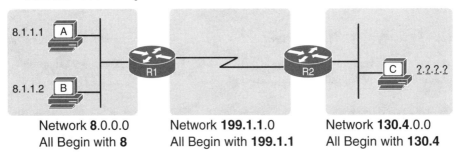

| Network **8.0.0.0** | Network **199.1.1**.0 | Network **130.4**.0.0 |
| All Begin with **8** | All Begin with **199.1.1** | All Begin with **130.4** |

Figure 4-5   *Sample TCP/IP Internetwork Using IPv4 Network Numbers*

The figure lists a network identifier (network ID) for each network, as well as a text description of the DDN values in each network. For example, the hosts in the Ethernet LAN on the far left use IP addresses that begin with a first octet of 8; the network ID happens to be 8.0.0.0. As another example, the serial link between R1 and R2 consists of only two interfaces—a serial interface on each router—and uses an IP address that begins with the three octets 199.1.1.

Figure 4-5 also serves as a good figure for discussing two important facts about how IPv4 groups IP addresses:

- All IP addresses in the same group must not be separated from each other by a router.
- IP addresses separated from each other by a router must be in different groups.

Take the first of the two rules, and look at hosts A and B on the left. Hosts A and B are in the same IP network and have IP addresses that begin with 8. Per the first rule, hosts A and B cannot be separated from each other by a router (and they are indeed not separated from each other by a router).

Next, take the second of the two rules and add host C to the discussion. Host C is separated from host A by at least one router, so host C cannot be in the same IP network as host A. Host C's address cannot begin with 8.

NOTE This example assumes the use of IP networks only, and no subnets, simply because the discussion has not yet dealt with the details of subnetting.

As mentioned earlier in this chapter, IP address grouping behaves similarly to ZIP codes. Everyone in my ZIP code lives in a little town in Ohio. If some addresses in my ZIP code were in California, some mail might be delivered to the wrong local post office, because the postal service delivers the letters based on the postal (ZIP) codes. The post system relies on all addresses in one postal code being near to each other.

Likewise, IP routing relies on all addresses in one IP network or IP subnet to be in the same location, specifically on a single instance of a LAN or WAN data link. Otherwise, the routers might deliver IP packets to the wrong locations.

For any TCP/IP internetwork, each LAN or WAN link will use either an IP network or an IP subnet. Next, this chapter looks more closely at the concepts behind IP networks, followed by IP subnets.

Class A, B, and C IP Networks

The IPv4 address space includes all possible combinations of numbers for a 32-bit IPv4 address. Literally 2^{32} different values exist with a 32-bit number, for more than 4 billion different numbers. With DDN values, these numbers include all combinations of the values 0 through 255 in all four octets: 0.0.0.0, 0.0.0.1, 0.0.0.2, and all the way up to 255.255.255.255.

IP standards first subdivide the entire address space into classes, as identified by the value of the first octet. Class A gets roughly half of the IPv4 address space, with all DDN numbers that begin with 1–126, as shown in Figure 4-6. Class B gets one-fourth of the address space, with all DDN numbers that begin with 128–191 inclusive, while Class C gets one-eighth of the address space, with all numbers that begin with 192–223.

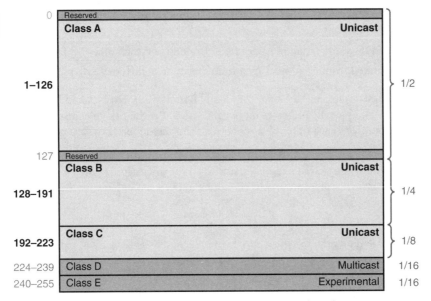

Figure 4-6 *Division of the Entire IPv4 Address Space by Class*

Figure 4-6 also notes the purpose for the five address classes. Classes A, B, and C define unicast IP addresses, meaning that the address identifies a single host interface. Class D defines multicast addresses, used to send one packet to multiple hosts, while Class E defines experimental addresses.

IPv4 standards also subdivide the Class A, B, and C unicast classes into predefined IP networks. Each IP network makes up a subset of the DDN values inside the class.

IPv4 uses three classes of unicast addresses so that the IP networks in each class can be different sizes and thus meet different needs. Class A networks each support a very large number of IP addresses (over 16 million host addresses per IP network). However, because each Class A network is so large, Class A holds only 126 networks. Class B defines IP networks that have 65,534 addresses per network, but with space for over 16,000 such networks. Class C defines much smaller IP networks, with 254 addresses each, as shown in Figure 4-7.

Figure 4-7 shows a visual perspective, as well as the literal numbers, for all the Class A, B, and C IPv4 networks in the entire world. The figure shows clouds for IP networks. It of course does not show one cloud for every possible network, but shows the general idea, with a small number of large clouds for Class A and a large number of small clouds for Class C.

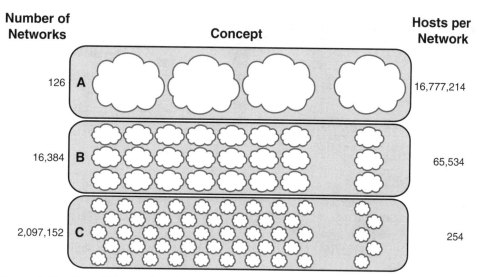

Figure 4-7 *Size of Network and Host Parts of Class A, B, and C Addresses*

The Actual Class A, B, and C IP Networks

Figure 4-7 shows the number of Class A, B, and C IP networks in the entire world. Eventually, you need to actually pick and use some of these IP networks to build a working TCP/IP internetwork, so you need to be able to answer the following question: What are the specific IP networks?

First, you must be able to identify each network briefly using a *network identifier* (network ID). The network ID is just one reserved DDN value per network that identifies the IP network. (The network ID cannot be used by a host as an IP address.) For example, Table 4-2 shows the network IDs that match Figure 4-5 (shown earlier).

Table 4-2 Network IDs Used in Figure 4-5

Concept	Class	Network ID
All addresses that begin with 8	A	8.0.0.0
All addresses that begin with 130.4	B	130.4.0.0
All addresses that begin with 199.1.1	C	199.1.1.0

NOTE   Many people use the term *network ID*, but others use the terms *network number* and *network address*. Be ready to use all three terms.

So, what are the actual Class A, B, and C IP networks, and what are their network IDs? First, consider the Class A networks. Per Figure 4-7, only 126 Class A networks exist. As it turns out, they consist of all addresses that begin with 1, all addresses that begin with 2, all addresses that begin with 3, and so on, up through the 126th such network, where "all addresses that begin with 126." Table 4-3 lists a few of these networks.

Table 4-3   Sampling of IPv4 Class A Networks

Concept	Class	Network ID
All addresses that begin with 8	A	8.0.0.0
All addresses that begin with 13	A	13.0.0.0
All addresses that begin with 24	A	24.0.0.0
All addresses that begin with 125	A	125.0.0.0
All addresses that begin with 126	A	126.0.0.0

Class B networks have a first octet value between 128 and 191, inclusive, but in a single Class B network, the addresses have the same value in the first two octets. For example, Figure 4-5 uses Class B network 130.4.0.0. The DDN value 130.4.0.0 must be in Class B, because the first octet is between 128 and 191, inclusive. However, the first two octets define the addresses in a single Class B network. Table 4-4 lists some sample IPv4 Class B networks.

Table 4-4   Sampling of IPv4 Class B Networks

Concept	Class	Network ID
All addresses that begin with 128.1	B	128.1.0.0
All addresses that begin with 172.20	B	172.20.0.0
All addresses that begin with 191.191	B	191.191.0.0
All addresses that begin with 150.1	B	150.1.0.0

Class C networks can also be easily identified, with a first octet value between 192 and 223, inclusive. With Class C networks and addresses, the first three octets define the group, with addresses in one Class C network having the same value in the first three octets. Table 4-5 shows some examples.

Table 4-5   Sampling of IPv4 Class C Networks

Concept	Class	Network ID
All addresses that begin with 199.1.1	C	199.1.1.0
All addresses that begin with 200.1.200	C	200.1.200.0
All addresses that begin with 223.1.10	C	223.1.10.0
All addresses that begin with 209.209.1	C	209.209.1.0

Listing all the Class A, B, and C networks would of course take too much space. For study review, Table 4-6 summarizes the first octet values that identify the class and summarizes the range of Class A, B, and C network numbers available in the entire IPv4 address space.

Table 4-6   All Possible Valid Network Numbers

Class	First Octet Range	Valid Network Numbers
A	1 to 126	1.0.0.0 to 126.0.0.0
B	128 to 191	128.0.0.0 to 191.255.0.0
C	192 to 223	192.0.0.0 to 223.255.255.0

NOTE   The term *classful IP network* refers to any Class A, B, or C network, because it is defined by Class A, B, or C rules.

4

IP Subnetting

Subnetting is one of the most important topics in the world of networking. You need to know how subnetting works and how to "do the math" to figure out issues when subnetting is in use, both in real life and on the exam. Part IV of this book covers the details of subnetting concepts, motivation, and math, but you should have a basic understanding of the concepts before covering the topics between here and Part IV.

Subnetting defines methods of further subdividing the IPv4 address space into groups that are smaller than a single IP network. IP subnetting defines a flexible way for anyone to take a single Class A, B, or C IP network and further subdivide it into even smaller groups of consecutive IP addresses. In fact, the name *subnet* is just shorthand for *subdivided network*. Then, in each location where you used to use an entire Class A, B, or C network, you can use a smaller subnet, wasting fewer IP addresses.

To make it clear how an internetwork can use both classful IPv4 networks as well as subnets of classful IPv4 networks, the next two figures show the same internetwork—one with classful networks only and one with subnets only. Figure 4-8 shows the first such example, which uses five Class B networks, with no subnetting.

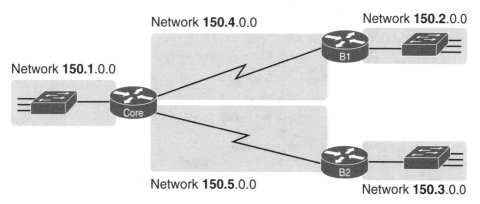

Figure 4-8   *Example That Uses Five Class B Networks*

The design in Figure 4-8 requires five groups of IP addresses, each of which is a Class B network in this example. Specifically, the three LANs each use a single Class B network, and the two serial links each use a Class B network.

Figure 4-8 wastes many IP addresses, because each Class B network has 2^{16} – 2 host addresses—far more than you will ever need for each LAN and WAN link. For example, the Ethernet on the left uses an entire Class B network, which supports 65,534 IP addresses that begin with 150.1. However, a single LAN seldom grows past a few hundred devices, so many of the IP addresses in Class B network 150.1.0.0 would be wasted. Even more waste occurs on the point-to-point serial links, which only need two IP addresses.

Figure 4-9 illustrates a more common design today—one that uses basic subnetting. Like the previous figure, this figure needs five groups of addresses. However, in this case, the figure uses five subnets of Class B network 150.9.0.0.

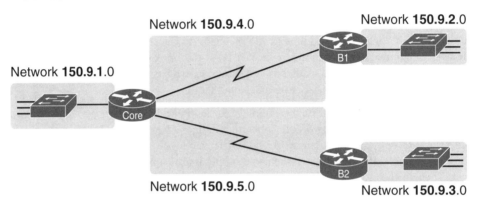

Figure 4-9   *Using Subnets for the Same Design as the Previous Figure*

Subnetting allows the network engineer for the TCP/IP internetwork to choose to use a longer part of the addresses that must have the same value. Subnetting allows quite a bit of flexibility, but Figure 4-9 shows one of the simplest forms of subnetting. In this case, each subnet includes the addresses that begin with the same value in the first three octets, as follows:

■ One group of the 254 addresses that begin with 150.9.1

■ One group of the 254 addresses that begin with 150.9.2

■ One group of the 254 addresses that begin with 150.9.3

■ One group of the 254 addresses that begin with 150.9.4

■ One group of the 254 addresses that begin with 150.9.5

As a result of using subnetting, the network engineer has saved many IP addresses. First, only a small part of Class B network 150.9.0.0 has been used so far. Each subnet has 254 addresses, which should be plenty of addresses for each LAN, and more than enough for the WAN links.

NOTE   All chapters of Part IV of this book explain the details of IP addressing, including the methods to choose an IP network and subnet it into smaller subnets.

In summary, you now know some of the details of IP addressing, with a focus on how it relates to routing. Each host and router interface will have an IP address. However, the IP addresses will not be randomly chosen, but will instead be grouped together to aid the routing process. The groups of addresses can be an entire Class A, B, or C network number or they can be a subnet.

IPv4 Routing

In the first section of this chapter ("Overview of Network Layer Functions"), you read about the basics of IPv4 routing using a network with three routers and two PCs. Armed with more knowledge of IP addressing, you now can take a closer look at the process of routing IP. This section begins with the simple two-part routing logic on the originating host, and then moves on to discuss how routers choose where to route or forward packets to the final destination.

IPv4 Host Routing

Hosts actually use some simple routing logic when choosing where to send a packet. If you assume that the design uses subnets (which is typical), this two-step logic is as follows:

Step 1.   If the destination IP address is in the same IP subnet as I am, send the packet directly to that destination host.

Step 2.   Otherwise, send the packet to my *default gateway*, also known as a *default router*. (This router has an interface on the same subnet as the host.)

For example, consider Figure 4-10 and focus on the Ethernet LAN on the left. When PC1 sends an IP packet to PC11 (150.9.1.11), PC1 first considers some match related to subnetting. PC1 concludes that PC11's IP address is in the same subnet as PC1, so PC1 ignores its default router (Core, 150.9.1.1), sending the packet directly to PC11, as shown in Step 1 of the figure.

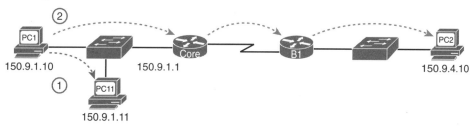

Figure 4-10   *Host Routing: Forwarding to a Host on the Same Subnet*

Alternatively, when PC1 sends a packet to PC2 (150.9.4.10), PC1 does the same kind of subnetting math, and realizes that PC2 is not on the same subnet. So, PC1 forwards the packet (Step 2) to its default gateway, 150.9.1.1, which then routes the packet to PC2.

Router Forwarding Decisions and the IP Routing Table

Earlier in this chapter, Figure 4-1 showed the network layer concepts of routing, while Figure 4-2 showed the data-link encapsulation logic related to routing. This next topic dives a little deeper into that same process, using an example with three routers forwarding (routing) one packet. But before we look at the example, the text first summarizes how a router thinks about forwarding a packet.

A Summary of Router Forwarding Logic

First, when a router receives a data-link frame addressed to its data link address, the router needs to think about processing the contents of the frame. When such a frame arrives, the router uses the following logic on the data-link frame:

Step 1.   Use the data-link Frame Check Sequence (FCS) field to ensure that the frame had no errors; if errors occurred, discard the frame.

Step 2.   Assuming that the frame was not discarded in Step 1, discard the old data-link header and trailer, leaving the IP packet.

Step 3.   Compare the IP packet's destination IP address to the routing table, and find the route that best matches the destination address. This route identifies the outgoing interface of the router, and possibly the next-hop router IP address.

Step 4.   Encapsulate the IP packet inside a new data-link header and trailer, appropriate for the outgoing interface, and forward the frame.

With these steps, each router forwards the packet to the next location, inside a data-link frame. With each router repeating this process, the packet reaches its final destination.

Although the router does all the steps in the list, Step 3 is the main routing or forwarding step. The packet has a destination IP address in the header, whereas the routing table lists slightly different numbers—typically a list of networks and subnets. To match a routing table entry, the router thinks like this:

Network numbers and subnet numbers represent a group of addresses that begin with the same prefix. Think about those numbers as groups of addresses. In which of the groups does this packet's destination address reside?

Next we'll look at a specific example of matching the routing table.

A Detailed Routing Example

The routing example uses Figure 4-11. In this example, all routers happen to use the Open Shortest Path First (OSPF) routing protocol, and all routers know routes for all subnets. In particular, PC2, at the bottom, sits in subnet 150.150.4.0, which consists of all addresses that begin with 150.150.4. In the example, PC1 sends an IP packet to 150.150.4.10, PC2's IP address.

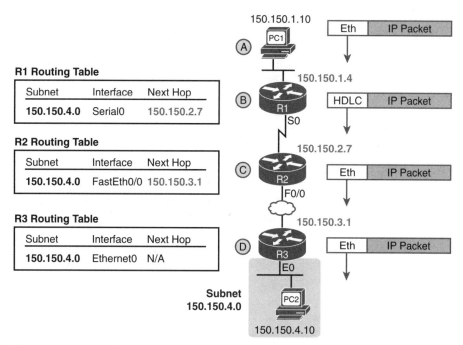

R1 Routing Table

Subnet	Interface	Next Hop
150.150.4.0	Serial0	150.150.2.7

R2 Routing Table

Subnet	Interface	Next Hop
150.150.4.0	FastEth0/0	150.150.3.1

R3 Routing Table

Subnet	Interface	Next Hop
150.150.4.0	Ethernet0	N/A

Figure 4-11   *Simple Routing Example, with IP Subnets*

> **NOTE**   Note that the routers all know in this case that "subnet 150.150.4.0" means "all addresses that begin with 150.150.4."

The following list explains the forwarding logic at each step in the figure. (Note that the text refers to Steps 1, 2, 3, and 4 of the routing logic shown in the previous section.)

Step A.   **PC1 sends the packet to its default router.** PC1 first builds the IP packet, with a destination address of PC2's IP address (150.150.4.10). PC1 needs to send the packet to R1 (PC1's default router) because the destination address is on a different subnet. PC1 places the IP packet into an Ethernet frame, with a destination Ethernet address of R1's Ethernet address. PC1 sends the frame onto the Ethernet. (Note that the figure omits the data-link trailers.)

Step B.   **R1 processes the incoming frame and forwards the packet to R2.** Because the incoming Ethernet frame has a destination MAC of R1's Ethernet MAC, R1 copies the frame off the Ethernet for processing. R1 checks the frame's FCS, and no errors have occurred (Step 1). R1 then discards the Ethernet header and trailer (Step 2). Next, R1 compares the packet's destination address (150.150.4.10) to the routing table and finds the entry for subnet 150.150.4.0—which includes addresses 150.150.4.0 through 150.150.4.255 (Step 3). Because the destination address is in this group, R1 forwards the packet out interface Serial0 to next-hop router R2 (150.150.2.7) after encapsulating the packet in a High-Level Data Link Control (HDLC) frame (Step 4).

Step C.   **R2 processes the incoming frame and forwards the packet to R3.** R2 repeats the same general process as R1 when it receives the HDLC frame. R2 checks the FCS field and finds that no errors occurred (Step 1). R2 then discards the HDLC header and trailer (Step 2). Next, R2 finds its route for subnet 150.150.4.0—which includes the address range 150.150.4.0–150.150.4.255— and realizes that the packet's destination address 150.150.4.10 matches that route (Step 3). Finally, R2 sends the packet out interface Fast Ethernet 0/0 to next-hop router 150.150.3.1 (R3) after encapsulating the packet in an Ethernet header (Step 4).

Step D.   **R3 processes the incoming frame and forwards the packet to PC2.** Like R1 and R2, R3 checks the FCS, discards the old data-link header and trailer, and matches its own route for subnet 150.150.4.0. R3's routing table entry for 150.150.4.0 shows that the outgoing interface is R3's Ethernet interface, but there is no next-hop router, because R3 is connected directly to subnet 150.150.4.0. All R3 has to do is encapsulate the packet inside a new Ethernet header and trailer, with a destination Ethernet address of PC2's MAC address, and forward the frame.

Next, this chapter briefly introduces the concepts behind IP routing protocols.

IPv4 Routing Protocols

The routing (forwarding) process depends heavily on having an accurate and up-to-date IP routing table on each router. This section takes another look at routing protocols, considers the goals of a routing protocol, the methods routing protocols use to teach and learn routes, and an example based on the same internetwork shown in the routing example in Figure 4-10.

First, consider the goals of a routing protocol, regardless of how the routing protocol works:

- To dynamically learn and fill the routing table with a route to each subnet in the internetwork.
- If more than one route to a subnet is available, to place the best route in the routing table.
- To notice when routes in the table are no longer valid, and to remove them from the routing table.
- If a route is removed from the routing table and another route through another neighboring router is available, to add the route to the routing table. (Many people view this goal and the preceding one as a single goal.)
- To work quickly when adding new routes or replacing lost routes. (The time between losing the route and finding a working replacement route is called *convergence* time.)
- To prevent routing loops.

Routing protocols all use some similar ideas to allow routers to learn routing information from each other. Of course, each routing protocol works differently; otherwise, you would not need more than one routing protocol. However, many routing protocols use the same general steps for learning routes:

Step 1. Each router, independent of the routing protocol, adds a route to its routing table for each subnet directly connected to the router.

Step 2. Each router's routing protocol tells its neighbors about the routes in its routing table, including the directly connected routes as well as routes learned from other routers.

Step 3. After learning a new route from a neighbor, the router's routing protocol adds a route to its IP routing table, with the next-hop router of that route typically being the neighbor from which the route was learned.

For example, Figure 4-12 shows the same sample network as in Figure 4-11, but now with a focus on how the three routers each learned about subnet 150.150.4.0. Note that routing protocols do more work than is implied in the figure; this figure just focuses on how the routers learn about subnet 150.150.4.0.

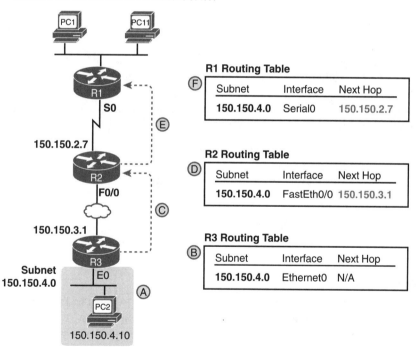

Figure 4-12   *Router R1 Learning About Subnet 150.150.4.0*

Follow items A through F shown in the figure to see how each router learns its route to 150.150.4.0. All references to Steps 1, 2, and 3 refer to the list just before Figure 4-12.

Step A. Subnet 150.150.4.0 exists as a subnet at the bottom of the figure, connected to router R3.

Step B.   R3 adds a connected route for 150.150.4.0 to its IP routing table (Step 1); this happens without help from the routing protocol.

Step C.   R3 sends a routing protocol message, called a *routing update*, to R2, causing R2 to learn about subnet 150.150.4.0 (Step 2).

Step D.   R2 adds a route for subnet 150.150.4.0 to its routing table (Step 3).

Step E.   R2 sends a similar routing update to R1, causing R1 to learn about subnet 150.150.4.0 (Step 2).

Step F.   R1 adds a route for subnet 150.150.4.0 to its routing table (Step 3). The route lists R1's own Serial0 as the outgoing interface and R2 as the next-hop router IP address (150.150.2.7).

Chapter 18, "IPv4 Routing Protocol Concepts," covers routing protocols in more detail. Next, the final major section of this chapter introduces several additional functions related to how the network layer forwards packets from source to destination through an internetwork.

Other Network Layer Features

The TCP/IP network layer defines many functions beyond the function defined by the IPv4 protocol. Sure, IPv4 plays a huge role in networking today, defining IP addressing and IP routing. However, other protocols and standards, defined in other RFCs, play an important role for network layer functions as well. For example, routing protocols such as OSPF exist as separate protocols, defined in separate RFCs.

This last short section of the chapter introduces three other network layer features that should be helpful to you when reading through the rest of this book. These last three topics fill in a few holes, give you some perspective, and help you make sense of later discussions:

- Domain Name System (DNS)
- Address Resolution Protocol (ARP)
- Ping

Using Names and the Domain Name System

Can you imagine a world in which every time you used an application, you had to think about the other computer and refer to it by IP address? Instead of using easy names such as google.com and facebook.com, you would have to remember and type IP addresses, such as 74.125.225.5. Certainly, that would not be user friendly and could drive some people away from using computers at all.

Thankfully, TCP/IP defines a way to use *host names* to identify other computers. The user either never thinks about the other computer or refers to the other computer by name. Then, protocols dynamically discover all the necessary information to allow communications based on that name.

For example, when you open a web browser and type in the host name **www.google.com**, your computer does not send an IP packet with destination IP address www.google.com; it sends an IP packet to an IP address used by the web server for Google. TCP/IP needs a way to let a computer find the IP address used by the listed host name, and that method uses the *Domain Name System (DNS)*.

Enterprises use the DNS process to resolve names into the matching IP address, as shown in the example in Figure 4-13. In this case, PC11, on the left, needs to connect to a server named Server1. At some point, the user either types in the name Server1 or some application on PC11 refers to that server by name. At Step 1, PC11 sends a DNS message—a DNS query—to the DNS server. At Step 2, the DNS server sends back a DNS reply that lists Server1's IP address. At Step 3, PC11 can now send an IP packet to destination address 10.1.2.3, the address used by Server1.

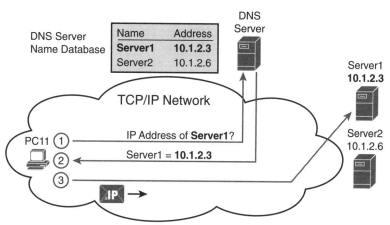

Figure 4-13 *Basic DNS Name Resolution Request*

Note that the example in Figure 4-13 shows a cloud for the TCP/IP network because the details of the network, including routers, do not matter to the name resolution process. Routers treat the DNS messages just like any other IP packet, routing them based on the destination IP address. For example, at Step 1 in the figure, the DNS query will list the DNS server's IP address as the destination address, which any routers will use to forward the packet.

Finally, DNS defines much more than just a few messages. DNS defines protocols, as well as standards for the text names used throughout the world, and a worldwide set of distributed DNS servers. The domain names that people use every day when web browsing, which look like www.example.com, follow the DNS naming standards. Also, no single DNS server knows all the names and matching IP addresses, but the information is distributed across many DNS servers. So, the DNS servers of the world work together, forwarding queries to each other, until the server that knows the answer supplies the desired IP address information.

The Address Resolution Protocol

IP routing logic requires that hosts and routers encapsulate IP packets inside data link layer frames. In fact, Figure 4-11 shows how every router de-encapsulates each IP packet and encapsulates the IP packet inside a new data link frame.

On Ethernet LANs, whenever a host or router needs to encapsulate an IP packet in a new Ethernet frame, the host or router knows all the important facts to build that header—except for the destination MAC address. The host knows the IP address of the next device, either another host IP address or the default router IP address. A router knows the IP route used for forwarding the IP packet, which lists the next router's IP address. However, the hosts and routers do not know those neighboring devices' MAC addresses beforehand.

TCP/IP defines the *Address Resolution Protocol (ARP)* as the method by which any host or router on a LAN can dynamically learn the MAC address of another IP host or router on the same LAN. ARP defines a protocol that includes the *ARP Request*, which is a message that asks the simple request "if this is your IP address, please reply with your MAC address." ARP also defines the *ARP Reply* message, which indeed lists both the original IP address and the matching MAC address.

Figure 4-14 shows an example that uses the same router and host from the bottom part of Figure 4-11 (shown earlier). The figure shows the ARP Request on the left as a LAN broadcast, so all hosts receive the frame. On the right, at Step 2, host PC2 sends back an ARP Reply, identifying PC2's MAC address. The text beside each message shows the contents inside the ARP message itself, which lets PC2 learn R3's IP address and matching MAC address, and R3 learn PC2's IP address and matching MAC address.

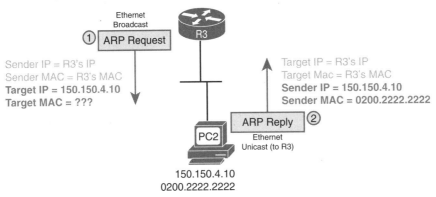

Figure 4-14 *Sample ARP Process*

Note that hosts remember the ARP results, keeping the information in their *ARP cache* or *ARP table*. A host or router only needs to use ARP occasionally, to build the ARP cache the first time. Each time a host or router needs to send a packet encapsulated in an Ethernet frame, it first checks its ARP cache for the correct IP address and matching MAC address. Hosts and routers will let ARP cache entries time out to clean up the table, so occasional ARP Requests can be seen.

NOTE You can see the contents of the ARP cache on most PC operating systems by using the **arp -a** command from a command prompt.

ICMP Echo and the ping Command

After you have implemented a TCP/IP internetwork, you need a way to test basic IP connectivity without relying on any applications to be working. The primary tool for testing basic network connectivity is the **ping** command.

Ping (Packet Internet Groper) uses the *Internet Control Message Protocol (ICMP)*, sending a message called an *ICMP echo request* to another IP address. The computer with that IP address should reply with an *ICMP echo reply*. If that works, you successfully have tested the IP network. In other words, you know that the network can deliver a packet from one host to the other and back. ICMP does not rely on any application, so it really just tests basic IP connectivity—Layers 1, 2, and 3 of the OSI model. Figure 4-15 outlines the basic process.

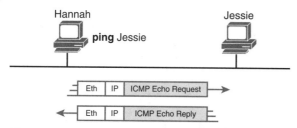

Figure 4-15   *Sample Network,* **ping** *Command*

Note that while the **ping** command uses ICMP, ICMP does much more. ICMP defines many messages that devices can use to help manage and control the IP network.

Exam Preparation Tasks

Review All the Key Topics

Review the most important topics from this chapter, noted with the Key Topic icon. Table 4-7 lists these key topics and where each is discussed.

Table 4-7   Key Topics for Chapter 4

Key Topic Element	Description	Page Number
List	Two statements about how IP expects IP addresses to be grouped into networks or subnets	147
Figure 4-6	Breakdown of IPv4 address space	148
Figure 4-7	Sizes of Class A, B, and C Networks	149
Table 4-6	List of the three types of unicast IP networks and the size of the network and host parts of each type of network	151
Figure 4-9	Conceptual view of how subnetting works	152
List	Two-step process of how hosts route (forward) packets	153
List	Four-step process of how routers route (forward) packets	154
List	Goals of IP routing protocols	156
Figure 4-13	Example that shows the purpose and process of DNS name resolution	159
Figure 4-14	Example of the purpose and process of ARP	160

Complete the Tables and Lists from Memory

Print a copy of Appendix C, "Memory Tables," or at least the section for this chapter, and complete the tables and lists from memory. Appendix D, "Memory Tables Answer Key," includes completed tables and lists for you to check your work.

Definitions of Key Terms

After your first reading of the chapter, try to define these key terms, but do not be concerned about getting them all correct at that time. Chapter 24, "Final Review," directs you in how to use these terms for late-stage preparation for the exam.

default router (default gateway), routing table, IP network, IP subnet, IP packet, routing protocol, dotted-decimal notation (DDN), IPv4 address, unicast IP address, subnetting, host name, DNS, ARP, ping

Part I Review

Keep track of your part review progress with the checklist shown in Table P1-1. Details on each task follow the table.

Table P1-1 Part I Review Checklist

Activity	First Date Completed	Second Date Completed
Repeat All DIKTA Questions		
Answer Part Review Questions		
Review Key Topics		

Repeat All DIKTA Questions: For this task, answer the "Do I Know This Already?" questions again for the chapters in this part of the book, using the PCPT software. Refer to the Introduction and find the section "How to View Only DIKTA Questions by Part" for help with how to make the PCPT software show you DIKTA questions for this part only.

Answer Part Review Questions: For this task, answer the Part Review questions for this part of the book, using the PCPT software. Refer to the Introduction and find the section "How to View Only Part Review Questions by Part" for help with how to make the PCPT software show you Part Review questions for this part only.

Review Key Topics: Browse back through the chapters and look for the Key Topic icons. If you do not remember some details, take the time to reread those topics.

The data networking components of today's data centers are typically built using Ethernet technology. Specifically, the physical links, data-link protocols, and networking devices, such as Ethernet LAN switches, follow Ethernet standards.

Part II begins with Chapter 5, which looks specifically at Cisco Nexus data center switches—how to access the user interface, how to configure administrative features, how to configure the devices to perform LAN switching, and how to make the devices perform many of the basic functions necessary for a data center LAN.

Chapters 6–9 then discuss two specific larger topics about how a Layer 2 data center LAN works: virtual LANs (VLANs) and Spanning Tree Protocol (STP).

Finally, Chapter 10 provides some historical perspectives on Ethernet, while focusing on the logic of how a Layer 2 switch forwards Ethernet frames.

Part II

Data Center Nexus Switching and Routing Fundamentals

This chapter covers the following exam topics:

2.0. Data center networking concepts

CHAPTER 5

Installing and Operating Nexus Switches

When you buy a Cisco Nexus switch, you can take it out of the box, power on the switch by connecting the power cable to the switch and a power outlet, and connect hosts to the switch using the correct UTP cables, and the switch works. You do not have to do anything else, and you certainly do not have to tell the switch to start forwarding Ethernet frames. The switch uses default settings so that all interfaces will work, assuming that the right cables and devices connect to the switch, and the switch forwards frames in and out of each interface.

However, most enterprises will want to be able to check on the switch's status, look at information about what the switch is doing, and possibly configure specific features of the switch. Engineers will also want to enable security features that allow them to securely access the switches without being vulnerable to malicious people breaking into the switches. To perform these tasks, a network engineer needs to connect to the switch's user interface.

This chapter explains the details of how to access a Cisco switch's user interface, how to use commands to find out how the switch is currently working, and how to configure the switch to tell it what to do. This chapter focuses on the processes and introduces several commands. The remaining chapters in Part II of the book focus on commands for performing particular tasks.

"Do I Know This Already?" Quiz

Use the "Do I Know This Already?" quiz to help decide whether you might want to skim this chapter, or a major section, moving more quickly to the "Exam Preparation Tasks" section near the end of the chapter. Table 5-1 lists the major headings in this chapter and their corresponding "Do I Know This Already?" quiz questions. For thorough explanations, see Appendix A, "Answers to the 'Do I Know This Already?' Quizzes."

Table 5-1 "Do I Know This Already?" Foundation Topics Section-to-Question Mapping

Foundation Topics Section	Questions
Accessing the Cisco Nexus Switch CLI	1–3
Configuring Cisco NX-OS Software	4–6

1. In what modes can you execute the command **show mac address-table?**

   a. EXEC command mode.

   b. Subinterface configuration command mode.

   c. Global configuration mode.

   d. All answers are correct.

2. In which user role can you issue the command **reload** to reboot the switch?

   a. Network-operator

   b. Network-admin

   c. Test user

   d. Interface user

3. Which of the following is a difference between Telnet and SSH as supported by a Cisco switch?

   a. SSH encrypts the passwords used at login, but not other traffic; Telnet encrypts nothing.

   b. SSH encrypts all data exchange, including login passwords; Telnet encrypts nothing.

   c. Telnet is used from Microsoft operating systems, and SSH is used from UNIX and Linux operating systems.

   d. Telnet encrypts only password exchanges; SSH encrypts all data exchanges.

4. What type of switch memory is used to store the running configuration?

   a. RAM

   b. ROM

   c. Flash

   d. NVRAM

   e. Bubble

5. What command copies the configuration from RAM into NVRAM?

   a. copy running-config tftp

   b. copy tftp running-config

   c. copy running-config start-up-config

   d. copy start-up-config running-config

   e. copy startup-config running-config

   f. copy running-config startup-config

6. A switch user is currently in console line configuration mode. Which of the following would place the user in EXEC mode? (Choose two answers.)

   a. Using the **exit** command once

   b. Using the **end** command once

   c. Pressing the Ctrl+Z key sequence once

   d. Using the **quit** command

Foundation Topics

Accessing the Cisco Nexus Switch CLI

Cisco uses the concept of a command-line interface (CLI) with its router products and most of its Nexus data center switch products. The CLI is a text-based interface in which the user, typically a network engineer, enters a text command and presses Enter. Pressing Enter sends the command to the switch, which tells the device to do something. The switch does what the command says, and in some cases, the switch replies with some messages stating the results of the command.

This book discusses only Cisco Nexus data center enterprise-class switches, and in particular how to use the Cisco CLI to monitor and control these switches. This first major section of the chapter first examines these Nexus switches in more detail and then explains how a network engineer can get access to the CLI to issue commands.

Cisco Nexus Switches and the 5500 Switch

Within the Cisco Nexus brand of data center switches, Cisco has produced multiple product families to meet a variety of customer needs. For example, there are four series of Nexus switches: the Nexus 7000, 7700, 9500 core, and aggregation switches; the Nexus 9300, 5500, 5600, and 6000 core, aggregation, and access switches; the Nexus 3000 aggregation, access, and low-latency switches; and the Nexus 2000 fabric extenders.

Figure 5-1 shows a photo of the Nexus 5548 switch series from Cisco, which we will use as our main reference in this chapter.

Figure 5-1 *Cisco 5500 Nexus Switch Series*

Cisco refers to a switch's physical connectors as either *interfaces* or *ports*. Each interface has a number in the style x/y, where x and y are two different numbers. On a Nexus 5500 series switch, the numbering of 1/10 gigabit interfaces starts at 1/1, the second is 1/2, and so on. Unlike the Catalyst series switches, which use descriptions for interfaces such as Gigabit 1/1 and 10 Gigabit 1/1, the Nexus series switches use a generic Ethernet naming convention regardless of the interface speed. For example, the first Ethernet interface on a Nexus 5500 switch would be interface Ethernet 1/1. The Nexus series switches support 100MB, 1GB, 10GB, 40GB, and 100GB interfaces based on the model chosen.

Accessing the Cisco NX-OS CLI

Like any other piece of computer hardware, Cisco switches need some kind of operating system (OS) software. Cisco calls this OS the Nexus Operating System (NX-OS).

Cisco NX-OS software for Nexus switches implements and controls logic and functions performed by a Cisco switch. Besides controlling the switch's performance and behavior,

Cisco NX-OS also defines an interface for humans called the *command-line interface* (CLI). The Cisco NX-OS CLI allows the user to use a terminal emulation program, which accepts text entered by the user. When the user presses Enter, the terminal emulator sends that text to the switch. The switch processes the text as if it is a command, does what the command says, and sends text back to the terminal emulator.

The switch CLI can be accessed through three popular methods: the console, Telnet, and Secure Shell (SSH). Two of these methods (Telnet and SSH) use the IP network in which the switch resides to reach the switch. The console is a physical port built specifically to allow access to the CLI. Figure 5-2 depicts the options.

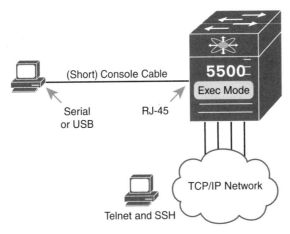

Figure 5-2 *CLI Access*

Console access requires both a physical connection between a PC (or other user device) and the switch's console port, in addition to some software on the PC. Telnet and SSH require software on the user's device, but they rely on the existing TCP/IP network to transmit data. The next few pages detail how to connect the console and set up the software for each method to access the CLI.

Cabling the Console Connection

The physical console connection, both old and new, uses three main components: the physical console port on the switch, a physical serial port on the PC, and a cable that works with the console and serial ports. However, the physical cabling details have changed slowly over time, mainly because of advances and changes with PC hardware.

Older console connections use a PC serial port, a console cable, and an RJ-45 connector on the switch. The PC serial port typically has a D-shell connector (roughly rectangular) with nine pins (often called a *DB-9*). Older switches, as well as some current models, use an RJ-45 connector for the console port. Figure 5-3 shows the cabling on the left.

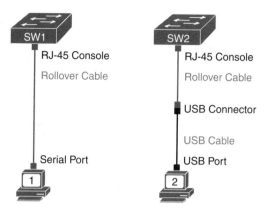

Figure 5-3 *Console Connection to a Switch*

You can use either a purpose-built console cable (which ships with new Cisco switches and routers) or make your own console cable using UTP cables and a standard RJ-45-to-DB-9 converter plug. You can buy the converter plug at most computer stores. Then, for the UTP cabling, the cable uses rollover cable pinouts, rather than any of the standard Ethernet cabling pinouts. Instead, it uses eight wires, rolling the wire at pin 1 to pin 8, pin 2 to pin 7, pin 3 to pin 6, and so on.

PCs have migrated away from using serial ports to instead use Universal Serial Bus (USB) ports for serial communications. Cisco has also begun building newer routers and switches with USB ports for console access as well.

The right side of the figure shows yet another common option. Many PCs no longer have serial ports, but many existing Cisco routers and switches have only an RJ-45 console port and no USB console port. To connect such a PC to a router or switch console, you need some kind of converter that converts from the older console cable to a USB connector, as shown in the middle of the right side of Figure 5-3.

NOTE When using the USB options, you typically also need to install a software driver so that your PC's OS knows that the device on the other end of the USB connection is the console of a Cisco device.

Configuring the Terminal Emulator for the Console

After the PC is physically connected to the console port, a terminal emulator software package must be installed and configured on the PC. The terminal emulator software treats all data as text. It accepts the text typed by the user and sends it over the console connection to the switch. Similarly, any bits coming into the PC over the console connection are displayed as text for the user to read.

The emulator must be configured to use the PC's serial port to match the settings on the switch's console port settings. The default console port settings on a switch are as follows. Note that the last three parameters are referred to collectively as *8N1*:

- 9600 bits/second

- No hardware flow control

- 8-bit ASCII

- No parity bits

- 1 stop bit

Figure 5-4 shows one such terminal emulator, Zterm Pro. The image shows the window created by the emulator software in the background, with some output of a **show** command. The foreground, in the upper left, shows a settings window that lists the same default console settings just listed.

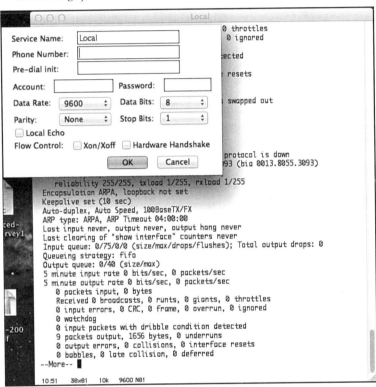

Figure 5-4   *Terminal Settings for Console Access*

Accessing the CLI with Telnet and SSH in NX-OS

The TCP/IP Telnet application allows a terminal emulator to communicate with another willing device. The process works much like what happens with an emulator on a PC connected to the console, except that the data flows over a TCP/IP network instead of over a console cable. However, Telnet uses an IP network to send and receive the data rather than a specialized cable and physical port on the device. The Telnet application protocols call the terminal emulator a Telnet client and the device that listens for commands and replies to them a Telnet server. Telnet is a TCP-based application layer protocol that uses well-known port 23.

To use Telnet, users must install a Telnet client software package on their PC. (As mentioned earlier, most terminal emulator software packages today include both Telnet and SSH client functions.) The Nexus switch disables Telnet server software by default, but the switch does need to have an IP address configured so that it can send and receive IP packets and be enabled for Telnet. (Chapter 10, "Configuring Ethernet Switching," covers switch IP address configuration in greater detail.) In addition, the network between the PC and switch needs to be up and working so that the PC and switch can exchange IP packets.

Many network engineers habitually use a Telnet client to monitor switches. Engineers can sit at their desks without having to walk to another part of the building (or go to another state or country) and still get into the CLI of that device.

While Telnet works well, many network engineers instead use SSH to overcome a serious security problem with Telnet. Telnet sends all data (including any username and password information for logging in to the switch) as clear-text data. SSH encrypts the contents of all messages, including the passwords, thus avoiding the possibility of someone capturing packets in the network and stealing the password to network devices.

SSH does the same basic things as Telnet, but with added security. The user uses a terminal emulator that supports SSH. Like Telnet, SSH uses TCP, using well-known port 22 instead of Telnet's 23. As with Telnet, the SSH server (on the switch) receives the text from each SSH client, processes the text as a command, and sends messages back to the client. Using SSH is the default enabled way to access a Cisco Nexus switch.

Management Interface

A Cisco Nexus switch has a dedicated management interface referred to as the *management 0* interface used for out-of-band management of any series of Cisco Nexus switches. Another characteristic to this interface as compared to other interfaces on the switch is it has by default been put in its own virtual routing and forwarding (VRF) instance called the *management VRF*. To access the switch for management via Telnet or SSH, you must assign an IP address, default mask, and default route to the Mgmt0 interface, as shown in Example 5-1.

Nexus switches use two VRFs by default for the purpose of separating management traffic from traffic between the servers in the data center and the rest of the network. By default, Nexus places the management interface into the management VRF and places all other interfaces into the default VRF. The Nexus switch does not forward frames between the management interface and the interfaces in the default VRF.

For the switch to communicate out of its management interface, it needs two things to be configured. First, you need to choose an IP address and subnet mask to apply to this interface from your management network. Second, you need to inform the switch of the default route to get to the rest of the network by applying an **ip route** statement under the VRF context for management to tell it what the next-hop Layer 3 device is. Figure 5-5 shows what VRF each interface is in by default on a Nexus switch.

Nexus Switch Internals: VRFs

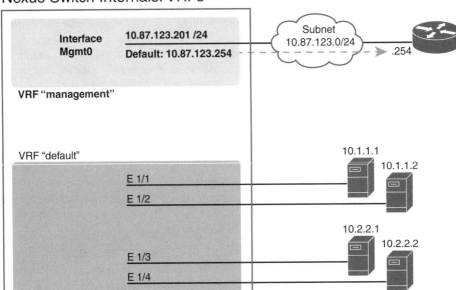

Figure 5-5   *VRF Settings on Nexus Switch by Default*

Example 5-1   *Configuration of the Management Interface and Context Default Route*

```
Certskills1# configure terminal
Enter configuration commands, one per line.    End with CNTL/Z.
Certskills1(config)# interface mgmt0
Certskills1(config-if)# ip address 10.87.123.201/24


Certskills1# configure terminal
Enter configuration commands, one per line.    End with CNTL/Z.
Certskills1(config)# vrf context management
Certskills1(config-vrf)# ip route 0.0.0.0/0 10.87.123.254
```

Password Security for CLI Access

A Cisco Nexus switch with default settings has a default Network-admin role with a user-name of admin; the default user cannot be deleted or changed at any time. This default user does not have a password and should be explicitly defined using a strong password. If the password is basic and easy to decipher, the switch will not accept the password, and you will be asked for a stronger password.

Be sure to configure a strong password for each user account. A strong password has the following characteristics:

■ At least eight characters long

- Does not contain many consecutive characters (such as abcd)

- Does not contain many repeating characters (such as aaabbb)

- Does not contain dictionary words

- Does not contain proper names

- Contains both uppercase and lowercase characters

- Contains numbers

Table 5-2 outlines CLI password configuration from the console.

Table 5-2   CLI Password Configuration: Console and Telnet

Access From	Password Type	Sample Configuration
Console, SSH, or Telnet (vty)	Console, SSH, or vty password	Username admin password Cisco123 role (network-operator/network-admin)
Privileged Mode (configure terminal)	Feature to enable Telnet or SSH	Feature SSH or Telnet

Cisco switches refer to the console as a *console line* (specifically, console line 0). Similarly, switches support 16 concurrent Telnet sessions, referenced as virtual terminal (vty) lines 0 through 15. (The term *vty* refers to an old name for terminal emulators.) The line vty configuration command tells the switch that the commands that follow apply to all 16 possible concurrent virtual terminal connections to the switch (0 through 15), which includes Telnet and SSH access.

NOTE: Most if not all of the NX-OS switches support 32 vty lines by default and can support up to 64, unlike IOS.

To enable user, role, and password authentication for SSH and Telnet, you have to use the **feature telnet** or **feature ssh** command for enabling the protocol you would like to use to communicate with for managing your Cisco Nexus switch. Console authentication, by default, is enabled to user authentication. After adding the configuration shown in Table 5-2, a user connecting to the console, Telnet, or SSH is prompted for a username and password, and the user must use Cisco123 for the password with admin as the username in this case.

User Settings

All three CLI access methods covered so far (console, Telnet, and SSH) place the user in an area of the CLI called user EXEC command mode. The *EXEC mode* part of the name refers to the fact that in this mode, when you enter a command, the switch executes the command and then displays messages that describe the command's results.

Cisco NX-OS supports restricting users from executing commands in EXEC mode based on their user role. For example, you can use the **reload** command, which tells the switch to reinitialize or reboot Cisco NX-OS, from network-admin role but not from network-operator mode.

NOTE   Unlike IOS, Cisco NX-OS does not store or use an enable-secret in the configuration. Each user account is created with its own password (stored locally or through AAA), and authorization levels are dictated by the role assigned to the account. It is important to secure all accounts by assigning the correct privileged access with the network-admin or vdc-admin roles. Using this method simplifies password management in NX-OS. Table 5-3 shows the predefined roles that can be assigned to a given username in NX-OS.

Table 5-3   NX-OS 5x00 Predefined User Roles

Role Name	Description
Network-admin (super user)	Complete read and write access to the entire switch
Network-operator	Complete read access to the switch
San-admin	Complete read and write access to Fibre Channel and Fibre Channel over Ethernet (FCoE) administrative tasks using SNMP or CLI

NOTE   Nexus 7000 and other switches do have additional default user roles, so be sure to reference each switch's configuration guide.

Example 5-2 shows the output that you could see in a Telnet window. In this case, the user connects with Telnet and tries the **reload** command. This command tells the switch to reinitialize or reboot Cisco NX-OS. NX-OS allows this powerful command, so in the example, NX-OS rejects the **reload** command if the user does not have the privileges to execute it (for example, the network-operator role).

Example 5-2   *Executing the* reload *Command in Different User Roles on Switch Certskills1*

```
Certskills1(config)# username test password Cisco123 role network-operator
Certskills1(config)# username admin password Cisco123 role network-admin


Nexus 5000 Switch
login: test
Password:
Cisco Nexus Operating System (NX-OS) Software
Certskills1# reload
% Permission denied for the role
Certskills1#


Nexus 5000 Switch
login: admin
Password:
Cisco Nexus Operating System (NX-OS) Software
Certskills1# reload
WARNING: There is unsaved configuration!!!
WARNING: This command will reboot the system
Do you want to continue? (y/n) [n] y
```

NOTE The commands that can be used in either user (EXEC) mode or enable (EXEC) mode are called *EXEC commands*.

This example is the first instance of this book showing you the output from the CLI, so it is worth noting a few conventions. The bold text represents what the user typed, and the non-bold text is what the switch sent back to the terminal emulator. Also, for security purposes, the typed passwords do not show up on the screen. Finally, note that this switch has been preconfigured with a hostname of Certskills1, so the command prompt on the left shows that hostname on each line.

So far, this chapter has pointed out some of the first things you should know when unpacking and installing a switch. The Nexus switch will work with a basic configuration; just plug in the power and Ethernet cables, enable the interfaces, and it works. However, you should at least connect to the switch console port and configure passwords for each user role. Next, this chapter examines some of the CLI features that exist regardless of how you access the CLI.

CLI Help Features

If you printed the Cisco NX-OS Command Reference documents, you would end up with a stack of paper several feet tall. No one should expect to memorize all the commands (and no one does). You can use several very easy, convenient tools to help you remember commands and save time typing. As you progress through your Cisco certifications, the exams will cover progressively more commands. However, you should know the methods of getting command help.

Table 5-4 summarizes command-recall help options available at the CLI. Note that in the first column, *command* represents any command. Likewise, *parm* represents a command's parameter. For example, the second row lists command ?, which means that commands such as **show ?** and **copy ?** would list help for the **show** and **copy** commands, respectively.

Table 5-4   Cisco NX-OS Software Command Help

What You Enter	What Help You Get
?	Help for all commands available in this mode.
command ?	Text help describing all the first parameter options for the command.
com?	A list of commands that start with "com".
command parm?	This style of help lists all parameters beginning with the parameter typed so far. (Notice that there is no space between *parm* and the question mark.)
command parm **\<Tab\>**	If you press the Tab key midword, the CLI either spells the rest of this parameter at the command line or does nothing. If the CLI does nothing, it means that this string of characters represents more than one possible next parameter, so the CLI does not know which one to spell out.
command parm1 ?	If a space is inserted before the question mark, the CLI lists all the next parameters and gives a brief explanation of each.

When you enter ?, the Cisco NX-OS CLI reacts immediately; that is, you don't need to press the Enter key or any other keys. The device running Cisco NX-OS also redisplays what you entered before the ? to save you some keystrokes. If you press Enter immediately after the ?, Cisco NX-OS tries to execute the command with only the parameters you have entered so far.

The information supplied by using help depends on the CLI mode. For example, when ? is entered in EXEC mode, the commands allowed in EXEC mode are displayed, but commands available only in global configuration mode are not displayed. Also, note that NX-OS enables you to run commands from less-specific modes in more-specific modes, but you cannot run commands from more-specific modes in less-specific modes. For example, you can run EXEC commands in global configuration mode, interface mode, or subinterface mode, but you are not allowed to run global, interface, or subinterface commands in EXEC mode.

Cisco NX-OS stores the commands you enter in a history buffer, storing ten commands by default. The CLI allows you to move backward and forward in the historical list of commands and then edit the command before reissuing it. These key sequences can help you use the CLI more quickly on the exams. Table 5-5 lists the commands used to manipulate previously entered commands.

Table 5-5   Key Sequences for Command Edit and Recall

Keyboard Command	What Happens
Up arrow or Ctrl+P	This displays the most recently used command. If you press it again, the next most recent command appears, until the history buffer is exhausted. (The P stands for previous.)
Down arrow or Ctrl+N	If you have gone too far back into the history buffer, these keys take you forward to the more recently entered commands. (The N stands for next.)
Left arrow or Ctrl+B	This moves the cursor backward in the currently displayed command without deleting characters. (The B stands for back.)
Right arrow or Ctrl+F	This moves the cursor forward in the currently displayed command without deleting characters. (The F stands for forward.)
Backspace	This moves the cursor backward in the currently displayed command, deleting characters.
Ctrl+A	This moves the cursor directly to the first character of the currently displayed command.
Ctrl+E	This moves the cursor directly to the end of the currently displayed command.
Ctrl+R	This redisplays the command line with all characters. It is useful when messages clutter the screen.
Ctrl+D	This deletes a single character.
Ctrl+Shift+6	Interrupts the current command.

The debug and show Commands

By far, the single most popular Cisco NX-OS command is the **show** command. The **show** command has a large variety of options, and with those options, you can find the status of almost every feature of Cisco NX-OS. Essentially, the **show** command lists the currently known facts about the switch's operational status. The only work the switch does in reaction to **show** commands is to find the current status and then list the information in messages sent to the user.

The **debug** command has a similar role as compared with the **show** command. Like the **show** command, **debug** has many options. However, instead of just listing messages about the current status, the **debug** command asks the switch to continue monitoring different processes in the switch. The switch then sends ongoing messages to the user when different events occur.

The effects of the **show** and **debug** commands can be compared to a photograph (**show** command) and a movie (**debug** command). A **show** command shows what's true at a single point in time, and it takes less effort. A **debug** command shows what's true over time, but it requires more effort. As a result, the **debug** command requires more CPU cycles, but it lets you watch what is happening in a switch while it is happening.

Cisco NX-OS handles the messages from the **show** and **debug** commands very differently. NX-OS sends the output of **show** commands to the user who issued the **show** command, and to no other users. However, NX-OS reacts to **debug** commands by creating log messages related to that command's options. Any user logged in can choose to view the log messages just by using the **terminal monitor** command from EXEC mode.

NX-OS also treats the **show** command as a very short-lived event and the **debug** command as an ongoing task. The options enabled by a single **debug** command are not disabled until the user takes action or until the switch is reloaded. A **reload** of the switch disables all currently enabled debug options. To disable a single debug option, repeat the same **debug** command with those options, prefaced by the word **no**. For example, if the **debug spanning-tree** command had been issued earlier, issue the **no debug spanning-tree** command to disable that same debug. Also, the **no debug all** and **undebug all** commands disable all currently enabled debugs.

Introduction to Cisco NX-OS

Cisco Nexus switches were created to provide the next generation of data center class features and functionality. To enable these features and functionalities, Cisco created a new OS called Cisco NX-OS. Cisco NX-OS was designed to support modularity, serviceability, and high availability, which are all required in today's data centers.

You gain several advantages when you use the Cisco NX-OS, as highlighted in the brief list that follows:

- Modularity in software
- Virtualization features
- Resiliency
- IPv4 and IPv6 feature-rich routing and multicast functionality

- Data center security, serviceability, and availability features
- Unified Fabric

Cisco NX-OS is a purpose-built OS for data centers of today. Cisco NX-OS is a combination of two well-known operating systems: SAN-OS and Internetwork Operating System (IOS). SAN-OS is the operating system that was used in the Fibre Channel storage area network (SAN) switches known as the *Cisco MDS*. IOS is the original operating system used and adapted over the years that runs on Cisco routers and Catalyst local area network (LAN) switches. IOS and SAN-OS merged to create Cisco NX-OS. Figure 5-6 shows the merger of the two operating systems that created NX-OS. Figure 5-7 shows the platforms on which NX-OS is supported.

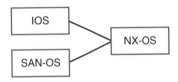

Figure 5-6 *NX-OS OS Merger*

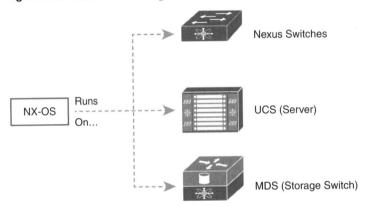

Figure 5-7 *NX-OS Platforms*

Software Modularity in Cisco NX-OS

The first step to understanding how Cisco NX-OS was built and provides an improvement for data center networks is to explore the software modularity that is provided. Cisco NX-OS was built with a mindset to provide the highest level of availability for data center networks. To do this, the team that created Cisco NX-OS focused on providing modular processes as a foundation to the operating system. When a feature is enabled in Cisco NX-OS, a process is started and system resources are then allocated to the given process. Each individual feature is enabled on demand and given its own protected memory space. Cisco NX-OS then uses a real-time preemptive scheduler that helps ensure the timely processing of critical functions. Example 5-3 shows enabling a feature on a Cisco NX-OS platform, as well as the output before and after the enablement.

Example 5-3 *Enabling VTP Feature Before and After*

```
Certskills1# show vtp
% Incomplete command at '^' marker.
Certskills1# show feature | include vtp
vtp                        1              disabled
Certskills1# configure terminal
Enter configuration commands, one per line.    End with CNTL/Z.
Certskills1(config)# feature vtp
Certskills1(config)# exit

Certskills1# show feature | include vtp
vtp                        1              enabled

Certskills1# show vtp ?
    counters      VTP statistics
    interface     VTP interface status and configuration
    internal      Show internal information
    password      VTP password
    status        VTP domain status

Certskills1# show vtp status
VTP Status Information
---------------------
VTP Version                          : 2 (capable)
Configuration Revision               : 0
Maximum VLANs supported locally : 1005
Number of existing VLANs             : 6
VTP Operating Mode          : Server
VTP Domain Name                   : <VTP domain not acquired/configured yet>
VTP Pruning Mode                  : Disabled (Operationally Disabled)
VTP V2 Mode                        : Disabled
VTP Traps Generation              : Disabled
MD5 Digest                         : 0x83 0x35 0xB0 0xD0 0x44 0x8B 0x5E 0x86
Configuration last modified by 10.87.123.230 at 0-0-00 00:00:00

Local updater ID is 10.87.123.230 on interface mgmt0 (first L3 interface found)
VTP version running          : 1
```

Service Restart in Cisco NX-OS

The Cisco NX-OS service restart feature enables you to restart a faulty service without restarting the supervisor. A system manager is in control of the overall function of the system; it monitors the services and system health. The system manager is in charge of instructing the system and service to take an action when an action is needed, such as instructing a service to do a stateful or stateless restart. A service can undergo either a stateful or stateless restart.

Not all services are designed for stateful restart. For example, Cisco NX-OS does not store runtime state information for all Layer 3 routing protocols. Some Layer 3 routing protocols rely on functions such as graceful restart (NSF).

Cisco NX-OS allows services to store runtime state information and messages for a stateful restart. In a stateful restart, the service can retrieve this stored state information and resume operations from the last checkpoint service state. In a stateless restart, the service can initialize and run as if it had just been started with no prior state. Stateful restarts of processes use a service enabled in Cisco NX-OS called *Persistent Storage Service* (PSS). PSS is used in many Cisco NX-OS services as a database to store and manage their runtime state information. This allows the services to create checkpoints of their state, and in case of a failure a service can use the checkpoint to recover to its last known operating manner statefully.

Software High Availability in Cisco NX-OS

Along with the service restart functionality of Cisco NX-OS, the software offers what are called *high availability (HA) policies*. Cisco NX-OS allows for each service to have an associated set of HA policies that specify what restart methodology will be used for a failed service. NX-OS supports HA policies that define how NX-OS restarts a service if it fails. The policies can be simple, like the default policy on a single supervisor Nexus switch: The switch simply resets the supervisor, restarting NX-OS. (On a dual-supervisor switch, the default HA policy causes a failover from the current supervisor to the standby supervisor, which does not cause an outage.)

NOTE Supervisor modules are particular to modular switches with multiple line card slots. For example, the Cisco Nexus 7000/7700/9500 series and the Cisco MDS 9500/9700 series have the capability to have multiple supervisor modules. Fixed-form factor switches, such as the Cisco Nexus 3000, 5500, 5600, 9300 and 6000, have built-in single supervisor modules.

In-Service Software Upgrades

With the modular architecture that Cisco NX-OS provides, it allows for a unique feature known as *in-service software upgrade* (ISSU). ISSUs enable the Nexus switching system to do a complete system software upgrade without disruption to the data plane. This functionality allows for complete system software upgrades to happen while the system will continue to forward packets. Figure 5-8 shows the process the system takes when performing an ISSU.

NOTE ISSU is done when dual supervisor modules are available in the systems. In special cases, it can be done across physical systems. It should only be done when the network is stable, and a change control window is recommended.

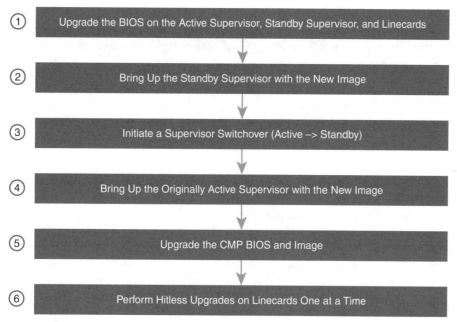

Figure 5-8 *NX-OS ISSU Steps*

Cisco NX-OS Licensing

So far in this chapter, we have discussed how Cisco NX-OS has been architected from its foundation to provide data center class software modularity and HA. Now that you are familiar with the NX-OS features, this section describes how the software licensing model supports the modular software architecture.

Cisco NX-OS is composed of two different images (except the Nexus 9000, which goes back to a single binary image): the kickstart image and the system image. When doing software upgrades, network administrators must download and install both of these images for the appropriate version they want to install or upgrade to. Note that administrators do not have to upgrade software or purchase a particular level of the operating system, because Cisco NX-OS is a universal image. Therefore, all the features available in a particular version are available in the operating system images they download. For certain features or functionality, they will have to purchase feature licenses, which are loaded into the system's flash and enabled for the system's use. Example 5-4 displays output that results from installing a license file on a Nexus switch.

Example 5-4 *Displaying and Installing an NX-OS License File*

```
Certskills1# show license host-id
License hostid: VDH=TBM14299862


Certskills1# dir bootflash:
              342        Mar 12 15:53:30 2012     LAN_ENT.lic
! some output omitted


Certskills1# install license bootflash:LAN_ENT.lic
Installing license ..done
```

NOTE Cisco NX-OS offers a 120-day grace period to test certain features. The grace period license can be enabled for a customer to test a feature license without purchase. To enable the grace period licensing, you issue the command **Certskills1(config)# license grace-period.**

After you have installed the appropriate license files needed for your Nexus switch, you issue the feature commands to enable their processes and start configuration of your Nexus switch.

Here is a link to the licensing guide:

http://www.cisco.com/c/en/us/td/docs/switches/datacenter/sw/nx-os/licensing/guide/ b_Cisco_NX-OS_Licensing_Guide/b_Cisco_NX-OS_Licensing_Guide_chapter_01.html

Cisco NX-OS and Cisco IOS Comparison

To finish up this introduction to Cisco NX-OS, this section describes how Cisco NX-OS and Cisco IOS differ. Cisco IOS and NX-OS are similar in many ways. From a feature and functionality standpoint, as well as from a configurations standpoint, many of the commands' structures are the same for working in both the IOS and NX-OS command-line interfaces. It is important to understand some of the differences between them, though, which will help you to navigate inside each operating system and lead to less confusion when switching between the two operating systems. Here are the main points to be aware of:

- Interfaces in NX-OS are all listed as Ethernet interfaces (for data interfaces). In contrast, IOS uses a description based on speed, such as Gigabit or 10 Gigabit.

- When you log in to IOS, you are prompted for an enable password to move from user EXEC mode into enable (also called privileged) EXEC mode. NX-OS does not have a user or enable mode, nor does it have an **enable** command. Instead, NX-OS associates a privilege level for each user based on a username/password combination, with all users considered to be in EXEC mode.

- NX-OS uses a universal image, and features are unlocked using license keys and feature-enablement commands. Cisco IOS originally required you to purchase, download, and install an operating system image that had the appropriate feature set for your enterprise needs. As of a couple of years ago, IOS has also adopted the universal image concept with license key enablement.

- NX-OS has a management Virtual Routing and Forwarding (VRF) instance per Nexus switch as well as a default VRF that all other interfaces belong to. To get access to remotely manage a Nexus switch, you must configure the Management interface (as covered later in this book).

- NX-OS uses two binary images per version of the operating system to be downloaded and installed (kickstart and system), except for Nexus 9000. Cisco IOS is a single binary image that is downloaded and installed by the network administrator.

- To enable features in NX-OS, the **feature** command is used per feature, such as **feature ospf** and **feature eigrp** to enable these Layer 3 routing protocols. In Cisco IOS, the command **ip routing** enables all the processes for every routing protocol a given operating system image will support.

There are also command differences between the two operating systems, but there are too many to list here. To compare the command differences, see the following website, which lists each command in Cisco IOS and how you can use it in NX-OS:

http://docwiki.cisco.com/wiki/Cisco_NX-OS/IOS_Software_Default_Configuration_Differences

Configuring Cisco NX-OS Software

You must understand how to configure a Cisco switch to succeed on the exam and in real networking jobs. This section covers the basic configuration processes, including the concept of a configuration file and the locations in which a configuration file can be stored. Although this section focuses on the configuration process, and not on the configuration commands themselves, you should know all the commands covered in this chapter for the exams, in addition to the configuration processes.

Commands entered in configuration mode update the active configuration file. These changes to the configuration occur immediately each time you press the Enter key at the end of a command. Be careful when you enter a configuration command!

Configuration Submodes and Contexts

Configuration mode itself contains a multitude of subcommand modes. Context-setting commands move you from one configuration subcommand mode, or context, to another. These context-setting commands tell the switch the topic about which you will enter the next few configuration commands.

> **NOTE** *Context setting* is not a Cisco term; it is just a term used here to help make sense of configuration mode. As mentioned earlier in the chapter, NX-OS enables you to enter commands that might be at a less-specific command mode with the ? character. For instance, you can be in interface command mode, enter (config-if)# **spanning-tree vlan ?**, and it will list the help for this global configuration command.

The **interface** command is one of the most commonly used context-setting configuration commands. For example, the CLI user could enter interface configuration mode by entering the **interface Ethernet 1/1** configuration command. Asking for help in interface configuration mode displays only commands that are useful when configuring Ethernet interfaces. Commands used in this context are called *subcommands* (or, in this specific case, *interface subcommands*). When you begin practicing with the CLI using real equipment, the navigation between modes can become natural. For now, consider Example 5-5, which shows the following:

- Movement from EXEC mode to global configuration mode by using the **configure terminal** EXEC command

- Using a **hostname Fred** global configuration command to configure the switch's name

- Movement from console configuration mode to interface configuration mode (using the **interface** command)

- Setting the speed to 10 Gigabit for interface Ethernet1/1 (using the **speed 10000** interface subcommand)

- Movement from interface configuration mode back to global configuration mode (using the **exit** command)

Example 5-5 *Navigating Between Different Configuration Modes*

```
Switch# configure terminal
Switch(config)# hostname Fred
Fred(config)# interface Ethernet 1/1
Fred(config-if)# speed 10000
Fred(config-if)# exit
Fred(config)#
```

The text inside parentheses in the command prompt identifies the configuration mode. For example, the first command prompt after you enter configuration mode lists (config), meaning global configuration mode. After the **interface Ethernet 1/1** command, the text expands to (config-if), meaning line configuration mode. Table 5-6 shows the most common command prompts in configuration mode, the names of those modes, and the context-setting commands used to reach those modes. NX-OS also has a **where** command that you can use from any mode to tell you what configuration modes you have gone through to get to the current configuration mode as well as which configuration mode you are currently in.

Table 5-6   Common Switch Configuration Modes

Prompt	Name of Mode	Context-Setting Commands to Reach This Mode
hostname(config)#	Global	None (first mode after configure terminal)
hostname(config-line)#	Line	`line console`, `line vty`
hostname(config-if)#	Interface	`interface` `type` `number`

You should practice until you become comfortable moving between the different configuration modes, back to EXEC mode, and then back into the configuration modes. However, you can learn these skills just doing labs about the topics in later chapters of the book. For now, Figure 5-9 shows most of the navigation between global configuration mode and the three configuration submodes listed in Table 5-6.

NOTE   You can also move directly from one configuration submode to another without first using the **exit** command to move back to global configuration mode. Just use the commands listed in bold in the center of the figure. To go directly back to enabled mode, you can type the **end** command from any submode.

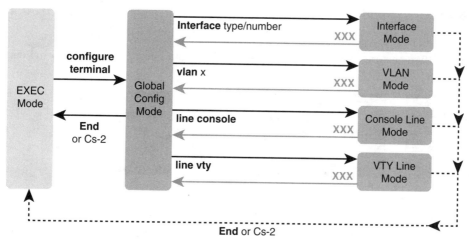

Figure 5-9 *Navigation In and Out of Switch Configuration Modes*

No set rules exist for what commands are global commands or subcommands. Generally, however, when multiple instances of a parameter can be set in a single switch, the command used to set the parameter is likely a configuration subcommand. Items that are set once for the entire switch are likely global commands. For example, the **hostname** command is a global command because there is only one host name per switch. Conversely, the **duplex** command is an interface subcommand to allow the switch to use a different setting on the different interfaces.

Storing Switch Configuration Files

When you configure a switch, it needs to use the configuration. It also needs to be able to retain the configuration in case the switch loses power. Cisco Nexus switches contain random access memory (RAM) to store data while Cisco NX-OS is using it, but RAM loses its contents when the switch loses power. To store information that must be retained when the switch loses power, Cisco switches use several types of more permanent memory, none of which has any moving parts. By avoiding components with moving parts (such as traditional disk drives), switches can maintain better uptime and availability.

The following list details the four main types of memory found in Cisco switches and the most common use of each type:

- **RAM:** Sometimes called DRAM (for dynamic random access memory), RAM is used by the switch just as it is used by any other computer: for working storage. The running (active) configuration file is stored here.

- **ROM:** Read-only memory stores a bootstrap (or boothelper) program that is loaded when the switch first powers on. This bootstrap program then finds the full Cisco NX-OS image and manages the process of loading Cisco NX-OS into RAM, at which point Cisco NX-OS takes over operation of the switch.

- **Flash memory:** Either a chip inside the switch or a removable memory card, flash memory stores fully functional Cisco NX-OS images and is the default location where the switch gets its Cisco NX-OS at boot time. Flash memory also can be used to store any other files, including backup copies of configuration files.

■ **NVRAM:** Nonvolatile RAM (NVRAM) stores the initial or startup configuration file that is used when the switch is first powered on and when the switch is reloaded.

Figure 5-10 summarizes this same information in a more convenient form for memorization and study.

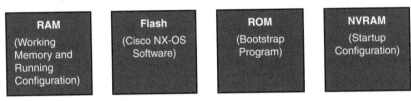

Figure 5-10   *Cisco Switch Memory Types*

Cisco NX-OS stores the collection of configuration commands in a configuration file. In fact, switches use multiple configuration files—one file for the initial configuration used when powering on, and another configuration file for the active, currently used running configuration as stored in RAM. Table 5-7 lists the names of these two files, their purpose, and their storage location.

Table 5-7   Names and Purposes of the Two Main Cisco NX-OS Configuration Files

Configuration Filename	Purpose	Where It Is Stored
Startup config	Stores the initial configuration used any time the switch reloads Cisco NX-OS.	NVRAM
Running config	Stores the currently used configuration commands. This file changes dynamically when someone enters commands in configuration mode.	RAM

Essentially, when you use configuration mode, you change only the running config file. This means that the configuration example earlier in this chapter (Example 5-2) updates only the running config file. However, if the switch were to lose power right after you complete the configuration shown in Example 5-2, all that configuration would be lost. If you want to keep that configuration, you have to copy the running config file into NVRAM, overwriting the old startup config file.

Example 5-6 demonstrates that commands used in configuration mode change only the running configuration in RAM. The example shows the following concepts and steps:

Step 1.   The original **hostname** command on the switch, with the startup config file matching the running config file.

Step 2.   The **hostname** command changes the hostname, but only in the running config file.

Step 3.   The **show running-config** and **show startup-config** commands are shown, with only the **hostname** commands displayed for brevity, to make the point that the two configuration files are now different.

Example 5-6 *How Configuration Mode Commands Change the Running Config File, Not the Startup Config File*

```
! Step 1 next (two commands)
!
hannah# show running-config
! (lines omitted)
hostname hannah
! (rest of lines omitted)


hannah# show startup-config
! (lines omitted)
hostname hannah
! (rest of lines omitted)
! Step 2 next. Notice that the command prompt changes immediately after
! the hostname command.
hannah# configure terminal
hannah(config)# hostname jessie
jessie(config)# exit
! Step 3 next (two commands)
!
jessie# show running-config
! (lines omitted)
hostname jessie
! (rest of lines omitted - notice that the running configuration reflects the
!    changed hostname)
jessie# show startup-config
! (lines omitted)
hostname hannah
! (rest of lines omitted - notice that the changed configuration is not
! shown in the startup config)
```

NOTE Cisco uses the term *reload* to refer to what most PC operating systems call rebooting or restarting. In each case, it is a reinitialization of the software. The reload EXEC command causes a switch to reload.

Copying and Erasing Configuration Files

If you want to keep the new configuration commands you add in configuration mode (so that the changes are present the next time the system is rebooted), like the **hostname jessie** command in Example 5-6, you need to use the command **copy running-config startup-config**. This command overwrites the current startup config file with what is currently in the running configuration file.

You can use the **copy** command to copy files in a switch, most typically a configuration file or a new version of Cisco NX-OS software. The most basic method for moving configuration files in and out of a switch is to use the **copy** command to copy files between RAM or NVRAM on a switch and a TFTP server. You can copy the files between any pair, as shown in Figure 5-11.

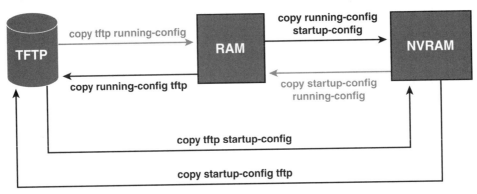

Figure 5-11   *Locations for Copying and Results from Copy Operations*

The commands for copying Cisco NX-OS configurations can be summarized as follows:

```
copy {tftp | running-config | startup-config} {tftp | running-config | startup-config}
```

The first set of parameters enclosed in braces ({ }) is the "from" location; the next set of parameters is the "to" location.

The **copy** command always replaces the existing file when the file is copied into NVRAM or into a TFTP server. In other words, it acts as if the destination file was erased and the new file completely replaced the old one. However, when the **copy** command copies a configuration file into the running config file in RAM, the configuration file in RAM is not replaced, but is merged instead. Effectively, any **copy** into RAM works just as if you entered the commands in the "from" configuration file in the order listed in the config file.

Who cares? Well, we do. If you change the running config and then decide that you want to revert to what's in the startup config file, the result of the **copy startup-config running-config** command might not cause the two files to actually match. One way to guarantee that the two configuration files match is to issue the **reload** command, which reloads, or reboots, the switch, which erases RAM and then copies the startup config into RAM as part of the reload process.

You can use the **write erase** command to erase the contents of NVRAM. Of course, if the switch is reloaded at this point, there is no initial configuration. Note that Cisco NX-OS does not have a command that erases the contents of the running config file. To clear out the running config file, simply erase the startup config file and then **reload** the switch.

NOTE   Making a copy of all current switch and router configurations should be part of any network's overall security strategy, mainly so that you can replace a device's configuration if an attack changes the configuration.

Initial Configuration (Setup Mode)

Cisco NX-OS software supports two primary methods of giving a switch an initial basic configuration: configuration mode (which has already been covered in this chapter) and setup mode. Setup mode leads a switch administrator by asking questions that prompt the administrator for basic configuration parameters. After the administrator answers the questions, NX-OS builds a configuration file, saves it as the startup config, and also loads it as the running config to start using the new configuration.

When a Cisco switch or router initializes, but the startup config file is empty, the switch or router asks the console user if he wants to use setup. Figure 5-12 shows the branches in the process. The left side of the figure, moving down, brings the user to the point at which NX-OS asks the user questions about what should be added to the configuration.

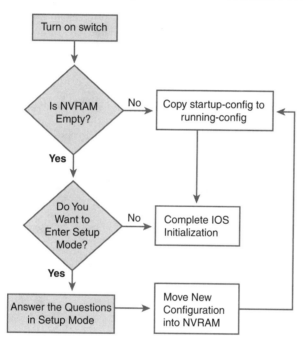

Figure 5-12   *Getting into Setup Mode*

Frankly, most network engineers never use setup mode, mainly because setup supports only a small percentage of modern switch configuration settings. However, you will still see some evidence of setup, because when you reload a switch or router that has no configuration, NX-OS will ask you whether you want to enter the "initial configuration dialog" (the official term for setup mode). Just answer no (which is the default), as shown in Example 5-7, and use configuration mode to configure the device.

Example 5-7   *Initial Configuration Dialog (Setup): Rejected*

```
--- System Configuration Dialog ---

Would you like to enter the initial configuration dialog? [yes/no]: no

Switch>
```

NX-OS Version and Other Reload Facts

To finish this first chapter about how Cisco NX-OS works, with the NX-OS CLI, this last topic looks at the switch **show version** command.

When a switch loads the NX-OS, it must do many tasks. The NX-OS software itself must be loaded into RAM. The NX-OS must become aware of the hardware available (for example, all the different interfaces on the switch). After the software is loaded, the NX-OS keeps track of some statistics related to the current operation of the switch, such as the amount of time since the NX-OS was last loaded and the reason why the NX-OS was most recently loaded.

The **show version** command lists these facts, plus many others. As you might guess from the command itself, the **show version** command does list information about the NX-OS, including the version of NX-OS software. As highlighted in Example 5-8, however, this command lists many other interesting facts as well.

Example 5-8   *Example of a* **show version** *Command on a Cisco Nexus Switch*

```
SW1# show version

Cisco Nexus Operating System (NX-OS) Software
TAC support: http://www.cisco.com/tac
Documents: http://www.cisco.com/en/US/products/ps9372/tsd_products_support_
series_home.html
Copyright (c) 2002-2013, Cisco Systems, Inc. All rights reserved.
The copyrights to certain works contained herein are owned by
other third parties and are used and distributed under license.
Some parts of this software are covered under the GNU Public
License. A copy of the license is available at
http://www.gnu.org/licenses/gpl.html.


Software
    BIOS:            version 3.6.0
    loader:        version N/A
    kickstart: version 6.0(2)N2(2)
    system:        version 6.0(2)N2(2)
    Power Sequencer Firmware:
                Module 1: version v1.0
                Module 2: version v1.0
                Module 3: version v5.0
```

```
    Microcontroller Firmware:                version v1.2.0.1
    SFP uC:          Module 1: v1.0.0.0
    QSFP uC:        Module not detected
    BIOS compile time:          05/09/2012
    kickstart image file is: bootflash:///n5000-uk9-kickstart.6.0.2.N2.2.bin
    kickstart compile time:    10/4/2013 12:00:00 [10/04/2013 16:04:23]
    system image file is:       bootflash:///n5000-uk9.6.0.2.N2.2.bin
    system compile time:         10/4/2013 12:00:00 [10/04/2013 18:23:49]


Hardware
    cisco Nexus5548 Chassis ("O2 32X10GE/Modular Universal Platform Supervisor")
    Intel(R) Xeon(R) CPU             with 8253856 kB of memory.
    Processor Board ID FOC153662P2


    Device name: 5K-L3-A
    bootflash:       2007040 kB

Kernel uptime is 32 day(s), 12 hour(s), 37 minute(s), 33 second(s)

Last reset
    Reason: Unknown
    System version: 6.0(2)N2(2)
    Service:


plugin
    Core Plugin, Ethernet Plugin, Fc Plugin, Virtualization Plugin
```

Working through the highlighted parts of the example, top to bottom, this command lists the following:

- The NX-OS kickstart and system image versions
- Hardware version and number of base interfaces
- Switch device name
- Time since last load of the NX-OS
- Reason for last load of the NX-OS

Exam Preparation Tasks

Review All Key Topics

Review the most important topics from this chapter, noted with the Key Topic icon in the outer margin of the page. Table 5-8 lists references for these key topics and the page number on which each is found.

Table 5-8   Key Topics for Chapter 5

Key Topic Element	Description	Page Number
List	Default switch console port settings	179
Table 5-6	Common switch configuration modes	188
Table 5-7	Names and purposes of the two main Cisco NX-OS configuration files	190

Definitions of Key Terms

After your first reading of the chapter, try to define these key terms, but do not be concerned about getting them all correct at that time. Chapter 24, "Final Review," directs you in how to use these terms for late-stage preparation for the exam.

command-line interface (CLI), Telnet, Secure Shell (SSH), EXEC mode, global configuration mode, startup config file, running config file

Command References

Table 5-9 lists and briefly describes the configuration commands used in this chapter.

Table 5-9   Chapter 5 Configuration Commands

Command	Mode and Purpose
`line console`	Global command that changes the context to console configuration mode.
`line vty`	Global command that changes the context to vty configuration mode.
`interface ethernet port-number`	Global command that changes the context to interface mode (for example, interface Ethernet 1/1).
`hostname name`	Global command that sets this switch's hostname, which is also used as the first part of the switch's command prompt.
`exit`	Moves back to the next higher mode in configuration mode.
`end`	Exits configuration mode and goes back to EXEC mode from any of the configuration submodes.
Ctrl+Z	This is not a command, but rather a two-key combination (pressing the Ctrl key and the letter Z) that together do the same thing as the `end` command.

Command	Mode and Purpose
`interface mgmt0`	Management interface. Using the command will enter you into interface command mode for the management interface.
`vrf context management`	Management Virtual Routing and Forwarding context. Using this command will allow you to enter and configure parameters of the management VRF.
`install license` `license file` `location and name`	Installs a license file for features a network admin would use on a Nexus switch.

Table 5-10 lists and briefly describes the EXEC commands used in this chapter.

Table 5-10   Chapter 5 EXEC Command Reference

Command	Purpose
`no debug all` `undebug all`	Disables all currently enabled debugs.
`terminal monitor`	Tells Cisco NX-OS to send a copy of all syslog messages, including debug messages, to the Telnet or SSH user who issues this command.
`reload`	Reboots the switch or router.
`copy from-location to-location`	Copies files from one file location to another. Locations include the startup config and running config files in RAM, TFTP, and RPC servers as well as in flash memory.
`copy running-config startup-config`	Saves the active config, replacing the startup config file used when the switch initializes.
`copy startup-config running-config`	Merges the startup config file with the currently active config file in RAM.
`show running-config`	Lists the contents of the running config file.
`exit`	Disconnects the user from the CLI session.
`show startup-config`	Lists the contents of the startup config (initial config) file.
`configure terminal`	Moves the user into configuration mode.
`show license host-id`	Displays the serial number (host ID) of the switch chassis to use for licensing.
`show feature`	Lists all the features available for use on a Cisco Nexus switch. Shows which features have been enabled or disabled.
`show vtp status`	Shows the status of VLAN Trunking Protocol (VTP) on a Nexus switch.

5

This chapter covers the following exam topics:

2.2. Describe classic Ethernet fundamentals

2.2.a. Forward

2.2.b. Filter

2.2.c. Flood

2.2.d. MAC address table

2.3 Describe switching concepts and perform basic configuration

2.3.a. STP

2.3.b. 802.1q

CHAPTER 6

VLAN and Trunking Concepts

At its heart, the Layer 2 switching logic on Ethernet switches receives Ethernet frames, makes decisions, and then forwards (switches) those Ethernet frames. That core logic revolves around MAC addresses, the interface in which the frame arrives, and the interfaces out which the switch forwards the frame.

Several switch features have some impact on an individual switch's decisions about where to forward frames, but of all the topics in this book, the virtual LAN (VLAN) easily has the biggest impact on those choices.

This chapter examines the concepts and configuration of VLANs. The first major section of the chapter explains the basics of VLANs and how to forward VLAN traffic over links called *trunks*. This first section explains Layer 2 forwarding, which includes considering the existence of VLANs. Next, the chapter adds the logic of how to forward data between two VLANs by using some form of routing, whether that routing is done by a device called a router or whether it is done by a switch that has the ability to also route packets.

The final section of the chapter explains the VLAN Trunking Protocol (VTP), which gives network engineers a tool to configure some VLAN settings on one LAN switch and have that configuration be pushed to the rest of the LAN switches.

> **NOTE** As promised in the Introduction's section "For Those Studying Routing & Switching," if you have already read *ICND1 100-101 Official Cert Guide*'s Chapter 9, "Implementing Ethernet Virtual LANs," you can skip the first half of this chapter. However, make sure you read this chapter's major section beginning with "VLAN Trunking Protocol" through the end of the chapter.

"Do I Know This Already?" Quiz

Use the "Do I Know This Already?" quiz to help decide whether you might want to skim this chapter, or a major section, moving more quickly to the "Exam Preparation Tasks" section near the end of the chapter. Table 6-1 lists the major headings in this chapter and their corresponding "Do I Know This Already?" quiz questions. For thorough explanations, see Appendix A, "Answers to the 'Do I Know This Already?' Quizzes."

Table 6-1 "Do I Know This Already?" Foundation Topics Section-to-Question Mapping

Foundation Topics Section	Questions
Virtual LANs and VLAN Trunks	1–4
VLAN and VLAN Trunking Configuration and Verification	5–7

1. In a LAN, which of the following terms best equates to the term *VLAN*?

    a. Collision domain

    b. Broadcast domain

    c. Subnet

    d. Single switch

    e. Trunk

2. Imagine a switch with three configured VLANs. How many IP subnets are required, assuming that all hosts in all VLANs want to use TCP/IP?

    a. 0.

    b. 1.

    c. 2.

    d. 3.

    e. You can't tell from the information provided.

3. Switch SW1 sends a frame to switch SW2 using 802.1Q trunking. Which of the answers describes how SW1 changes or adds to the Ethernet frame before forwarding the frame to SW2?

    a. It inserts a 4-byte header and changes the MAC addresses.

    b. It inserts a 4-byte header and does not change the MAC addresses.

    c. It encapsulates the original frame behind an entirely new Ethernet header

    d. None of the other answers is correct.

4. For an 802.1Q trunk between two Ethernet switches, which answer most accurately defines which frames do not include an 802.1Q header?

    a. Frames in the native VLAN (only one)

    b. Frames in extended VLANs

    c. Frames in VLAN 1 (not configurable)

    d. Frames in all native VLANs (multiple allowed)

5. A Nexus switch has some ports assigned to VLAN 11 and some to VLAN 12. Which of the following devices, acting as described in the answers, can forward data between ports in different VLANs? (Choose two answers.)

    a. The Nexus switch when acting as a Layer 2 switch

    b. The Nexus switch when acting as a Layer 3 switch

    c. An external router

    d. An external bridge

6. A network engineer wants to use VTP to distribute VLAN configuration information to all switches in a data center so that all switches learn a new VLAN configuration when a VLAN configuration change is made. Which of the following modes cannot be used on any of the switches? (Choose two answers.)

   a. Server

   b. Off

   c. Transparent

   d. Client

7. Which of the following answers list configuration information that VTP distributes? (Choose two answers.)

   a. VLAN name

   b. VLAN assigned to a switch port

   c. Ports on which 802.1Q is enabled

   d. VLAN ID

6

Foundation Topics

Virtual LANs and VLAN Trunks

Before understanding VLANs, you must first have a specific understanding of the definition of a LAN. For example, from one perspective, a LAN includes all the user devices, servers, switches, routers, cables, and wireless access points in one location. However, an alternative narrower definition of a LAN can help in understanding the concept of a virtual LAN:

A LAN includes all devices in the same broadcast domain.

A broadcast domain includes the set of all LAN-connected devices so that when any of the devices sends a broadcast frame, all the other devices get a copy of the frame. So, from one perspective, you can think of a LAN and a broadcast domain as being basically the same thing.

Without VLANs, a switch considers all its interfaces to be in the same broadcast domain. That is, for one switch, when a broadcast frame enters one switch port, the switch forwards that broadcast frame out all other ports. With that logic, to create two different LAN broadcast domains, you have to buy two different Ethernet LAN switches, as shown in Figure 6-1.

Figure 6-1 *Creating Two Broadcast Domains with Two Physical Switches and No VLANs*

With support for VLANs, a single switch can accomplish the same goal of the design in Figure 6-1—that is, to create two broadcast domains. With VLANs, a switch can configure some interfaces into one broadcast domain and some into another, thus creating multiple broadcast domains. These individual broadcast domains created by the switch are called *virtual LANs* (VLANs).

For example, in Figure 6-2, the single switch creates two VLANs, treating the ports in each VLAN as being completely separate. The switch would never forward a frame sent by Dino (in VLAN 1) over to either Wilma or Betty (in VLAN 2).

Figure 6-2 *Creating Two Broadcast Domains Using One Switch and VLANs*

Designing campus LANs to use more VLANs, each with a smaller number of devices, often helps improve the LANs in many ways. For example, a broadcast sent by one host in a VLAN will be received and processed by all the other hosts in the VLAN—but not by hosts in a different VLAN. Limiting the number of hosts that receive a single broadcast frame reduces the number of hosts that waste effort processing unneeded broadcasts. It also reduces security risks, because fewer hosts see frames sent by any one host. These are just a few reasons for separating hosts into different VLANs. The following list summarizes the most common reasons for choosing to create smaller broadcast domains (VLANs):

- To reduce CPU overhead on each device by reducing the number of devices that receive each broadcast frame

- To reduce security risks by reducing the number of hosts that receive copies of frames that the switches flood (broadcasts, multicasts, and unknown unicasts)

- To improve security for hosts that send sensitive data by keeping those hosts on a separate VLAN

- To create more flexible designs that group users by department, or by groups that work together, instead of by physical location

- To solve problems more quickly, because the failure domain for many problems is the same set of devices as those in the same broadcast domain

- To reduce the workload for the Spanning Tree Protocol (STP) by limiting a VLAN to a single access switch

This chapter does not examine all the reasons for VLANs in more depth. However, know that most enterprise networks use VLANs quite a bit. The rest of this chapter looks closely at the mechanics of how VLANs work across multiple Cisco switches. To that end, the next section examines VLAN trunking, a feature required when installing a VLAN that exists on more than one LAN switch.

Creating Multiswitch VLANs Using Trunking

Configuring VLANs on a single switch requires only a little effort: You simply configure each port to tell it the VLAN number to which the port belongs. With multiple switches, you have to consider additional concepts about how to forward traffic between the switches.

When you use VLANs in networks that have multiple interconnected switches, which, of course, is typical in a data center LAN, the switches need to use *VLAN trunking* on the links between the switches. VLAN trunking causes the switches to use a process called *VLAN tagging*, by which the sending switch adds another header to the frame before sending it over the trunk. This extra trunking header includes a VLAN identifier (VLAN ID) field so that the sending switch can associate the frame with a particular VLAN ID, and the receiving switch can then know in what VLAN each frame belongs.

Figure 6-3 shows an example that demonstrates VLANs that exist on multiple switches, but it does not use trunking. First, the design uses two VLANs: VLAN 10 and VLAN 20. Each switch has two ports assigned to each VLAN, so each VLAN exists in both switches. To forward traffic in VLAN 10 between the two switches, the design includes a link between switches, with that link fully inside VLAN 10. Likewise, to support VLAN 20 traffic between switches, the design uses a second link between switches, with that link inside VLAN 20.

VLAN 10

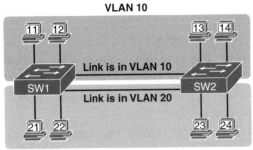

VLAN 20

Figure 6-3 *Multiswitch VLAN Without VLAN Trunking*

The design in Figure 6-3 functions perfectly. For example, PC11 (in VLAN 10) can send a frame to PC14. The frame flows into SW1, over the top link (the one that is in VLAN 10), and over to SW2.

However, although the design shown in Figure 6-3 works, it simply does not scale very well. It requires one physical link between switches to support every VLAN. If a design needs 10 or 20 VLANs, you would need 10 or 20 links between switches, and you would use 10 or 20 switch ports (on each switch) for those links.

VLAN trunking creates one link between switches that supports as many VLANs as you need. As a VLAN trunk, the switches treat the link as if it were a part of all the VLANs. At the same time, the trunk keeps the VLAN traffic separate, so frames in VLAN 10 would not go to devices in VLAN 20, and vice versa, because each frame is identified by VLAN number as it crosses the trunk. Figure 6-4 shows the idea, with a single physical link between the two switches.

VLAN 10

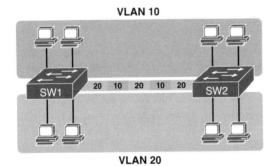

VLAN 20

Figure 6-4 *Multiswitch VLAN with Trunking*

The use of trunking allows switches to pass frames from multiple VLANs over a single physical connection by adding a small header to the Ethernet frame. For example, Figure 6-5 shows PC11 sending a broadcast frame on interface Fa0/1 at Step 1. To flood the frame, switch SW1 needs to forward the broadcast frame to switch SW2. However, SW1 needs to let SW2 know that the frame is part of VLAN 10, so that after the frame is received, SW2 will flood the frame only into VLAN 10, and not into VLAN 20. So, as shown at Step 2, before sending the frame, SW1 adds a VLAN header to the original Ethernet frame, with the VLAN header listing a VLAN ID of 10 in this case.

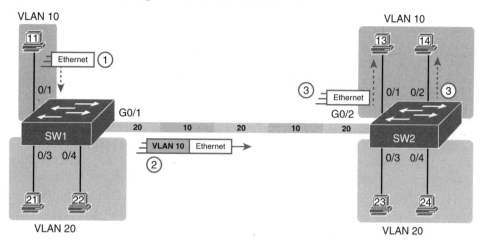

Figure 6-5 *VLAN Trunking Between Two Switches*

When SW2 receives the frame, it understands that the frame is in VLAN 10. SW2 then removes the VLAN header, forwarding the original frame out its interfaces in VLAN 10 (Step 3).

For another example, consider the case when PC21 (in VLAN 20) sends a broadcast. SW1 sends the broadcast out port Fa0/4 (because that port is in VLAN 20) and out Gi0/1 (because it is a trunk, meaning that it supports multiple different VLANs). SW1 adds a trunking header to the frame, listing a VLAN ID of 20. SW2 strips off the trunking header after noticing that the frame is part of VLAN 20, so SW2 knows to forward the frame out only ports Fa0/3 and Fa0/4, because they are in VLAN 20, and not out ports Fa0/1 and Fa0/2, because they are in VLAN 10.

The 802.1Q and ISL VLAN Trunking Protocols

Cisco has supported two different trunking protocols over the years: Inter-Switch Link (ISL) and IEEE 802.1Q. Cisco created the ISL protocol long before 802.1Q, in part because the IEEE had not yet defined a VLAN trunking standard. Years later, the IEEE completed work on the 802.1Q standard, which defines a different way to do trunking. Today, 802.1Q has become the more popular trunking protocol; in fact, the Nexus series of switches supports only 802.1Q, and not ISL.

Both ISL and 802.1Q tag each frame with the VLAN ID, but the details differ. 802.1Q inserts an extra 4-byte 802.1Q VLAN header into the original frame's Ethernet header, as shown at the top of Figure 6-6. As for the fields in the 802.1Q header, only the 12-bit VLAN ID field inside the 802.1Q header matters for the topics discussed in this book. This 12-bit field supports a theoretical maximum of 2^{12} (4096) VLANs, while in practice, it supports a maximum of 4094. (Both 802.1Q and ISL use 12 bits to tag the VLAN ID, with two reserved values [0 and 4095].)

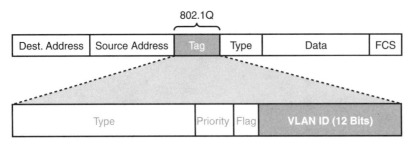

Figure 6-6 *802.1Q Trunking*

802.1Q also defines one special VLAN ID on each trunk as the *native VLAN* (defaulting to use VLAN 1). By definition, 802.1Q simply does not add an 802.1Q header to frames in the native VLAN. When the switch on the other side of the trunk receives a frame that does not have an 802.1Q header, the receiving switch knows that the frame is part of the native VLAN. Note that because of this behavior, both switches must agree on which VLAN is the native VLAN.

The 802.1Q native VLAN provides some interesting functions, mainly to support connections to devices that do not understand trunking. For example, a Cisco switch could be cabled to a switch that does not understand 802.1Q trunking. The Cisco switch could send frames in the native VLAN—meaning that the frame has no trunking header—so that the other switch would understand the frame. The native VLAN concept gives switches the capability of at least passing traffic in one VLAN (the native VLAN), which can allow some basic functions, such as reachability to telnet into a switch.

Forwarding Data Between VLANs

If you create a LAN that contains many VLANs, you typically still need all devices to be able to send data to all other devices; however, Layer 2 switching logic purposefully does not forward Ethernet frames between VLANs. The solution? Routing, which is a Layer 3 function. This next topic discusses some concepts about how to route data between VLANs.

First, it helps to know a few terms about some categories of LAN switches. Most of the Ethernet switch functions described in this book so far use the details and logic defined by OSI Layer 2 protocols. For example, Chapter 3 "Fundamentals of Ethernet LANs," discussed how LAN switches receive Ethernet frames (a Layer 2 concept), look at the destination Ethernet MAC address (a Layer 2 address), and forward the Ethernet frame out some other interface. This chapter has already discussed the concept of VLANs as broadcast domains, which is yet another Layer 2 concept.

Some switches, including many in the Cisco Nexus series of data center switches, combine Layer 2 switching features with Layer 3 routing features. These basically route IP packets and use IP routing protocols, as introduced back in Chapter 4, "Fundamentals of IPv4 Addressing and Routing." Switches that can also route packets go by the name *multilayer switch* or *Layer 3 switch*. The next few pages discuss the options for routing packets between VLANs, first with a router, and then with a multilayer switch.

Routing Packets Between VLANs with a Router

When including VLANs in a campus LAN design, the devices in a VLAN need to be in the same subnet. Following the same design logic, devices in different VLANs need to be in different subnets. For example, in Figure 6-7, the two PCs on the left sit in VLAN 10, in subnet 10. The two PCs on the right sit in a different VLAN (20), with a different subnet (20).

VLAN 10
Subnet 10

Dino

Fred

SW1

Wilma

Betty

VLAN 20
Subnet 20

Figure 6-7   *Layer 2 Switch Does Not Route Between the VLANs*

NOTE   The figure refers to subnets somewhat generally, like subnet 10, just so the subnet numbers do not distract. Also, note that the subnet numbers do not have to be the same number as the VLAN numbers.

Layer 2 switches will not forward data between two VLANs. In fact, one goal of VLANs is to separate traffic in one VLAN from another, preventing frames in one VLAN from leaking over to other VLANs. For example, when Dino (in VLAN 10) sends any Ethernet frame, if SW1 is a Layer 2 switch, that switch will not forward the frame to the PCs on the right in VLAN 20.

The network as a whole needs to support traffic flowing into and out of each VLAN, even though the Layer 2 switch does not forward frames outside a VLAN. The job of forwarding data into and out of a VLAN falls to routers. Instead of switching Layer 2 Ethernet frames between the two VLANs, the network must route Layer 3 packets between the two subnets.

That previous paragraph has some very specific wording related to Layers 2 and 3, so take a moment to reread and reconsider it. The Layer 2 logic does not let the Layer 2 switch forward the Layer 2 protocol data unit (L2PDU), the Ethernet frame, between VLANs. However, routers can route Layer 3 PDUs (L3PDUs [packets]) between subnets as their normal job in life.

For example, Figure 6-8 shows a router that can route packets between subnets 10 and 20. The figure shows the same Layer 2 switch as shown in Figure 6-7, with the same PCs and with the same VLANs and subnets. Now router R1 has one LAN physical interface connected to the switch and assigned to VLAN 10, and a second physical interface connected to the switch and assigned to VLAN 20. With an interface connected to each subnet, the Layer 2 switch can keep doing its job (forwarding frames inside a VLAN) while the router can do its job (routing IP packets between the subnets).

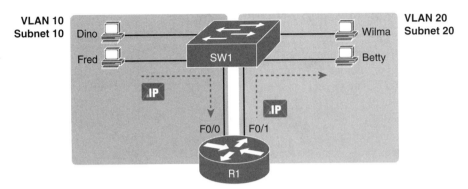

Figure 6-8 *Routing Between Two VLANs on Two Physical Interfaces*

The figure shows an IP packet being routed from Fred, which sits in one VLAN/subnet, to Betty, which sits in the other. The Layer 2 switch forwards two different Layer 2 Ethernet frames: one in VLAN 10, from Fred to R1's F0/0 interface, and the other in VLAN 20, from R1's F0/1 interface to Betty. From a Layer 3 perspective, Fred sends the IP packet to its default router (R1), and R1 routes the packet out another interface (F0/1) into another subnet where Betty resides.

The design shown in Figure 6-8 works, but it uses too many physical interfaces, one per VLAN. A much less-expensive (and much preferred) option uses a VLAN trunk between the switch and router, requiring only one physical link between the router and switch, while supporting all VLANs. Trunking can work between any two devices that choose to support it: between two switches, between a router and a switch, or even between server hardware and a switch.

Figure 6-9 shows the same design idea as Figure 6-8, with the same packet being sent from Fred to Betty, except now R1 uses VLAN trunking instead of a separate link for each VLAN.

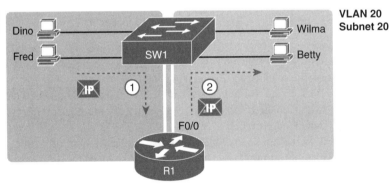

Figure 6-9 *Routing Between Two VLANs Using a Trunk on the Router*

NOTE Because the router has a single physical link connected to the LAN switch, this design is sometimes called a *router-on-a-stick* or a *one-armed router*.

As a brief aside about terminology, many people describe the concept in Figures 6-8 and 6-9 as "routing packets between VLANs." You can use that phrase, and people know what you mean. However, for exam preparation purposes, note that this phrase is not literally true, because it refers to routing packets (a Layer 3 concept) and VLANs (a Layer 2 concept). It just takes fewer words to say something like "routing between VLANs" rather than the literally true but long "routing Layer 3 packets between Layer 3 subnets, with those subnets each mapping to a different Layer 2 VLAN."

Routing Packets with a Layer 3 Switch

Routing packets using a physical router, even with the VLAN trunk in the router-on-a-stick model shown in Figure 6-9, still has one significant problem: performance. The physical link puts an upper limit on how many bits can be routed, and less-expensive routers tend to be less powerful, and might not be able to route a large enough number of packets per second (pps) to keep up with the traffic volumes.

The ultimate solution moves the routing functions inside the LAN switch hardware. Vendors long ago started combining the hardware and software features of their Layer 2 LAN switches, plus their Layer 3 routers, creating products called *Layer 3 switches* (also known as *multilayer switches*). Layer 3 switches can be configured to act only as a Layer 2 switch, or they can be configured to do both Layer 2 switching and Layer 3 routing.

Today, many data centers, as well as medium- to large-sized enterprise campus LANs, use Layer 3 switches to route packets between subnets (VLANs).

In concept, a Layer 3 switch works a lot like the original two devices on which the Layer 3 switch is based: a Layer 2 LAN switch and a Layer 3 router. In fact, if you take the concepts and packet flow shown in Figure 6-8, with a separate Layer 2 switch and Layer 3 router, and then imagine all those features happening inside one device, you have the general idea of what a Layer 3 switch does. Figure 6-10 shows that exact concept, repeating many details of Figure 6-8, but with an overlay that shows the one Layer 3 switch doing the Layer 2 switch functions and the separate Layer 3 routing function.

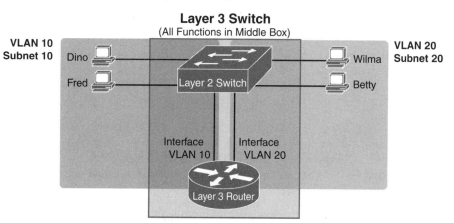

Figure 6-10 *Multilayer Switch: Layer 2 Switching with Layer 3 Routing in One Device*

This chapter introduces the core concepts of routing IP packets between VLANs (or more accurately, between the subnets on the VLANs). Chapter 18, "IPv4 Routing Protocol Concepts," discusses routing and Layer 3 switching in more depth, after you have read more about IPv4 addressing and subnetting.

VLAN Trunking Protocol

VLAN Trunking Protocol (VTP) gives engineers a convenient way to distribute some VLAN configuration information among switches. VTP defines a messaging protocol and related processes, so that VLAN configuration made on one switch is then advertised to other switches.

For instance, if a LAN had 40 switches, and VLAN 11 needed to be supported on those switches, the configuration to create and name VLAN 11 could be done on one switch only. Then, VTP, running on all the switches, would send messages so that the other 39 switches could dynamically learn the configuration using VTP.

NOTE Even though the *T* in VTP stands for *trunking*, VTP is not a trunking protocol like 802.1Q.

This final of three major sections in this chapter discusses the main concepts behind VTP. This section begins with a discussion of exactly what functions VTP provides, before moving on to show how VTP messages and processes advertise VLAN configuration information. This section ends with a discussion of how to avoid using VTP by using either VTP transparent mode or by disabling VTP.

VTP Functions

In Nexus and Catalyst switches, a VLAN must exist in the switch's configuration before the switch can do any work with that VLAN. Specifically, the VLAN must exist on a switch before that switch can forward frames in that VLAN. Once a VLAN is configured, the switch can assign access interfaces to that VLAN, support that VLAN on trunk interfaces, and forward frames in that VLAN.

VTP distributes some VLAN configuration information from one switch to the rest of the switches in a VTP domain. Specifically, the configuration includes the following:

- The VLAN ID
- The VLAN name

Note that VTP does advertise about each VLAN, but does not advertise the VLAN associated with each access port. For example, VTP does advertise the existence of a VLAN 11, named Payroll; however, VTP does not advertise the configuration that switch SW1's E1/2 port has been assigned to VLAN 11.

VTP can also group switches together using a concept called *VTP domains*. For instance, a data center might separate the LAN to support accounting functions in one part of the network and sales functions in another. VTP can be configured to use VTP domains with different names (for example, Accounting or Sales) so that VLANs configured in the Sales domain are learned only by other switches inside that domain and are not learned by the Accounting domain's switches, as shown in Figure 6-11.

VTP Sales   VTP Accounting

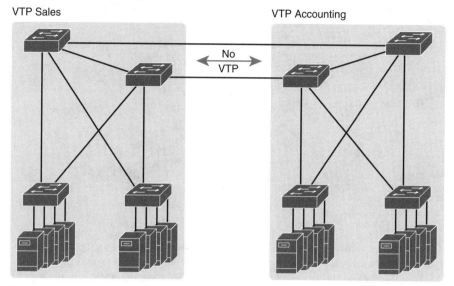

Figure 6-11 *VTP Domains Remain Separate*

VTP can be a powerful tool, but it is also a potentially dangerous tool. It does reduce the configuration effort, and it reduces the chances of making a typo in the VLAN name, because it is only typed once. However, a configuration mistake, such as deleting a VLAN that is still in use, automatically deletes the VLAN from all the switches in the same VTP domain. Once a VLAN is deleted, each switch can no longer forward frames in that VLAN. Other less-obvious mistakes can also lead to unintentionally deleting VLANs as well, so some installations simply avoid the dangers of VTP by just not using VTP.

This section next looks at how VTP works if you decide to use VTP, followed by a discussion of a few different ways to disable VTP.

Making VTP Work with VTP Servers and Clients

To use VTP, a network engineer must make a few design choices, such as the following:

- Which switches to put in the same VTP domain; that is, which switches need to know the same set of VLANs.

- A text name for the domain.

- A VTP password for the domain. (Switches ignore incoming VTP messages unless both the domain name and password match with the local switch's configuration.)

- Which switches will act as VTP servers and which will act as VTP clients.

For example, imagine a small network, as shown in Figure 6-12. In this case, the engineer chose to put all switches in the same VTP domain, using a domain name of MyCompany and a password of MyPassw0rd. The engineer also chose to make the two switches at the top of the figure (EoR1 and EoR2) VTP servers, and the other switches VTP clients.

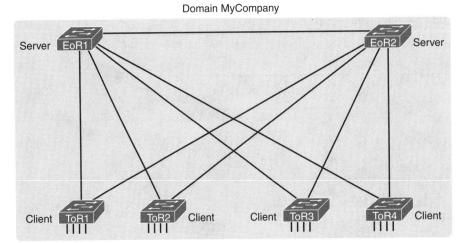

Figure 6-12 *VTP Domain MyCompany with Two VTP Servers*

Most of the choices shown in Figure 6-12 relate to the business needs, but the choice of VTP server and client relates more to the features of VTP. VTP defines several modes of operation, including server mode and client mode. The VTP mode determines how the switch acts with VTP, with VTP servers and clients being active participants in VTP.

VTP servers and clients can both learn about an updated configuration by listening for a VTP message, processing the message, and then forwarding the message. However, only VTP servers can be used to configure VLANs—that is, creating a VLAN, giving it a name, and deleting it—whereas VTP client switches cannot. A VTP client switch literally rejects the configuration commands to create a VLAN because of the fact that the switch is a VTP client.

Figure 6-13 shows the process of what happens on a smaller LAN than shown in Figure 6-12. This updated LAN drawing has a different topology, but fewer links, just so the VTP features are more obvious; the design in Figure 6-13 is not a typical design. In this scenario, new VLAN configuration is added to EoR1, which then sends VTP messages to inform the other switches about the new VLAN.

The figure shows the following the steps:

Step 1.   An engineer configures VLAN 11 on EoR1.

Step 2.   EoR1 sends a new VTP update out its trunks to ToR1 and EoR2.

Step 3.   ToR1 receives the VTP update, learns about new VLAN 11, and adds VLAN 11 to its local configuration.

Step 4.   EoR2 also receives the VTP update, learns about new VLAN 11, and adds VLAN 11 to its local configuration.

Step 5.   EoR2 forwards the VTP update to ToR4.

Step 6.   ToR4 then learns about VLAN 11.

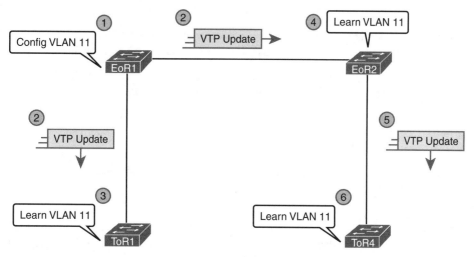

Figure 6-13 *A VTP Example of Configuring and Synchronizing for New VLAN 11*

This example shows the basic process. The switches forward the VTP messages so they reach all the switches, following the spanning-tree path, as discussed in upcoming chapters. Both the VTP client and VTP server switches react, updating their configuration. By the end of the process, all four switches once again have a consistent configuration of the VLAN IDs and VLAN names.

The example in Figure 6-13 shows the basics, but VTP does more than what is shown in that example. To round out the discussion, note that the VTP update actually holds the *VLAN database*, which is the entire list of VLAN IDs and names. That is, when a configuration change is made, the server sends the entire database. Once the process has completed, each switch has an updated copy of the database.

The VTP process also makes use of a VTP revision number, which is a revision number for the VLAN database. Each VTP update message lists the revision number of the current database. When a configuration change occurs, the VTP server adds one to the revision number and then sends a new VTP update. The other switches can notice the change to the revision number and know that the VLAN database has changed.

As an example, suppose that the VTP update message in Figure 6-13 was revision 7. Then imagine the following process happening over the next few days:

Step 1. For 3 days, no one changes the VLAN configuration. So, EoR1 and EoR2 independently send VTP updates every 5 minutes, with revision number 7.

Step 2. The engineer makes a VLAN configuration change on EoR1. The resulting VTP update, sent by EoR1 (as shown in Figure 6-13), lists revision 8.

Step 3. All the other switches in the domain receive the VTP update with revision 8 and know that the previous message listed revision 7, so each switch uses VTP messages to learn about the VLAN configuration changes and to update their local copy of the VLAN database.

Step 4. Both VTP servers now have a copy of the VLAN database based on revision 8.

Step 5. Another day passes with no configuration changes; EoR1 and EoR2 independently send VTP updates, every 5 minutes, with revision 8.

Step 6. Next, the engineer happens to make a configuration change from EoR2 instead of EoR1. EoR2 sends a VTP update with revision 9.

Step 7. All the other switches process the revision 9 update, realizing that a configuration change happened because of the revision number change from 8 to 9.

Step 8. Both VTP servers (EoR1 and EoR2) now have a copy of the database based on revision 9.

As you can see, all the clients and servers track the revision number of the VLAN database as a way to synchronize, so that all switches use the same version of the VLAN database—in other words, the same version of the VLAN configuration.

Disabling VTP

VTP supports two other modes that provide different levels of disabling VTP:

■ VTP transparent mode works in subtle ways, and it's most useful when an engineer wants to use VTP for some switches and not use VTP for others.

■ VTP off mode is straightforward, disabling VTP completely, and makes more sense when the engineer does not want to use VTP on any of the switches in the LAN.

VTP off mode disables *all* VTP processes on the switch. The switch does not originate VTP messages or process received VTP messages, and, importantly, it does not forward VTP messages. In designs that simply want to avoid VTP on all switches, off mode should be used.

VTP transparent mode disables *most* VTP processing, but not all, making a switch be transparent to the working (server and client) switches. To see how transparent mode is useful, consider the following requirements for a design:

■ Use VTP for some switches in the data center.

■ Purposefully do not use VTP on one switch and instead configure VLANs directly on that switch.

■ The switches should all have trunks connected to each other, which is useful for the VTP traffic to be able to pass through the transparent mode switch to other VTP servers and clients.

Figure 6-14 shows just such an example, using the same initial action as shown in Figure 6-13. In this case, the engineer wants to make switch EoR2 not use VTP, but the other three switches will use VTP. With EoR2 configured in VTP transparent mode, the engineer adds VLAN 11 configuration at EoR1, with the behavior of EoR2 differing from the example in Figure 6-13.

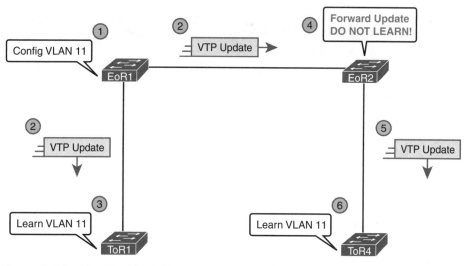

Figure 6-14 *The Need for VTP Transparent Mode*

With EoR2 in VTP transparent mode, the switch acts just like VTP off mode, except that it can forward the VTP update sent by EoR1. As shown in Steps 4 and 5, EoR2 (in transparent mode) ignores the contents of the VTP update but forwards the update to ToR4. If EoR2 had been in VTP off mode, it would not have forwarded the VTP update.

> **NOTE**   VTP transparent mode switches must also be configured with a matching VTP domain name and password to be willing to forward the VTP updates for a given domain.

VTP transparent and off-mode switches also have the added advantage of supporting more VLANs than VTP servers and clients. Servers and clients support VLANs 1–1005 only (called *normal* or *standard VLANs*). On Nexus switches, VTP transparent and off-mode switches support extended VLANs 1006–4094. (Note that 3968–4047 and 4094 are reserved and cannot be deleted.)

Summary of VTP Features

Table 6-2 summarizes the key comparison points of the different VTP modes. Using VTP with server and client mode has some great advantages for ease of configuration; however, it limits the VLANs that can be used in each switch, and it creates a potential danger when misused.

VTP off mode works very well for simply avoiding VTP altogether for all switches, enabling the use of many more switches, and is the preferred method to disable VTP when the design chooses to completely avoid using VTP. VTP transparent mode should be used as a tactic to support designs that call for use of VTP in some but not all switches.

Table 6-2 Comparisons of VTP Modes

	Server	Client	Transparent	Off
Can be used to configure a VLAN	Yes	No	Yes	Yes
Supports VLAN IDs	1–1005	1–1005	1–4094[1]	1–4094[1]
Originates VTP updates	Yes	No	No	No
Forwards VTP updates[2]	Yes	Yes	Yes	No
Synchronizes its VLAN database based on the received VTP updates	Yes	Yes	No	No

1 VLANs 3968–4047 and 4094 are reserved for internal use.
2 When configured with a matching VTP domain name and password.

Exam Preparation Tasks

Review All Key Topics

Review the most important topics from this chapter, noted with the Key Topic icon in the outer margin of the page. Table 6-3 lists references for these key topics and the page number on which each is found.

Table 6-3   Key Topics for Chapter 6

Key Topic Element	Description	Page Number
Figure 6-2	Basic VLAN concept	202
List	Reasons for using VLANs	203
Figure 6-5	Diagram of VLAN trunking	205
Figure 6-6	802.1Q header	206
Figure 6-9	Routing between VLANs with router-on-a-stick	208
Figure 6-10	Routing between VLANs with a Layer 3 switch	209
Figure 6-13	Basic VTP synchronization example	213
Table 6-2	VTP mode comparisons	216

6

Complete the Tables and Lists from Memory

Print a copy of Appendix C, "Memory Tables," or at least the section for this chapter, and complete the tables and lists from memory. Appendix D, "Memory Tables Answer Key," includes completed tables and lists to check your work.

Definitions of Key Terms

After your first reading of the chapter, try to define these key terms, but do not be concerned about getting them all correct at that time. Chapter 24, "Final Review," directs you in how to use these terms for late-stage preparation for the exam.

802.1Q, trunk, trunking administrative mode, trunking operational mode, VLAN, VTP, VTP client mode, VTP server mode, VTP transparent mode, Layer 3 switch, access interface, trunk interface

This chapter covers the following exam topics:

2.3. Describe switching concepts and perform basic configuration

2.3.a. STP

2.4.b. 802.1q

2.3.c. Port channels

CHAPTER 7

VLAN Trunking and Configuration

As you learned in Chapter 6, "VLAN and Trunking Concepts," VLANs are a way for us to segment different networks and decrease the size of our broadcast and collision domains. This chapter delves into how to enable VLANs from a configuration perspective on our Nexus data center switches.

This chapter examines the configuration of VLANs. The major section of the chapter explains how to configure VLANs and VLAN trunks as well as how to statically assign interfaces to a VLAN. This chapter also provides detailed information about VLAN Trunking Protocol (VTP) configuration and verification.

NOTE As mentioned in the Introduction's section "For Those Studying Routing & Switching," we suggest reading this entire chapter. Although the *ICND1 100-101 Official Cert Guide* also discusses VLAN and VLAN trunking configuration, and the NX-OS commands are often identical or similar, this chapter includes enough differences that it is worth your time to read and review it in full.

"Do I Know This Already?" Quiz

Use the "Do I Know This Already?" quiz to help decide whether you might want to skim this chapter, or a major section, moving more quickly to the "Exam Preparation Tasks" section near the end of the chapter. Table 7-1 lists the major headings in this chapter and their corresponding "Do I Know This Already?" quiz questions. For thorough explanations, see Appendix A, "Answers to the 'Do I Know This Already?' Quizzes."

Table 7-1 "Do I Know This Already?" Foundation Topics Section-to-Question Mapping

Foundation Topics Section	Questions
VLAN Configuration and Verification	1–2
VLAN Trunking Configuration and Verification	3–4
VTP Configuration and Verification	5

1. Imagine that on Switch 1 you are told to configure port Ethernet 1/1 to participate in VLAN 10. Which commands would enable interface Ethernet 1/1 to participate in VLAN 10? (Choose two answers.)
   a. switchport mode trunk
   b. switchport access vlan 10
   c. no shutdown
   d. access vlan 10
   e. vlan 10 access

2. A Nexus switch has just arrived from Cisco. The switch has never been configured

with any VLANs, but VTP has been disabled. An engineer gets into configuration mode and issues the **vlan 22** command, followed by the **name Evans-VLAN** command. Which of the following are true? (Choose two answers.)

    a. VLAN 22 is listed in the output of the **show vlan brief** command.

    b. VLAN 22 is listed in the output of the **show running-config** command.

    c. VLAN 22 is not created by this process.

    d. VLAN 22 does not exist in that switch until at least one interface is assigned to that VLAN.

3. Which of the following commands identify switch interfaces as being trunking interfaces—interfaces that currently operate as VLAN trunks? (Choose two answers.)

    a. show interface

    b. show interface switchport

    c. show interface trunk

    d. show trunks

4. Imagine that you are told that switch 1 is configured with the **switchport mode trunk** parameter for trunking on its Eth1/5 interface, which is connected to switch 2. You have to configure switch 2. Which of the following settings for trunking could allow trunking to work? (Choose two answers.)

    a. switchport mode trunk

    b. shutdown

    c. no shutdown

    d. access

    e. None of the answers are correct.

5. A Nexus switch has just arrived from Cisco. The switch has never been configured. An engineer would like to configure VLAN Trunking Protocol (VTP) in client mode. Which commands would he enter in configuration mode to do this? (Choose two answers.)

    a. feature vtp

    b. vlan 33 mode client

    c. vtp client

    d. vtp mode client

Foundation Topics

Cisco Nexus switches require minimal configuration to work, as you have seen in the previous chapters. When you purchase a Cisco Nexus switch, install devices with the correct cabling, and turn on the switch, the switch defaults all the interfaces into a single VLAN, known as VLAN 1. You would never need to configure the switch with any more details than the base configuration if all devices were in a single VLAN 1, and it would work fine until you needed more than one VLAN. But if you want to use VLANs—and most every enterprise network does—you need to make some configurations.

This chapter separates the VLAN configuration details into three major sections:

- The first looks at how to configure access interfaces—interfaces used for host connections generally.

- The second part shows how to configure interfaces that do use VLAN trunking between multiple switches to extend VLANs beyond a single switch.

- The third describes the VLAN Trunking Protocol (VTP), which is a Layer 2 messaging protocol used to distribute the VLAN information between multiple switches.

VLAN Configuration and Verification

This section provides an overview of VLAN support on Nexus switches, including guidelines for VLAN numbering, creating VLANs, assigning access VLANs to an interface, and two VLAN configuration examples.

VLAN Guidelines for Cisco Nexus Switches

Cisco Nexus switches support 4094 VLANs, by default; however, VLANs 3968–4094 are considered reserved for system use. When you are creating VLANs on Nexus switches, it is important not to use one in this reserved range. Table 7-2 outlines some other considerations that are important to note when creating or configuring VLANs on a Nexus switch.

Table 7-2   Considerations for Creating/Configuring VLANs on a Nexus Switch

VLAN Numbers	Range	Usage
1	Normal	Cisco default. You can use this VLAN, but you cannot modify or delete it.
2–1005	Normal	You can create, use, modify, and delete these VLANs.
1006–4094	Extended	You can create, name, and use these VLANs. You cannot change the following parameters: State is always active. VLAN is always enabled. You cannot shut down these VLANs.
3968–4047 and 4094	Internally allocated	These 80 VLANs, plus VLAN 4094, are allocated for internal use. You cannot create, delete, or modify any VLANs within the block reserved for internal use.

Creating VLANs and Assigning Access VLANs to an Interface

This section shows how to create a VLAN, give the VLAN a name, and assign interfaces to the VLAN. To focus on these basic details, this section shows examples using a single switch, so VLAN trunking is not needed.

For a Cisco Nexus switch to forward frames in a particular VLAN, the switch must be configured to believe that the VLAN exists. In addition, the switch must have nontrunking interfaces (called *access interfaces*) assigned to the VLAN, and/or trunks that support the VLAN. The configuration steps for access interfaces are as follows, with the trunk configuration shown later in the section "VLAN Trunking Configuration and Verification":

Step 1.   To configure a new VLAN, follow these steps:

   A. From configuration mode, use the **vlan** *vlan-id* global configuration command to create the VLAN and to move the user into VLAN configuration mode.

   B. (Optional) Use the **name** *name* VLAN subcommand to assign a name for the VLAN. If not configured, the VLAN name is VLANZZZZ, where ZZZZ is the four-digit decimal VLAN ID.

Step 2.   For each access interface (each interface that does not trunk, but instead belongs to a single VLAN), follow these steps:

   A. Use the **interface** command to move into interface configuration mode for each desired interface.

   B. Use the **switchport access vlan** *id-number* interface subcommand to specify the VLAN number associated with that interface.

   C. (Optional) To disable trunking on that same interface, so that the interface does not negotiate to become a trunk, use the **switchport mode access** interface subcommand.

While the list might look a little daunting, the process on a single switch is actually pretty simple. For example, if you want to put the switch's ports in three VLANs—11, 12, and 13—you just add three **vlan** commands: **vlan 11**, **vlan 12**, and **vlan 13**. Then, for each interface, add a **switchport access vlan 11** (or **12** or **13**) command to assign that interface to the proper VLAN.

VLAN Configuration Example 1: Full VLAN Configuration

Example 7-1 shows the configuration process of adding a new VLAN and assigning access interfaces to that VLAN. Figure 7-1 shows the network used in the example, with one LAN switch (SW1) and two hosts in each of three VLANs (1, 2, and 3). The example shows the details of the two-step process for VLAN 2 and the interfaces in VLAN 2. The configuration of VLAN 3 is deferred until the next example.

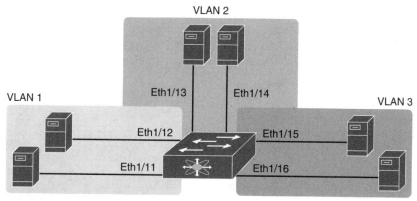

Figure 7-1 *Network with One Switch and Three VLANs*

Example 7-1 *Configuring VLANs and Assigning VLANs to Interfaces*

```
SW1# show vlan brief
VLAN Name                             Status    Ports
---- -------------------------------- --------- -------------------------------
1         default                     active    Eth1/1, Eth1/2, Eth1/3, Eth1/4
                                                 Eth1/5, Eth1/6, Eth1/7, Eth1/8
                                                 Eth1/9, Eth1/10, Eth1/11, Eth1/12
                                                 Eth1/13, Eth1/14, Eth1/15, Eth1/16
                                                 Eth1/17, Eth1/18, Eth1/19, Eth1/20
                                                 Eth1/21, Eth1/22, Eth1/23, Eth1/24
                                                 Eth1/25, Eth1/26, Eth1/27, Eth1/28,
                                                 Eth1/29, Eth1/30, Eth1/31, Eth1/32
! Above, VLANs 2 and 3 do not yet exist. Below, VLAN 2 is added, with name Freds-vlan,
! with two interfaces assigned to VLAN 2.

SW1# configure terminal
Enter configuration commands, one per line.    End with CNTL/Z.
SW1(config)# vlan 2
SW1(config-vlan)# name Freds-vlan
SW1(config-vlan)# exit
SW1(config)# interface Ethernet 1/13 - 14
SW1(config-if)# switchport access vlan 2
SW1(config-if)# end

! Below, the show running-config command lists the interface subcommands on
! interfaces Eth1/13 and Eth1/14.
SW1# show running-config
! Many lines omitted for brevity
! Early in the output:
vlan 2
 name Freds-vlan
```

```
!
! more lines omitted for brevity
interface Ethernet1/13
 switchport access vlan 2
 switchport mode access
!
interface Ethernet1/14
 switchport access vlan 2
 switchport mode access
!

SW1# show vlan brief

VLAN Name                     Status    Ports
---- -------------------- --------- ------------------------------
1    default              active    Eth1/1, Eth1/2, Eth1/3, Eth1/4
                                    Eth1/5, Eth1/6, Eth1/7, Eth1/8
                                    Eth1/9, Eth1/10, Eth1/11, Eth1/12
                                    Eth1/15, Eth1/16, Eth1/17, Eth1/18
                                    Eth1/19, Eth1/20, Eth1/21, Eth1/22
                                    Eth1/23, Eth1/24, Eth1/25, Eth1/26,
                                    Eth1/27, Eth1/28, Eth1/29, Eth1/30,
                                    Eth1/31, Eth1/32
2    Freds-vlan           active    Eth1/13, Eth1/14

SW1# show vlan id 2
VLAN Name                           Status    Ports
---- -------------------------- --------- ------------------------------
2    Freds-vlan                     active    Eth1/13, Eth1/14

VLAN Type   Vlan-mode
---- ----- ----------
2           enet            CE
```

After the configuration has been added, to list the new VLAN, the example repeats the **show vlan brief** command (highlighted in gray). Note that this command lists VLAN 2, named Freds-vlan, and the interfaces assigned to that VLAN (Eth1/13 and Eth1/14).

The example surrounding Figure 7-1 uses six switch ports, all of which need to operate as access ports. That is, each port should not use trunking, but instead should be assigned to a single VLAN, as assigned by the **switchport access vlan** *vlan-id* command.

For ports that should always act as access ports, add the optional interface subcommand **switchport mode access**. This command tells the switch to only allow the interface to be an access interface. The upcoming section "VLAN Trunking Configuration and Verification" discusses more details about the commands that allow a port to negotiate whether it should use trunking.

VLAN Configuration Example 2: Shorter VLAN Configuration

Example 7-1 showed several of the optional configuration commands, with a side effect of being a bit longer than is required. Example 7-2 shows a much briefer alternative configuration, picking up the story where Example 7-1 ended and showing the addition of VLAN 3 (refer to Figure 7-1). Note that SW1 does not know about VLAN 3 at the beginning of this example.

Example 7-2 *Shorter VLAN Configuration Example (VLAN 3)*

```
SW1# configure terminal
Enter configuration commands, one per line.   End with CNTL/Z.
SW1(config)# interface Ethernet 1/15 - 16
SW1(config-if-range)# switchport access vlan 3
% Access VLAN does not exist. Creating vlan 3
SW1(config-if-range)# ^Z

SW1# show vlan brief

VLAN    Name                              Status    Ports
----    ------------------------------    --------  ------------------------------
1       default                           active    Eth1/1, Eth1/2, Eth1/3, Eth1/4
                                                    Eth1/5, Eth1/6, Eth1/7, Eth1/8
                                                    Eth1/9, Eth1/10, Eth1/11, Eth1/12
                                                    Eth1/17, Eth1/18, Eth1/19, Eth1/20
                                                    Eth1/21, Eth1/22, Eth1/23, Eth1/24
                                                    Eth1/25, Eth1/26, Eth1/27, Eth1/28,
                                                    Eth1/29, Eth1/30, Eth1/31, Eth1/32
2       Freds-vlan                        active    Eth1/13, Eth1/14
3       VLAN0003                          active    Eth1/15, Eth1/16
```

Example 7-2 shows how a switch can dynamically create a VLAN—the equivalent of the **vlan** *vlan-id* global config command—when the **switchport access vlan** interface subcommand refers to a currently unconfigured VLAN. This example begins with SW1 not knowing about VLAN 3. When the **switchport access vlan 3** interface subcommand was used, the switch realized that VLAN 3 did not exist, and as noted in the shaded message in the example, the switch created VLAN 3, using a default name (VLAN0003). No other steps are required to create the VLAN. At the end of the process, VLAN 3 exists in the switch, and interfaces Eth1/15 and Eth1/16 are in VLAN 3, as noted in the shaded part of the **show vlan brief** command output.

VLAN Trunking Configuration and Verification

So far, we have discussed configuring a single switch with multiple VLANs. The next step is to see how we can extend a single VLAN or multiple VLANs between multiple switches using VLAN trunking. Trunking configuration between two Cisco switches can be very simple if you just statically configure trunking. NX-OS trunking requires only some straightforward configuration. Because Cisco Nexus switches support only the more modern trunking option

(802.1Q), NX-OS does not need a configuration command to define the type of trunking. You could literally add one interface subcommand for the switch interface on each side of the link (**switchport mode trunk**), and you would create a VLAN trunk that supports all the VLANs known to each switch.

> **NOTE** Some IOS switches support DOT1Q and the ISL trunking encapsulation methodology; they can be configured using the **switchport trunk encapsulation** command. Because NX-OS only supports the standards-based DOT1Q trunking encapsulation, this command is not available in NX-OS.

However, trunking configuration on Cisco Nexus switches includes many more options, including several options for what VLANs can be carried across the trunk as well as whether the trunk will be going to an end host such as a virtualized server that might need VLANs trunked down to it or to another switch.

Cisco Nexus switches support only 802.1Q trunking, as previously mentioned, and so in the configurations of a Cisco Nexus switch, there is no **encapsulation** command, only a **mode trunk** command to enable 802.1Q trunking. It's important to note this difference from other switches where we would have to configure the trunking encapsulation methodology like with Cisco Catalyst switches. Table 7-3 references the two switchport administrative mode commands available in Cisco Nexus switches.

Table 7-3   Trunking Administrative Mode Options with the **switchport mode** Command

Command Option	Description
access	Always act as an access (nontrunk) port
trunk	Always act as a trunk port

> **NOTE** This note is for you CCNA R&S folks: Unlike IOS on Catalyst switches, NX-OS does not dynamically negotiate whether to trunk. As a result, the NX-OS **switchport trunk** command does not have options that tell the Nexus switch to negotiate the trunking state.

For example, consider the two switches shown in Figure 7-2. This figure shows an expansion of the network of Figure 7-1, with a trunk to a new switch (SW2) and with parts of VLANs 1 and 3 on ports attached to SW2. The two switches use Ethernet link for the trunk. In this case, the trunk has been enabled because both Cisco Nexus switches default to an administrative mode of *access*, meaning that neither switch initiates the trunk negotiation process. By changing both switches to use *trunk* mode, which does initiate the negotiation, the switches negotiate to use trunking, specifically 802.1Q, because the 5548s support only 802.1Q. This is done on interface Ethernet 1/1 in Figure 7-2.

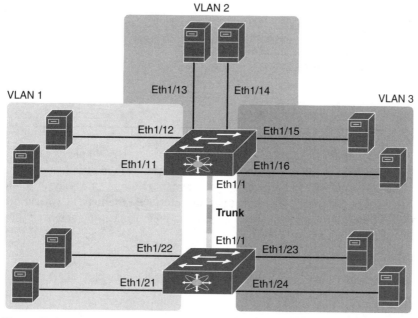

Figure 7-2 *Network with Two Switches and Three VLANs*

Example 7-3 show the basic configuration of setting up a trunk on interface Ethernet 1/1 based on Figure 7-2.

Example 7-3 *Trunk Configuration and Verification*

```
SW1# show running-config interface Ethernet 1/1

--some lines omitted--

interface Ethernet 1/1
    switchport mode trunk

SW1# show interface Ethernet 1/1 switchport
Name: Ethernet 1/1
    Switchport: Enabled
    Switchport Monitor: Not enabled
    Operational Mode: trunk
    Access Mode VLAN: 1 (default)
    Trunking Native Mode VLAN: 1 (default)
    Trunking VLANs Allowed: 1-4094
    Voice VLAN: none
    Extended Trust State : not trusted [COS = 0]
    Administrative private-vlan primary host-association: none
    Administrative private-vlan secondary host-association: none
    Administrative private-vlan primary mapping: none
```

```
Administrative private-vlan secondary mapping: none
Administrative private-vlan trunk native VLAN: none
Administrative private-vlan trunk encapsulation: dot1q
Administrative private-vlan trunk normal VLANs: none
Administrative private-vlan trunk private VLANs: none
Operational private-vlan: none
Unknown unicast blocked: disabled
Unknown multicast blocked: disabled
```

As you can see in the output of Example 7-3, the configuration is pretty simple: We get into interface configuration mode and use the command **switchport mode trunk** under Ethernet 1/1. This command will enable trunking on Ethernet 1/1 for all VLANs enabled on SW1 to traverse this link. You verify this using the **show interface Ethernet 1/1 switchport** command to look at the interface's trunking characteristics. By looking at the output of this command, you see a couple of key things to note:

- The operational mode is trunk.
- That the switch is trunking with a native VLAN of 1 (more on native VLAN in the note that follows).

If you use only the **switchport mode trunk** command, the switch, by default, will send all or allow any and all VLANs that have been configured on the switch. You see in the output highlighted in gray that the allowed VLANs are 1–4094, which means that all are allowed.

NOTE   Native VLAN is by default 1 on all Cisco switches, including Nexus. Native VLAN frames are not encapsulated with any method and are known as *untagged*, which means that any host on this VLAN can see these frames. Cisco Discovery Protocol (CDP), VTP, and other types of control plane messaging are always sent on the native VLAN 1 by default. You can configure the native VLAN as another VLAN if you want, and in this case, all the frames would be untagged. If you do change the native from its default of 1, it is best practice to do so on other switches as well.

Controlling Which VLANs Can Be Supported on a Trunk

Now that you know how to configure an interface to trunk VLANs from one switch to another, it is important to understand how to control which VLANs are allowed between them. The *allowed VLAN list* feature provides a mechanism for engineers to administratively disable a VLAN from a trunk. By default, switches include all possible VLANs (1–4094) in each trunk's allowed VLAN list. However, the engineer can then limit the VLANs allowed on the trunk by using the following interface subcommand:

```
switchport trunk allowed vlan {add | all | except | remove|none} vlan-list
```

This command provides a way to easily add and remove VLANs from the list. For example, the **add** option permits the switch to add VLANs to the existing allowed VLAN list, and the **remove** option permits the switch to remove VLANs from the existing list. The **all** option means all VLANs, so you can use it to reset the switch to its original default setting (permitting VLANs 1–4094 on the trunk). The **except** option is rather tricky; it adds all VLANs to the list that are not part of the command. For example, the **switchport trunk allowed vlan except 100-200** interface subcommand adds VLANs 1 through 99 and 201 through 4094 to the existing allowed VLAN list on that trunk.

In addition to the allowed VLAN list, a switch has other reasons to prevent a particular VLAN's traffic from crossing a trunk. All five reasons are summarized in the following list:

- A VLAN has been removed from the trunk's *allowed VLAN* list.
- A VLAN does not exist in the switch's configuration (as seen with the **show vlan** command).
- A VLAN does exist, but has been administratively disabled (**shutdown**).
- A VLAN has been automatically pruned by VTP. (VTP is discussed later in this chapter.)
- A VLAN's STP instance has placed the trunk interface into a blocking state.

This section has already discussed the first reason (the allowed VLAN list), so let's consider the next two reasons in the list. If a switch does not know that a VLAN exists—for example, if the switch does not have a **vlan** *vlan-id* command configured, as confirmed by the output of the **show vlan** command—the switch will not forward frames in that VLAN over any interface. In addition, a VLAN can exist in a switch's configuration, but also be administratively shut down either by using the **shutdown vlan** *vlan-id* global configuration command or by using the **shutdown** command in VLAN configuration mode. When disabled, a switch will no longer forward frames in that VLAN, even over trunks. So, switches do not forward frames in nonexistent VLANs or a shutdown VLAN over any of the switch's trunks.

This book has a motive for listing the reasons for limiting VLANs on a trunk: The **show interface trunk** command lists VLAN ID ranges as well, based on these same reasons. This command includes a progression of three lists of the VLANs supported over a trunk. These three lists are as follows:

- VLANs allowed on the trunk (1–4094, by default)
- VLANs from the first group that are also in an RSTP forwarding state
- VLANs from the second group that are not VTP pruned and not STP blocked

To get an idea of these three lists inside the output of the **show interfaces trunk** command, Example 7-4 shows how VLANs might be disallowed on a trunk for various reasons. The command output is taken from SW1 in Figure 7-2, after the completion of the configuration, as shown in all the earlier examples in this chapter. In other words, VLANs 1 through 3 exist in SW1's configuration and are not shut down. Trunking is operational between SW1 and SW2. Then, during the example, the following items are configured on SW1:

Step 1.   VLAN 4 is configured.

Step 2.   VLAN 2 is shut down, which causes RSTP to use a disabled state for all ports in VLAN 2.

Step 3.   VLAN 3 is removed from the trunk's allowed VLAN list.

Example 7-4 *Allowed VLAN List and the List of Active VLANs*

```
! The three lists of VLANs in the next command list allowed VLANs (1-4094),
! Allowed and active VLANs (1-3), and allowed/active/not pruned/STP forwarding
! VLANs (1-3)
SW1# show interfaces trunk


--------------------------------------------------------------------------------
Port                    Native                    Status              Port
                                          Vlan                              Channel
--------------------------------------------------------------------------------
Eth1/1                  1                         trunking               -


          --------------------------------------------------------------------------------
Port                    Vlans Allowed on Trunk
--------------------------------------------------------------------------------
Eth1/1                  1-4094



--------------------------------------------------------------------------------
Port                    Vlans Err-disabled on Trunk
--------------------------------------------------------------------------------
Eth1/1                  none



--------------------------------------------------------------------------------
Port                    STP Forwarding
--------------------------------------------------------------------------------
Eth1/1                  1-3


--------------------------------------------------------------------------------
Port                    Vlans in spanning tree forwarding state and not pruned
--------------------------------------------------------------------------------
Eth1/1                  1-3


--Some Lines Omitted for Brevity--


! Next, the switch is configured with new VLAN 4; VLAN 2 is shutdown;
! and VLAN 3 is removed from the allowed VLAN list on the trunk.
SW1# configure terminal
Enter configuration commands, one per line.    End with CNTL/Z.
SW1(config)# vlan 4
SW1(config-vlan)# vlan 2
SW1(config-vlan)# shutdown
SW1(config-vlan)# interface Eth1/1
```

```
SW1(config-if)# switchport trunk allowed vlan remove 3
SW1(config-if)# ^Z


! The three lists of VLANs in the next command list allowed VLANs (1-2, 4-4094),
! allowed and active VLANs (1,4), and allowed/active/not pruned/STP forwarding
! VLANs (1,4)
SW1# show interfaces trunk


-------------------------------------------------------------------------------
Port                    Native                  Status          Port
                                        Vlan
Channel
-------------------------------------------------------------------------------
Eth1/1                  1                       trunking                        -


  ! VLAN 3 is omitted next, because it was removed from the allowed VLAN list.
      -------------------------------------------------------------------------
Port                    Vlans Allowed on Trunk
-------------------------------------------------------------------------------
Eth1/1                  1-2,4-4094



-------------------------------------------------------------------------------
Port                    Vlans Err-disabled on Trunk
-------------------------------------------------------------------------------
Eth1/1                  none

! Since VLAN 2 is shutdown, RSTP considers all ports to be in a disabled state, so the
! switch omits VLAN 2 from the "STP Forwarding" List. VLANs 5-4094 are omitted below
! because SW1 does not have them configured.
-------------------------------------------------------------------------------
Port                    STP Forwarding
-------------------------------------------------------------------------------
Eth1/1                  1,4



-------------------------------------------------------------------------------
Port                    Vlans in spanning tree forwarding state and not pruned
-------------------------------------------------------------------------------
Eth1/1                  1,4


--Some Lines Omitted for Brevity--
```

VTP Configuration and Verification

Now that you know how to enable and control the extension of VLANs between switches, let's explore a tool created to help ease the pain of configuring VLANs across every switch of your data center; this older Cisco protocol and tool is called the VLAN Trunking Protocol (VTP). VTP is a Cisco proprietary tool on Cisco switches that advertises each VLAN configured in one switch (with the **vlan** *number* command) so that all the other switches learn about that VLAN. However, for various reasons, many enterprises choose not to use VTP. If you do choose to use VTP, we want you to understand how to utilize it best for your data center, so we explore what it is and how to use it with your Cisco Nexus switches.

VTP is a Layer 2 messaging protocol that maintains VLAN consistency by managing the addition, deletion, and renaming of VLANs within a VTP domain. A VTP domain is made up of one or more network devices that share the same VTP domain name and that are connected with trunk interfaces. Each network device can be in only one VTP domain. Figure 7-3 shows how VTP is used in a switch network.

VTP Features

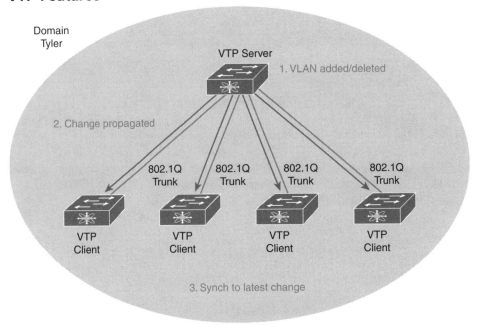

Figure 7-3   *VTP Operation*

Enabling VTP

VTP is disabled by default on the device. You can enable and configure VTP using the command-line interface (CLI). When VTP is disabled, the device does not relay any VTP protocol packets. To enable VTP on a Nexus switch, use the command **feature vtp**. By default, the switch will then be in VTP server mode. Example 7-5 shows the enabling and verification of VTP.

Example 7-5   *VTP Enablement and Verification*

```
SW1# show vtp
% Invalid command at '^' marker.
SW1# configure terminal
SW1(config)# feature vtp
SW1(config)# show vtp status
VTP Status Information
----------------------
VTP Version                            : 2 (capable)
Configuration Revision           : 0
Maximum VLANs supported locally : 1005
Number of existing VLANs         : 3
VTP Operating Mode                  : Server
VTP Domain Name                     : <VTP domain not acquired/configured yet>
VTP Pruning Mode                     : Disabled (Operationally Disabled)
VTP V2 Mode                          : Disabled
VTP Traps Generation            : Disabled
MD5 Digest                          : 0xB2 0xCC 0x45 0x18 0x7F 0x01 0xCD 0xD7
Configuration last modified by 10.0.128.203 at 0-0-00 00:00:00
Local updater ID is 10.0.128.203
VTP version running                  : 1
```

As you can see in the output of Example 7-5, VTP is disabled by default, so there are no associated VTP commands available to you to verify its configuration. To enable VTP, you must use the command **feature vtp**. After enabling VTP, you can see the default settings by using the **show vtp status** command. You can see in the output that by default you are in server mode and currently running in version 1. Let's look at some of the differences between version 2 and version 1 of VTP.

> **NOTE**   A newer version of VTP (VTP version 3) is currently supported in some of the Cisco Nexus Switches platform. Here are the major benefits of VTPv3:
>
> - VTPv3 creates a new mechanism to reduce unintended changes to the database, by introducing the concept of a "primary server." The primary server is the only device that is allowed to update other devices.
> - VTPv3 adds support to the entire spectrum of VLANs defined in 802.1Q 1–4095. It also adds support for private VLANs (PVANs).
> - VTPv3 adds support for the MST database.
>
> VTP maintains a list of trunk ports in the Spanning Tree Protocol (STP) forwarding state by querying STP at boot and listening to the notifications it generates. VTP sets a trunk port to the pruned or joined state by interacting with STP. STP notifies VTP when a trunk port goes to the blocking or forwarding state. VTP notifies STP when a trunk port becomes pruned or joined.

VTP Version 2 supports the following features not supported in VTP Version 1:

■ **Token Ring support:** VTP Version 2 supports Token Ring LAN switching and VLANs.

■ **Unrecognized Type-Length-Value (TLV) support:** A VTP server or client propagates configuration changes to its other trunks, even for TLVs that it is not able to parse. The unrecognized TLV is saved in NVRAM.

■ **Version-dependent transparent mode:** In VTP Version 1, a VTP transparent network device inspects VTP messages for the domain name and version and forwards a message only if the version and domain name match. Because only one domain is supported, VTP Version 2 forwards VTP messages in transparent mode without checking the version.

■ **Consistency checks:** In VTP Version 2, VLAN consistency checks (such as VLAN names and values) are performed only when you enter new information through the CLI or SNMP. Consistency checks are not performed when new information is obtained from a VTP message or when information is read from NVRAM. If the digest on a received VTP message is correct, its information is accepted without consistency checks.

Each switch can use one of three VTP modes: server, client, or transparent (mentioned earlier). Switches use either VTP server or client mode when the switch wants to use VTP for its intended purpose of dynamically advertising VLAN configuration information. Figure 7-4 describes each mode and its properties.

VTP Features

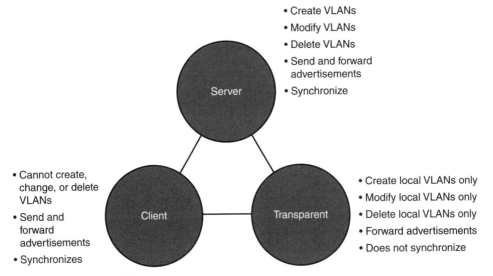

Figure 7-4 *VTP Modes and Descriptions*

It is always a best practice to configure a domain and password pair for your VTP environment to protect against rogue devices attaching to the network with the same domain name and a higher revision number, which would rewrite the VLANs already distributed with whatever was configured on the switch. Example 7-6 shows how to change the domain and password for your VTP environment. Also, you can configure the switch to use VTP Version 1 or 2. By default, it runs in Version 1.

Example 7-6   *VTP Version, Domain, and Password Configuration*

```
SW1# configure terminal
SW1(config)# vtp domain Tyler
SW1(config)# vtp password Evan
SW1(config)# vtp version 2
SW1(config)# show vtp status
VTP Status Information
----------------------
VTP Version                              : 2 (capable)
Configuration Revision          : 1
Maximum VLANs supported locally : 1005
Number of existing VLANs        : 3
VTP Operating Mode                  : Server
VTP Domain Name                     : Tyler
VTP Pruning Mode                    : Disabled (Operationally Disabled)
VTP V2 Mode                             : Enabled
VTP Traps Generation            : Disabled
MD5 Digest                          : 0x46 0xE0 0x71 0x5A 0x6E 0x2D 0x2C 0x4B
Configuration last modified by 10.0.128.203 at 6-9-14 23:13:21
Local updater ID is 10.0.128.203
VTP version running                 : 2
```

Limiting VTP Using Pruning

Because you now have a tool to distribute the VLANs across multiple different switches, you also need a tool to control and minimize the risks associated with doing so. This tool is VTP pruning. VTP pruning optimizes the usage of network bandwidth by restricting the flooded traffic to only those trunk ports that can reach all the active network devices. When this protocol is in use, a trunk port does not receive the flooded traffic that is meant for a certain VLAN unless an appropriate join message is received. Figure 7-5 demonstrates how VTP pruning works.

VTP Pruning

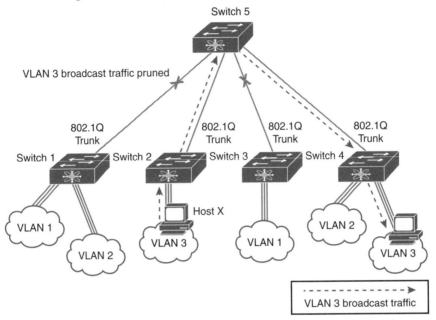

Figure 7-5 *VTP Pruning*

VTP pruning, as shown in Figure 7-5, is a way to determine which VLANs are present and being used on a particular switch (have active hosts). If an active host is not present, you can prune the VLANs off of the trunk links to avoid these switches from having to process flooded traffic from any unused VLANs. This helps from both a bandwidth and CPU perspective. To enable VTP pruning, use the **vtp pruning** command in global configuration mode.

NOTE VTP pruning is a way to use VTP to determine whether VLANs are active and then remove them if needed. Another and more popular way of doing this is by using the **switchport trunk allowed vlan** command. Using the allowed VLAN solution hard-codes what VLANs are allowed on a trunk link and in turn does not send flooded traffic on a trunk for VLANs that are not allowed. VTP pruning is currently supported only on Nexus 7000s.

Exam Preparation Tasks

Review All Key Topics

Review the most important topics from this chapter, noted with the Key Topic icon in the outer margin of the page. Table 7-4 lists a reference for these key topics and the page number on which each is found.

Table 7-4   Key Topics for Chapter 7

Key Topic Element	Description	Page Number
Table 7-2	VLAN creation guidelines	221
List	VLAN creation and assignment	222
Table 7-3	Trunking administrative mode options with the switchport mode command	226
Figure 7-3	VTP operation	232
Example 7-5	VTP enablement and verification	233
Figure 7-4	VTP modes and descriptions	234
Figure 7-5	VTP pruning	236

Command Reference to Check Your Memory

Although you should not necessarily memorize the information in Tables 7-5 and 7-6, this section does include a reference for the configuration and EXEC commands covered in this chapter. Practically speaking, you should memorize the commands as a side effect of reading the chapter and doing all the activities in this exam preparation section. To check and see how well you have memorized the commands as a side effect of your other studies, cover the left side of the table with a piece of paper, read the descriptions in the right side, and see whether you remember the command.

Table 7-5   Chapter 7 Configuration Command Reference

Command	Description
vlan *vlan-id*	Global config command that both creates the VLAN and puts the CLI into VLAN configuration mode
name *vlan-name*	VLAN subcommand that names the VLAN
[no] **shutdown**	VLAN mode subcommand that enables (**no shutdown**) or disables (**shutdown**) the VLAN
[no] **shutdown vlan** *vlan-id*	Global config command that has the same effect as the [no] **shutdown** VLAN mode subcommands
feature vtp	Enables VTP on a Cisco Nexus switch
vtp mode {server | client | transparent | off}	Global config command that defines the VTP mode
switchport mode {access | trunk}	Interface subcommand that configures the trunking administrative mode on the interface
switchport trunk allowed vlan {add | all | except | remove | none} *vlan-list*	Interface subcommand that defines the list of allowed VLANs
switchport access vlan *vlan-id*	Interface subcommand that statically configures the interface into that one VLAN
switchport trunk native vlan *vlan-id*	Interface subcommand that defines the native VLAN for a trunk port
vtp pruning	Enables VTP pruning on a Cisco Nexus switch (Nexus 7x00)

Table 7-6 Chapter 7 EXEC Command Reference

Command	Description
show interface *interface-id* switchport	Lists information about any interface regarding administrative settings and its operational state
show interface *interface-id* trunk	Lists information about all operational trunks (but no other interfaces), including a list of VLANs that can be forwarded over the trunk
show vlan [brief | id *vlan-id* | name *vlan-name* | summary]	Lists information about the VLAN
show vlan name [*vlan*]	Displays VLAN information
show vtp status	Lists VTP configuration and status information

7

This chapter covers the following exam topics:

2.0. Basic data center networking concepts

2.3. Describe switching concepts and perform basic configuration

2.3.a. STP

CHAPTER 8

Spanning Tree Protocol Concepts

Spanning Tree Protocol (STP) allows Ethernet LANs to have the added benefit of redundant links while overcoming the known problems that occur when those extra links are added. Redundant links in a LAN design allow the LAN to keep working even when some links fail or even when entire switches fail. Proper LAN design should add enough redundancy so that no single point of failure crashes the LAN; STP allows the design to use redundancy without causing some other problems.

This chapter discusses the concepts behind STP. In particular, it discusses why LANs need STP, what STP does to solve certain problems in LANs with redundant links, and how STP does its work.

This chapter breaks the STP discussions into three major sections. The first examines the oldest version of STP as defined by the IEEE, based on the 802.1D standard, and is generally referred to as *STP*. The second major section looks at various improvements to 802.1D STP over the years, including Port-Channel and PortFast.

> **NOTE** As mentioned in the Introduction's section "For Those Studying Routing & Switching," you need to read this chapter. This chapter's content is not found in the *ICND1 100-101 Official Cert Guide*, and it ends with a discussion of 802.1w Rapid Spanning Tree Protocol (RSTP).

"Do I Know This Already?" Quiz

Use the "Do I Know This Already?" quiz to help decide whether you might want to skim this chapter, or a major section, moving more quickly to the "Exam Preparation Tasks" section near the end of the chapter. Table 8-1 lists the major headings in this chapter and their corresponding "Do I Know This Already?" quiz questions. For thorough explanations, see Appendix A, "Answers to the 'Do I Know This Already?' Quizzes."

Table 8-1 "Do I Know This Already?" Foundation Topics Section-to-Question Mapping

Foundation Topics Section	Questions
Spanning Tree Protocol (IEEE 802.1D)	1–3
Optional STP Features	5
Rapid STP (IEEE 802.1w)	6, 7

1. Which of the following IEEE 802.1D port states are stable states used when STP has completed convergence? (Choose three answers.)

   a. Blocking

   b. Forwarding

   c. Listening

   d. Learning

   e. Discarding

2. Which of the following are transitory IEEE 802.1D port states used only during the process of STP convergence? (Choose two answers.)

   a. Blocking

   b. Forwarding

   c. Listening

   d. Learning

   e. Discarding

3. Which of the following bridge IDs win election as root, assuming that the switches with these bridge IDs are in the same network?

   a. 32769:0200.1111.1111

   b. 32769:0200.2222.2222

   c. 4097:0200.1111.1111

   d. 4097:0200.2222.2222

   e. 40961:0200.1111.1111

4. Which of the following facts determines how often a nonroot switch sends an 802.1D STP hello BPDU message?

   a. The hello timer as configured on that switch.

   b. The hello timer as configured on the root switch.

   c. It is always every 2 seconds.

   d. The switch reacts to BPDUs received from the root switch by sending another BPDU 2 seconds after receiving the root BPDU.

5. What STP feature causes an interface to be placed in the forwarding state as soon as the interface is physically active?

   a. STP

   b. Port-Channel

   c. Root Guard

   d. PortFast

6. Switch S1 sits in a LAN that uses RSTP. SW1's E1/1 port is its root port, with E1/2 as the only other port connected to other switches. SW1 knows that it will use E1/2 as its root port if E1/1 fails. If SW1's E1/1 interface fails, which of the following is true?

   a. SW1 waits 10 times the hello timer (default 10 x 2 = 20 seconds) before reacting.

   b. SW1 waits three times the hello timer (default 3 x 2 = 6 seconds) before reacting.

   c. SW1 does not wait but makes E1/2 the root port and puts it in a learning state.

   d. SW1 does not wait but makes E1/2 the root port and puts it in a forwarding state.

7. Switch SW1 sits in a LAN that uses RSTP. SW1 has 24 RSTP edge ports and is also receiving hello BPDUs on two point-to-point ports, E1/1 and E1/2. SW1 chooses E1/1 as its root port. Which of the following about the RSTP port role of E1/2 is true?

   a. Backup role

   b. Blocking role

   c. Discarding role

   d. Alternate role

8

Foundation Topics

Spanning Tree Protocol (IEEE 802.1D)

A LAN with redundant links would cause Ethernet frames to loop for an indefinite period of time unless some other mechanism stops the frames from looping. The fundamental frame-forwarding logic in a switch does not prevent such loops.

Historically, Spanning Tree Protocol (STP) was the first loop-prevention mechanism for Ethernet networks that used bridges and later switches. With STP enabled, some switches block ports so that these ports do not forward frames. In effect, the LAN can have redundant links for backup purposes, but STP logically stops using some links to remove the loops from the network.

STP intelligently chooses which ports to block, with two goals in mind:

- All devices in a VLAN can send frames to all other devices. In other words, STP does not block too many ports, cutting off some parts of the LAN from other parts.
- Frames have a short life and do not loop around the network indefinitely.

STP strikes a balance, allowing frames to be delivered to each device, without causing the problems that occur when frames loop through the network over and over again.

STP prevents looping frames by adding an additional check on each interface before a switch uses it to send or receive user traffic. That check works like this: If the port is in STP forwarding state in that VLAN, use it as normal; if it is in STP blocking state, however, block all user traffic and do not send or receive user traffic on that interface in that VLAN.

Note that these STP states do not change the other information you already know about switch interfaces. The interface's state of connected/notconnect does not change. The interface's operational state as either an access or trunk port does not change. STP adds this additional STP state, with the blocking state basically disabling the interface.

In many ways, those last two paragraphs sum up what STP does. However, the details of how STP does its work can take a fair amount of study and practice. This first major section of the chapter begins by explaining the need for STP and the basic ideas of what STP does to solve the problem of looping frames. The majority of this section looks at how STP goes about choosing which switch ports to block to accomplish its goals.

The Need for Spanning Tree

STP prevents three common problems in Ethernet LANs that would occur if the LAN were to have redundant links and STP were not used. All three problems are actually side effects of the fact that without STP, some Ethernet frames would loop around the network for a long time (hours, days, or literally forever if the LAN devices and links never failed).

Just one frame that loops around a network causes what is called a *broadcast storm*. Broadcast storms happen when broadcast frames, multicast frames, or unknown-destination unicast frames loop around a LAN indefinitely. Broadcast storms can saturate all the links with copies of that one single frame, crowding out good frames, as well as significantly impacting end-user PC performance by making the PCs process too many broadcast frames.

To help you understand how this occurs, Figure 8-1 shows a sample network in which Bob sends a broadcast frame. The dashed lines show how the switches forward the frame when STP does not exist.

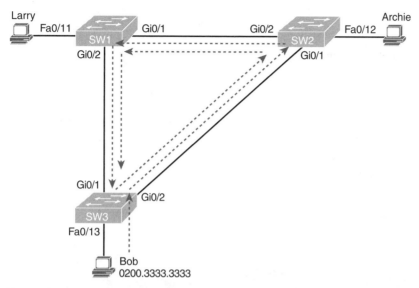

Figure 8-1   *Broadcast Storm*

NOTE   Bob's original broadcast would also be forwarded around the other direction as well, with SW3 sending a copy of the original frame out its Gi0/1 port. The figure does not show that frame just to reduce the clutter.

8

Remember the LAN switching logic from back in Chapter 3, "Fundamentals of Ethernet LANs"? That logic tells switches to flood broadcasts out all interfaces in the same VLAN except the interface in which the frame arrived. In the figure, that means SW3 forwards Bob's frame to SW2, SW2 forwards the frame to SW1, SW1 forwards the frame back to SW3, and SW3 forwards it back to SW2 again.

When broadcast storms happen, frames like the one in Figure 8-1 keep looping until something changes—someone shuts down an interface, reloads a switch, or does something else to break the loop. Also note that the same event happens in the opposite direction. When Bob sends the original frame, SW3 also forwards a copy to SW1, SW1 forwards it to SW2, and so on.

Looping frames also cause a *MAC table instability* problem. MAC table instability means that the switches' MAC address tables keep changing the information listed for the source MAC address of the looping frame. For example, SW3 begins Figure 8-1 with a MAC table entry for Bob, at the bottom of the figure, as follows:

  0200.3333.3333   Fa0/13   VLAN 1

However, now think about the switch-learning process that occurs when the looping frame goes to SW2, then SW1, and then back into SW3's Gi0/1 interface. SW3 thinks, "Hmm…

the source MAC address is 0200.3333.3333, and it came in my Gi0/1 interface. Update my MAC table!" This results in the following entry on SW3:

0200.3333.3333   Gi0/1   VLAN 1

At this point, SW3 itself cannot correctly deliver frames to Bob's MAC address. At that instant, if a frame arrives at SW3 destined for Bob—a different frame than the looping frame that causes the problems—SW3 incorrectly forwards the frame out Gi0/1 to SW1.

The looping frames also cause a third problem: Multiple copies of the frame arrive at the destination. Consider a case in which Bob sends a frame to Larry but none of the switches know Larry's MAC address. Switches flood frames sent to unknown destination unicast MAC addresses. When Bob sends the frame destined for Larry's MAC address, SW3 sends a copy to both SW1 and SW2. SW1 and SW2 also flood the frame, causing copies of the frame to loop. SW1 also sends a copy of each frame out Fa0/11 to Larry. As a result, Larry gets multiple copies of the frame, which may result in an application failure, if not more pervasive networking problems.

Table 8-2 summarizes the main three classes of problems that occur when STP is not used in a LAN with redundancy.

Table 8-2   Three Classes of Problems Caused by Not Using STP in Redundant LANs

Problem	Description
Broadcast storms	The forwarding of a frame repeatedly on the same links, consuming significant parts of the links' capacities
MAC table instability	The continual updating of a switch's MAC address table with incorrect entries, in reaction to looping frames, resulting in frames being sent to the wrong locations
Multiple frame transmission	A side effect of looping frames in which multiple copies of one frame are delivered to the intended host, thus confusing the host

What IEEE 802.1D Spanning Tree Does

STP prevents loops by placing each switch port in either a forwarding state or a blocking state. Interfaces in the forwarding state act as normal, forwarding and receiving frames. However, interfaces in a blocking state do not process any frames except STP messages (and some other overhead messages). Interfaces that block do not forward user frames, do not learn MAC addresses of received frames, and do not process received user frames.

Figure 8-2 shows a simple STP tree that solves the problem shown in Figure 8-1 by placing one port on SW3 in the blocking state.

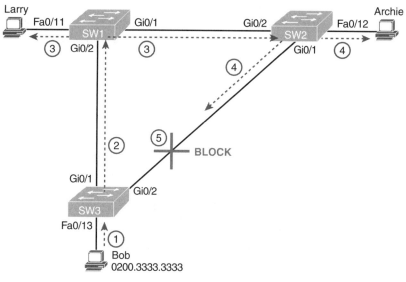

Figure 8-2   *What STP Does: Blocks a Port to Break the Loop*

Now when Bob sends a broadcast frame, the frame does not loop. As shown in the steps in the figure:

Step 1.   Bob sends the frame to SW3.

Step 2.   SW3 forwards the frame only to SW1, but not out Gi0/2 to SW2, because SW3's Gi0/2 interface is in a blocking state.

Step 3.   SW1 floods the frame out both Fa0/11 and Gi0/1.

Step 4.   SW2 floods the frame out Fa0/12 and Gi0/1.

Step 5.   SW3 physically receives the frame, but it ignores the frame received from SW2 because SW3's Gi0/2 interface is in a blocking state.

With the STP topology in Figure 8-2, the switches simply do not use the link between SW2 and SW3 for traffic in this VLAN, which is the minor negative side effect of STP. However, if either of the other two links fails, STP converges so that SW3 forwards instead of blocks on its Gi0/2 interface.

> **NOTE**   The term *STP convergence* refers to the process by which the switches collectively realize that something has changed in the LAN topology and so the switches might need to change which ports block and which ports forward.

That completes the description of what STP does, placing each port into either a forwarding or blocking state. The more interesting question, and the one that takes a lot more work to understand, is the question of how and why STP makes its choices. How does STP manage to make switches block or forward on each interface? And how does it converge to change state from blocking to forwarding to take advantage of redundant links in response to network outages? The following sections answer these questions.

How Spanning Tree Works

The STP algorithm creates a spanning tree of interfaces that forward frames. The tree structure of forwarding interfaces creates a single path to and from each Ethernet link, just like you can trace a single path in a living, growing tree from the base of the tree to each leaf.

> **NOTE**   STP was created before LAN switches even existed. In those days, Ethernet bridges used STP. Today, switches play the same role as bridges, implementing STP. However, many STP terms still refer to *bridge*. For the purposes of STP and this chapter, consider the terms *bridge* and *switch* synonymous.

The process used by STP, sometimes called the *spanning-tree algorithm* (STA), chooses the interfaces that should be placed into a forwarding state. For any interfaces not chosen to be in a forwarding state, STP places the interfaces in blocking state. In other words, STP simply picks which interfaces should forward, and any interfaces left over go to a blocking state.

STP uses three criteria to choose whether to put an interface in forwarding state:

■ STP elects a *root switch*. STP puts all working interfaces on the root switch in forwarding state.

■ Each nonroot switch considers one of its ports to have the least administrative cost between itself and the root switch. The cost is called that switch's *root cost*. STP places its port that is part of the least-root-cost path, called that switch's *root port* (RP), in forwarding state.

■ Many switches can attach to the same Ethernet segment, but in modern networks, normally two switches connect to each link. The switch with the lowest root cost, as compared with the other switches attached to the same link, is placed in forwarding state. That switch is the designated switch, and that switch's interface, attached to that segment, is called the *designated port* (DP) .

> **NOTE**   The real reason the root switch places all working interfaces in a forwarding state is that all its interfaces will become DPs, but it is easier to just remember that all the root switch's working interfaces will forward frames.

All other interfaces are placed in a blocking state. Table 8-3 summarizes the reasons STP places a port in forwarding or blocking state.

Table 8-3   STP: Reasons for Forwarding or Blocking

Characterization of Port	STP State	Description
All the root switch's ports	Forwarding	The root switch is always the designated switch on all connected segments.
Each nonroot switch's root port	Forwarding	The port through which the switch has the least cost to reach the root switch (lowest root cost).
Each LAN's designated port	Forwarding	The switch forwarding the hello on to the segment, with the lowest root cost, is the designated switch for that segment.
All other working ports	Blocking	The port is not used for forwarding user frames, nor are any frames received on these interfaces considered for forwarding.

NOTE   STP only considers working interfaces (those in a connected state). Failed interfaces (for example, interfaces with no cable installed) or administratively shutdown interfaces are instead placed into an STP disabled state. Therefore, this section uses the term *working ports* to refer to interfaces that could forward frames if STP placed the interface into a forwarding state.

The STP Bridge ID and Hello BPDU

STP begins with an election of one switch to be the root switch. To better understand this election process, you need to understand the STP messages sent between switches as well as the concept and format of the identifier used to uniquely identify each switch.

The STP bridge ID (BID) is an 8-byte value unique to each switch. The BID consists of a 2-byte priority field and a 6-byte system ID, with the system ID being based on a universal (burned-in) MAC address in each switch. Using a burned-in MAC address ensures that each switch's BID will be unique.

STP defines messages called *bridge protocol data units* (BPDUs), which switches use to exchange information with each other. The most common BPDU, called a hello BPDU, lists many details, including the sending switch's BID. Switches can tell which switch sent which hello BPDU via its BID. Table 8-4 lists some of the key information in the hello BPDU.

Table 8-4   Fields in the STP Hello BPDU

Field	Description
Root BID	The BID of the switch the sender of this hello currently believes to be the root switch
Sender's BID	The BID of the switch sending this hello BPDU
Sender's root cost	The STP cost between this switch and the current root
Timer values on the root switch	Includes the hello timer, MaxAge timer, and forward delay timer

For the time being, just keep the first three items from Table 8-4 in mind, as the following sections work through the three steps for how STP chooses the interfaces to place into a forwarding state. Next, the text examines the three main steps in the STP process.

Electing the Root Switch

Switches elect a root switch based on the BIDs in the BPDUs. The root switch is the switch with the lowest numeric value for the BID. Because the two-part BID starts with the priority value, essentially the switch with the lowest priority becomes the root. For example, if one switch has priority 4096, and another switch has priority 8192, the switch with priority 4096 wins, regardless of what MAC address was used to create the BID for each switch.

If a tie occurs based on the priority portion of the BID, the switch with the lowest MAC address portion of the BID is the root. No other tiebreaker should be needed because switches use one of their own universal (burned-in) MAC addresses as the second part of their BIDs. So if the priorities tie, and one switch uses a MAC address of 0200.0000.0000 as part of the BID and the other uses 0911.1111.1111, the first switch (MAC 0200.0000.0000) becomes the root switch.

STP elects a root switch in a manner not unlike a political election. The process begins with all switches claiming to be the root by sending hello BPDUs listing their own BID as the root BID. If a switch hears a hello that lists a better (lower) BID, that switch stops advertising itself as root and starts forwarding the superior hello. The hello sent by the better switch lists the better switch's BID as the root. It works like a political race in which a less-popular candidate gives up and leaves the race, throwing his support behind the more popular candidate. Eventually, everyone agrees which switch has the best (lowest) BID, and everyone supports the elected switch—which is where the political race analogy falls apart.

> **NOTE**   A better hello, meaning that the listed root's BID is better (numerically lower), is called a *superior hello*; a worse hello, meaning that the listed root's BID is not as good (numerically higher), is called an *inferior hello*.

Figure 8-3 shows the beginning of the root election process. In this case, SW1 has advertised itself as root, as have SW2 and SW3. However, SW2 now believes that SW1 is a better root, so SW2 is now forwarding the hello originating at SW1. So, at this point, the figure shows SW1 is saying hello, claiming to be root; SW2 agrees, and is forwarding SW1's hello that lists SW1 as root; but, SW3 is still claiming to be best, sending its own hello BPDUs, listing SW3's BID as the root.

Two candidates still exist in Figure 8-3: SW1 and SW3. So who wins? Well, from the BID, the lower-priority switch wins; if a tie occurs, the lower MAC address wins. As shown in the figure, SW1 has a lower BID (32769:0200.0001.0001) than SW3 (32769:0200.0003.0003), so SW1 wins, and SW3 now also believes that SW1 is the better switch. Figure 8-4 shows the resulting hello messages sent by the switches.

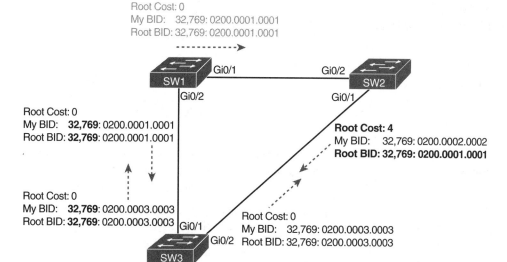

Figure 8-3 *Beginnings of the Root Election Process*

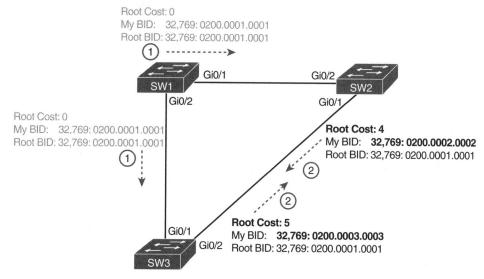

Figure 8-4 *SW1 Wins the Election*

After the election is complete, only the root switch continues to originate STP hello BPDU messages. The other switches receive the hellos, update the sender's BID field (and root cost field), and forward the hellos out other interfaces. The figure reflects this fact, with SW1 sending hellos at Step 1, and SW2 and SW3 independently forwarding the hello out their other interfaces at Step 2.

Summarizing, the root election happens through each switch claiming to be root, with the best switch being elected based on the numerically lowest BID. Breaking down the BID into its components, the comparisons can be made as follows:

- The lowest priority
- If that ties, the lowest switch MAC address

Choosing Each Switch's Root Port

The second part of the STP process occurs when each nonroot switch chooses its one and only root port. A switch's RP is its interface through which it has the least STP cost to reach the root switch (least root cost).

The idea of a switch's cost to reach the root switch can be easily seen for humans. Just look at a network diagram that shows the root switch, lists the STP cost associated with each switch port, and the nonroot switch in question. Switches use a different process than looking at a network diagram, of course, but using a diagram can make it easier to learn the idea.

Figure 8-5 shows just such a diagram, with the same three switches shown in the last several figures. SW1 has already won the election as root, and the figure considers the cost from SW3's perspective.

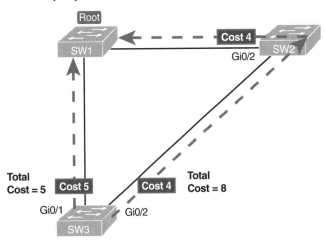

Figure 8-5   *How a Human Might Calculate STP Cost from SW3 to the Root (SW1)*

SW3 has two possible physical paths to send frames to the root switch: the direct path to the left, and the indirect path to the right through switch SW2. The cost is the sum of the costs of all the *switch ports the frame would exit* if it flowed over that path. (The calculation ignores the inbound ports.) As you can see, the cost over the direct path out SW3's G0/1 port has a total cost of 5, and the other path has a total cost of 8. SW3 picks its G0/1 port as root port because it is the port that is part of the least-cost path to send frames to the root switch.

Switches come to the same conclusion, but using a different process. Instead, they add their local interface STP cost to the root cost listed in each received hello BPDU. The STP port cost is simply an integer value assigned to each interface, per VLAN, for the purpose of providing an objective measurement that allows STP to choose which interfaces to add to the STP topology. The switches also look at their neighbor's root cost, as announced in the hello BPDUs received from each neighbor.

Figure 8-6 shows an example of how switches calculate their best root cost and then choose their root port, using the same topology and STP costs as shown in Figure 8-5. STP on SW3 calculates its cost to reach the root over the two possible paths by adding the advertised cost (in hello messages) to the interface costs listed in the figure.

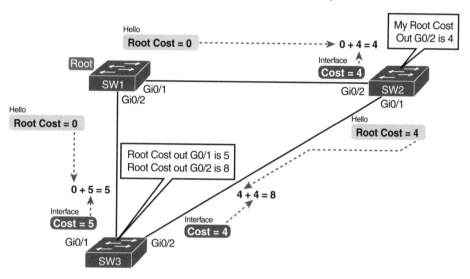

Figure 8-6 *How STP Actually Calculates the Cost from SW3 to the Root*

Focus on the process for a moment. The root switch sends hellos, with a listed root cost of 0. The idea is that the root's cost to reach itself is 0.

Next, look on the left of the figure. SW3 takes the received cost (0) from the hello sent by SW1, adds the interface cost (5) of the interface on which that hello was received. SW3 calculates that the cost to reach the root switch, out that port (G0/1), is 5.

On the right side, SW2 has realized its best cost to reach the root is cost 4. So, when SW2 forwards the hello toward SW3, SW2 lists a root cost of 4. SW3's STP port cost on port G0/2 is 4, so SW3 determines a total cost of 8 to reach the root out its G0/2 port.

As a result of the process depicted in Figure 8-6, SW3 chooses Gi0/1 as its RP, because the cost to reach the root switch through that port (5) is lower than the other alternative (Gi0/2, cost 8). Similarly, SW2 chooses Gi0/2 as its RP, with a cost of 4 (SW1's advertised cost of 0 plus SW2's Gi0/2 interface cost of 4). Each switch places its root port into a forwarding state.

Tiebreakers for Root Port

In some cases, a switch must use a tiebreaker when choosing its root port. The reason is simple: The root cost might be equal over more than one path to the root.

In most cases, the first tiebreaker solves the problem—the lowest neighbor BID. For instance, if you refer to Figure 8-6 in the previous section, imagine that SW3's root cost tied over both paths to reach the root (SW1). SW3 then looks at the BIDs of its two neighbors (SW1 and SW2) and picks the one that is lowest. In Figure 8-6, SW1's BID is lowest, so SW3 would choose as its root port the port connected to that neighbor—namely, SW3's G0/1 port.

8

In some other cases, STP needs even more tiebreakers. Specifically, when two switches connect with multiple links, as shown in Figure 8-7, the neighbor's BID will be equal.

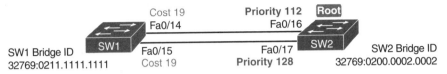

Figure 8-7   *The Need for Additional Root Port Tiebreakers*

In this particular example, SW2 becomes the root, and SW1 needs to choose its RP. SW1's port costs tie, at 19 each, so SW1's root cost ties over each path at cost 19. SW2 sends hellos over each link to SW1, so SW1 cannot break the tie based on the neighbor BID, because both neighbor BIDs list SW2's BID. So, SW1 has to consider the other two tiebreakers, in order: the neighboring switch ports' port priority, and if that ties, the neighboring switch ports' internal port number (with lowest being best).

In Figure 8-7, SW1 would see that the hello that entered its F0/14 port has a neighbor's port priority of 112, better than the other port's priority of 128, so SW1 would choose F0/14 as its root port.

The following list summarizes the criteria for choosing a root port, with all the tiebreakers listed:

1. Choose based on the least cost path to the root. If a tie occurs…
2. Choose based on the lowest BID of the neighboring bridge. If a tie occurs…
3. Choose based on the lowest port priority of the neighboring switch ports. If a tie occurs…
4. Choose based on the lowest internal port number on the neighboring switch ports.

Choosing the Designated Port on Each LAN Segment

STP's final step in choosing the STP topology is to choose the designated port on each LAN segment. The designated port (DP) on each LAN segment is the switch port that advertises the lowest-cost hello on to a LAN segment. When a nonroot switch forwards a hello, the nonroot switch sets the root cost field in the hello to that switch's cost to reach the root. In effect, the switch with the lower cost to reach the root, among all switches connected to a segment, becomes the DP on that segment.

For example, earlier Figure 8-4 showed in bold text the parts of the hello messages from both SW2 and SW3 that determine the choice of DP on that segment. Note that both SW2 and SW3 list their respective cost to reach the root switch (cost 4 on SW2 and cost 5 on SW3). SW2 lists the lower cost, so SW2's Gi0/1 port is the designated port on that LAN segment.

All DPs are placed into a forwarding state; so in this case, SW2's Gi0/1 interface will be in a forwarding state.

If the advertised costs tie, the switches break the tie by choosing the switch with the lower BID. In this case, SW2 would also have won, with a BID of 32769:0200.0002.0002 versus SW3's 32769:0200.0003.0003.

NOTE Two additional tiebreakers are needed in some cases, although these would be unlikely today. A single switch can connect two or more interfaces to the same collision domain by connecting to a hub. In that case, the one switch hears its own BPDUs. So, if a switch ties with itself, two additional tiebreakers are used: the lowest interface STP priority on the local switch and, if that ties, the lowest internal interface number on the local switch.

The only interface that does not have a reason to be in a forwarding state on the three switches in the examples shown in Figures 8-3 through 8-6 is SW3's Gi0/2 port. So, the STP process is now complete. Table 8-5 outlines the state of each port and shows why it is in that state.

Table 8-5   State of Each Interface

Switch Interface	State	Reason for That Interface State
SW1, Gi0/1	Forwarding	The interface is on the root switch, so it becomes the DP on that link.
SW1, Gi0/2	Forwarding	The interface is on the root switch, so it becomes the DP on that link.
SW2, Gi0/2	Forwarding	The root port of SW2.
SW2, Gi0/1	Forwarding	The designated port on the LAN segment to SW3.
SW3, Gi0/1	Forwarding	The root port of SW3.
SW3, Gi0/2	Blocking	Not the root port and not the designated port.

Influencing and Changing the STP Topology

Switches do not just use STP once and never again. The switches continually watch for changes. Those changes can be due to a link or switch failing or because a new link can now be used. The configuration can change in a way that changes the STP topology. This section briefly discusses the kinds of things that change the STP topology, either through configuration or through changes in the status of devices and links in the LAN.

Making Configuration Changes to Influence the STP Topology

The network engineers can choose to change the STP settings to then change the choices STP makes in a given LAN. The two main tools available to the engineer are to configure the BID and to change STP port costs.

Switches have a way to create a default BID, by taking a default priority value and adding a universal MAC address that comes with the switch hardware. However, engineers typically want to choose which switch becomes the root. Chapter 9, "Cisco Nexus Spanning Tree Protocol Implementation," shows how to configure a Cisco switch to override its default BID setting to make a switch become root.

Port costs also have default values, per port, per VLAN. You can configure these port costs, or you can use the default values. Table 8-6 lists the default port costs defined by IEEE; Cisco uses these same defaults.

Table 8-6   Default Port Costs According to IEEE

Ethernet Speed	IEEE Cost
10 Mbps	100
100 Mbps	19
1 Gbps	4
10 Gbps	2
40 Gbps	1

With STP enabled, all working switch interfaces will settle into an STP forwarding or blocking state, even access ports. For switch interfaces connected to hosts or routers, which do not use STP, the switch still forwards hellos on to those interfaces. By virtue of being the only device sending a hello on to that LAN segment, the switch is sending the least-cost hello on to that LAN segment, making the switch become the designated port on that LAN segment. So, STP puts working access interfaces into a forwarding state as a result of the designated port part of the STP process.

Reacting to State Changes That Affect the STP Topology

After the engineer has finished all STP configuration, the STP topology should settle into a stable state and not change, at least until the network topology changes. This section examines the ongoing operation of STP while the network is stable, and then it covers how STP converges to a new topology when something changes.

The root switch sends a new hello BPDU every 2 seconds by default. Each nonroot switch forwards the hello on all DPs, but only after changing the items listed in the hello. The switch sets the root cost to that local switch's calculated root cost. The switch also sets the "sender's bridge ID" field to its own BID. (The root's BID field is not changed.)

By forwarding the received (and changed) hellos out all DPs, all switches continue to receive hellos every 2 seconds. The following steps summarize the steady-state operation when nothing is currently changing in the STP topology:

Step 1.   The root creates and sends a hello BPDU, with a root cost of 0, out all its working interfaces (those in a forwarding state).

Step 2.   The nonroot switches receive the hello on their root ports. After changing the hello to list their own BID as the sender's BID, and listing that switch's root cost, the switches forward the hello out all designated ports.

Step 3.   Steps 1 and 2 repeat until something changes.

Each switch relies on these periodic received hellos from the root as a way to know that its path to the root is still working. When a switch ceases to receive the hellos, or receives a hello that lists different details, something has failed, so the switch reacts and starts the process of changing the spanning-tree topology.

How Switches React to Changes with STP

For various reasons, the convergence process requires the use of three timers. Note that all switches use the timers as dictated by the root switch, which the root lists in its periodic hello BPDU messages. Table 8-7 describes the timers.

Table 8-7 STP Timers

Timer	Description	Default Value
Hello	The time period between hellos created by the root.	2 seconds
MaxAge	How long any switch should wait, after ceasing to hear hellos, before trying to change the STP topology.	10 times hello
Forward delay	Delay that affects the process that occurs when an interface changes from blocking state to forwarding state. A port stays in an interim listening state, and then an interim learning state, for the number of seconds defined by the forward delay timer.	15 seconds

If a switch does not get an expected hello BPDU within the hello time, the switch continues as normal. However, if the hellos do not show up again within the MaxAge time, the switch reacts by taking steps to change the STP topology. With default settings, MaxAge is 20 seconds (10 times the default hello timer of 2 seconds). So, a switch would go 20 seconds without hearing a hello before reacting.

After MaxAge expires, the switch essentially makes all its STP choices again, based on any hellos it receives from other switches. It reevaluates which switch should be the root switch. If the local switch is not the root, it chooses its RP. And it determines whether it is the DP on each of its other links. The best way to describe STP convergence is to show an example using the same familiar topology. Figure 8-8 shows the same familiar figure, with SW3's Gi0/2 in a blocking state, but SW1's Gi0/2 interface has just failed.

SW3 reacts to the change because SW3 fails to receive its expected hellos on its Gi0/1 interface. However, SW2 does not need to react because SW2 continues to receive its periodic hellos in its Gi0/2 interface. In this case, SW3 reacts either when the MaxAge time passes without hearing the hellos, or as soon as SW3 notices that interface Gi0/1 has failed. (If the interface fails, the switch can assume that the hellos will not be arriving in that interface anymore.)

Now that SW3 can act, it begins by reevaluating the choice of root switch. SW3 still receives the hellos from SW2, as forwarded from the root (SW1). SW1 still has a lower BID than SW3; otherwise, SW1 would not have already been the root. So, SW3 decides that SW1 is still the best switch and that SW3 is not the root.

Next, SW3 reevaluates its choice of RP. At this point, SW3 is receiving hellos on only one interface: Gi0/2. Whatever the calculated root cost, Gi0/2 becomes SW3's new RP. (The cost would be 8, assuming the STP costs had no changes since Figures 8-5 and 8-6.)

SW3 then reevaluates its role as DP on any other interfaces. In this example, no real work needs to be done. SW3 was already the DP on interface Fa0/13, and it continues to be the DP because no other switches connect to that port.

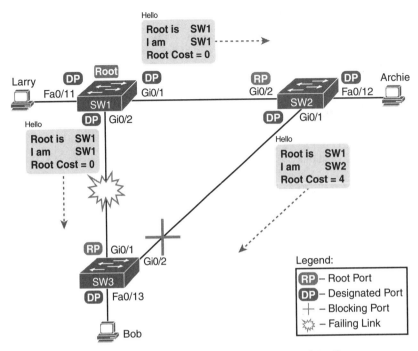

Figure 8-8 *Initial STP State Before the SW1–SW3 Link Fails*

Changing Interface States with STP

STP uses the idea of roles and states. Roles, such as root port and designated port, relate to how STP analyzes the LAN topology. States, such as forwarding and blocking, tell a switch whether to send or receive frames. When STP converges, a switch chooses new port roles, and the port roles determine the state (forwarding or blocking).

Switches can simply move immediately from forwarding to blocking state, but they must take extra time to transition from blocking state to forwarding state. For instance, when a switch formerly used port G0/1 as its RP (a role), that port was in a forwarding state. After convergence, G0/1 might be neither an RP nor a DP; the switch can immediately move that port to a blocking state.

When a port that was formerly blocked needs to transition to forwarding, the switch first puts the port through two intermediate interface states. These temporary states help prevent temporary loops:

- **Listening:** Like in the blocking state, the interface does not forward frames. The switch removes old, stale (unused) MAC table entries for which no frames are received from each MAC address during this period. These stale MAC table entries could be the cause of the temporary loops.

- **Learning:** Interfaces in this state still do not forward frames, but the switch begins to learn the MAC addresses of frames received on the interface.

STP moves an interface from blocking to listening, then to learning, and then to forwarding state. STP leaves the interface in each interim state for a time equal to the forward delay timer, which defaults to 15 seconds. As a result, a convergence event that causes an interface to change from blocking to forwarding requires 30 seconds to transition from blocking to forwarding. In addition, a switch might have to wait MaxAge seconds before even choosing to move an interface from blocking to forwarding state.

For example, follow what happens with the initial STP topology shown in Figures 8-3 through 8-6, with the SW1-to-SW3 link failing, as shown in Figure 8-8. If SW1 simply quit sending hello messages to SW3, but the link between the two did not fail, SW3 would wait MaxAge seconds before reacting (20 seconds by default). SW3 would actually quickly choose its ports' STP roles, but then wait 15 seconds each in the listening and learning states on interface Gi0/2, resulting in a 50-second convergence delay.

Table 8-8 summarizes spanning tree's various interface states for easier review.

Table 8-8   IEEE 802.1D Spanning-Tree States

State	Forwards Data Frames?	Learns MACs Based on Received Frames?	Transitory or Stable State?
Blocking	No	No	Stable
Listening	No	No	Transitory
Learning	No	Yes	Transitory
Forwarding	Yes	Yes	Stable
Disabled	No	No	Stable

Optional STP Features

The first major section of this chapter defines STP as standardized in the IEEE standard 802.1D. STP, as described in that first section, has been around for about 30 years. Cisco switches today still support and use STP. And other than changes to the default cost values, the description of STP in this chapter so far works like the original STP as created all those years ago.

Even with such an amazingly long life, STP has gone through several changes over these decades—some small, some large. For instance, Cisco added proprietary features to make improvements to STP. In some cases, the IEEE added these same improvements, or something like them, to later IEEE standards, whether as a revision of the 802.1D standard or as an additional standard. And STP has gone through one major revision that improves convergence, called the Rapid Spanning Tree Protocol (RSTP), as originally defined in IEEE 802.1w.

This final of three major sections of this chapter briefly discusses the basics of several of these optional features that go beyond the base 802.1D STP concepts, including Port-Channel, PortFast, and BPDU Guard.

NOTE   Even though STP has enjoyed a long life, many data center LANs have moved past STP to alternative protocols and technologies. The DCICN exam includes the details of STP, whereas the DCICT exam covers a wide variety of alternatives in the data center. These include Fabric Extension, Fabric Path, and virtual Port Channels (vPCs), to name a few.

8

Port-Channel

One of the best ways to lower STP's convergence time is to avoid convergence altogether. Port-Channel provides a way to prevent STP convergence from being needed when only a single port or cable failure occurs.

Port-Channel combines multiple parallel segments of equal speed between the same pair of switches, bundled into a Port-Channel. The switches treat the Port-Channel as a single interface with regard to STP. As a result, if one of the links fails, but at least one of the links is up, STP convergence does not have to occur. For example, Figure 8-9 shows the familiar three-switch network, but now with two Gigabit Ethernet connections between each pair of switches.

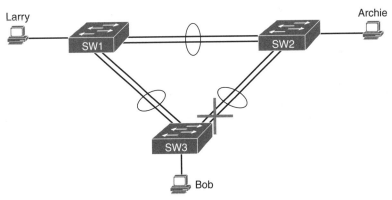

Figure 8-9   *Two-Segment Port-Channels Between Switches*

With each pair of Ethernet links configured as a Port-Channel, STP treats each Port-Channel as a single link. In other words, both links to the same switch must fail for a switch to need to cause STP convergence. Without Port-Channel, if you have multiple parallel links between two switches, STP blocks all the links except one. With Port-Channel, all the parallel links can be up and working at the same time, while reducing the number of times STP must converge, which in turn makes the network more available.

When a switch makes a forwarding decision to send a frame out a Port-Channel, the switch then has to take an extra step in logic: Out which physical interface does it send the frame? The switches have load-balancing logic that let them pick an interface for each frame, with a goal of spreading the traffic load across all active links in the channel. As a result, a LAN design that uses Port-Channel makes much better use of the available bandwidth between switches, while also reducing the number of times that STP must converge.

PortFast

PortFast allows a switch to immediately transition from blocking to forwarding state, bypassing the listening and learning states. However, the only ports on which you can safely enable PortFast are the ones to which you know no bridges, switches, or other STP-speaking devices are connected. Otherwise, using PortFast risks creating loops, the very thing that the listening and learning states are intended to avoid.

PortFast is most appropriate for connections to end-user devices. If you turn on PortFast on ports connected to end-user devices, when an end-user PC boots, the switch port can move to an STP forwarding state and forward traffic as soon as the PC NIC is active. Without PortFast, each port must wait while the switch confirms that the port is a DP, and then wait while the interface sits in the temporary listening and learning states before settling into the forwarding state.

BPDU Guard

STP opens up the LAN to several different types of possible security exposures. For example:

- An attacker could connect a switch to one of these ports, one with a low STP priority value, and become the root switch. The new STP topology could have worse performance than the desired topology.

- The attacker could plug into multiple ports, into multiple switches, become root, and actually forward much of the traffic in the LAN. Without the networking staff realizing it, the attacker could use a LAN analyzer to copy large numbers of data frames sent through the LAN.

- Users could innocently harm the LAN when they buy and connect an inexpensive consumer LAN switch (one that does not use STP). Such a switch, without any STP function, would not choose to block any ports and would likely cause a loop.

The Cisco BPDU Guard feature helps defeat these kinds of problems by disabling a port if any BPDUs are received on the port. So, this feature is particularly useful on ports that should be used only as an access port and never connected to another switch.

In addition, the BPDU Guard feature helps prevent problems with PortFast. PortFast should be enabled only on access ports that connect to user devices, not to other LAN switches. Using BPDU Guard on these same ports makes sense because if another switch connects to such a port, the local switch can disable the port before a loop is created.

Rapid STP (IEEE 802.1w)

As mentioned earlier in this chapter, the IEEE defines STP in the 802.1D IEEE standard. The IEEE has improved the 802.1D protocol with the definition of Rapid Spanning Tree Protocol (RSTP), as defined in standard 802.1w.

RSTP (802.1w) works just like STP (802.1D) in several ways:

- It elects the root switch using the same parameters and tiebreakers.
- It elects the root port on nonroot switches with the same rules.
- It elects designated ports on each LAN segment with the same rules.
- It places each port in either forwarding or blocking state, although RSTP calls the blocking state the discarding state.

RSTP can be deployed alongside traditional 802.1D STP switches, with RSTP features working in switches that support it, and traditional 802.1D STP features working in the switches that support only STP.

With all these similarities, you might be wondering why the IEEE bothered to create RSTP in the first place. The overriding reason is convergence. STP takes a relatively long time to converge (50 seconds with the default settings when all the wait times must be followed). RSTP improves network convergence when topology changes occur, usually converging within a few seconds, or in poor conditions, in about 10 seconds.

IEEE 802.1w RSTP changes and adds to IEEE 802.1D STP in ways that avoid waiting on STP timers, resulting in quick transitions from forwarding to blocking state, and vice versa. Specifically, RSTP, compared to STP, defines more cases in which the switch can avoid waiting for a timer to expire. For example:

■ It adds a new mechanism to replace the root port without any waiting to reach a forwarding state (in some conditions).

■ It adds a new mechanism to replace a designated port, without any waiting to reach a forwarding state (in some conditions).

RSTP also lowers the waiting times for cases in which it must wait.

For instance, when a link remains up, but hello BPDUs simply stop arriving regularly on a port, STP requires a switch to wait for MaxAge seconds. STP defines the MaxAge timers based on 10 times the hello timer, or 20 seconds, by default. RSTP shortens this timer, defining MaxAge as three times the hello timer.

The best way to get a sense for these mechanisms is to see how the RSTP alternate port and the backup port both work. RSTP uses the term *alternate port* to refer to a switch's other ports that could be used as the root port if the root port ever fails. The *backup port* concept provides a backup port on the local switch for a designated port, but only applies to some topologies that frankly do not happen often with a modern data center design. However, both are instructive about how RSTP works. Table 8-9 lists these RSTP port roles.

Table 8-9 Port Roles in 802.1w RSTP

Function	Port Role
Nonroot switch's best path to the root	Root port
Replaces the root port when the root port fails	Alternate port
Switch port designated to forward onto a collision domain	Designated port
Replaces a designated port when a designated port fails	Backup port
Port that is administratively disabled	Disabled port

RSTP and the Alternate (Root) Port

With STP, each nonroot switch places one port in the STP root port (RP) role. RSTP follows that same convention, with the same exact rules for choosing the RP. RSTP then takes another step, naming other possible RPs, identifying them as *alternate ports*.

To be an alternate port, that switch port must also be hearing a hello BPDU that declares the same switch to be the root switch. For instance, in Figure 8-10, SW1 is the root. SW3 will receive hello BPDUs on two ports: G0/1 and G0/2. Both hellos list SW1's BID as the root switch, so whichever port is not the root port meets the criteria to be an alternate port. SW3 picks G0/1 as its root port in this case, and then makes G0/2 an alternate port.

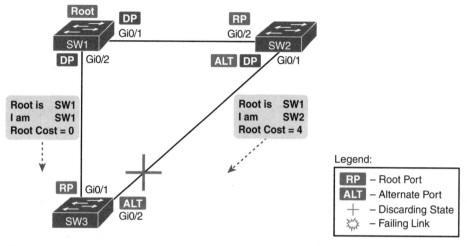

Figure 8-10   *Example of SW3 Making G0/2 Become an Alternate Port*

An alternate port basically works like the second-best option for the root port. The alternate port can take over for the former root port, often very rapidly, without requiring a wait in other interim RSTP states. For instance, when the root port fails, or when hellos stop arriving on the original root port, the switch moves the original root port to a disabled role, and transitions to a discarding state (the equivalent of STP's blocking state). Without waiting on any timers, the best alternate port then becomes the new root port. That new root port also does not need to spend time in other states, such as the learning state, instead moving immediately to the forwarding state.

Figure 8-11 shows an example of RSTP convergence in which the link between SW1 and SW3 fails. The figure begins with Step 1 being the event that causes the link to fail.

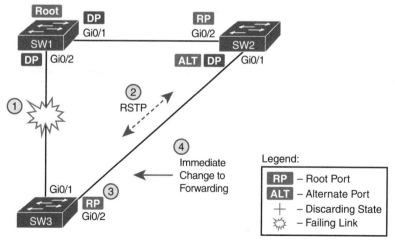

Figure 8-11   *Convergence Events with SW3 G0/1 Failure*

The following are the steps shown in the figure:

Step 1.   The link between SW1 and SW3 fails.

Step 2.   SW3 and SW2 exchange RSTP messages to confirm that SW3 will now transition its former alternate port to be the root port. This action causes SW2 to flush the required MAC table entries.

Step 3.   SW3 transitions G0/1 to the disabled role and G0/2 to the root port role.

Step 4.   SW3 transitions G0/2 to a forwarding state immediately, without using the learning state, because this is one case in which RSTP knows the transition will not create a loop.

Once SW3 realizes its G0/1 interface has failed, the process shown in the figure takes very little time. None of the processes rely on timers, so as soon as the work can be done, the convergence completes. (This particular convergence example takes about one second in a lab.)

RSTP States and Processes

The depth of the example does not point out all the details of RSTP, of course; however, the example does show enough details to discuss RSTP states and internal processes.

Both STP and RSTP use *port states*, but with some differences. First, RSTP keeps both the learning and forwarding states, as compared with STP, for the same purposes. However, RSTP does not even define a listening state, finding it unnecessary. Also, RSTP renames the blocking state to the discarding state and redefines its use slightly.

RSTP uses the discarding state for what 802.1D defines as two states: disabled state and blocking state. Blocking should be somewhat obvious by now: The interface can work physically, but STP/RSTP chooses to not forward traffic to avoid loops. STP's disabled state simply means that the interface is administratively disabled. RSTP simply combines those into a single discarding state.

Table 8-10 shows the list of STP and RSTP states for comparison purposes.

Table 8-10   Port States Compared: 802.1D STP and 802.1w RSTP

Function	802.1D State	802.1w State
Port is administratively disabled.	Disabled	Discarding
Stable state that ignores incoming data frames and is not used to forward data frames.	Blocking	Discarding
Interim state without MAC learning and without forwarding.	Listening	Not used
Interim state with MAC learning and without forwarding.	Learning	Learning
Stable state that allows MAC learning and forwarding of data frames.	Forwarding	Forwarding

RSTP also changes its algorithm processes and message content (compared to STP) to speed convergence. STP waits for a time (forward delay) in both listening and learning states. The reason for this delay in STP is that, at the same time, the switches have all been told to time out their MAC table entries. When the topology changes, the existing MAC table entries may actually cause a loop. With STP, the switches all tell each other (with BPDU messages) that the topology has changed, and to time out any MAC table entries using the forward delay timer. This removes the entries, which is good, but it causes the need to wait in both the listening and learning states for forward delay time (default 15 seconds each).

RSTP, to converge more quickly, avoids relying on timers. RSTP switches tell each other (using messages) that the topology has changed. Those messages also direct neighboring switches to flush the contents of their MAC tables in a way that removes all the potentially loop-causing entries, without a wait. As a result, RSTP creates more scenarios in which a formerly discarding port can immediately transition to a forwarding state, without waiting, and without using the learning state, as shown in the example surrounding Figure 8-11.

RSTP Backup (Designated) Ports

To complete the discussion, next consider the idea of a backup for a designated port. This concept, called a *backup port*, can be a bit confusing at first, because it only happens in designs that are a little unlikely today. The reason? The design must use hubs, which then allows the possibility that one switch connects more than one port to the same collision domain.

Figure 8-12 shows an example. SW3 and SW4 both connect to the same hub. SW4's port E1/1 happens to win the election as the designated port (DP). The other port on SW4 that connects to the same collision domain, E1/2, acts as a backup port.

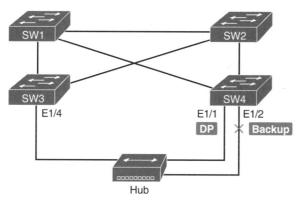

Figure 8-12 *RSTP Backup Port Example*

With a backup port, if the current designated port fails, SW4 can start using the backup port with rapid convergence. For instance, if SW4's E1/1 interface fails, SW4 could transition E1/2 to the DP role, without any delay in moving from the discarding state to the forwarding state.

Exam Preparation Tasks

Review All the Key Topics

Review the most important topics from this chapter, noted with the Key Topic icon in the outer margin of the page. Table 8-11 lists a reference for these key topics and the page numbers on which each is found.

Table 8-11   Key Topics for Chapter 8

Key Topic Element	Description	Page Number
Table 8-2	Lists the three main problems that occur when not using STP in a LAN with redundant links	246
Table 8-3	Lists the reasons why a switch chooses to place an interface into the forwarding or blocking state	249
Table 8-4	Lists the most important fields in hello BPDU messages	249
List	Logic for the root switch election	252
Figure 8-6	Shows how switches calculate their root cost	253
List	Logic for choosing a nonroot switch's root port	254
Table 8-6	Lists the original and current default STP port costs for various interface speeds	256
Step list	A summary description of steady-state STP operations	256
Table 8-7	STP timers	257
List	Definitions of what occurs in the listening and learning states	258
Table 8-8	Summary of 802.1D states	259
Table 8-9	Port Roles in 802.1w RSTP	262
Table 8-10	Comparison of port states for 802.1D STP and 802.1w RSTP	264

Complete the Tables and Lists from Memory

Print a copy of Appendix C, "Memory Tables," or at least the section for this chapter, and complete the tables and lists from memory. Appendix D, "Memory Tables Answer Key," includes completed tables and lists to check your work.

Definitions of Key Terms

After your first reading of the chapter, try to define these key terms, but do not be concerned about getting them all correct at that time. Chapter 24, "Final Review," directs you in how to use these terms for late-stage preparation for the exam.

blocking state, BPDU Guard, bridge ID, bridge protocol data unit (BPDU), designated port, Port-Channel, forward delay, forwarding state, hello BPDU, IEEE 802.1D, learning state, listening state, MaxAge, PortFast, root port, root switch, root cost, Spanning Tree Protocol (STP), Rapid STP (RSTP), IEEE 802.1w, alternate port, backup port, discarding state

8

This chapter covers the following exam topics:

2.3. Describe switching concepts and perform basic configuration

2.3.b. VLAN

2.3.a. STP

CHAPTER 9

Cisco Nexus Spanning Tree Protocol Implementation

Cisco Nexus switches enable Spanning Tree Protocol (STP) by default on all interfaces in every VLAN. However, network engineers who work with medium-size to large-size data centers usually want to configure at least some STP settings, with the goal of influencing the choices made by STP. For instance, when all switches and links work, the engineer knows which switch is the root and which ports block. The configuration can also be set so that when links or switches fail, the engineer can predict the STP topology in those cases as well.

This chapter discusses the configuration options for STP. The first major section details how to change different settings, per VLAN, with the **show** commands to reveal the current STP status affected by each configuration command. The second major section of this chapter looks at how to improve STP operations, which includes a deeper examination of the STP rules discussed in Chapter 8, "Spanning Tree Protocol Concepts," plus more discussion of various switch **show** commands.

"Do I Know This Already?" Quiz

Use the "Do I Know This Already?" quiz to help decide whether you might want to skim this chapter, or a major section, moving more quickly to the "Exam Preparation Tasks" section near the end of the chapter. Table 9-1 lists the major headings in this chapter and their corresponding "Do I Know This Already?" quiz questions. For thorough explanations, see Appendix A, "Answers to the 'Do I Know This Already?' Quizzes."

Table 9-1 "Do I Know This Already?" Foundation Topics Section-to-Question Mapping

Foundation Topics Section	Questions
STP Configuration and Verification	1–3
Improving STP Operations	4–6

1. On a Nexus switch, which of the following commands change the value of the bridge ID? (Choose two answers.)
   a. spanning-tree bridge-id *value*
   b. spanning-tree vlan *vlan-number* root {primary | secondary}
   c. spanning-tree vlan *vlan-number* priority *value*
   d. set spanning-tree priority *value*

2. Examine the following extract from the **show spanning-tree** command on a Cisco Nexus switch:

```
Spanning tree enabled protocol rstp
    Root ID        Priority        8193
          Address          c84c.75fa.601e
          This bridge is the root
          Hello Time    2    sec    Max Age 20 sec    Forward Delay 15 sec

    Bridge ID    Priority        8193        (priority 8192 sys-id-ext 1)
          Address          c84c.75fa.601e
          Hello Time    2    sec    Max Age 20 sec    Forward Delay 15 sec


Interface    Role Sts Cost      Prio.Nbr Type
----------   ---- --- --------- -------- --------------------------------
Po15         Desg FWD 1                  128.4110 (vPC) P2p
Po16         Desg FWD 1                  128.4111 (vPC) P2p
```

Which of the following answers is true about the switch on which this command output was gathered?

a. The information is about the STP instance for VLAN 1.

b. The information is about the STP instance for VLAN 3.

c. The command output confirms that this switch cannot possibly be the root switch.

d. The command output confirms that this switch is currently the root switch.

3. A switch's Eth1/1 interface, a trunk that supports VLANs 1–10, has a speed of 10 Gbps. The switch currently has all default settings for STP. Which of the following actions result in the switch using an STP cost of 2 for that interface in VLAN 3? (Choose two answers.)

a. spanning-tree cost 2

b. spanning-tree port-cost 19

c. spanning-tree vlan 3 port-cost 19

d. Adding no configuration

4. An engineer configures a switch to put interfaces Eth1/1 and Eth1/2 into the same PortChannel. Which of the following terms is used in the configuration commands?

```
interface port-channel1
  switchport mode trunk
  mtu 9216
  vpc 1
```

a. Port-Channel

b. Virtual PortChannel

c. Ethernet-Channel

d. Channel-group

5. Switch SW3 is receiving only two hello BPDUs, both from the same root switch, received on the two interfaces listed as follows:

```
SW3# show interfaces status
Port          Name     Status        Vlan     Duplex     Speed      Type
Eth1/13                connected     1        full       10G        10Gbase-SR
Eth1/1                 connected     1        full       10G        10Gbase-SR
```

SW3 has no STP-related configuration commands. The hello received on Eth1/13 lists root cost 10, and the hello received on Eth1/1 lists root cost 20. Which of the following is true about STP on SW3?

a. SW3 will choose Eth1/13 as its root port.

b. SW3 will choose Eth1/1 as its root port.

c. SW3's Eth1/13 will become a designated port.

d. SW3's Eth1/1 will become a designated port.

6. Which of the following commands list a nonroot switch's root cost? (Choose two answers.)

a. show spanning-tree root

b. show spanning-tree root cost

c. show spanning-tree bridge

d. show spanning-tree

9

Foundation Topics

STP Configuration and Verification

By default, all Cisco Nexus switches are enabled for Rapid Per-VLAN Spanning Tree (Rapid-PVST/802.1w), which is backward compatible with Per-VLAN Spanning Tree (PVST/802.1D) for interoperability and migration purposes. You can buy some Cisco switches and connect them with Ethernet cables in a redundant topology, and STP will ensure that frames do not loop. And you never even have to think about changing any settings.

This chapter focuses on only Rapid-PVST (802.1w). As mentioned earlier, Cisco Nexus switches default to using Rapid-PVST, but to set a switch to use this mode, use the **spanning-tree mode rapid-pvst** global command. Alternatively, Cisco Nexus switches allow Multiple Spanning Tree (MST) with the **spanning-tree mode mst** command. We do not cover MST because it is a more advanced concept and out of scope for DCICN.

Although Rapid-PVST works without any configuration, all data centers regardless of size benefit from some Rapid-PVST configuration. With all defaults set, the switches choose the root based on the lowest burned-in MAC address on the switches because they all default to use the same STP priority. As a better option, configure the switches so that the root is predictable.

For instance, Figure 9-1 shows a typical data center design model, with two distribution/aggregation layer switches (D1 and D2). The design may have dozens of access layer switches that connect to servers; the figure shows just three access switches (A1, A2, and A3). For a variety of reasons, most network engineers make the distribution layer switches be the root. For instance, the configuration could make D1 be the root by having a lower priority, with D2 configured with the next lower priority, so it becomes root if D1 fails.

This first section of the chapter examines a variety of topics that somehow relate to STP configuration. It begins with a look at STP configuration options, as a way to link the concepts of Chapter 8 to the configuration choices in this chapter. Following that, this section introduces some **show** commands for the purpose of verifying the default STP settings before changing any configuration. At that point, this section shows examples of how to configure core STP features and some of the optional STP features.

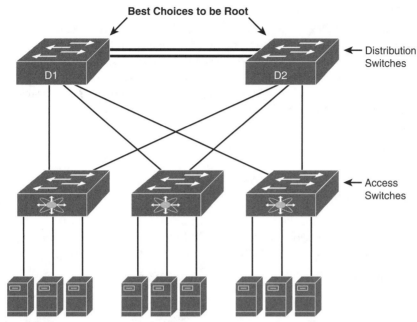

Figure 9-1   *Typical Configuration Choice: Making the Distribution/Aggregation Switch Be Root*

Connecting STP Concepts to STP Configuration Options

If you think back to the details of STP operation in Chapter 8, you'll recall that STP uses two types of numbers for most of its decisions: the bridge ID (BID) and STP port costs. Focusing on those two types of numbers, consider this summary of what STP does behind the scenes:

■ It uses the BID to elect the root switch, electing the switch with the numerically lowest BID.

■ It uses the total STP cost in each path to the root, when each nonroot switch chooses its own root port (RP).

■ It uses each switch's root cost, which is in turn based on STP port costs, when switches decide which switch port becomes the designated port (DP) on each LAN segment.

Unsurprisingly, Cisco switches let you configure part of a switch's BID and the STP port cost, which in turn influences the choices each switch makes with STP.

9

Per-VLAN Configuration Settings

Beyond supporting the configuration of the BID and STP port costs, Cisco switches support configuring both settings per VLAN. Cisco Nexus switches implement Rapid-PVST (often abbreviated as simply RPVST today), and RPVST creates a different instance of Spanning Tree for each VLAN. The main difference between PVST+ and Rapid PVST is the convergence time when using RPVST has been greatly reduced. So, before looking at the tunable STP parameters, you need to have a basic understanding of RPVST+, because the configuration settings can differ for each instance of STP.

RPVST+ gives engineers a load-balancing tool with STP. By changing some STP configuration parameters differently for the various VLANs, the engineer could cause switches to pick different RPs and DPs in different VLANs. As a result, some traffic in some VLANs can be forwarded over one trunk, and traffic for other VLANs can be forwarded over a different trunk.

Figure 9-2 shows the basic idea, with SW3 forwarding odd-numbered VLAN traffic over the left trunk (Eth1/1) and even-numbered VLANs over the right trunk (Eth1/2).

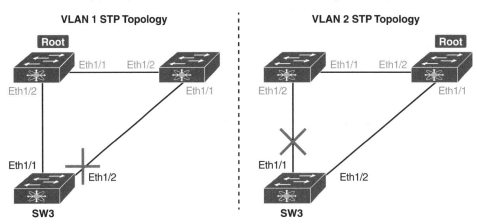

Figure 9-2 *Load Balancing with PVST+*

The next few pages look specifically at how to change the BID and STP port cost settings, per VLAN, when using the default RPVST+ mode.

The Bridge ID and System ID Extension

Originally, combining the switch's 2-byte priority and its 6-byte MAC address formed a switch's BID. Later, the IEEE changed the rules, splitting the original Priority field into two separate fields, as shown in Figure 9-3: a 4-bit Priority field and a 9-bit subfield called the *System ID Extension* (which represents the VLAN ID).

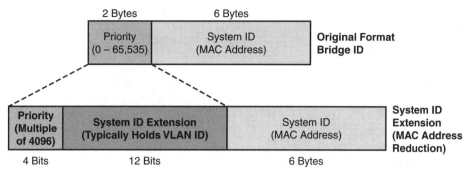

Figure 9-3 *STP System ID Extension*

Cisco switches let you configure the BID, but only the priority part. The switch fills in its universal (burned-in) MAC address as the system ID. It also plugs in the VLAN ID of a VLAN in the 12-bit System ID Extension field. The only part configurable by the network engineer is the 4-bit Priority field.

Configuring the number to put in the Priority field, however, is one of the strangest things to configure on a Cisco router or switch. As shown at the top of Figure 9-3, the Priority field was originally a 16-bit number, which represented a decimal number from 0 to 65,535. Because of that history, the current configuration command (**spanning-tree vlan** *vlan-id* **priority** *x*) requires a decimal number between 0 and 65,535. And not just any number in that range, either: It must be a multiple of 4096: 0, 4096, 8192, 12288, and so on, up through 61,440.

The switch still sets the first 4 bits of the BID based on the configured value. As it turns out, of the 16 allowed multiples of 4096, from 0 through 61,440, each has a different binary value in its first 4 bits: 0000, 0001, 0010, and so on, up through 1111. The switch sets the true 4-bit priority based on the first 4 bits of the configured value.

Although the history and configuration might make the BID priority idea seem a bit convoluted, having an extra 12-bit field in the BID works well in practice because it can be used to identify the VLAN ID. VLAN IDs range from 1 to 4094, requiring 12 bits. Cisco switches place the VLAN ID into the System ID Extension field, so each switch has a unique BID per VLAN.

For example, a switch configured with VLANs 1 through 4, with a default base priority of 32,768, has a default STP priority of 32,769 in VLAN 1; 32,770 in VLAN 2; 32,771 in VLAN 3, and so on. So, you can view the 16-bit priority as a base priority (as configured on the **spanning-tree vlan** *vlan-id* **priority** *x* command) plus the VLAN ID.

Per-VLAN Port Costs

Each switch interface defaults its per-VLAN STP cost based on the IEEE recommendations listed in Table 2-6 in Chapter 2, "The TCP/IP and OSI Networking Models." On interfaces that support multiple speeds, Cisco switches base the cost on the current actual speed. So, if an interface negotiates to use a lower speed, the default STP cost reflects that lower speed. If the interface negotiates to use a different speed, the switch dynamically changes the STP port cost as well.

Alternatively, you can configure a switch's STP port cost with the **spanning-tree** [**vlan** *vlan-id*] **cost** *cost* interface subcommand. You see this command most often on trunks because setting the cost on trunks has an impact on the switch's root cost, whereas setting STP costs on access ports does not.

The command itself can include the VLAN ID, or not. The command only needs a **vlan** parameter on trunk ports to set the cost per VLAN. On a trunk, if the command omits the **vlan** parameter, it sets the STP cost for all VLANs whose cost is not set by a **spanning-tree vlan** *x* **cost** command.

STP Configuration Option Summary

Table 9-2 summarizes the default settings for both the BID and the port costs, and it lists the optional configuration commands covered in this chapter.

Table 9-2   STP Defaults and Configuration Options

Setting	Default	Command(s) to Change Default
BID priority	Base: 32,768	`spanning-tree vlan `*`vlan-id`*` root {primary | secondary}`
		`spanning-tree vlan `*`vlan-id`*` priority `*`priority`*
Interface cost	100 for 10 Mbps	`spanning-tree vlan `*`vlan-id`*` cost `*`cost`*
	19 for 100 Mbps	
	4 for 1 Gbps	
	2 for 10 Gbps	
PortFast	Not enabled	`spanning-tree portfast`
BPDU Guard	Not enabled	`spanning-tree bpduguard enable`

Next, the configuration section shows how to examine the operation of STP in a simple network, along with how to change these optional settings.

Verifying STP Operation

Before taking a look at how to change the configuration, let's first consider a few STP verification commands. Looking at these commands first will help reinforce the default STP settings. In particular, the examples in this section use the network shown in Figure 9-4.

Example 9-1 begins the discussion with a useful command for STP: the **show spanning-tree vlan 10** command. This command identifies the root switch and lists settings on the local switch. Example 9-1 lists the output of this command on both SW1 and SW2, as explained following the example.

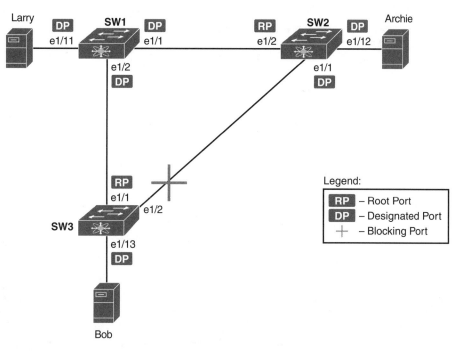

Figure 9-4 *Sample Topology for STP Configuration and Verification Examples*

Example 9-1 *STP Status with Default STP Parameters on SW1 and SW2*

```
SW1# show spanning-tree vlan 10


VLAN0010
    Spanning tree enabled protocol rstp
  Root ID      Priority       8193
                    Address         c84c.75fa.6014
                    This bridge is the root
                    Hello Time    2 sec  Max Age 20 sec   Forward Delay 15 sec


   Bridge ID    Priority       8193     (priority 8192 sys-id-ext 1)
                    Address         c84c.75fa.6014
                    Hello Time    2 sec  Max Age 20 sec   Forward Delay 15 sec


Interface                    Role Sts Cost        Prio.Nbr Type
------------------- ---- --- --------- -------- --------------------------------
Eth1/11                      Desg FWD 4              128.11      P2p Edge
Eth1/1                       Desg FWD 2              128.25      P2p
Eth1/2                       Desg FWD 2              128.26      P2p
SW2# show spanning-tree vlan 10
```

```
VLAN0010
    Spanning tree enabled protocol rstp
    Root ID          Priority         32778
                     Address          c84c.75fa.6014
                     Cost              2
                     Port              26 (Ethernet1/2)
                     Hello Time    2 sec  Max Age 20 sec   Forward Delay 15 sec


    Bridge ID        Priority         32778   (priority 32768 sys-id-ext 10)
                     Address          c84c.75fa.6014
                     Hello Time    2 sec  Max Age 20 sec   Forward Delay 15 sec



Interface                    Role Sts Cost        Prio.Nbr Type
------------------- ---- --- --------- -------- --------------------------------
Eth1/12                      Desg FWD 4               128.12    P2p
Eth1/1                       Desg FWD 2               128.25    P2p
Eth1/2                       Root FWD 2               128.26    P2p
```

Example 9-1 begins with the output of the **show spanning-tree vlan 10** command on SW1. This command first lists three major groups of messages: one group of messages about the root switch, followed by another group about the local switch, and ending with interface role and status information. In this case, SW1 lists its own BID as the root, with even a specific statement that "This bridge is the root," confirming that SW1 is now the root of the VLAN 10 STP topology.

Next, compare the highlighted lines of the same command on SW2 in the lower half of the example. SW2 lists SW1's BID details as the root; in other words, SW2 agrees that SW1 has won the root election. SW2 does not list the phrase "This bridge is the root." SW1 then lists its own (different) BID details in the lines after the details about the root's BID.

The output also confirms a few default values. First, each switch lists the priority part of the BID as a separate number: 32778. This value comes from the default priority of 32768, plus VLAN 10, for a total of 32778. The output also shows the interface cost of Ten Gigabit Ethernet interfaces, defaulting to 2.

Finally, the bottom of the output from the **show spanning-tree** command lists each interface in the VLAN, including trunks, with the STP port role and port state listed. For instance, on switch SW1, the output lists three interfaces, with a role of Desg for designated port (DP) and a state of FWD for forwarding. SW2 lists three interfaces, two DPs, and one root port, so all three are in an FWD or forwarding state.

Example 9-1 shows a lot of good STP information, but two other commands, shown in Example 9-2, work better for listing BID information in a shorter form. The first, **show spanning-tree root**, lists the root's BID for each VLAN. This command also lists other details, such as the local switch's root cost and root port. The other command, **show spanning-tree vlan 10 bridge**, breaks out the BID into its component parts. In this example, it shows SW2's priority as the default of 32768, the VLAN ID of 10, and the MAC address.

Example 9-2 *Listing Root Switch and Local Switch BIDs on Switch SW2*

```
SW2# show spanning-tree root

                                          Root       Hello Max Fwd
Vlan            Root ID              Cost  Time  Age  Dly  Root Port
-------------   ---------------- --------- ----- --- --- -------------
VLAN0001        32769 c84c.75fa.6014    23     2   20  15   Eth1/1
VLAN0010        32778 c84c.75fa.6014     4     2   20  15   Eth1/2
VLAN0020        32788 c84c.75fa.6014     4     2   20  15   Eth1/2
VLAN0030        32798 c84c.75fa.6014     4     2   20  15   Eth1/2
VLAN0040        32808 c84c.75fa.6014     4     2   20  15   Eth1/2

SW2# show spanning-tree vlan 10 bridge


Hello    Max    Fwd
Vlan           Bridge ID                     Time  Age  Dly  Protocol
-----------    -----------------------------  ----- --- --- --------
VLAN0010       32778 (32768,     10) c84c.75fa.6014  2    20   15   rstp
```

Note that both the commands in Example 9-2 have a VLAN option: **show spanning-tree**
[**vlan** *x*] **root** and **show spanning-tree** [**vlan** *x*] **bridge**, respectively. Without the VLAN
listed, each command lists one line per VLAN; with the VLAN, the output lists the same
information, but just for that one VLAN.

Improving STP Operation

In the previous section we discussed how to configure STP on Cisco Nexus switches. To
round out this chapter, we will now dig in to how to improve Spanning Tree for optimal use
in data center networks.

Configuring STP Port Costs

Changing the STP port costs requires a simple interface subcommand: **spanning-tree** [**vlan**
x] **cost** *x*. To show how it works, consider Example 9-3, where we change the spanning-tree
port cost on SW3 from Figure 9-5. We will then examine what changes in Example 9-4.

Back in Figure 9-4, with default settings, SW1 became root, and SW3 blocked on its Eth1/2
interface. A brief scan of the figure, based on the default STP cost of 2 for Ten Gigabit
interfaces, shows that SW3 should have found a cost-2 path and a cost-4 path to reach the
root, as shown in Figure 9-5.

To show the effects of changing the port cost, Example 9-3 shows a change to SW3's configuration, setting its Eth1/1 port cost higher so that the better path to the root goes out
SW3's Eth1/2 port instead.

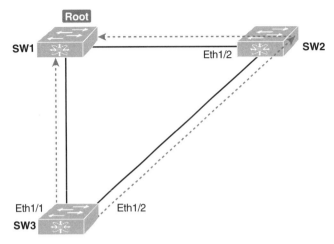

Figure 9-5 *Analysis of SW3's Current Root Cost of 4 with Defaults*

Example 9-3 *Manipulating STP Port Cost*

```
SW3# configure terminal
Enter configuration commands, one per line.    End with CNTL/Z.
SW3(config)# interface Ethernet1/1
SW3(config-if)# spanning-tree vlan 10 cost 30
SW3(config-if)# ^Z
```

This example shows the configuration to change SW3's port cost, in VLAN 10, to 30, with the **spanning-tree vlan 10 cost 30** interface subcommand. Based on the figure, the root cost through SW3's Eth1/1 will now be 30 instead of 4. As a result, SW3's best cost to reach the root is cost 4, with SW3's Eth1/2 as its root port.

Using **show** commands later can confirm the same choice by SW3, to now use its Eth1/2 port as its RP. Example 9-4 shows the new STP port cost setting on SW3, along with the new root port and root cost, using the **show spanning-tree vlan 10** command. Note that Eth1/2 is now listed as the root port. The top of the output lists SW3's root cost as 4, matching the analysis shown in Figure 9-5.

Example 9-4 *New STP Status and Settings on SW3*

```
SW3# show spanning-tree vlan 10


VLAN0010
    Spanning tree enabled protocol ieee
    Root ID        Priority        32778
                   Address         1833.9d7b.0e80
                   Cost            4
                   Port            26 (Ethernet1/2)
                   Hello Time   2 sec  Max Age 20 sec   Forward Delay 15 sec
```

```
    Bridge ID     Priority        32778    (priority 32768 sys-id-ext 10)
                         Address          f47f.35cb.d780
                         Hello Time       2 sec  Max Age 20 sec  Forward Delay 15 sec


Interface            Role   Sts   Cost      Prio.Nbr  Type
------------------   ----   ---   --------- --------- ----
Eth1/23             Desg   FWD     4        128.23    P2p
Eth1/1              Altn   BLK    30        128.25    P2p
Eth1/2              Root   FWD     2        128.26    P2p
```

Configuring Priority to Influence the Root Election

The other big STP configuration option is to influence the root election by changing the priority of a switch. The priority can be set explicitly with the **spanning-tree vlan** *vlan-id* **priority** *value* global configuration command, which sets the base priority of the switch. (This is the command that requires a parameter of a multiple of 4096.)

However, Cisco gives us a better configuration option than configuring a specific priority value. In most designs, the network engineers pick two switches to be root: one to be root if all switches are up, and another to take over if the first switch fails. Switch IOS supports this idea with the **spanning-tree vlan** *vlan-id* **root primary** and **spanning-tree vlan** *vlan-id* **root secondary** commands.

The **spanning-tree vlan** *vlan-id* **root primary** command tells the switch to set its priority low enough to become root right now. The switch looks at the current root in that VLAN, and at the root's priority. Then the local switch chooses a priority value that causes the local switch to take over as root.

Remembering that Cisco switches use a default base priority of 32,768, this command chooses the base priority as follows:

- If the current root has a base priority higher than 24,576, *the local switch uses a base priority of 24,576.*

- If the current root's base priority is 24,576 or lower, the local switch sets its base priority to the highest multiple of 4096 that still results in the local switch becoming root.

For the switch intended to take over as the root if the first switch fails, use the **spanning-tree vlan** *vlan-id* **root secondary** command. This command is much like the **spanning-tree vlan** *vlan-id* **root primary** command, but with a priority value worse than the primary switch but better than all the other switches. This command sets the switch's base priority to 28,672 regardless of the current root's current priority value.

For example, in Figures 9-4 and 9-5, SW1 was the root switch, and as shown in various commands, all three switches defaulted to use a base priority of 32,768. Example 9-5 shows a configuration that makes SW2 the primary root, and SW1 the secondary, just to show the role move from one to the other. These commands result in SW2 having a base priority of 24,576 and SW1 having a base priority of 28,672.

9

Example 9-5   *Making SW2 Become Root Primary and SW1 Root Secondary*

```
! First, on SW2:
SW2# configure terminal
Enter configuration commands, one per line.    End with CNTL/Z.
SW2(config)# spanning-tree vlan 10 root primary
SW2(config)# ^Z
! Next, SW1 is configured to back-up SW1
SW1# configure terminal
Enter configuration commands, one per line.    End with CNTL/Z.
SW1(config)# spanning-tree vlan 10 root secondary
SW1(config)# ^Z
SW1#


! The next command shows the local switch's BID (SW1)
SW1# show spanning-tree vlan 10 bridge


Hello    Max    Fwd
Vlan             Bridge ID                        Time    Age    Dly    Protocol
---------------- -------------------------------- -----   ---    ---    --------
VLAN0010         28682 (28672, 10) 1833.9d7b.0e80   2      20     15    rstp

! The next command shows the root's BID (SW2)
SW1# show spanning-tree vlan 10 root


                                                         Root    Hello Max Fwd
Vlan             Root ID              Cost  Time   Age  Dly  Root Port
---------------- -------------------- ----  -----  ---  ---  ------------
VLAN0010         24586 1833.9d7b.1380   4     2    20    15   Eth1/1
```

The two **show** commands in the output clearly point out the resulting priority values on each switch. First, the **show spanning-tree bridge** command lists the local switch's BID information, while the **show spanning-tree root** command lists the root's BID, plus the local switch's root cost and root port (assuming it is not the root switch). So, SW1 lists its own BID, with priority 28,682 (base 28,672, with VLAN 10), via the **show spanning-tree bridge** command. Still on SW1, the output lists the root's priority as 24,586 in VLAN 10, implied as base 24,576 plus 10 for VLAN 10, with the **show spanning-tree root** command.

Note that alternatively you could have configured the priority settings specifically. SW1 could have used the **spanning-tree vlan 10 priority 28672** command, with SW2 using the **spanning-tree vlan 10 priority 24576** command. In this particular case, both options would result in the same STP operation.

Spanning-Tree Port Types

Cisco NX-OS provides three basic switch port types to ease configuration. These port types bundle in extensions or features that are commonly configured on a particular type of interface:

- **Network ports:** Network ports define connections between two bridges or switches. By default, a feature called *Bridge Assurance* is enabled on these ports.

- **Normal ports:** A switch port is a normal port in respect to Spanning Tree and has no added configuration. These ports operate in standard bridging mode.

- **Edge ports:** Because these ports are used to connect to non-bridging Layer 2 devices, such as hosts, they transition immediately into forwarding state, bypassing the listening and learning states. They enable a feature known as *PortFast* to accomplish this.

> **NOTE**   Bridge Assurance (BA) is a new feature that allows all ports to send and receive bridge protocol data units (BPDUs) on all VLANs regardless of their state. This creates a bidirectional keepalive so that if a malfunctioning bridge stops sending BPDUs, the ports on the BA-enabled switch will be placed into an inconsistent state. This helps prevent a malfunctioning bridge from creating loops. Bridge Assurance is enabled by default on all interfaces in the Spanning Tree port type of network.

Configuring PortFast and BPDU Guard

In Chapter 8, you learned about the functionality and benefits of using PortFast and BPDU Guard on a host interface. Here you learn how to configure them on Nexus switches.

You can easily configure the PortFast and BPDU Guard features on any interface, but with two different configuration options. One option works best when you only want to enable these features on a few ports, and the other works best when you want to enable these features on most every access port.

First, to enable the features on just one port at a time, use the **spanning-tree port type edge** command to enable PortFast and the **spanning-tree bpduguard enable** interface subcommands. Example 9-6 shows an example of the process, with SW3's Eth1/4 interface having both these features enabled. (Also, note the long warning message NX-OS lists when enabling PortFast; using PortFast on a port connected to other switches can indeed cause serious problems.)

Example 9-6   *Enabling PortFast and BPDU Guard on One Interface*

```
SW3# configure terminal
Enter configuration commands, one per line.    End with CNTL/Z.
SW3(config)# interface Ethernet1/4
SW3(config-if)# spanning-tree port type edge
Warning: Edge port type (portfast) should only be enabled on ports connected to a
single host. Connecting hubs, concentrators, switches, bridges, etc… to this interface
when edge port type (portfast) is enabled, can cause temporary bridging loops.
 Use with CAUTION
```

9

```
Edge Port Type (Portfast) has been configured on Ethernet1/4 but will only
 have effect when the interface is in a non-trunking mode.
SW3(config-if)# spanning-tree bpduguard ?
    disable    Disable BPDU guard for this interface
    enable     Enable BPDU guard for this interface


SW3(config-if)# spanning-tree bpduguard enable
SW3(config-if)# ^Z
SW3#
*Mar   1 07:53:47.808: %SYS-5-CONFIG_I: Configured from console by console
SW3# show running-config interface Eth1/4
Building configuration…


Current configuration : 138 bytes
!
interface Ethernet1/4
 switchport access vlan 104
 spanning-tree port type edge
 spanning-tree bpduguard enable
end


SW3# show spanning-tree interface Ethernet1/4 edge
VLAN0104                            enabled
```

The second half of the example confirms the configuration on the interface and the
PortFast status. The **show running-config** command simply confirms that the switch record-
ed the two configuration commands. The **show spanning-tree interface Ethernet1/4 edge**
command lists the PortFast status of the interface; note that the status only shows up as
enabled if PortFast is configured and the interface is up.

The alternative configuration works better when most of a switch's ports need PortFast and
BPDU Guard. By default, switches disable both features on each interface. The alternative
configuration lets you reverse the default, making the default for PortFast and BPDU Guard
to be enabled on each interface. Then you have the option to disable the features on a port-
by-port basis.

To change the defaults, use these two global commands:

- **spanning-tree port type edge default**
- **spanning-tree port type edge bpduguard default**

Then, to override the defaults, to disable the features, use these interface subcommands:

- **no spanning-tree port type edge**
- **spanning-tree bpduguard disable**

Configuring Port-Channel

As introduced back in Chapter 2 two neighboring switches can treat multiple parallel links between each other as a single logical link called a *Port-Channel*. STP operates on the Port-Channel, instead of the individual physical links, so that STP either forwards or blocks on the entire logical Port-Channel for a given VLAN. As a result, a switch in a forwarding state can then load-balance traffic over all the physical links in the Port-Channel. Without Port-Channel, only one of the parallel links between two switches would be allowed to forward traffic, with the rest of the links blocked by STP.

Port-Channel may be one of the most challenging switch features to make work. First, the configuration has several options, so you have to remember the details of which options work together. Second, the switches also require a variety of other interface settings to match among all the links in the channel, so you have to know those settings as well.

This section focuses on the correct Port-Channel configuration. The later section titled "Troubleshooting Port-Channel" looks at many of the potential problems with Port-Channel, including all those other configuration settings that a switch checks before allowing the Port-Channel to work.

Configuring a Manual Port-Channel

The simplest way to configure a Port-Channel is to add the correct **channel-group** configuration command to each physical interface, on each switch, all with the **on** keyword. The **on** keyword tells the switches to place a physical interface into a Port-Channel.

Before getting into the configuration and verification, however, we need to start using three terms as synonyms: *Port-Channel*, *PortChannel*, and *channel-group*. NX-OS uses the **channel-group** configuration command, but then to display its status, NX-OS uses the **show port-channel summary** command.

To configure a Port-Channel manually, follow these steps:

Step 1.   Add the **channel-group** *number* **mode on** interface subcommand under each physical interface that should be in the channel.

Step 2.   Use the same number for all commands on the same switch, but the channel-group number on the neighboring switch can differ.

Example 9-7 simply shows two links between switches SW1 and SW2, as illustrated in Figure 9-6. The configuration shows SW1's two interfaces placed into channel-group 1, with two **show** commands to follow.

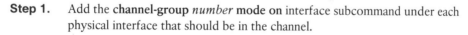
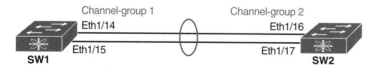

Figure 9-6   *Sample Data Center Used in the Port-Channel Example*

Example 9-7 *Configuring and Monitoring a Port-Channel*

```
SW1# configure terminal
Enter configuration commands, one per line.    End with CNTL/Z.
SW1(config)# interface Eth1/14
SW1(config-if)# channel-group 1 mode on
SW1(config)# interface Eth1/15
SW1(config-if)# channel-group 1 mode on
SW1(config-if)# ^Z


SW1# show spanning-tree vlan 3


VLAN0003
    Spanning tree enabled protocol ieee
    Root ID      Priority        28675
                 Address         0019.e859.5380
                 Cost            4
                 Port            72 (Port-channel1)
                 Hello Time   2 sec  Max Age 20 sec   Forward Delay 15 sec

     Bridge ID   Priority       28675   (priority 28672 sys-id-ext 3)
                 Address        0019.e86a.6f80
                 Hello Time   2 sec  Max Age 20 sec   Forward Delay 15 sec
                 Aging Time 300


Interface        Role Sts  Cost  Prio.Nbr  Type
---------------- ---- ---  ----- --------  --------------
Po1              Root FWD   12    128.64   P2p Peer(STP)


SW1# show port-channel summary
Flags:    D - Down          P - Up in port-channel (members)
          I - Individual    H - Hot-standby (LACP only)
          s - Suspended     r - Module-removed
          S - Switched      R - Routed
          U - Up (port-channel)
          M - Not in use. Min-links not met
-------------------------------------------------------------------------
Group    Port-      Type     Protocol               Member Ports
         Channel
1        Po1(SU)      Eth       NONE       Eth1/14(P)   Eth1/15(P)
```

Take a few moments to look at the output in the two **show** commands in the example as
well. First, the **show spanning-tree** command lists Po1, short for PortChannel1, as an interface. This interface exists because of the **channel-group** commands using the **1** parameter.
STP no longer operates on physical interfaces Eth1/14 and Eth1/15, instead operating on
the PortChannel1 interface, so only that interface is listed in the output.

Next, note the output of the **show port-channel 1 summary** command. It lists as a heading "Port-channel," with Po1 below it. It also shows both Eth1/14 and Eth1/15 in the list of ports, with a (P) beside each. Per the legend, the *P* means that the ports are bundled in the PortChannel, which is a code that means these ports have passed all the configuration checks and are valid to be included in the channel.

Configuring Dynamic Port-Channels

Cisco switches support two different protocols that allow them to negotiate whether a particular link becomes part of a Port-Channel. Basically, the configuration enables the protocol for a particular channel-group number. At that point, the switch can use the protocol to send messages to/from the neighboring switch and discover whether their configuration settings pass all checks. If a given physical link passes, the link is added to the Port-Channel and used; if not, it is placed in a down state, and not used, until the configuration inconsistency can be resolved.

For now, this section focuses on how to make it work, with the later "Troubleshooting Port-Channel" section focusing on the specific settings that can make it fail.

Cisco switches support the Cisco proprietary Port Aggregation Protocol (PAgP) and the IEEE standard Link Aggregation Control Protocol (LACP), based on IEEE standard 802.3ad. Although differences exist between the two, to the depth discussed here, they both accomplish the same task: negotiate so that only links that pass the configuration checks are actually used in a Port-Channel. Cisco NX-OS only supports LACP or manual configuration of channels, as shown before.

To configure the LACP protocol, the **channel-group** configuration commands are used on each switch, but with a keyword that means either "use this protocol and begin negotiations" (**active**) or "use this protocol and wait for the other switch to begin negotiations" (**passive**). As shown in Figure 9-7, the **active** and **passive** keywords enable LACP. With these options, at least one side has to begin the negotiations. In other words, with LACP, at least one of the two sides must use **active**.

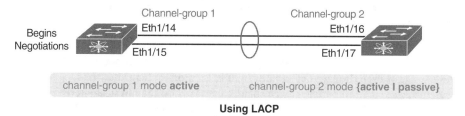

Figure 9-7 *Correct Port-Channel Configuration Combinations*

> **NOTE** Do not use the **on** parameter on one end and either **active** or **passive** on the neighboring switch. The **on** option does not use LACP, so a configuration that uses **on**, with LACP options on the other end, would prevent the Port-Channel from working.

For instance, you could replace the configuration in Example 9-7 with **channel-group 1 mode active** for both interfaces, with SW2 using **channel-group 2 mode passive.** In NX-OS, we would need to enable the feature for LACP to work. Example 9-8 shows the enabling of LACP.

Example 9-8   *Enabling Feature Set for LACP*

```
SW1(config)# feature lacp
SW1(config)# show feature | inc lacp
lacp                                  1                    enabled
```

Troubleshooting Port-Channel

Port-Channels can prove particularly challenging to troubleshoot for a couple of reasons. First, you have to be careful to match the correct configuration, and there are many more incorrect configuration combinations than there are correct combinations. Second, many interface settings must match on the physical links, both on the local switch and on the neighboring switch, before a switch will add the physical link to the channel. This last topic in the chapter works through both sets of issues.

Incorrect Options on the channel-group Command

Earlier, the section titled "Configuring Port-Channel" listed the small set of working configuration options on the **channel-group** command. Those rules can be summarized as follows, for a single Port-Channel:

- On the local switch, all the **channel-group** commands for all the physical interfaces must use the same channel-group number.
- The **channel-group** number can be different on the neighboring switches.
- If you use the **on** keyword, you must use it on the corresponding interfaces of both switches.
- If you use the **active** keyword on one switch, the switch uses LACP; the other switch must use either **active** or **passive.**

These rules summarize the correct configuration options, but the options actually leave many more incorrect choices. The following list shows some incorrect configurations that the switches allow, even though they would result in the Port-Channel not working. The list compares the configuration on one switch to another based on the physical interface configuration. Each lists the reasons why the configuration is incorrect:

- Configuring the **on** keyword on one switch, and **active** or **passive** on the other switch. The **on** keyword does not enable LACP, and the other options rely on LACP.
- Configuring the **passive** keyword on both switches. Both use LACP, but both wait on the other switch to begin negotiations.

Example 9-9 is an example that matches the last item in the list. In this case, SW1's two ports (Eth1/14 and Eth1/15) have been configured with the **passive** keyword, and SW2's matching Eth1/16 and Eth1/17 have been configured with the **passive** keyword. This example lists some telling status information about the failure, with notes following the example.

Example 9-9 *Ruling Out Switches as Root Based on Having a Root Port*

```
SW1# show port-channel summary
Flags:    D - Down          P - Up in port-channel (members)
          I - Individual    H - Hot-standby (LACP only)
          s - Suspended     r - Module-removed
          S - Switched      R - Routed
          U - Up (port-channel)
          M - Not in use. Min-links not met
---------------------------------------------------------------------
Group Port-           Type        Protocol    Member Ports
        Channel
---------------------------------------------------------------------
1       Po1(SD)        Eth         LACP        Eth1/14(I)    Eth1/15(I)

SW1# show interfaces status | include Po|14|15
Port         Name     Status       Vlan       Duplex   Speed   Type
Eth1/14               connected    301        full     10G     10Gbase-SR
Eth1/15               connected    301        full     10G     10Gbase-SR
Po1                   notconnect   unassigned auto     auto
```

Start at the top, in the legend of the **show port-channel summary** command. The *D* code letter means that the channel itself is down, with *S* meaning that the channel is a Layer 2 Port-Channel. Code *I* means that the physical interface is working independently from the Port-Channel (described as "stand-alone"). Then, the bottom of that command's output highlights Port-Channel (Po1) as a Layer 2 Port-Channel in a down state (SD), with Eth1/14 and Eth1/15 as standalone interfaces (I).

Interestingly, because the problem is a configuration mistake, the two physical interfaces still operate independently, as if the PortChannel did not exist. The last command in the example shows that while the PortChannel1 interface is down, the two physical interfaces are in a connected state.

> **NOTE**   As a suggestion for attacking Port-Channel problems on the exam, rather than memorizing all the incorrect configuration options, concentrate on the list of correct configuration options. Then look for any differences between a given question's configuration as compared to the known correct configurations and work from there.

Configuration Checks Before Adding Interfaces to Port-Channels

Even when the **channel-group** commands have all been configured correctly, other configuration settings can cause problems as well. This last topic examines those configuration settings and their impact.

First, a local switch checks each new physical interface that is configured to be part of a Port-Channel, comparing each new link to the existing links. That new physical interface's settings must be the same as the existing links; otherwise, the switch does not add the new link to the list of approved and working interfaces in the channel. That is, the physical interface remains configured as part of the Port-Channel, but it is not used as part of the channel, often being placed into some nonworking state.

Here's a list of some items the switch checks:

- Speed
- Duplex
- Operational access or trunking state (all must be access, or all must be trunks.)
- If an access port, the access VLAN
- If a trunk port, the allowed VLAN list (per the **switchport trunk allowed** command)
- If a trunk port, the native VLAN
- STP interface settings

In addition, switches check the settings on their neighboring switches. To do so, the switches either use LACP (if already in use) or Cisco Discovery Protocol (CDP, if using manual configuration). The neighbor must match on all parameters in this list except the STP settings.

As an example, SW1 and SW2 again use two links in one Port-Channel. Before configuring the Port-Channel, SW1's Eth1/15 was given a different STP port cost than Eth1/14. Example 9-10 picks up the story just after the correct **channel-group** commands have been configured, when the switch is deciding whether to use Eth1/14 or Eth1/15 in this Port-Channel.

Example 9-10 *Local Interfaces Fail in Port-Channel Because of Mismatched STP Cost*

```
*Mar    1 23:18:56.132: %PM-4-ERR_DISABLE: channel-misconfig (STP) error detected on
Po1, putting Eth1/14 in err-disable state
*Mar    1 23:18:56.132: %PM-4-ERR_DISABLE: channel-misconfig (STP) error detected on
Po1, putting Eth1/15 in err-disable state
*Mar    1 23:18:56.132: %PM-4-ERR_DISABLE: channel-misconfig (STP) error detected on
Po1, putting Po1 in err-disable state
*Mar    1 23:18:58.120: %LINK-3-UPDOWN: Interface Ethernet1/14, changed state to down
*Mar    1 23:18:58.137: %LINK-3-UPDOWN: Interface Port-channel1, changed state to down
*Mar    1 23:18:58.137: %LINK-3-UPDOWN: Interface Ethernet1/15, changed state to down


SW1# show port-channel summary
Flags:    D - Down          P - Up in port-channel (members)
          I - Individual   H - Hot-standby (LACP only)
          s - Suspended     r - Module-removed
          S - Switched      R - Routed
          U - Up (port-channel)
          M - Not in use. Min-links not met
-------------------------------------------------------------------------------
Group Port-     Type         Protocol   Member Ports
      Channel
-------------------------------------------------------------------------------
1       Po1(SD)       Eth          NONE        Eth1/14(D)       Eth1/15(D)
```

The messages at the top of the example specifically state what the switch does when thinking about whether the interface settings match. In this case, SW1 detects the different STP costs. SW1 does not use Eth1/14, does not use Eth1/15, and even places them into an err-disabled state. The switch also puts the PortChannel into an err-disabled state. As a result, the PortChannel is not operational, and the physical interfaces are also not operational.

To solve this problem, you must reconfigure the physical interfaces to use the same STP settings. In addition, you must use **shutdown** and then **no shutdown** on the PortChannel and physical interfaces, to recover from the err-disabled state. (Note that when a switch applies the **shutdown** and **no shutdown** commands to a PortChannel, it applies those same commands to the physical interfaces as well; therefore, you can just do the **shutdown/no shutdown** on the PortChannel interface.)

9

Exam Preparation Tasks

Review All the Key Topics

Review the most important topics from this chapter, noted with the Key Topic icon in the outer margin of the page. Table 9-3 lists references for these key topics and the page number on which each is found.

Table 9-3   Key Topics for Chapter 9

Key Topic Element	Description	Page Number
Figure 9-1	Typical design choice for which switches should be made to be root	273
Figure 9-2	Conceptual view of load-balancing benefits of PVST+	274
Figure 9-3	Shows the format of the system ID extension of the STP Priority field	275
Table 9-2	Lists default settings for STP optional configuration settings and related configuration commands	276
List	Configuring priority to influence the root election	281
List	Steps to manually configure a Port-Channel	285
List	Troubleshooting a Port-Channel	288
List	Interface settings that must match with other interfaces on the same switch for an interface to be included in a Port-Channel	290

Definitions of Key Terms

After your first reading of the chapter, try to define these key terms, but do not be concerned about getting them all correct at that time. Chapter 24, "Final Review," directs you in how to use these terms for late-stage preparation for the exam.

Rapid PVST+, PVST+, System ID Extension, PAgP, LACP, PortChannel, channel-group

Command Reference to Check Your Memory

Although you should not necessarily memorize the information in Tables 9-4 and 9-5, this section does include a reference for the configuration and EXEC commands covered in this chapter. Practically speaking, you should memorize the commands as a side effect of reading the chapter and doing all the activities in this exam preparation section. To check to see how well you have memorized the commands as a side effect of your other studies, cover the left side of the table with a piece of paper, read the descriptions on the right side, and see whether you remember the command.

Table 9-4   Chapter 9 Configuration Command Reference

Command	Description
`spanning-tree mode { rapid-pvst	mst }`	Global configuration command to set the STP mode.
`spanning-tree vlan vlan-number root primary`	Global configuration command that changes this switch to the root switch. The switch's priority is changed to the lower of either 24,576 or 4096 less than the priority of the current root bridge when the command was issued.
`spanning-tree vlan vlan-number root secondary`	Global configuration command that sets this switch's STP base priority to 28,672.
`spanning-tree [vlan vlan-id] {priority priority}`	Global configuration command that changes the bridge priority of this switch for the specified VLAN.
`spanning-tree [vlan vlan-number] cost cost`	Interface subcommand that changes the STP cost to the configured value.
`spanning-tree [vlan vlan-number] port-priority priority`	Interface subcommand that changes the STP port priority in that VLAN (0 to 240, in increments of 16).
`channel-group channel-group-number mode { active	passive	on}`	Interface subcommand that enables Port-Channel on the interface.
`spanning-tree port type edge`	Interface subcommand that enables PortFast on the interface.
`spanning-tree bpduguard enable`	Interface subcommand to enable BPDU Guard on an interface.
`spanning-tree port type edge default`	Global command that changes the switch default for PortFast on access interfaces from disabled to enabled.
`spanning-tree portfast bpduguard default`	Global command that changes the switch default for BPDU Guard on access interfaces from disabled to enabled.
`No spanning-tree port type edge`	Interface subcommand that disables PortFast on the interface.
`spanning-tree bpduguard disable`	Interface subcommand to disable BPDU Guard on an interface.

9

Table 9-5 Chapter 9 EXEC Command Reference

Command	Description
`show spanning-tree`	Lists details about the state of STP on the switch, including the state of each port
`show spanning-tree interface` `interface-id`	Lists STP information only for the specified port
`show spanning-tree vlan` `vlan-id`	Lists STP information for the specified VLAN
`show spanning-tree [vlan vlan-id]` `root`	Lists information about each VLAN's root or for just the specified VLAN
`show spanning-tree [vlan vlan-id]` `bridge`	Lists STP information about the local switch for each VLAN or for just the specified VLAN
`debug spanning-tree events`	Causes the switch to provide informational messages about changes in the STP topology
`show spanning-tree interface` `type number` `portfast`	Lists a one-line status message about PortFast on the listed interface
`show port-channel` `[channel-group-number]` `{brief` `|detail| port|port-channel|` `summary}`	Lists information about the state of Port-Channels on this switch

This chapter covers the following exam topics:

2.2. Describe classic Ethernet fundamentals

2.2.a. Forward

2.2.b. Filter

2.2.c. Flood

2.2.d. MAC address table

2.3. Describe switching concepts and perform basic configuration

CHAPTER 10

Configuring Ethernet Switching

Cisco Nexus switches are designed to have robust Layer 2 Ethernet switching features in addition to feature-rich Layer 3 routing functionality. This product family is known as a multilayer type of switch because it has the hardware and software capable of using both forwarding methods exclusively (Layer 2 only switch or Layer 3 only router) or it can act as a Layer 3 router and a Layer 2 switch at the same time.

This chapter explains a large variety of Layer 2 switching features, broken into two parts. The first half of the chapter explains many switch administrative features that happen to work the same way on all models of Nexus switches; this chapter keeps these common features together so that you can easily refer to them later when working with the different models within the Nexus product family. The second half of the chapter shows how to configure some switch-specific features on the Cisco Nexus platforms series of switches, many of which impact how a switch forwards frames.

"Do I Know This Already?" Quiz

Use the "Do I Know This Already?" quiz to help decide whether you might want to skim this chapter, or a major section, moving more quickly to the "Exam Preparation Tasks" section near the end of the chapter. Table 10-1 lists the major headings in this chapter and their corresponding "Do I Know This Already?" quiz questions. For thorough explanations, see Appendix A, "Answers to the 'Do I Know This Already?' Quizzes."

Table 10-1 "Do I Know This Already?" Foundation Topics Section-to-Question Mapping

Foundation Topics Section	Questions
Configuration of Features in Common on All Nexus Models	1–3
Nexus Switch Configuration and Operation	4–5

1. Which command enables you to configure a user named Fred to have read-only access to the Nexus switch CLI?

   a. username Fred read-only

   b. username Fred password Cisco123 role network-admin

   c. username Fred password Cisco123 role network-operator

   d. user Fred password Cisco123 role read-only

2. An engineer had formerly configured a Cisco Nexus switch to allow Telnet access so that the switch expected a password of mypassword from the Telnet user admin with the role of network-admin. The engineer then changed the configuration to support Secure Shell. Which of the following commands could have been part of the new configuration? (Choose two answers.)

   a. A **username** *name* **password** *password* vty mode subcommand.

   b. A **username** *name* **password** *password* global configuration command.

   c. A **login local** vty mode subcommand.

   d. None of these answers is correct.

3. The following command was copied and pasted into configuration mode when a user was telnetted into a Cisco switch:

   ```
   banner motd    #this is the login banner #
   ```

   Which of the following is true about what occurs the next time a user logs in from the console?

   a. No banner text is displayed.

   b. The banner text "this is" is displayed.

   c. The banner text "this is the login banner" is displayed.

   d. The banner text "Login banner configured, no text defined" is displayed.

4. Which of the following describes what VRF context the management interface (mgmt0) is in on a Nexus switch by default?

   a. In the Management Virtual Routing and Forwarding (VRF) instance.

   b. In the Default Virtual Routing and Forwarding (VRF) instance.

   c. Not in a Virtual Routing and Forwarding (VRF) instance.

   d. None of the answers is correct.

5. In which of the following modes of the CLI could you configure the speed setting for interface Ethernet 1/5?

   a. User mode

   b. Enable mode

   c. Global configuration mode

   d. VLAN mode

   e. Interface configuration mode

Foundation Topics

Configuration of Features in Common on All Nexus Switches

This is the first of the two major sections of this chapter. It examines the configuration of several features, all done the exact same way on all Nexus switches. In particular, this section examines how to secure access to the command-line interface (CLI) and also covers various settings for the console. Note that although this section refers to only switches, and not routers, the commands apply to both.

Securing the Switch CLI

The first step in securing a switch is to secure access to the CLI. Securing the CLI includes protecting access to the Cisco Nexus switch's network-admin role, because from the network-admin role, an attacker could reload the switch or change the configuration.

For example, consider a user who accesses a switch from the console. The default console configuration settings allow a console user to access the Nexus switch with a default username of admin in the network-admin role, with no password required. These defaults make some sense, because when you use the console, you are typically sitting near or next to the switch. If you can touch the switch, even if the console has all the available password protections, you can still perform the switch password recovery/reset procedure in 5 minutes and get into the switch. So, by default, console access is open; however, most network engineers add login security to the switch for all access methods by providing a strong password for the admin account. A strong password is one that is not easy to decipher.

> **NOTE**   To see the password recovery/reset procedures, go to Cisco.com and search for the phrase "password recovery procedure for Cisco NX-OS."

This section examines many of the configuration details related to accessing EXEC mode on a Cisco Nexus switch. Management interface IP configuration was covered in Chapter 5, "Installing and Operating Nexus Switches," in the section "Management Interface."

In particular, this section covers the following topics:

- Secure Shell (SSH)
- Basics of secure access with authentication servers

Securing Access with Local Usernames and Passwords

Cisco Nexus switches support other login authentication methods that use a username and password so that each user has unique login details that do not have to be shared. One method configures the username/password pairs locally on the switch, and the other relies on an external server called an authentication, authorization, and accounting (AAA) server. (The server could be the same server used for logins for other servers in the network.) This book covers the configuration using locally configured usernames/passwords.

10

In addition to the username and password, each user can be assigned to a role, as discussed in Chapter 5. Based on the username and password provided and the role assigned by the administrator, the user is given access to the entire switch configuration and verification commands or just a subset.

When a Telnet or SSH user connects to the switch configured as shown in Figure 10-1, the user is prompted first for a username and then for a password. The username/password pair must be from the list of local usernames; otherwise, the login is rejected.

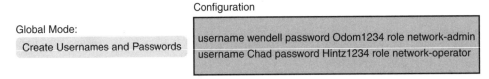

Figure 10-1 *Configuring Switches to Use Local Username Login Authentication*

NOTE The default admin username cannot be deleted or modified and always belongs to the network-admin role.

Securing Access with External Authentication Servers

Using a local list of usernames and passwords on a switch or router works well in small networks. However, using locally configured username/password pairs means that every switch and router needs the configuration for all users who might need to log in to the devices. Then, when any changes need to happen, like an occasional change to the passwords, the configuration of all devices must be changed.

Cisco switches and routers support an alternative way to keep track of valid usernames and passwords by using an external AAA server. When using a AAA server for authentication, the switch (or router) simply sends a message to the AAA server asking whether the username and password are allowed, and the AAA server replies. Figure 10-2 shows an example, with the user first supplying his username and password, the switch asking the AAA server whether they are valid, and the server replying to the switch stating that the username/password pair is valid.

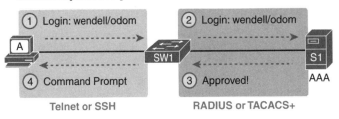

Figure 10-2 *Basic Authentication Process with an External AAA Server*

While the figure shows the general idea, note that the information flows with a couple of different protocols. On the left, the connection between the user and the switch or router uses Telnet or SSH. On the right, the switch and AAA server typically use either the RADIUS or TACACS+ protocol, both of which encrypt the passwords as they traverse the network.

Configuring Secure Shell

The switch already runs an SSH server by default, accepting incoming SSH connections from SSH clients. In addition, the switch is already configured with a cryptography key, used to encrypt the data. Because the Nexus switch is already configured for SSH, recommended practice dictates that you provide a strong password to the default admin user and create any additional usernames and roles that are needed to access the Cisco Nexus switch. The following list details the steps for a Cisco Nexus switch to change any of the default SSH configurations using local usernames.

Step 1. Configure the switch with local usernames, passwords, and roles on the AAA server.

Step 2. Disable the SSH feature:

```
(config)# no feature ssh
```

Step 3. Configure the switch to generate a matched public and private key pair to use for encryption, using one command in config mode:

```
ssh key (dsa | rsa (bits) (force)
```

Step 4. Enable the SSH feature:

```
(config)# feature ssh
```

Seeing the configuration happen in configuration mode, step by step, can be particularly helpful with SSH. Note in particular that the **ssh key** command actually prompts the user for more information and generates some messages while the key is being generated. Example 10-1 shows the commands being configured, with the encryption key as the final step.

Example 10-1 *SSH Configuration Process*

```
Switch# configure terminal
Enter configuration commands, one per line.    End with CNTL/Z.
! Step 1's username command happens next
Switch(config)# username admin passwordCisc0123 role Network-admin
Switch(config)# username chad passwordCisc0123 role Network-operator
!
! Step 2's feature commands happen next
    Switch(config)# no feature ssh
XML interface to system may become unavailable since ssh is disabled
!
      ! Step 3's key command happens next
   Switch(config)# ssh key rsa ?
      <CR>
        <1024-2048>    Enter number of bits (in multiples of 8)
        Switch(config)# ssh key rsa 2048
   generating rsa key(2048 bits).....
....
      generated rsa key
!
! Step 4's feature command happens next
      Switch(config)# feature ssh
      Switch(config)# exit
```

10

Two key commands give some information about the status of SSH on the switch. First, the **show ssh server** command lists status information about the SSH server itself. The **show ssh** command then lists information about each SSH client currently connected into the switch. Example 10-2 shows samples of each, with user Wendell currently connected to the switch.

Example 10-2 *Displaying SSH Status*

```
        Switch# show ssh server
        ssh version 2 is enabled


Switch# show ssh key
****************************************
rsa Keys generated:Thu Jan 30 00:08:15 2014


ssh-rsa AAAAB3NzaC1yc2EAAAADAQABAAABAQDICL7II0e18J4pEbgJZ2LnXrKG7xakmhKnIlwf5SRM
lYc3++H5ysdD7dVY2oYYV7lpEjmeAn1lATcn/pvRX+DmqJhl+u9ExQPx9IFVx5fKDQh8MTEKKxIGaISC
ihRYDQFGKGYS3vB1y6uWagXre177XBQKEL9yZ5XXgnYHk9z2OVhE7xa/6mZBUXqb40Id0rheU4GAib5R
TW8S+SFbM59UUXea/09Z4a8v6nSvz7pbSuWzbTfKHieqF5HQSGNb40NJcZUD38jhNq8HnEY1/Y1QhT1i
DoPHnqrkh6h0Dyit8DEWY5Y0aDLA/dTOKP9wQ0/7Uy7DPRNP9nYPdtZB4sEL


bitcount:2048
fingerprint:
ad:0d:54:95:ea:5e:f8:94:ae:28:3e:4d:37:a8:c7:47
```

Note that this example is using SSH Version 2 rather than Version 1; it is the only version of SSH that NX-OS supports. SSH v2 improves the underlying security algorithms over SSH v1 and adds some other small advantages, such as banner support.

Banners

Cisco Nexus switches can display a banner to notify users they are attempting to log in to a device. This banner appears prior to the user authentication process and serves as a warning to deter unauthorized users from attempting to log in. A banner is simply some text that appears on the screen for the user. You can configure a Cisco Nexus switch to display a banner for use with all login methods (vty, console), before login.

The **banner motd** global configuration command can be used to configure a banner to be displayed before login for all login types. NX-OS only provides one banner type called Message of the Day (MOTD). IOS has three different types for different login types: console, SSH, and Telnet. The first nonblank character after the banner type is called a *beginning delimiter character*. The banner text can span several lines, with the CLI user pressing **Enter** at the end of each line. The CLI knows that the banner has been configured as soon as the user enters the same delimiter character again.

Example 10-3 shows the configuration process for banner MOTD on a Cisco Nexus switch. The banner in Example 10-3 uses a **Z** as the delimiter character to start and end the message. It is important to know that any character can be used with the exception of the quote (") or percentage (%) character. Also, the last **banner** command shows multiple lines of banner text.

Key Topic

Example 10-3 *Banner MOTD Configuration*

```
7K-B# configure terminal
Enter configuration commands, one per line.    End with CNTL/Z.
7K-B(config)# banner motd Z
Enter TEXT message. End with the character 'Z'.
> Authorized Access Only!
> Z


! Below, the user of this Nexus switch exits the Telnet connection, and logs back in,
! seeing the MOTD banner, then the password prompt,
        7K-B# exit
Connection closed by foreign host.
telnet 1.1.1.1
Authorized Access Only!
login: admin
Password:
Cisco Nexus Operating System (NX-OS) Software
TAC support: http://www.cisco.com/tac
Copyright (c) 2002-2013, Cisco Systems, Inc. All rights reserved.
The copyrights to certain works contained in this software are
owned by other third parties and used and distributed under
license. Certain components of this software are licensed under
the GNU General Public License (GPL) version 2.0 or the GNU
Lesser General Public License (LGPL) Version 2.1. A copy of each
such license is available at
http://www.opensource.org/licenses/gpl-2.0.php and
http://www.opensource.org/licenses/lgpl-2.1.php
7K-B#
```

History Buffer Commands

When you enter commands from the CLI, the last several commands are saved in the history buffer. As mentioned in Chapter 5, you can use the up-arrow key, or press Ctrl+P, to move back in the history buffer stack to retrieve a command you entered a few commands ago. This feature makes it very easy and fast to use a set of commands repeatedly. Table 10-2 lists some of the key commands related to the history buffer.

Table 10-2   Commands Related to the History Buffer

Command	Description
show cli history	Lists the commands currently held in the history buffer
show cli history X	Lists the last number of commands held in history buffer
show cli history unformatted	Shows how to display unformatted command history

10

The logging synchronous and exec-timeout Commands

This next short section looks at a couple of ways to make using the console a little more user friendly, by asking the switch to not interrupt with log messages and by controlling how long you can be connected to the console before getting forced out.

The console automatically receives copies of all unsolicited syslog messages on a switch. The idea is that if the switch needs to tell the network administrator some important and possibly urgent information, the administrator might be at the console and might notice the message.

The display of these messages at the console can be disabled and enabled with the **no logging console** and **logging console** global commands, respectively. For example, when working from the console, if you want to temporarily not be bothered by log messages, you can disable the display of these messages with the **no logging console** global configuration command, and then when finished, you can enable them again.

Another way to improve the user experience is to control timeouts from the console. By default, the Cisco Nexus switch's timeout setting is 0, which means it never times out. The **exec-timeout** *minutes seconds* line subcommand lets you set the length of that inactivity timer.

Example 10-4 shows the syntax for these two commands, both on the console line. Note that both can be applied to the vty lines as well, for the same reasons.

Example 10-4 *Defining Console Inactivity Timeouts and When to Display Log Messages*

```
line console
exec-timeout 5
```

Nexus Switch Configuration and Operation

Cisco switches work very well when received from the factory, without any configuration added. Cisco Nexus Platforms leave the factory with default settings, with all interfaces enabled (a default configuration of **no shutdown**) and with auto-negotiation enabled for ports that can use it (a default configuration of **duplex auto** and **speed auto**). All interfaces default to be part of VLAN 1 (**switchport access vlan 1**). All you have to do with a new Cisco switch is make all the physical connections—Ethernet cables and power cord—and the switch starts working.

In most enterprise networks, you will want the switch to operate with some different settings as compared with the factory defaults. The second half of this chapter discusses some of those settings, with Chapter 7, "VLAN Trunking and Configuration," discussing more. (Also note that the details in this section differ from the configuration on a router.) In particular, this section covers the following topics:

- Switched virtual interface (SVI)
- Interface configuration (including speed and duplex)
- Securing unused switch interfaces
- Predicting the contents of the MAC address table

Switched Virtual Interface Concept Inside a Switch

A typical Layer 2 Cisco Nexus Platforms switch can use only one Layer 3 VLAN interface (SVI) without a Layer 3 module or license, but the network engineer can choose which VLAN interface to enable this on (typically VLAN 1). All interfaces on a Cisco Nexus switch belong to a Virtual Routing and Forwarding (VRF) instance called Default, except for the management interface, which belongs to the Management VRF. Within the "default" VRF, the network engineer can configure a single Layer 3 interface called a *switched virtual interface* (SVI). Example 10-5 shows the configuration of an SVI on VLAN 1.

> **NOTE**   Some Cisco switches, called Layer 2 switches, forward Ethernet frames, as discussed in depth in Chapter 3, "Fundamentals of Ethernet LANs." Other Cisco switches, called multilayer switches or Layer 3 switches, can also route IP packets using the Layer 3 logic normally used by routers. Layer 3 switches configure IP addresses on more than one VLAN interface at a time. This chapter assumes all switches are Layer 2 switches. Chapter 6, "VLAN and Trunking Concepts," further defines the differences between these types of Nexus switches.

Configuring IPv4 on a Cisco Nexus Switch

A switch configures its IPv4 address and mask on this special NIC-like *VLAN interface.* The following steps list the commands used to configure IPv4 on a switch, assuming that the IP address is configured to be in VLAN 1, with Example 10-5, which follows, showing a configuration example.

Step 1.   Enable the SVI feature on the switch using the **feature interface-vlan** command.

Step 2.   Enter VLAN 1 configuration mode using the **interface vlan 1** global configuration command.

Step 3.   Assign an IP address and mask using the **ip address** *ip-address mask* interface subcommand.

Step 4.   If not already enabled, enable the VLAN 1 interface using the **no shutdown** interface subcommand.

Step 5.   (Optional) Add the **ip name-server** *ip-address1 ip-address2...* global command to configure the switch to use DNS to resolve names into their matching IP address.

Example 10-5   *Switch Static IP Address Configuration*

```
Switch# configure terminal
Switch(config)# feature interface-vlan
Switch(config)# interface vlan 1
Switch(config-if)# ip address 192.168.1.200 255.255.255.0
   or…
Switch(config-if)# ip address 192.168.1.200/24
```

```
Switch(config-if)# no shutdown
00:25:07: %LINK-3-UPDOWN: Interface Vlan1, changed state to up
00:25:08: %LINEPROTO-5-UPDOWN: Line protocol on Interface Vlan1, changed
    state to up
Switch(config-if)# exit
```

As a side note, this example shows a particularly important and common command: the [no] shutdown command. To administratively enable an interface on a switch, use the no shutdown interface subcommand; to disable an interface, use the shutdown interface subcommand. The messages shown in Example 10-5, immediately following the no shutdown command, are syslog messages generated by the switch stating that the switch did indeed enable the interface.

Verifying IPv4 on a Switch

The switch IPv4 configuration can be checked in several places. First, you can always look at the current configuration using the show running-config command. Second, you can look at the IP address and mask information using the show interface vlan *x* command, which shows detailed status information about the VLAN interface in VLAN *x*. Example 10-6 shows sample output from these commands to match the configuration in Example 10-5.

Example 10-6 *Verifying DHCP-Learned Information on a Switch*

```
Switch# show interface vlan 1
Vlan1 is up, line protocol is up
    Hardware is EtherSVI, address is     0026.980b.55c1
    Internet Address is 192.168.1.200/24
    MTU 1500 bytes, BW 1000000 Kbit, DLY 10 usec,
       reliability 255/255, txload 1/255, rxload 1/255
! lines omitted for brevity
```

The output of the show interfaces vlan 1 command lists two very important details related to switch IP addressing. First, this show command lists the interface status of the VLAN 1 interface—in this case, up and up. If the VLAN 1 interface is not up, the switch cannot use its IP address to send and receive traffic. Notably, if you forget to issue the no shutdown command, the VLAN 1 interface remains in its default shutdown state and is listed as administratively down in the show command output.

Second, note that the output lists the interface's IP address on the third line. If you statically configure the IP address, as in Example 10-5, the IP address will always be listed.

Configuring Switch Interfaces

NX-OS uses the term *interface* to refer to physical ports used to forward data to and from other devices. Each interface can be configured with several settings, each of which might differ from interface to interface.

NX-OS uses interface subcommands to configure these settings. For example, interfaces can be configured to use the duplex and speed interface subcommands to configure those settings statically, or an interface can use auto-negotiation (the default). Example 10-7 shows how to configure duplex and speed, as well as the **description** command, which is simply a text description that can be configured by the administrator.

Example 10-7 *Interface Configuration Basics*

```
Switch# configure terminal
Enter configuration commands, one per line.    End with CNTL/Z.
Switch(config)# interface Ethernet 1/2
Switch(config-if)# duplex full
Switch(config-if)# speed 10000
Switch(config-if)# description Server1 connects here
Switch(config-if)# exit
Switch(config)# interface Ethernet 1/11 - 20
Switch(config-if-range)# description end-users connect_here
Switch(config-if-range)# duplex full
Switch(config-if-range)# speed 10000
Switch(config-if-range)# ^Z
Switch#
Switch# show interface status
Port    Name                  Status       Vlan     Duplex   Speed    Type
---------------------------------------------------------------------------------
Eth1/1   --                   connected    f-path   full     10G      SFP-H10GB-C
Eth1/2   Server1 connects here connected 1          full     10G      10Gbase-SR
Eth1/3   --                   sfpAbsent 1           full     10G      --
Eth1/4   --                   sfpAbsent 1           full     10G      --
Eth1/5   --                   sfpAbsent 1           full     10G      --
Eth1/6   --                   sfpAbsent 1           full     10G      --
Eth1/7   --                   sfpAbsent 1           full     10G      --
Eth1/8   --                   sfpAbsent 1           full     10G      --
Eth1/9   --                   sfpAbsent trunk       full     10G      --
Eth1/10  --                   sfpAbsent 1           full     10G      --
Eth1/11 servers-connect-here  sfpAbsent 1           full     10G      --
Eth1/12 servers-connect-here  sfpAbsent 1           full     10G      --
Eth1/13 servers-connect-here  sfpAbsent 1           full     10G      --
Eth1/14 servers-connect-here  sfpAbsent 1           full     10G      --
Eth1/15 servers-connect-here  vpcPeerLn t           full     10G      SFP-H10GB-C
Eth1/16 servers-connect-here  vpcPeerLn             full     10G      SFP-H10GB-C
Eth1/17 servers-connect-here  connected             full     10G      SFP-H10GB-C
Eth1/18 servers-connect-here  connected             full     10G      SFP-H10GB-C
Eth1/19 servers-connect-here  sfpAbsent 1           full     10G      --
Eth1/20 servers-connect-here  sfpAbsent 1           full     10G      --
! lines omitted for brevity
```

10

You can see some of the details of interface configuration with both the **show running-config** command (not shown in the example) and the handy **show interfaces status** command. This command lists a single line for each interface, the first part of the interface description, and the speed and duplex settings. Some of the early entries in the output purposefully show some differences, as follows:

Ethernet 1/2 (Eth1/2): This output lists the configured speed of 100 and duplex full; however, it lists a status of connected. The connected status means that the physical link is currently working, which means it has been enabled with a cable connection and the **no shutdown** command.

Also, note that for the sake of efficiency, you can configure a command on a range of interfaces at the same time using the **interface** command. In the example, the **interface Ethernet 1/11 - 20** command tells NX-OS that the next subcommand(s) applies to interfaces Eth1/11 through Eth1/20. You can also use a range of interfaces that are not contiguous, such as interface Ethernet 1/11, 2/20, 2/22.

> **NOTE** Configuring both the speed and duplex on a Cisco switch interface disables auto-negotiation.

Securing Unused Switch Interfaces

The default settings on Cisco switches work great if you want to buy a switch, unbox it, plug it in, and have it immediately work without any other effort. Those same defaults have an unfortunate side effect of worse security. With an all-default configuration, unused interfaces might be used by an attacker to gain access to the LAN. So, Cisco makes some general recommendations to override the default interface settings to make the unused ports more secure, as follows:

- Administratively disable the interface using the **shutdown** interface subcommand.
- Prevent VLAN trunking by making the port a nontrunking interface using the **switchport mode access** interface subcommand.
- Assign the port to an unused VLAN using the **switchport access vlan** *number* interface subcommand.
- Set the native VLAN to not be VLAN 1, but to instead be an unused VLAN, using the **switchport trunk native vlan** *vlan-id interface* subcommand. (The native VLAN is discussed in Chapter 6.)

Frankly, if you just shut down the interface, the security exposure goes away, but the other tasks prevent any immediate problems if someone else comes around and enables the interface by configuring a **no shutdown** command.

Predicting the Contents of the MAC Address Table

As explained in Chapter 3, switches learn MAC addresses and then use the entries in the MAC address table to make a forwarding/filtering decision for each frame. To know exactly how a particular switch will forward an Ethernet frame, you need to examine the MAC address table on a Cisco Nexus switch. To derive how this is done, we will use Figure 10-3 and manually build what we believe to be a MAC address table for each switch. It is important to understand how the switch will utilize the MAC address table to forward flows. Your task is to take out a piece of paper and try to build what you believe to be the MAC address table on each Nexus switch.

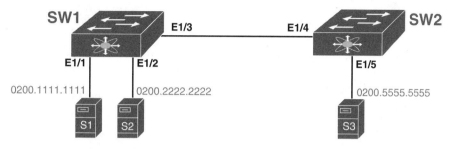

Figure 10-3 *Predicting the MAC Address Table*

Now that we have built our MAC address tables manually, you need to validate whether you got it right. The best way to validate what your MAC address tables contain is to use the command **show mac-address table**. Figure 10-4 shows the MAC address table for each switch. Let's break this down to understand how it was built and how the switch will use it to forward on a Layer 2 network between the servers in the figure.

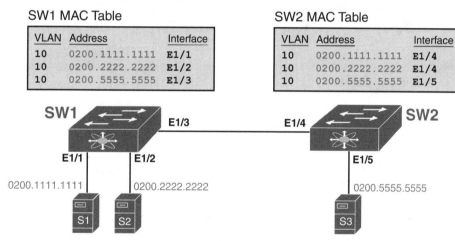

Figure 10-4 *Contents of the MAC Address Table*

The MAC table entries you predict in this case define where you think frames will flow. Even though the sample network in Figure 10-3 shows only one physical path through the Ethernet LAN, the exercise should be worthwhile because it forces you to correlate what you would expect to see in the MAC address table with how the switches forward frames. Figure 10-4 shows the resulting MAC table entries for servers. Let's work through some scenarios where we want to understand how the switch will forward frames between S1 and S2 as well as S1 and S3.

Scenario 1: Communication Between S1 and S2

When S1 sends a frame destined to the MAC address of S2, the frame will be received in on interface Ethernet 1/1 on Switch 1. The list that follows outlines the steps that the switch will take to get the frame to its destination of S2 on the same network (VLAN 10):

Step 1.   Switch 1 will do a lookup for the destination MAC address of 0200.2222.2222 in its MAC address table.

Step 2.   Switch 1 sees that the destination address of S2 is learned through its Ethernet 1/2 interface.

Step 3.   Switch 1 forwards the frame sourced from S1 to the destination of S2 out of the interface of Ethernet 1/2, which is where the MAC address of S2 has been learned.

Step 4.   S2 receives the frame from S1.

In this scenario, one lookup is done on the Switch 1 MAC address table and is sent to the output interface where the destination MAC address was learned.

Scenario 2: Communication from S1 to S3

The list that follows outlines the detailed steps that happen across the communication path between S1 and S3 on VLAN 10 when S1 sends a frame into interface Ethernet 1/1:

Step 1.   Switch 1 will do a lookup for the destination MAC address of 0200.5555.5555 of S3 in its MAC address table.

Step 2.   Switch 1 sees that the destination address of S3 is learned through its Ethernet 1/3 interface.

Step 3.   Switch 1 forwards the frame sourced from S1 to the destination of S3 out of the interface of Ethernet 1/3, which is where Switch 1 has learned the MAC address of S3.

Step 4.   Switch 2 receives the frame from Switch 1 on its Ethernet 1/4 interface with a source address of S1's MAC address and a destination address of S3's MAC address.

Step 5.   Switch 2 will do a lookup for the destination MAC address of 0200.5555.5555 of S3 in its MAC address table and see that it has learned this MAC address on interface Ethernet 1/5.

Step 6.   Switch 2 will forward the frame sourced from S1 to S3 out of interface Ethernet 1/5 to reach S3.

Step 7.   S3 will receive the frame from S1.

As you can see in the table outputs created by learning the MAC addresses of the servers across the data center LAN in Figure 10-3, switches will always make their forwarding decision based on the destination address. Switches will learn the address of the host or servers (in our case, across their interswitch links) and label this interface between the switches and the path to get to the remote MAC addresses.

Exam Preparation Tasks

Review All Key Topics

Review the most important topics from this chapter, noted with the Key Topic icon in the outer margin of the page. Table 10-3 lists references for these key topics and the page number on which each is found.

> **NOTE**   There is no need to memorize any configuration step list referenced as a key topic; these lists are just study aids.

Table 10-3   Key Topics for Chapter 10

Key Topic Element	Description	Page Number
Example 10-1	SSH configuration process	301
Example 10-3	Configuring banner MOTD	303
Example 10-5	Switch static IP address configuration	305
Figure 10-4	Contents of the MAC address table	309
Scenario 1	Communication between S1 and S2	310
Scenario 2	Communication between S1 and S3	310

Definitions of Key Terms

After your first reading of the chapter, try to define these key terms, but do not be concerned about getting them all correct at that time. Chapter 24, "Final Review," directs you in how to use these terms for late-stage preparation for the exam.

Telnet, SSH, local username, VLAN interface

Command References

Tables 10-4 through 10-7 list the configuration commands used in this chapter, by general topic. Table 10-8, at the very end of the chapter, lists the EXEC commands from this chapter.

Table 10-4   Console, Telnet, and SSH Login Commands

Command	Mode/Purpose/Description
line console	Changes the context to console configuration mode.
line vty	Changes the context to vty configuration mode for the range of vty lines listed in the command.
(no)feature ssh	Enables or disables the SSH feature on a Cisco Nexus switch.

10

Command	Mode/Purpose/Description
username *name* **password** *pass-value* **role** *role-value*	Global command. Defines one of possibly multiple usernames and associated passwords, used for user authentication. Used when the **login local** line configuration command has been used.
ssh key rsa/ dsa key value (1024-2048)	Global command. Creates and stores (in a hidden location in flash memory) the keys required by SSH.

Table 10-5 Switch IPv4 Configuration

Command	Mode/Purpose/Description
(no) feature interface-vlan	Enables or disables the feature interface VLAN (SVI) on a Cisco Nexus switch.
interface vlan *number*	Changes the context to VLAN interface mode. For VLAN 1, allows the configuration of the switch's IP address.
ip address *ip-address subnet-mask*	VLAN interface mode. Statically configures the switch's IP address and mask.
ip name-server *server-ip-1 server-ip-2 ...*	Global command. Configures the IP addresses of DNS servers, so any commands when logged in to the switch will use the DNS for name resolution.

Table 10-6 Switch Interface Configuration

Command	Mode/Purpose/Description
interface *Ethernet port-number*	Changes context to interface mode. The possible port numbers vary depending on the model of switch (for example, Eth1/1 or Eth1/2).
shutdown **no shutdown**	Interface mode. Disables or enables the interface, respectively.
speed {1000 | 10000 | auto}	Interface mode. Manually sets the speed to the listed speed or, with the **auto** setting, automatically negotiates the speed.
duplex {auto | full | half}	Interface mode. Manually sets the duplex to half or full, or to auto-negotiate the duplex setting.
description *text*	Interface mode. Lists any information text that the engineer wants to track for the interface, such as the expected device on the other end of the cable.

Table 10-7   Other Switch Configuration

Command	Mode/Purpose/Description
hostname *name*	Global command. Sets this switch's hostname, which is also used as the first part of the switch's command prompt.
exec-timeout *minutes [seconds]*	Console or vty mode. Sets the inactivity timeout, so that after the defined period of no action, NX-OS closes the current user login session.
switchport access vlan *vlan-number*	Interface subcommand that defines the VLAN in which the interface resides.
banner motd *delimiter banner-text delimiter*	Global command that defines a banner that is displayed at different times when users log in to the Cisco Nexus switch.

Table 10-8   Chapter 10 EXEC Command Reference

Command	Purpose
show running-config	Lists the currently used configuration
show running-config | begin line vty	Pipes (sends) the command output to the **begin** command, which only lists output beginning with the first line that contains the text "line vty"
show mac address-table dynamic	Lists the dynamically learned entries in the switch's address (forwarding) table
show ssh key rsa	Lists the public and shared key created for use with SSH using the **ssh key rsa** global configuration command
show ssh server	Lists status information for the SSH server, including the SSH version
show ssh key	Lists the key enabled by SSH
show interfaces status	Lists one output line per interface, noting the description, operating state, and settings for duplex and speed on each interface
show interfaces vlan 1	Lists the interface status, the switch's IP address and mask, and much more
show cli history {x/ unformatted}	Lists the commands in the current history buffer
(no) logging console	Enables or disables logging messages to the console interface

10

Part II Review

Keep track of your part review progress with the checklist shown in Table P2-1. Details on each task follow the table.

Table P2-1 Part II Review Checklist

Activity	First Date Completed	Second Date Completed
Repeat All DIKTA Questions		
Answer Part Review Questions		
Review Key Topics		

Repeat All DIKTA Questions: For this task, answer the "Do I Know This Already?" questions again for the chapters in this part of the book, using the PCPT software. Refer to the Introduction and find the section "How to View Only DIKTA Questions by Part" for help with how to make the PCPT software show you DIKTA questions for this part only.

Answer Part Review Questions: For this task, answer the Part Review questions for this part of the book, using the PCPT software. Refer to the Introduction and find the section "How to View Only Part Review Questions by Part" for help with how to make the PCPT software show you Part Review questions for this part only.

 Review Key Topics: Browse back through the chapters and look for the Key Topic icons. If you do not remember some details, take the time to reread those topics.

Subnetting is a fundamental part of networking and a great way to segment and carve up your networks to make your overall networking journey easier.

Chapter 11 starts with the perspectives of subnetting IPv4. In Chapters 12 through 14 we dig deeper into understanding subnetting and its best practices.

Finally, the fundamental concepts of IPv6 are introduced in Chapter 15.

Part III

IPv4/IPv6 Subnetting

This chapter covers the following exam topics:

2.0. Basic data center networking concepts

Perspectives on IPv4 Subnetting

Most entry-level networking jobs require you to operate and troubleshoot a network using a preexisting IP addressing and subnetting plan. The CCNA Data Center certification requires you to be ready to analyze preexisting IP addressing and subnetting information to perform typical operations tasks, such as monitoring the network, reacting to possible problems, and troubleshooting those problems.

However, some exam questions, as well as many real-life issues at work, require that you understand the design of the network so that you can better operate it. The process of monitoring any network requires that you continually answer the question, "Is the network working as *designed*?" If a problem exists, you must consider questions such as, "What happens when the network works normally, and what is different right now?" Both questions require you to understand the intended design of the network, including details of the IP addressing and subnetting design.

This chapter provides some perspectives and answers for the bigger issues in IPv4 addressing. What addresses can be used so that they work properly? What addresses should be used? When you are told to use certain numbers, what does that tell you about the choices made by some other network engineer? How do these choices impact the practical job of configuring switches, routers, and hosts as well as operating the network on a daily basis? This chapter hopes to answer these questions while revealing details of how IPv4 addresses work.

> **NOTE** As promised in the Introduction's section "For Those Studying Routing & Switching," readers of the *ICND1 100-101 Official Cert Guide* (Chapter 11 of that book) can skip most of this chapter. However, do review this chapter's section titled "Subnet Rules with Layer 3 Switches," plus the text surrounding Figure 11-8.

"Do I Know This Already?" Quiz

Use the "Do I Know This Already?" quiz to help decide whether you might want to skim this chapter, or a major section, moving more quickly to the "Exam Preparation Tasks" section near the end of the chapter. Table 11-1 lists the major headings in this chapter and their corresponding "Do I Know This Already?" quiz questions. For thorough explanations, see Appendix A, "Answers to the 'Do I Know This Already?' Quizzes."

Table 11-1 "Do I Know This Already?" Foundation Topics Section-to-Question Mapping

Foundation Topics Section	Questions
Analyze Subnetting and Addressing Needs	1–3
Make Design Choices	4–8

1. Host A is a PC, connected to switch SW1 and assigned to VLAN 1. Which of the following are typically assigned an IP address in the same subnet as Host A? (Choose two answers.)

   a. The local router's WAN interface

   b. The local router's LAN interface

   c. All other hosts attached to the same switch

   d. Other hosts attached to the same switch and also in VLAN 1

2. Why does the formula for the number of hosts per subnet ($2^H - 2$) require the subtraction of two hosts?

   a. To reserve two addresses for redundant default gateways (routers)

   b. To reserve the two addresses required for DHCP operation

   c. To reserve addresses for the subnet ID and default gateway (router)

   d. To reserve addresses for the subnet broadcast address and subnet ID

3. A Class B network needs to be subnetted such that it supports 100 subnets and 100 hosts per subnet. Which of the following answers list a workable combination for the number of network, subnet, and host bits? (Choose two answers.)

   a. Network = 16, subnet = 7, host = 7

   b. Network = 16, subnet = 8, host = 8

   c. Network = 16, subnet = 9, host = 7

   d. Network = 8, subnet = 7, host = 17

4. Which of the following are private IP networks? (Choose two answers.)

   a. 172.31.0.0

   b. 172.32.0.0

   c. 192.168.255.0

   d. 192.1.168.0

   e. 11.0.0.0

5. Which of the following are public IP networks? (Choose three answers.)

   a. 9.0.0.0

   b. 172.30.0.0

   c. 192.168.255.0

   d. 192.1.168.0

   e. 1.0.0.0

6. Before Class B network 172.16.0.0 is subnetted by a network engineer, what parts of the structure of the IP addresses in this network already exist, with a specific size? (Choose two answers.)

   a. Network

   b. Subnet

   c. Host

   d. Broadcast

7. A network engineer spends time thinking about the entire Class B network 172.16.0.0 and how to subnet that network. He then chooses how to subnet this Class B network and creates an addressing and subnetting plan, on paper, showing his choices. If you compare his thoughts about this network before subnetting the network, to his thoughts about this network after mentally subnetting the network, which of the following occurred to the parts of the structure of addresses in this network?

   a. The subnet part got smaller.

   b. The host part got smaller.

   c. The network part got smaller.

   d. The host part was removed.

   e. The network part was removed.

8. Which of the following terms are *not* used to reference the one number in each subnet used to uniquely identify the subnet? (Choose two answers.)

   a. Subnet ID

   b. Subnet number

   c. Subnet broadcast

   d. Subnet name

   e. Subnet address

11

Foundation Topics

Introduction to Subnetting

Suppose you just happen to be at the sandwich shop when they are selling the world's longest sandwich. You're pretty hungry, so you go for it. Now you have one sandwich, but at more than 2 kilometers (about 1.25 miles) long, you realize it's a bit more than you need for lunch all by yourself. To make the sandwich more useful (and more portable), you chop the sandwich into meal-size pieces, and give the pieces to other folks around you, who are also ready for lunch.

Huh? Well, subnetting, at least the main concept, is similar to this sandwich story. You start with one network, but it is just one large network. As a single large entity, it might not be useful, and it is probably far too large. To make it useful, you chop it into smaller pieces, called subnets, and assign those subnets to be used in different parts of the enterprise internetwork.

This short section introduces IP subnetting. First, it shows the general ideas behind a completed subnet design that indeed chops (or "subnets") one network into subnets. The rest of this section describes the many design steps you would take to create just such a subnet design. By the end of this section, you should have the right context to then read through the subnetting design steps introduced throughout the rest of this chapter.

> **NOTE**   In this book, only Chapter 15, "Fundamentals of IP Version 6," discusses IPv6 to any depth. So, in this chapter and Chapter 12, "Analyzing Classful IPv4 Networks," Chapter 13, "Analyzing Subnet Masks," and Chapter 14, "Analyzing Existing Subnets," all references to *IP* refer to IPv4 unless otherwise stated.

Subnetting Defined Through a Simple Example

An IP network—in other words, a Class A, B, or C network—is simply a set of consecutively numbered IP addresses that follows some preset rules. These Class A, B, and C rules, first introduced back in Chapter 4, "Fundamentals of IPv4 Addressing and Routing," in the section "Class A, B, and C IP Networks," define that for a given network, all the addresses in the network have the same value in some of the octets of the addresses. For example, Class B network 172.16.0.0 consists of all IP addresses that begin with 172.16: 172.16.0.0, 172.16.0.1, 172.16.0.2, and so on, through 172.16.255.255. Another example: Class A network 10.0.0.0 includes all addresses that begin with 10.

An IP subnet is simply a subset of a Class A, B, or C network. In fact, the word *subnet* is a shortened version of the phrase *subdivided network*. For example, one subnet of Class B network 172.16.0.0 could be the set of all IP addresses that begin with 172.16.1 and would include 172.16.1.0, 172.16.1.1, 172.16.1.2, and so on, up through 172.16.1.255. Another subnet of that same Class B network could be all addresses that begin 172.16.2.

To give you a general idea, Figure 11-1 shows some basic documentation from a completed subnet design that could be used when an engineer subnets Class B network 172.16.0.0.

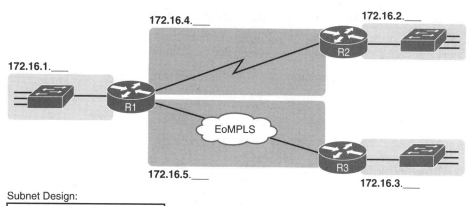

Subnet Design:

> **Class B 172.16.0.0**
> **First 3 Octets are Equal**

Figure 11-1 *Sample Subnet Plan Document*

The design shows five subnets: one for each of the three LANs and one each for the two WAN links. The small text note shows the rationale used by the engineer for the subnets: Each subnet includes addresses that have the same value in the first three octets. For example, for the LAN on the left, the number shows 172.16.1.__, meaning "all addresses that begin with 172.16.1." Also, note that the design, as shown, does not use all the addresses in Class B network 172.16.0.0, so the engineer has left plenty of room for growth.

Operational View Versus Design View of Subnetting

Most IT jobs require you to work with subnetting from an operational view. That is, someone else, before you got the job, designed how IP addressing and subnetting would work for that particular enterprise network. You need to interpret what someone else has already chosen.

To fully understand IP addressing and subnetting, you need to think about subnetting from both a design perspective and operational perspective. For example, Figure 11-1 simply states that in all these subnets, the first three octets must be equal. Why was that convention chosen? What alternatives exist? Would those alternatives be better for your internetwork today? All these questions relate more to subnetting design rather than to operation. To help you see both perspectives, the explanations in this part of the book often point out whether you should take an operational approach to the topic or a design approach.

The remainder of this chapter breaks the topics into three major topics, in the sequence noted in Figure 11-2.

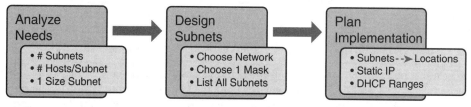

Figure 11-2 *Subnet Planning, Design, and Implementation Tasks*

Analyze Subnetting and Addressing Needs

This section discusses the meaning of four basic questions that can be used to analyze the addressing and subnetting needs for any new or changing enterprise network:

1.   Which hosts should be grouped together into a subnet?

2.   How many subnets does this network require?

3.   How many host IP addresses does each subnet require?

4.   Will we use a single subnet size for simplicity, or not?

Rules About Which Hosts Are in Which Subnet

Every device that connects to an IP internetwork needs to have an IP address. These devices include computers used by end users, servers, mobile phones, laptops, IP phones, tablets, and networking devices such as routers, switches, and firewalls (in short, any device that uses IP to send and receive packets needs an IP address).

> **NOTE**   In discussing IP addressing, the term *network* has a specific meaning: a Class A, B, or C IP network. To avoid confusion with that use of the term *network*, this book uses the terms *internetwork* and *enterprise network* when referring to a collection of hosts, routers, switches, and so on.

The IP addresses must be assigned according to some basic rules, and for good reasons. To make routing work efficiently, IP addressing rules group addresses into groups called subnets. The rules are as follows:

■   Addresses in the same subnet are not separated by a router.

■   Addresses in different subnets are separated by at least one router.

Figure 11-3 shows the general concept, with hosts A and B in one subnet and host C in another. In particular, note that hosts A and B are not separated from each other by any routers. However, host C, separated from A and B by at least one router, must be in a different subnet.

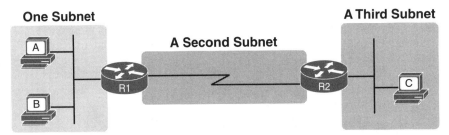

Figure 11-3   *PC A and B in One Subnet, and PC C in a Different Subnet*

The idea that hosts on the same link must be in the same subnet is much like the postal code concept. All mailing addresses in the same town use the same postal code (ZIP codes in the United States). Addresses in another town, whether relatively nearby or on the other side of the country, have a different postal code. The postal code gives the postal service a better ability to automatically sort the mail to deliver it to the right location. For the same general reasons, hosts on the same LAN are in the same subnet, and hosts in different LANs are in different subnets.

Note that the point-to-point WAN link in the figure also needs a subnet. Figure 11-3 shows router R1 connected to the LAN subnet on the left and to a WAN subnet on the right. Router R2 connects to that same WAN subnet. To do so, both R1 and R2 will have IP addresses on their WAN interfaces, and the addresses will be in the same subnet. (An Ethernet over Multiprotocol Label Switching [EoMPLS] WAN link has the same IP addressing needs, with each of the two routers having an IP address in the same subnet.)

The Ethernet LANs in Figure 11-3 also show a slightly different style of drawing, using simple lines with no Ethernet switch. When drawing Ethernet LANs and the details of the LAN switches do not matter, you simply show each device connected to the same line, as seen in Figure 11-3. (This kind of drawing mimics the original Ethernet cabling before switches and hubs existed.)

Finally, because the routers' main job is to forward packets from one subnet to another, routers typically connect to multiple subnets. For example, in this case, router R1 connects to one LAN subnet on the left and one WAN subnet on the right. To do so, R1 will be configured with two different IP addresses, one per interface. These addresses will be in different subnets because the interfaces connect the router to different subnets.

Subnet Rules with Layer 3 Switches

Thinking about subnets when using Layer 3 switches requires a little more work. When a network diagram uses router icons, there is a clear division of where the IP subnets will be needed, as demonstrated previously in Figure 11-3. By contrast, consider Figure 11-4, which shows a Nexus switch, which can be configured as a Layer 3 switch. Which of the four servers should be in the same subnet, and which should be in different subnets?

Figure 11-4   *The Lack of Information Makes It Unclear Which Servers Are in Which Subnets*

To know where subnets should exist when using Layer 3 switches, you must know what VLANs exist. The devices in a VLAN should be in the same IP subnet. The concept of a VLAN and an IP subnet are different. A VLAN is a Layer 2 concept, whereas a subnet is a Layer 3 concept; but they group the same devices together.

As a reminder, devices in different VLANs (and therefore different subnets) can communicate, but only if a router or Layer 3 switch is configured to forward traffic between the two subnets. For instance, Figure 11-5 repeats the same network as shown in Figure 11-4, but with VLANs and subnets shown. The figure represents the Layer 3 switching logic inside the Nexus switch with a router icon. IP packets that flow from the subnet on the left to the subnet on the right must be processed by the Layer 3 switching logic—routing logic if you will—inside the Nexus switch.

11

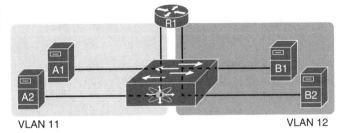

VLAN 11   VLAN 12

Figure 11-5 *Nexus Layer 3 Switch (Routing) Sits Between Two Subnets*

Figure 11-5 also shows enough internals of a Layer 3 switch to connect back to the subnet design rules: Devices separated by a router are in different subnets. For instance, server A1 is separated from server B1 by a routing function (that is, the Layer 3 switching function configured on the Nexus switch). Therefore, A1 and B1 would be in different subnets. However, A1 and A2, not separated by a Layer 3 switching function, would be in the same subnet.

Determine the Number of Subnets

To determine the number of subnets required, you must think about the internetwork as documented and apply the following rules. To do so, you require access to (1) network diagrams, (2) VLAN configuration details, and (3) if Frame Relay WANs are used, details about the permanent virtual circuits (PVCs). Based on this info, you should use these rules and plan for one subnet for every

- VLAN
- Point-to-point serial link
- Ethernet emulation WAN link (EoMPLS)
- Frame Relay PVC

> **NOTE** WAN technologies such as MPLS and Frame Relay allow subnetting options other than one subnet per pair of routers on the WAN, but this book only uses WAN technologies that have one subnet for each point-to-point WAN connection between two routers.

For example, imagine that as the network planner, you only have Figure 11-6 on which to base the subnet design.

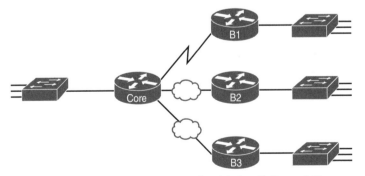

Figure 11-6 *Four-Site Internetwork with Small Central Site*

The number of subnets required cannot be fully predicted with only this figure. Certainly, three subnets will be needed for the WAN links (one per link). However, each LAN switch can be configured with a single VLAN or with multiple VLANs. You can be certain that you need at least one subnet for the LAN at each site, but you might need more.

Next, consider the more detailed version of the same figure shown in Figure 11-7. In this case, the figure shows VLAN counts in addition to the same Layer 3 topology (the routers and the links connected to the routers). It also shows that the central site has many more switches, but the key fact on the left, regardless of how many switches exist, is that the central site has a total of 12 VLANs. Similarly, the figure lists each branch as having two VLANs. Along with the same three WAN subnets, this internetwork requires 21 subnets.

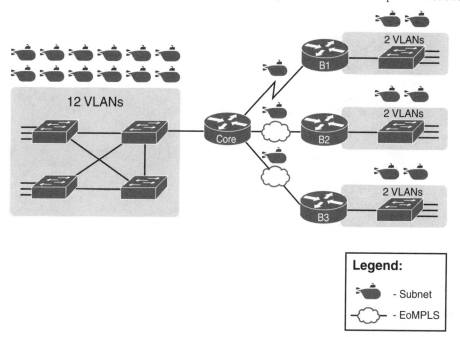

Figure 11-7   *Four-Site Internetwork with Larger Central Site*

Data centers also use subnets for Port-Channel and single Ethernet links in the Layer 3 parts of the design. The links that connect Nexus switches configured as Layer 3 switches, and that also connect the Layer 3 switches to any WAN routers, also use a subnet.

For example, consider the partial network diagram shown in Figure 11-8. The diagram shows two routers at the top, with the WAN (not shown) above the routers. Six links connect between the two WAN routers and the two End of Row (EoR) Nexus switches, which are configured to provide Layer 3 switching. The two Layer 3 switches both route packets for the ten subnets for the ten VLANs for the servers at the bottom of the figure.

WAN

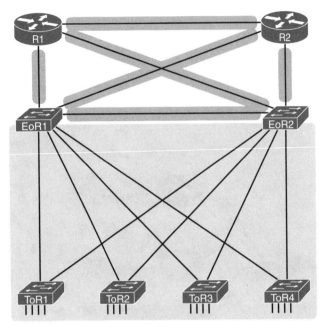

10 Server VLANs

Figure 11-8 *Subnets Used for Router and Layer 3 Switch Links*

Finally, in a real job, you would consider the needs today as well as how much growth you expect in the internetwork over time. Any subnetting plan should include a reasonable estimate of the number of subnets required to meet future needs.

Determine the Number of Hosts per Subnet

Determining the number of hosts per subnet requires knowing a few simple concepts and then doing a lot of research and questioning. Every device that connects to a subnet needs an IP address. For a totally new network, you can look at business plans—numbers of people at the site, devices on order, and so on—to get some idea of the possible devices. When expanding an existing network to add new sites, you can use existing sites as a point of comparison, and then find out which sites will get bigger or smaller. And don't forget to count the router interface IP address in each subnet and the switch IP address used to remotely manage the switch.

Instead of gathering data for each and every site, planners often just use a few typical sites for planning purposes. For example, maybe you have some large sales offices and some small sales offices. You might dig in and learn a lot about only one large sales office and only one small sales office. Add that analysis to the fact that point-to-point links need a subnet with just two addresses, plus any analysis of more one-of-a-kind subnets, and you have enough information to plan the addressing and subnetting design.

For example, in Figure 11-9, the engineer has built a diagram that shows the number of hosts per LAN subnet in the largest branch, B1. For the two other branches, the engineer did not bother finding out the number of required hosts. As long as the number of required IP addresses at sites B2 and B3 stays below the estimate of 50, based on the larger site B1, the engineer can plan for 50 hosts in each branch LAN subnet and have plenty of addresses per subnet.

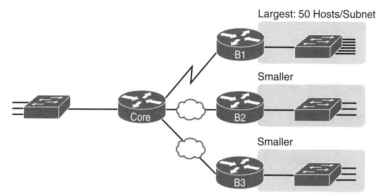

Figure 11-9 *Large Branch B1 with 50 Hosts/Subnet*

One Size Subnet Fits All (Or Not)

The final choice in the initial planning step is to decide whether you will use a simpler design by using a one-size-subnet-fits-all philosophy. A subnet's size, or length, is simply the number of usable IP addresses in the subnet. A subnetting design can either use one size subnet or varied sizes of subnets, with pros and cons for each choice.

Defining the Size of a Subnet

Now think for a moment like the person who chooses the subnet design. To do so, the engineer assigns each subnet a *subnet mask*, and that mask, among other things, defines the size of that subnet. The mask sets aside a number of *host bits* whose purpose is to number different host IP addresses in that subnet. Because you can number 2^x things with x bits, if the mask defines H host bits, the subnet contains 2^H unique numeric values.

However, the subnet's size is not 2^H. It's $2^H - 2$, because two numbers in each subnet are reserved for other purposes. Each subnet reserves the numerically lowest value for the *subnet number* and the numerically highest value as the *subnet broadcast address*. As a result, the number of usable IP addresses per subnet is $2^H - 2$.

> **NOTE** The terms *subnet number*, *subnet ID*, and *subnet address* all refer to the number that represents or identifies a subnet.

Figure 11-10 shows the general concept behind the three-part structure of an IP address, focusing on the host part and the resulting subnet size.

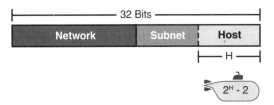

Figure 11-10 *Subnet Size Concepts*

One Size Subnet Fits All

To choose to use a single-size subnet in an enterprise network, you must use the same mask for all subnets, because the mask defines the size of the subnet. But which mask?

One requirement to consider when choosing that one mask is this: The mask must provide enough host IP addresses to support the largest subnet. To do this, the number of host bits (H) defined by the mask must be large enough so that $2^H - 2$ is larger than (or equal to) the number of host IP addresses required in the largest subnet.

For example, consider Figure 11-11. It shows the required number of hosts per LAN subnet. (The figure ignores the subnets on the WAN links, which require only two IP addresses each.) The branch LAN subnets require only 50 host addresses, but the main site LAN subnet requires 200 host addresses. To accommodate the largest subnet, you need at least 8 host bits. Seven host bits would not be enough, because $2^7 - 2 = 126$. Eight host bits would be enough, because $2^8 - 2 = 254$, which is more than enough to support 200 hosts in a subnet.

What's the big advantage when using a single-size subnet? Operational simplicity. In other words, keeping it simple. Everyone on the IT staff who has to work with networking can get used to working with one mask—and one mask only. They will be able to answer all subnetting questions more easily, because everyone gets used to doing subnetting math with that one mask.

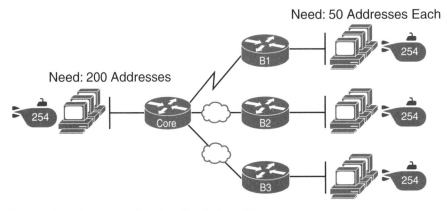

Figure 11-11 *Network Using One Subnet Size*

The big disadvantage for using a single-size subnet is that it wastes IP addresses. For example, in Figure 11-8, all the branch LAN subnets support 254 addresses, but the largest branch subnet needs only 50 addresses. The WAN subnets only need two IP addresses, but each supports 254 addresses, again wasting more IP addresses.

The wasted IP addresses do not actually cause a problem in most cases, however. Most organizations use private IP networks in their enterprise internetworks, and a single Class A or Class B private network can supply plenty of IP addresses, even with the waste.

Multiple Subnet Sizes (Variable-Length Subnet Masks)

To create multiple sizes of subnets in one Class A, B, or C network, the engineer must create some subnets using one mask, some with another, and so on. Different masks mean different numbers of host bits, and a different number of hosts in some subnets based on the $2^H - 2$ formulas.

For example, consider the requirements listed earlier in Figure 11-11. It showed one LAN subnet on the left that needs 200 host addresses, three branch subnets that need 50 addresses, and three WAN links that need two addresses. To meet those needs, while wasting fewer IP addresses, three subnet masks could be used, creating subnets of three different sizes, as shown in Figure 11-12.

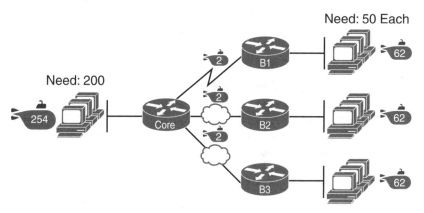

Figure 11-12   *Three Masks, Three Subnet Sizes*

The smaller subnets now waste fewer IP addresses compared to the design seen earlier in Figure 11-8. The subnets on the right that need 50 IP addresses have subnets with 6 host bits, for $2^6 - 2 = 62$ available addresses per subnet. The WAN links use masks with 2 host bits, for $2^2 - 2 = 2$ available addresses per subnet.

However, some are still wasted, because you cannot set the size of the subnet as some arbitrary size. All subnets will be a size based on the $2^H - 2$ formula, with H being the number of host bits defined by the mask for each subnet. For the most part, this book explains subnetting using designs that use a single mask, creating a single subnet size for all subnets. Why? First, it makes the process of learning subnetting easier. Second, some types of analysis that you can do about a network—specifically, calculating the number of subnets in the classful network—only make sense when a single mask is used.

Make Design Choices

Now that you know how to analyze the IP addressing and subnetting needs, the next major step examines how to apply the rules of IP addressing and subnetting to those needs and mask some choices. In other words, now that you know how many subnets you need and

11

how many host addresses you need in the largest subnet, how do you create a useful subnetting design that meets those requirements? The short answer is that you need to do the three tasks shown on the right side of Figure 11-13.

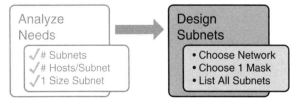

Figure 11-13 *Input to the Design Phase, and Design Questions to Answer*

Choose a Classful Network

In the original design for what we know of today as the Internet, companies used registered *public classful IP networks* when implementing TCP/IP inside the company. By the mid-1990s, an alternative became more popular: *private IP networks*. This section discusses the background behind these two choices, because it impacts the choice of what IP network a company will then subnet and implement in its enterprise internetwork.

Public IP Networks

The original design of the Internet required that any company that connected to the Internet had to use a *registered public IP network*. To do so, the company would complete some paperwork, describing the enterprise's internetwork and the number of hosts existing, plus plans for growth. After submitting the paperwork, the company would receive an assignment of either a Class A, B, or C network.

Public IP networks, and the administrative processes surrounding them, ensure that all the companies that connect to the Internet use unique IP addresses. In particular, after a public IP network is assigned to a company, only that company should use the addresses in that network. That guarantee of uniqueness means that Internet routing can work well, because there are no duplicate public IP addresses.

For example, consider the example shown in Figure 11-14. Company 1 has been assigned public Class A network 1.0.0.0, and company 2 has been assigned public Class A network 2.0.0.0. Per the original intent for public addressing in the Internet, after these public network assignments have been made, no other companies can use addresses in Class A networks 1.0.0.0 and 2.0.0.0.

This original address assignment process ensured unique IP addresses across the entire planet. The idea is much like the fact that your telephone number should be unique in the universe, your postal mailing address should also be unique, and your email address should also be unique. If someone calls you, your phone rings, not someone else's. Similarly, if Company 1 is assigned Class A network 1.0.0.0, and it assigns address 1.1.1.1 to a particular PC, that address should be unique in the universe. A packet sent through the Internet, to destination 1.1.1.1, should only arrive at this one PC inside Company 1, instead of being delivered to some other host.

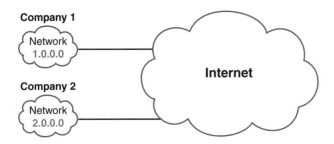

Figure 11-14 *Two Companies with Unique Public IP Networks*

Growth Exhausts the Public IP Address Space

By the early 1990s, the world was running out of public IP networks that could be assigned. During most of the 1990s, the number of hosts newly connected to the Internet was growing at a double-digit pace, *per month*. Companies kept following the rules, asking for public IP networks, and it was clear that the current address-assignment scheme could not continue without some changes. Simply put, the number of Class A, B, and C networks supported by the 32-bit address in IP Version 4 (IPv4) was not enough to support one public classful network per organization, while also providing enough IP addresses in each company.

> **NOTE**   From one perspective, the universe ran out of public IPv4 addresses in early 2011. IANA, which assigns public IPv4 address blocks to the five Internet registries around the globe, assigned the last of the IPv4 address space in early 2011.

The Internet community worked hard during the 1990s to solve this problem, coming up with several solutions, including the following:

- A new version of IP (IPv6), with much larger addresses (128 bit)
- Assigning a subset of a public IP network to each company, instead of an entire public IP network, to reduce waste
- Network Address Translation (NAT), which allows the use of private IP networks

These three solutions matter to real networks today. However, to stay on the topic of subnet design, this chapter focuses on the third option, and in particular, the private IP networks that can be used by an enterprise when also using NAT.

NAT allows multiple companies to use the exact same *private IP network*, using the same IP addresses as other companies, while still connecting to the Internet. For example, Figure 11-15 shows the same two companies connecting to the Internet as in Figure 11-14, but now with both using the same private Class A network 10.0.0.0.

11

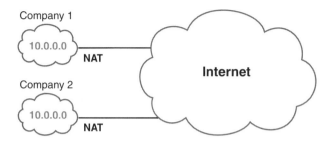

Figure 11-15   *Reusing the Same Private Network 10.0.0.0, with NAT*

Both companies use the same classful IP network (10.0.0.0). Both companies can implement their subnet design internal to their respective enterprise internetworks, without discussing their plans. The two companies can even use the exact same IP addresses inside network 10.0.0.0. And amazingly, at the same time, both companies can even communicate with each other through the Internet.

The technology called *Network Address Translation* (NAT) makes it possible for companies to reuse the same IP networks, as shown in Figure 11-15. NAT does this by translating the IP addresses inside the packets as they go from the enterprise to the Internet, using a small number of public IP addresses to support tens of thousands of private IP addresses.

> **NOTE**   Although this book does not detail how NAT works, or how to configure NAT, if you're interested in more information, refer to books about the Cisco CCNA Routing and Switching certification, which does cover NAT.

Private IP Networks

RFC 1918 defines the set of private IP networks, as listed in Table 11-2. By definition, these private IP networks

■ Will never be assigned to an organization as a public IP network

■ Can be used by organizations that will use NAT when sending packets into the Internet

■ Can also be used by organizations that never need to send packets into the Internet

So, when using NAT—and almost every organization that connects to the Internet uses NAT—the company can simply pick one or more of the private IP networks from the list of reserved private IP network numbers. RFC 1918 defines the list, which is summarized in Table 11-2.

Table 11-2   RFC 1918 Private Address Space

Class of Networks	Private IP Networks	Number of Networks
A	10.0.0.0	1
B	172.16.0.0 through 172.31.0.0	16
C	192.168.0.0 through 192.168.255.0	256

Choose an IP Network During the Design Phase

Today, some organizations use private IP networks along with NAT, and some use public IP networks. Most new enterprise internetworks use private IP addresses throughout the network, along with NAT, as part of the connection to the Internet. Those organizations that already have registered public IP networks—often obtained before the addresses started running short in the early 1990s—can continue to use those public addresses throughout their enterprise networks.

After the choice to use a private IP network has been made, just pick one that has enough IP addresses. You can have a small internetwork and still choose to use private Class A network 10.0.0.0. It might seem wasteful to choose a Class A network, which has more than 16 million IP addresses, especially if you only need a few hundred. However, there's no penalty or problem with using a private network that is too large for your current or future needs.

For the purposes of this book, most examples use private IP network numbers. For the design step to choose a network number, just choose a private Class A, B, or C network from the list of RFC 1918 private networks.

Regardless, from a math and concept perspective, the methods to subnet a public IP network versus a private IP network are the same.

Choose the Mask

If a design engineer followed the topics in this chapter so far, in order, he would know the following:

- The number of subnets required
- The number of hosts/subnet required
- That a choice was made to use only one mask for all subnets, so that all subnets are the same size (same number of hosts/subnet)
- The classful IP network number that will be subnetted

This section completes the design process, at least the parts described in this chapter, by discussing how to choose that one mask to use for all subnets. First, this section examines default masks, used when a network is not subnetted, as a point of comparison. Next, the concept of borrowing host bits to create subnet bits is explored. Finally, this section ends with an example of how to create a subnet mask based on the analysis of the requirements.

Classful IP Networks Before Subnetting

Before an engineer subnets a classful network, the network is a single group of addresses. In other words, the engineer has not yet subdivided the network into many smaller subsets called *subnets*.

In an unsubnetted classful network, the addresses have only two parts: the network part and the host part. When comparing any two addresses in the classful network, you see the following:

- The addresses have the same value in the network part.
- The addresses have different values in the host part.

The actual sizes of the network and host parts of the addresses in a network can be easily predicted, as shown in Figure 11-16.

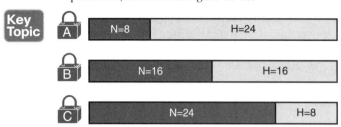

Figure 11-16   *Format of Unsubnetted Class A, B, and C Networks*

In Figure 11-16, N and H represent the number of network and host bits, respectively. Class rules define the number of network octets (1, 2, or 3) for Classes A, B, and C, respectively; the figure shows these values as a number of bits. The number of host octets is 3, 2, or 1, respectively.

Continuing the analysis of classful network before subnetting, the number of addresses in one classful IP network can be calculated with the same $2^H - 2$ formula previously discussed. In particular, the size of an unsubnetted Class A, B, or C network is as follows:

- **Class A:** $2^{24} - 2 = 16,777,214$
- **Class B:** $2^{16} - 2 = 65,534$
- **Class C:** $2^{8} - 2 = 254$

Borrow Host Bits to Create Subnet Bits

To subnet a network, the designer thinks about the network and host parts, as shown in Figure 11-13, and then he adds a third part in the middle: the subnet part. However, the designer cannot change the size of the network part or the size of the entire address (32 bits). To create a subnet part of the address structure, the engineer borrows bits from the host part. Figure 11-17 shows the general idea.

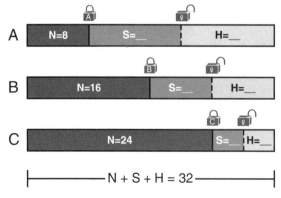

Figure 11-17   *Concept of Borrowing Host Bits*

Figure 11-17 shows a rectangle that represents the subnet mask. N, representing the number of network bits, remains locked at 8, 16, or 24, depending on the class. Conceptually, the designer moves a (dashed) dividing line into the host field, with subnet bits (S) between the network and host parts, and the remaining host bits (H) on the right. The three parts must add up to 32, because IPv4 addresses consist of 32 bits.

Choose Enough Subnet and Host Bits

The design process requires a choice of where to place the dashed line shown in Figure 11-14. But what is the right choice? How many subnet and host bits should the designer choose? The answers hinge on the requirements gathered in the early stages of the planning process:

- Number of subnets required
- Number of hosts/subnet

The bits in the subnet part create a way to uniquely number the different subnets that the design engineer wants to create. With 1 subnet bit, you can number 2^1 (or two) subnets. With 2 bits, 2^2 (or four) subnets, with 3 bits, 2^3 (or eight) subnets, and so on. The number of subnet bits must be large enough to uniquely number all the subnets, as determined during the planning process.

At the same time, the remaining number of host bits must also be large enough to number the host IP addresses in the largest subnet. Remember, in this chapter, we assume the use of a single mask for all subnets. This single mask must support both the required number of subnets and the required number of hosts in the largest subnet. Figure 11-18 shows the concept.

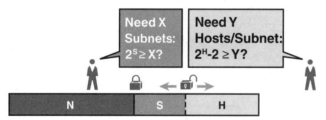

Figure 11-18   *Borrowing Enough Subnet and Host Bits*

Figure 11-18 shows the idea of the designer choosing a number of subnet (S) and host (H) bits and then checking the math. 2^S must be more than the number of required subnets, or the mask will not supply enough subnets in this IP network. Also, $2^H - 2$ must be more than the required number of hosts/subnet.

> **NOTE**   The idea of calculating the number of subnets as 2^S applies only in cases where a single mask is used for all subnets of a single classful network, as is being assumed in this chapter.

To effectively design masks, or to interpret masks that were chosen by someone else, you need a good working memory of the powers of 2. Table 11-3 lists the powers of 2 up through 2^{12}, along with a column with $2^H - 2$, for perspective when calculating the number of hosts/subnet. Appendix I, "Numeric Reference Tables," lists a table with powers of 2 up through 2^{24} for your reference.

11

Table 11-3   Powers of 2 Reference for Designing Masks

Number of Bits	2^x	$2^x - 2$
1	2	0
2	4	2
3	8	6
4	16	14
5	32	30
6	64	62
7	128	126
8	256	254
9	512	510
10	1024	1022
11	2048	2046
12	4096	4094

Design Example: 172.16.0.0, 200 Subnets, 200 Hosts

To help make sense of the theoretical discussion so far, consider an example that focuses on the design choice for the subnet mask. In this case, the planning and design choices so far tell us the following:

- Use a single mask for all subnets.
- Plan for 200 subnets.
- Plan for 200 host IP addresses per subnet.
- Use private Class B network 172.16.0.0.

To choose the mask, you would ask this question:

How many subnet (S) bits do I need to number 200 subnets?

From Table 11-3, you can see that S = 7 is not large enough (2^7 = 128), but S = 8 is enough (2^8 = 256). So, you need *at least* 8 subnet bits.

Next, you would ask a similar question, based on the number of hosts per subnet:

How many host (H) bits do I need to number 200 hosts per subnet?

The math is basically the same, but the formula subtracts 2 when counting the number of hosts/subnet. From Table 11-3, you can see that H = 7 is not large enough ($2^7 - 2$ = 126), but H = 8 is enough ($2^8 - 2$ = 254).

Only one possible mask meets all the requirements in this case. First, the number of network bits (N) must be 16, because the design uses a Class B network. The requirements tell us that the mask needs at least 8 subnet bits and at least 8 host bits. The mask only has 32 bits in it; Figure 11-19 shows the resulting mask.

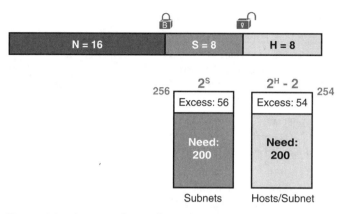

Figure 11-19   *Sample Mask Choice: N = 16, S = 8, H = 8*

Masks and Mask Formats

Although engineers think about IP addresses in three parts when making design choices (network, subnet, and host), the subnet mask gives engineers a way to communicate those design choices to all the devices in the subnet.

The subnet mask is a 32-bit binary number with a number of binary 1s on the left and with binary 0s on the right. By definition, the number of binary 0s equals the number of host bits—in fact, that is exactly how the mask communicates the idea of the size of the host part of the addresses in a subnet. The beginning bits in the mask equal binary 1, with those bit positions representing the combined network and subnet parts of the addresses in the subnet.

Because the network part always comes first, then the subnet part, and then the host part, the subnet mask, in binary form, cannot have interleaved 1s and 0s. Each subnet mask has one unbroken string of binary 1s on the left, with the rest of the bits as binary 0s.

After you choose the classful network and the number of subnet and host bits in a subnet, creating the binary subnet mask is easy. Just write down N 1s, S 1s, and then H 0s (assuming that N, S, and H represent the number of network, subnet, and host bits). Figure 11-20 shows the mask based on the previous example, which subnets a Class B network by creating 8 subnet bits, leaving 8 host bits.

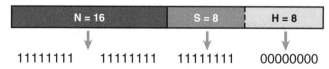

11

Figure 11-20   *Creating the Subnet Mask – Binary – Class B Network*

In addition to the binary mask shown in Figure 11-20, masks can also be written in two other formats: the familiar dotted-decimal notation (DDN) seen in IP addresses and the even briefer *prefix* notation. Chapter 13 discusses these formats and how to convert between them.

Build a List of All Subnets

This final task of the subnet design step determines the actual subnets that can be used, based on all the earlier choices. The earlier design work determined the Class A, B, or C network to use, and the (one) subnet mask to use that supplies enough subnets and enough host IP addresses per subnet. But what are those subnets? How do you identify or describe a subnet? This section answers these questions.

A subnet consists of a group of consecutive numbers. Most of these numbers can be used as IP addresses by hosts. However, each subnet reserves the first and last numbers in the group, and these two numbers cannot be used as IP addresses. In particular, each subnet contains the following:

- **Subnet number:** Also called the *subnet ID* or *subnet address*, this number identifies the subnet. It is the numerically smallest number in the subnet. It cannot be used as an IP address by a host.
- **Subnet broadcast:** Also called the *subnet broadcast address* or *directed broadcast address*, this is the last (numerically highest) number in the subnet. It also cannot be used as an IP address by a host.
- **IP addresses:** All the numbers between the subnet ID and the subnet broadcast address can be used as a host IP address.

For example, consider the earlier case in which the design results were as follows:

Network: 172.16.0.0 (Class B)

Mask: 255.255.255.0 (for all subnets)

With some math, the facts about each subnet that exists in this Class B network can be calculated. In this case, Table 11-4 shows the first ten such subnets. It then skips many subnets and shows the last two (numerically largest) subnets.

Table 11-4   First Ten Subnets, Plus the Last Two, from 172.16.0.0, 255.255.255.0

Subnet Number	IP Addresses	Broadcast Address
172.16.0.0	172.16.0.1 – 172.16.0.254	172.16.0.255
172.16.1.0	172.16.1.1 – 172.16.1.254	172.16.1.255
172.16.2.0	172.16.2.1 – 172.16.2.254	172.16.2.255
172.16.3.0	172.16.3.1 – 172.16.3.254	172.16.3.255
172.16.4.0	172.16.4.1 – 172.16.4.254	172.16.4.255
172.16.5.0	172.16.5.1 – 172.16.5.254	172.16.5.255
172.16.6.0	172.16.6.1 – 172.16.6.254	172.16.6.255
172.16.7.0	172.16.7.1 – 172.16.7.254	172.16.7.255
172.16.8.0	172.16.8.1 – 172.16.8.254	172.16.8.255
172.16.9.0	172.16.9.1 – 172.16.9.254	172.16.9.255
Skipping many…		
172.16.254.0	172.16.254.1 – 172.16.254.254	172.16.254.255
172.16.255.0	172.16.255.1 – 172.16.255.254	172.16.255.255

Plan the Implementation

The next step, planning the implementation, is the last step before actually configuring the devices to create a subnet. You first need to choose where to use each subnet. For example, at a branch office in a particular city, which subnet from the subnet planning chart (Table 11-4) should be used for each VLAN at that site? Also, for any interfaces that require static IP addresses, which addresses should be used in each case? Finally, what range of IP addresses from inside each subnet should be configured in the DHCP server, to be dynamically leased to hosts for use as their IP address? Figure 11-21 summarizes the list of implementation planning tasks.

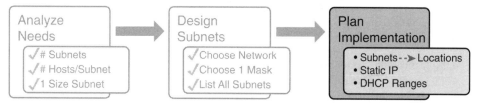

Figure 11-21   *Facts Supplied to the Plan Implementation Step*

Assign Subnets to Different Locations

The job is simple: Look at your network diagram, identify each location that needs a subnet, and pick one from the table you made of all the possible subnets. Then, track it so that you know which ones you use, and where, using a spreadsheet or some other purpose-built subnet-planning tool. That's it! Figure 11-22 shows a completed design example using Table 11-4, which happens to match the initial design example shown way back in Figure 11-1.

Although this design could have used any five subnets from Table 11-4, in real networks, engineers usually give more thought to some strategy for assigning subnets. For example, you might assign all LAN subnets lower numbers and WAN subnets higher numbers. Or you might slice off large ranges of subnets for different divisions of the company. Or you might follow that same strategy, but ignore organizational divisions in the company, paying more attention to geographies.

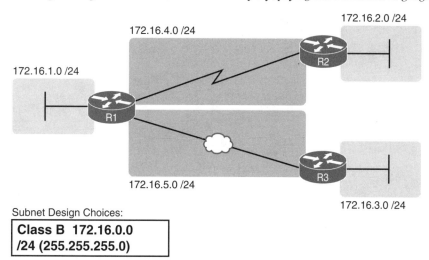

Figure 11-22   *Example of Subnets Assigned to Different Locations*

Choose Static and Dynamic Ranges per Subnet

Devices receive their IP address and mask assignment in one of two ways: dynamically by using Dynamic Host Control Protocol (DHCP) or statically through configuration. For DHCP to work, you must tell the DHCP server the subnets for which it must assign IP addresses. In addition, that configuration limits the DHCP server to only a subset of the addresses in the subnet. For static addresses, you simply configure the device to tell it what IP address and mask to use.

To keep things as simple as possible, most shops use a strategy to separate the static IP addresses on one end of each subnet, and the DHCP-assigned dynamic addresses on the other. It does not really matter whether the static addresses sit on the low end of the range of addresses or the high end.

For example, imagine that an engineer decides that, for the LAN subnets in Figure 11-22, the DHCP pool comes from the high end of the range—namely, addresses that end in .101 through .254. (The address that ends in .255 is, of course, reserved.) The engineer also assigns static addresses from the lower end, with addresses ending in .1 through .100. Figure 11-23 shows the idea.

Figure 11-23 shows all three routers with statically assigned IP addresses that end in .1. The only other static IP address in the figure is assigned to the server on the left, with address 172.16.1.11 (abbreviated simply as .11 in the figure).

On the right, each LAN has two PCs that use DHCP to dynamically lease their IP addresses. DHCP servers often begin by leasing the addresses at the bottom of the range, so in each LAN the hosts have leased addresses that end in .101 and .102, which are at the low end of the range chosen by design.

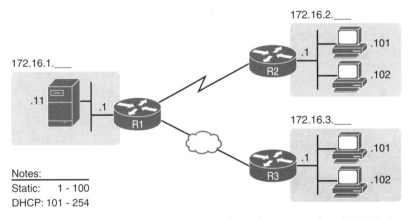

Figure 11-23 *Using Static Assignment from the Low End and DHCP from the High End*

Exam Preparation Tasks

Review All the Key Topics

Review the most important topics from this chapter, noted with the Key Topic icon. Table 11-5 lists these key topics and where each is discussed.

Table 11-5 Key Topics for Chapter 11

Key Topic Element	Description	Page Number
List	Key facts about subnets	324
Figure 11-5	Conceptual figure of subnets with a Layer 3 switch	326
List	Rules about what places in a network topology need a subnet	326
Figure 11-10	Locations of the network, subnet, and host parts of an IPv4 address	330
List	Features that extended the life of IPv4	333
Figure 11-16	Formats of Class A, B, and C addresses when not subnetted	336
Figure 11-17	Formats of Class A, B, and C addresses when subnetted	336
Figure 11-18	General logic when choosing the size of the subnet and host parts of addresses in a subnet	337
List	Items that together define a subnet	340

Complete the Tables and Lists from Memory

Print a copy of Appendix C, "Memory Tables," or at least the section for this chapter, and complete the tables and lists from memory. Appendix D, "Memory Tables Answer Key," includes completed tables and lists for you to check your work.

Definitions of Key Terms

After your first reading of the chapter, try to define these key terms, but do not be concerned about getting them all correct at that time. Chapter 24, "Final Review," directs you in how to use these terms for late-stage preparation for the exam.

subnet, network, classful network, network part, subnet part, host part, public IP network, private IP network, subnet mask

11

This chapter covers the following exam topics:

2.0. Basic Data Center Networking Concepts

CHAPTER 12

Analyzing Classful IPv4 Networks

When operating a network, you often start investigating a problem based on an IP address and mask. Based on the IP address alone, you should be able to determine several facts about the Class A, B, or C network in which the IP address resides. These facts can be useful when troubleshooting some networking problems.

This chapter lists the key facts about classful IP networks and explains how to discover these facts. Following that, this chapter lists some practice problems. Before moving to the next chapter, you should practice until you can consistently determine all these facts, quickly and confidently, based on an IP address.

> **NOTE** As promised in the Introduction's section, "For Those Studying Routing & Switching," this chapter covers the same content as the *ICND1 100-101 Official Cert Guide*'s Chapter 12. Feel free to skim or skip this chapter if you have already read that chapter in the other book.

"Do I Know This Already?" Quiz

Use the "Do I Know This Already?" quiz to help decide whether you might want to skim this chapter, or a major section, moving more quickly to the "Exam Preparation Tasks" section near the end of the chapter. Table 12-1 lists the major headings in this chapter and their corresponding "Do I Know This Already?" quiz questions. For thorough explanations, see Appendix A, "Answers to the 'Do I Know This Already?' Quizzes."

Table 12-1 "Do I Know This Already?" Foundation Topics Section-to-Question Mapping

Foundation Topics Section	Questions
Classful Network Concepts	1–6

1. Which of the following are not valid Class A network IDs? (Choose two answers.)

   a. 1.0.0.0

   b. 130.0.0.0

   c. 127.0.0.0

   d. 9.0.0.0

2. Which of the following are not valid Class B network IDs?

   a. 130.0.0.0.

   b. 191.255.0.0.

   c. 128.0.0.0.

   d. 150.255.0.0.

   e. All are valid Class B network IDs.

3. Which of the following are true about IP address 172.16.99.45's IP network? (Select two answers.)

   a. The network ID is 172.0.0.0.

   b. The network is a Class B network.

   c. The default mask for the network is 255.255.255.0.

   d. The number of host bits in the unsubnetted network is 16.

4. Which of the following are true about IP address 192.168.6.7's IP network? (Select two answers.)

   a. The network ID is 192.168.6.0.

   b. The network is a Class B network.

   c. The default mask for the network is 255.255.255.0.

   d. The number of host bits in the unsubnetted network is 16.

5. Which of the following is a network broadcast address?

   a. 10.1.255.255

   b. 192.168.255.1

   c. 224.1.1.255

   d. 172.30.255.255

6. Which of the following is a Class A, B, or C network ID?

   a. 10.1.0.0

   b. 192.168.1.0

   c. 127.0.0.0

   d. 172.20.0.1

Foundation Topics

Classful Network Concepts

Imagine you have a job interview for your first IT job. As part of the interview, you're given an IPv4 address and mask: 10.4.5.99, 255.255.255.0. What can you tell the interviewer about the classful network (in this case, the Class A network) in which the IP address resides?

This section, the first of two major sections in this chapter, reviews the concepts of *classful IP networks* (in other words, Class A, B, and C networks). In particular, this chapter examines how to begin with a single IP address and then determine the following facts:

- Class (A, B, or C)
- Default mask
- Number of network octets/bits
- Number of host octets/bits
- Number of host addresses in the network
- Network ID
- Network broadcast address
- First and last usable address in the network

IPv4 Network Classes and Related Facts

IP version 4 (IPv4) defines five address classes. Three of the classes, Classes A, B, and C, consist of unicast IP addresses. Unicast addresses identify a single host or interface so that the address uniquely identifies the device. Class D addresses serve as multicast addresses, so that one packet sent to a Class D multicast IPv4 address can actually be delivered to multiple hosts. Finally, Class E addresses are experimental.

The class can be identified based on the value of the first octet of the address, as shown in Table 12-2.

Table 12-2   IPv4 Address Classes Based on First Octet Values

Class	First Octet Values	Purpose
A	1–126	Unicast (large networks)
B	128–191	Unicast (medium-sized networks)
C	192–223	Unicast (small networks)
D	224–239	Multicast
E	240–255	Experimental

The exam focuses on the unicast classes (A, B, and C) rather than Classes D and E. After you identify the class as either A, B, or C, many other related facts can be derived just through memorization. Table 12-3 lists that information for reference and later study; each of these concepts is described in this chapter.

Table 12-3   Key Facts for Classes A, B, and C

	Class A	Class B	Class C
First octet range	1 – 126	128 – 191	192 – 223
Valid network numbers	1.0.0.0 – 126.0.0.0	128.0.0.0 – 191.255.0.0	192.0.0.0 – 223.255.255.0
Total networks	$2^7 - 2 = 126$	$2^{14} = 16,384$	$2^{21} = 2,097,152$
Hosts per network	$2^{24} - 2$	$2^{16} - 2$	$2^8 - 2$
Octets (bits) in network part	1 (8)	2 (16)	3 (24)
Octets (bits) in host part	3 (24)	2 (16)	1 (8)
Default mask	255.0.0.0	255.255.0.0	255.255.255.0

Actual Class A, B, and C Networks

Table 12-3 lists the range of Class A, B, and C network numbers. However, some key points can be lost just referencing a table of information. This section examines the Class A, B, and C network numbers, focusing on the more important points and the exceptions and unusual cases.

First, the number of networks from each class significantly differs. Only 126 Class A networks exist: network 1.0.0.0, 2.0.0.0, 3.0.0.0, and so on, up through network 126.0.0.0. However, 16,384 Class B networks exist, with over 2 million Class C networks.

Next, note that the size of networks from each class also significantly differs. Each Class A network is relatively large—over 16 million host IP addresses per network—so these networks were originally intended to be used by the largest companies and organizations. Class B networks are smaller, with over 65,000 hosts per network. Finally, Class C networks, intended for small organizations, have 254 hosts in each network. Figure 12-1 summarizes these facts.

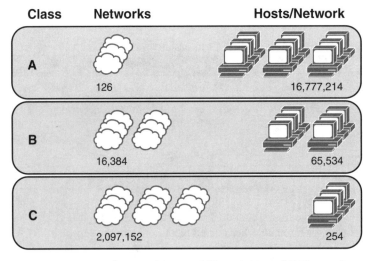

Figure 12-1   *Numbers and Sizes of Class A, B, and C Networks*

Address Formats

In some cases, an engineer might need to think about a Class A, B, or C network as if the network has not been subdivided through the subnetting process. In such a case, the addresses in the classful network have a structure with two parts: the *network part* (sometimes called the *prefix*) and the *host part*. Then, comparing any two IP addresses in one network, the following observations can be made:

The addresses in the same network have the same values in the network part.

The addresses in the same network have different values in the host part.

For example, in Class A network 10.0.0.0, by definition, the network part consists of the first octet. As a result, all addresses have an equal value in the network part, namely a 10 in the first octet. If you then compare any two addresses in the network, the addresses have a different value in the last three octets (the host octets). For example, IP addresses 10.1.1.1 and 10.1.1.2 have the same value (10) in the network part, but different values in the host part.

Figure 12-2 shows the format and sizes (in number of bits) of the network and host parts of IP addresses in Class A, B, and C networks, before any subnetting has been applied.

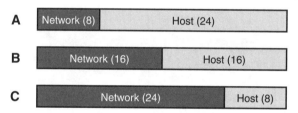

Figure 12-2 *Sizes (Bits) of the Network and Host Parts of Unsubnetted Classful Networks*

Default Masks

Although we humans can easily understand the concepts behind Figure 12-2, computers prefer numbers. To communicate those same ideas to computers, each network class has an associated *default mask* that defines the size of the network and host parts of an unsubnetted Class A, B, and C network. To do so, the mask lists binary 1s for the bits considered to be in the network part and binary 0s for the bits considered to be in the host part.

For example, Class A network 10.0.0.0 has a network part of the first single octet (8 bits) and a host part of the last three octets (24 bits). As a result, the Class A default mask is 255.0.0.0, which in binary is

11111111 00000000 00000000 00000000

Figure 12-3 shows default masks for each network class, both in binary and dotted-decimal format.

12

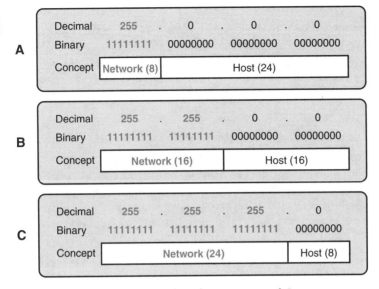

Figure 12-3 *Default Masks for Classes A, B, and C*

NOTE Decimal 255 converts to the binary value 11111111. Decimal 0, converted to 8-bit binary, is 00000000. See Appendix I, "Numeric Reference Tables," for a conversion table.

Number of Hosts per Network

Calculating the number of hosts per network requires some basic binary math. First, consider a case where you have a single binary digit. How many unique values are there? There are, of course, two values: 0 and 1. With 2 bits, you can make four combinations: 00, 01, 10, and 11. As it turns out, the total combination of unique values you can make with N bits is 2^N.

Host addresses—the IP addresses assigned to hosts—must be unique. The host bits exist for the purpose of giving each host a unique IP address by virtue of having a different value in the host part of the addresses. So, with H host bits, 2^H unique combinations exist.

However, the number of hosts in a network is not 2^H; instead, it is $2^H - 2$. Each network reserves two numbers that would have otherwise been useful as host addresses, but have instead been reserved for special use: one for the network ID and one for the network broadcast address. As a result, the formula to calculate the number of host addresses per Class A, B, or C network is

$2^H - 2$

where H is the number of host bits.

Deriving the Network ID and Related Numbers

Each classful network has four key numbers that describe the network. You can derive these four numbers if you start with just one IP address in the network. The numbers are as follows:

- Network number
- First (numerically lowest) usable address
- Last (numerically highest) usable address
- Network broadcast address

First, consider both the network number and first usable IP address. The *network number*, also called the *network ID* or *network address*, identifies the network. By definition, the network number is the numerically lowest number in the network. However, to prevent any ambiguity, the people who made up IP addressing added the restriction that the network number cannot be assigned as an IP address. So, the lowest number in the network is the network ID. Then, the first (numerically lowest) host IP address is *one larger than* the network number.

Next, consider the network broadcast address along with the last (numerically highest) usable IP address. The TCP/IP RFCs define a network broadcast address as a special address in each network. This broadcast address could be used as the destination address in a packet, and the routers would forward a copy of that one packet to all hosts in that classful network. Numerically, a network broadcast address is always the highest (last) number in the network. As a result, the highest (last) number usable as an IP address is the address that is simply *one less than* the network broadcast address.

Simply put, if you can find the network number and network broadcast address, finding the first and last usable IP addresses in the network is easy. For the exam, you should be able to find all four values with ease; the process is as follows:

Step 1.   Determine the class (A, B, or C) based on the first octet.

Step 2.   Mentally divide the network and host octets based on the class.

Step 3.   To find the network number, change the IP address's host octets to 0.

Step 4.   To find the first address, add 1 to the fourth octet of the network ID.

Step 5.   To find the broadcast address, change the network ID's host octets to 255.

Step 6.   To find the last address, subtract 1 from the fourth octet of the network broadcast address.

12

The written process actually looks harder than it is. Figure 12-4 shows an example of the process, using Class A IP address 10.17.18.21, with the circled numbers matching the process.

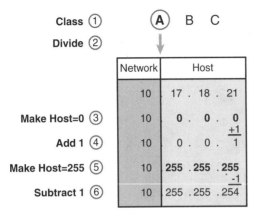

Figure 12-4   *Example of Deriving the Network ID and Other Values from 10.17.18.21*

Figure 12-4 shows the identification of the class as Class A (Step 1) and the number of network/host octets as 1 and 3, respectively. So, to find the network ID at Step 3, the figure copies only the first octet, setting the last three (host) octets to 0. At Step 4, just copy the network ID and add 1 to the fourth octet. Similarly, to find the broadcast address at Step 5, copy the network octets, but set the host octets to 255. Then, at Step 6, subtract 1 from the fourth octet to find the last (numerically highest) usable IP address.

Just to show an alternative example, consider IP address 172.16.8.9. Figure 12-5 shows the process applied to this IP address.

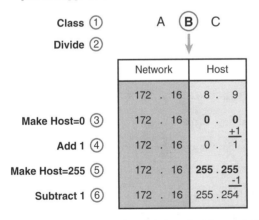

Figure 12-5   *Example Deriving the Network ID and Other Values from 172.16.8.9*

Figure 12-5 shows the identification of the class as Class B (Step 1) and the number of network/host octets as 2 and 2, respectively. So, to find the network ID at Step 3, the figure copies only the first two octets, setting the last two (host) octets to 0. Similarly, Step 5 shows the same action, but with the last two (host) octets being set to 255.

Unusual Network IDs and Network Broadcast Addresses

Some of the more unusual numbers in and around the Class A, B, and C network ranges can cause some confusion. This section lists some examples of numbers that cause many people to make the wrong assumptions about the meaning of a number.

For Class A, the first odd fact is that the range of values in the first octet omits the numbers 0 and 127. As it turns out, what would be Class A network 0.0.0.0 was originally reserved for some broadcasting requirements, so all addresses that begin with 0 in the first octet are reserved. What would be Class A network 127.0.0.0 is still reserved because of a special address used in software testing, called the loopback address (127.0.0.1).

For Class B (and C), some of the network numbers can look odd, particularly if you fall into a habit of thinking that 0s at the end means the number is a network ID, and 255s at the end means it's a network broadcast address. First, Class B network numbers range from 128.0.0.0 to 191.255.0.0, for a total of 2^{14} networks. However, even the very first (lowest number) Class B network number (128.0.0.0) looks a little like a Class A network number, because it ends with three 0s. However, the first octet is 128, making it a Class B network with a two-octet network part (128.0).

For another Class B example, the high end of the Class B range also might look strange at first glance (191.255.0.0), but this is indeed the numerically highest of the valid Class B network numbers. This network's broadcast address, 191.255.255.255, might look a little like a Class A broadcast address because of the three 255s at the end, but it is indeed the broadcast address of a Class B network.

Other valid Class B network IDs that look unusual include 130.0.0.0, 150.0.0.0, 155.255.0.0, and 190.0.0.0. All of these follow the convention of a value from 128 to 191 in the first octet, a value from 0 to 255 in the second octet, and two more 0s, so they are indeed valid Class B network IDs.

Class C networks follow the same general rules as Class B, but with the first three octets defining the network. The network numbers range from 192.0.0.0 to 223.255.255.0, with all addresses in a single network sharing the same value in the first three octets.

Similar to Class B networks, some of the valid Class C network numbers do look strange. For example, Class C network 192.0.0.0 looks a little like a Class A network because of the last three octets being 0, but because it is a Class C network, it consists of all addresses that begin with three octets equal to 192.0.0. Similarly, Class C network 223.255.255.0, another valid Class C network, consists of all addresses that begin with 223.255.255.

Other valid Class C network IDs that look unusual include 200.0.0.0, 220.0.0.0, 205.255.255.0, and 199.255.255.0. All of these follow the convention of a value from 192 to 223 in the first octet, a value from 0 to 255 in both the second and third octets, and a 0 in the fourth octet.

Practice with Classful Networks

As with all areas of IP addressing and subnetting, you need to practice to be ready for the exams. Before the exam, you should master the concepts and processes in this chapter and be able to get the right answer every time—with speed. I cannot overemphasize the importance of mastering IP addressing and subnetting for the exams: Know the topics, and know them well.

However, you do not need to completely master everything in this chapter right now. You should practice some now to make sure you understand the processes, but you can use your notes, use this book, or whatever. After you practice enough to confirm you can get the right answers using any help available, you understand the topics in this chapter well enough to move to the next chapter.

Then, before the exam, practice until you master the topics in this chapter and can move pretty fast. Table 12-4 summarizes the key concepts and suggestions for this two-phase approach.

Table 12-4   Keep-Reading and Take-Exam Goals for This Chapter's Topics

Time Frame	After Reading This Chapter	Before Taking the Exam
Focus On...	Learning how	Being correct and fast
Tools Allowed	All	Your brain and a notepad
Goal: Accuracy	90% correct	100% correct
Goal: Speed	Any speed	10 seconds

Practice Deriving Key Facts Based on an IP Address

Practice finding the various facts that can be derived from an IP address, as discussed throughout this chapter. To do so, complete Table 12-5.

Table 12-5   Practice Problems: Find the Network ID and Network Broadcast

	IP Address	Class	Number of Network Octets	Number of Host Octets	Network ID	Network Broadcast Address
1	1.1.1.1					
2	128.1.6.5					
3	200.1.2.3					
4	192.192.1.1					
5	126.5.4.3					
6	200.1.9.8					
7	192.0.0.1					
8	191.255.1.47					
9	223.223.0.1					

The answers are listed in the section "Answers to Earlier Practice Problems," later in this chapter.

Practice Remembering the Details of Address Classes

Tables 12-2 and 12-3, shown earlier in this chapter, summarized some key information about IPv4 address classes. Tables 12-6 and 12-7 show sparse versions of these same tables. To practice recalling those key facts, particularly the range of values in the first octet that identifies the address class, complete these tables. Then, refer to Tables 12-2 and 12-3 to check your answers. Repeat this process until you can recall all the information in the tables.

Table 12-6   Sparse Study Table Version of Table 12-2

Class	First Octet Values	Purpose
A		
B		
C		
D		
E		

Table 12-7   Sparse Study Table Version of Table 12-3

	Class A	Class B	Class C
First octet range			
Valid network numbers			
Total networks			
Hosts per network			
Octets (bits) in network part			
Octets (bits) in host part			
Default mask			

Additional Practice

For additional practice with classful networks, consider the following:

■ Appendix E, "Practice for Chapter 12: Analyzing Classful IPv4 Networks," has additional practice problems. This appendix also includes explanations about how to find the answer for each problem.

■ Create your own problems. You can randomly choose any IP address and try to find the same information asked for by the practice problems in this section. Then, to check your work, use any subnet calculator. Most subnet calculators list the class and network ID.

12

Exam Preparation Tasks

Review All Key Topics

Review the most important topics from this chapter, noted with the Key Topic icon. Table 12-8 lists these key topics and where each is discussed.

Table 12-8   Key Topics for Chapter 12

Key Topic Elements	Description	Page Number
Table 12-2	Address classes	347
Table 12-3	Key facts about Class A, B, and C networks	348
List	Comparisons of network and host parts of addresses in the same classful network	349
Figure 12-3	Default masks	350
Paragraph	Function to calculate the number of hosts per network	350
List	Steps to find information about a classful network	351

Complete the Tables and Lists from Memory

Print a copy of Appendix C, "Memory Tables," or at least the section for this chapter, and complete the tables and lists from memory. Appendix D, "Memory Tables Answer Key," includes completed tables and lists for you to check your work.

Definitions of Key Terms

After your first reading of the chapter, try to define these key terms, but do not be concerned about getting them all correct at that time. Chapter 24, "Final Review," directs you in how to use these terms for late-stage preparation for the exam.

network, classful network, network number, network ID, network address, network broadcast address, first address, last address, network part, host part, default mask

Practice

If you have not done so already, practice discovering the details of a classful network as discussed in this chapter. Refer to the earlier section "Practice with Classful Networks" for suggestions.

Answers to Earlier Practice Problems

Table 12-5, shown earlier, listed several practice problems. Table 12-9 lists the answers.

Table 12-9 Practice Problems: Find the Network ID and Network Broadcast

	IP Address	Class	Number of Network Octets	Number of Host Octets	Network ID	Network Broadcast
1	1.1.1.1	A	1	3	1.0.0.0	1.255.255.255
2	128.1.6.5	B	2	2	128.1.0.0	128.1.255.255
3	200.1.2.3	C	3	1	200.1.2.0	200.1.2.255
4	192.192.1.1	C	3	1	192.192.1.0	192.192.1.255
5	126.5.4.3	A	1	3	126.0.0.0	126.255.255.255
6	200.1.9.8	C	3	1	200.1.9.0	200.1.9.255
7	192.0.0.1	C	3	1	192.0.0.0	192.0.0.255
8	191.255.1.47	B	2	2	191.255.0.0	191.255.255.255
9	223.223.0.1	C	3	1	223.223.0.0	223.223.0.255

The class, number of network octets, and number of host octets all require you to look at the first octet of the IP address to determine the class. If a value is between 1 and 126, inclusive, the address is a Class A address, with one network octet and three host octets. If a value is between 128 and 191, inclusive, the address is a Class B address, with two network and two host octets. If a value is between 192 and 223, inclusive, it is a Class C address, with three network octets and one host octet.

The last two columns can be found based on Table 12-3, specifically the number of network and host octets along with the IP address. To find the network ID, copy the IP address, but change the host octets to 0. Similarly, to find the network broadcast address, copy the IP address, but change the host octets to 255.

The last three problems can be confusing, and were included on purpose so that you could see an example of these unusual cases, as follows.

Answers to Practice Problem 7 (from Table 12-5)

Consider IP address 192.0.0.1. First, 192 is on the lower edge of the first octet range for Class C; as such, this address has three network octets and one host octet. To find the network ID, copy the address, but change the single host octet (the fourth octet) to 0, for a network ID of 192.0.0.0. It looks strange, but it is indeed the network ID.

The network broadcast address choice for problem 7 can also look strange. To find the broadcast address, copy the IP address (192.0.0.1) but change the last octet (the only host octet) to 255, for a broadcast address of 192.0.0.255. In particular, if you decide that the broadcast should be 192.255.255.255, you might have fallen into a trap of logic, like "Change all 0s in the network ID to 255s," which is not the correct logic. Instead, change all host octets in the IP address (or network ID) to 255s.

12

Answers to Practice Problem 8 (from Table 12-5)

The first octet of problem 8 (191.255.1.47) sits on the upper edge of the Class B range for the first octet (128–191). As such, to find the network ID, change the last two octets (host octets) to 0, for a network ID of 191.255.0.0. This value sometimes gives people problems, because they are used to thinking that 255 somehow means the number is a broadcast address.

The broadcast address, found by changing the two host octets to 255, means that the broadcast address is 191.255.255.255. It looks more like a broadcast address for a Class A network, but it is actually the broadcast address for Class B network 191.255.0.0.

Answers to Practice Problem 9 (from Table 12-5)

The last problem with IP address 223.223.0.1 is that it's near the high end of the Class C range. As a result, only the last (host) octet is changed to 0 to form the network ID 223.223.0.0. It looks a little like a Class B network number at first glance, because it ends in two octets of 0. However, it is indeed a Class C network ID (based on the value in the first octet).

This chapter covers the following exam topics:

2.0. Basic data center networking concepts

2.1. Compare and contrast the OSI and the TCP/IP models

CHAPTER 13

Analyzing Subnet Masks

The subnet mask used in one or many subnets in an IP internetwork says a lot about the intent of the subnet design. First, the mask divides addresses into two parts: *prefix* and *host*, with the host part defining the size of the subnet. Then, the class (A, B, or C) further divides the structure of addresses in a subnet, breaking the prefix part into the *network* and *subnet* parts. The subnet part defines the number of subnets that could exist inside one classful IP network, assuming that one mask is used throughout the classful network.

The subnet mask holds the key to understanding several important subnetting design points. However, to analyze a subnet mask, you first need some basic math skills with masks. The math converts masks between the three different formats used to represent a mask:

Binary

Dotted-decimal notation (DDN)

Prefix (also called CIDR)

This chapter has two major sections. The first focuses totally on the mask formats and the math used to convert between the three formats. The second section explains how to take an IP address and its subnet mask and analyze those values. In particular, it shows how to determine the three-part format of the IPv4 address and describes the facts about the subnetting design that are implied by the mask.

Note As promised in the Introduction's section "For Those Studying Routing & Switching," this chapter covers the same content as Chapter 13 in the *ICND1 100-101 Official Cert Guide*. Feel free to skim or skip this chapter if you have already read that chapter in the other book.

"Do I Know This Already?" Quiz

Use the "Do I Know This Already?" quiz to help decide whether you might want to skim this chapter, or a major section, moving more quickly to the "Exam Preparation Tasks" section near the end of the chapter. Table 13-1 lists the major headings in this chapter and their corresponding "Do I Know This Already?" quiz questions. For thorough explanations, see Appendix A, "Answers to the 'Do I Know This Already?' Quizzes."

Table 13-1 "Do I Know This Already?" Foundation Topics Section-to-Question Mapping

Foundation Topics Section	Questions
Subnet Mask Conversion	1–4
Identifying Subnet Design Choices Using Masks	5–9

1. Which of the following answers lists the prefix (CIDR) format equivalent of 255.255.254.0?

   a. /19

   b. /20

   c. /23

   d. /24

   e. /25

2. Which of the following answers lists the prefix (CIDR) format equivalent of 255.255.255.240?

   a. /26

   b. /28

   c. /27

   d. /30

   e. /29

3. Which of the following answers lists the dotted-decimal notation (DDN) equivalent of /24?

   a. 255.255.240.0

   b. 255.255.252.0

   c. 255.255.255.0

   d. 255.255.255.192

   e. 255.255.255.240

4. Which of the following answers lists the dotted-decimal notation (DDN) equivalent of /30?

   a. 255.255.255.192

   b. 255.255.255.252

   c. 255.255.255.240

   d. 255.255.254.0

   e. 255.255.255.0

5. While working at the help desk, you receive a call and learn a user's PC IP address and mask (10.55.66.77, mask 255.255.255.0). When thinking about this using classful logic, you determine the number of network (N), subnet (S), and host (H) bits. Which of the following is true in this case?

   a. N=12

   b. S=12

   c. H=8

   d. S=8

   e. N=24

6. While working at the help desk, you receive a call and learn a user's PC IP address and mask (192.168.9.1/27). When thinking about this using classful logic, you determine the number of network (N), subnet (S), and host (H) bits. Which of the following is true in this case?

   a. N=24

   b. S=24

   c. H=8

   d. H=7

7. An engineer is thinking about the following IP address and mask using classless IP addressing logic: 10.55.66.77, 255.255.255.0. Which of the following statements are true when using classless addressing logic? (Choose two.)

   a. The network part's size is 8 bits.

   b. The prefix length is 24 bits.

   c. The prefix length is 16 bits.

   d. The host part's size is 8 bits.

8. Which of the following statements is true about classless IP addressing?

   a. It uses a 128-bit IP address.

   b. It applies only to Class A and B networks.

   c. It separates IP addresses into network, subnet, and host parts.

   d. It ignores Class A, B, and C network rules.

9. Which of the following masks, when used as the only mask within a Class B network, would supply enough subnet bits to support 100 subnets? (Choose two.)

   a. /24

   b. 255.255.255.252

   c. /20

   d. 255.255.252.0

13

Foundation Topics

Subnet Mask Conversion

This section describes how to convert between different formats for the subnet mask. You can then use these processes when you practice. If you already know how to convert from one format to the other, go ahead and move on to the section "Practice Converting Subnet Masks," later in this chapter.

Three Mask Formats

Subnet masks can be written as 32-bit binary numbers, but not just any binary number. In particular, the binary subnet mask must follow these rules:

- The value must not interleave 1s and 0s.
- If 1s exist, they are on the left.
- If 0s exist, they are on the right.

For example, the following values would be illegal. The first is illegal because the value interleaves 0s and 1s, and the second is illegal because it lists 0s on the left and 1s on the right:

    10101010 01010101 11110000 00001111

    00000000 00000000 00000000 11111111

The following two binary values meet the requirements, in that they have all 1s on the left, followed by all 0s, with no interleaving of 1s and 0s:

    11111111 00000000 00000000 00000000

    11111111 11111111 11111111 00000000

Two alternate subnet mask formats exist so that we humans do not have to work with 32-bit binary numbers. One format, *dotted-decimal notation (DDN)*, converts each set of 8 bits into the decimal equivalent. For example, the two previous binary masks would convert to the following DDN subnet masks, because binary 11111111 converts to decimal 255, and binary 00000000 converts to decimal 0:

    255.0.0.0

    255.255.255.0

Although the DDN format has been around since the beginning of IPv4 addressing, the third mask format was added later, in the early 1990s: the *prefix* format. This format takes advantage of the rule that the subnet mask starts with some number of 1s, and then the rest of the digits are 0s. Prefix format lists a slash (/) followed by the number of binary 1s in the binary mask. Using the same two examples as earlier in this section, the prefix format equivalent masks are as follows:

    /8

    /24

Note that although the terms *prefix* or *prefix mask* can be used, the terms *CIDR mask* or *slash mask* can also be used. This newer prefix style mask was created around the same time as the *classless interdomain routing (CIDR)* specification back in the early 1990s, and the acronym CIDR grew to be used for anything related to CIDR, including prefix-style masks. Additionally, the term *slash mask* is sometimes used because the value includes a slash mark (/).

You need to be able to think about masks in different formats. The rest of this section examines how to convert between the three formats.

Converting Between Binary and Prefix Masks

Converting between binary and prefix masks should be relatively intuitive after you know that the prefix value is simply the number of binary 1s in the binary mask. For the sake of completeness, the processes to convert in each direction are as follows:

Binary to prefix: Count the number of binary 1s in the binary mask, and write the total, in decimal, after a slash mark (/).

Prefix to binary: Write P binary 1s, where P is the prefix value, followed by as many binary 0s as required to create a 32-bit number.

Tables 13-2 and 13-3 show some examples.

Table 13-2 Sample Conversions: Binary to Prefix

Binary Mask	Logic	Prefix Mask
11111111 11111111 11000000 00000000	Count 8 + 8 + 2 = 18 binary 1s	/18
11111111 11111111 11111111 11110000	Count 8 + 8 + 8 + 4 = 28 binary 1s	/28
11111111 11111000 00000000 00000000	Count 8 + 5 = 13 binary 1s	/13

Table 13-3 Sample Conversions: Prefix to Binary

Prefix Mask	Logic	Binary Mask
/18	Write 18 1s, then 14 0s, total 32	11111111 11111111 11000000 00000000
/28	Write 28 1s, then 4 0s, total 32	11111111 11111111 11111111 11110000
/13	Write 13 1s, then 19 0s, total 32	11111111 11111000 00000000 00000000

Converting Between Binary and DDN Masks

By definition, a *dotted-decimal notation (DDN)* used with IPv4 addressing contains four decimal numbers, separated by dots. Each decimal number represents 8 bits. So, a single DDN shows four decimal numbers that together represent some 32-bit binary number.

Conversion from a DDN mask to the binary equivalent is relatively simple to describe, but can be laborious to perform. First, to do the conversion, the process is as follows:

For each octet, perform a decimal-to-binary conversion.

13

However, depending on your comfort level with doing decimal-to-binary conversions, that process can be difficult or time-consuming. If you want to think about masks in binary for the exam, consider picking one of the following methods to do the conversion and practicing until you can do it quickly and accurately:

■ Do the decimal-binary conversions, and practice until you get fast at them. If you choose this path, consider the Cisco Binary Game, which you can find by searching its name at the Cisco Learning Network (CLN; http://learningnetwork.cisco.com).

■ Although this chapter teaches you how to convert the masks quickly, if you are weak at basic numeric conversions, take the time to practice binary-hex and binary-decimal conversions as ends unto themselves.

■ Use the decimal-binary conversion chart in Appendix I, "Numeric Reference Tables." This lets you find the answer more quickly now, but you cannot use the chart on exam day.

■ Memorize the nine possible decimal values that can be in a decimal mask, and practice using a reference table with those values.

The third method, which is the method recommended in this book, takes advantage of the fact that any and every DDN mask octet must be one of only nine values. Why? Well, remember how a binary mask cannot interleave 1s and 0s, and the 0s must be on the right? It turns out that only nine different 8-bit binary numbers conform to these rules. Table 13-4 lists the values, along with other relevant information.

Table 13-4   Nine Possible Values in One Octet of a Subnet Mask

Binary Mask Octet	Decimal Equivalent	Number of Binary 1s
00000000	0	0
10000000	128	1
11000000	192	2
11100000	224	3
11110000	240	4
11111000	248	5
11111100	252	6
11111110	254	7
11111111	255	8

Many subnetting processes can be done with or without binary math. Some of those processes—mask conversion included—use the information in Table 13-4. You should plan to memorize the information in the table. We recommend making a copy of the table to keep handy while you practice. (You will likely memorize the contents of this table simply by practicing the conversion process enough to get both good and fast at the conversions.)

Using the table, the conversion processes in each direction with binary and decimal masks are as follows:

Binary to decimal: Organize the bits into four sets of eight. For each octet, find the binary value in the table and write down the corresponding decimal value.

Decimal to binary: For each octet, find the decimal value in the table and write down the corresponding 8-bit binary value.

Tables 13-5 and 13-6 show some examples.

Table 13-5   Sample Conversions: Binary to Decimal

Binary Mask	Logic	Decimal Mask
11111111 11111111 11000000 00000000	11111111 maps to 255. 11000000 maps to 192. 00000000 maps to 0.	255.255.192.0
11111111 11111111 11111111 11110000	11111111 maps to 255. 11110000 maps to 240.	255.255.255.240
11111111 11111000 00000000 00000000	11111111 maps to 255. 11111000 maps to 248. 00000000 maps to 0.	255.248.0.0

Table 13-6   Sample Conversions: Decimal to Binary

Decimal Mask	Logic	Binary Mask
255.255.192.0	255 maps to 11111111. 192 maps to 11000000. 0 maps to 00000000	11111111 11111111 11000000 00000000
255.255.255.240	255 maps to 11111111. 240 maps to 11110000	11111111 11111111 11111111 11110000
255.248.0.0	255 maps to 11111111. 248 maps to 11111000. 0 maps to 00000000.	11111111 11111000 00000000 00000000

Converting Between Prefix and DDN Masks

When you're learning, the best way to convert between the prefix and decimal formats is to first convert to binary. For example, to move from decimal to prefix, first convert decimal to binary and then binary to prefix.

For the exams, set a goal to master these conversions doing the math in your head. While learning, you will likely want to use paper. To train yourself to do all this without writing it down, instead of writing each octet of binary, just write the number of binary 1s in that octet.

Figure 13-1 shows an example with a prefix-to-decimal conversion. The left side shows the conversion to binary as an interim step. For comparison, the right side shows the binary interim step in shorthand, which just lists the number of binary 1s in each octet of the binary mask.

13

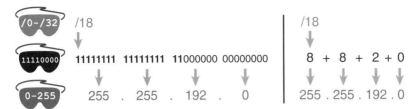

Figure 13-1 *Conversion from Prefix to Decimal: Full Binary Versus Shorthand*

Similarly, when converting from decimal to prefix, mentally convert to binary along the way, and as you improve, just think of the binary as the number of 1s in each octet. Figure 13-2 shows an example of such a conversion.

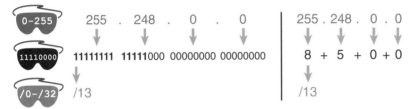

Figure 13-2 *Conversion from Decimal to Prefix: Full Binary Versus Shorthand*

Note that Appendix I has a table that lists all 33 legal subnet masks, with all three formats shown.

Practice Converting Subnet Masks

Before moving to the second half of this chapter, and thinking about what these subnet masks mean, first do some practice. Practice the processes discussed in this chapter until you get the right answer most of the time. Use any tools you want, and take all the time you need, until you meet the goal in Table 13-7 for being ready to move on to the next section. Later, before taking the exam, practice more until you master the topics in this chapter and can move pretty fast, as outlined in the right column of Table 13-7.

Table 13-7 The Keep-Reading and Take-Exam Goals for This Chapter's Topics

Time Frame	Before Moving to the Next Section	Before Taking the Exam
Focus on...	Learning how	Being correct and fast
Tools allowed	All	Your brain and a notepad
Goal: accuracy	90% correct	100% correct
Goal: speed	Any speed	10 seconds

Table 13-8 lists eight practice problems. The table has three columns—one for each mask format. Each row lists one mask, in one format. Your job is to find the mask's value in the other two formats for each row. Table 13-11, located in the section "Answers to Earlier Practice Problems," later in this chapter, lists the answers.

Table 13-8   Practice Problems: Find the Mask Values in the Other Two Formats

Prefix	Binary Mask	Decimal
	11111111 11111111 11000000 00000000	
		255.255.255.252
/25		
/16		
		255.0.0.0
	11111111 11111111 11111100 00000000	
		255.254.0.0
/27		

For additional practice converting subnet masks, consider the following:

■ Appendix F, "Practice for Chapter 13: Analyzing Subnet Masks," has some additional practice problems listed. This section also includes explanations as to how to find the answer to each problem.

■ Create your own problems. Only 33 legal subnet masks exist, so pick one and convert that mask to the other two formats. Then check your work based on Appendix I, which lists all mask values in all three formats. (Recommendation: Think of a prefix and convert it to binary and then decimal. Then, think of a DDN mask and convert it to binary and to prefix format.)

Note that many other subnetting problems will require you to do these conversions, so you will get extra practice as well.

Identifying Subnet Design Choices Using Masks

Subnet masks have many purposes. In fact, you would likely get a variety of true answers if you asked ten experienced network engineers, "What is the purpose of a subnet mask?" That's because a subnet mask plays several roles.

This chapter focuses on one particular use of a subnet mask: defining the prefix part of the IP addresses in a subnet. The prefix part must be the same value for all addresses in a subnet. In fact, a single subnet can be defined as all IPv4 addresses that have the same value in their prefix part.

Although the previous paragraph might sound a bit formal, the idea is relatively basic, as shown in Figure 13-3. The figure shows a network diagram, focusing on two subnets: a subnet of all addresses that begin with 172.16.2 and another subnet made up of all addresses that begin with 172.16.3. In this example, the prefix—the part that has the same value in all the addresses in the subnet—is the first three octets.

13

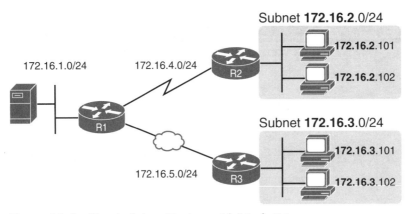

Figure 13-3   *Simple Subnet Design, with Mask /24*

Whereas people can sit around a conference table and talk about how a prefix is three octets long, computers communicate that same concept using a subnet mask. In this case, the subnets use a subnet mask of /24, which means that the prefix part of the addresses is 24 bits (three octets) long.

This section explains more about how to use a subnet mask to understand this concept of a prefix part of an IPv4 address, along with these other uses for a subnet mask (note that this section discusses the first five items in the list):

- Defines the size of the prefix (combined network and subnet) part of the addresses in a subnet

- Defines the size of the host part of the addresses in the subnet

- Can be used to calculate the number of hosts in the subnet

- Provides a means for the network designer to communicate the design details—the number of subnet and host bits—to the devices in the network

- Under certain assumptions, can be used to calculate the number of subnets in the entire classful network

- Can be used in binary calculations of both the subnet ID and the subnet broadcast address

Masks Divide the Subnet's Addresses into Two Parts

The subnet mask subdivides the IP addresses in a subnet into two parts: the *prefix (or subnet) part* and the *host part*.

The prefix part identifies the addresses that reside in the same subnet, because all IP addresses in the same subnet have the same value in the prefix part of their addresses. The idea is much like the postal code (ZIP Codes in the United States) in mailing addresses. All mailing addresses in the same town have the same postal code. Likewise, all IP addresses in the same subnet have identical values in the prefix part of their addresses.

The host part of an address identifies the host uniquely inside the subnet. If you compare any two IP addresses in the same subnet, their host parts will differ, even though the prefix parts of their addresses have the same value. Here's a summary of these key comparisons:

Prefix (subnet) part: Equal in all addresses in the same subnet.

Host part: Different in all addresses in the same subnet.

For example, imagine a subnet that, in concept, includes all addresses whose first three octets are 10.1.1. Thus, the following list shows several addresses in this subnet:

10.1.1.**1**

10.1.1.**2**

10.1.1.**3**

In this list, the prefix or subnet part (the first three octets of 10.1.1) are equal. The host part (the last octet, shown in bold) are different. So, the prefix or subnet part of the address identifies the group, and the host part identifies the specific member of the group.

The subnet mask defines the dividing line between the prefix and the host part. To do so, the mask creates a conceptual line between the binary 1s in the binary mask and the binary 0s in the mask. In short, if a mask has P binary 1s, the prefix part is P bits long and the rest of the bits are host bits. Figure 13-4 shows the general concept.

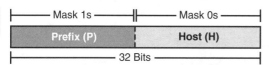

Figure 13-4 *Prefix (Subnet) and Host Parts Defined by Masks 1s and 0s*

Figure 13-5 shows a specific example using mask 255.255.255.0. Mask 255.255.255.0 (/24) has 24 binary 1s, for a prefix length of 24 bits.

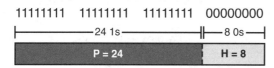

Figure 13-5 *Mask 255.255.255.0: P=24, H=8*

Masks and the Class Divide Addresses into Three Parts

In addition to the two-part view of IPv4 addresses, you can also think about IPv4 addresses as having three parts. To do so, just apply Class A, B, and C rules to the address format to define the network part at the beginning of the address. This added logic divides the prefix into two parts: the *network* part and the *subnet* part. The class defines the length of the network part, with the subnet part simply being the rest of the prefix. Figure 13-6 shows the idea.

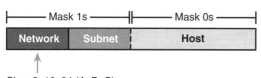

Figure 13-6 *Class Concepts Applied to Create Three Parts*

The combined network and subnet parts act like the prefix because all addresses in the same subnet must have identical values in the network and subnet parts. The size of the host part remains unchanged, regardless of whether the addresses are viewed as having two parts or three parts.

To be complete, Figure 13-7 shows the same example as in the previous section, with the subnet of "all addresses that begin with 10.1.1." In that example, the subnet uses mask 255.255.255.0, and the addresses are all in Class A network 10.0.0.0. The class defines 8 network bits, and the mask defines 24 prefix bits, meaning that 16 subnet bits exist (that is, 24 − 8 = 16). The host part remains as 8 bits per the mask.

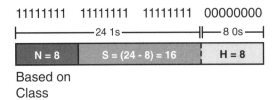

Figure 13-7   *Subnet 10.1.1.0, Mask 255.255.255.0: N=8, S=16, H=8*

Classless and Classful Addressing

The terms *classless addressing* and *classful addressing* refer to the two different ways to think about IPv4 addresses, as described so far in this chapter. Classful addressing means that you think about Class A, B, and C rules, so the prefix is separated into the network and subnet parts, as shown earlier in Figures 13-6 and 13-7. Classless addressing means that you ignore the Class A, B, and C rules and treat the prefix part as one part, as shown earlier in Figures 13-4 and 13-5. The following more formal definitions are listed for reference and study:

Classless addressing: The concept that an IPv4 address has two parts—the prefix part plus the host part—as defined by the mask, with *no consideration of the class* (A, B, or C).

Classful addressing: The concept that an IPv4 address has three parts—network, subnet, and host—as defined by the mask and Class A, B, and C rules.

> **NOTE**   Networking includes two other related topics that are (unfortunately) also referenced as *classless* and *classful*. In addition to the classless and classful addressing described here, each routing protocol can be categorized as either a *classless routing protocol* or a *classful routing protocol*. Additionally, the terms *classless routing* and *classful routing* refer to some details of how Cisco routers forward (route) packets using the default route in some cases (which is outside the scope of this book). As a result, these terms can be easily confused and misused. So, when you see the words *classless* and *classful*, be careful to note the context: addressing, routing, or routing protocols.

Calculations Based on the IPv4 Address Format

After you know how to break an address down using both classless and classful addressing rules, you can easily calculate a couple of important facts using some basic math formulas.

First, for any subnet, after you know the number of host bits, you can calculate the number of host IP addresses in the subnet. Next, if you know the number of subnet bits (using classful addressing concepts) and you know that only one subnet mask is used throughout the network, you can also calculate the number of subnets in the network. The formulas just require that you know the powers of 2:

Hosts in the subnet: $2^H - 2$, where H is the number of host bits.

Subnets in the network: 2^S, where S is the number of subnet bits. Only use this formula if only one mask is used throughout the network.

> **NOTE**   The section "Choose the Mask" in Chapter 11, "Perspectives on IPv4 Subnetting," details many concepts related to masks, including comments about this assumption of one mask throughout a single Class A, B, or C network.

The sizes of the parts of IPv4 addresses can also be calculated. The math is basic, but the concepts are important. Keeping in mind that IPv4 addresses are 32 bits long, and the two parts with classless addressing must add up to 32 (P + H = 32). With classful addressing, the three parts must add up to 32 (N + S + H = 32). Figure 13-8 shows the relationships.

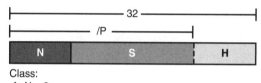

Class:
A: N = 8
B: N = 16
C: N = 24

Figure 13-8   *Relationship Between /P, N, S, and H*

You often begin with an IP address and mask. Based on the information in this chapter and earlier chapters, you should be able to find all the information in Figure 13-8 and then calculate the number of hosts per subnet and the number of subnets in the network. For reference, the following process spells out the steps:

Step 1.   Convert the mask to prefix format (/P) as needed. (See the earlier section "Practice Converting Subnet Masks" for review.)

Step 2.   Determine N based on the class. (See Chapter 12, "Analyzing Classful IPv4 Networks," for review.)

Step 3.   Calculate S = P − N.

Step 4.   Calculate H = 32 − P.

Step 5.   Calculate the hosts per subnet: $2^H - 2$.

Step 6.   Calculate the number of subnets: 2^S.

13

For example, consider the case of IP address 8.1.4.5 with a mask of 255.255.0.0. Here is the process:

Step 1. 255.255.0.0 = /16, so P = 16.

Step 2. 8.1.4.5 is in the range 1–126 in the first octet, so it is Class A; therefore, N = 8.

Step 3. S = P – N = 16 – 8 = 8.

Step 4. H = 32 – P = 32 – 16 = 16.

Step 5. 2^{16} – 2 = 65,534 hosts/subnet.

Step 6. 2^8 = 256 subnets.

Figure 13-9 shows a visual analysis of the same problem.

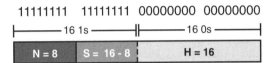

11111111   11111111   00000000   00000000

— 16 1s —   — 16 0s —

N = 8   S = 16 - 8   H = 16

Figure 13-9   *Visual Representation of the Problem: 8.1.4.5, 255.255.0.0*

For another example, consider address 200.1.1.1, mask 255.255.255.252. Here is the process:

Step 1. 255.255.255.252 = /30, so P = 30.

Step 2. 200.1.1.1 is in the range 192–223 in the first octet, so it is Class C; therefore, N = 24.

Step 3. S = P – N = 30 – 24 = 6.

Step 4. H = 32 – P = 32 – 30 = 2.

Step 5. 2^2 – 2 = 2 hosts/subnet.

Step 6. 2^6 = 64 subnets.

This example uses a popular mask for serial links, because serial links only require two host addresses, and the mask supports only two host addresses.

Practice Analyzing Subnet Masks

Before moving to the next chapter, practice until you get the right answer most of the time, but use any tools you want and take all the time you need. Then, you can move on with your reading.

However, before taking the exam, practice until you master the topics in this chapter and can move pretty fast. As for time, you should be able to find the entire answer—the size of the three parts, plus the formulas to calculate the number of subnets and hosts—in around 15 seconds. Table 13-9 summarizes the key concepts and suggestions for this two-phase approach.

Table 13-9   Goals: To Keep Reading and to Take the Exam

Time Frame	Before Moving to the Next Chapter	Before Taking the Exam
Focus on...	Learning how	Being correct and fast
Tools allowed	All	Your brain and a notepad
Goal: accuracy	90% correct	100% correct
Goal: speed	Any speed	15 seconds

On a piece of scratch paper, answer the following questions. In each case:

- Determine the structure of the addresses in each subnet based on the class and mask, using classful IP addressing concepts. In other words, find the size of the network, subnet, and host parts of the addresses.
- Calculate the number of hosts in the subnet.
- Calculate the number of subnets in the network, assuming that the same mask is used throughout.

1. 8.1.4.5, 255.255.254.0
2. 130.4.102.1, 255.255.255.0
3. 199.1.1.100, 255.255.255.0
4. 130.4.102.1, 255.255.252.0
5. 199.1.1.100, 255.255.255.224

The answers are listed in the section "Answers to Earlier Practice Problems," later in this chapter.

For additional practice analyzing subnet masks, consider the following:

- Appendix F has some additional practice problems listed. This appendix also includes explanations as to how to find the answer to each problem.
- Appendix G, "Practice for Chapter 14: Analyzing Existing Subnets," has another 25 practice problems related to this chapter. Although Appendix F focuses on the topics in this chapter, the problems in both Appendix F and Appendix G begin with an IP address and mask. Therefore, Appendix G also includes commentary and answers for items such as the number of network, subnet, and host bits, and other topics related to this chapter.
- Create your own problems. Many subnet calculators show the number of network, subnet, and host bits when you type in an IP address and mask, so make up an IP address and mask on paper, and then find N, S, and H. Then, to check your work, use any subnet calculator. Most subnet calculators list the class and network ID.

Exam Preparation Tasks

Review All the Key Topics

Review the most important topics from this chapter, noted with the Key Topic icon. Table 13-10 lists these key topics and where each is discussed.

Table 13-10   Key Topics for Chapter 13

Key Topic Element	Description	Page Number
List	Rules for binary subnet mask values	364
List	Rules to convert between binary and prefix masks	365
Table 13-4	Nine possible values in a decimal subnet mask	366
List	Rules to convert between binary and DDN masks	367
List	Some functions of a subnet mask	370
List	Comparisons of IP addresses in the same subnet	371
Figure 13-4	Two-part classless view of an IP address	371
Figure 13-6	Three-part classful view of an IP address	371
List	Definitions of classful addressing and classless addressing	372
List	Formal steps to analyze masks and calculate values	373

Complete the Tables and Lists from Memory

Print a copy of Appendix C, "Memory Tables," or at least the section for this chapter, and complete the tables and lists from memory. Appendix D, "Memory Tables Answer Key," includes completed tables and lists for you to check your work.

Definitions of Key Terms

After your first reading of the chapter, try to define these key terms, but do not be concerned about getting them all correct at that time. Chapter 24, "Final Review," directs you in how to use these terms for late-stage preparation for the exam.

binary mask, dotted-decimal notation (DDN), decimal mask, prefix mask, slash mask, CIDR mask, classful addressing, classless addressing

Practice

If you have not done so already, practice converting and analyzing subnet masks as discussed in this chapter. Refer to the earlier sections "Practice Converting Subnet Masks" and "Practice Analyzing Subnet Masks" for suggestions.

Answers to Earlier Practice Problems

Table 13-8, shown earlier, listed several practice problems for converting subnet masks; Table 13-11 lists the answers.

Table 13-11   Answers to Problems in Table 13-8

Prefix	Binary Mask	Decimal
/18	11111111 11111111 11000000 00000000	255.255.192.0
/30	11111111 11111111 11111111 11111100	255.255.255.252
/25	11111111 11111111 11111111 10000000	255.255.255.128
/16	11111111 11111111 00000000 00000000	255.255.0.0
/8	11111111 00000000 00000000 00000000	255.0.0.0
/22	11111111 11111111 11111100 00000000	255.255.252.0
/15	11111111 11111110 00000000 00000000	255.254.0.0
/27	11111111 11111111 11111111 11100000	255.255.255.224

Table 13-12 lists the answers to the practice problems from the earlier section "Practice Analyzing Subnet Masks."

Table 13-12   Answers to Problems from Earlier in the Chapter

	Problem	/P	Class	N	S	H	2^S	$2^H - 2$
1	8.1.4.5 255.255.254.0	23	A	8	15	9	32,768	510
2	130.4.102.1 255.255.255.0	24	B	16	8	8	256	254
3	199.1.1.100 255.255.255.0	24	C	24	0	8	N/A	254
4	130.4.102.1 255.255.252.0	22	B	16	6	10	64	1022
5	199.1.1.100 255.255.255.224	27	C	24	3	5	8	30

The following list reviews the problems:

1. For 8.1.4.5, the first octet (8) is in the 1–126 range, so it is a Class A address with 8 network bits. Mask 255.255.254.0 converts to /23, so P – N = 15, for 15 subnet bits. H can be found by subtracting /P (23) from 32, for 9 host bits.

2. 130.4.102.1 is in the 128–191 range in the first octet, making it a Class B address with N = 16 bits. 255.255.255.0 converts to /24, so the number of subnet bits is 24 – 16 = 8. With 24 prefix bits, the number of host bits is 32 – 24 = 8.

13

3. The third problem purposely shows a case where the mask does not create a subnet part of the address. The address 199.1.1.100 has a first octet between 192 and 223, making it a Class C address with 24 network bits. The prefix version of the mask is /24, so the number of subnet bits is 24 – 24 = 0. The number of host bits is 32 minus the prefix length (24), for a total of 8 host bits. So, in this case, the mask shows that the network engineer is using the default mask, which creates no subnet bits and no subnets.

4. With the same address as the second problem, 130.4.102.1 is a Class B address with N = 16 bits. This problem uses a different mask, 255.255.252.0, which converts to /22. This makes the number of subnet bits 22 – 16 = 6. With 22 prefix bits, the number of host bits is 32 – 22 = 10.

5. With the same address as the third problem, 199.1.1.100 is a Class C address with N = 24 bits. This problem uses a different mask, 255.255.255.224, which converts to /27. This makes the number of subnet bits 27 – 24 = 3. With 27 prefix bits, the number of host bits is 32 – 27 = 5.

This chapter covers the following exam topics:

1.3. Use the OSI and TCP/IP models and their associated protocols to explain how data flows in a network

1.3.a. IP

3.1. Describe the operation and benefits of using private and public IP addressing

3.1.a. Classful IP addressing

3.1.b. RFC 1918

3.2. Describe the difference between IPv4 and IPv6 addressing scheme

3.2.a. Comparative address space

CHAPTER 14

Analyzing Existing Subnets

Often, a networking task begins with the discovery of the IP address and mask used by some host. Then, to understand how the internetwork routes packets to that host, you must find key pieces of information about the subnet—specifically the following:

- Subnet ID
- Subnet broadcast address
- Subnet's range of usable unicast IP addresses

This chapter discusses the concepts and math for taking a known IP address and mask and then fully describing a subnet by finding the values in this list. These specific tasks might well be the most important IP skills in the entire IP addressing and subnetting topics in this book, because these tasks might be the most commonly used tasks when operating and troubleshooting real networks.

> **NOTE** As promised in the Introduction's section "For Those Studying Routing & Switching," this chapter covers the same content as Chapter 14 in the *ICND1 100-101 Official Cert Guide*. Feel free to skim or skip this chapter if you have already read that chapter in the other book.

"Do I Know This Already?" Quiz

Use the "Do I Know This Already?" quiz to help decide whether you might want to skim this chapter, or a major section, moving more quickly to the "Exam Preparation Tasks" section near the end of the chapter. Table 14-1 lists the major headings in this chapter and their corresponding "Do I Know This Already?" quiz questions. For thorough explanations, see Appendix A, "Answers to the 'Do I Know This Already?' Quizzes."

Table 14-1 "Do I Know This Already?" Foundation Topics Section-to-Question Mapping

Foundation Topics Section	Questions
Defining a Subnet	1
Analyzing Existing Subnets: Binary	2
Analyzing Existing Subnets: Decimal	3–7

1. When you're thinking about an IP address using classful addressing rules, the address can have three parts: network, subnet, and host. If you examined all the addresses in one subnet, in binary, which of the following answers correctly states which of the three parts of the addresses will be equal among all addresses? (Pick the best answer.)

    a. Network part only

    b. Subnet part only

    c. Host part only

    d. Network and subnet parts

    e. Subnet and host parts

2. Which of the following statements are true regarding the binary subnet ID, subnet broadcast address, and host IP address values in any single subnet? (Choose two.)

    a. The host part of the broadcast address is all binary 0s.

    b. The host part of the subnet ID is all binary 0s.

    c. The host part of a usable IP address can have all binary 1s.

    d. The host part of any usable IP address must not be all binary 0s.

3. Which of the following is the resident subnet ID for IP address 10.7.99.133/24?

    a. 10.0.0.0

    b. 10.7.0.0

    c. 10.7.99.0

    d. 10.7.99.128

4. Which of the following is the resident subnet for IP address 192.168.44.97/30?

    a. 192.168.44.0

    b. 192.168.44.64

    c. 192.168.44.96

    d. 192.168.44.128

5. Which of the following is the subnet broadcast address for the subnet in which IP address 172.31.77.201/27 resides?

    a. 172.31.201.255

    b. 172.31.255.255

    c. 172.31.77.223

    d. 172.31.77.207

6. A fellow engineer tells you to configure the DHCP server to lease the last 100 usable IP addresses in subnet 10.1.4.0/23. Which of the following IP addresses could be leased as a result of your new configuration?

   a.   10.1.4.156

   b.   10.1.4.254

   c.   10.1.5.200

   d.   10.1.7.200

   e.   10.1.255.200

7. A fellow engineer tells you to configure the DHCP server to lease the first 20 usable IP addresses in subnet 192.168.9.96/27. Which of the following IP addresses could be leased as a result of your new configuration?

   a.   192.168.9.126

   b.   192.168.9.110

   c.   192.168.9.1

   d.   192.168.9.119

Foundation Topics

Defining a Subnet

An IP subnet is a subset of a classful network, created by choice of some network engineer. However, that engineer cannot pick just any arbitrary subset of addresses; instead, the engineer must follow certain rules, such as the following:

- The subnet contains a set of consecutive numbers.

- The subnet holds 2^H numbers, where H is the number of host bits defined by the subnet mask.

- Two special numbers in the range cannot be used as IP addresses:

  - The first (lowest) number acts as an identifier for the subnet (*subnet ID*).

  - The last (highest) number acts as a *subnet broadcast address*.

- The remaining addresses, whose values sit between the subnet ID and subnet broadcast address, are used as *unicast IP addresses*.

This section reviews and expands on the basic concepts of the subnet ID, subnet broadcast address, and range of addresses in a subnet.

An Example with Network 172.16.0.0 and Four Subnets

Imagine that you work at a customer support center, where you receive all initial calls from users who have problems with their computer. You coach a user through finding her IP address and mask: 172.16.150.41, mask 255.255.192.0. One of the first and most common tasks you will do based on that information is to find the subnet ID of the subnet in which that address resides. (In fact, this subnet ID is sometimes called the *resident subnet*, because the IP address exists in or resides in that subnet.)

Before getting into the math, examine the mask (255.255.192.0) and classful network (172.16.0.0) for a moment. From the mask, based on what you learned in Chapter 13, "Analyzing Subnet Masks," you can find the structure of the addresses in the subnet, including the number of host and subnet bits. That analysis tells you that 2 subnet bits exist, meaning that there should be four (2^2) subnets. (If these concepts are not yet clear, review Chapter 13's section "Identifying Subnet Design Choices Using Masks.") Figure 14-1 shows the idea.

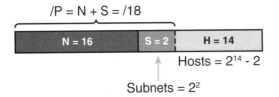

Figure 14-1   *Address Structure: Class B Network, /18 Mask*

NOTE   This chapter, like the others in this part of the book, assumes that one mask is used throughout an entire classful network.

Because each subnet uses a single mask, all subnets of this single IP network must be the same size, because all subnets have the same structure. In this example, all four subnets will have the structure shown in the figure, so all four subnets will have $2^{14} - 2$ host addresses.

Next, consider the big picture of what happens with this sample subnet design: The one Class B network now has four subnets of equal size. Conceptually, if you represent the entire Class B network as a number line, each subnet consumes one-fourth of the number line, as shown in Figure 14-2. Each subnet has a subnet ID—the numerically lowest number in the subnet—that sits on the left of the subnet. And each subnet has a subnet broadcast address—the numerically highest number in the subnet—that sits on the right side of the subnet.

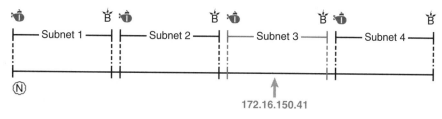

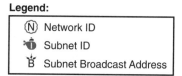

Legend:

(N) Network ID

Subnet ID

B Subnet Broadcast Address

Figure 14-2 *Network 172.16.0.0, Divided into Four Equal Subnets*

The rest of this chapter focuses on how to take one IP address and mask and discover the details about that one subnet in which the address resides. In other words, you see how to find the resident subnet of an IP address. Again, using IP address 172.16.150.41 and mask 255.255.192.0 as an example, Figure 14-3 shows the resident subnet, along with the subnet ID and subnet broadcast address that bracket the subnet.

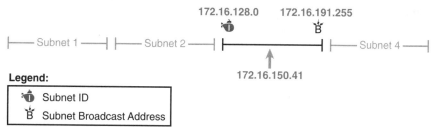

Legend:

Subnet ID

B Subnet Broadcast Address

Figure 14-3 *Resident Subnet for 172.16.150.41, 255.255.192.0*

Subnet ID Concepts

A subnet ID is simply a number used to succinctly represent a subnet. When listed along with its matching subnet mask, the subnet ID identifies the subnet and can be used to derive the subnet broadcast address and range of addresses in the subnet. Rather than having to write down all these details about a subnet, you simply need to write down the subnet ID and mask, and you have enough information to fully describe the subnet.

The subnet ID appears in many places, but it is seen most often in IP routing tables. For example, when an engineer configures a router with its IP address and mask, the router calculates the subnet ID and puts a route into its routing table for that subnet. The router typically then advertises the subnet ID/mask combination to neighboring routers with some IP routing protocol. Eventually, all the routers in an enterprise learn about the subnet—again using the subnet ID and subnet mask combination—and display it in their routing tables. (You can display the contents of a router's IP routing table using the **show ip route** command.)

Unfortunately, the terminology related to subnets can sometimes cause problems. First, the terms *subnet ID*, *subnet number*, and *subnet address* are synonyms. Additionally, people sometimes simply say *subnet* when referring to both the idea of a subnet and the number that is used as the subnet ID. When talking about routing, people sometimes use the term *prefix* instead of *subnet*. The term *prefix* refers to the same idea as *subnet*—it just uses terminology from the classless addressing way to describe IP addresses, as discussed in Chapter 13's section "Classless and Classful Addressing."

The biggest terminology confusion arises between the terms *network* and *subnet*. In the real world, people often use these terms synonymously, and that is perfectly reasonable in some cases. In other cases, the specific meaning of these terms, and their differences, matter to what is being discussed.

For example, people often might say, "What is the network ID?" when they really want to know the subnet ID. In another case, they might want to know the Class A, B, or C network ID. Suppose an engineer asks you something like, "What's the net ID for 172.16.150.41 slash 18?" In this case, you can use the context to figure out whether he wants the literal classful network ID (172.16.0.0, in this case) or the literal subnet ID (172.16.128.0, in this case).

For the exams, be ready to notice when the terms *subnet* and *network* are used, and then use the context to figure out the specific meaning of the term in that case.

Table 14-2 summarizes the key facts about the subnet ID, along with the possible synonyms, for easier review and study.

Table 14-2 Summary of Subnet ID Key Facts

Definition	Number that represents the subnet
Numeric Value	First (smallest) number in the subnet
Literal Synonyms	Subnet number, subnet address, prefix, resident subnet
Common-Use Synonyms	Network, network ID, network number, network address
Typically Seen In...	Routing tables, documentation

Subnet Broadcast Address

The subnet broadcast address has two main roles: to be used as a destination IP address for the purpose of sending packets to all hosts in the subnet, and as a means to find the high end of the range of addresses in a subnet.

The original purpose for the subnet broadcast address was to give hosts a way to send one packet to all hosts in a subnet, and to do so efficiently. For example, a host in subnet A could send a packet with a destination address of subnet B's subnet broadcast address. The routers would forward this one packet just like a packet sent to a host in subnet B. After the packet arrives at the router connected to subnet B, that last router would then forward the packet to all hosts in subnet B, typically by encapsulating the packet in a data link layer broadcast frame. As a result, all hosts in host B's subnet would receive a copy of the packet.

The subnet broadcast address also helps you find the range of addresses in a subnet, because the broadcast address is the last (highest) number in a subnet's range of addresses. To find the low end of the range, calculate the subnet ID; to find the high end of the range, calculate the subnet broadcast address.

Table 14-3 summarizes the key facts about the subnet broadcast address, along with the possible synonyms, for easier review and study.

Table 14-3 Summary of Subnet Broadcast Address Key Facts

Definition	A reserved number in each subnet that, when used as the destination address of a packet, causes the routers to forward the packet to all hosts in that subnet
Numeric Value	Last (highest) number in the subnet
Literal Synonyms	Directed broadcast address
Broader-Use Synonyms	Network broadcast
Typically Seen In...	Calculations of the range of addresses in a subnet

Range of Usable Addresses

The engineers implementing an IP internetwork need to know the range of unicast IP addresses in each subnet. Before you can plan which addresses to use as statically assigned IP addresses, which to configure to be leased by the DHCP server, and which to reserve for later use, you need to know the range of usable addresses.

To find the range of usable IP addresses in a subnet, first find the subnet ID and the subnet broadcast address. Then, just add 1 to the fourth octet of the subnet ID to get the first (lowest) usable address, and subtract 1 from the fourth octet of the subnet broadcast address to get the last (highest) usable address in the subnet.

For example, Figure 14-3 showed subnet ID 172.16.128.0, mask /18. The first usable address is simply 1 more than the subnet ID (in this case, 172.16.128.1). That same figure showed a subnet broadcast address of 172.16.191.255, so the last usable address is 1 less, or 172.16.191.254.

Now that this section has described the concepts behind the numbers that collectively define a subnet, the rest of this chapter focuses on the math used to find these values.

Analyzing Existing Subnets: Binary

What does it mean to "analyze a subnet"? For this book, it means that you should be able to start with an IP address and mask and then define key facts about the subnet in which that address resides. Specifically, that means discovering the subnet ID, subnet broadcast address, and range of addresses. The analysis can also include the calculation of the number of addresses in the subnet, as discussed in Chapter 13, but this chapter does not review those concepts.

Many methods exist to calculate the details about a subnet based on the address/mask. This section begins by discussing some calculations that use binary math, with the next section showing alternatives that use only decimal math. Although many people prefer the decimal method for going fast on the exams, the binary calculations ultimately give you a better understanding of IPv4 addressing. In particular, if you plan to move on to attain Cisco routing and switching certifications, you should take the time to understand the binary methods discussed in this section, even if you use the decimal methods for the exams.

Finding the Subnet ID: Binary

To start this section that uses binary, first consider a simple decimal math problem: Find the smallest three-digit decimal number that begins with 4. The answer, of course, is 400. And although most people would not have to break down the logic into steps, you know that 0 is the lowest-value digit you can use for any digit in a decimal number. You know that the first digit must be a 4, and the number is a three-digit number, so you just use the lowest value (0) for the last two digits, and find the answer: 400.

This same concept, applied to binary IP addresses, gives you the subnet ID. You have seen all the related concepts in other chapters, so if you already intuitively know how to find the subnet ID in binary, great! If not, the following key facts should help you see the logic:

All numbers in the subnet (subnet ID, subnet broadcast address, and all usable IP addresses) have the same value in the prefix part of the numbers.

The subnet ID is the lowest numeric value in the subnet, so its host part, in binary, is all 0s.

To find the subnet ID in binary, you take the IP address in binary and change all host bits to binary 0. To do so, you need to convert the IP address to binary. You also need to identify the prefix and host bits, which can be easily done by converting the mask (as needed) to prefix format. (Note that Appendix I, "Numeric Reference Tables," includes a decimal-to-binary conversion table.) Figure 14-4 shows the idea, using the same address/mask as in the earlier examples in this chapter: 172.16.150.41, mask /18.

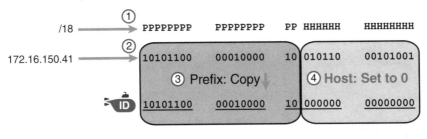

Legend:

 Subnet ID

Figure 14-4 *Binary Concept: Convert the IP Address to the Subnet ID*

Starting at the top of Figure 14-4, the format of the IP address is represented with 18 prefix (P) and 14 host (H) bits in the mask (Step 1). The second row (Step 2) shows the binary version of the IP address, converted from the dotted-decimal notation (DDN) value 172.16.150.41. (If you have not used the conversion table in Appendix I yet, it might be useful to double-check the conversion of all four octets based on the table.)

The next two steps show the action to copy the IP address's prefix bits (Step 3) and give the host bits a value of binary 0 (Step 4). This resulting number is the subnet ID (in binary).

The last step, not shown in Figure 14-4, is to convert the subnet ID from binary to decimal. This book shows that conversion as a separate step, in Figure 14-5, mainly because many people make a mistake at this step in the process. When converting a 32-bit number (such as an IP address or IP subnet ID) back to an IPv4 DDN, you must follow this rule:

Convert 8 bits at a time from binary to decimal, regardless of the line between the prefix and host parts of the number.

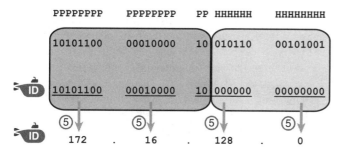

Figure 14-5 *Converting the Subnet ID from Binary to DDN*

Figure 14-5 shows this final step. Note that the third octet (the third set of 8 bits) has 2 bits in the prefix and 6 bits in the host part of the number, but the conversion occurs for all 8 bits.

NOTE   You can do the numeric conversions in Figures 14-4 and 14-5 by relying on the conversion table in Appendix I. To convert from DDN to binary, for each octet, find the decimal value in the table and then write down the 8-bit binary equivalent. To convert from binary back to DDN, for each octet of 8 bits, find the matching binary entry in the table and write down the corresponding decimal value. For example, 172 converts to binary 10101100, and 00010000 converts to decimal 16.

Finding the Subnet Broadcast Address: Binary

Finding the subnet broadcast address uses a similar process. To find the subnet broadcast address, use the same binary process used to find the subnet ID, but instead of setting all the host bits to the lowest value (all binary 0s), set the host part to the highest value (all binary 1s). Figure 14-6 shows the concept.

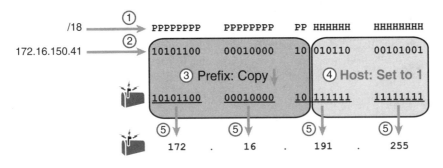

Figure 14-6   *Finding a Subnet Broadcast Address: Binary*

The process in Figure 14-6 demonstrates the same first three steps shown in Figure 14-4. Specifically, it shows the identification of the prefix and host bits (Step 1), the results of converting the IP address 172.16.150.41 to binary (Step 2), and the copying of the prefix bits (first 18 bits, in this case). The difference occurs in the host bits on the right, changing all host bits (the last 14, in this case) to the largest possible value (all binary 1s). The final step converts the 32-bit subnet broadcast address to DDN format. Also, remember that with any conversion from DDN to binary, or vice versa, the process always converts using 8 bits at a time. In particular, in this case, the entire third octet of binary 10111111 is converted back to decimal 191.

Binary Practice Problems

Figures 14-4 and 14-5 demonstrate a process to find the subnet ID using binary math. The following process summarizes those steps in written form for easier reference and practice:

Step 1.   Convert the mask to prefix format to find the length of the prefix (/P) and the length of the host part (32 – P).

Step 2.   Convert the IP address to its 32-bit binary equivalent.

Step 3.   Copy the prefix bits of the IP address.

Step 4.   Write down 0s for the host bits.

Step 5.   Convert the resulting 32-bit number, 8 bits at a time, back to decimal.

The process to find the subnet broadcast address is exactly the same, except in Step 4, you set the bits to 1s, as seen in Figure 14-6.

Take a few moments and run through the following five practice problems on scratch paper. In each case, find both the subnet ID and subnet broadcast address. Also, record the prefix style mask:

1. 8.1.4.5, 255.255.0.0
2. 130.4.102.1, 255.255.255.0
3. 199.1.1.100, 255.255.255.0
4. 130.4.102.1, 255.255.252.0
5. 199.1.1.100, 255.255.255.224

Tables 14-4 through 14-8 show the results for the five different examples. The tables show the host bits in bold, and they include the binary version of the address and mask as well as the binary version of the subnet ID and subnet broadcast address.

Table 14-4   Subnet Analysis for Subnet with Address 8.1.4.5, Mask 255.255.0.0

Prefix Length	/16	11111111 11111111 00000000 00000000
Address	8.1.4.5	00001000 00000001 00000100 00000101
Subnet ID	8.1.0.0	00001000 00000001 00000000 00000000
Broadcast Address	8.1.255.255	00001000 00000001 11111111 11111111

Table 14-5   Subnet Analysis for Subnet with Address 130.4.102.1, Mask 255.255.255.0

Prefix Length	/24	11111111 11111111 11111111 00000000
Address	130.4.102.1	10000010 00000100 01100110 00000001
Subnet ID	130.4.102.0	10000010 00000100 01100110 00000000
Broadcast Address	130.4.102.255	10000010 00000100 01100110 11111111

Table 14-6   Subnet Analysis for Subnet with Address 199.1.1.100, Mask 255.255.255.0

Prefix Length	/24	11111111 11111111 11111111 00000000
Address	199.1.1.100	11000111 00000001 00000001 01100100
Subnet ID	199.1.1.0	11000111 00000001 00000001 00000000
Broadcast Address	199.1.1.255	11000111 00000001 00000001 11111111

Table 14-7   Subnet Analysis for Subnet with Address 130.4.102.1, Mask 255.255.252.0

Prefix Length	/22	11111111 11111111 11111100 00000000
Address	130.4.102.1	10000010 00000100 01100110 00000001
Subnet ID	130.4.100.0	10000010 00000100 01100100 00000000
Broadcast Address	130.4.103.255	10000010 00000100 01100111 11111111

Table 14-8   Subnet Analysis for Subnet with Address 199.1.1.100, Mask 255.255.255.224

Prefix Length	/27	11111111 11111111 11111111 11100000
Address	199.1.1.100	11000111 00000001 00000001 01100100
Subnet ID	199.1.1.96	11000111 00000001 00000001 01100000
Broadcast Address	199.1.1.127	11000111 00000001 00000001 01111111

Shortcut for the Binary Process

The binary process described in this section so far requires that all four octets be converted to binary and then back to decimal. However, you can easily predict the results in at least three of the four octets, based on the DDN mask. You can then avoid the binary math in all but one octet and reduce the number of binary conversions you need to do.

First, consider an octet, and that octet only, whose DDN mask value is 255. The mask value of 255 converts to binary 11111111, which means that all 8 bits are prefix bits. Thinking through the steps in the process, at Step 2, you convert the address to some number. At Step 3, you copy the number. At Step 4, you convert the same 8-bit number back to decimal. All you did in those three steps, in this one octet, is convert from decimal to binary and convert the same number back to the same decimal value!

In short, the subnet ID (and subnet broadcast address) is equal to the IP address in octets for which the mask is 255.

For example, the resident subnet ID for 172.16.150.41, mask 255.255.192.0 is 172.16.128.0. The first two mask octets are 255. Rather than think about the binary math, you could just start by copying the address's value in those two octets: 172.16.

Another shortcut exists for octets whose DDN mask value is decimal 0, or binary 00000000. With a decimal mask value of 0, the math always results in a decimal 0 for the subnet ID, no matter the beginning value in the IP address. Specifically, just look at Steps 4 and 5 in this case: At Step 4, you would write down eight binary 0s, and at Step 5, convert 00000000 back to decimal 0.

The following revised process steps take these two shortcuts into account. However, when the mask is neither 0 nor 255, the process requires the same conversions. At most, you have to do only one octet of the conversions. To find the subnet ID, apply the logic in these steps for each of the four octets:

Step 1.   If the mask = 255, copy the decimal IP address for that octet.

Step 2.   If the mask = 0, write down a decimal 0 for that octet.

Step 3.   If the mask is neither 0 nor 255 in this octet, use the same binary logic as shown in the section "Finding the Subnet ID: Binary," earlier in this chapter.

Figure 14-7 shows an example of this process, again using 172.16.150.41, 255.255.192.0.

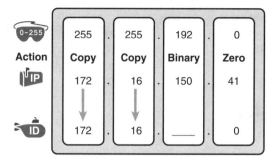

Figure 14-7 *Binary Shortcut Example*

A similar shortcut exists when finding the subnet broadcast address. For DDN mask octets equal to decimal 0, set the decimal subnet broadcast address value to 255 instead of 0, as noted in the following list:

Step 1.   If the mask = 255, copy the decimal IP address for that octet.

Step 2.   If the mask = 0, write down a decimal 255 for that octet.

Step 3.   If the mask is neither 0 nor 255 in this octet, use the same binary logic as shown in the section "Finding the Subnet Broadcast Address: Binary," earlier in this chapter.

Brief Note About Boolean Math

So far, this chapter has described how humans can use binary math to find the subnet ID and subnet broadcast address. However, computers typically use an entirely different binary process to find the same values, using a branch of mathematics called *Boolean Algebra*. Computers already store the IP address and mask in binary form, so they do not have to do any conversions to and from decimal. Then, certain Boolean operations allow the computers to calculate the subnet ID and subnet broadcast address with just a few CPU instructions.

You do not need to know Boolean math to have a good understanding of IP subnetting. However, in case you are interested, computers use the following Boolean logic to find the subnet ID and subnet broadcast address, respectively:

Perform a *Boolean AND* of the IP address and mask. This process converts all host bits to binary 0.

Invert the mask, and then perform a *Boolean OR* of the IP address and inverted subnet mask. This process converts all host bits to binary 1s.

Finding the Range of Addresses

Finding the range of usable addresses in a subnet, after you know the subnet ID and subnet broadcast address, requires only simple addition and subtraction. To find the first (lowest) usable IP address in the subnet, simply add 1 to the fourth octet of the subnet ID. To find the last (highest) usable IP address, simply subtract 1 from the fourth octet of the subnet broadcast address.

Analyzing Existing Subnets: Decimal

Analyzing existing subnets using the binary process works well. However, some of the math takes time for most people, particularly the decimal-to-binary conversions. And you need to do the math quickly for the exam. When using binary methods, most people require a lot of practice to be able to find these answers, even when using the abbreviated binary process.

This section discusses how to find the subnet ID and subnet broadcast address using only decimal math. Most people can find the answers more quickly using this process, at least after a little practice, as compared with the binary process. However, the decimal process does not tell you anything about the meaning behind the math. So, if you have not read the earlier section "Analyzing Existing Subnets: Binary," it is worthwhile to read it for the sake of understanding subnetting. This section focuses on getting the right answer using a method that, after you have practiced, should be faster.

Analysis with Easy Masks

With three easy subnet masks in particular, finding the subnet ID and subnet broadcast address requires only easy logic and literally no math. Three easy masks exist:

255.0.0.0

255.255.0.0

255.255.255.0

These easy masks have only 255 and 0 in decimal. In comparison, difficult masks have one octet that has neither a 255 nor a 0 in the mask, which makes the logic more challenging.

> **NOTE**   The terms *easy mask* and *difficult mask* are created for use in this book to describe the masks and the level of difficulty when working with each.

When the problem uses an easy mask, you can quickly find the subnet ID based on the IP address and mask in DDN format. Just use the following process for each of the four octets to find the subnet ID:

Step 1.   If the mask octet = 255, copy the decimal IP address.

Step 2.   If the mask octet = 0, write a decimal 0.

A similar simple process exists to find the subnet broadcast address, as follows:

Step 1.   If the mask octet = 255, copy the decimal IP address.

Step 2.   If the mask octet = 0, write a decimal 255.

Before moving to the next section, take some time to fill in the blanks in Table 14-9. Check your answers against Table 14-14 in the section "Answers to Earlier Practice Problems," later in this chapter. Complete the table by listing the subnet ID and subnet broadcast address.

Table 14-9   Practice Problems: Find Subnet ID and Broadcast, Easy Masks

	IP Address	Mask	Subnet ID	Broadcast Address
1	10.77.55.3	255.255.255.0		
2	172.30.99.4	255.255.255.0		
3	192.168.6.54	255.255.255.0		
4	10.77.3.14	255.255.0.0		
5	172.22.55.77	255.255.0.0		
6	1.99.53.76	255.0.0.0		

Predictability in the Interesting Octet

Although three masks are easier to work with (255.0.0.0, 255.255.0.0, and 255.255.255.0), the rest make the decimal math a little more difficult, so we call these masks difficult masks. With difficult masks, one octet is neither a 0 nor a 255. The math in the other three octets is easy and boring, so this book calls the one octet with the more difficult math the *interesting octet*.

If you take some time to think about different problems and focus on the interesting octet, you will begin to see a pattern. This section takes you through that examination so that you can learn how to predict the pattern, in decimal, and find the subnet ID.

First, the subnet ID value has a predictable decimal value because of the assumption that a single subnet mask is used for all subnets of a single classful network. The chapters in this part of the book assume that, for a given classful network, the design engineer chooses to use a single subnet mask for all subnets.

To see that predictability, consider some planning information written down by a network engineer, as shown in Figure 14-8. The figure shows four different masks the engineer is considering using in an IPv4 network, along with Class B network 172.16.0.0. The figure shows the third-octet values for the subnet IDs that would be created when using masks 255.255.128.0, 255.255.192.0, 255.255.224.0, and 255.255.240.0, from top to bottom in the figure.

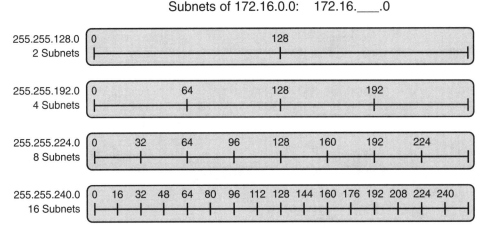

Subnets of 172.16.0.0:   172.16.___.0

Figure 14-8 *Numeric Patterns in the Interesting Octet*

First, to explain the figure further, look at the top row of the figure. If the engineer uses 255.255.128.0 as the mask, the mask creates two subnets, with subnet IDs 172.16.0.0 and 172.16.128.0. If the engineer uses mask 255.255.192.0, the mask creates four subnets, with subnet IDs 172.16.0.0, 172.16.64.0, 172.16.128.0, and 172.16.192.0.

If you take the time to look at the figure, the patterns become obvious:

   Mask: 255.255.128.0, Pattern: multiples of 128

   Mask: 255.255.192.0, Pattern: multiples of 64

   Mask: 255.255.224.0, Pattern: multiples of 32

   Mask: 255.255.240.0, Pattern: multiples of 16

To find the subnet ID, you just need a way to figure out what the pattern is. If you start with an IP address and mask, just find the subnet ID closest to the IP address, without going over, as discussed in the next section.

Finding the Subnet ID: Difficult Masks

The following written process lists all the steps for finding the subnet ID using only decimal math. This process adds to the earlier process used with easy masks. For each octet, follow these steps:

Step 1.   If the mask octet = 255, copy the decimal IP address.

Step 2.   If the mask octet = 0, write a decimal 0.

Step 3.   If the mask is neither, refer to this octet as the *interesting octet*:

   A. Calculate the *magic number* as 256 – mask.

   B. Set the subnet ID's value to the multiple of the magic number that is closest to the IP address without going over.

The process uses two new terms created for this book: *magic number* and *interesting octet*. The term *interesting octet* refers to the octet identified at Step 3 in the process; in other words, it is the octet with the mask that is neither 255 nor 0. Step 3A then uses the term *magic number*, which is derived from the DDN mask. Conceptually, the magic number is the number you add to one subnet ID to get the next subnet ID in order, as shown in Figure 14-8. Numerically, it can be found by subtracting the DDN mask's value, in the interesting octet, from 256, as mentioned in Step 3A.

You can use the examples over the next few pages that show the process being used on paper. Then, follow the practice opportunities outlined in the section "Practice Analyzing Existing Subnets," later in this chapter.

Resident Subnet Example 1

For example, consider the requirement to find the resident subnet for IP address 130.4.102.1, mask 255.255.240.0. The process does not require you to think about prefix bits versus host bits, convert the mask, think about the mask in binary, or convert the IP address to and from binary. Instead, for each of the four octets, choose an action based on the value in the mask. Figure 14-9 shows the results; the circled numbers in the figure refer to the step numbers in the written process to find the subnet ID, as listed in the previous few pages.

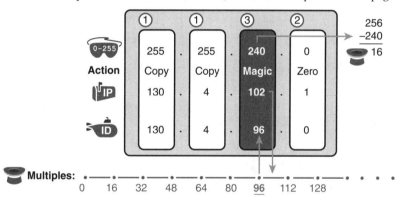

Figure 14-9   *Find the Subnet ID: 130.4.102.1, 255.255.240.0*

First, examine the three uninteresting octets (1, 2, and 4, in this example). The process keys on the mask, and the first two octets have a mask value of 255, so simply copy the IP address to the place where you intend to write down the subnet ID. The fourth octet has a mask value of 0, so write down a 0 for the fourth octet of the subnet ID.

The most challenging logic occurs in the interesting octet, which is the third octet in this example, because of the mask value 240 in that octet. For this octet, Step 3A asks you to calculate the magic number as 256 − mask. That means you take the mask's value in the interesting octet (240, in this case) and subtract it from 256: 256 − 240 = 16. The subnet ID's value in this octet must be a multiple of decimal 16, in this case.

Step 3B then asks you to find the multiples of the magic number (16, in this case) and choose the one closest to the IP address without going over. Specifically, that means you should mentally calculate the multiples of the magic number, starting at 0. (Do not forget to start at 0!) Thus, you count 0, 16, 32, 48, 64, 80, 96, 112, and so on. Then, you find the multiple closest to the IP address value in this octet (102, in this case), without going over 102.

So, as shown in Figure 14-9, you make the third octet's value 96 to complete the subnet ID of 130.4.96.0.

Resident Subnet Example 2

Consider another example: 192.168.5.77, mask 255.255.255.224. Figure 14-10 shows the results.

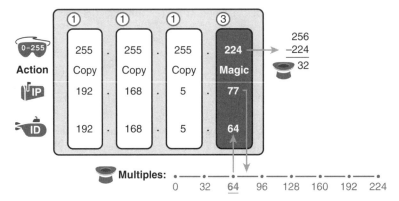

Figure 14-10 *Resident Subnet for 192.168.5.77, 255.255.255.224*

The three uninteresting octets (1, 2, and 3, in this case) require only a little thought. For each octet, each with a mask value of 255, just copy the IP address.

For the interesting octet, at Step 3A, the magic number is 256 – 224 = 32. The multiples of the magic number are 0, 32, 64, 96, and so on. Because the IP address value in the fourth octet is 77, in this case, the multiple must be the number closest to 77 without going over; therefore, the subnet ID ends with 64, for a value of 192.168.5.64.

Resident Subnet Practice Problems

Before moving to the next section, take some time to fill in the blanks in Table 14-10. Check your answers against Table 14-15 in the section "Answers to Earlier Practice Problems," later in this chapter. Complete the table by listing the subnet ID in each case. The text following Table 14-15 also lists explanations for each problem.

Table 14-10 Practice Problems: Find Subnet ID, Difficult Masks

Problem	IP Address	Mask	Subnet ID
1	10.77.55.3	255.248.0.0	
2	172.30.99.4	255.255.192.0	
3	192.168.6.54	255.255.255.252	
4	10.77.3.14	255.255.128.0	
5	172.22.55.77	255.255.254.0	
6	1.99.53.76	255.255.255.248	

Finding the Subnet Broadcast Address: Difficult Masks

To find a subnet's broadcast address, a similar process can be used. For simplicity, this process begins with the subnet ID, rather than the IP address. If you happen to start with an IP address instead, use the processes in this chapter to first find the subnet ID, and then use the following process to find the subnet broadcast address for that same subnet. For each octet, follow these steps:

Step 1. If the mask octet = 255, copy the subnet ID.

Step 2. If the mask octet = 0, write a 255.

Step 3. If the mask is neither, identify this octet as the *interesting octet*:

    A. Calculate the *magic number* as 256 – mask.

    B. Take the subnet ID's value, add the magic number, and subtract 1 (ID + magic number – 1).

As with the similar process used to find the subnet ID, you have several options for how to best learn and internalize the process. Look at the examples in this section, which show the process being used on paper. Then, follow the practice opportunities outlined in the section "Additional Practice."

Subnet Broadcast Example 1

The first example continues the first example from the section "Finding the Subnet ID: Difficult Masks," earlier in this chapter, as demonstrated in Figure 14-9. That example started with the IP address 130.4.102.1 and the mask 255.255.240.0, and showed how to find subnet ID 130.4.96.0. Figure 14-11 now begins with that subnet ID and the same mask.

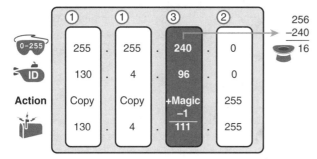

Figure 14-11 *Find the Subnet Broadcast: 130.4.96.0, 255.255.240.0*

First, examine the three uninteresting octets (1, 2, and 4). The process keys on the mask, and the first two octets have a mask value of 255, so simply copy the subnet ID to the place where you intend to write down the subnet broadcast address. The fourth octet has a mask value of 0, so write down a 255 for the fourth octet.

The logic related to the interesting octet occurs in the third octet in this example, because of the mask value 240. First, Step 3A asks you to calculate the magic number, as 256 – mask. (If you had already calculated the subnet ID using the decimal process in this book, you should already know the magic number.) At Step 3B, you take the subnet ID's value

(96), add the magic number (16), and subtract 1, for a total of 111. That makes the subnet broadcast address 130.4.111.255.

Subnet Broadcast Example 2

Again, this example continues an earlier example, from the section "Resident Subnet Example 2," as demonstrated in Figure 14-10. That example started with the IP address 192.168.5.77 and the mask 255.255.255.224, and showed how to find subnet ID 192.168.5.64. Figure 14-12 now begins with that subnet ID and the same mask.

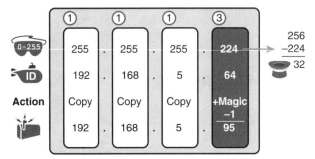

Figure 14-12   *Find the Subnet Broadcast: 192.168.5.64, 255.255.255.224*

First, examine the three uninteresting octets (1, 2, and 3). The process keys on the mask, and the first three octets have a mask value of 255, so simply copy the subnet ID to the place where you intend to write down the subnet broadcast address.

The interesting logic occurs in the interesting octet, which is the fourth octet in this example, because of the mask value 224. First, Step 3A asks you to calculate the magic number as 256 – mask. (If you had already calculated the subnet ID, it is the same magic number, because the same mask is used.) At Step 3B, you take the subnet ID's value (64), add the magic number (32), and subtract 1, for a total of 95. That makes the subnet broadcast address 192.168.5.95.

Subnet Broadcast Address Practice Problems

Before moving to the next section, take some time to do several practice problems on a scratch piece of paper. Go back to Table 14-10, which lists IP addresses and masks, and practice by finding the subnet broadcast address for all the problems in that table. Then check your answers against Table 14-16 in the section "Answers to Earlier Practice Problems," later in this chapter.

Practice Analyzing Existing Subnets

Before moving on to the next chapter, practice until you get the right answer most of the time—but use any tools you want and take all the time you need. Then, you can move on with your reading.

However, before taking the exam, practice until you master the topics in this chapter and can move pretty fast. As for time, you should be able to find the subnet ID, based on an IP address and mask, in around 15 seconds. You should also strive to start with a subnet ID/mask and find the broadcast address and range of addresses in another 15 seconds. Table 14-11 summarizes the key concepts and suggestions for this two-phase approach.

Table 14-11   The Keep-Reading and Take-Exam Goals for This Chapter's Topics

Time Frame	Before Moving to the Next Chapter	Before Taking the Exam
Focus on...	Learning how	Being correct and fast
Tools allowed	All	Your brain and a notepad
Goal: accuracy	90% correct	100% correct
Goal: speed	Any speed	30 seconds

A Choice: Memorize or Calculate

As described in this chapter, the decimal processes to find the subnet ID and subnet broadcast address do require some calculations, including the calculation of the magic number (256 – mask). The processes also use a DDN mask, so if an exam question gives you a prefix-style mask, you need to convert to DDN format before using the process in this book.

Over the years, some people have told me they prefer to memorize a table to find the magic number. These tables could list the magic number for different DDN masks and prefix masks, so you avoid converting from the prefix mask to DDN. Table 14-12 shows an example of such a table. Feel free to ignore this table, use it, or make your own.

Table 14-12   Reference Table: DDN Mask Values, Binary Equivalent, Magic Numbers, and Prefixes

Prefix, interesting octet 2	/9	/10	/11	/12	/13	/14	/15	/16
Prefix, interesting octet 3	/17	/18	/19	/20	/21	/22	/23	/24
Prefix, interesting octet 4	/25	/26	/27	/28	/29	/30		
Magic number	128	64	32	16	8	4	2	1
DDN mask in the interesting octet	128	192	224	240	248	252	254	255

Additional Practice

This section lists several options for additional practice:

- Appendix G, "Practice for Chapter 14: Analyzing Existing Subnets," has some additional practice problems. This appendix also includes explanations about how to find the answer of each problem.

- Create your own problems. Many subnet calculators list the number of network, subnet, and host bits when you type in an IP address and mask, so make up an IP address and mask on paper, and find the subnet ID and range of addresses. Then, to check your work, use any subnet calculator. (Check the author's web pages for this book, as listed in the Introduction, for some suggested calculators.)

Exam Preparation Tasks

Review All the Key Topics

Review the most important topics from this chapter, noted with the Key Topic icon. Table 14-13 lists these key topics and where each is discussed.

Table 14-13   Key Topics for Chapter 14

Key Topic Element	Description	Page Number
List	Definition of a subnet's key numbers	384
Table 14-2	Key facts about the subnet ID	386
Table 14-3	Key facts about the subnet broadcast address	387
List	Steps to use binary math to find the subnet ID	390
List	General steps to use binary and decimal math to find the subnet ID	392
List	Steps to use decimal and binary math to find the subnet broadcast address	393
List	Steps to use only decimal math to find the subnet ID	396
List	Steps to use only decimal math to find the subnet broadcast address	399

Complete the Tables and Lists from Memory

Print a copy of Appendix C, "Memory Tables," or at least the section for this chapter, and complete the tables and lists from memory. Appendix D, "Memory Tables Answer Key," includes completed tables and lists for you to check your work.

Definitions of Key Terms

After your first reading of the chapter, try to define these key terms, but do not be concerned about getting them all correct at that time. Chapter 24, "Final Review," directs you in how to use these terms for late-stage preparation for the exam.

resident subnet, subnet ID, subnet number, subnet address, subnet broadcast address

Practice

If you have not done so already, practice finding the subnet ID, range of addresses, and subnet broadcast address associated with an IP address and mask. Refer to the earlier section "Practice Analyzing Existing Subnets" for suggestions.

Answers to Earlier Practice Problems

This chapter includes practice problems spread around different locations in the chapter. The answers are located in Tables 14-14, 14-15, and 14-16.

Table 14-14   Answers to Problems in Table 14-9

	IP Address	Mask	Subnet ID	Broadcast Address
1	10.77.55.3	255.255.255.0	10.77.55.0	10.77.55.255
2	172.30.99.4	255.255.255.0	172.30.99.0	172.30.99.255
3	192.168.6.54	255.255.255.0	192.168.6.0	192.168.6.255
4	10.77.3.14	255.255.0.0	10.77.0.0	10.77.255.255
5	172.22.55.77	255.255.0.0	172.22.0.0	172.22.255.255
6	1.99.53.76	255.0.0.0	1.0.0.0	1.255.255.255

Table 14-15   Answers to Problems in Table 14-10

	IP Address	Mask	Subnet ID
1	10.77.55.3	255.248.0.0	10.72.0.0
2	172.30.99.4	255.255.192.0	172.30.64.0
3	192.168.6.54	255.255.255.252	192.168.6.52
4	10.77.3.14	255.255.128.0	10.77.0.0
5	172.22.55.77	255.255.254.0	172.22.54.0
6	1.99.53.76	255.255.255.248	1.99.53.72

The following list explains the answers in Table 14-15:

1. The second octet is the interesting octet, with magic number 256 – 248 = 8. The multiples of 8 include 0, 8, 16, 24, ..., 64, 72, and 80. 72 is closest to the IP address value in that same octet (77) without going over, making the subnet ID 10.72.0.0.

2. The third octet is the interesting octet, with magic number 256 – 192 = 64. The multiples of 64 include 0, 64, 128, and 192. 64 is closest to the IP address value in that same octet (99) without going over, making the subnet ID 172.30.64.0.

3. The fourth octet is the interesting octet, with magic number 256 – 252 = 4. The multiples of 4 include 0, 4, 8, 12, 16, ..., 48, 52, and 56. 52 is the closest to the IP address value in that same octet (54) without going over, making the subnet ID 192.168.6.52.

4. The third octet is the interesting octet, with magic number 256 – 128 = 128. Only two multiples exist that matter: 0 and 128. 0 is the closest to the IP address value in that same octet (3) without going over, making the subnet ID 10.77.0.0.

5. The third octet is the interesting octet, with magic number 256 – 254 = 2. The multiples of 2 include 0, 2, 4, 6, 8, and so on—essentially all even numbers. 54 is closest to the IP address value in that same octet (55) without going over, making the subnet ID 172.22.54.0.

6. The fourth octet is the interesting octet, with magic number 256 – 248 = 8. The multiples of 8 include 0, 8, 16, 24, ..., 64, 72, and 80. 72 is closest to the IP address value in that same octet (76) without going over, making the subnet ID 1.99.53.72.

Table 14-16 Answers to Problems in the Section "Subnet Broadcast Address Practice Problems"

	Subnet ID	Mask	Broadcast Address
1	10.72.0.0	255.248.0.0	10.79.255.255
2	172.30.64.0	255.255.192.0	172.30.127.255
3	192.168.6.52	255.255.255.252	192.168.6.55
4	10.77.0.0	255.255.128.0	10.77.127.255
5	172.22.54.0	255.255.254.0	172.22.55.255
6	1.99.53.72	255.255.255.248	1.99.53.79

The following list explains the answers in Table 14-16:

1. The second octet is the interesting octet. Completing the three easy octets means that the broadcast address in the interesting octet will be 10.___.255.255. With a magic number of 256 − 248 = 8, the second octet will be 72 (from the subnet ID), plus 8, minus 1, or 79.

2. The third octet is the interesting octet. Completing the three easy octets means that the broadcast address in the interesting octet will be 172.30.___.255. With a magic number of 256 − 192 = 64, the interesting octet will be 64 (from the subnet ID), plus 64 (the magic number), minus 1, for 127.

3. The fourth octet is the interesting octet. Completing the three easy octets means that the broadcast address in the interesting octet will be 192.168.6.___. With a magic number of 256 − 252 = 4, the interesting octet will be 52 (the subnet ID value), plus 4 (the magic number), minus 1, or 55.

4. The third octet is the interesting octet. Completing the three easy octets means that the broadcast address will be 10.77.___.255. With a magic number of 256 − 128 = 128, the interesting octet will be 0 (the subnet ID value), plus 128 (the magic number), minus 1, or 127.

5. The third octet is the interesting octet. Completing the three easy octets means that the broadcast address will be 172.22.___.255. With a magic number of 256 − 254 = 2, the broadcast address in the interesting octet will be 54 (the subnet ID value), plus 2 (the magic number), minus 1, or 55.

6. The fourth octet is the interesting octet. Completing the three easy octets means that the broadcast address will be 1.99.53.___. With a magic number of 256 − 248 = 8, the broadcast address in the interesting octet will be 72 (the subnet ID value), plus 8 (the magic number), minus 1, or 79.

This chapter covers the following exam topics:

2.0. Basic data center networking concepts

2.1. Compare and contrast the OSI and the TCP/IP models

CHAPTER 15

Fundamentals of IP Version 6

Much of the work to standardize IP Version 4 (IPv4) occurred in the 1970s—an era when most families did not own a computer and when a home computer with 16 kilobytes of RAM was considered a lot of RAM. At the time, a 32-bit IPv4 address, which could number more than 4 billion hosts, seemed ridiculously large. However, by the early 1990s, the IPv4-based Internet not only showed signs of running out of addresses, but it also risked running out of addresses very soon—endangering the emergence of the global Internet as a world-wide network available to all.

The Internet community came together to create both short-term and long-term solutions. The biggest short-term solution, Network Address Translation (NAT), reduced the number of unique IPv4 addresses needed by each company, thus putting off the day when the world would run out of IPv4 addresses. The long-term solution required a new version of IP, called IP Version 6 (IPv6).

IPv6 solves the long-term addressing problem with a mind-staggering 128-bit address, providing a little more than 3.4×10^{38} IPv6 addresses. For perspective, that number is far larger than most estimates for the number of grains of sand on Earth, and for the number of stars in the entire universe.

This chapter introduces IPv6, with comparisons to IPv4.

"Do I Know This Already?" Quiz

Use the "Do I Know This Already?" quiz to help decide whether you might want to skim this chapter, or a major section, moving more quickly to the "Exam Preparation Tasks" section near the end of the chapter. Table 15-1 lists the major headings in this chapter and their corresponding "Do I Know This Already?" quiz questions. For thorough explanations, see Appendix A, "Answers to the 'Do I Know This Already?' Quizzes."

Table 15-1 "Do I Know This Already?" Foundation Topics Section-to-Question Mapping

Foundation Topics Section	Questions
Introduction to IP Version 6	1–4
IPv6 Addressing and Subnetting	5–7
Implementing IPv6	8

1. Of the following list of motivations for the Internet community to create IPv6 to replace IPv4, which was the most important reason?

   a. To remove the requirement to use NAT when connecting to the Internet

   b. To simplify the IP header to simplify router-forwarding CPU time

   c. To improve support to allow mobile devices to move into a network

   d. To provide more addresses to relieve the address-exhaustion problem

2. Which of the following is the shortest valid abbreviation for FE80:0000:0000:0100:00 00:0000:0000:0123?

   a. FE80::100::123

   b. FE8::1::123

   c. FE80::100:0:0:0:123:4567

   d. FE80:0:0:100::123

3. Which of the following is the shortest valid abbreviation for 2000:0300:0040:0005:60 00:0700:0080:0009?

   a. 2:3:4:5:6:7:8:9

   b. 2000:300:40:5:6000:700:80:9

   c. 2000:300:4:5:6000:700:8:9

   d. 2000:3:4:5:6:7:8:9

4. Which of the following is the prefix for address 2000:0000:0000:0005:6000:0700:008 0:0009, assuming a mask of /64?

   a. 2000::5::/64

   b. 2000::5:0:0:0:0/64

   c. 2000:0:0:5::/64

   d. 2000:0:0:5:0:0:0:0/64

5. Which of the following IPv6 addresses appears to be a global unicast address, based on its first few hex digits?

   a. 3123:1:3:5::1

   b. FE80::1234:56FF:FE78:9ABC

   c. FDAD::1

   d. FF00::5

6. When subnetting an IPv6 address block, an engineer shows a drawing that breaks the address structure into three pieces. Comparing this concept to a three-part IPv4 address structure, which part of the IPv6 address structure is most like the IPv4 network part of the address?

   a. Subnet

   b. Interface ID

   c. Network

   d. Global routing prefix

   e. Subnet router anycast

7. When subnetting an IPv6 address block, an engineer shows a drawing that breaks the address structure into three pieces. Assuming that all subnets use the same prefix length, which of the following answers lists the name of the field on the far right side of the address?

   a. Subnet

   b. Interface ID

   c. Network

   d. Global routing prefix

   e. Subnet router anycast

8. Host PC1 dynamically learns its IPv6 settings using stateless address autoconfiguration (SLAAC). Think about the host's unicast address as two parts: the prefix and the interface ID. Which of the answers list a way that SLAAC learns or builds the value of the interface ID portion of the host's address? (Choose two answers.)

   a. Learned from a DHCPv6 server

   b. Built by the host using EUI-64 rules

   c. Learned from a router using NDP RS/RA messages

   d. Built by the host using a random value

15

Foundation Topics

Introduction to IP Version 6

IP Version 6 (IPv6) serves as the replacement protocol for IP Version 4 (IPv4). And although IPv6 has many benefits compared to IPv4, the overwhelming motivation to create IPv6 was to solve the shortage of IPv4 addresses by creating a new IP protocol with many more addresses.

This introductory section of the chapter begins by discussing the motivations and effects of the world's migration from IPv4 to IPv6. The rest of the introduction then examines the IPv6 addresses and prefixes that solve the primary issue of not having enough IPv4 addresses.

The Need and Effect of a New Internet Protocol

In the past 40 years, the Internet has gone from its infancy to being a huge influence in the world. It first grew through research at universities, from the ARPANET beginnings of the Internet in the late 1960s into the 1970s. The Internet kept growing fast in the 1980s, with its growth still primarily driven by research and the universities that joined in that research. By the early 1990s, the Internet began to transform to allow commerce, enabling people to sell services and products, which drove yet another steep spike upward in the growth of the Internet. Figure 15-1 shows some of these major milestones.

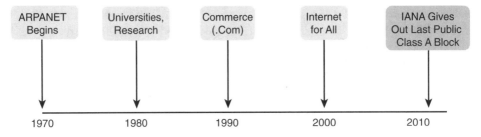

Figure 15-1 *Some Major Events in the Growth of the Internet*

Note that the figure ends the timeline with an event in which IANA/ICANN, the groups that assign public IPv4 addresses, gave out the last public IPv4 address blocks. IANA/ICANN assigned the final Class A networks to each of the Regional Internet Registries (RIRs) in February 2011. This event was an important one for the Internet, bringing us closer to the day when a company simply cannot get new IPv4 public address blocks.

In other words, one day, a company could be rejected when attempting to connect to the Internet, all because no more public IPv4 addresses exist.

Even though the press made a big deal about running out of IPv4 addresses in 2011, those who care about the Internet knew about this potential problem since the late 1980s. The problem, generally called the *IPv4 address-exhaustion* problem, could literally have caused the huge growth of the Internet in the 1990s to have come to a screeching halt! Something had to be done.

The IETF came up with several short-term solutions to make IPv4 last longer, hoping to put off the day when the world ran out of public IPv4 addresses. The two primary short-term solutions were Network Address Translation/Port Address Translation (NAT/PAT) and classless interdomain routing (CIDR). Both worked wonderfully. At the time, the Internet community hoped to extend the life of IPv4 for a few more years. In practice, these tools helped extend IPv4's life another couple of decades, as shown in the timeline of Figure 15-2.

15

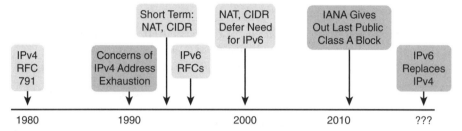

Figure 15-2 *Timeline for IPv4 Address Exhaustion and Short/Long-Term Solutions*

NOTE   The website www.potaroo.net, by Geoff Huston, shows many interesting statistics about the growth of the Internet, including IPv4 address exhaustion.

While the short-term solutions to IPv4 address exhaustion gave us all a few more decades to use IPv4, IPv6 gives the world a long-term solution. IPv6 replaces IPv4 as the core Layer 3 protocol, with a new IPv6 header and new IPv6 addresses. These addresses support a huge number of addresses, solving the address-shortage problem for generations (we hope).

NOTE   You may wonder why the next version of IP is not called IP Version 5. There was an earlier effort to create a new version of IP, and it was numbered version 5. IPv5 did not progress to the standards stage. However, to prevent any issues, because version 5 had been used in some documents, the next effort to update IP was numbered as version 6.

Additional Motivations for IPv6

While the need for more addresses drove the need for a new standard, IPv6 provides other benefits as well. For example, the designers of IPv6 acted on the decades of experience with IPv4 to make other improvements. The IPv6 header is actually simpler than the IPv4 header, streamlining the work routers do when forwarding packets. IPv6 supports some security and device mobility processes much more naturally than IPv4 as well.

Another big advantage for IPv6 is that enterprises no longer have to use NAT at the point of the enterprise's connection to the Internet. Today, most every company must use NAT, because without it, the Internet would have run out of IPv4 addresses a long time ago. Unfortunately, NAT happens to cause problems for some applications. IPv6 removes the requirement for NAT, solving a variety of problems with different applications.

A variety of other small motivations existed as well. IPv6 improved security, added new address autoconfiguration options, offered improvements to support device mobility more easily, and several others.

Many Protocols Updated

The upgrade to IPv6 begins with a new protocol called IP Version 6, but it includes many more new standards as well.

First, IPv6 does have a new protocol definition, as defined in RFC 2460. This RFC defines familiar concepts: a packet concept, addresses for those packets, and the role of hosts and routers. These rules allow the devices to forward IPv6 packets, sourced by IPv6 hosts, through multiple IPv6 routers, so that they arrive at the correct destination IPv6 host. (Those same concepts are defined for IPv4 in RFC 791.)

As you might imagine, IPv4 touches many other protocols as well, so an upgrade of IP from IPv4 to IPv6 required many other protocols to be upgraded, too. Some other RFCs define how to migrate from IPv4 to IPv6. Others define new versions of familiar protocols, or replace old protocols with new ones. Here are some examples:

- **Older OSPF Version 2 Upgraded to OSPF Version 3:** The older OSPF Version 2 works for IPv4, but not for IPv6, so a newer version, OSPF Version 3, was created to support IPv6.

- **ICMP Upgraded to ICMP Version 6:** ICMP worked well with IPv4 but needed to be changed to support IPv6. The new name is ICMPv6.

- **ARP Replaced by Neighbor Discovery Protocol:** For IPv4, ARP discovers the MAC address used by neighbors. IPv6 replaces ARP with a more general Neighbor Discovery Protocol (NDP).

NOTE If you go to any website that lists the RFCs, such as www.rfc-editor.org, you can find almost 300 RFCs that have IPv6 in the title.

Introduction to IPv6 Addresses and Prefixes

The other chapters in Part IV of this book have explained many details of how IPv4 addressing and subnetting work. For instance, with IPv4, you need to be able to interpret IPv4 addresses, such as 172.21.73.14. You need to be able to work with prefix-style masks, such as /25, and interpret what they mean when used with a particular IPv4 address. And you need to be able to take an address and mask, such as 172.21.73.14/25, and find the subnet ID.

The next few pages introduce the equivalent work with IPv6. Thankfully, even though the IPv6 addresses are much longer, the math is typically much more obvious and easier to do. In particular, this section looks at the following:

- How to write and interpret unabbreviated IPv6 addresses (32 hex digits in length)

- How to abbreviate IPv6 addresses, and how to interpret abbreviated addresses

- How to interpret the IPv6 prefix length mask

- How to find the IPv6 prefix (subnet ID), based on an address and prefix length mask

The biggest challenge with these tasks lies in the sheer size of the numbers. Thankfully, the math to find the subnet ID—often a challenge for IPv4—is easier for IPv6, at least to the depth discussed in this book.

Representing Full (Unabbreviated) IPv6 Addresses

IPv6 uses a convenient hexadecimal (hex) format for addresses. To make it more readable, IPv6 uses a format with eight sets of four hex digits, with each set of four digits separated by a colon. Here's an example:

2340:1111:AAAA:0001:1234:5678:9ABC:1234

> **NOTE**   For convenience, the term *quartet* is used for one set of four hex digits, with eight quartets in each IPv6 address. Note that the IPv6 RFCs do not use this term.

> **NOTE**   The IPv6 address format shown here may be referred to as *delimited hexadecimal*.

IPv6 addresses have a binary format as well, but thankfully, most of the time you do not need to look at the binary version of the addresses. However, in those cases, converting from hex to binary is relatively easy. Just change each hex digit to the equivalent 4-bit value, as listed in the hexadecimal-binary conversion table in Appendix I, "Numeric Reference Tables."

Abbreviating IPv6 Addresses

IPv6 also defines ways to abbreviate or shorten how you write or type an IPv6 address. Why? Although using a 32-digit hex number works much better than working with a 128-bit binary number, 32 hex digits is still a lot of digits to remember, recognize in command output, and type on a command line. The IPv6 address abbreviation rules let you shorten these numbers.

> **NOTE**   Computers and routers typically use the shortest abbreviation, even if you type all 32 hex digits of the address. So, even if you would prefer to use the longer unabbreviated version of the IPv6 address, you need to be ready to interpret the meaning of an abbreviated IPv6 address as listed by a router or host.

To be ready for the exam, you should be ready to abbreviate a full 32-digit IPv6 address, and to do the reverse: expand an abbreviated address back to its full 32 digits. Two basic rules let you, or any computer, shorten or abbreviate an IPv6 address:

1. Inside each quartet of four hex digits, remove the leading 0s (0s on the left side of the quartet) in the three positions on the left. (Note that at this step, a quartet of 0000 will leave a single 0.)

2. Find any string of two or more consecutive quartets of all hex 0s, and replace that set of quartets with a double colon (::). The :: means "two or more quartets of all 0s." However, you can only use :: once in a single address, because otherwise the exact IPv6 address might not be clear.

For example, consider the following IPv6 address, in which the bold digits represent the digits where the address could be abbreviated:

FE00:**0000:0000:0001:0000:0000:0000:00**56

Applying the first rule, you would look at all eight quartets independently. In each, remove all the leading 0s. Note that five of the quartets have four 0s, so for these, only remove three 0s, thus leaving the following value:

FE00:**0:0:1:0:0:0:**56

This abbreviation is valid, but the address can be abbreviated more using the second rule. In this case, two instances exist where more than one quartet in a row has only a 0. Pick the longest such sequence and replace it with ::, giving you the shortest legal abbreviation:

FE00:0:0:1::56

FE00:0:0:1::56 is indeed the shortest abbreviation, but this example happens to make it easier to see the two most common mistakes when abbreviating IPv6 addresses. First, never remove trailing 0s in a quartet (0s on the right side of the quartet). In this case, the first quartet of FE00 cannot be shortened at all, because the two 0s are trailing 0s. Therefore, the following address, which begins now with only FE in the first quartet, is not a correct abbreviation of the original IPv6 address:

FE:0:0:1::56

The second common mistake is to replace all series of all 0 quartets with a double colon. For instance, the following abbreviation would be incorrect for the original IPv6 address listed in this discussion:

FE00::1::56

The reason this abbreviation is incorrect is because now you do not know how many quartets of all 0s to substitute into each :: to find the original unabbreviated address.

Expanding IPv6 Addresses

To expand an IPv6 address back into its full unabbreviated 32-digit number, use two similar rules. The rules basically reverse the logic of the previous two rules.

1. In each quartet, add leading 0s as needed until the quartet has four hex digits.
2. If a double colon (::) exists, count the quartets currently shown; the total should be less than eight. Replace the :: with multiple quartets of 0000 so that eight total quartets exist.

The best way to get comfortable with these addresses and abbreviations is to do some yourself. Table 15-2 lists some practice problems, with the full 32-digit IPv6 address on the left and the best abbreviation on the right. The table gives you either the expanded or abbreviated address, and you need to supply the opposite value. You can find the answers at the end of the chapter, under the heading "Answers to Earlier Practice Problems."

Table 15-2   IPv6 Address Abbreviation and Expansion Practice

Full	Abbreviation
2340:0000:0010:0100:1000:ABCD:0101:1010	
	30A0:ABCD:EF12:3456:ABC:B0B0:9999:9009
2222:3333:4444:5555:0000:0000:6060:0707	
	3210::
210F:0000:0000:0000:CCCC:0000:0000:000D	
	34BA:B:B::20
FE80:0000:0000:0000:DEAD:BEFF:FEEF:CAFE	
	FE80::FACE:BAFF:FEBE:CAFE
FE80:000F:00E0:0D00:FACE:BAFF:FE00:0000	
	FE80:800:0:40:CAFE:FF:FE00:1

You will become more comfortable with these abbreviations as you get more experience. The "Exam Preparation Tasks" section at the end of this chapter lists several suggestions for getting more practice.

Representing the Prefix Length of an Address

IPv6 uses a mask concept, called *the prefix length*, similar to IPv4 subnet masks. Similar to the IPv4 prefix-style mask, the IPv6 prefix length is written as a slash mark (/) followed by a decimal number. The prefix length defines how many bits of the IPv6 address make up the IPv6 prefix, which is basically the same concept as the IPv4 subnet ID.

When you're writing IPv6 addresses, if the prefix length matters, the prefix length follows the IPv6 address. For example, use either of these for an address with a 64-bit prefix length:

2222:1111:0:1:A:B:C:D/64

2222:1111:0:1:A:B:C:D /64

Finally, note that the prefix length is a number of bits, so with IPv6, the legal value range is 0 through 128, inclusive.

Calculating the IPv6 Prefix (Subnet ID)

With IPv4, you can take an IP address and the associated subnet mask and then calculate the subnet ID. With IPv6 subnetting, you can take an IPv6 address and the associated prefix length and then calculate the IPv6 equivalent of the subnet ID: an *IPv6 prefix*.

Each IPv6 prefix, or *subnet* if you prefer, has a number that represents the group. Per the IPv6 RFCs, the number itself is also called the *prefix*, but many people just call it a subnet number or subnet ID, using the same terms as IPv4.

Like with different IPv4 subnet masks, some IPv6 prefix lengths make for an easy math problem to find the IPv6 prefix, and some prefix lengths make the math more difficult. For many good reasons, almost every subnet uses a prefix length of /64. And even better, a /64 prefix length makes the math to find the IPv6 prefix incredibly simple.

More generally, for any prefix length, you follow some basic rules to find the IPv6 subnet based on the IPv6 address and prefix length. If the prefix length is /P, use these rules:

1. Copy the first P bits.

2. Change the rest of the bits to 0.

However, because this book assumes that only /64 is used, the process can be even further simplified. Simply put, copy the first half of the address and then change the second half to all hexadecimal 0s. Figure 15-3 shows an example.

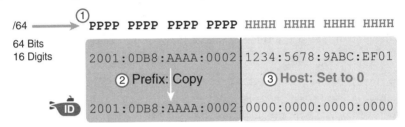

Legend:

⌐🔲 ID⌐ Subnet ID

Figure 15-3 *Creating the IPv6 Prefix from an Address/Length*

After you find the IPv6 prefix, you should also be ready to abbreviate the IPv6 prefix using the same rules you use to abbreviate IPv6 addresses. However, pay extra attention to the end of the prefix, because it often has several octets of all 0 values. As a result, the abbreviation typically ends with two colons (::).

For example, consider the following IPv6 address that is assigned to a host on a LAN:

2000:1234:5678:9ABC:1234:5678:9ABC:1111/64

This example shows an IPv6 address that itself cannot be abbreviated. After you calculate the prefix for the subnet in which the address resides, by zeroing out the last 64 bits (16 digits) of the address, you find the following prefix value:

2000:1234:5678:9ABC:**0000:0000:0000:0000**/64

This value can be abbreviated, with four quartets of all 0s at the end, as follows:

2000:1234:5678:9ABC::/64

To get better at the math, take some time to work through finding the prefix for several practice problems, as listed in Table 15-3. You can find the answers at the end of the chapter, under the heading "Answers to Earlier Practice Problems."

Table 15-3   Finding the IPv6 Prefix from an Address/Length Value

Address/Length	Prefix
2340:0:10:100:1000:ABCD:101:1010/64	
30A0:ABCD:EF12:3456:ABC:B0B0:9999:9009/64	
2222:3333:4444:5555::6060:707/64	
3210::ABCD:101:1010/64	
210F::CCCC:B0B0:9999:9009/64	
34BA:B:B:0:5555:0:6060:707/64	
3124::DEAD:CAFE:FF:FE00:1/64	
2BCD::FACE:BEFF:FEBE:CAFE/64	
3FED:F:E0:D00:FACE:BAFF:FE00:0/64	
3BED:800:0:40:FACE:BAFF:FE00:0/64	

Assigning Unique IPv6 Prefixes Across the Globe

IPv6 global unicast addresses allow IPv6 to work more like the original design of the IPv4 Internet. In other words, each organization asks for a block of IPv6 addresses that no one else can use. That organization further subdivides the address block into smaller chunks, called *subnets*. Finally, to determine what IPv6 address to use for any host, the engineer chooses an address from the right subnet.

That reserved block of IPv6 addresses—a set of unique addresses that only one company can use—is called a *global routing prefix*. Each organization that wants to connect to the Internet, and use IPv6 global unicast addresses, should ask for and receive a global routing prefix. Very generally, you can think of the global routing prefix like an IPv4 Class A, B, or C network number from the range of public IPv4 addresses.

The term *global routing prefix* might not make you think of a block of IPv6 addresses at first. The term actually refers to the idea that Internet routers can have one route that refers to all the addresses inside the address block, without a need to have routes for smaller parts of that block. For instance, Figure 15-4 shows three companies, with three different IPv6 global routing prefixes; the router on the right (R4) has one IPv6 route for each global routing prefix.

The global routing prefix sets those IPv6 addresses apart for use by that one company, just like a public IPv4 network or CIDR address block does in IPv4. All IPv6 addresses inside that company should begin with that global routing prefix, to avoid using other companies' IPv6 addresses. No other companies should use IPv6 addresses with that same prefix. And thankfully, IPv6 has plenty of space to allow all companies to have a global routing prefix, with plenty of addresses.

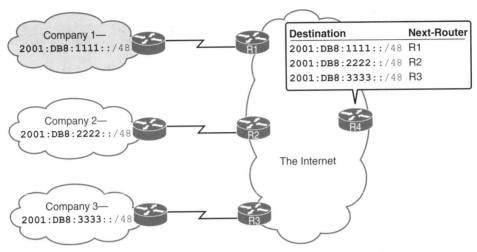

Figure 15-4   *Three Global Routing Prefixes, with One Route per Prefix*

Both the IPv6 and IPv4 address assignment process rely on the same organizations: IANA (along with ICANN), the RIRs, and ISPs. For example, an imaginary company, Company 1, received the assignment of a global routing prefix. The prefix means "All addresses whose first 12 hex digits are 2001:0DB8:1111," as represented by prefix 2001:0DB8:1111::/48. In order for Company 1 to receive that assignment, the process shown in Figure 15-5 had to happen.

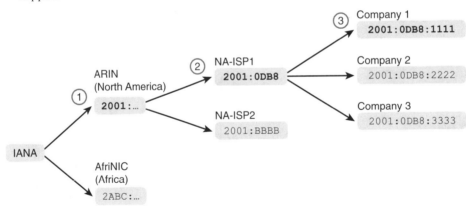

Figure 15-5   *Prefix Assignment with IANA, RIRs, and ISPs*

The event timeline in the figure uses a left-to-right flow; in other words, the event on the far left must happen first. Following the left-to-right flow in the figure, we have the following events occurring:

1.   **IANA gives ARIN prefix 2001::/16:** ARIN (the RIR for North America) asks IANA for the assignment of a large block of addresses. In this imaginary example, IANA gives ARIN a prefix of "all addresses that begin 2001," or 2001::/16.

2. **ARIN gives NA-ISP1 prefix 2001:0DB8::/32:** NA-ISP1, an imaginary ISP based in North America, asks ARIN for a new IPv6 prefix. ARIN takes a subset of its 2001::/16 prefix, specifically all addresses that begin with the 32 bits (8 hex digits) 2001:0DB8, and gives it to the ISP.

3. **NA-ISP1 gives Company 1 2002:0DB8:1111::/48:** Company 1 decides to start supporting IPv6, so they go to their ISP, NA-ISP1, to ask for a block of global unicast addresses. NA-ISP1 gives Company 1 a "small" piece of NA-ISP1's address block, in this case the addresses that begin with the 48 bits (12 hex digits) of 2001:0DB8:1111 (2001:0DB8:1111::/48).

Once a company has its IPv6 global routing prefix, the network engineers in that company can begin to divide that block of addresses into subnets usable inside the company, as described later in this chapter in the section titled "Global Unicast Addresses and IPv6 Subnetting."

Now that you know a few of the basics of IPv6, the next section dives into more detail about IPv6 addressing.

IPv6 Addressing and Subnetting

IPv6 defines many types of addresses. For instance, all the earlier examples in this chapter use *global unicast* addresses. The word *unicast* refers to the fact that each address represents a single host interface. The word *global* refers to the fact that with proper address assignment, the addresses should be unique across the globe. In other words, IPv6 global unicast addresses basically act like the equivalent of public IPv4 addresses.

This second of three major sections of this chapter examines several types of addresses. In particular, this section looks at the two major types of unicast addresses—global unicast addresses and unique local addresses—plus several types of specialized IPv6 addresses as well. Note that each type of address can be identified by the first few hex digits of the address, as noted in Table 15-4.

Table 15-4   Some Types of IPv6 Addresses and Their First Hex Digit(s)

Address Type	First Hex Digits
Global unicast	2 or 3 (originally); today, all addresses not otherwise reserved
Unique local	FD
Multicast	FF
Link local	FE80

Note that this discussion also covers IPv6 subnetting, in the same section that explains global unicast addressing.

Global Unicast Addresses and IPv6 Subnetting

Global unicast addresses give the world a way to give each and every IPv6 host a unique IPv6 address, without having to reuse the same addresses inside each company with something like IPv4 private addresses.

The process to give each host a global unicast address that is unique in the universe is relatively basic. As discussed earlier in the section titled "Assigning Unique IPv6 Prefixes Across the Globe," each company can apply for and receive a unique IPv6 prefix. (This prefix comes from the range of global unicast addresses, by the way.) The prefix gives the company a block of addresses—that is, all the addresses that begin with that prefix. Then, the engineers at the company further subdivide the address block into IPv6 subnets. Finally, each host can be assigned a unique address from the correct IPv6 subnet. Following this process gives each host a unique address.

The next few pages walk through the process described in the previous paragraph.

> **NOTE**   If the IPv4 subnetting concepts seem a little vague to you, you might want to reread Chapter 11, "Perspectives on IPv4 Subnetting," which discusses the subnetting concepts for IPv4.

IPv6 Subnetting Concepts

First, IPv6 and IPv4 both use the same concepts about where a subnet is needed: one for each VLAN, one for each point-to-point WAN connection (serial and Ethernet over Multiprotocol Label Switching [EoMPLS]), and so on. Figure 15-6 shows an example of the idea, using the small enterprise internetwork of Company 1. Company 1 needs one subnet for the branch office LAN on the left, one subnet for the point-to-point serial link connecting the sites, and two subnets for the two server VLANs at the central site on the right.

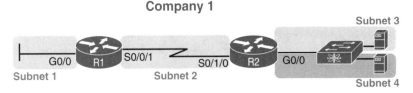

Figure 15-6   *Locations for IPv6 Subnets*

Next, think like the network engineer at Company 1, just after receiving the assignment of a global routing prefix from some ISP. The global routing prefix is a prefix, but it also represents a block of global unicast addresses. For instance, 2001:0DB8:1111 means "the block of addresses that begins 2001:0DB8:1111."

With IPv4, to create subnets of a network, you add a subnet field just after the network field in the IPv4 address structure. That subnet field can be used to number and identify different subnets. With IPv6, you do the same thing, adding a subnet field after the global routing prefix, as shown in Figure 15-7.

Just think about the general idea in Figure 15-7, compared with IPv4 subnetting with the network, subnet, and host parts of an IPv4 address. The IPv6 global routing prefix acts like the IPv4 network part of the address structure. The IPv6 subnet part acts like the IPv4 subnet part. And the right side of the IPv6 address, formally called the *interface ID* (short for interface identifier), acts like the IPv4 host field.

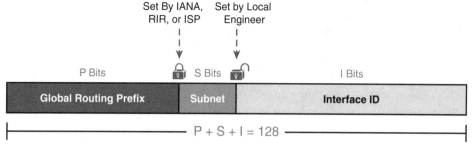

Figure 15-7 *Structure of Subnetted IPv6 Global Unicast Addresses*

The size of the fields will vary from company to company; however, most every company chooses to use a 64-bit interface ID field. As you will learn later in this chapter, a 64-bit interface ID field fits nicely with some of the other IPv6 protocols. Because most installations use a 64-bit interface ID, this book shows all the global unicast addresses with a 64-bit interface ID.

The length of the global routing prefix will also vary from company to company, as set by the organization that assigns the prefix to the company. For instance, one company might receive a global routing prefix from an ISP, with a prefix length of /40; another company might receive a slightly smaller block, with a /48 prefix length.

Finally, the subnet field sits in the bits between the global routing prefix and the interface ID. For instance, bringing the general concepts into an example, consider the structure of a specific global unicast IPv6 address, 2001:0DB8:1111:0001:0000:0000:0000:0001, as shown in Figure 15-8. In this case:

- The company was assigned prefix 2001:0DB8:1111, with a prefix length of /48.
- The company uses the usual 64-bit interface ID.
- The company has a subnet field of 16 bits, allowing for 2^{16} IPv6 subnets.

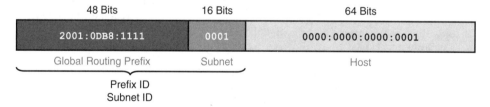

Figure 15-8 *Address Structure for Company 1 Example*

The example in Figure 15-8, along with a little math, shows one reason why so many companies use a /64 prefix length for all subnets. With this structure, Company 1 can support 2^{16} possible subnets (65,536). Very few companies need that many subnets. Then, each subnet supports over 1018 addresses (2^{64}, minus some reserved values). So, for both subnets and hosts, the address structure supports far more than are needed. Plus, the /64 prefix length for all subnets makes the math simple, because it cuts the 128-bit IPv6 address in half, so that the IPv6 subnet ID in this case would be as follows:

2001:DB8:1111:1::/64

NOTE   The IPv6 subnet ID, more formally called the *subnet router anycast address*, is reserved, and should not be used as an IPv6 address for any host.

Assigning Subnets and Addresses

The network engineer can determine all the IPv6 subnet IDs and then plan which subnet ID to use on each link that needs an IPv6 subnet. Just like with IPv4, each VLAN, each serial link, each EoMPLS link, and many other data-link instances need an IPv6 subnet. Figure 15-9 shows just such an example, with the same Company 1 network shown earlier in Figure 15-6. The figure shows four subnet IDs.

Company 1

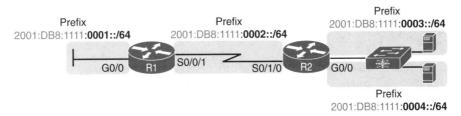

Figure 15-9   *Subnets in Company 1, with a Global Routing Prefix of 2001:0DB8:1111::/48*

NOTE   In IPv6, you can use two terms to refer to the groups of addresses as shown in Figure 15-9: prefix and subnet. Similarly, the last field in the structure of the address can be called either the *interface ID* or *host*. The pairs of terms include the traditional IPv4 terms as well as the newer terms specific to IPv6.

Now that the engineer has planned which IPv6 subnet will be used in each location, the individual IPv6 addressing can be planned and implemented. Each address must be unique, in that no other host interface uses the same IPv6 address. Also, the hosts cannot use the subnet ID itself.

Engineers can simply statically assign the addresses, as shown in Figure 15-10. Static assignment is common for devices in the control of IT, such as routers, switches, and servers. Addresses can be configured statically, along with the prefix length, default router, and DNS servers' IPv6 addresses. Figure 15-10 shows the interfaces that will be assigned different addresses for three of the IPv6 subnets; note that the addresses in the same subnet (per Figure 15-9) have the same 64-bit prefix values, which puts them in the same subnet.

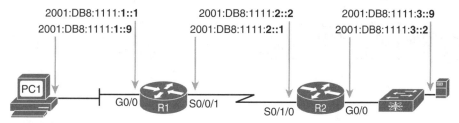

Figure 15-10 *Example of Static IPv6 Addresses Based on the Subnet Design of Figure 15-9*

The Actual Global Unicast Addresses

IANA reserves certain parts of the entire range of IPv6 addresses for different types of addresses. IANA originally reserved a large part of the entire IPv6 address space—all addresses that begin with hex 2 or hex 3—for global unicast addresses. IANA later expanded that range even further, stating that addresses not otherwise reserved for some other purpose were included in the range of global addresses.

> **NOTE**   You may see the idea "all addresses that begin with hex 2 or 3" written as the prefix 2000::/3. This prefix means "all addresses whose first three bits match hex 2000." If you look at the value in binary, you would see that the values include all hex IPv6 addresses that begin with a 2 or 3.

Unique Local Unicast Addresses

When a company decides to implement IPv6, they can choose to use global unicast addresses. To do so, they obtain a prefix from an ISP, do some subnet planning as just discussed in this chapter, and start using the addresses.

Alternately, a company can choose to not use global unicast addresses, but instead use *unique local* unicast addresses. These unique local addresses act somewhat like private IPv4 addresses, in that the company's network engineer can pick some values to use without registering any public addresses with an ISP or other organization. So, although not the literal equivalent of private IPv4 addresses, they can serve the same overall purpose.

Although the network engineer creates unique local addresses without any registration or assignment process, the addresses still need to follow some rules, as detailed next:

- Use FD as the first two hex digits (as required by IANA).
- Choose a unique 40-bit global ID.
- Append the 40-bit global ID behind the FD to create a 48-bit prefix, used as the prefix for all of that company's addresses.
- Use the next 16 bits as a subnet field.
- Note that the structure leaves a convenient 64-bit interface ID field.

Figure 15-11 shows the format of these unique local unicast addresses.

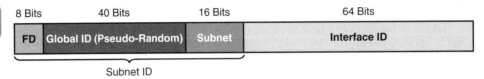

Figure 15-11   *IPv6 Unique Local Unicast Address Format*

> **NOTE**   Just to be completely exact, IANA actually reserves prefix FC00::/7, and not
> FD00::/8, for these addresses. FC00::/7 includes all addresses that begin with hex FC and
> FD. However, RFC 4193 requires that the eighth bit of these addresses to be set to 1, mak-
> ing the first two hex digits FD. Therefore, in practice today, the unique local addresses all
> begin with their first two digits as FD.

After the engineer has determined the 48-bit prefix to use inside the company, the rest of
the subnetting and address assignment concepts work exactly like they do with global unicast addresses.

Link Local Addresses

IPv6 uses both global unicast and unique local addresses for the same purposes as IPv4
addresses. Hosts use one of these types of IPv6 addresses for their interfaces, routers use
one per interface, and packets use these addresses as the source and destination of IPv6
packets that flow from end to end through the network.

IPv6 also defines *link local* addresses: a completely new type of unicast address that is not
used for normal user traffic, but is instead used for some special types of IPv6 packets. As
the name implies, packets that use a link local address stay on the local link and are not
routed by a router to the next subnet. Instead, IPv6 uses link local addresses for some overhead protocols and for routing. Some examples are shown over the next few pages.

For instance, routers use link local addresses as the next-hop IP addresses in IPv6 routes, as
shown in Figure 15-12. IPv6 hosts also use a default router (default gateway) concept, like
IPv4, but instead of the default router address being in the same subnet, hosts refer to the
router's link local address. The next-hop address in IPv6 routing tables also lists the neighboring router's link local address.

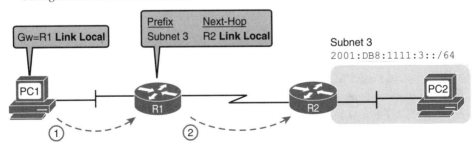

Figure 15-12   *IPv6 Using Link Local Addresses as the Next-Hop Address*

Link local addresses also solve some initialization issues. Hosts can calculate a complete link local address to use even before they dynamically learn their other (global unicast or unique local) address that they use for user traffic. Having an IPv6 address that can be used when sending packets on the local link helps the operation of several overhead protocols.

The following list summarizes the key facts about link local addresses:

Unicast (not multicast): Link local addresses represent a single host (in other words, it is a unicast address), and packets sent to a link local address should be processed by only that one IPv6 host.

Forwarding scope is the local link only: Packets flow on-link only, because routers do not forward packets with link local destination addresses.

Automatically generated: Every IPv6 host interface (and router interface) can create its own link local address automatically, solving some initialization problems for hosts before they learn a dynamically learned global unicast address.

Common Uses: Used for some overhead protocols that stay local to one subnet, and as the next-hop address for IPv6 routes.

IPv6 hosts and routers can calculate their own link local address, for each interface, using some basic rules. First, all link local addresses start with the same prefix, as shown on the left side of Figure 15-13. By definition, the first 10 bits must match prefix FE80::/10, meaning that the first three hex digits will be either FE8, FE9, FEA, or FEB. However, when following the RFC, the next 54 bits should be binary 0, so the link local address should always start with FE80:0000:0000:0000 as the first four unabbreviated quartets.

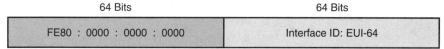

Figure 15-13 *Link Local Address Format*

The second half of the link local address, in practice, can be formed with different rules. It can be randomly generated, statically configured, or set based on the interface MAC address using EUI-64 rules. The upcoming section "Dynamic Assignment of the Interface ID with EUI-64" discusses the automatic process based on the EUI-64 rules.

IPv6 Multicast Addresses

IPv6 does not define or use the concept of a broadcast IPv6 address, but it does define and use many types of IPv6 multicast addresses. Multicast addresses have an advantage for the network because only a subset of the hosts in the network will receive and process a packet sent to a multicast address, whereas packets sent to an IPv4 broadcast address arrive at all hosts.

IPv6 defines different types of multicast addresses based on the scope of where the packets should flow. In some cases, multicast messages need to stay within one subnet, but in other cases, they need to be able to flow to many subnets. To aid that logic, IPv6 defines some ranges of multicast addresses so that a packet sent to that address should stay on the link; these addresses have a *link local* scope. Multicast addresses that allow the packets to be routed to other subnets inside the enterprise have an *organization local* scope.

Table 15-5 shows a sampling of some link-local-scope multicast addresses. IANA defines all multicast addresses from within the range of addresses that begin with FF, or more formally, prefix FF00::/8. IANA reserves the more specific range of addresses that begin with FF02 (formally, FF02::/16) for link-local-scope multicast addresses.

Table 15-5   Key IPv6 Local Scope Multicast Addresses

Short Name	Multicast Address	Meaning	IPv4 Equivalent
All-nodes	FF02::1	All nodes (all interfaces that use IPv6 that are on the link)	A subnet broadcast address
All-routers	FF02::2	All routers (all IPv6 router interfaces on the link)	None
RIPng routers	FF02::9	All RIPng routers	224.0.0.9
All-OSPF, All-OSPF-DR	FF02::5, FF02::6	All OSPF routers and all OSPF designated routers, respectively	224.0.0.5, 224.0.0.6
EIGRPv6 routers	FF02::A	All routers using EIGRP for IPv6 (EIGRPv6)	224.0.0.10

The table mentions a few routing protocols with familiar-looking names. RIP, OSPF, and EIGRP all have IPv6-compatible versions. RIP for IPv6 goes by the name RIPng, for RIP next generation. OSPF Version 3 (OSPFv3) is simply the next version of OSPF (the normal OSPF version used with IPv4 happens to be OSPF Version 2). EIGRP for IPv6 may be called EIGRPv6 in reference to IPv6, although there is no published EIGRP version number.

Miscellaneous IPv6 Addresses

To round out the discussion, two other special IPv6 addresses exist that can be commonly seen even with basic implementations of IPv6:

■ The unknown (unspecified) IPv6 address, ::, or all 0s

■ The loopback IPv6 address, ::1, or 127 binary 0s with a single 1

The unknown address (::) can be used by a host when its own IPv6 address is not yet known or when the host wonders if its own IPv6 address may have problems. For instance, hosts use the unknown address during the early stages of dynamically discovering their IPv6 address. When a host does not yet know what IPv6 address to use, it can use the :: address as its source IPv6 address.

The IPv6 loopback address gives each IPv6 host a way to test its own protocol stack. Just like the IPv4 127.0.0.1 loopback address, packets sent to ::1 do not leave the host, but are instead simply delivered down the stack to IPv6 and back up the stack to the application on the local host.

Implementing IPv6

IPv6 implementation often begins with the simple act of enabling IPv6 on an interface by giving it an IPv6 address. This final of three major sections of the chapter introduces the available options for giving IPv6 addresses to hosts, ranging from fully automated processes to simply typing the address into the configuration of the device.

This section closes with a brief introduction to one of the big questions each installation must ask when implementing IPv6: how do you migrate from IPv4 and have IPv6 coexist with IPv4 while the migration takes place?

IPv6 Address Assignment

To implement IPv6, routers, user devices, servers, switches, and other devices need IPv6 addresses. For instance, the entire IPv6 address and prefix length can simply be configured. The process works much like it does for IPv4, from a graphical interface on most user operating systems, to the **ipv6 address** command on most Cisco platforms. The next few pages review the methods of assigning IPv6 addresses that require more than simply typing the information, emphasizing the differences between IPv4 and IPv6.

Dynamic Assignment of the Interface ID with EUI-64

Stop for a moment and think about the subnet planning process versus the process of choosing the specific IPv6 address for each host and router interface. Some network engineer must plan which subnet ID to use for each location in the network. Once chosen, the IPv6 addresses inside a given subnet must have the same prefix value as well as a unique value in the interface ID (host) part of the address.

In fact, most engineers do not care what specific interface ID each host in a subnet uses, as long as it is unique among all hosts in the same subnet.

The EUI-64 option gives devices a way to automatically generate a unique interface ID. Someone statically configures the prefix, lets the device create a unique interface ID, and the process is complete.

The process to create the interface ID uses another unique number: the interface's MAC address. The process works as follows:

1. Split the 6-byte (12-hex-digit) MAC address in two halves (6 hex digits each).

2. Insert FFFE in between the two, making the interface ID now have a total of 16 hex digits (64 bits).

3. Invert the seventh bit of the interface ID.

Figure 15-14 shows the major pieces of how the address is formed.

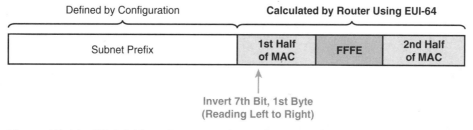

Figure 15-14 *IPv6 Address Format with Interface ID and EUI-64*

Although it might seem a bit convoluted, it works. Also, with a little practice, you can look at an IPv6 address and quickly notice the FFFE in the middle of the interface ID, and then easily find the two halves of the corresponding interface's MAC address. But you need to be ready to do the same math, in this case to predict the EUI-64-formatted IPv6 address on an interface.

For example, if you ignore the final step of inverting the seventh bit, the rest of the steps just require that you move the pieces around. Figure 15-15 shows two examples, just so you see the process.

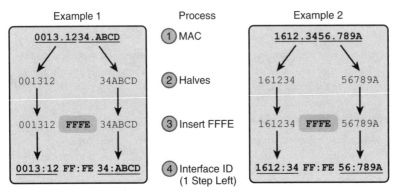

Figure 15-15   *Two Examples of Most of the EUI-64 Interface ID Process*

Both examples follow the same process. Each starts with the MAC address, breaking it into two halves (Step 2). The third step inserts FFFE in the middle, and the fourth step inserts a colon every four hex digits, keeping with IPv6 conventions.

The examples in Figure 15-15 show most of the steps, but they omit the final step of inverting the seventh bit. Figure 15-16 completes the work, showing the conversion of the first byte (first two hex digits) to binary, flipping the bit, and converting back to hexadecimal.

NOTE   If you do not have those steps handy in your memory, take a few moments to look at Table I-2 in Appendix I.

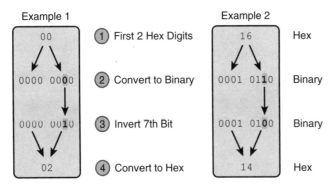

Figure 15-16   *Inverting the Seventh Bit of an EUI-64 Interface ID Field*

To summarize, these two examples translate the MAC addresses into the 64-bit (16 hex digit) interface ID values as follows:

MAC 0013.1234.ABCD results in interface ID 0213:12FF:FE34:ABCD.

MAC 1612.3456.789A results in interface ID 1412:34FF:FE56:789A.

Discovering the IPv6 Prefix with SLAAC

In some cases, the network engineer may want to configure the prefix and let the device create its own unique interface ID value, as just shown. However, in other cases, the engineer may want the device to create its entire IPv6 address automatically. IPv4 lets hosts lease an IPv4 address from a DHCP server, and IPv6 supports an equivalent process also using Dynamic Host Control Protocol (DHCP). However, IPv6 supports another automatic process, called *stateless address autoconfiguration*, or *SLAAC*.

A host using SLAAC relies on two key processes. First, the host learns the subnet prefix from a router that sits on the same subnet, using the IPv6 Neighbor Discovery Protocol (NDP). The second process is familiar: The host calculates the interface ID using EUI-64 rules.

NDP defines several features, including a process to discover the existence of IPv6 routers and to discover some basic information from the router. The NDP Router Solicitation (RS) message generally means something like this: "IPv6 routers, tell me information that you know!" The Router Advertisement (RA) message gives IPv6 routers a means to distribute the information: "Here is the information that I know!" Figure 15-17 shows one fact learned through the RS and RA messages—namely, the IPv6 address of the IPv6 router.

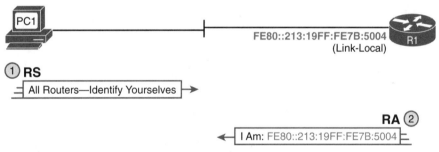

Figure 15-17 *Using NDP RS/RA to Discover the Prefix/Length on the LAN*

> **NOTE** IPv6 allows multiple prefixes and multiple default routers to be listed in the RA message; the figure just shows one of each for simplicity's sake.

Pulling these ideas together, when using SLAAC, a host does not lease its IPv6 address, or even learn its IPv6 address from some other device. Instead, the host learns part of the address—the prefix—and then makes up the rest of its own IPv6 address. Specifically, a host using SLAAC to choose its own IPv6 address uses the following steps:

1. Learn the IPv6 prefix used on the link, from any router, using NDP RS/RA messages.

2. Choose a unique interface ID, either randomly or using EUI-64 rules.

Before leaving SLAAC, take a moment to stop and think about the bigger picture of IPv6 implementation on all devices. With SLAAC, routers supplied the prefix information, so the routers have to have some way to first know the prefixes. To make that happen, most routers and Layer 3 switches are either configured with static IPv6 addresses or are statically configured with the prefix while using EUI-64 to derive the router's interface ID. In other words, the router knows the prefix because the network engineer typed that information into the configuration. SLAAC makes more sense as a tool for end-user devices, with the SLAAC process relying on the prefix information known by the routers and Layer 3 switches.

Dynamic Configuration Using Stateful DHCP

DHCP for IPv6 (DHCPv6) gives an IPv6 host a way to learn host IPv6 configuration settings, using the same general concepts as DHCP for IPv4. The host exchanges messages with a DHCP server, and the server supplies the host with configuration information, including a lease of an IPv6 address, along with prefix length and DNS server address information.

> **NOTE** The DHCP version is not actually version 6; the name just ends in v6 in reference to the support for IPv6.

More specifically, stateful DHCPv6 works like the more familiar DHCP for IPv4 in many other general ways, as follows:

- DHCP clients on a LAN send messages that flow only on the local LAN, hoping to find a DHCP server.
- If the DHCP server sits on the same LAN as the client, the client and server can exchange DHCP messages directly, without needing help from a router.
- If the DHCP server sits on another link as compared to the client, the client and server rely on a router to forward the DHCP messages.
- The router that forwards messages from one link to a server in a remote subnet must be configured as a DHCP relay agent, with knowledge of the DHCP server's IPv6 address.
- Servers have a configuration that lists pools of addresses for each subnet from which the server allocates addresses.
- Servers offer a lease of an IP address to a client from the pool of addresses for the client's subnet; the lease lasts a set time period (usually days or weeks).
- The server tracks state information, specifically a client identifier (often based on the MAC address), along with the address that is currently leased to that client.

DHCPv6 also updates the protocol messages to use IPv6 packets instead of IPv4 packets, with new messages and fields as well. For instance, Figure 15-18 shows the names of the DHCPv6 messages, which replace the DHCPv4 Discover, Offer, Request, and Acknowledgment (DORA) messages. Instead, DHCPv6 uses the Solicit, Advertise, Request, and Reply messages.

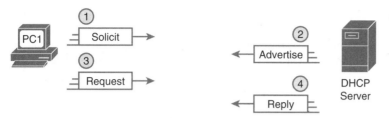

Figure 15-18 *Four Stateful DHCPv6 Messages Between Client and Server*

The four DHCPv6 messages work in two matched pairs with the same general flow as the similar DHCPv4 messages. The Solicit and Advertise messages complete the process of the client searching for the IPv6 address of a DHCPv6 server (the Solicit message), and the server advertising an address (and other configuration settings) for the client to possibly use (the Advertise message). The Request and Reply messages let the client ask to lease the address, with the server confirming the lease in the Reply message.

NOTE This section describes the operation of DHCPv6 called stateful DHCP. DHCPv6 can also operate as stateless DHCP, which is a useful function when SLAAC is also being used. Stateless DHCP is not discussed in this book.

IPv6 Transition and Coexistence

IPv4 exists on most every electronic device on the planet. Most every PC, tablet, phone, and server use IPv4. Most consumer electronics have support for IPv4 as well, with IPv4 commonly used in game systems and televisions. And with the emergence of the concept called the Internet of Things, in which a large number of physical devices connect to the Internet, the need for addresses will grow even more.

Transitioning a world that uses IPv4 on most every existing network-connected device cannot happen overnight, or even in a single year. In fact, such a transition cannot happen quickly even inside a single company. To deal with the challenges of migration, IPv6 defines several transition and coexistence strategies that allow the Internet and enterprises to add IPv6 support, operate a network with some IPv4 and some IPv6, and eventually, one day, complete a migration to using only IPv6.

Dual Stack

One way to begin the migration to IPv6 requires the addition of IPv6 to all Layer 3 devices (routers and Layer 3 switches). The routers and Layer 3 switches continue to support IPv4 as always, with IPv6 configuration added. For each interface on which a router formerly supported IPv4, the router now supports both IPv4 and IPv6. This transition method is called *dual stack*.

Once the routers can route both IPv4 packets and IPv6 packets, then the end-user devices, servers, and other devices can migrate to IPv6. Those devices can also add support for IPv6, keeping the old support for IPv4. Eventually, over time, all devices can migrate to IPv6, so at some point, IPv4 support can finally be disabled.

The process of running both IPv4 and IPv6 is called dual stack, and Figure 15-19 reinforces the idea. The PCs and the routers all support both IPv4 and IPv6. On the top, PC1 has sent an IPv4 packet to Server 1's IPv4 address, with router R1 forwarding the packet to the next router. PC2 then sends an IPv6 packet to that same server. R1 and the other routers, running IPv6, support the ability to route the IPv6 packet through the network to reach the server.

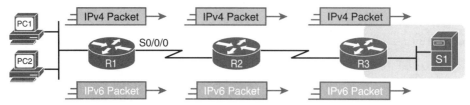

Figure 15-19 *Dual Stack Implemented on Three Routers*

Tunneling IPv6 Inside IPv4

IPv6 also provides several different coexistence tools in which the IPv6 packets tunnel through the IPv4 network. The general idea works like this:

1. The user devices and servers at some locations can begin to support IPv6.

2. The router directly connected to each user or server subnet runs dual stack, but the routers in between do not.

3. The routers directly connected to the user or server subnets create tunnels between each other.

4. The routers forward IPv6 packets by encapsulating them in an IPv4 packet, forwarding the IPv4 packet to another dual-stack router, which removes the original IPv6 packet.

An example surely helps in this case. Figure 15-20 shows just such an example, in which PC1 and server S1 both now support IPv6. Routers R1 and R3 also now support IPv6, and they create a tunnel through the IPv4 network. Note that all other routers between R1 and R3, such as router R2 in the figure, can still use only IPv4, and have no knowledge of IPv6.

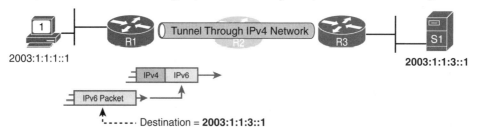

Figure 15-20 *Tunneling IPv6 in IPv4 as a Coexistence Method*

By reading the figure from left to right, we see that PC1 sends an IPv6 packet to the server. When the IPv6 packet arrives at router R1, R1 encapsulates the IPv6 packet behind an IPv4 header. R1 and R2 forward this IPv4 packet to R3, as an IPv4 packet, so that R3 can remove the original IPv6 packet and forward it to server S1.

IPv6 supports several different tunneling methods to meet different transition needs.

Exam Preparation Tasks

Review All the Key Topics

Review the most important topics from this chapter, noted with the Key Topic icon. Table 15-6 lists these key topics and where each is discussed.

15

Table 15-6   Key Topics for Chapter 15

Key Topic Element	Description	Page Number
List	Rules to abbreviate IPv6 addresses	413
List	Rules to expand an abbreviated IPv6 address	414
Figure 15-5	Description of the IPv6 prefix (address block) assignment process	418
Table 15-4	List of address types and their initial digits	419
Figure 15-7	Structure of a subnetted global unicast address	421
Figure 15-11	Structure of a unique local address	424
List	Uses for link local addresses	425
Figure 15-14	Summary of EUI-64 structure and logic	427
List	Summary of SLAAC rules	429
List	Comparison points for DHCPv4 versus DHCPv6	430

Complete the Tables and Lists from Memory

Print a copy of Appendix C, "Memory Tables," or at least the section for this chapter, and complete the tables and lists from memory. Appendix D, "Memory Tables Answer Key," includes completed tables and lists for you to check your work.

Definitions of Key Terms

After your first reading of the chapter, try to define these key terms, but do not be concerned about getting them all correct at that time. Chapter 24, "Final Review," directs you in how to use these terms for late-stage preparation for the exam.

IP version 6, Network Address Translation, IPv4 address exhaustion, global unicast address, unique local address, global routing prefix, link local address, EUI-64, stateless address autoconfiguration (SLAAC), DHCP, dual stack, tunneling, OSPF Version 3 (OSPFv3), EIGRP Version 6 (EIGRPv6), prefix, prefix length, quartet

Answers to Earlier Practice Problems

This chapter includes practice problems spread around different locations in the chapter. The answers are located in Tables 15-7 and 15-8.

Table 15-7   Answers to Questions in Table 15-2

Full	Abbreviation
2340:0000:0010:0100:1000:ABCD:0101:1010	2340:0:10:100:1000:ABCD:101:1010
30A0:ABCD:EF12:3456:0ABC:B0B0:9999:9009	30A0:ABCD:EF12:3456:ABC:B0B0:9999:9009
2222:3333:4444:5555:0000:0000:6060:0707	2222:3333:4444:5555::6060:707
3210:0000:0000:0000:0000:0000:0000:0000	3210::
210F:0000:0000:0000:CCCC:0000:0000:000D	210F::CCCC:0:0:D
34BA:000B:000B:0000:0000:0000:0000:0020	34BA:B:B::20
FE80:0000:0000:0000:DEAD:BEFF:FEEF:CAFE	FE80::DEAD:BEFF:FEEF:CAFE
FE80:0000:0000:0000:FACE:BAFF:FEBE:CAFE	FE80::FACE:BAFF:FEBE:CAFE
FE80:000F:00E0:0D00:FACE:BAFF:FE00:0000	FE80:F:E0:D00:FACE:BAFF:FE00:0
FE80:0800:0000:0040:CAFE:00FF:FE00:0001	FE80:800:0:40:CAFE:FF:FE00:1

Table 15-8   Answers to Questions in Table 15-3

Address/Length	Prefix
2340:0:10:100:1000:ABCD:101:1010/64	2340:0:10:100::/64
30A0:ABCD:EF12:3456:ABC:B0B0:9999:9009/64	30A0:ABCD:EF12:3456::/64
2222:3333:4444:5555::6060:707/64	2222:3333:4444:5555::/64
3210::ABCD:101:1010/64	3210::/64
210F::CCCC:B0B0:9999:9009/64	210F::/64
34BA:B:B:0:5555:0:6060:707/64	34BA:B:B::/64
3124::DEAD:CAFE:FF:FE00:1/64	3124:0:0:DEAD::/64
2BCD::FEED:FACE:BEEF:FEBE:CAFE/64	2BCD:0:0:FEED::/64
3FED:F:E0:D00:FACE:BAFF:FE00:0/64	3FED:F:E0:D00::/64
3BED:800:0:40:FACE:BAFF:FE00:0/64	3BED:800:0:40::/64

Part III Review

Keep track of your part review progress with the checklist shown in Table P3-1. Details on each task follow the table.

Table P3-1 Part III Review Checklist

Activity	First Date Completed	Second Date Completed
Repeat All DIKTA Questions		
Answer Part Review Questions		
Review Key Topics		

Repeat All DIKTA Questions: For this task, answer the "Do I Know This Already?" questions again for the chapters in this part of the book, using the PCPT software. Refer to the Introduction and find the section "How to View Only DIKTA Questions by Part" for help with how to make the PCPT software show you DIKTA questions for this part only.

Answer Part Review Questions: For this task, answer the Part Review questions for this part of the book, using the PCPT software. Refer to the Introduction and find the section "How to View Only Part Review Questions by Part" for help with how to make the PCPT software show you Part Review questions for this part only.

Review Key Topics: Browse back through the chapters and look for the Key Topic icons. If you do not remember some details, take the time to reread those topics.

Parts II and III of this book focused on Ethernet technologies, with most of that discussion related to Layer 2 (data link) processing. Part IV now changes the focus of this book from Layer 2 to Layer 3 (network), setting the foundation for examining IP routing.

Part IV creates a foundation for understanding Layer 3 processing on both routers and Layer 3 switches by explaining IP Version 4 (IPv4) routing. This part also introduces the use of First Hop Redundancy Protocols (FHRPs) and finishes off with creating IPv4 access control lists (ACLs) to control what traffic is allowed to traverse your Layer 3 networks.

Part IV

IPv4 Routing

This chapter covers the following exam topics:

4.1. Describe and configure basic routing concepts

4.1.a. Packet forwarding

4.1.b. Router look-up process (exec mode, exec commands, configuration mode)

4.2. Describe the operation of Cisco routers

4.2.a. Router boot-up process

4.2.b. POST

4.3.c. Router components

CHAPTER 16

IPv4 Routing Concepts

Routers route IPv4 packets. That simple statement actually carries a lot of hidden meaning. For routers to route packets, routers follow a routing process. That routing process relies on information called *IP routes*. Each IP route lists a destination—an IP network, IP subnet, or some other group of IP addresses. Each route also lists instructions that tell the router where to forward packets sent to addresses in that IP network or subnet. For routers to do a good job of routing packets, they need to have a detailed, accurate list of IP routes.

Routers use three methods to add IPv4 routes to their IPv4 routing tables. Routers first learn *connected routes*, which are routes for subnets attached to a router interface. Routers can also use *static routes*, which are routes created through a configuration command (**ip route**) that tells the routers what route to put in the IPv4 routing table. And routers can use a routing protocol, in which routers tell each other about all their known routes, so that all routers can learn and build routes to all networks and subnets.

This chapter begins by reintroducing the IP routing process that relies on these routes. This IP routing discussion reviews the concepts from Chapter 4, "Fundamentals of IPv4 Addressing and Routing," as well as takes the concepts deeper, including showing information needed in a single IP route. Then, the second major section in this chapter discusses connected routes, including variations of connected routes such as VLANs connected to a router's VLAN trunk, and for connected routes on Layer 3 switches.

NOTE As promised in the Introduction's section "For Those Studying Routing & Switching," you have already read about the concepts in the first major heading of this chapter, which comprises most of the chapter. The first major heading covers generic routing, and the second gets into Cisco Nexus specifics.

"Do I Know This Already?" Quiz

Use the "Do I Know This Already?" quiz to help decide whether you might want to skim this chapter, or a major section, moving more quickly to the "Exam Preparation Tasks" section near the end of the chapter. Table 16-1 lists the major headings in this chapter and their corresponding "Do I Know This Already?" quiz questions. For thorough explanations, see Appendix A, "Answers to the 'Do I Know This Already?' Quizzes."

Table 16-1 "Do I Know This Already?" Foundation Topics Section-to-Question Mapping

Foundation Topics Section	Questions
IP Routing	1–2
Cisco Nexus Switch Operation with Routing	3–5

1. A user on a PC opens a command prompt and uses the **ipconfig** command to see that the PC's IP address and mask are 192.168.4.77 and 255.255.255.224, respectively. The user then runs a test using the **ping 192.168.4.117** command. Which of the following answers is the most likely to happen?

   a. The PC sends packets directly to the host with address 192.168.4.117.

   b. The PC sends packets to its default gateway.

   c. The PC sends a DNS query for 192.168.4.117.

   d. The PC sends an ARP looking for the MAC address of the DHCP server.

2. Router R1 lists a route in its routing table. Which of the following answers list a fact from a route, that the router then compares to the packet's destination address? (Choose two answers.)

   a. Mask

   b. Next-hop router

   c. Subnet ID

   d. Outgoing interface

3. Which implementation on a Cisco Nexus switch turns off all Layer 2 protocol functions on an interface?

   a. Routed interface

   b. Switched virtual interface (SVI)

   c. Switchport access interface

   d. Switchport trunk interface

4. Which interface is preferred if you want to support both Layer 2 and Layer 3 for a VLAN on a Cisco Nexus switch?

   a. Trunk

   b. Access

   c. Switched virtual interface (SVI)

   d. Switchport

5. Which interface implementation on a Cisco Nexus switch allows for the faster interface or link down detection when router peering?

   a. Switched virtual interface (SVI)

   b. Routed interface

   c. Trunk

   d. ISL

Foundation Topics

IP Routing

IP routing—the process of forwarding IP packets—delivers packets across entire TCP/IP networks, from the device that originally builds the IP packets to the device that is supposed to receive the packets. In other words, IP routing delivers IP packets from the sending host to the destination host.

The complete end-to-end routing process relies on network layer logic on hosts and on routers. The sending host uses Layer 3 concepts to create an IP packet, forwarding the IP packet to the host's default gateway (default router). The process requires Layer 3 logic on the routers as well, by which the routers compare the destination address in the packet to their routing tables, to decide where to forward the IP packet next.

The routing process also relies on the data link and physical details at each link. IP routing relies on serial links, Ethernet LANs, wireless LANs, and many other networks that implement data link and physical layer standards. These lower-layer devices and protocols move the IP packets around the TCP/IP network by encapsulating and transmitting the packets inside data link layer frames.

The previous two paragraphs summarized the key concepts about IP routing as introduced back in Chapter 4. The rest of this section takes the discussion of IP routing another step or two deeper, taking advantage of the additional depth of knowledge you gained in Parts II and III of this book.

NOTE   Some references also incorrectly claim that the term *IP routing* includes the function of dynamically learning routes with IP routing protocols. Although IP routing protocols play an important role, the term *IP routing* refers to the packet-forwarding process only.

IPv4 Routing Process Reference

Because you have already seen the basics back in Chapter 4, this section collects the routing process into steps for reference. The steps use many specific terms discussed in Parts II and III of this book. The upcoming descriptions and examples then discuss these summaries of routing logic to make sure that each step is clear.

The routing process starts with the host that creates the IP packet. First, the host asks the question: Is the destination IP address of this new packet in my local subnet? The host uses its own IP address/mask to determine the range of addresses in the local subnet. Based on its own opinion of the range of addresses in the local subnet, a LAN-based host acts as follows:

Step 1.   If the destination is local, send directly:

A. Find the destination host's MAC address. Use the already known Address Resolution Protocol (ARP) table entry, or use ARP messages to learn the information.

B. Encapsulate the IP packet in a data-link frame, with the destination data-link address of the *destination host*.

Step 2.   If the destination is not local, send to the default gateway:

    A. Find the default gateway's MAC address. Use the already known ARP table entry, or use ARP messages to learn the information.

    B. Encapsulate the IP packet in a data-link frame, with the destination data-link address of the *default gateway*.

Figure 16-1 summarizes these same concepts. In the figure, host A sends a local packet directly to host D. However, for packets to host B, on the other side of a router and there-fore in a different subnet, host A sends the packet to its default router (R1). (As a reminder, the terms *default gateway* and *default router* are synonyms.)

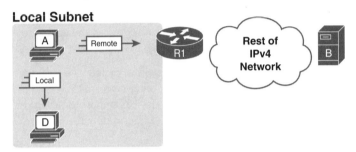

Figure 16-1   *Host Routing Logic Summary*

Routers have a little more routing work to do as compared to hosts. Whereas the host logic begins with an IP packet sitting in memory, a router has some work to do before getting to that point. In the following five-step summary of a router's routing logic, the router takes the first two steps just to receive the frame and extract the IP packet, before even thinking about the packet's destination address at Step 3.

1. For each received data-link frame, choose whether or not to process the frame. Process it if

    A. The frame has no errors (per the data-link trailer Frame Check Sequence, or FCS, field)

    B. The frame's destination data-link address is the router's address (or an appropriate multicast or broadcast address).

2. If choosing to process the frame at Step 1, de-encapsulate the packet from inside the data-link frame.

3. Make a routing decision. To do so, compare the packet's destination IP address to the routing table and find the route that matches the destination address. This route iden-tifies the outgoing interface of the router and possibly the next-hop router.

4. Encapsulate the packet into a data-link frame appropriate for the outgoing interface. When forwarding out LAN interfaces, use ARP as needed to find the next device's MAC address.

5. Transmit the frame out the outgoing interface, as listed in the matched IP route.

NOTE The fact that this list has five steps, instead of breaking the logic into some other number of steps, does not matter. The concepts inside each step matter a lot, so be sure you know them. However, for the exams, there is no need to memorize which piece of logic goes with a particular step number.

This routing process summary lists many details, but sometimes you can think about the routing process in simpler terms. For example, leaving out some details, this paraphrase of the step list details the same big concepts:

> The router receives a frame, removes the packet from inside the frame, decides where to forward the packet, puts the packet into another frame, and then sends the frame.

To give you a little more perspective on these steps, Figure 16-2 breaks down the same five-step routing process as a diagram. The figure shows a packet arriving from the left, entering a router Ethernet interface, with an IP destination of host C. The figure shows the packet arriving, encapsulated inside an Ethernet frame (both header and trailer).

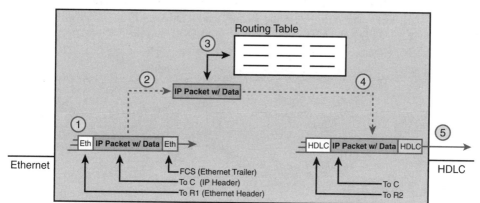

Figure 16-2 *Router Routing Logic Summary*

Router R1 processes the frame and packet, as shown with the numbers in the figure matching the same five-step process described just before the figure, as follows:

1. Router R1 notes that the received Ethernet frame passes the FCS check, and that the destination Ethernet MAC address is R1's MAC address, so R1 processes the frame.

2. R1 de-encapsulates the IP packet from inside the Ethernet frame's header and trailer.

3. R1 compares the IP packet's destination IP address to R1's IP routing table.

4. R1 encapsulates the IP packet inside a new data-link frame—in this case, inside a High-Level Data Link Control (HDLC) header and trailer.

5. R1 transmits the IP packet, inside the new HDLC frame, out the serial link on the right.

> **NOTE**   This chapter uses several figures that show an IP packet encapsulated inside a data link layer frame. These figures often show both the data-link header as well as the data-link trailer, with the IP packet in the middle. The IP packets all include the IP header, plus any encapsulated data.

An Example of IP Routing

The next several pages walk you through an example that discusses each routing step, in order, through multiple devices. This example uses a case in which host A (172.16.1.9) sends a packet to host B (172.16.2.9), with host routing logic and the five steps showing how R1 forwards the packet.

Figure 16-3 shows a typical IP addressing diagram for an IPv4 network with typical address abbreviations. A diagram can get a little too messy if it lists the full IP address for every router interface. Therefore, when possible, these diagrams will list the subnet and then the last octet or two of the individual IP addresses—just enough so that you know the IP address, but with less clutter. For example, host A uses IP address 172.16.1.9, taking from subnet 172.16.1.0/24 (in which all addresses begin 172.16.1), and the ".9" beside the host A icon. As another example, R1 uses address 172.16.1.1 on its LAN interface, 172.16.4.1 on one serial interface, and 172.16.5.1 on the other serial interface.

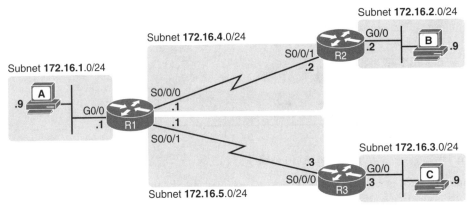

Figure 16-3   *IPv4 Network Used to Show Five-Step Routing Example*

Now on to the example, with host A (172.16.1.9) sending a packet to host B (172.16.2.9).

Host Forwards the IP Packet to the Default Router (Gateway)

In this example, host A uses some application that sends data to host B (172.16.2.9). After host A has the IP packet sitting in memory, host A's logic reduces to the following:

- My IP address/mask is 172.16.1.9/24, so my local subnet contains numbers 172.16.1.0–172.16.1.255 (including the subnet ID and subnet broadcast address).

- The destination address is 172.16.2.9, which is clearly not in my local subnet.

- Send the packet to my default gateway, which is set to 172.16.1.1.

- To send the packet, encapsulate it in an Ethernet frame. Make the destination MAC address be R1's G0/0 MAC address (host A's default gateway).

Figure 16-4 pulls these concepts together, showing the destination IP address and destination MAC address in the frame and packet sent by host A in this case.

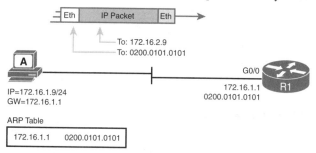

Figure 16-4   *Host A Sends Packet to Host B*

Note that the figure shows the Ethernet LAN as simple lines, but the LAN can include any of the devices discussed in Part II of this book. The LAN could be a single cable between host A and R1, or it could be 100 LAN switches connected across a huge campus of buildings. Regardless, host A and R1 sit in the same VLAN, and the Ethernet LAN then delivers the Ethernet frame to R1's G0/0 interface.

Routing Step 1: Decide Whether to Process the Incoming Frame

Routers receive many frames in an interface, particularly LAN interfaces. However, a router can and should ignore some of those frames. So, the first step in the routing process begins with a decision of whether a router should process the frame or silently discard (ignore) the frame.

First, the router does a simple but important check (Step 1A in the process summary) so that the router ignores all frames that had bit errors during transmission. The router uses the data-link header's Frame Check Sequence (FCS) field to check the frame, and if errors occurred in transmission, the router discards the frame. (The router makes no attempt at error recovery; that is, the router does not ask the sender to retransmit the data.)

The router also checks the destination data-link address (Step 1B in the summary) to decide whether the frame is intended for the router. For example, frames sent to the router's unicast MAC address for that interface are clearly sent to that router. However, a router can actually receive a frame sent to some other unicast MAC address, and routers should ignore these frames.

For example, routers will receive some unicast frames sent to other devices in the VLAN just because of how LAN switches work. Think back to how LAN switches forward unknown unicast frames: frames for which the switch does not list the destination MAC address in the MAC address table. The LAN switch floods those frames. The result? Routers sometimes receive frames destined for some other device, with some other device's MAC address listed as the destination MAC address. Routers should ignore those frames.

In this example, host A sends a frame destined for R1's MAC address. So, after the frame is received, and after R1 confirms with the FCS that no errors occurred, R1 confirms that the frame is destined for R1's MAC address (0200.0101.0101 in this case). All checks have been passed, so R1 will process the frame, as shown in Figure 16-5. (Note that the large rectangle in the figure represents the internals of router R1.)

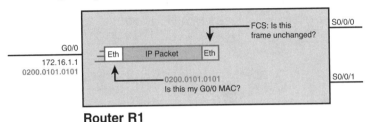

Router R1

Figure 16-5 *Routing Step 1, on Router R1: Checking FCS and Destination MAC*

Routing Step 2: De-encapsulate the IP Packet

After the router knows that it ought to process the received frame (per Step 1), the next step is a relatively simple one: de-encapsulate the packet. In router memory, the router no longer needs the original frame's data-link header and trailer, so the router removes and discards them, leaving the IP packet, as shown in Figure 16-6. Note that the destination IP address remains unchanged (172.16.2.9).

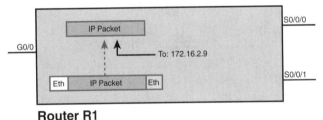

Router R1

Figure 16-6 *Routing Step 2 on Router R1: De-encapsulating the Packet*

Routing Step 3: Choose Where to Forward the Packet

Routing Step 2 required little thought, but Step 3 requires the most thought of all the steps. At this point, the router needs to make a choice about where to forward the packet next. That process uses the router's IP routing table, with some matching logic to compare the packet's destination address with the table.

First, an IP routing table lists multiple routes. Each individual route contains several facts, which in turn can be grouped as shown in Figure 16-7. Part of each route is used to match the destination address of the packet, while the rest of the route lists forwarding instructions: where to send the packet next.

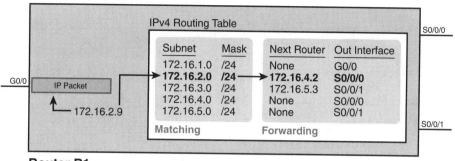

Router R1

Figure 16-7 *Routing Step 3 on Router R1: Matching the Routing Table*

Focus on the entire routing table for a moment, and notice the fact that it lists five routes. Earlier, Figure 16-3 showed the entire sample network, with five subnets, so R1 has a route for each of the five subnets.

Next, look at the part of the five routes that router R1 will use to match packets. To fully define each subnet, each route lists both the subnet ID and the subnet mask. When matching the IP packet's destination with the routing table, the router looks at the packet's destination IP address (172.16.2.9) and compares it to the range of addresses defined by each subnet. Specifically, the router looks at the subnet and mask information, and with a little math, the router can figure out in which of those subnets 172.16.2.9 resides (the route for subnet 172.16.2.0/24).

Finally, look to the right side of the figure, to the forwarding instructions for these five routes. After the router matches a specific route, the forwarding information in the route tells the router where to send the packet next. In this case, the router matched the route for subnet 172.16.2.0/24, so R1 will forward the packet out its own interface, S0/0/0, to router R2 next, listed with its next-hop router IP address of 172.16.4.2.

> **NOTE** Routes for remote subnets typically list both an outgoing interface and next-hop router IP address. Routes for subnets that connect directly to the router list only the outgoing interface, because packets to these destinations do not need to be sent to another router.

Routing Step 4: Encapsulate the Packet in a New Frame

At this point, the router knows how it will forward the packet. However, routers cannot forward a packet without first wrapping a data-link header and trailer around it (encapsulation).

Encapsulating packets for serial links does not require a lot of thought because of the simplicity of the HDLC and PPP protocols. Because serial links have only two devices on the link—the sender and the then-obvious receiver—the data-link addressing does not matter. In this example, R1 forwards the packet out S0/0/0, after encapsulating the packet inside an HDLC frame, as shown in Figure 16-8.

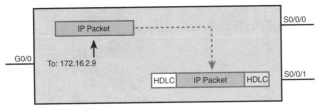

Router R1

Figure 16-8 *Routing Step 4 on Router R1: Encapsulating the Packet*

Note that with some other types of data links, the router has a little more work to do at this routing step. For example, sometimes a router forwards packets out an Ethernet interface. To encapsulate the IP packet, the router would need to build an Ethernet header, and that Ethernet header's destination MAC address would need to list the correct value.

For example, consider this different sample network, with an Ethernet WAN link between routers R1 and R2. R1 matches a route that tells R1 to forward the packet out R1's G0/1 Ethernet interface to 172.16.6.2 (R2) next. R1 needs to put R2's MAC address in the header, and to do that, R1 uses its IP ARP table information, as shown in Figure 16-9. If R1 did not have an ARP table entry for 172.16.6.2, it would first have to use ARP to learn the matching MAC address.

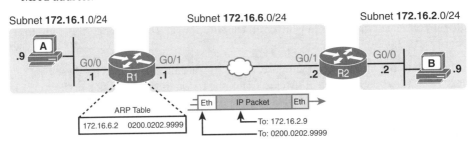

Figure 16-9 *Routing Step 4 on Router R1 with a LAN Outgoing Interface*

Routing Step 5: Transmit the Frame

After the frame has been prepared, the router simply needs to transmit it. The router might have to wait, particularly if other frames are already waiting their turn to exit the interface.

Internal Processing on Cisco Routers

The next topic looks a little deeper at how Cisco actually implements IP routing internal to a router. The discussion so far in this chapter has been fairly generic, but it matches an early type of internal processing on Cisco routers called *process switching*. This section discusses the issues that drove Cisco to improve the internal routing process, while having the same result: A packet arrives inside one frame, a choice is made, and it exits the router inside another frame.

Potential Routing Performance Issues

When you're learning about IP routing, it helps to think through all the particulars of the routing process, as discussed over the last few pages. However, routers barely spend any processing time in routing a single IP packet. In fact, even slower routers need to forward tens of thousands of packets per second; to do that, they cannot spend a lot of effort processing each one.

The process of matching a packet's destination address with the IP routing table can actually take a lot of CPU time. The example in this chapter (Figure 16-7) listed only five routes, but enterprise networks routinely have thousands of IP routes, and routers in the core of the Internet have hundreds of thousands of routes. Now think about a router CPU that needs to search a list that's 100,000 entries long, for every packet, for a router that needs to forward hundreds of thousands of packets per second! And what if the router had to do subnetting math each time, calculating the range of addresses in each subnet for each route? Those actions would take too many CPU cycles.

Over the years, Cisco has created several ways to optimize the internal process of how routers forward packets. Some methods tie to a specific model series of router. Layer 3 switches do the forwarding in application-specific integrated circuits (ASIC), which are computer chips built for the purpose of forwarding frames or packets. All these optimizations take the basic logic from the five-step list here in the book, but work differently inside the router hardware and software, in an effort to use fewer CPU cycles and reduce the overhead of forwarding IP packets.

Cisco Router Fast Switching and CEF

Historically, Cisco has had three major variations of internal routing logic that apply across the entire router product family. First, Cisco routers used internal logic called *process switching* in the early days, dating back to the late 1980s and early 1990s. Process switching works basically like the routing process detailed so far in this chapter, without any of the extra optimizations.

Next, in the early 1990s, Cisco introduced alternate internal routing logic called *fast switching*. Fast switching made a couple of optimizations compared to the older process-switching logic. First, it kept another list in addition to the routing table, listing specific IP addresses for recently forwarded packets. This fast-switching cache also kept a copy of the new data-link headers used when forwarding packets to each destination, so rather than build a new data-link header for each packet destined for a particular IP address, the router saved a little effort by copying the old data-link header.

Cisco improved on fast switching with the introduction of Cisco Express Forwarding (CEF) later in the 1990s. Like fast switching, CEF uses additional tables for faster searches, and it saves outgoing data-link headers. However, CEF organizes its tables for all routing table destinations ahead of time, not just for some of the specific destination IP addresses. CEF also uses much more sophisticated search algorithms and binary tree structures as compared to fast switching. As a result, the CEF table lookups that replace the routing table matches take even less time than with fast switching. And CEF caches the data-link headers as well.

Today, current models of Cisco routers, and current IOS versions, use CEF by default. Table 16-2 lists a summary of the key comparison points between process switching, fast switching, and CEF.

Table 16-2   Comparisons of Packet Switching, Fast Switching, and CEF

Improves Routing Efficiency By...	Process Switching	Fast Switching	CEF
Saving data-link headers used for encapsulating packets	No	Yes	Yes
Using other tables, with faster lookup time, before looking at the routing table	No	Yes	Yes
Organizing the tables using tree structures for very fast searches and less time to route packets	No	No	Yes

Cisco Nexus Switch Operations with Routing

A multilayer switch is essentially a switch at Layer 2 that has routing functionality. Multilayer switches traditionally have been built to give you the ability to have multiple VLANs on a given switch and route between them if needed without the need for an external dedicated router. Also, multilayer switches are primarily created in the same manner as traditional Layer 2 switches, where they only have Ethernet interfaces ranging from 10 Mb to 100 Gigabit Ethernet based on the switch chosen. Switches use ASICs to provide forwarding in hardware to accelerate the process of packet switching and routing, in comparison to the original routers, which did this primarily in software.

The second major difference between multilayer and Layer 2 switches is based on how routing is implemented or configured on them. On a Layer 3 switch, you can implement a switched virtual interface (SVI) or a Layer 3 routed interface (sometimes referred to as a *routed interface*). Let's explore each one a little deeper to understand the difference.

NOTE   Cisco Nexus switches have both Layer 2 and Layer 3 functionality and are considered to be multilayer switches. Throughout the rest of this section, we refer to them as Cisco Nexus switches.

The first thing to understand is how a Cisco Nexus switch implements the logical routed interface known as an SVI and when you would want to use it in your data center. Figure 16-10 shows what an SVI looks like logically in a Nexus switch.

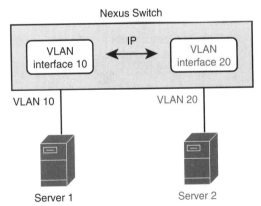

Figure 16-10   *SVI Logically Represented on a Nexus Switch*

As you can see, the Nexus switch in Figure 16-10 creates a VLAN for both hosts to communicate and then enables an interface for VLANs 10 and 20 that has IP connectivity enabled.
The top layer of this figure is representative of a logical router that is created for each
VLAN (10 and 20, respectively) and assigned an IP address. This allows for many Layer 2
interfaces to be part of either of these networks and also enables the Cisco Nexus switch to
route between them if communication is needed using the SVI interfaces. In the past, when
there were no multilayer switches like a Cisco Nexus switch, you had to attach separate
physical routers to your switched network and send packets up to them to route between
different networks, as shown in Figure 16-11.

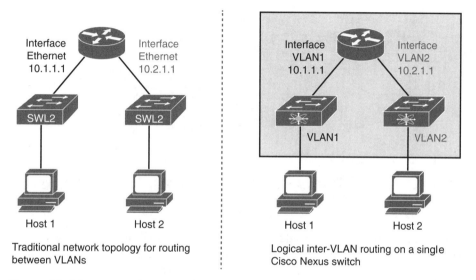

Traditional network topology for routing
between VLANs

Logical inter-VLAN routing on a single
Cisco Nexus switch

Figure 16-11   *SVI Replacing Dedicated Routers for Inter-VLAN Communication*

Now with Cisco Nexus switches being able to perform both routing and switching simultaneously, you can enable SVIs or logical routers on them and allow for inter-VLAN routing
without having to go to another external device. The typical use case for this in the data
center is at the distribution or access layer, where you need to do inter-VLAN routing and
support many downstream Layer 2 networks at the same time, as shown in Figure 16-12.

In Figure 16-12, we would enable SVIs on R3 and R4 for any Layer 2 networks below them
or off of SW1 and SW2. This allows for multiple devices to join these networks by being
assigned to a VLAN and for inter-VLAN communication to happen at R3 and R4.

The second way to implement routing on a Cisco Nexus switch is by using a routed interface—which is implemented when you configure an interface on a Layer 3 switch to not
have any switching functionality. Figure 16-12 shows these between R1, R2, R3, and R4. As
mentioned previously, a routed interface does not have any Layer 2 functionality enabled
on it and is typically used for Cisco Nexus-to-Nexus connections as peering points for routing or when directly connecting to a separate physical router over a strictly Layer 3 interconnect.

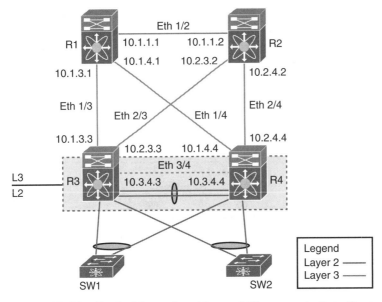

Figure 16-12 *Typical Layer 3 and Layer 2 Placement in Data Center*

The question that now usually gets asked is, "When do I use an SVI versus a routed interface?" We have answered this question already, but let's now review when it might be good to use them and look at a few considerations when using an SVI or a routed interface.

The SVI is most useful when you need to support Layer 2 and Layer 3 simultaneously for a given subnet. You're probably wondering what that means. If you refer to Figure 16-12, you'll see that in a typical data center design we have an aggregation layer where all the Layer 2–connected devices live, but we need to provide default gateways for them as dedicated routers normally would if connected to a switched network in the past. Using an SVI here lets us run Layer 2 protocols such as Spanning Tree Protocol (STP) and run a logical router that acts as the default gateway for a VLAN or many VLANs. (Each VLAN has its own logical router or SVI interface.) This enables us to add devices to this Layer 2 network and point them to their gateway (SVI or logical router) to talk to other networks.

So, when should you use a routed interface? A routed interface is useful when you don't need any Layer 2 devices on a routed segment, such as when you want to peer from a routing perspective with another router or multilayer switch. In this case, you create a small subnet (usually a /30) between the devices and dedicate an interface for peering, because no other devices will live on this segment except the peering routers, which do not need to support Layer 2 because you use routed interfaces for this connection.

> **NOTE** One benefit from using routed interfaces when dedicating them for router peering is that they provide faster downtime detection of a failed interface or link. If you are using SVI peering, it takes longer from the time the interface or link fails for the router to, in turn, shut down the SVI than it would if it were a routed interface.

Exam Preparation Tasks

Review All the Key Topics

Review the most important topics from this chapter, noted with the Key Topic icon. Table 16-3 lists these key topics and where each is discussed.

Table 16-3   Key Topics for Chapter 16

Key Topic Element	Description	Page Number
List	Steps taken by a host when forwarding IP packets	443
List	Steps taken by a router when forwarding IP packets	444
Figure 16-2	Diagram of five routing steps taken by a router	445
Figure 16-7	Breakdown of IP routing table with matching and forwarding details	449
Figure 16-10	SVI logically represented on a Nexus switch	452
Figure 16-12	Typical Layer 3 and Layer 2 placement in the data center	454
Paragraph	SVI versus routed interface discussion	454

Definitions of Key Terms

After your first reading of the chapter, try to define these key terms, but do not be concerned about getting them all correct at that time. Chapter 24, "Final Review," directs you in how to use these terms for late-stage preparation for the exam.

default gateway/router, ARP table, routing table, next-hop router, outgoing interface, subinterface, VLAN interface, multilayer switch, Cisco Express Forwarding (CEF), connected route, static route, default route, zero subnet, switched virtual interface (SVI), routed interface, inter-VLAN routing

This chapter covers the following exam topics:

4.1. Describe and configure basic routing concepts

4.1.a. Packet forwarding

4.1.b. Router look-up process (exec mode, exec commands, configuration mode)

CHAPTER 17

Cisco Nexus IPv4 Routing Configuration

This chapter focuses on how to implement or configure IPv4 routing on a Cisco Nexus switch. The chapter begins by exploring two forms of connected routes you often see on a Nexus switch: direct and local.

The final major section then looks at static routes, which let the engineer tell the router what route(s) to add to the router's IP routing table. The static route section also shows how to configure a static default route that is used when no other route matches an IP packet. Dynamic routing, using the Open Shortest Path First (OSPF) routing protocol, awaits in Chapter 19, "Nexus Routing Protocol Configuration."

NOTE As promised in the Introduction's section "For Those Studying Routing & Switching," you need to read this whole chapter. While many of the commands in this chapter mirror the same function in IOS, small differences exist, especially in **show** command output and in Layer 3 switching configuration, so take the time to read the entire chapter.

"Do I Know This Already?" Quiz

Use the "Do I Know This Already?" quiz to help decide whether you might want to skim this chapter, or a major section, moving more quickly to the "Exam Preparation Tasks" section near the end of the chapter. Table 17-1 lists the major headings in this chapter and their corresponding "Do I Know This Already?" quiz questions. For thorough explanations, see Appendix A, "Answers to the 'Do I Know This Already?' Quizzes."

Table 17-1 "Do I Know This Already?" Foundation Topics Section-to-Question Mapping

Foundation Topics Section	Questions
Configuring Connected Routes on Cisco Nexus Switches	1–4
Configuring Static Routes	5–6

1. Which implementation on a Cisco Nexus switch turns off all Layer 2 protocol functions on an interface?

   a. **no switchport** under the interface configuration mode

   b. **interface vlan 1** under the interface configuration mode

   c. **ip address** under the interface configuration mode

   d. **router ospf** under the routing process

2. Which command under an interface on a Layer 3 switch enables a VLAN 10 to be assigned to it?

   a. no switchport vlan 10

   b. switchport trunk allowed vlan 10

   c. switchport access vlan 10

   d. vlan 10 switchport

3. Which implementation on a Cisco Nexus switch allows for an IP address to be assigned to a switched virtual interface (SVI) for VLAN 10 if the **feature interface-vlan** command has already been enabled?

   a. **ip address** command under a physical interface assigned to a VLAN 10

   b. **ip address** command under the **interface vlan 10** configuration mode

   c. **ip address** command under the **interface** configuration mode

   d. **ip address** command assigned to VLAN 10 under the **vlan** configuration mode

4. A Layer 3 switch has been configured to route IP packets between VLANs 1, 2, and 3, which connect to subnets 172.20.1.0/25, 172.20.2.0/25, and 172.20.3.0/25, respectively. The engineer issues a **show ip route** command on the Layer 3 switch, listing the connected routes. Which of the following answers lists a piece of information that should be in at least one of the routes?

   a. Interface Ethernet 1/1

   b. Next-hop router 172.20.4.1

   c. Interface VLAN 2

   d. Mask 255.255.255.0

5. An engineer configures a static IPv4 route on router R1. Which of the following pieces of information should not be listed as a parameter in the configuration command that creates this static IPv4 route?

   a. The destination subnet's subnet ID

   b. The next-hop router's IP address

   c. The next-hop router's neighboring interface

   d. The subnet mask

6. Which of the following commands correctly configures a static route?

   a. ip route 10.1.3.0 255.255.255.0

   b. ip route 10.1.3.0 Ethernet 1/1

   c. ip route 10.1.3.0 0.0.0.255

   d. ip route 10.1.3.0 /24 Ethernet 1/2

Foundation Topics

Configuring Connected Routes on Cisco Nexus Switches

When routers and Layer 3 switches configure IP addresses on their interfaces, the devices know about the subnets connected, based on what has been configured. The devices then use these subnets to build a routing table for any subnet that is directly connected to one of its interfaces. Although Cisco Nexus switches enable IPv4 routing globally, you must enable particular routing features in Nexus L3–enabled products to enable the appropriate feature. Table 17-2 shows the feature commands for basic routing and the associated functionality they enable.

Table 17-2   Basic Routing Feature Commands for Cisco Nexus

Feature Command	Description
(no) **feature interface-vlan**	Enables/disables the ability to configure SVIs using an **interface vlan** x command
(no) **ip address**	Enables IP address on an interface or SVI
ip route	Enables a static route with a destination network and next-hop router address or outgoing interface

To make the router be ready to route packets on a particular interface, the router must be configured with an IP address, and the interface must be configured such that it comes up, reaching a "line status up, line protocol up" state. Only at that point can routers route IP packets in and out a particular interface.

After a router can route IP packets out one or more interfaces, the router needs some routes. Routers can add routes to their routing tables through three methods:

- **Connected routes:** Added because of the configuration of the **ip address** interface sub-command on the local router

- **Static routes:** Added because of the configuration of the **ip route** global command on the local router

- **Routing protocols:** Added as a function by configuration on all routers, resulting in a process by which routers dynamically tell each other about the network so that they all learn routes

This chapter discusses how to use connected and static routes. Chapter 19 then covers how you can configure routing protocols for use with Cisco Nexus switches.

Direct and Local Routes and the ip address Command

A Cisco Nexus L3 switch automatically adds two routes to its routing table based on the IPv4 address configured for an interface, assuming that the following two facts are true:

- The interface is in a working state—in other words, the interface status in the **show interfaces** command lists a line status of up and a protocol status of up.

- The interface has an IP address assigned through the **ip address** interface subcommand.

The two routes, called a *direct route* and a *local route*, route packets to the subnet directly connected to that interface. The router, of course, needs to know the subnet number used on the physical network connected to each of its interfaces, so it can route packets to that subnet. The router can simply do the math, taking the interface IP address and mask, and calculate the subnet ID. However, the router needs that route only when the interface is up and working, so the router includes a directly connected route in the routing table only when the interface is working.

Example 17-1 shows the direct and local routes on router R1 in Figure 17-1. The first part of the example shows the configuration of IP addresses on all three of R1's interfaces. The end of the example lists the output from the **show ip route** command, which lists these routes with "direct" or "local" as the route code, meaning *connected*.

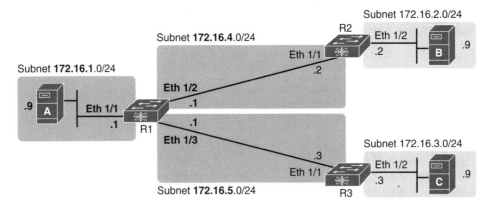

Figure 17-1 *Sample Network to Show Connected Routes*

Example 17-1 *Connected and Local Routes on R1*

```
! Excerpt from show running-config follows...
!
interface Ethernet1/1
 no switchport
 ip address 172.16.1.1/24
 no shutdown
!
interface Ethernet 1/2
 no switchport
 no shutdown
 ip address 172.16.4.1/24
!
interface Ethernet 1/3
 no switchport
 no shutdown
```

```
    ip address 172.16.5.1/24

R1# show ip route
IP Route Table for VRF """"""""""""default"
''''''''''''*' denotes best ucast next-hop
'**' denotes best mcast next-hop
'[x/y]' denotes [preference/metric]
'%<string>' in via output denotes VRF <string>
172.16.1.0/24, ubest/mbest: 1/0, attached
    *via 172.16.1.1, Eth1/1, [0/0], 2w0d, direct
172.16.1.1/32, ubest/mbest: 1/0, attached
    *via 172.16.1.1, Eth1/1, [0/0], 2w0d, local
172.16.4.0/24, ubest/mbest: 1/0, attached
    *via 172.16.4.1, Eth1/1, [0/0], 2w0d, direct
172.16.4.1/32, ubest/mbest: 1/0, attached
    *via 172.16.4.1, Eth1/1, [0/0], 2w0d, local
172.16.5.0/24, ubest/mbest: 1/0, attached
    *via 172.16.5.1, Eth1/1, [0/0], 2w0d, direct
172.16.5.1/32, ubest/mbest: 1/0, attached
    *via 172.16.5.1, Eth1/1, [0/0], 2w0d, local
```

17

Focus on the lists with highlights, which focus on the direct and local routes related to R1's E1/1 interface. First, the output shows a route to subnet 172.16.1.0/24—the subnet off R1's E1/1 interface—with an ending word of *direct*. This route represents the entire directly connected subnet. R1 will use this route when forwarding packets to other hosts in subnet 172.16.1.0/24.

The second highlighted route, the local route, lists 172.16.1.1/32. Look back to the top of the example, to R1's configuration on interface E1/1. Because the configuration shows 172.16.1.1 as the exact IP address on that interface, R1 adds a route with a /32 prefix length for that address, with outgoing interface E1/1. This route matches packets sent to 172.16.1.1 only. R1 then lists this route as a local route, as noted at the end of the second line for that route.

In the configuration in Example 17-1, notice the **no switchport** command, which is high-lighted under each Ethernet interface. You learned in Chapter 16, "IPv4 Routing Concepts," that there are two ways to configure routing on a Cisco Nexus switch:

- **A routed interface:** This is enabled by using the **no switchport** command. Remember that when using this command, we are disabling any Layer 2 functionality on an interface.

- **A switched virtual interface (SVI):** You use this when you route between VLANs and support Layer 2 with Layer 3 simultaneously.

Routing Between Subnets on VLANs

Almost all enterprise networks use VLANs. To route IP packets in and out of those VLANs—or more accurately, the subnets that sit on each of those VLANs—some router needs to have an IP address in each subnet and have a connected route to each of those subnets. Then the hosts in each subnet can use the router IP addresses as their default gateways, respectively.

Three options exist for connecting a router to each subnet on a VLAN. However, the first option requires too many interfaces and links, and is mentioned only to make the list complete:

■ Use a router, with one router LAN interface and cable connected to the switch for each and every VLAN (typically not used).

■ Use a router, with a VLAN trunk connecting to a LAN switch.

■ Use a Layer 3 switch.

The other option for routing traffic to VLANs uses a device called a *Layer 3 switch* or *multilayer switch*. As introduced back in Chapter 6, "VLAN and Trunking Concepts," a Layer 3 switch is one device that performs two primary functions: Layer 2 LAN switching and Layer 3 IP routing. The Layer 2 switch function forwards frames inside each VLAN, but it will not forward frames between VLANs. The Layer 3 forwarding logic—routing—forwards IP packets between VLANs.

The configuration of a Layer 3 switch mostly looks like the Layer 2 switching configuration, with a small bit of configuration added for the Layer 3 functions. The Layer 3 switching function needs a virtual interface connected to each VLAN internal to the switch. These VLAN interfaces act like router interfaces, with an IP address and mask. The Layer 3 switch has an IP routing table, with connected routes off each of these VLAN interfaces. (These interfaces are also referred to as SVIs.)

Figure 17-2 shows the Layer 3 switch function with a router icon inside the switch, to emphasize that the switch routes the packets. The data center has three server VLANs, so the Layer 3 switch needs one VLAN interface for each VLAN.

Key Topic

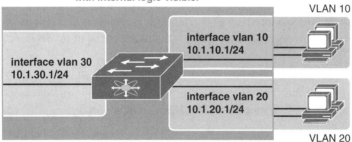

Figure 17-2 *Routing on VLAN Interfaces in a Layer 3 Switch*

The following steps show how to configure Cisco Nexus Layer 3 switching. Note that on some switches (such as the 5500 switches used for the examples in this book), the ability to route IPv4 packets requires the addition of a Layer 3 module with associated licensing, with a **reload** of the switch required to enable the feature. The rest of the steps after Step 1 would apply to all models of Cisco switches that are capable of doing Layer 3 switching.

Step 1. Enable the feature for configuring interface VLANs (**feature interface-vlan**).

Step 2. Create a VLAN interface for each VLAN for which the Layer 3 switch is routing packets (**interface vlan** *vlan_id*).

Step 3. Configure an IP address and mask on the VLAN interface (in interface configuration mode for that interface), enabling IPv4 on that VLAN interface (**ip address** *address mask*).

Step 4. If the switch defaults to placing the VLAN interface in a disabled (shutdown) state, enable the interface (**no shutdown**).

Example 17-2 shows the configuration to match Figure 17-2. In this case, the switch is a Cisco Nexus switch. The example shows the related configuration on all three VLAN interfaces.

Example 17-2 *VLAN Interface Configuration for Layer 3 Switching*

```
feature Interface-vlan
!
interface vlan 10
 ip address 10.1.10.1/24
!
interface vlan 20
 ip address 10.1.20.1/24
!
interface vlan 30
 ip address 10.1.30.1/24
```

With the VLAN configuration shown here, the switch is ready to route packets between the VLANs, as shown in Figure 17-2. To support the routing of packets, the switch adds connected IP routes, as shown in Example 17-3. Note that each route is listed as being direct to a different VLAN interface.

Example 17-3 *Connected Routes on a Layer 3 Switch*

```
SW1# show ip route
! legend omitted for brevity
10.1.10.0/24, ubest/mbest: 1/0, attached
    *via 10.1.10.1, Vlan 0010, [0/0], 2w0d, direct
10.1.10.1/32, ubest/mbest: 1/0, attached
    *via 10.1.10.1, Vlan 0010, [0/0], 2w0d, local
10.1.20.0/24, ubest/mbest: 1/0, attached
    *via 10.1.20.1, Vlan0020, [0/0], 1w6d, direct
10.1.20.1/32, ubest/mbest: 1/0, attached
    *via 10.1.20.1, Vlan0020, [0/0], 1w6d, local
10.1.30.0/24, ubest/mbest: 1/0, attached
    *via 10.1.30.1, Vlan0020, [0/0], 1w6d, direct
10.1.30.1/32, ubest/mbest: 1/0, attached
    *via 10.1.30.1, Vlan0020, [0/0], 1w6d, local
```

The switch also needs additional routes to the rest of the network shown in Figure 17-2, possibly using static routes, as discussed in the final major section of this chapter.

Configuring Static Routes

All routers add connected routes, as discussed in the previous section. Then, most networks use dynamic routing protocols to cause each router to learn the rest of the routes in an internetwork. Networks use static routes—routes added to a routing table through direct configuration—much less often than dynamic routing. However, static routes can be useful at times, and they happen to be useful learning tools as well. This last of two major sections in the chapter discusses static routes.

Static Route Configuration

NX-OS allows the definition of individual static routes using the **ip route** global configuration command. Every **ip route** command defines a destination that can be matched, usually with a subnet ID and mask. The command also lists the forwarding instructions, typically listing either the outgoing interface or the next-hop router's IP address. NX-OS then takes that information and adds that route to the IP routing table.

As an example, Figure 17-3 shows a small IP network. The figure shows only the details related to a static route on R1, for subnet 172.16.2.0/24, which sits on the far right. To create that static route on R1, R1 will configure the subnet ID and mask, and either R1's outgoing interface (Ethernet 1/1), or R2 as the next-hop router IP address (172.16.4.2).

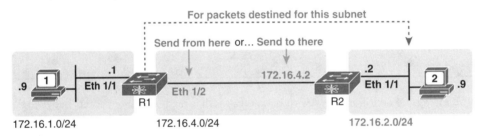

Figure 17-3 *Static Route Configuration Concept*

Example 17-4 shows the configuration of a couple of sample static routes. In particular, it shows routes on R1 in Figure 17-4, for the two subnets on the right side of the figure.

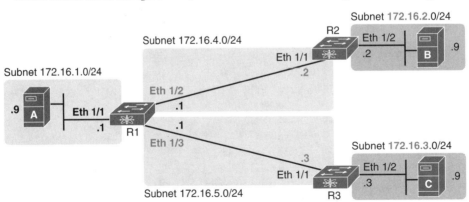

Figure 17-4 *Sample Network Used in Static Route Configuration Examples*

Example 17-4 *Static Routes Added to R1*

```
ip route 172.16.2.0 255.255.255.0 172.16.4.2
ip route 172.16.3.0 255.255.255.0 Ethernet 1/1
```

The two sample **ip route** commands show the two different styles. The first command shows subnet 172.16.2.0, mask 255.255.255.0, which sits in the data center near Nexus R2. That same first command lists 172.16.4.2, R2's IP address, as the next-hop router. This route basically says this: To send packets to the subnet off Nexus R2, send them to R2.

The second route has the same kind of logic, but instead of identifying the next router by IP address, it lists the local router's outgoing interface. This route basically states the following: To send packets to the subnet off router R3, send them out my own local Ethernet 1/1 interface (which happens to connect to R3).

The routes created by these two **ip route** commands actually look a little different in the IP routing table. Both are static routes. However, the route that used the outgoing interface configuration is also noted as a connected route; this is just a quirk of the output of the **show ip route** command.

Example 17-4 lists these two routes using the **show ip route static** command. This command lists the details of static routes only, but it also lists a few statistics about all IPv4 routes. For example, the example shows two lines, for the two static routes configured in Example 17-5, but statistics state that this route has routes for ten subnets.

Example 17-5 *Static Routes Added to R1*

```
R1# show ip route static
IP Route Table for VRF "default"
'*' denotes best ucast next-hop
'**' denotes best mcast next-hop
'[x/y]' denotes [preference/metric]
'%<string>' in via output denotes VRF <string>
172.16.2.0//24, ubest/mbest: 1/0
    *via 172.16.4.2 [1/0], 00:00:05, static
172.16.3.0/24, ubest/mbest: 1/0, attached
    *via Ethernet1/1, [1/0], 00:00:05, static
```

NX-OS adds and removes these static routes dynamically over time, based on whether the outgoing interface is working. For example, in this case, if R1's Ethernet 1/1 interface fails, R1 removes the static route to 172.16.3.0/24 from the IPv4 routing table. Later, when the interface comes up again, NX-OS adds the route back to the routing table.

Finally, if static routes are used, and dynamic routing protocols are not used at all, all routers would need to have some static routes configured. For example, at this point, in the network in Figure 17-4, PC A would not be able to receive packets back from PC B because router R2 does not have a route for PC A's subnet. R2 would need static routes for other subnets, as would R3.

Static Default Routes

When a router tries to route a packet, the router might not match the packet's destination IP address with any route. When that happens, the router normally just discards the packet.

Routers can be configured so that they use either a statically configured or a dynamically learned default route. The default route matches all packets, so that if a packet does not match any other more specific route in the routing table, the router can at least forward the packet based on the default route.

NX-OS allows the configuration of a static default route by using special values for the subnet and mask fields in the **ip route** command: 0.0.0.0 and 0.0.0.0. For example, the command **ip route 0.0.0.0 0.0.0.0 vlan 16** creates a static default route on a Cisco Nexus switch—a route that matches all IP packets—and sends those packets out SVI VLAN 16.

Example 17-6 shows a static default route using a Cisco Nexus switch.

Example 17-6 *Adding a Static Default Route on Cisco Nexus Switch*

```
SW1# configure terminal
Enter configuration commands, one per line. End with CNTL/Z.
R2(config)# ip route 0.0.0.0 0.0.0.0 Vlan 16
R2(config)# ^Z
SW1# sh ip route
IP Route Table for VRF "default"
'*' denotes best ucast next-hop
'**' denotes best mcast next-hop
'[x/y]' denotes [preference/metric]
'%<string>' in via output denotes VRF <string>
0.0.0.0/0, ubest/mbest: 1/0, attached
```

Exam Preparation Tasks

Review All the Key Topics

Review the most important topics from this chapter, noted with the Key Topic icon. Table 17-3 lists these key topics and where each is discussed.

Table 17-3   Key Topics for Chapter 17

Key Topic Element	Description	Page Number
Table 17-2	Basic routing feature commands for Cisco Nexus switches	459
Figure 17-2	Layer 3 switching concept and configuration	462
List	Layer 3 switching configuration	463
Example 17-3	Connected routes on a Layer 3 switch	463
Figure 17-4	Static route configuration concept	464

17

Definitions of Key Terms

After your first reading of the chapter, try to define these key terms, but do not be concerned about getting them all correct at that time. Chapter 24, "Final Review," directs you in how to use these terms for late-stage preparation for the exam.

VLAN interface, Layer 3 switch, connected route, static route, default route, local route, direct route, **feature interface-vlan**, **show ip route**

Command Reference to Check Your Memory

Although you should not necessarily memorize the information in Tables 17-4 and 17-5, this section does include a reference for the configuration and EXEC commands covered in this chapter. Practically speaking, you should memorize the commands as a side effect of reading the chapter and doing all the activities in this exam preparation section. To check to see how well you have memorized the commands as a side effect of your other studies, cover the left side of the table with a piece of paper, read the descriptions on the right side, and see whether you remember the commands.

Table 17-4   Chapter 17 Configuration Command Reference

Command	Description
ip address *ip-address mask* [secondary]	Interface subcommand that assigns the interface's IP address and optionally makes the address a secondary address
(no) feature interface-vlan	Global command that enables (**ip routing**) or disables (**no ip routing**) the routing of IPv4 packets on a Nexus Layer 3 switch
interface vlan *vlan_id*	Global command on a Layer 3 switch to create a VLAN interface and to enter configuration mode for that VLAN interface
ip route *prefix mask* {*ip-address* | *interface-type interface-number*} [*distance*] [**permanent**]	Global configuration command that creates a static route

Table 17-5   Chapter 17 EXEC Command Reference

Command	Description
show ip route	Lists the router's entire routing table
show ip route [connected | static | ospf]	Lists a subnet of the IP routing table
show ip route *ip-address*	Lists detailed information about the route that a router matches for the listed IP address
show vlans	Lists VLAN configuration and statistics for VLAN trunks configured on routers

This chapter covers the following exam topics:

4.1. Describe and configure basic routing concepts

4.1.a. Packet forwarding

4.2. Describe the operation of Cisco routers

4.2.c. Router components

CHAPTER 18

IPv4 Routing Protocol Concepts

Routers and Layer 3 switches add IP routes to their routing tables using three methods: connected routes, static routes, and routes learned by using *dynamic routing protocols*. The routing process forwards IP packets, but if a router does not have any routes in its IP routing table that match a packet's destination address, the router discards the packet. Routers need routing protocols so that they can learn all the possible routes and add them to the routing table. Thus, the routing process can forward (route) routable protocols such as IP.

IPv4 supports several different routing protocols, some of which are primarily used inside one company, while one is meant primarily for use between companies to create the Internet. This chapter introduces the concepts behind Interior Gateway Protocols (IGPs), typically used inside one company. In particular, this chapter discusses the theory behind types of routing protocols, including distance vector and link-state logic. The chapter also introduces the Routing Information Protocol (RIP), Enhanced Interior Gateway Routing Protocol (EIGRP), and Open Shortest Path First (OSPF) routing protocol.

> **NOTE** As promised in the Introduction's section "For Those Studying Routing & Switching," you need to read this chapter. It contains a variety of topics not found in the ICND1 book.

"Do I Know This Already?" Quiz

Use the "Do I Know This Already?" quiz to help decide whether you might want to skim this chapter, or a major section, moving more quickly to the "Exam Preparation Tasks" section near the end of the chapter. Table 18-1 lists the major headings in this chapter and their corresponding "Do I Know This Already?" quiz questions. For thorough explanations, see Appendix A, "Answers to the 'Do I Know This Already?' Quizzes."

Table 18-1 "Do I Know This Already?" Foundation Topics Section-to-Question Mapping

Foundation Topics Section	Questions
Introduction to Routing Protocols	1–2
RIP Concepts and Operation	3–4
EIGRP Concepts and Operation	5–6
OSPF Concepts and Operation	7–8

1. Which of the following distance vector features prevents routing loops by causing the routing protocol to advertise only a subset of known routes, as opposed to the full routing table, under normal stable conditions?

   a. Route poisoning

   b. Dijkstra SPF

   c. Hello

   d. Split horizon

2. Which of the following distance vector features prevents routing loops by advertising an infinite metric route when a route fails?

   a. Dijkstra SPF

   b. Hello

   c. Split horizon

   d. Route poisoning

3. Which of the following is true about both RIPv1 and RIPv2? (Choose two answers.)

   a. Uses a hop-count metric

   b. Sends update messages to multicast address 224.0.0.9

   c. Supports authentication

   d. Uses split horizon

4. Router R1 uses RIPv1 and learns one possible route to reach subnet 10.1.1.0/24. That route would have a metric of 15 from R1's perspective. Which of the following is true?

   a. R1 cannot use the route, because metric 15 is considered to be infinity.

   b. R1 will add the route to its routing table.

   c. The cumulative bandwidth between R1 and subnet 10.1.1.0/24 is 15 Mbps.

   d. The slowest bandwidth of the links between R1 and subnet 10.1.1.0/24 is 15 Kbps.

5. Routers A and B use EIGRP. How does router A watch for the status of router B so that router A can react if router B fails?

   a. By using EIGRP hello messages, with A needing to receive periodic hello messages to believe B is still working.

   b. By using EIGRP update messages, with A needing to receive periodic update messages to believe B is still working.

   c. Using a periodic ping of B's IP address based on the EIGRP neighbor timer.

   d. None of the other answers is correct.

6. Which of the following affect the calculation of EIGRP metrics when all possible default values are used? (Choose two answers.)

    a. Bandwidth

    b. Delay

    c. Load

    d. Reliability

    e. Hop count

7. Which of the following routing protocols is considered to use link-state logic?

    a. RIPv1

    b. RIPv2

    c. EIGRP

    d. OSPF

8. Which of the following is true about how a router using a link-state routing protocol chooses the best route to reach a subnet?

    a. The router finds the best route in the link-state database.

    b. The router calculates the best route by running the SPF algorithm against the information in the link-state database.

    c. The router compares the metrics listed for that subnet in the updates received from each neighbor and picks the best (lowest) metric route.

    d. The router uses the path that has the lowest hop count.

18

Foundation Topics

Introduction to Routing Protocols

Many IP routing protocols exist, in part due to the long history of IP; however, if you compare all the IP routing protocols, they all have some core features in common. Each routing protocol causes routers (and Layer 3 switches) to do the following:

1. Learn routing information about IP subnets from other neighboring routers.

2. Advertise routing information about IP subnets to other neighboring routers.

3. Choose the best route among multiple possible routes to reach one subnet, based on that routing protocol's concept of a metric.

4. React and converge to use a new choice of best route for each destination subnet when the network topology changes—for example, when a link fails.

All the routing protocols discussed in this chapter do these same four functions, but the protocols differ in other ways. The rest of this chapter works through enough of the logic and features of each routing protocol so that you can see the differences, while understanding the basics of how each routing protocol learns routes, advertises routes, picks the best route, and converges when the network changes.

History of Interior Gateway Protocols

Historically speaking, RIP Version 1 (RIPv1) was the first popularly used IP routing protocol, with the Cisco-proprietary Interior Gateway Routing Protocol (IGRP) being introduced a little later, as shown in Figure 18-1.

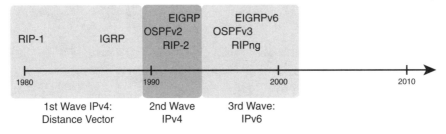

Figure 18-1 *Timeline for IP IGPs*

By the early 1990s, business and technical factors pushed the IPv4 world toward a second wave of better routing protocols. RIPv1 and IGRP had some technical limitations, even though they were great options for the technology levels of the 1980s. The huge movement toward TCP/IP in the 1990s drove the need for better IPv4 routing protocols. In the 1990s, many enterprises migrated from older vendor-proprietary networks to networks built with routers, LANs, and TCP/IP. These businesses needed better performance from their routing protocols, including better metrics and better convergence. All these factors led to the introduction of a new wave of IPv4 Interior Routing Protocols: RIP Version 2 (RIPv2), OSPF Version 2 (OSPFv2), and EIGRP.

NOTE   As an aside, many documents refer to EIGRP's support for learning IPv4 routes simply as EIGRP, and EIGRP support for IPv6 as EIGRPv6. This book follows that same convention. OSPF RFCs define specific versions: OSPF Version 2 (OSPFv2) for learning IPv4 routes, and OSPF Version 3 (OSPFv3) for learning IPv6 routes.

Comparing IGPs

What is an IGP in the first place? All the routing protocols mentioned so far in this chapter happen to be categorized as Interior Gateway Protocols (IGPs) rather than as Exterior Gateway Protocols (EGPs). First, the term *gateway* was used instead of *router* in the early days of IP routing, so the terms IGP and EGP really do refer to routing protocols. The designers of some routing protocols intended them for use inside one company or organization (IGP), with other routing protocols intended for use between companies and between Internet service providers (ISPs) in the Internet (EGPs).

This chapter falls back to using the term IGP when talking about all the routing protocols mentioned in this chapter.

When deploying a new network, the network engineer can choose between a variety of IGPs. Today, most enterprises use EIGRP and OSPFv2. RIPv2 has fallen away as a serious competitor, in part due to its less robust hop-count metric, and in part due to its slower (worse) convergence time. This chapter discusses enough of the fundamentals of all of these IGPs so that you get a sense of some of the basic trade-offs when comparing them. Here are a few key comparison points:

- **The underlying routing protocol algorithm:** Specifically, whether the routing protocol uses logic referenced as distance vector (DV) or link state (LS).

- **The usefulness of the metric:** The routing protocol chooses which route is best based on its metric; so the better the metric, the better the choices made by that routing protocol.

- **The speed of convergence:** How long does it take all the routers to learn about a change in the network and update their IPv4 routing tables? That concept, called *convergence time*, varies depending on the routing protocol.

- **Whether the protocol is a public standard or a vendor-proprietary function:** RIP and OSPF happen to be standards, defined by RFCs. EIGRP happens to be defined by Cisco, and until 2013, was kept private.

For example, RIP uses a basic metric of hop count. Hop count treats each router as a hop, so the hop count is the number of other routers between a router and some remote subnet. RIP's hop-count metric means that RIP picks the route with the smallest number of links and routers. However, that shortest route may have the slowest links; a routing protocol that uses a metric based in part on link speed (called *bandwidth*) might make a better choice. In contrast, EIGRP's metric calculation uses a math formula that gives routes with slow links a higher (worse) metric, and routes with fast links a lower (better) metric, so EIGRP prefers faster routes.

For example, Figure 18-2 shows two copies of the same topology. The topology shows three Nexus switches configured to act as Layer 3 switches. The figure focuses on router B's route to a subnet off router A. As you can see on the left in the figure, RIP on router B chooses

18

the shorter hop route over the top of the network, over the single link, even though that link runs at 1 Gbps. EIGRP, on the right side of the figure, chooses the route that happens to have more links through the network, but both links have a faster bandwidth of 10 Gbps.

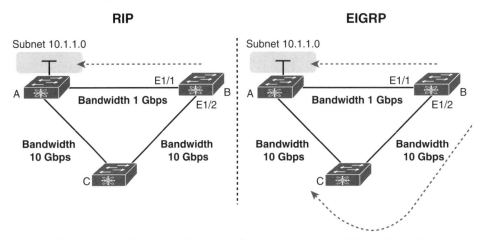

Figure 18-2   *EIGRP Choosing the Longer but Better Route to Subnet 10.1.1.0*

On another comparison point, the biggest negative about EIGRP has traditionally been that it requires Cisco routers. That is, using EIGRP locks you into using Cisco products, because Cisco kept EIGRP as a Cisco proprietary protocol. In an interesting change, Cisco published EIGRP as an informational RFC in 2013, meaning that now other vendors can choose to implement EIGRP as well. In the past, many companies chose to use OSPF rather than EIGRP to give themselves options for what router vendor to use for future router hardware purchases. In the future, it might be that you can buy some routers from Cisco, some from other vendors, and still run EIGRP on all routers.

For reference and study, Table 18-2 lists several features of OSPFv2 and EIGRP, as well as RIPv1/2. Note that the table includes a few features that have not yet been introduced (but will be introduced before the end of the chapter).

Table 18-2   Interior IP Routing Protocols Compared

Feature	RIPv1	RIPv2	EIGRP	OSPF
Distance vector (DV) or link state (LS).	DV	DV	DV[1]	LS
Default metrics based on link bandwidth.	No	No	Yes	Yes
Convergence time.	Slow	Slow	Fast	Fast
Originally Cisco proprietary.	No	No	Yes	No
Uses areas for design.	No	No	No	Yes
Routing updates are sent to a multicast IP address.	No	Yes	Yes	Yes
Classless/supports VLSM.	No	Yes	Yes	Yes

1. EIGRP is often described as a balanced hybrid routing protocol, instead of LS or DV. Some documents refer to EIGRP as an advanced distance vector protocol.

Distance Vector Basics

Each IGP can be categorized based on its internal logic, either DV or LS. As a starting point to better understand IGPs, the next few pages explain more about how a DV protocol actually exchanges routing information. These pages use RIP as an example, showing RIP's simple hop-count metric, which, although a poor option in real networks today, is a much simpler option for learning.

The Concept of a Distance and a Vector

The term *distance vector* describes what a router knows about each route. At the end of the process, when a router learns about a route to a subnet, all the router knows is some measurement of distance (the metric) as well as the next-hop router and outgoing interface to use for that route (a vector, or direction).

Figure 18-3 shows a view of both the vector and the distance as learned with RIP. The figure shows the flow of RIP messages that cause R1 to learn some IPv4 routes, specifically three routes to reach subnet X:

- The four-hop route through R2
- The three-hop route through R5
- The two-hop route through R7

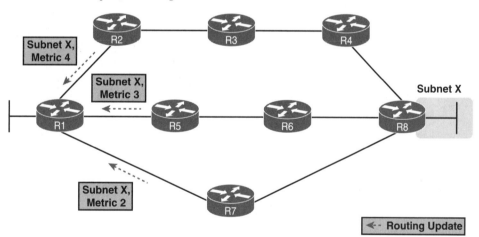

Figure 18-3   *Information Learned Using DV Protocols*

DV protocols learn two pieces of information about a possible route to reach a subnet:

- The distance (metric)
- The vector (the next-hop router)

In Figure 18-3, R1 learns three routes to reach subnet X, through three different neighboring routers. If R1 had learned only one route to subnet X, R1 would use that route. However, having learned three routes to subnet X, R1 picks the two-hop route through next-hop router R7 because that route has the lowest RIP metric.

Whereas Figure 18-3 shows how R1 learns the routes with RIP updates, Figure 18-4 gives a better view into R1's DV logic. The figure shows R1's three competing routes to subnet X as vectors, with longer vectors for routes with larger metrics. R1 knows three routes, each with the following information:

Distance: The metric for a possible route

Vector: The direction, based on the next-hop router for a possible route

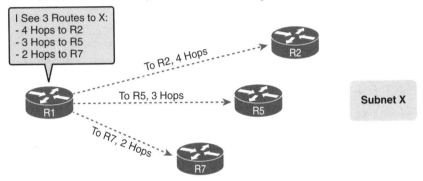

Figure 18-4 *Graphical Representation of the DV Concept*

Full Update Messages and Split Horizon

Some DV protocols, such as RIP (both RIPv1 and RIPv2), send periodic full routing updates based on a relatively short timer. Specifically, *full update* means that a router advertises all its routes, using one or more RIP update messages, regardless of whether the route has changed or not. So, even if a route does not change for months, the router keeps advertising that same route over and over.

Figure 18-5 illustrates this concept in an internetwork with two Nexus switches configured as Layer 3 switches, with four total subnets. The figure shows both routers' full routing tables, and lists the periodic full updates sent by each router.

This figure shows a lot of information, so take the time to work through the details. For example, consider what switch S1 learns for subnet 172.30.22.0/24, which is the subnet connected to S2's E1/4 interface:

1. S2 interface E1/4 has an IP address, and is in an up/up state.

2. S2 adds a connected route for 172.30.22.0/24, off interface E1/4, to R2's routing table.

3. S2 advertises its route for 172.30.22.0/24 to S1, with a metric of 1, meaning that S1's metric to reach this subnet will be metric 1 (hop count 1).

4. S1 adds a route for subnet 172.30.22.0/24, listing it as an RIP-learned route with a metric of 1.

Also, take a moment to focus more on the route learned at Step 4 (the bold route in S1's routing table). This route is for 172.30.22.0/24, as learned from S2. It lists S1's local E1/2 interface as the outgoing interface because S1 receives the update on that interface. It also lists S2's IP address of 172.30.1.2 as the next-hop router because that's the IP address from which S1 learned the route.

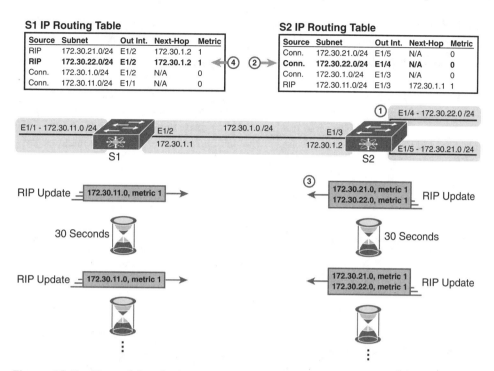

S1 IP Routing Table

Source	Subnet	Out Int.	Next-Hop	Metric
RIP	172.30.21.0/24	E1/2	172.30.1.2	1
RIP	**172.30.22.0/24**	**E1/2**	**172.30.1.2**	**1**
Conn.	172.30.1.0/24	E1/2	N/A	0
Conn.	172.30.11.0/24	E1/1	N/A	0

S2 IP Routing Table

Source	Subnet	Out Int.	Next-Hop	Metric
Conn.	172.30.21.0/24	E1/5	N/A	0
Conn.	**172.30.22.0/24**	**E1/4**	**N/A**	**0**
Conn.	172.30.1.0/24	E1/3	N/A	0
RIP	172.30.11.0/24	E1/3	172.30.1.1	1

Figure 18-5 *Normal Steady-State RIP Operations: Full Update with Split Horizon*

Monitoring Neighbor State with Periodic RIP Updates

RIPv1 and RIPv2 also send *periodic updates*, as shown at the bottom of Figure 18-5. This means that each router sends a new update (a full update) on a relatively short time period (30 seconds with RIP).

Many of the early DV protocols used this short periodic timer, repeating their full updates, as a way to let each router know whether a neighbor had failed. Routers need to react when a neighboring router fails or if the link between two routers fails. If both routers on a link must send updates every 30 seconds, when a local router no longer receives those updates, it knows that a problem has occurred, and it can react to converge to use alternate routes.

Note that newer DV protocols, such as EIGRP, do not require routers to keep sending updates for the purpose of tracking the state of the neighbor. Instead, they both define a simple hello protocol that allows the routers to send short messages to each other, instead of the long full routing updates, for the purpose of knowing when a neighbor fails.

Split Horizon

Figure 18-5 also shows a common DV feature called *split horizon*. Note that both routers list all four subnets in their IP routing tables. However, the RIP update messages do not list four subnets. The reason? Split horizon.

Split horizon is a DV feature that tells a router to omit some routes from an update sent out an interface. Which routes are omitted from an update sent out interface X? The routes that would like interface X as the outgoing interface. Those routes that are not advertised on an interface usually include the routes learned in routing updates received on that interface.

Split horizon is difficult to learn by reading words, and much easier to learn by seeing an example. Figure 18-6 continues the same example as Figure 18-5, but focusing on S1's RIP update sent out S1's E1/2 interface to S2. Figure 18-6 shows S1's routing table with three light-colored routes, all of which list E1/2 as the outgoing interface. When building the RIP update to send out E1/2, split-horizon rules tell S1 to ignore those light-colored routes. Only the bold route, which does not list E1/2 as an outgoing interface, can be included in the RIP update sent out E1/2.

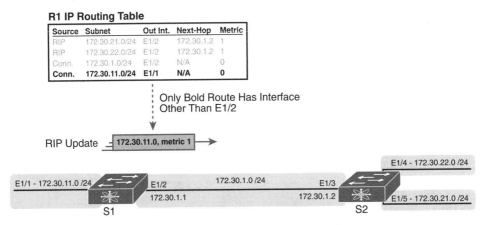

Figure 18-6 *R1 Does Not Advertise Three Routes Due to Split Horizon*

Route Poisoning

DV protocols help prevent routing loops by ensuring that every router learns that the route has failed, through every means possible, as quickly as possible. One of these features, *route poisoning*, helps all routers know for sure that a route has failed.

Route poisoning refers to the practice of advertising a failed route, but with a special metric value called *infinity*. Routers consider routes advertised with an infinite metric to have failed.

Figure 18-7 shows an example of route poisoning with RIP, with S2's E1/4 interface failing, meaning that S2's route for 172.30.22.0/24 has failed. RIP defines infinity as 16.

Figure 18-7 shows the following process:

1. S2's E1/4 interface fails.

2. S2 removes its connected route for 172.30.22.0/24 from its routing table.

3. S2 advertises 172.30.22.0 with an infinite metric (which for RIP is 16).

4. Depending on other conditions, S1 either immediately removes the route to 172.30.22.0 from its routing table, or marks the route as unusable (with an infinite metric) for a few minutes before removing the route.

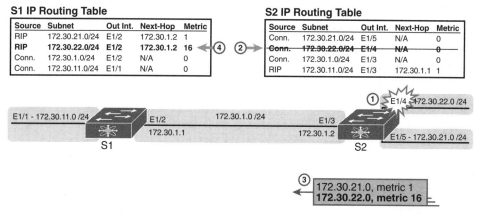

S1 IP Routing Table

Source	Subnet	Out Int.	Next-Hop	Metric
RIP	172.30.21.0/24	E1/2	172.30.1.2	1
RIP	**172.30.22.0/24**	**E1/2**	**172.30.1.2**	**16**
Conn.	172.30.1.0/24	E1/2	N/A	0
Conn.	172.30.11.0/24	E1/1	N/A	0

S2 IP Routing Table

Source	Subnet	Out Int.	Next-Hop	Metric
Conn.	172.30.21.0/24	E1/5	N/A	0
~~Conn.~~	~~172.30.22.0/24~~	~~E1/4~~	~~N/A~~	~~0~~
Conn.	172.30.1.0/24	E1/3	N/A	0
RIP	172.30.11.0/24	E1/3	172.30.1.1	1

Figure 18-7 *Route Poisoning*

By the end of this process, router S1 knows for sure that its old route for subnet 172.30.22.0/24 has failed, which helps S1 avoid introducing looping IP routes.

Each routing protocol has its own definition of an infinite metric. RIP uses 16, as shown in the figure, with 15 being a valid metric for a usable route. EIGRP has long used $2^{32} - 1$ as infinity (a little more than 4 billion), with some Cisco products bumping that value to $2^{56} - 1$ (more than 10^{16}). OSPFv2 uses $2^{24} - 1$ as infinity.

The previous few pages focused on DV concepts, using RIP as an example. This chapter next turns the focus to the particulars of both RIPv1 and RIPv2.

RIP Concepts and Operation

The Routing Information Protocol (RIP) was the first commonly used IGP in the history of TCP/IP. Organizations used RIP inside their networks commonly in the 1980s and into the 1990s. RIPv2, created in the mid-1990s, improved RIPv2, giving engineers an option for easy migration and co-existence to move from RIPv1 to the better RIPv2.

This second of four major sections of the chapter compares RIPv1 and RIPv2, while discussing a few of the core features that apply to both.

Features of Both RIPv1 and RIPv2

Like all IGPs, both RIPv1 and RIPv2 perform the same core features. That is, when using either RIPv1 or RIPv2, a router advertises information to help other routers learn routes; a router learns routes by listening to messages from other routers; a router chooses the best route to each subnet by looking at the metric of the competing routes; and the routing protocol converges to use new routes when something changes about the network.

RIPv1 and RIPv2 use the same logic to achieve most of those core functions. The similarities include the following:

■ Both send regular full periodic routing updates on a 30-second timer, with *full* meaning that the update messages include all known routes.

■ Both use split-horizon rules, as shown in Figure 18-6.

- Both use hop count as the metric.

- Both allow a maximum hop count of 15.

- Both use route poisoning as a loop-prevention mechanism (see Figure 18-7), with a hop count of 16 used to imply an unusable route with an infinite metric.

Although you might be puzzled why the creators of RIPv2 made it so much like RIPv1, the goal was simple: interoperability. A network that used RIPv1 could slowly migrate to RIPv2, enabling RIPv2 on some routers on one weekend, some more on the next, and so on. Done correctly, the network could migrate over time. The fact that both RIPv1 and RIPv2 used the same metric, as well as same loop-prevention mechanisms, allowed for a smooth migration.

Differences Between RIPv1 and RIPv2

Of course, RIPv2 needed to be better than RIPv1 in some ways; otherwise, what is the point of having a new version of RIP? RIPv2 made many changes to RIPv1: solutions to known problems, improved security, and new features as well. However, while RIPv2 improved RIP beyond RIPv1, it did not compete well with OSPF and EIGRP, particularly due to somewhat slow convergence compared to OSPF and EIGRP. However, for the sake of completeness, the next few pages walk through a few of the differences.

First, RIPv1 had one protocol feature that prevented it from using variable-length subnet masks (VLSMs). To review, VLSM means that inside one classful network (one Class A, B, or C network) more than one subnet mask is used. For instance, in Figure 18-8, all the subnets are from Class A network 10.0.0.0, but some subnets use a /24 mask, whereas others use a /30 mask.

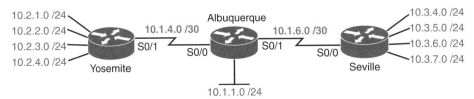

Figure 18-8 *An Example of VLSM*

RIPv1 could not support a network that uses VLSM because RIPv1 did not send mask information in the RIPv1 update message. Basically, RIPv1 routers had to guess what mask applied to each advertised subnet, and a design with VLSM made routers guess wrong. RIPv2 solved that problem by using an improved update message, which includes the subnet mask with each route, removing any need to guess what mask to use, so RIPv2 correctly supports VLSM.

RIPv2 fixed a couple of other perceived RIPv1 shortcomings as well. RIPv2 added authentication (RIPv1 had none), which can avoid cases in which an attacker introduces incorrect routes into a router's routing table. RIPv2 changed from using IP broadcasts sent to the 255.255.255.255 broadcast address (as in RIPv1) to instead sending updates to the 224.0.0.9 IPv4 multicast address. Using multicasts means that RIP messages can be more easily ignored by other devices, thus wasting less CPU on those devices.

Table 18-3 summarizes some of the key features of RIPv1 and RIPv2.

Table 18-3   Key Features of RIPv1 and RIPv2

Feature	RIPv1	RIPv2
Hop-count metric	Yes	Yes
Sets 15 as the largest metric for a working route	Yes	Yes
Sends full routing updates	Yes	Yes
Uses split horizon	Yes	Yes
Uses route poisoning, with metric 16	Yes	Yes
Sends mask in routing update	No	Yes
Supports noncontiguous classful networks	No	Yes
Sends updates to 224.0.0.9 multicast address	No	Yes
Supports authentication	No	Yes

18

EIGRP Concepts and Operation

Enhanced Interior Gateway Routing Protocol (EIGRP) went through a similar creation process as compared to RIP, but with the work happening inside Cisco. Cisco had already created the Interior Gateway Routing Protocol (IGRP) in the 1980s, and the same needs that drove people to create RIPv2 and OSPF drove Cisco to improve IGRP as well. Instead of naming the original IGRP Version 1, and the new one IGRP Version 2, Cisco named the new version Enhanced IGRP (EIGRP).

EIGRP acts a little like a DV protocol, and a little like no other routing protocol. Frankly, over the years, different Cisco documents and different books have characterized EIGRP as either its own category, called a *balanced hybrid routing protocol*, or as some kind of advanced DV protocol.

Regardless of what label you put on EIGRP, the protocol uses several features that work like basic DV protocols such as RIP, or work similarly enough. Routers that use EIGRP send messages so that other routers learn routes, they listen for messages to learn routes, they choose the best route among multiple routes to the same subnet based on a metric, and they react and converge when the network topology changes.

Of course, EIGRP works differently in several ways as compared to RIPv2. This third of four sections of the chapter discusses some of those similarities and differences, so you get a sense of how EIGRP works. Note that this section does not attempt to mention all the features of EIGRP, but instead gives some highlights that point out some of EIGRP's unique features compared to other IGPs. Regardless, at the end of the day, once you enable EIGRP on all your routers and Layer 3 switches, the devices will learn good routes for all the subnets in the network.

EIGRP Maintains Neighbor Status Using Hello

Unlike RIP, EIGRP does not send full or partial update messages based on a periodic timer. When a router first comes up, it advertises known routing information. Then, over time, as facts change, the router simply reacts, sending partial updates with the new information.

The fact that EIGRP does not send routing information on a short periodic timed basis greatly reduces EIGRP overhead traffic, but it also means that EIGRP cannot rely on these updates to monitor the state of neighboring routers. Instead, EIGRP defines the concept of a neighbor relationship, using EIGRP hello messages to monitor that relationship. The EIGRP hello message and protocol define that each router should send a periodic hello message on each interface, so that all EIGRP routers know that the router is still working. Figure 18-9 shows the idea.

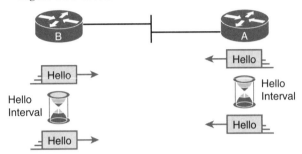

Figure 18-9 *EIGRP Hello Packets*

The routers use their own independent hello interval, which defines the time period between each EIGRP hello. For instance, routers R1 and R2 do not have to send their hellos at the same time. Routers also must receive a hello from a neighbor with a time value called the *hold interval*, with a default setting of three times the hello interval.

For instance, imagine both R1 and R2 use default settings of 5 and 15 for their hello and hold intervals, respectively. Under normal conditions, R1 receives hellos from R2 every 5 seconds, well within R1's hold interval (15 seconds) before R1 would consider R2 to have failed. If R2 does fail, R2 no longer sends hello messages. R1 notices that 15 seconds pass without receiving a hello from R2, so then R1 can choose new routes that do not use R2 as a next-hop router.

EIGRP Topology and the Metric Calculation

One of the most compelling reasons to consider using EIGRP instead of other IGPs is the strength of the EIGRP metric. EIGRP uses a math function to calculate the metric. More importantly, that function uses two input variables by default:

■ The slowest link in the end-to-end route

■ The cumulative delay for all links in the route

As a result, EIGRP defines the concept of the best route based on the constraining bandwidth (speed) of the links in the route, plus the total delay in the route.

The words *bandwidth* and *delay* have specific meaning with EIGRP. *Bandwidth* refers to the perceived speed of each link. *Delay* refers to the router's perception of the time it takes to send a frame over the link. Both bandwidth and delay are settings on router interfaces; although routers do have default values for both bandwidth and delay on each interface, the settings can be configured as well.

EIGRP calls the calculated metric value the *composite metric*, with the individual inputs into the formula being the metric components. The formula itself is not as important as the effect of the metric components on the calculation:

■ A smaller bandwidth yields a larger composite metric because less bandwidth is worse than more bandwidth.

■ A smaller delay yields a smaller composite metric because less delay is better than more delay.

Using these two inputs gives EIGRP a much better metric than RIP. Basically, EIGRP prefers routes with faster links, avoiding routes with slower links. Slow links, besides the obvious negative of being slow, also may experience more congestion, with packets waiting longer to get a turn to cross the link. For example, EIGRP could prefer a route with multiple 10Gbps links rather than a single-hop route over a 1Gbps or 100Mbps link.

EIGRP Convergence

Another compelling reason to choose EIGRP as an IGP has to do with EIGRP's much better convergence time as compared with RIP. EIGRP converges more quickly than RIP in all cases, and in some cases, EIGRP converges much more quickly.

For perspective, with RIPv2 in normal operation, convergence could take several minutes. During those minutes, some user traffic is not delivered to the correct destination, even though a physical path exists. With EIGRP, those same worst cases typically experience convergence of less than a minute, often less than 20 seconds, with some cases taking a second or two.

EIGRP does loop avoidance completely differently than RIP by keeping some basic topological information. The EIGRP topology database on each router holds some information about the local router, plus some information about the next-hop router in each possible route for each known subnet. That extra topology information lets EIGRP on each router take the following approach for all the possible routes to reach one subnet:

■ Similar to how other routing protocols work, a local router calculates the metric for each possible route to reach a subnet and chooses the best route based on the best metric.

■ Unlike how other routing protocols work, the local router uses that extra topology information to look at the routes that were not chosen as the best route, to find all alternate routes that, if the best route fails, could be immediately used without causing a loop.

That second bullet reveals the key to understanding how EIGRP converges very quickly. Without getting into all the details, a simple example of the power of this fast EIGRP convergence can help. To begin, consider Figure 18-10, which focuses on router E's three possible routes to reach subnet 1 on the right.

18

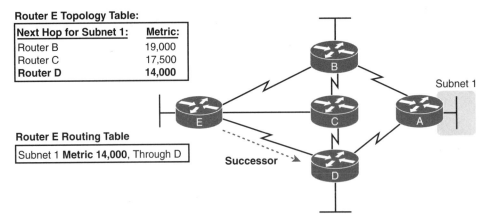

Figure 18-10   *Route Through Router D Is the Successor Route to Subnet 1*

The upper left shows router E's topology table information about the three competing routes to reach subnet 1: a route through router B, another through router C, and yet another through router D. The metrics in the upper left are shown from router E's perspective, so router E chooses the route with the smallest metric: the route through next-hop router D. EIGRP on router E places that route, with next-hop router D, into its IP routing table, represented on the lower left of the figure.

Note   EIGRP calls the best route to reach a subnet the successor route.

At the same time, EIGRP on router E uses additional topology information to decide whether either of the other routes—the routes through B and C—could be used if the route through router D fails, without causing a loop. Ignoring the details of how router E decides, imagine that router E does that analysis, and decides that its route for subnet 1 through router B could be used without causing a loop, but the route through router C could not. Router E would call that route through router B a *feasible successor* route, as noted in Figure 18-11.

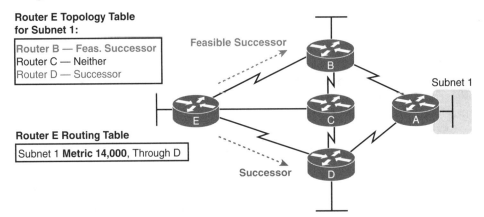

Figure 18-11   *Route Through Router B Is a Feasible Successor*

As long as the network stays stable, router E has chosen the best route, and is ready to act, as follows:

- Router E uses the successor route as its only route to subnet 1, as listed in the IPv4 routing table.

- Router E lists the route to subnet 1, through router B, as a feasible successor, as noted in the EIGRP topology table.

Later, when convergence to a new route to subnet 1 needs to occur—days later, weeks later, or whenever—the convergence is almost instant. As soon as router E realizes that the current route through router D has failed, router E can immediately remove the old route from its IPv4 routing table and then add a route to subnet 1 listing router B as the next-hop router.

EIGRP Summary

As you can see, EIGRP provides many advantages over both RIPv1 and RIPv2. Most significantly, it uses a much better metric, and it converges much more quickly than does RIP.

The biggest downside to EIGRP has traditionally been that EIGRP was a Cisco proprietary protocol. That is, to run EIGRP, you had to use Cisco products only. Interestingly, Cisco published EIGRP as an informational RFC in 2013, so now other vendors can choose to add EIGRP support to their products. Over time, maybe this one negative about EIGRP will fade away.

The next topic introduces the final routing protocol for this chapter, OSPF, which has always been a public standard.

Understanding the OSPF Link-State Routing Protocol

To complete this chapter, this final major section examines one more routing protocol: the Open Shortest Path First (OSPF) protocol. Like EIGRP, OSPF converges quickly. Like EIGRP, OSPF bases its metric by default on link bandwidth, so that OSPF makes a better choice than simply relying on the router hop-count metric used by RIP. But OSPF uses much different internal logic, being a link-state routing protocol rather than a distance vector protocol.

This section introduces OSPF, first by listing some of the more obvious similarities and differences between OSPF and EIGRP. The rest of this section then explains a few of the internals of OSPF to give you some insights into a few key differences between OSPF and other IGPs.

OSPF Comparisons with EIGRP

Like all the IGPs discussed in this chapter, OSPF causes routers to learn routes, choose the best route to each subnet based on a metric, and to converge to choose new best routes when the network changes.

Although EIGRP uses DV logic, and OSPF uses LS logic, OSPF and EIGRP have three major activities that, from a general perspective, appear to be the same:

1. Both OSPF and EIGRP use a hello protocol to find neighboring routers, maintain a list of working neighbors, monitor ongoing hello messages to make sure the neighbor is still reachable, and notice when the path to a neighbor has failed.

2. Both OSPF and EIGRP exchange topology data, which each router stores locally in a topology database. The topology database describes facts about the network but is a different entity than the router's IPv4 routing table.

3. Both OSPF and EIGRP cause each router to process its topology database, from which the router can choose the current best route (lowest metric route) to reach each subnet, adding those best routes to the IPv4 routing table.

For instance, in a network that uses Nexus Layer 3 switches, you could use OSPF or EIGRP. If using OSPF, you could display a Layer 3 switch's OSPF neighbors (**show ip ospf neighbor**), the OSPF database (**show ip ospf database**), and the IPv4 routing table (**show ip route**). Alternatively, if you instead used EIGRP, you could display the equivalent in EIGRP: EIGRP neighbors (**show ip eigrp neighbor**), the EIGRP topology database (**show ip eigrp topology**), and the IPv4 routing table (**show ip route**).

However, if you dig a little deeper, OSPF and EIGRP clearly use different conventions and logic. The protocols, of course, are different, with EIGRP being created inside Cisco and OSPF developed as an RFC. The topology databases differ significantly, with OSPF collecting much more detail about the topology, and with EIGRP collecting just enough to make choices about successor and feasible successor routes. The method of processing the database, which then determines the best route for each subnet, differs significantly as well.

Most of the similarities end here, with OSPF, as an LS protocol, simply using an entirely different approach to choosing the currently best route for each subnet. The rest of this section describes LS behavior, using OSPF as the example.

Building the OSPF LSDB and Creating IP Routes

Link-state protocols build IP routes with a couple of major steps. First, the routers build a detailed database of information about the network and flood that so that all routers have a copy of the same information. (The information is much more detailed than the topology data collected by EIGRP.) That database, called the *link-state database* (LSDB), gives each router the equivalent of a roadmap for the network, showing all routers, all router interfaces, all links between routers, and all subnets connected to routers. Second, each router runs a complex mathematical formula (the details of which we can all ignore) to calculate the best route to reach each subnet.

The next few pages walk through both parts of the process: building the LSDB, and then processing the LSDB to choose the best routes.

Topology Information and LSAs

Routers using LS routing protocols need to collectively advertise practically every detail about the internetwork to all the other routers. At the end of the process of *flooding* the information to all routers, every router in the internetwork has the exact same information about the internetwork. Flooding a lot of detailed information to every router sounds like a lot of work, and relative to DV routing protocols, it is.

OSPF, the most popular LS IP routing protocol, organizes topology information using link-state advertisements (LSAs) and the link-state database (LSDB). Figure 18-12 represents the ideas. Each LSA is a data structure with some specific information about the network topology—for instance, each router must be described by a separate LSA. The LSDB holds the collection of all the LSAs known to a router. Think of the LSDB as having one LSA for every router, one for every link, with several other types as well.

Link State Database (LSDB)

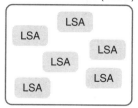

Figure 18-12 *LSA and LSDB Relationship*

LS protocols rely on having all routers knowing the same view of the network topology and link status (link state) by all having a copy of the LSDB. The idea is like giving all routers a copy of the same updated roadmap. If all routers have the exact same roadmap, and they base their choices of best routes on that same roadmap, then the routers, using the same algorithm, will never create any routing loops.

To create the LSDB, each router will create some of the LSAs needed. Each router floods both the LSAs it creates, plus others learned from neighboring routers, so that all the routers have a copy of each LSA. Figure 18-13 shows the general idea of the flooding process, with R8 creating and flooding an LSA that describes itself (called a *router LSA*). The router LSA for router R8 describes the router itself, including the existence of subnet 172.16.3.0/24, as shown on the right side of the figure. (Note that Figure 18-13 actually shows only a subset of the information in R8's router LSA.)

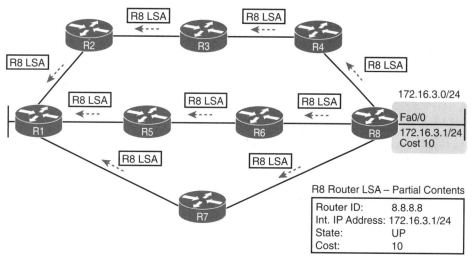

Figure 18-13 *Flooding LSAs Using an LS Routing Protocol*

Figure 18-13 shows the rather basic flooding process, with R8 sending the original LSA for itself and with the other routers flooding the LSA by forwarding it until every router has a copy. The flooding process has a way to prevent loops so that the LSAs do not get flooded around in circles. Basically, before sending an LSA to yet another neighbor, routers communicate and ask "do you already have this LSA?" Then they avoid flooding the LSA to neighbors that already have it.

Applying Dijkstra SPF Math and OSPF Metrics to Find the Best Routes

Although incredibly detailed and useful, the LSDB does not explicitly state each router's best route to reach a destination. Instead, it lists the data from which a router can derive its currently best route to reach each subnet, by doing some math.

All LS protocols use a type of math algorithm called the Dijkstra shortest path first (SPF) algorithm to process the LSDB. That algorithm analyzes (with math) the LSDB and then builds the routes that the local router should add to the IP routing table—routes that list a subnet number and mask, an outgoing interface, and a next-hop router IP address.

Although engineers do not need to know the details of how SPF does the math, you can easily predict what SPF will choose, given some basic information about the network. The key is that once SPF has identified a route, it calculates the metric for a route as follows:

The OSPF metric for a route is the sum of the interface costs for all outgoing interfaces in the route. By default, a router's OSPF interface cost is actually derived from the interface bandwidth: The faster the bandwidth, the lower the cost. So, a lower OSPF cost means that the interface is better than an interface with a higher OSPF cost.

Armed with the facts in the previous few paragraphs, you can look at the example in Figure 18-14 and predict how the OSPF SPF algorithm will analyze the available routes and choose a best route. This figure features the logic on router R1, with its three competing routes to subnet X (172.16.3.0/24) at the bottom of the figure.

> **NOTE** OSPF considers the costs of the outgoing interfaces (only) in each route. It does not add the cost for incoming interfaces in the route.

Table 18-4 lists the three routes shown in Figure 18-14, with their cumulative costs, showing that R1's best route to 172.16.3.0/24 starts by going through R5.

Table 18-4   Comparing R1's Three Alternatives for the Route to 172.16.3.0/24

Route	Location in Figure 18-14	Cumulative OSPF Cost
R1–R7–R8	Left	10 + 180 + 10 = 200
R1–R5–R6–R8	Middle	20 + 30 + 40 + 10 = 100
R1–R2–R3–R4–R8	Right	30 + 60 + 20 + 5 + 10 = 125

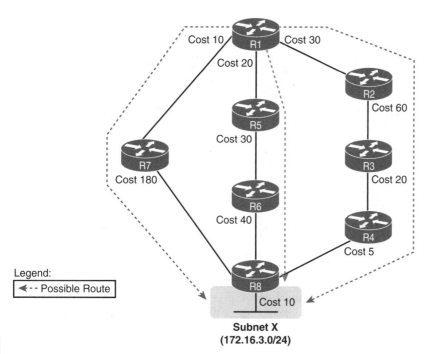

Figure 18-14 *SPF Tree to Find R1's Route to 172.16.3.0/24*

As a result of the SPF algorithm's analysis of the LSDB, R1 adds a route to subnet 172.16.3.0/24 to its routing table, with the next-hop router of R5.

> **NOTE** OSPF calculates costs using different processes depending on the area design. The example shown in Figure 18-14 best matches OSPF's logic when a single area design is used.

Scaling OSPF Through Hierarchical Design

OSPF can be used in some networks with very little thought about design issues. You just turn on OSPF in all the routers, and it works! However, in large networks, engineers need to think about and plan how to use several OSPF features that allow OSPF to scale well. For instance, the OSPF design in Figure 18-15 uses a single OSPF area, because this small inter-network does not need the scalability benefits of OSPF areas.

Using a single OSPF area for smaller internetworks, as in Figure 18-15, works well. The configuration is simple, and some of the hidden details in how OSPF works remain simple. In fact, with a small OSPF internetwork, you can just enable OSPF, with all interfaces in the same area, and mostly ignore the idea of an OSPF area.

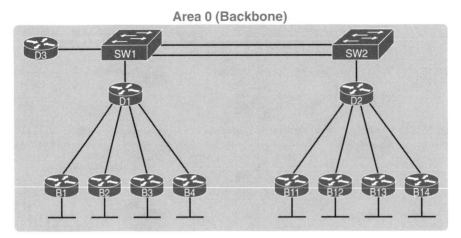

Figure 18-15 *Single-Area OSPF*

Now imagine a network with 900 routers (instead of only 11) and several thousand subnets. In that size of network, the sheer amount of processing required to run the complex SPF algorithm might cause convergence time to be slow due to how long it takes each router to process all the math. Also, the routers might experience memory shortages. The problems can be summarized as follows:

- A larger topology database requires more memory on each router.

- The router CPU time required to run the SPF algorithm grows exponentially with the size of the LSDB.

- With a single area, a single interface status change (up to down, or down to up) forces every router to run SPF again!

OSPF provides a way to manage the size of the LSDB by breaking up a larger network into smaller pieces using a concept called OSPF *areas*. The engineer places some links in one area, some in another, others in yet a third area, and so on. OSPF then creates a separate and smaller LSDB per area, rather than one huge LSDB for all links and routers in the internetwork. With smaller topology databases, routers consume less memory and take less processing time to run SPF.

An OSPF multi-area design puts all ends of a link—a serial link, a VLAN, and so on—inside an area. To make that work, some routers (called area border routers, or ABRs) sit at the border between multiple areas. Routers D1 and D2 serve as ABRs in the area design shown in Figure 18-16, which shows the same network as Figure 18-15, but with three OSPF areas (0, 1, and 2).

Figure 18-16 shows a sample area design and some terminology related to areas, but it does not show the power and benefit of the areas. By using areas, the OSPF SPF algorithm ignores the details of the topology in the other areas. For example, OSPF on router B1 (area 1), when doing the complex SPF math processing, ignores the topology information about area 0 and area 2. Each router has much less SPF work to do, so each router more quickly finishes its SPF work, finding the current best OSPF routes.

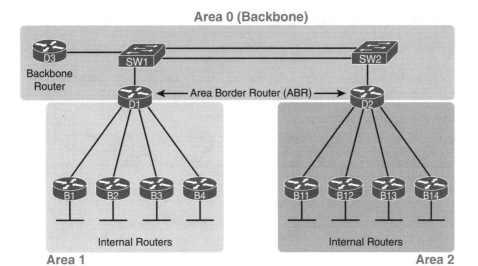

Figure 18-16   *Three-Area OSPF*

Exam Preparation Tasks

Review All the Key Topics

Review the most important topics from this chapter, noted with the Key Topic icon. Table 18-5 lists these key topics and where each is discussed.

Table 18-5   Key Topics for Chapter 18

Key Topic Element	Description	Page Number
Table 18-3	Key features of RIPv1 and RIPv2	483
Paragraph	How SPF calculates the metric for a route	490
Figure 18-14	How OSPF's SPF algorithm analyzes and selects the best route	491

Complete the Tables and Lists from Memory

Print a copy of Appendix C, "Memory Tables," or at least the section for this chapter, and complete the tables and lists from memory. Appendix D, "Memory Tables Answer Key," includes completed tables and lists for you to check your work.

Definitions of Key Terms

After your first reading of the chapter, try to define these key terms, but do not be concerned about getting them all correct at that time. Chapter 24, "Final Review," directs you in how to use these terms for late-stage preparation for the exam.

convergence, distance vector, Interior Gateway Protocol (IGP), partial update, poisoned route, split horizon, feasible successor, successor, shortest path first (SPF) algorithm, link state, link-state advertisement (LSA), link-state database (LSDB)

This chapter covers the following exam topics:

4.1. Describe and configure basic routing concepts

4.1a. Packet forwarding

4.2. Describe the operation of Cisco routers

4.2c. Route components

CHAPTER 19

Nexus Routing Protocol Configuration

As you learned in Chapter 18, "IPv4 Routing Protocol Concepts," there are three main types of routing protocols for IPv4:

- Distance vector, such as RIPv2
- Link state, as in the case of OSPF
- A hybrid of the two with EIGRP

This chapter shows you how each of these three routing protocols is configured in NX-OS on Cisco Nexus switches that have Layer 3 capabilities. To do this, the chapter provides examples of how to configure these routing protocols and verify their operation, and it covers the troubleshooting basics. The chapter starts with Routing Information Protocol Version 2 (RIPv2), moves on to Enhanced Interior Gateway Routing Protocol (EIGRP), and finishes up with the Open Shortest Path First (OSPF) protocol in a single area. Each routing protocol is applied to a single network topology with two configuration examples.

"Do I Know This Already?" Quiz

Use the "Do I Know This Already?" quiz to help decide whether you might want to skim this chapter, or a major section, moving more quickly to the "Exam Preparation Tasks" section near the end of the chapter. Table 19-1 lists the major headings in this chapter and their corresponding "Do I Know This Already?" quiz questions. For thorough explanations, see Appendix A, "Answers to the 'Do I Know This Already?' Quizzes."

Table 19-1 "Do I Know This Already?" Foundation Topics Section-to-Question Mapping

Foundation Topics Section	Questions
RIP Version 2 Configuration on NX-OS	1–2
OSPF Configuration on NX-OS	3
EIGRP Configuration on NX-OS	4–5

1. RIP is what type of routing protocol?

   a. Link state

   b. Hybrid

   c. Distance vector

   d. Single hop

2. Which command shows you all of your RIP-specific configuration on a Cisco Nexus Layer 3 switch?

   a. **show interface status**

   b. **show running-config rip**

   c. **show ip route**

   d. **show routing process rip**

3. What is the default interface type for OSPF on an Ethernet interface?

   a. Point to point

   b. Nonbroadcast multiaccess

   c. Broadcast

   d. Point to multipoint

4. Which two K values does EIGRP enable by default?

   a. K1 bandwidth

   b. K5 MTU

   c. K3 delay

   d. K12 pipe density

5. Which command under an EIGRP routing process enables you to manually set the identity of Router 2 across the network?

   a. **routing process identifier 2**

   b. **router 2**

   c. **router-id 2.2.2.2**

   d. **routing-id 2.2.2.2**

Foundation Topics

The Cisco Nexus switches have the capability to be enabled for IP Version 4 and 6 routing protocols; this chapter focuses on IPv4 routing protocol configurations. When you're implementing these protocols on a Cisco Nexus switch, it is important to understand the fundamentals of routing on any Cisco Layer 3 switch. First, two different types of interfaces can participate in Layer 3 operations. One is referred to as a *routed interface*, where you disable switching on this interface using the **no switchport** command and dedicate it for Layer 3 operations. Example 19-1 shows how you would configure a routed interface on a Cisco Nexus Layer 3 switch.

Example 19-1   *"Routed" Interface Configuration*

```
R2# configure terminal
Enter configuration commands, one per line. End with CNTL/Z.
R2# configure terminal
R2(config)# interface Ethernet1/1
R2(config-if)# no switchport
R2(config-if)# ip address 10.1.1.1/24
R2(config-if)# no shutdown
```

The second interface that can participate in Layer 3 operations is a switched virtual interface (SVI), which was discussed in Chapter 16, "IPv4 Routing Concepts," and Chapter 17, "Cisco Nexus IPv4 Routing Configuration," where a group of Layer 2 interfaces are associated with a VLAN and then a Layer 3 SVI is configured for routing over this VLAN. Example 19-2 shows the enabling of an SVI on a Cisco Nexus Layer 3 switch. After configuring these two options, you then enable IPv4 routing protocols to allow participation with the routing protocol of your choice.

Example 19-2   *"SVI" Interface Configuration*

```
R2# configure terminal
R2(config)# interface Ethernet 1/3
R2(config-if)# switchport
R2(config-if)# switchport access vlan 88
R2(config-if)# exit
R2(config)# interface Vlan 88
R2(config-if)# ip address 10.8.1.1/24
R2(config-if)# no shutdown
```

Another fundamental to note in NX-OS, which is different from previous Cisco operating systems, is that you enable the routing instance on each interface or SVI that you would like to have participating in the routing process. This is important to note for two reasons:

- In older versions of IOS, when enabling IPv4 routing protocols, you would specify the networks under the **router** *protocol tag*, which in some cases enabled the routing process for multiple interfaces, especially on Layer 3 switches that had an IP address in that subnet range. This is important because in Layer 3 routing protocols, you want to minimize

19

the amount of adjacencies per routing protocol to aid in the stability, recovery, and convergence of the network. By enabling under the interface, you can be more granular on which interface/subnets will participate or be advertised to neighbors.

■ The second benefit is that in earlier IOS versions, when you enabled a **network** statement under the routing process that covered multiple interface addresses, the router would also start sending hello messages out of those interfaces. To limit the number of neighbor adjacencies, you would use the **passive** *interface* command to limit which interfaces would send hellos. NX-OS simplifies this because you enable the routing process only under the interfaces with their associated subnets; in turn, you only have to add the **passive** *interface* command under the interfaces you don't want to form neighbor adjacencies on but would like their subnets advertised to neighbors.

Example 19-3 shows IOS-based configuration versus NX-OS configuration of the EIGRP routing process.

Example 19-3   *Routing Process Enablement IOS and NX-OS with Passive Interface*

```
IOS
R1# configure terminal
R1(config)# ip routing
R1(config)# router eigrp 1
R1(config-router)# network 10.0.0.0
R1(config-router)# passive-interface vlan 13
R1(config-router)# passive-interface vlan 14
R1(config)# interface vlan 12
R1(config-if)# ip address 10.1.1.1/24
R1(config-if)# no shutdown
R1(config)# interface vlan 13
R1(config-if)# ip address 10.1.3.1/24
R1(config-if)# no shutdown
R1(config)# interface vlan 14
R1(config-if)# ip address 10.1.4.1/24
R1(config-if)# no shutdown
```

```
NX-OS
R1# Configure terminal
R1(config)# feature eigrp
R1(config)# feature interface-vlan
R1(config)# router eigrp 1
R1(config)# interface vlan 12
R1(config-if)# ip address 10.1.1.1/24
R1(config-if)# no shutdown
R1(config-if)# ip router eigrp 1
R1(config)# interface vlan 13
R1(config-if)# ip address 10.1.3.1/24
R1(config-if)# no shutdown
R1(config-if)# ip router eigrp 1
R1(config-if)# ip passive-interface eigrp 1
```

```
R1(config)# interface vlan 14
R1(config-if)# ip address 10.1.4.1/24
R1(config-if)# no shutdown
R1(config-if)# ip router eigrp 1
R1(config-if)# ip passive-interface eigrp 1
```

Before we get into our three different routing protocol configurations, we need to explore a common tool you will use to troubleshoot and verify routing in your network no matter what routing protocol you use—the routing table. You have learned about this in previous chapters, but let's spend some time looking at the routing table and what you need to look at to verify your networks are working the way you expect them to. Example 19-4 shows a sample routing table on a Nexus switch.

Example 19-4   *Sample Routing Table*

```
SW1# show ip route
IP Route Table for VRF "default"
'*' denotes best ucast next-hop
'**' denotes best mcast next-hop
'[x/y]' denotes [preference/metric]
'%<string>' in via output denotes VRF <string>
0.0.0.0/0, ubest/mbest: 1/0
        *via 172.16.31.6, Eth1/8, [170/3328], 1d01h, eigrp-1, external
10.0.0.0/24, ubest/mbest: 1/0, attached
        *via 10.0.0.252, Vlan500, [0/0], 1d01h, direct
10.0.0.252/32, ubest/mbest: 1/0, attached
        *via 10.0.0.252, Vlan500, [0/0], 1d01h, local
10.0.0.254/32, ubest/mbest: 1/0
        *via 10.0.0.254, Vlan500, [0/0], 1d01h, hsrp
10.0.2.0/24, ubest/mbest: 1/0, attached
        *via 10.0.2.154, Vlan502, [0/0], 1d01h, direct
10.0.2.154/32, ubest/mbest: 1/0, attached
        *via 10.0.2.154, Vlan502, [0/0], 1d01h, local
10.0.2.254/32, ubest/mbest: 1/0
        *via 10.0.2.254, Vlan502, [0/0], 1d01h, hsrp
10.0.3.0/24, ubest/mbest: 1/0, attached
        *via 10.0.3.154, Vlan503, [0/0], 1d01h, direct
10.0.3.154/32, ubest/mbest: 1/0, attached
        *via 10.0.3.154, Vlan503, [0/0], 1d01h, local
10.0.3.254/32, ubest/mbest: 1/0
        *via 10.0.3.254, Vlan503, [0/0], 1d01h, hsrp
10.0.128.103/32, ubest/mbest: 3/0
        *via 10.0.0.253, Vlan500, [90/130816], 1d01h, eigrp-1, internal
        *via 10.0.2.54, Vlan502, [90/130816], 1d01h, eigrp-1, internal
        *via 10.0.3.54, Vlan503, [90/130816], 1d01h, eigrp-1, internal
```

19

In the output, you see a couple of highlighted areas that are important to note when you verify your networking by looking at the routing table. First, you can see the route highlighted in the top left (10.0.0.0/24), which is a destination you have the capability to route to. Just below that, as part of the routing table output, you see that you can reach this network via 10.0.0.252 and that it is a direct route. A *direct* route means that you have an interface directly connected on this device that lives in that network. To see a network to which you have access that is not directly connected to this Cisco Nexus switch (see the route for 10.0.128.103/32 highlighted), you can reach this route through three different paths. You can see that the admin cost of 90 is associated, letting you know it is an EIGRP route. You can also see that it is an EIGRP route at the end of the same line. Whichever routing protocol you use, viewing the **show ip route** command output can provide a great amount of detail of how your network and routers see the network, which can assist in verification and troubleshooting. If you want to look just at routes learned from a particular routing protocol, you can also use a more specific **show ip route** command by adding the routing protocol name at the end of the command; for example, **show ip route** (**rip/eigrp/ospf**).

RIP Version 2 Configuration on NX-OS

As you learned in Chapter 16, RIP is a distance vector routing protocol. This section describes how to enable RIPv2 (the default version on Cisco Nexus switches), validate configuration, and perform basic troubleshooting. Figure 19-1 shows routing between four Nexus switches—a topology common in today's data centers. You will use this topology to configure RIPv2 in two ways:

- RIPv2 enabled via routed interfaces
- Based on SVI being enabled as the Layer 3 interface for routing protocol participation

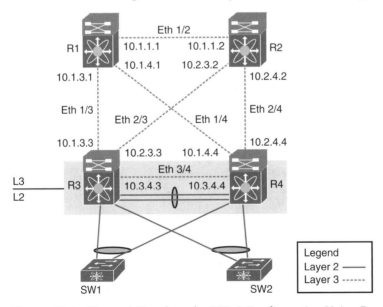

Figure 19-1 *Network Topology for RIPv2 Configuration Using Routed Interfaces*

Example 19-5 shows the configuration steps to enable RIPv2 on R1 and R2 of the Nexus switches connected via Layer 3 interfaces at the top of the topology.

Example 19-5   *RIPv2 Configuration on R1 and R2 Using Routed Interface*

```
R1 Configuration
R1# configure terminal
R1(config)# feature rip
R1(config)# interface Ethernet1/2
R1(config-if)# no switchport
R1(config-if)# ip address 10.1.1.1/24
R1(config-if)# no shutdown
R1(config-if)# ip router rip enterprise
R1(config)# interface Ethernet1/3
R1(config-if)# no switchport
R1(config-if)# ip address 10.1.3.1/24
R1(config-if)# no shutdown
R1(config-if)# ip router rip enterprise
R1(config)# interface Ethernet1/4
R1(config-if)# no switchport
R1(config-if)# ip address 10.1.4.1/24
R1(config-if)# no shutdown
R1(config-if)# ip router rip enterprise
R1(config)# router rip enterprise
```

```
R2 Configuration
R2# Configure terminal
R2(config)# feature rip
R2(config)# interface Ethernet1/2
R2(config-if)# no switchport
R2(config-if)# ip address 10.1.1.2/24
R2(config-if)# no shutdown
R2(config-if)# ip router rip enterprise
R2(config)# interface Ethernet2/3
R2(config-if)# no switchport
R2(config-if)# ip address 10.2.3.2/24
R2(config-if)# no shutdown
R2(config-if)# ip router rip enterprise
R2(config)# interface Ethernet2/4
R2(config-if)# no switchport
R2(config-if)# ip address 10.2.4.2/24
R2(config-if)# no shutdown
R2(config-if)# ip router rip enterprise
R2(config)# router rip enterprise
```

As shown in the configurations in Example 19-5, each Nexus, R1 through R4, would have similar configurations for **feature rip** being enabled globally, with **no switchport** under the physical interface to put the interfaces into a strict L3-only mode (no switching). From there, you enable the routing process for RIP using the **ip router rip enterprise** command. Also, you would need to enable the **router rip** *instance-tag*; this example uses **enterprise** as the instance tag to identify the routing process to be enabled on the interfaces.

> **NOTE** Nexus 7000 series switches by default have all physical interfaces in **no switchport** or Layer 3 mode, while Nexus 5000 series switches have switchport enabled on each physical interface by default.

So far, you have learned how to configure RIPv2 on a Nexus Layer 3 routed interface. The next task is to learn how to do this using interface VLAN or switched virtual interface (SVI) at Layer 3. Figure 19-2 uses the same basic topology as Figure 19-1, but peers R1 and R2 over a VLAN using RIPv2.

> **NOTE** Nexus 5000s have all of the interface enabled or in a no shutdown state, whereas Nexus 7000s by default have them disabled or in a shutdown state. It is important to check this while configuring your 7000 or 5000.

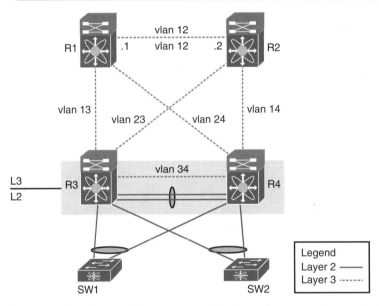

Figure 19-2 *Network Topology for RIPv2 Configuration Using SVIs*

Example 19-6 shows the configuration for SVI configuration and enabling RIPv2.

Example 19-6   *RIPv2 Configuration on R1 and R2 Using SVI*

```
R1 Configuration
R1# configure terminal
R1(config)# feature rip
R1(config)# router rip enterprise
R1(config)# feature interface-vlan
R1(config)# interface vlan 12
R1(config-if)# ip address 10.1.1.1/24
R1(config-if)# no shutdown
R1(config-if)# ip router rip enterprise
R1(config)# interface vlan 13
R1(config-if)# ip address 10.1.3.1/24
R1(config-if)# no shutdown
R1(config-if)# ip router rip enterprise
R1(config)# interface vlan 14
R1(config-if)# ip address 10.1.4.1/24
R1(config-if)# no shutdown
R1(config-if)# ip router rip enterprise
R2 Configuration
R2# configure terminal
R2(config)# feature rip
R2(config)# router rip enterprise
R2(config)# feature interface-vlan
R2(config)# interface vlan 12
R2(config-if)# ip address 10.1.1.2/24
R2(config-if)# no shutdown
R2(config-if)# ip router rip enterprise
R2(config)# interface vlan 23
R2(config-if)# ip address 10.2.3.2/24
R2(config-if)# no shutdown
R2(config-if)# ip router rip enterprise
R2(config)# interface vlan 24
R2(config-if)# ip address 10.2.4.2/24
R2(config-if)# no shutdown
R2(config-if)# ip router rip enterprise
```

19

Finally, you need to verify that your RIP configuration is correct, followed by some basic troubleshooting for RIPv2 2 on Cisco Nexus switches. Example 19-7 uses **show** commands to validate that the neighboring Layer 3 Nexus switches are communicating with each other and learning routing via the RIPv2 routing protocol.

Example 19-7 *RIPv2 Verification on R1*

```
R1# show ip rip
Process Name "rip-enterprise" VRF "default"
RIP port 520, multicast-group 224.0.0.9
Admin-distance: 120
Updates every 30 sec, expire in 180 sec
Collect garbage in 120 sec
Default-metric: 1
Max-paths: 8
Process is up and running
    Interfaces supported by ipv4 RIP :
        Vlan 12
        Vlan 13
        Vlan 14
R1# show running-config rip
        feature rip
router rip enterprise
interface Vlan12
    ip router rip enterprise
interface Vlan13
    ip router rip enterprise
interface Vlan14
    ip router rip enterprise
R1# show ip rip neighbor
Process Name "rip-enterprise" VRF "default"
RIP Neighbor Information (number of neighbors = 3)
('dead' means more than 300 seconds ago)
10.1.1.2, Vlan12
        Last Response sent/received: 00:00:20/00:00:08
        Last Request   sent/received: 00:04:58/never
        Bad Pkts Received: 0
        Bad Routes Received: 0
10.1.3.3, Vlan13
        Last Response sent/received: 00:00:22/00:00:10
        Last Request   sent/received: 00:04:58/never
        Bad Pkts Received: 0
        Bad Routes Received: 0
10.1.4.4, Vlan14
        Last Response sent/received: 00:00:28/00:00:16
        Last Request   sent/received: 00:04:59/never
        Bad Pkts Received: 0
        Bad Routes Received: 0
```

Example 19-7 highlights a few lines from each **show** command to enable you to understand the values and how they can validate or troubleshoot what you have configured on R1.

These same commands would validate both of the configuration examples, whether for a routed interface or SVI.

From the **show ip rip** command output, you can validate on the local Layer 3 switch which interfaces are enabled for IPv4 RIP, whether the process is enabled on the Layer 3 switch, as well as confirm the configured process name. From the **show running-config rip** command output, the highlighted items isolate what interfaces have been configured for the RIP process. **show running-config rip** is an important command for ensuring that you globally configured the instance-tag correctly and on the interfaces you want enabled for RIP. The final **show** command in Example 19-7 is **show ip rip neighbor**, which enables you to see that the neighbors have come up, the IP addresses with which you are peering, and how many you have. If you see that you do not have the number of neighbors in comparison to the interfaces/SVIs with which you have enabled RIP, this provides a good indication of which interfaces on R1 and the adjacent Layer 3 switch for which you need to validate the configuration.

As you can see, using these three **show** commands individually and together, you can validate and troubleshoot your configurations of RIP on the Cisco Nexus switches.

EIGRP Configuration on NX-OS

Enhanced Interior Gateway Routing Protocol (EIGRP) is as the name says—an enhanced version of the original IGRP. EIGRP is sometimes referred to as an *advanced* version of a distance vector routing protocol because it brings some of the benefits of a link-state routing protocol but also has some characteristics of a standard distance vector routing protocol. This section of the chapter demonstrates the ways to configure EIGRP on SVIs and routed interfaces as well as how to verify/troubleshoot the configuration of EIGRP. Through this verification and configuration, you will be able to see why EIGRP is seen as an advanced distance vector routing protocol.

Refer to Figure 19-1 for the routed interface example and Figure 19-2 for the SVI example. Example 19-8 shows the configuration of EIGRP on NX-OS using the routed interface example based on Figure 19-1. Example 19-9 shows configuration of EIGRP on NX-OS using SVIs based on Figure 19-2.

Example 19-8 *EIGRP Configuration: Routed Interface (R1 and R2)*

```
R1 Configuration
R1# configure terminal
R1(config)# feature eigrp
R1(config)# router eigrp 1
R1(config-router)# router-id 1.1.1.1
R1(config)# interface Ethernet1/2
R1(config-if)# no switchport
R1(config-if)# ip address 10.1.1.1/24
R1(config-if)# no shutdown
R1(config-if)# ip router eigrp 1
R1(config)# interface Ethernet1/3
R1(config-if)# no switchport
```

```
R1(config-if)# ip address 10.1.3.1/24
R1(config-if)# no shutdown
R1(config-if)# ip router eigrp 1
R1(config)# interface Ethernet1/4
R1(config-if)# no switchport
R1(config-if)# ip address 10.1.4.1/24
R1(config-if)# no shutdown
R1(config-if)# ip router eigrp 1
```

```
R2 Configuration
R2# configure terminal
R2(config)# feature eigrp
R2(config)# router eigrp 1
R2(config-router)# router-id 2.2.2.2
R2(config)# interface Ethernet1/2
R2(config-if)# no switchport
R2(config-if)# ip address 10.1.1.2/24
R2(config-if)# no shutdown
R2(config-if)# ip router eigrp 1
R2(config)# interface Ethernet2/3
R2(config-if)# no switchport
R2(config-if)# ip address 10.2.3.2/24
R2(config-if)# no shutdown
R2(config-if)# ip router eigrp 1
R2(config)# interface Ethernet2/4
R2(config-if)# no switchport
R2(config-if)# ip address 10.2.4.2/24
R2(config-if)# no shutdown
R2(config-if)# ip router eigrp 1
```

Key Topic

Example 19-9 *EIGRP Configuration: SVI (R1 and R2)*

```
R1 Configuration
R1# configure terminal
R1(config)# feature eigrp
R1(config)# feature interface-vlan
R1(config)# router eigrp 1
R1(config-router)# router-id 1.1.1.1
R1(config)# interface vlan 12
R1(config-if)# ip address 10.1.1.1/24
R1(config-if)# no shutdown
R1(config-if)# ip router eigrp 1
R1(config)# interface vlan 13
R1(config-if)# ip address 10.1.3.1/24
R1(config-if)# no shutdown
R1(config-if)# ip router eigrp 1
R1(config)# interface vlan 14
```

```
R1(config-if)# ip address 10.1.4.1/24
R1(config-if)# no shutdown
R1(config-if)# ip router eigrp 1
R2 Configuration
R2# configure terminal
R2(config)# feature eigrp
R2(config)# feature interface-vlan
R2(config)# router eigrp 1
R2(config-router)# router-id 2.2.2.2
R2(config)# interface vlan 12
R2(config-if)# ip address 10.1.1.2/24
R2(config-if)# no shutdown
R2(config-if)# ip router eigrp 1
R2(config)# interface vlan 23
R2(config-if)# ip address 10.2.3.2/24
R2(config-if)# no shutdown
R2(config-if)# ip router eigrp 1
R2(config)# interface vlan 24
R2(config-if)# ip address 10.2.4.2/24
R2(config-if)# no shutdown
R2(config-if)# ip router eigrp 1
```

As you can see, these configurations are very similar to how RIP was configured in the previous section. Because EIGRP is still a distance vector routing protocol, its implementation is almost exactly the same as other distance vector routing protocols. One new command that differs in the configurations for EIGRP is the use of the **router-id** *x.x.x.x* under the **router eigrp 1** process. Router IDs are important for identifying the router with a unique identifier in the routing protocol; each router will have a unique router ID that can be manually configured or dynamically assigned based on a selection process. In NX-OS, the process for selecting the router ID is as follows:

1. A router ID has been manually configured under the routing process (preferred).
2. The highest local IP address is selected, and loopback interfaces are preferred.
3. If no loopback interfaces are configured, use the highest IP address of a local interface.

Example 19-10 showcases some **show** commands used to validate and troubleshoot the EIGRP configurations from Examples 19-8 and 19-9. As mentioned earlier in the RIP section, the validation is the same whether you use SVI or routed interface configurations. Example 19-10 shows three different **show** commands and their output for validating and troubleshooting.

Example 19-10 *EIGRP Configuration on NX-OS: Validation and Troubleshooting*

```
R1# show running-config eigrp
feature eigrp
router eigrp 1
    autonomous-system 1
    router-id 1.1.1.1

interface Vlan12
     ip router eigrp 1
interface Vlan13
    ip router eigrp 1
interface Vlan14
    ip router eigrp 1
    R1#show ip eigrp
IP-EIGRP AS 1 ID 1.1.1.1 VRF default
    Process-tag: 1
    Instance Number: 1
    Status: running
    Authentication mode: none
    Authentication key-chain: none
    Metric weights: K1=1 K2=0 K3=1 K4=0 K5=0
    IP proto: 88 Multicast group: 224.0.0.10
    Int distance: 90 Ext distance: 170
    Max paths: 8
    Number of EIGRP interfaces: 3 (0 loopbacks)
    Number of EIGRP passive interfaces: 0
    Number of EIGRP peers: 3
    Graceful-Restart: Enabled
    Stub-Routing: Disabled
    NSF converge time limit/expiries: 120/0
    NSF route-hold time limit/expiries: 240/1
    NSF signal time limit/expiries: 20/0
    Redistributed max-prefix: Disabled
R1#sh ip eigrp neighbors 10.1.1.2
IP-EIGRP neighbors for process 1 VRF default
H     Address        Interface     Hold    Uptime    SRTT     RTO     Q     Seq
                                                     (sec)                  (ms)Cnt Num

0     10.1.1.2       Vlan12        11      4d02h     1        50      0     14
```

In the output for the SVI configuration in Example 19-9, you see three different **show** command outputs from R1, each of which needs to be looked at individually and together to help you make sure you have configured the routing protocol correctly. Start by taking a look at the first **show** command and identify the key parts of the output that can help validate or troubleshoot your configurations. From the **show running-config eigrp** command, you see the configuration output of what you have configured in particular to EIGRP on this Nexus device. Notice that the EIGRP autonomous system ID of 1 is the same for the **router eigrp 1** command as it is for the **ip router eigrp 1** subinterface command. This tells you that you have configured the correct EIGRP process on each interface for the global routing process, which is key to validating that your configuration is correct. You can execute these same commands on each Layer 3 switch to confirm correct configurations are in place.

NOTE EIGRP uses what is known as an *autonomous system ID*. This number must match for the routers to form as neighbors. In our example, number 1 is the autonomous system number (between 1 and 65,535), which must be the same on all EIGRP-speaking routers in the network that would like to communicate and share routing information.

The last two **show** commands, **show ip eigrp** and **show ip eigrp neighbors**, enable you to validate or troubleshoot that you have formed neighbor relationships with other Layer 3 switches and that they are communicating/sharing information. The highlighted output from **show ip eigrp** focuses on some key information. First, you can again validate that the process ID is configured correctly (also referred to as autonomous system ID if a number is used), and you can also see that the status is running. The next piece of key information is based on information you learned in Chapter 16. The K values in EIGRP are referring to what makes up the composite metric. By default, EIGRP uses bandwidth and delay with K value modifiers to calculate this metric to choose the best route to install in the routing table (successor) for any given destination. We do not go deep into this calculation here, but it is important to note that K1 is the bandwidth modifier for calculation and K3 is the delay modifier for calculation, so by default in your output, you should see K1 and K3 set to 1 and all other K values set to 0.

Finally, you see the number of neighbors (peers) and interfaces participating. Though these numbers for peers and interfaces do not always match, as in the case of peering with multiple neighbors on a local area network over one interface, it can help you understand the peering and interface configurations. In the final output from **show ip eigrp neighbors 10.1.1.2**, you can validate that the neighbors are up, how long they have been up, their IP address, and the interface in which the peering happened. Note one final thing about EIGRP (which you can see in the outputs) that differentiates it from other distance vector routing protocols: its hello and update methodology. As explained in Chapter 16, and as the examples show, EIGRP does certainly qualify as more of an advanced distance vector routing protocol.

OSPF Configuration on NX-OS

The Open Shortest Path First (OSPF) protocol is the final routing protocol to look at from a configuration perspective. In comparison to RIP and EIGRP, OSPF is considered a link-state routing protocol, and the following examples point out the differences in configuration, validation, and troubleshooting of this routing protocol compared to RIPv2 and EIGRP.

Again, refer to Figures 19-1 and 19-2 for the coverage of how to implement OSPF on NX-OS. Example 19-11 shows the configuration of a single area (0) with routed interfaces, and Example 19-12 explores configuring OSPF using SVIs for a single area (0).

19

Example 19-11   *OSPF Configuration on NX-OS with Routed Interfaces in a Single Area (0)*

```
R1 Configuration
R1# configure terminal
R1(config)# feature ospf
R1(config)# router ospf 1
R1(config-router)# router-id 1.1.1.1
R1(config)# interface Ethernet1/2
R1(config-if)# no switchport
R1(config-if)# ip address 10.1.1.1/24
R1(config-if)# no shutdown
R1(config-if)# ip router ospf 1 area 0
R1(config)# interface Ethernet1/3
R1(config-if)# no switchport
R1(config-if)# ip address 10.1.3.1/24
R1(config-if)# no shutdown
R1(config-if)# ip router ospf 1 area 0
R1(config)# interface Ethernet1/4
R1(config-if)# no switchport
R1(config-if)# ip address 10.1.4.1/24
R1(config-if)# no shutdown
R1(config-if)# ip router ospf 1 area 0
R2 Configuration
R2# configure terminal
R2(config)# feature ospf
R2(config)# router ospf 1
R2(config-router)# router-id 2.2.2.2
R2(config)# interface Ethernet1/2
R2(config-if)# no switchport
R2(config-if)# ip address 10.1.1.2/24
R2(config-if)# no shutdown
R2(config-if)# ip router ospf 1 area 0
R2(config)# interface Ethernet2/3
R2(config-if)# no switchport
R2(config-if)# ip address 10.2.3.2/24
R2(config-if)# no shutdown
R2(config-if)# ip router ospf 1 area 0
R2(config)# interface Ethernet2/4
R2(config-if)# no switchport
R2(config-if)# ip address 10.2.4.2/24
R2(config-if)# no shutdown
R2(config-if)# ip router ospf 1 area 0
```

Example 19-12 *OSPF Configuration on NX-OS with SVIs in a Single Area (0)*

```
R1 Configuration
R1# Configure terminal
R1(config)# feature ospf
R1(config)# router ospf 1
R1(config-router)# router-id 1.1.1.1
R1(config)# feature interface-vlan
R1(config)# interface vlan 12
R1(config-if)# ip address 10.1.1.1/24
R1(config-if)# no shutdown
R1(config-if)# ip router ospf 1 area 0
R1(config)# interface vlan 13
R1(config-if)# ip address 10.1.3.1/24
R1(config-if)# no shutdown
R1(config-if)# ip router ospf 1 area 0
R1(config)# interface vlan 14
R1(config-if)# ip address 10.1.4.1/24
R1(config-if)# no shutdown
R1(config-if)# ip router ospf 1 area 0
R2 Configuration
R2# Configure terminal
R2(config)# feature ospf
R2(config)# router ospf 1
R2(config-router)# router-id 2.2.2.2
R2(config)# feature interface-vlan
R2(config)# interface vlan 12
R2(config-if)# ip address 10.1.1.2/24
R2(config-if)# no shutdown
R2(config-if)# ip router ospf 1 area 0
R2(config)# interface vlan 23
R2(config-if)# ip address 10.2.3.2/24
R2(config-if)# no shutdown
R2(config-if)# ip router ospf 1 area 0
R2(config)# interface vlan 24
R2(config-if)# ip address 10.2.4.2/24
R2(config-if)# no shutdown
R2(config-if)# ip router ospf 1 area 0
```

19

Both of these examples show one difference from the RIP and EIGRP examples: the **area** tag at the end of the **ip router ospf 1 area 0** command. As mentioned in depth in Chapter 16, OSPF uses the concept of *areas* to segment and build hierarchy with the routed environment. This is a key attribute to scaling OSPF implementations, so it is important to note that each interface on a router or Layer 3 switch can belong to the same or different areas based on the network design you are using.

NOTE   OSPF uses what is known as a *process ID*. This number does not have to match for the routers to form as neighbors. Unlike EIGRP, which uses this as an autonomous system number, the process ID for OSPF is locally significant.

Next, look at the output of the **show** commands to again validate and troubleshoot the configurations in Examples 19-11 and 19-12. Example 19-13 focuses on three **show** commands commonly used for troubleshooting and validating OSPF configuration on NX-OS.

Example 19-13   *OSPF Configuration Troubleshooting and Validation on NX-OS*

```
R1# show running-config ospf
feature ospf
router ospf 1
    router-id 1.1.1.1


interface Vlan12
        ip router ospf 1 area 0
interface Vlan13
    ip router ospf 1 area 0
interface Vlan14
    ip router ospf 1 area 0
R1# sh ip ospf 1
        Routing Process 1 with ID 1.1.1.1 VRF default
 Routing Process Instance Number 1
 Stateful High Availability enabled
 Graceful-restart is configured
     Grace period: 60 state: Inactive
     Last graceful restart exit status: None
 Supports only single TOS(TOS0) routes
 Supports opaque LSA
 Administrative distance 110
 Reference Bandwidth is 40000 Mbps
 SPF throttling delay time of 200.000 msecs,
     SPF throttling hold time of 1000.000 msecs,
     SPF throttling maximum wait time of 5000.000 msecs
 LSA throttling start time of 0.000 msecs,
     LSA throttling hold interval of 5000.000 msecs,
     LSA throttling maximum wait time of 5000.000 msecs
 Minimum LSA arrival 1000.000 msec
 LSA group pacing timer 10 secs
 Maximum paths to destination 8
 Number of external LSAs 0, checksum sum 0
 Number of opaque AS LSAs 0, checksum sum 0
 Number of areas is 1, 1 normal, 0 stub, 0 nssa
 Number of active areas is 1, 1 normal, 0 stub, 0 nssa
 Install discard route for summarized external routes.
 Install discard route for summarized internal routes.
```

```
        Area BACKBONE(0.0.0.0) (Active)
                Area has existed for 03:49:02
                Interfaces in this area: 3 Active interfaces: 3
                Passive interfaces: 0    Loopback interfaces: 0
                No authentication available
                SPF calculation has run 2 times
                  Last SPF ran for 0.000256s
                Area ranges are
                Number of LSAs: 1, checksum sum 0xba7e
R1# sh ip ospf interface vlan 12
    Vlan12 is up, line protocol is up
        IP address 10.1.1.1/24, Process ID 1 VRF default, area 0.0.0.0
        Enabled by interface configuration
        State DR, Network type BROADCAST, cost 40
        Index 3, Transmit delay 1 sec, Router Priority 1
        Designated Router ID: 1.1.1.1, address: 10.1.1.1
        No backup designated router on this network
        Timer intervals: Hello 10, Dead 40, Wait 40, Retransmit 5
            Hello timer due in 00:00:03
        No authentication
        Number of opaque link LSAs: 0, checksum sum 0
R1# sh ip ospf neighbor vlan 12
Neighbor ID      Pri      State        Dead Time      Address      Interface
2.2.2.2           1      FULL/BDR       00:00:34       10.1.1.2      vlan 12
```

The **show running-config ospf** command is the same command used with the other routing protocols, the difference being **ospf** at the end. This **show** command is your first step in verifying that the configuration you think you have implemented is as you think it should be. The highlighted parts of this first **show** command emphasize what you want to focus on—that your process ID for the **router ospf command** of 1 is the same implemented on each interface. In addition, you want to make sure you have enabled the interfaces in the correct area (in this case, area 0, which you can confirm by finding **ip router ospf 1 area 0** under the interfaces or SVIs).

The **show ip ospf 1** command is one of the more powerful commands as far as what it helps you to understand is happening on R1 with the OSPF configuration you have applied. The highlighted parts of this output show the router ID. If the router ID was not manually configured, it shows what was given through the selection process. Further down in the output, you see how many areas this router or Layer 3 switch is participating in. You also see how many associated interfaces are within a given area, which is important information to validate that you have configured the device correctly. The last **show** command, **sh ip ospf interface vlan 12**, is valuable to show how OSPF is running on each interface or SVI. The highlighted parts of this **show** command reveal whether the interface or SVI is physically up and also up from a line protocol perspective. In addition, it shows what has been chosen by default as an interface type by OSPF. In this case, it is a broadcast interface, which you normally see on LANs or Layer 3 switch implementations. Because of the interface being broadcast, as you learned in Chapter 16, a designated router is needed in this OSPF area. As you can see, the last highlighted line of output shows the router ID of this designated router. The last output shows the neighbors what state they are in and their IP address.

Exam Preparation Tasks

Review All the Key Topics

Review the most important topics from this chapter, noted with the Key Topic icon. Table 19-2 lists these key topics and where each is discussed.

Table 19-2   *Key Topics for Chapter 19*

Key Topic Element	Description	Page Number
Example 19-1	Routed interface configuration	499
Example 19-2	SVI interface configuration	499
Example 19-3	Routing process enablement IOS and NX-OS with passive interface	500
Example 19-4	Routing table example	501
Example 19-5	RIPv2 configuration on R1 and R2 using a routed interface	503
Example 19-6	RIPv2 configuration on R1 and R2 using an SVI interface	505
Example 19-8	EIGRP configuration: routed interface (R1 and R2)	507
Example 19-9	EIGRP configuration: SVI (R1 and R2)	508
List	Router ID selection process for EIGRP	509
Example 19-10	EIGRP configuration on NX-OS: validation and troubleshooting	510
Example 19-11	OSPF configuration on NX-OS with routed interfaces in a single area (0)	512
Example 19-13	OSPF configuration troubleshooting and validation on NX-OS	514

Definitions of Key Terms

After your first reading of the chapter, try to define these key terms, but do not be concerned about getting them all correct at that time. Chapter 24, "Final Review," directs you in how to use these terms for late-stage preparation for the exam.

distance vector, autonomous system ID, link state, process ID, instance tag, cost, K values

Command Reference to Check Your Memory

Although you should not necessarily memorize the information in Tables 19-3 and 19-4, this section does include a reference for the configuration and EXEC commands covered in this chapter. Practically speaking, you should memorize the commands as a side effect of reading the chapter and doing all the activities in this exam preparation section. To check to see how well you have memorized the commands as a side effect of your other studies, cover the left side of the table with a piece of paper, read the description on the right side, and see whether you remember the command.

Table 19-3 Chapter 19 Configuration Command Reference

Command	Description
feature interface-vlan	Enables you to configure SVIs on a Nexus switch

Table 19-4 Chapter 19 EXEC Command Reference

Command	Description
feature rip	Enables RIPv2 process on a Cisco Nexus switch
feature eigrp	Enables EIGRP process on a Cisco Nexus switch
feature ospf	Enables OSPFv2 process on a Cisco Nexus switch
no switchport	Disables Layer 2 functionality on a physical interface
show running-config rip	Show only the RIP configuration in the running configuration
show running-config eigrp	Show only the EIGRP configuration in the running configuration
show running-config ospf	Show only the OSPF configuration in the running configuration
show eigrp neighbors	Displays the active EIGRP neighbors
show ospf neighbors	Displays the active OSPF neighbors
show ip rip	Displays the local router's RIP process information
show ospf 1	Displays the local router's OSPF process information

19

This chapter covers the following exam topics:

3.2. Compare and contrast the First-Hop Redundancy Protocols

3.2.a. VRRP

3.2.b. GLBP

3.2.c. HSRP

CHAPTER 20

Nexus First-Hop Redundancy Protocols and Configurations

This chapter begins by describing the importance of the default gateway in the network and how network devices determine whether or not they need to use a default gateway. The chapter then covers the different methods in order to provide redundancy to the default gateway by introducing what it is called a First-Hop Redundancy Protocol (FHRP). The following FHRPs are covered in this book:

- Hot Standby Routing Protocol (HSRP) for IPv4
- Hot Standby Routing Protocol (HSRP) for IPv6
- Virtual Router Redundancy Protocol (VRRP)
- Virtual Port Channel (vPC) with First-Hop Protocol
- Gateway Load Balancing Protocol (GLBP)

This chapter also includes how to configure and troubleshoot these FHRP methods and the difference between them.

By the end of this chapter, you should be able to understand why the default gateway is important in the network and to determine the difference between the listed protocols.

"Do I Know This Already?" Quiz

Use the "Do I Know This Already?" quiz to help decide whether you might want to skim this chapter, or a major section, moving more quickly to the "Exam Preparation Tasks" section near the end of the chapter. Table 20-1 lists the major headings in this chapter and their corresponding "Do I Know This Already?" quiz questions. For thorough explanations, see Appendix A, "Answers to the 'Do I Know This Already?' Quizzes."

Table 20-1 "Do I Know This Already?" Foundation Topics Section-to-Question Mapping

Foundation Topics Section	Questions
What Is the Default Gateway?	None
First-Hop Redundancy Protocols	1–5

1. What is the primary function of the default gateway?
   a. To forward traffic to different subnets
   b. To forward traffic to the same subnet
   c. To drop traffic that it is not destined to the default gateway
   d. None of the above

2. What are some of the FHRPs that Cisco Nexus switches support?

   a. OSPF

   b. EIGRP

   c. VRRP

   d. HSRP

   e. All of the above

   f. A and B

   g. C and D

3. What multicast address does HSRP leverage?

   a. 224.0.0.2

   b. 224.0.0.1

   c. 224.0.0.102

   d. All of the above

   e. A and C

4. What is the function of the coup message in HSRP?

   a. Coup messages are sent by the standby router when the router wishes to become the active router.

   b. Coup messages are sent by the active router when the router wishes to become the active router.

   c. Coup doesn't exist in HSRP; it only exists in VRRP.

   d. Coup messages are sent by the active router when it no longer wants to be the active router.

5. What Cisco feature was introduced in a vPC environment to protect against third-party devices that cache the switch MAC address instead of the virtual MAC address?

   a. peer-gateway

   b. HSRP

   c. peer-hsrp

   d. peer-hsrp-third-party

Foundation Topics

This chapter introduces the concepts of First-Hop Redundancy Protocols (FHRPs) and how to configure them. We will be covering the following FHRPs in this chapter:

- Hot Standby Routing Protocol (HSRP) for IPv4
- Hot Standby Routing Protocol (HSRP) for IPv6
- Virtual Router Redundancy Protocol (VRRP)
- Gateway Load Balancing Protocol (GLBP)
- Virtual Port Channel (vPC) with First-Hop Protocol

The default gateway (DG) is one of the most important concepts in networking because that's how network devices are able to communicate when they are not in the same subnet/ local area network (LAN).

What Is the Default Gateway?

The default gateway (DG) is a critical component in networking because it provides the function of forwarding packets to different subnets. It is important to understand that the DG is not leverage when two hosts are in the same subnet and want to communicate with each other. The configuration of the default gateway is a key component in designing a network, just like it is with IP allocation. This is because it allows the hosts in the network to only have to configure the default gateway instead of the entire routing table or network topology. This is how the hosts are able to reach the hosts in other subnets.

In Figure 20-1, the communication between these hosts does not leverage the default gateway because Host A and Host B are in the same subnet.

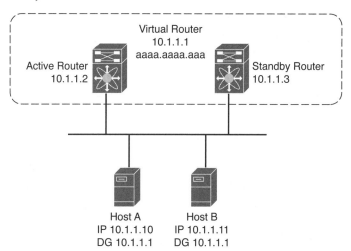

Figure 20-1 *Communication Between Two Hosts in the Same Subnet*

In Figure 20-2, the communication between these hosts does leverage the default gateway because Host A and Host B are in different subnets.

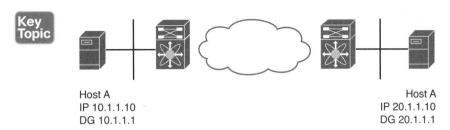

Figure 20-2 *Communications Between Two Hosts in Different Subnets*

It is important that every network engineer understands how the hosts in the network know whether or not to send packets to the default gateway. This is based on the IP addresses and subnets configured in the host. In order to understand how this function is performed, you need to understand some binary operations.

Figures 20-3 and 20-4 show the binary AND and XOR operations taking 2 bits and returning 1 bit. The AND operation will return 1 only if both inputs are 1; otherwise, the operation will return 0. In the case of the XOR operation, the result will be 1 *if and only if* one of the inputs is 1 and the other is 0; otherwise, if both inputs are the same, the operation returns 0.

a	b	A&b
0	0	0
0	1	0
1	0	0
1	1	1

Figure 20-3 *AND Operator (&)*

In order to determine whether or not the host needs to send the packets to the default gateway, the IP stack of the host will perform an XOR of the IP configured with the destination it is trying to reach. After the XOR calculation is done, the result is calculated by using the AND with the local subnet mask. If the result is 0, the destination is in the local network. If the result is different, the destination is not local and the packet needs to be sent to the default gateway.

a	b	a^b
0	0	0
0	1	1
1	0	1
1	1	0

Figure 20-4 *XOR (Exclusive Or)*

Figure 20-5 shows where Host A and Host B are in the same subnet with a virtual router IP address of 10.1.1.1, since the hosts are in the same subnet. These hosts do not need to leverage the default gateway.

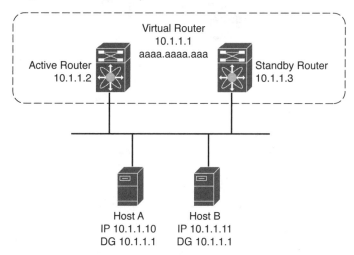

Figure 20-5 *Two Hosts in the Same Subnet*

Figure 20-6 shows the manipulation of the bits to determine how the network stack decides whether or not it needs to leverage the DG. Because the two hosts are in the same subnet or in the same LAN, they will create the packet with the MAC address of Host B. Host A learns the MAC address via ARP.

Because the final AND result is 0, the destination is local. Hence, the host doesn't
send the packet to the default gateway.

Figure 20-6   *Bitwise Operations*

In Figure 20-7, because the hosts are in different subnets, Host A will create the packet with
the destination MAC of the default gateway. The DG will get the packet and then forward
it to the next hop based on the routing table.

Host A
IP 10.1.1.10
DG 10.1.1.1

Host A
IP 20.1.1.10
DG 20.1.1.1

Figure 20-7   *Two Hosts in Different Subnets*

Figure 20-8 shows the manipulation of the bits to determine how the network stack decides
whether or not it needs to leverage the DG. Because the two hosts are in different subnets,
the network stack will send the packets to the DG.

Because the final AND result doesn't equal 0.0.0.0, the destination is not local and
the packets should be routed (that is, the packets are sent to the default gateway).

Figure 20-8   *Bitwise Operations*

The default gateway becomes critical when designing networks because every host in the network must be configured with a default gateway in order to be able to communicate outside its own LAN.

In the current example, there is only a single default gateway. Therefore, the question you should be asking yourself is, *what happens if the default gateway fails? How can we introduce redundancy into the environment and maintain the default gateway?*

This is why First-Hop Redundancy Protocol (FHRP) was created.

First-Hop Redundancy Protocol

The importance of the default gateway in the network was explained previously. However, it is equally important to provide a level of redundancy for the hosts in case of failures. This is why the First-Hop Redundancy Protocol (FHRP) definition was created. FHRP is the networking protocol that provides the level of redundancy needed in the network in order to provide redundancy for the default gateway by allowing two or more routers to provide backup in case of failures. Here's a list of the FHRPs covered in this chapter:

■ Hot Standby Routing Protocol (HSRP) for IPv4

■ Hot Standby Routing Protocol (HSRP) for IPv6

■ Virtual Router Redundancy Protocol (VRRP)

■ Gateway Load Balancing Protocol (GLBP)

■ Virtual Port Channel (vPC)

Hot Standby Routing Protocol

The Hot Standby Routing Protocol (HSRP) was developed by Cisco in the middle of the 1990s to provide the level of redundancy needed for high-demand networks. The idea behind HSRP is to provide a redundant mechanism for the default gateway in case of any failures by ensuring the traffic from the host is immediately switched over to the redundant default gateway. As previously mentioned, the default gateway provides a crucial function in the network by enabling hosts in the subnet to communicate outside their own subnet.

HSRP works by sharing the virtual IP (VIP) address and the MAC address between two or more routers in order to act as a "single virtual default gateway." An election process occurs whereby the router with the highest priority will be the "active default gateway." By default, this priority is set to 100. It is important to know that the host must configure its default gateway to the VIP address via static configuration or DHCP.

The routers or members participating in the same HSRP group have a mechanism to exchange their status in order to guarantee that there is always a default gateway available for the hosts in the local subnet. The "Hello HSRP" packets are sent to and received by a multicast UDP address. The active router is continuously sending these "hello packets" in case the active router is not able to send them. The standby router will become active after a configurable period of time. It is important to mention that the hosts will never notice a change in the network and will continue forwarding the traffic as they were previously doing.

NOTE: RFC 2281 defines the Hot Standby Routing Protocol.

In Figure 20-9, the hosts send their traffic to the virtual router based on a configuration obtained statically or via DHCP.

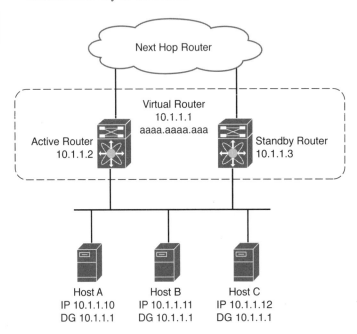

Figure 20-9 *HSRP Topology*

To enable HSRP in Cisco NX-OS, **feature hsrp** must be enabled globally, as shown in Example 20-1.

Example 20-1 *Enabling HSRP*

```
nexus# conf t
Enter configuration commands, one per line. End with CNTL/Z.
nexus (config)# feature hsrp
nexus (config)# sh run | in hsrp
feature hsrp
```

HSRP Versions

Table 20-2 describes the two HSRP versions currently supported in Cisco NX-OS.

Table 20-2   HSRP Versions

	Version 1	Version 2	
IP Protocol	IPv4	IPv4	IPv6
Group Number Range	0–255	0–4095	0–4095
Multicast Address	224.0.0.2	224.0.0.102	FF02::66
Virtual MAC Address Range	0000.0C07.AC00– 0000.0C07.ACFF	0000.0C9F.F000– 0000.0C9F.FFFF	0005.73A0.0000– 0005.73A0.0FFF
MD5	No	Yes	Yes
UDP Port	1985	1986	2029
Millisecond Support	No	Yes	Yes

> **NOTE**   By default, Cisco NX-OS supports HSRP version 1, and the packet formats are different between the two versions. HSRP version 2's packet format leverages type-length-value (TLV).

HSRP for IPv4

For networks that are running IPv4, the user must decide which version of HSRP they want to use. This is done via the command shown in Example 20-2.

Example 20-2   *Configuring the HSRP Version*

```
nexus# conf t
Enter configuration commands, one per line. End with CNTL/Z.
nexus (config)# interface vlan 1
nexus (config-if)# hsrp version ?
  1  Version 1
  2  Version 2
nexus (config-if)# hsrp version 2
```

Based on the HSRP version configured, the routers will start sending and receiving HSRP hello packets (once the HSRP is completed—but it is important to cover the concept of a virtual MAC address at this point). These packets will vary depending on the HSRP version, as previously stated in Table 20-2. The active router will send the HSRP hello packets to 224.0.0.2 or 224.0.0.102 (depending on the HSRP version) with the HSRP virtual MAC address, while the standby router(s) will source the HSRP hellos with the interface MAC address.

20

Example 20-3 *IPv4 HSRP Configuration*

```
nexus(config-if)# sh run int e1/1

version 7.0(3)I2(1)

interface Ethernet1/1
  no switchport
  ip address 10.1.1.2/24
  no shutdown
  hsrp version 2 ipv4
  hsrp 1
    ip 10.1.1.1
```

For Version 1, the virtual MAC address is the derived virtual MAC address in Table 20-2.

Example 20-4 *HSRP Verification and Virtual MAC Address for Group 1*

```
nexus(config-if-hsrp)# sh hsrp
Vlan1 - Group 1 (HSRP-V1) (IPv4)
  Local state is Listen, priority 100 (Cfged 100)
    Forwarding threshold(for vPC), lower: 0 upper: 100
  Hellotime 3 sec, holdtime 10 sec
  Virtual IP address is 10.1.1.1 (Cfged)
  Active router is local
  Standby router is 10.1.1.3
  Authentication text "cisco"
  Virtual mac address is 0000.0c07.ac01 (Default MAC)
  0 state changes, last state change never
  IP redundancy name is hsrp-Vlan1-1 (default)
```

HSRP for IPv6

When HSRP is configured for IPv6, the virtual MAC address is obtained from the HSRP group number in Table 20-2, and the virtual IPv6 link-local address is derived by the default from the HSRP virtual MAC address. The default virtual MAC address for an HSRP IPv6 group is always used from the virtual IPv6 link-local address, regardless of the actual virtual MAC address used by the group.

NOTE When you're configuring HSRP for IPv6, the version of HSRP must be set to Version 2.

Example 20-5 shows the running configuration for HSRP when using IPv6, and Example 20-6 shows the verification process.

Example 20-5   *IPv6 HSRP Configuration*

```
nexus(config-if)# sh run int e1/1


!Command: show running-config interface Ethernet1/1


version 7.0(3)I2(1)


interface Ethernet1/1
  no switchport
  ipv6 address ::ffff:10.1.1.2/4
  no shutdown
  hsrp version 2
hsrp 1 ipv6
    ip autoconfig
    ip ::ffff:10.1.1.1
```

Example 20-6   *HSRP Verification and Virtual MAC Address for Group 1*

```
nexus(config-if-hsrp)# sh hsrp
Vlan1 - Group 1 (HSRP-V2) (IPv6)
  Local state is Listen, priority 100 (Cfged 100)
    Forwarding threshold(for vPC), lower: 0 upper: 100
  Hellotime 3 sec, holdtime 10 sec
  Virtual IP address is fe80::5:73ff:fea0:1 (Auto)
  Active router is local
  Standby router is ::ffff:10.1.1.3
  Authentication text "cisco"
Virtual mac address is 0005.73a0.0001 (Default MAC)
  0 state changes, last state change never
  IP redundancy name is hsrp-Vlan1-1 (default)
  Secondary VIP(s):
                  ::ffff:10.1.1.1
```

HSRP Messages: Op Code

The HSRP protocol defines three types of op-codes in the type of message that is contained in the packet:

- **Hello:** This is op-code 0; hello messages are sent by the routers participating in HSRP to indicate that they are capable of becoming the active or standby router.

- **Coup:** This is op-code 1; coup messages are sent by the standby router when the router wishes to become the active router.

- **Resign:** This is op-code 2; this particular message is sent by the active router when it no longer wants to be the active router.

Here are some examples when a router will send these types of messages:

■ The active router is about to shut down.

■ When the active router receives a hello packet with a higher priority.

■ When the active router receives a coup message.

HSRP Authentication

In order to provide security from HSRP spoofing, HSRP version 2 introduces HSRP Message Digest 5 (MD5) algorithm authentication and plain-text authentication, as shown in Example 20-7. HSRP includes the IPv4 or IPv6 address in the authentication TLVs.

Example 20-7 *Authentication Enablement and Verification*

```
Nexus(config-if-hsrp)# authentication md5 ?
  key-chain   Set key chain
  key-string  Set key string


Nexus(config-if-hsrp)# authentication md5 key-string hsrp-authentication

Nexus(config-if-hsrp)# sh run interface Ethernet 1/1
interface Ethernet1/1
  no switchport
  ip address 10.1.1.2/24
  no shutdown
  hsrp version 2
  hsrp 1
    authentication md5 key-string hsrp-authentication
    ip 10.1.1.1


Nexus(config-if-hsrp)# sh hsrp
Ethernet1/1 - Group 1 (HSRP-V2) (IPv4)
  Local state is Active, priority 100 (Cfged 100)
    Forwarding threshold(for vPC), lower: 0 upper: 100
  Hellotime 3 sec, holdtime 10 sec
  Next hello sent in 2.231000 sec(s)
  Virtual IP address is 10.1.1.1 (Cfged)
  Active router is local
  Standby router is 10.1.1.3
  Authentication MD5, key-string "hsrp-authentication"
  Virtual mac address is 0000.0c9f.f001 (Default MAC)
  2 state changes, last state change 00:04:03
  IP redundancy name is hsrp-Eth1/1-1 (default)
```

HSRP Object Tracking

The object tracking feature in Cisco NX-OS allows for "tracking" an interface based on its operational state in order to modify the HSRP priority. This feature is widely leveraged in today's network to modify how HSRP behaves.

Figure 20-10 shows that both routers are connected to the outside world via Eth1/1. But what happens if the active router, E1/1, goes down? The HSRP state has not changed because the active and the standby routers are still exchanging hellos. In this particular scenario, the hosts in the LAN will still continue sending packets to the active router, and then the active router will send the packets to the standby router to go outside the LAN (assuming that the standby router is sending the routes to the outside world).

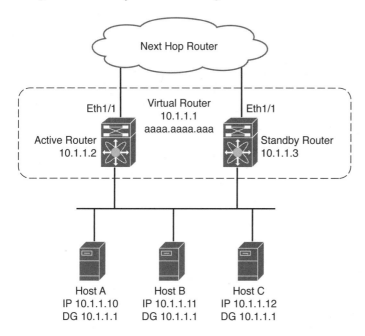

Figure 20-10 *Object Tracking*

Because of this failure, the packets from the hosts to the outside will have an extra hop penalty, which is the reason why object tracking was introduced. The primary function of this feature is to track the interface of the active routers in case of any failures. In this particular example, in case the active router interface Eth1/1 goes down, the router will detect this failure and decrease the standby priority to be lower than the standby router, which will cause the standby router to become the active router.

In Example 20-8, the router is tracking Ethernet 1/2 line-protocol to see if the interface is up. If the router detects that the interface is down, it will lower its HSRP priority by 20, which is lower than the standby router (remember, the default priority is 100). This will trigger the standby router to become the active router. Once interface 1/2 comes back online, the router will detect it and increase the priority by 20, for a total of 120. Now, because we have introduced the command **preempt**, the router will send a "coup" message and it will take over as the active router.

Example 20-8 *HSRP Object Tracking Enablement and Verification*

```
nexus(config-if)# sh run

version 7.0(3)I2(1)

track 1 interface Ethernet 1/2 line-protocol

interface Ethernet1/1
 no switchport
  ip address 10.1.1.2/24
  no shutdown
  hsrp version 2 ipv4
  hsrp 1
    preempt
    ip 10.1.1.1
    track 1 decrement 20

nexus(config-if-hsrp)# sh hsrp
Ethernet1/1 - Group 1 (HSRP-V2) (IPv4)
  Local state is Active, priority 80 (Cfged 100), may preempt
    Forwarding threshold(for vPC), lower: 0 upper: 100
  Hellotime 3 sec, holdtime 10 sec
  Next hello sent in 0.851000 sec(s)
  Virtual IP address is 10.1.1.1 (Cfged)
  Active router is local
  Standby router is 10.1.1.3
  Authentication MD5, key-string "hsrp-authentication"
  Virtual mac address is 0000.0c9f.f001 (Default MAC)
  2 state changes, last state change 00:10:21
    Track object 1 state DOWN decrement 20
  IP redundancy name is hsrp-Eth1/1-1 (default)
```

Virtual Router Redundancy Protocol

Virtual Router Redundancy Protocol (VRRP) is an open-standard alternative to Cisco's HSRP, providing almost identical functionality. RFC 3768 defines VRRP as follows:

"VRRP specifies an election protocol that dynamically assigns responsibility for a virtual router to one of the VRRP routers on a LAN. The VRRP router controlling the IP address(es) associated with a virtual router is called the Master, and forwards packets sent to these IP addresses. The election process provides dynamic failover in the forwarding responsibility should the Master become unavailable. This allows any of the virtual router IP addresses on the LAN to be used as the default first hop router by end-hosts. The advantage gained from using VRRP is a higher availability default path without requiring configuration of dynamic routing or router discovery protocols on every end-host."

The other routers participating in the VRRP process will become the backups. Only the VRRP master sends periodic advertisements using a multicast address of 224.0.0.18 with an IP protocol of 112. The advertisement announcements communicate the priority and state of the master.

As you can see, HSRP and VRRP are very similar. The main idea is to provide an appropriate redundancy level to the default gateway.

In Figure 20-11, the hosts send their traffic to the virtual router based on a configuration obtained statically or via DHCP.

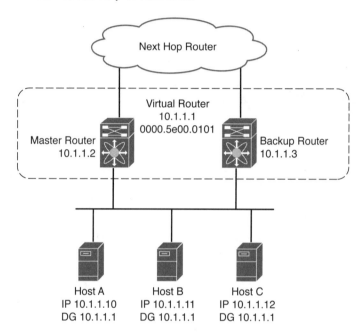

Figure 20-11 *VRRP Topology*

To enable VRRP in Cisco NX-OS, you must enable **feature vrrp** globally, as shown in Example 20-9.

Example 20-9 *Enabling VRRP*

```
nexus# conf t
Enter configuration commands, one per line. End with CNTL/Z.
nexus (config)# feature vrrp
nexus (config)# sh run | in vrrp
feature vrrp
```

The virtual MAC address for VRRP is derived from the range 0000.5e00.0000 to 0000.5e00.00ff, which will provide up to 255 VRRP mappings per router in the network, as shown in Example 20-10.

Example 20-10 *Virtual MAC for Group 1*

```
nexus# show vrrp detail

Ethernet1/1 - Group 1 (IPV4)
     State is Master
     Virtual IP address is 10.1.1.1
     Priority 255, Configured 100
     Forwarding threshold(for VPC), lower: 1 upper: 100
     Advertisement interval 1
     Preemption enabled
     Virtual MAC address is 0000.5e00.0101
     Master router is Local
```

Example 20-11 *IPv4 VRRP Configuration*

```
nexus(config-if)# sh run int e1/1

!Command: show running-config interface Ethernet1/1

version 7.0(3)I2(1)

interface Ethernet1/1
  no switchport
  no shutdown
  ip address 10.1.1.2/24
vrrp 1
     address 10.1.1.1
```

VRRP Authentication

VRRP supports only plain-text authentication, as you can see in Example 20-12.

Example 20-12 *MD5 Options*

```
Nexus(config-if-vrrp)# authentication ?
    text  Set the authentication password (8 char max)
```

VRRP Object Tracking

Similar to HSRP, VRRP supports object tracking, with the configuration shown in Example 20-13.

Example 20-13 *IPv4 VRRP Object Tracking*

```
nexus(config-if)# sh run

version 7.0(3)I2(1)

track 1 interface Ethernet 1/2 line-protocol

interface Ethernet1/1
  no switchport
  ip address 10.1.1.2/24
  no shutdown
  vrrp 1
    ip 10.1.1.1
    track 1 decrement 20
```

Gateway Load Balancing Protocol

Gateway Load Balancing Protocol (GLBP) is a Cisco technology that improves the functionality of HSRP and VRRP. Currently HSRP and VRRP behave in such a way where they allow multiple routers to be part of the same virtual group. But the problem is that only one active router acts as the default gateway and the rest of the routers do not forward packets to the virtual IP address until there is a failure in the active router.

GLBP introduces a load-balancing mechanism over multiple routers by leveraging a single virtual IP address and multiple MAC addresses. GLBP takes advantage of every router in the virtual group in order to share the forwarding of the traffic, which is different from HSRP and VRRP. The GLBP members communicate by using a hello message, which uses a multicast address of 224.0.0.102 with UDP port of 3222.

> **NOTE** Check the latest release notes in order to find out the GLBP support in the Nexus platform.

GLBP elects an active virtual gateway (AVG) if multiple gateways have the same priority; the router with the highest real IP address becomes the AVG. The rest of the members are put into a listen state. The function of the AVG is to assign the virtual MAC address to each member of the GLBP group. Then, each router in the virtual group will become an active virtual forwarder (AVF) for its assigned virtual MAC address; it will be responsible for forwarding packets sent to its assigned virtual MAC address. This means that each member of the GLBP group becomes the virtual forwarder (VF) for the assigned MAC address; this is called the *primary virtual forwarder* (PVF).

Another function of the AVG is to answer the ARP requests sent to the virtual IP address. The AVG will "load balance" the virtual MAC addresses' responses between the routers in the virtual group. If the AVG fails, the standby virtual gateway (VG) takes over.

As mentioned, the AVG responds to the ARP request sent to the virtual IP address. The AVG has three different configurable types of algorithm:

- **Round-robin:** This is the default method. In this method, the AVG cycles through all the members in the virtual group.
- **Weighted:** In this method, AVG takes into consideration the amount of load directed to an AVF, which is dependent on the weight advertised by the gateway. A higher weight means that the AVG directs more traffic to the AVF.
- **Host dependent:** The MAC address of the host is used to determine which virtual MAC addresses the host is directed to. This algorithm guarantees that a host gets the same virtual MAC address as long as the number of virtual forwarders remains the same.

In Figure 20-12, the Ethernet 1/2 interface on Router 1 is the gateway for Host 1 (the AVF for virtual MAC address, vMAC1), whereas Ethernet 2/2 on Router 2 acts as a secondary virtual forwarder for Host 1. Ethernet 1/2 tracks Ethernet 3/1, which is the network connection for Router 1. If Ethernet 3/1 goes down, the weighting for Ethernet 1/2 drops to 90, and Ethernet 2/2 on Router 2 preempts Ethernet 1/2 and takes over as AVF because it has the default weighting of 100 and is configured to preempt the AVF.

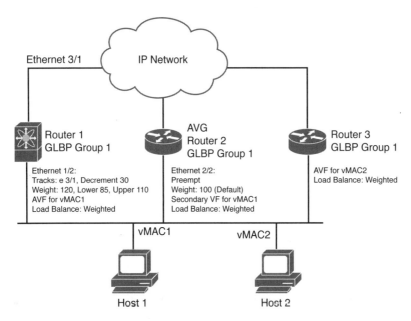

Figure 20-12   *GLBP Topology*

To enable GLBP in Cisco NX-OS, enable **feature glbp** globally, which is shown in Example 20-14.

Example 20-14 *Enabling GLBP*

```
nexus# conf t
Enter configuration commands, one per line. End with CNTL/Z.
nexus (config)# feature glbp
nexus (config)# sh run | in glbp
feature glbp
```

Example 20-15 shows how to configure GLBP on a Nexus switch.

Example 20-15 *IPv4 GLBP Configuration*

```
nexus(config-if)# sh run int e1/1

!Command: show running-config interface Ethernet1/1

version 7.0(3)I2(1)

interface Ethernet1/1
  no switchport
  no shutdown
  ip address 10.1.1.2/24
glbp 1
    ip 10.1.1.1
    load-balancing round-robin
```

20

As with HSRP and VRRP, GLBP also supports the object-tracking function in order to track line-protocol or IP routing. The configuration is identical to HSRP and VRRP.

Virtual Port Channel and HSRP

Let's start with a quick overview of virtual Port Channel (vPC). vPC is a Cisco technology that allows two Cisco switches running NX-OS to work together in order to show "downstream" devices such as other Cisco switches or third-party devices to appear as a single port channel. Here are the advantages of running vPC in the network:

- It eliminates the need to run Spanning Tree Protocol (STP).
- It provides a loop-free topology.
- Because we are no longer running STP, every link is leveraged.
- It improves high availability.
- It allows downstream devices to be connected to two separate devices, thus providing more redundancy.

Figure 20-13 shows a standard physical topology leveraging vPC, where two Nexus switches are connected to a server. The important thing about vPC is that the server doesn't have any knowledge that it is connected to two separate switches.

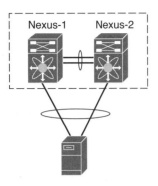

Figure 20-13 *vPC Topology*

Because we have created a vPC, we need to provide a default gateway to the host. In order to do this, the HSRP configuration doesn't change. The only recommendation is to make sure the active HSRP is in the primary vPC peer device and the standby HSRP is in the vPC secondary.

This configuration will work in the majority of the cases, but unfortunately some third-party vendors will ignore the HSRP virtual MAC and cache the source of the MAC address of the physical interface of the Cisco Nexus switches. In a vPC environment, the packets that use this source MAC address might be sent across the vPC peer link, potentially causing a packet to be dropped.

Cisco introduced a new feature in order to address this behavior: the **peer-gateway** command. This command allows for the handling of the packets that are sent to the local vPC peer MAC address and the remote vPC address, as well as the HSRP virtual MAC address.

Example 20-16 shows an example of the **peer-gateway** command.

Example 20-16 *vPC Peer Gateway*

```
nexus# conf t
Enter configuration commands, one per line. End with CNTL/Z.
nexus (config)# vpc domain 1
nexus (config-vpc-domain)# peer-gateway
```

Exam Preparation Tasks

Review All the Key Topics

Review the most important topics from this chapter, noted with the Key Topic icon. Table 20-3 lists these key topics and shows where each is discussed.

> **NOTE** There is no need to memorize any configuration steps referenced as a key topic; these steps are just study aids.

Table 20-3 Key Topics for Chapter 20

Key Topic Element	Description	Page Number
Figure 20-1 through Figure 20-8	Show the functionality of the default gateway	521-524
Figure 20-9	Shows the concepts of HSRP	526
Table 20-2	Provides definitions of the various versions of HSRP supported in the Cisco Nexus switches	527

Command References

Table 20-4 shows the most common commands used when covering FHRP.

Table 20-4 Chapter 20 FHRP Configuration and Verification commands

Command	Mode and Purpose
feature hsrp	Global command to enable HSRP in the Cisco Nexus switch.
feature vrrp	Global command to enable VRRP in the Cisco Nexus switch.
feature glbp	Global command to enable GLBP in the Cisco Nexus switch.
hsrp version {1 | 2}	Configures the HSRP version. Version 1 is the default.
authentication text *string*	Configures clear-text authentication for HSRP on this interface.
authentication md5 { key-chain key-chain | key-string{ 0 | 7 } text [timeoutseconds]}	Configures MD5 authentication for HSRP on this interface. You can use a key chain or key string. If you use a key string, you can optionally set the timeout for when HSRP only accepts a new key. The range is from 0 to 32,767 seconds.
track object-id interfaceinterface-type number {{ ip lipv6 } routing | line-protocol}	Configures the interface that this HSRP interface tracks. Changes in the state of the interface affect the priority of this HSRP interface as follows: ■ You configure the interface and corresponding object number that you use with the **track** command in HSRP configuration mode. ■ The **line-protocol** keyword tracks whether the interface is up. The **ip** keyword also checks that IP routing is enabled on the interface and an IP address is configured.
preempt [delay [minimumseconds] [reload seconds] [sync seconds]]	Configures the router to take over as the active router for an HSRP group if it has a higher priority than the current active router. This command is disabled by default. The range is from 0 to 3600 seconds.
show hsrp [group group-number]	Displays the HSRP status for all groups or one group.
show vrrp	To show information about the Virtual Router Redundancy Protocol (VRRP).

20

This chapter covers the following exam topics:

4.1. Describe and configure basic routing concepts

4.1a. Packet forwarding

CHAPTER 21

IPv4 Access Control Lists on Cisco Nexus Switches

Most every other topic in the scope of CCNA-DC focuses on achieving a core goal of any TCP/IP network: delivering IPv4 packets from the source host to the destination host. This chapter focuses instead on preventing a subset of those packets from being allowed to reach their destinations, by using IPv4 access control lists (ACLs).

IPv4 ACLs have many uses, but the CCNA-DC exam focuses on their most commonly known use: as packet filters. You want hosts in one subnet to be able to communicate throughout your corporate network, but perhaps there is a pocket of servers with sensitive data that must be protected. Maybe government privacy rules require you to further secure and protect access, not just with usernames and login, but through protecting the ability to deliver a packet to the protected host or server. IP ACLs provide a useful solution to achieve those goals.

This chapter discusses the basics of IPv4 ACLs on Nexus switches. This chapter starts by covering the basics and types of ACLs supported by Cisco Nexus switches. The second part of the chapter completes the discussion by describing IPv4 ACLs basics and configurations.

NOTE IPv6 ACLs exist as well, but they are not included in this book. It is important to check release notes/configuration guides to ensure ACL feature support because it can vary across some of the Nexus products based on ASIC usage.

"Do I Know This Already?" Quiz

Use the "Do I Know This Already?" quiz to help decide whether you might want to skim this chapter, or a major section, moving more quickly to the "Exam Preparation Tasks" section near the end of the chapter. Table 21-1 lists the major headings in this chapter and their corresponding "Do I Know This Already?" quiz questions. For thorough explanations, see Appendix A, "Answers to the 'Do I Know This Already?' Quizzes."

Table 21-1 "Do I Know This Already?" Foundation Topics Section-to-Question Mapping

Foundation Topics Section	Questions
IPv4 Access Control List Basics	1–4
Practice Cisco Nexus IPv4 ACLs	5
Basics of AAA	6

1. Barney is a host with IP address 10.1.1.1 in subnet 10.1.1.0/24. Which of the following are things that a standard IP ACL could be configured to do? (Choose two answers.)

   a. Match the exact source IP address.

   b. Match IP addresses 10.1.1.1 through 10.1.1.4 with one **access-list** command without matching other IP addresses.

   c. Match all IP addresses in Barney's subnet with one **access-list** command without matching other IP addresses.

   d. Match only the packet's destination IP address.

2. Which of the following wildcard masks is most useful for matching all IP packets in subnet 10.1.128.0, mask 255.255.255.0?

   a. 0.0.0.0

   b. 0.0.0.31

   c. 0.0.0.240

   d. 0.0.0.255

   e. 0.0.15.0

   f. 0.0.248.255

3. Which of the following masks is most useful for matching all IP packets in subnet 10.1.128.0, mask 255.255.240.0?

   a. 0.0.0.0

   b. 0.0.0.31

   c. 0.0.0.240

   d. 0.0.0.255

   e. 0.0.15.255

   f. 0.0.248.255

4. ACL 1 has three statements, in the following order, with address and mask values as follows: 1.0.0.0/8, 1.1.0.0/16, and 1.1.1.0/24. If a router tried to match a packet sourced from IP address 1.1.1.1 using this ACL, which ACL statement does a router consider the packet to have matched?

   a. First

   b. Second

   c. Third

   d. Implied deny at the end of the ACL

5. On a Cisco Nexus switch, what command will allow only host 10.1.1.1 to talk with host 192.168.1.3 for web traffic that is unencrypted for ACL web subcommands?

   a. permit tcp host 10.1.1.1 host 192.168.1.3 eq 80

   b. permit ip 10.1.1.0/24 host 192.168.1.3

   c. permit tcp 10.1.1.0/24 192.168.1.0/24 eq 80

   d. permit ip any any

6. Which AAA method allows a user after login to access to a certain configuration level on a Cisco network device?

   a. Authentication

   b. Access-List

   c. Authorization

   d. Accounting

21

Foundation Topics

IPv4 Access Control List Basics

IPv4 access control lists (IP ACLs) give network engineers a way to identify different types of packets. To do so, the ACL configuration lists values that the routed interfaces can see in the IP, TCP, UDP, and other headers. For example, an ACL can match packets whose source IP address is 1.1.1.1, or packets whose destination IP address is some address in subnet 10.1.1.0/24, or packets with a destination port of TCP port 23 (Telnet).

IPv4 ACLs perform many functions in Cisco routers, with the most common use as a packet filter. Engineers can enable ACLs on a router so that the ACL sits in the forwarding path of packets as they pass through the router. After it is enabled, the router considers whether each IP packet will either be discarded or allowed to continue as if the ACL did not exist.

However, ACLs can be used for many other IOS features as well. For example, ACLs can be used to match packets for applying quality of service (QoS) features. QoS allows a router to give some packets better service and other packets worse service. For example, packets that hold digitized voice need to have very low delay, so ACLs can match voice packets with QoS logic, in turn forwarding voice packets more quickly than forwarding data packets.

This first section introduces IP ACLs as used for packet filtering, focusing on these aspects of ACLs: the locations and direction in which to enable ACLs, matching packets by examining headers, and taking action after a packet has been matched.

ACL Location and Direction

Cisco Nexus can apply ACL logic to packets at the point at which the IP packets enter an interface or the point at which they exit an interface. In other words, the ACL becomes associated with an interface and for a direction of packet flow (either in or out). That is, the ACL can be applied inbound to the router, before the router makes its forwarding (routing) decision, or outbound, after the router makes its forwarding decision and has determined the exit interface to use.

The arrows in Figure 21-1 show the locations at which you could filter packets, flowing left to right in the topology. Suppose, for instance, that you want to allow packets sent by host A to server S1, but to discard packets sent by host B to server S1. Each arrowed line represents a location and direction at which a router could apply an ACL, filtering the packets sent by host B.

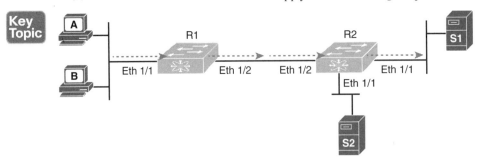

Figure 21-1 *Locations to Filter Packets from Hosts A and B Going Toward Server S1*

The four arrowed lines in the figure point out the location and direction for the routed interfaces used to forward the packet from host B to server S1. In this particular example, those interfaces and directions are as follows:

■ Inbound on R1's Eth1/1 interface

■ Outbound on R1's Eth1/2 interface

■ Inbound on R2's Eth1/2 interface

■ Outbound on R2's Eth1/1 interface

If, for example, you were to enable an ACL on R2's Eth1/1 interface, in either direction, that ACL could not possibly filter the packet sent from host B to server S1, because R2's Eth1/1 interface is not part of the route from B to S1.

In short, to filter a packet, you must enable an ACL on an interface that processes the packet, in the same direction the packet flows through that interface.

When enabled, the router then processes every inbound or outbound IP packet using that ACL. For example, if an ACL is enabled on R1 for packets inbound on interface Eth1/1, R1 would compare every inbound IP packet on Eth1/1 to the ACL to decide that packet's fate: to continue unchanged or to be discarded.

Matching Packets

When you think about the location and direction for an ACL, you must already be thinking about what packets you plan to filter (discard) and which ones you want to allow through. To tell the router those same ideas, you must configure the router with an IP ACL that matches packets. Matching packets refers to how to configure the ACL commands to look at each packet, listing how to identify which packets should be discarded and which should be allowed through.

Each IP ACL consists of one or more configuration commands, with each command listing details about values to look for inside a packet's headers. Generally, an ACL command uses logic like "look for these values in the packet header, and if found, discard the packet." (The action could instead be to allow the packet, rather than discard.) Specifically, the ACL looks for header fields you should already know well, including the source and destination IP addresses, plus TCP and UDP port numbers.

For instance, consider the example shown in Figure 21-2, where you want to allow packets from host A to server S1, but to discard packets from host B going to that same server. The hosts all now have IP addresses, and the figure shows pseudocode for an ACL on R2. Figure 21-2 also shows the chosen location to enable the ACL: inbound on R2's Eth1/2 interface.

Figure 21-2 shows a two-line ACL in a rectangle at the bottom, with simple matching logic: Both statements just look to match the source IP address in the packet. When the ACL is enabled, R2 looks at every inbound IP packet on that interface and compares each packet to those two ACL commands. Packets sent by host A (source IP address 10.1.1.1) are allowed through, and those sent by host B (source IP address 10.1.1.2) are discarded.

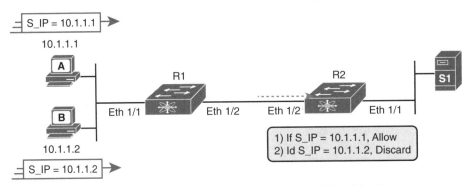

Figure 21-2 *Pseudocode to Demonstrate ACL Command-Matching Logic*

Taking Action when a Match Occurs

When IP ACLs are used to filter packets, only one of two actions can be chosen. The configuration commands use keywords **deny** and **permit**, and they mean (respectively) to discard the packet or to allow it to keep going as if the ACL did not exist.

This book focuses on using ACLs to filter packets, but NX-OS uses ACLs for many more features. Those features typically use the same matching logic. However, in other cases, the **deny** and **permit** keywords imply some other action.

Types of IP ACLs

Cisco IOS has supported IP ACLs since the early days of Cisco routers. Beginning with the original standard numbered IP ACLs in the early days of IOS, which could enable the logic shown earlier around Figure 21-2, Cisco has added many ACL features, including the following:

■ Standard numbered ACLs (1–99)

■ Extended numbered ACLs (100–199)

■ Additional ACL numbers (1300–1999 standard, 2000–2699 extended)

■ Named ACLs

■ Improved editing with sequence numbers

This chapter focuses solely on the Cisco Nexus implementation of IPv4 ACLs, which are extended named ACLs. Briefly, IP ACLs will be either numbered or named, in that the configuration identifies the ACL either using a number or a name. ACLs will also be either standard or extended, with extended ACLs having much more robust abilities in matching packets. Figure 21-3 summarizes the big ideas related to categories of IP ACLs when they were used in IOS.

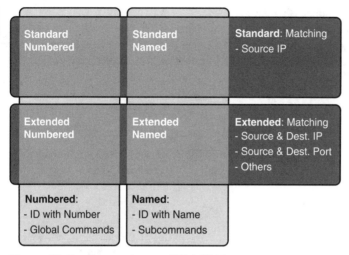

Figure 21-3 *Comparisons of IP ACL Types*

List Logic with IP ACLs

A single ACL is a single entity and, at the same time, a list of one or more configuration commands. In the case of an ACL as a single entity, the configuration enables the entire ACL on an interface, in a specific direction, as shown earlier around Figure 21-1. In the case of an ACL as a list of commands, each command has different matching logic that the router must apply to each packet when filtering using that ACL.

When doing ACL processing, the router processes the packet, compared to the ACL, as follows:

The ACL uses first-match logic. Once a packet matches one line in the ACL, the router takes the action listed in that line of the ACL and stops looking further in the ACL.

To see exactly what this means, consider the example built around Figure 21-4. The figure shows ACL 1 with three lines of pseudocode. This example applies ACL 1 on R2's Eth1/2 interface, inbound (the same location as in Figure 21-2, earlier).

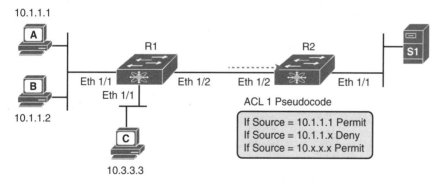

Figure 21-4 *Backdrop for Discussion of List Process with IP ACLs*

Consider the first-match ACL logic for a packet sent by host A to server S1. The source IP address will be 10.1.1.1, and it will be routed so that it enters R2's Eth 1/2 interface, driving R2's ACL 1 logic. R2 compares this packet to the ACL, matching the first item in the list with a permit action. Therefore, this packet should be allowed through, as shown in Figure 21-5, on the left.

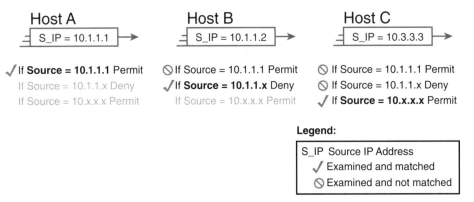

Figure 21-5 *ACL Items Compared for Packets from Hosts A, B, and C in Figure 21-4*

Next, consider a packet sent by host B, source IP address 10.1.1.2. When the packet enters R2's Eth1/2 interface, R2 compares the packet to ACL 1's first statement and does not make a match (10.1.1.1 is not equal to 10.1.1.2). R2 then moves to the second statement, which requires some clarification. The ACL pseudocode, back in Figure 21-4, shows 10.1.1.x, which is meant to be shorthand for "any value can exist in the last octet." Comparing only the first three octets, R2 decides that this latest packet does have a source IP address that begins with first three octets 10.1.1, so R2 considers that to be a match on the second statement. R2 takes the listed action (deny), discarding the packet. R2 also stops ACL processing on the packet, ignoring the third line in the ACL.

Finally, consider a packet sent by host C, again to server S1. The packet has source IP address 10.3.3.3, so when it enters R2's Eth1/2 interface, and drives ACL processing on R2, R2 looks at the first command in ACL 1. R2 does not match the first ACL command (10.1.1.1 in the command is not equal to the packet's 10.3.3.3). R2 looks at the second command, compares the first three octets (10.1.1) to the packet source IP address (10.3.3), and still no match. R2 then looks at the third command. In this case, the wildcard means ignore the last three octets, and just compare the first octet (10), so the packet matches. R2 then takes the listed action (permit), allowing the packet to keep going.

This sequence of processing an ACL as a list happens for any type of NX-OS ACL: IP and other protocols.

Finally, if a packet does not match any of the items in the ACL, the packet is discarded. The reason is because every IP ACL has a **deny all** statement implied at the end of the ACL. It does not exist in the configuration, but if a router keeps searching the list, and no match is made by the end of the list, IOS considers the packet to have matched an entry that has a deny action.

Matching Logic and Command Syntax

NX-OS IP ACLs use the following global command:

```
Switch(config)# ip access-list name
Switch(config-ip-acl)# [sequence-number] {permit | deny} protocol source destination
```

Each NX-OS IPv4 ACL has one or more access list entry commands, with an associated sequence number for each entry so they can be reordered if needed (whole number between 1 and 4,294,967,295).

Besides the ACL sequence number, each **ip access-list** subcommand also lists the action (**permit** or **deny**), plus the matching logic. The rest of this section examines how to configure the matching parameters for NX-OS IPv4 ACLs.

To match a specific source IP address, all you have to do is type that IP address with a /32 mask at the end of the command. For example, the previous example uses pseudocode for "permit if source = 10.1.1.1." The following command configures that logic with correct syntax using an ACL named sample-acl:

```
Switch(config)# ip access-list sample-acl
Switch(config-ip-acl)# permit ip 10.1.1.1/32 any
```

Matching the exact full IP address is that simple. Another option is to use the **host** keyword instead of using the /32, as seen in the following sample ACL sample-acl-host:

```
Switch(config)# ip access-list sample-acl-host
Switch(config-ip-acl)# permit ip host 10.1.1.1 any
```

NOTE An important thing to understand from this example is that all ACLs in NX-OS have what is referred to as an *explicit deny*. If you applied this ACL to an interface only, host 10.1.1.1 would be able to communicate because at the end of each ACL is an implicit deny statement of **ip any any**, which denies anything that has not been permitted using the ACL entries.

Matching TCP and UDP Port Numbers

Cisco Nexus ACLs can also examine parts of the TCP and UDP headers, particularly the source and destination port number fields. The port numbers identify the application that sends or receives the data.

The most useful ports to check are the well-known ports used by servers. For example, web servers use well-known port 80 by default. Figure 21-6 shows the location of the port numbers in the TCP header, following the IP header.

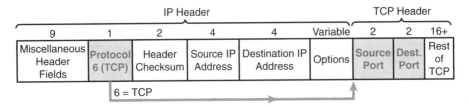

Figure 21-6 *IP Header, Followed by a TCP Header and Port Number Fields*

When a Cisco Nexus ACL command includes either the **tcp** or **udp** keyword, that command can optionally reference the source/destination port. To make these comparisons, the syntax uses keywords for equal, not equal, less than, greater than, and for a range of port numbers. In addition, the command can use either the literal decimal port numbers or more convenient keywords for some well-known application ports. Figure 21-7 shows the positions of the source and destination port fields in the **access-list** command and these port number keywords.

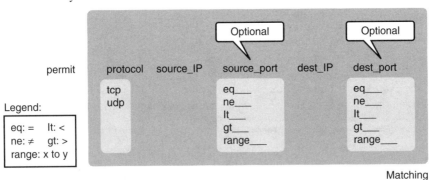

Figure 21-7 *Cisco Nexus ACL Syntax with Port Numbers Enabled Using Protocol TCP or UDP*

For example, consider the simple network shown in Figure 21-8. The FTP server sits on the right, with the client on the left. The figure shows the syntax of an ACL that matches the following:

- Packets that include a TCP header
- Packets sent from the client subnet
- Packets sent to the server subnet
- Packets with TCP destination port 21 (FTP server control port)

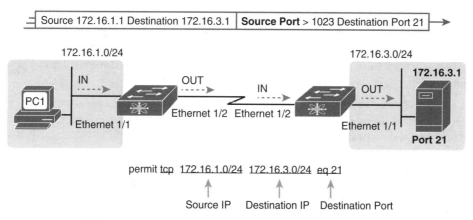

Figure 21-8 *Filtering Packets Based on Destination Port*

To fully appreciate the matching of the destination port with the **eq 21** parameters, consider packets moving from left to right, from PC1 to the server. Assuming the server uses well-known port 21 (FTP control port), the packet's TCP header has a destination port value of 21. The ACL syntax includes the **eq 21** parameters after the destination IP address. The position after the destination address parameters is important: That position identifies the fact that the **eq 21** parameters should be compared to the packet's destination port. As a result, the ACL statement shown in Figure 21-8 would match this packet, and the destination port of 21, if used in any of the four locations implied by the four dashed arrowed lines in the figure.

Conversely, Figure 21-9 shows the reverse flow, with a packet sent by the server back toward PC1. In this case, the packet's TCP header has a source port of 21, so the ACL must check the source port value of 21, and the ACL must be located on different interfaces. In this case, the **eq 21** parameters follow the source address field but come before the destination address field.

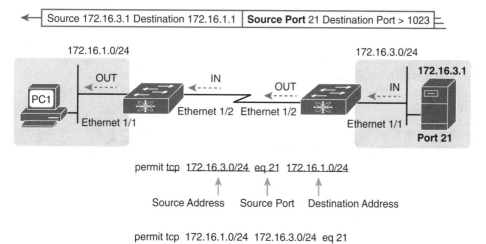

permit tcp 172.16.1.0/24 172.16.3.0/24 eq 21

Figure 21-9 *Filtering Packets Based on Source Port*

21

For exam questions that require ACLs and matching of port numbers, first consider the location and direction in which the ACL will be applied. That direction determines whether the packet is being sent to the server or from the server. At that point, you can decide whether you need to check the source or destination port in the packet, assuming that you want to check the well-known port used by that service.

For reference, Table 21-2 lists many of the popular port numbers and their transport layer protocols and applications. Note that the syntax of the **access-list** commands accepts both the port numbers and a shorthand version of the application name.

Table 21-2   Popular Applications and Their Well-Known Port Numbers

Port Number(s)	Protocol	Application	access-list Command Keyword
20	TCP	FTP data	ftp-data
21	TCP	FTP control	ftp
22	TCP	SSH	—
23	TCP	Telnet	telnet
25	TCP	SMTP	smtp
53	UDP, TCP	DNS	domain
67, 68	UDP	DHCP	nameserver
69	UDP	TFTP	tftp
80	TCP	HTTP (WWW)	www
110	TCP	POP3	pop3
161	UDP	SNMP	snmp
443	TCP	SSL	—
16,384–32,767	UDP	RTP-based voice (VoIP) and video	—

Table 21-3 lists several sample **access-list** commands that match based on port numbers. Cover the right side of the table and try to characterize the packets matched by each command. Then, check the right side of the table to see if you agree with the assessment.

Table 21-3   Extended **access-list** Command Examples and Logic Explanations

access-list Statement	What It Matches
deny tcp any gt 1023 host 10.1.1.1 eq 23	Packets with a TCP header, any source IP address, with a source port greater than (gt) 1023, a destination IP address of exactly 10.1.1.1, and a destination port equal to (eq) 23.
deny tcp any host 10.1.1.1 eq 23	The same as the preceding example, but any source port matches, because that parameter is omitted in this case.

access-list Statement	What It Matches
deny tcp any host 10.1.1.1 eq telnet	The same as the preceding example. The **telnet** keyword is used instead of port 23.
deny udp 1.0.0.0 0.255.255.255 lt 1023 any	A packet with a source in network 1.0.0.0/8, using UDP with a source port less than (lt) 1023, with any destination IP address.

Implementing Cisco Nexus IPv4 ACLs

This chapter has already introduced all the configuration steps in bits and pieces. This section summarizes those pieces as a configuration process. The process also refers to the **access-list** command, whose generic syntax is repeated here for reference:

```
ip access-list name
```

Step 1.   Configure one or more **access-list** subconfiguration commands to create the ACL, keeping the following in mind:

   A. The list is searched sequentially, using first-match logic.

   B. The default action, if a packet does not match any of the **access-list** commands, is to deny (discard) the packet.

Step 2.   Enable the ACL on the chosen interface (port/routed/VACL), in the correct direction, using the **ip access-group/** *number* {**in** | **out**} interface subcommand.

NOTE   IPv4 ACLs can be applied in three different manners: port for Layer 2 interfaces in the direction of in, as a standard Layer 3 ACL for both in and out, and as a VLAN access control list (VACL) by being a match in the VLAN access class list. The following example focuses on routed interface applications.

The rest of this section shows a couple of examples.

ACL Example 1

The first example shows the configuration for the same requirements, demonstrated with Figure 21-4 and Figure 21-5. Restated, the requirements for this ACL are as follows:

   1.   Enable the ACL inbound on R2's Eth1/2 interface.

   2.   Permit packets coming from host A.

   3.   Deny packets coming from other hosts in host A's subnet.

   4.   Permit packets coming from any other address in Class A network 10.0.0.0.

   5.   The original example made no comment about what to do by default; so, simply deny all other traffic.

Example 21-1 shows a completed correct configuration, starting with the configuration process, followed by output from the **show running-config** command.

Example 21-1 *Standard ACL Example 1 Configuration*

```
R2# configure terminal
Enter configuration commands, one per line. End with CNTL/Z.
R2(config)# ip access-list standard-acl
R2(config-ip-acl)#permit ip 10.1.1.1/32 any
R2(config-ip-acl)#deny ip 10.1.1.0/24 any
R2(config-ip-acl)#permit ip 10.0.0.0/8 any
R2(config)# interface Ethernet 1/2
R2(config-if)# ip access-group standard-acl in
R2(config-if)# ^Z
R2# show ip access-lists
! Lines omitted for brevity
      IP access list standard-acl
            10 permit ip 10.1.1.1 255.255.255.255 any
            20 deny ip 10.1.1.0 255.255.255.0 any
            30 permit ip 10.0.0.0 255.0.0.0 any
```

First, pay close attention to the configuration process at the top of the example. Note that the **ip access-list** command does change the command prompt from the global configuration mode prompt, because the **ip access-list** command enters a sub IP ACL configuration mode. Then, compare that to the output of the **show running-config** command: The details are identical compared to the commands that were added in configuration and subconfiguration mode. Finally, make sure to note the **ip access-group standard-acl in** command, under R2's Eth1/2 interface, which enables the ACL logic (both location and direction).

ACL Example 2

The second example, Example 21-2, shows the configuration for a slightly more advanced ACL configuration. This example configures an ACL named advanced-acl on R2 that only allows FTP from host 10.1.1.1 to anyone and HTTP from the 10.1.1.0/24 to anyone.

Example 21-2 *Advanced ACL Example 2 Configuration*

```
R2# configure terminal
Enter configuration commands, one per line. End with CNTL/Z.
R2(config)# ip access-list advanced-acl
R2(config-ip-acl)# permit tcp 10.1.1.1/32 any eq ftp
R2(config-ip-acl)# permit tcp 10.1.1.1/32 any eq ftp-data
R2(config-ip-acl)# permit tcp 10.1.1.0/24 any eq http
R2(config-ip-acl)# permit tcp 10.1.1.0/24 any eq https
      R2(config)# interface Ethernet 1/2
R2(config-if)# ip access-group advanced-acl in
R2(config-if)# ^Z
```

This example shows a more advanced ACL configuration, using an ACL to only allow certain TCP ports out from a single host or subnet. In this case, you are limiting it to FTP traffic from host 10.1.1.1 and allowing the 10.1.1.1.0/24 network the ability to use the Web. The example uses a source, destination, port, and protocol to determine what can communicate in the advanced ACL. This example demonstrates the power you have to lock down communication using this type of ACL within your own network.

Practice Cisco Nexus IPv4 ACLs

Some CCNA-DC topics, such as subnetting, simply require more drills and practice than others. You can also benefit from doing practice drills with ACLs in part because ACLs require you to think of parameters to match ranges of numbers, and that, of course, requires some use of math and some use of processes.

This section provides some practice problems and tips, from two perspectives. First, this section asks you to build one-line ACLs to match some packets. Second, this section asks you to interpret existing ACL commands to describe what packets the ACL will match. Both skills are useful for the exams.

Practice Building access-list Commands

This section provides some practice in getting comfortable with the syntax of the **ip access-list** command, particularly with choosing the correct matching logic. These skills will prove helpful when reading about ACLs.

First, the following list summarizes some important tips to consider when choosing matching parameters to any **access-list** command:

Key Topic

- To match a specific address, just list the address.
- To match any and all addresses, use the **any** keyword.
- To match based only on the first one, two, or three octets of an address, use the subnet masks, respectively. Also, make sure that the source (address) parameter has the correct subnet masks.
- To match a subnet, use the subnet ID as the source, and find the subnet mask prefix by using the "/" prefix length.

Table 21-4 lists the criteria for several practice problems. Your job: Create a one-line standard ACL that matches the packets..

Table 21-4   Building IPv4 ACLs: Practice

Problem	Criteria
1	Packets from 172.16.5.4
2	Packets from hosts with 192.168.6 as the first three octets
3	Packets from hosts with 192.168 as the first two octets
4	Packets from any host
5	Packets from subnet 10.1.200.0 255.255.248.0

Problem	Criteria
6	Packets from subnet 10.1.200.0 255.255.255.224
7	Packets from subnet 172.20.112.0 255.255.255.254
8	Packets from subnet 172.20.112.0 255.255.255.192
9	Packets from subnet 192.168.9.64 255.255.255.240
10	Packets from subnet 192.168.9.64 255.255.255.252

Authentication, Authorization & Accounting (AAA) Basics

When trying to secure the management of your Cisco nexus product line, a key component to understand is Authentication, Authorization & Accounting (referred to as AAA). So let's break down each one of the components of AAA and describe its use in securing the management of your Cisco Nexus devices.

What is AAA?

When it comes to network management security, AAA is a requirement. Here is what each of these are used for and why you should care:

Authentication: Identifies users by login and password using challenge and response methodology before the user even gains access to the network. This can be usernames and passwords stored locally on the networking device or authenticated using an Access Control Server such as Cisco ACS. The primary methods outside of locally stored username and passwords to authenticate a user are RADIUS or TACACS+. Here is a link to Cisco's website describing the differences:

http://www.cisco.com/c/en/us/support/docs/security-vpn/remote-authentication-dial-user-service-radius/13838-10.html

Authorization: After initial authentication, authorization looks at what that authenticated user has access to do. RADIUS or TACACS+ security servers perform authorization for specific privileges by defining attribute-value (AV) pairs, which would be specific to the individual user rights. In the Cisco NX-OS, you can define AAA authorization with a named list or authorization method.

Accounting: Accounting provides a way of collecting security information that you can use for billing, auditing, and reporting. You can use accounting to see what users do once they are authenticated and authorized. For example, with accounting, you could get a log of when users logged in and when they logged out.

Exam Preparation Tasks

Review All the Key Topics

Review the most important topics from this chapter, noted with the Key Topic icon. Table 21-5 lists these key topics and where each is discussed.

Table 21-5   Key Topics for Chapter 21

Key Topic Element	Description	Page Number
Figure 21-1	Locations to filter packets from hosts A and B going toward server S1	544
Paragraph	Summary of the general rule of the location and direction for an ACL	545
Figure 21-3	Summary of four main categories of IPv4 ACLs in Cisco IOS	547
Paragraph	Summary of first-match logic used by all ACLs	547
Figure 21-7	Cisco Nexus ACL syntax with port numbers enabled using protocol TCP or UDP	550
Table 21-2	Popular applications and their well-known port numbers	552
List	Steps to plan and implement a standard IP ACL	553
List	Tips for creating matching logic for the source address field in the **access-list** command	555

Definitions of Key Terms

After your first reading of the chapter, try to define these key terms, but do not be concerned about getting them all correct at that time. Chapter 24, "Final Review," directs you in how to use these terms for late-stage preparation for the exam.

standard access list, wildcard mask

Appendix H Practice Problems

Appendix H, "Practice for Chapter 21: IPv4 Access Control Lists on Cisco Nexus Switches," lists additional practice problems and answers.

Command Reference to Check Your Memory

Although you should not necessarily memorize the information in Tables 12-6 and 12-7, this section includes a reference for the configuration and EXEC commands covered in this chapter. Practically speaking, you should memorize the commands as a side effect of reading this chapter and doing all the activities in this "Exam Preparation Tasks" section. To see how well you have memorized the commands as a side effect of your other studies, cover the left side of the table, read the description on the right side, and see whether you remember the command.

Table 21-6   Chapter 21 Configuration Command Reference

Command	Description
ip access-list *name* (config-ip-acl)# [*sequence-number*] {**permit** | **deny**} *protocol source destination*	Global command for IPv4 access lists. Use subcommands for permit and deny functions.
ip access-group name {**in** | **out**}	Interface subcommand to enable access lists.

Table 21-7   Chapter 21 EXEC Command Reference

Command	Description
show ip interface [*type number*]	Includes a reference to the access lists enabled on the interface
show ip access-list [*access-list-number* | *access-list-name*]	Shows IP access lists

Part IV Review

Keep track of your part review progress with the checklist shown in Table P4-1. Details on each task follow the table.

Table P4-1 Part IV Review Checklist

Activity	First Date Completed	Second Date Completed
Repeat All DIKTA Questions		
Answer Part Review Questions		
Review Key Topics		

Repeat All DIKTA Questions: For this task, answer the "Do I Know This Already?" questions again for the chapters in this part of the book, using the PCPT software. Refer to the Introduction and find the section "How to View Only DIKTA Questions by Part" for help with how to make the PCPT software show you DIKTA questions for this part only.

Answer Part Review Questions: For this task, answer the Part Review questions for this part of the book, using the PCPT software. Refer to the Introduction and find the section "How to View Only Part Review Questions by Part" for help with how to make the PCPT software show you Part Review questions for this part only.

Review Key Topics: Browse back through the chapters and look for the Key Topic icons. If you do not remember some details, take the time to reread those topics.

Part V

Data Center Storage Technologies

Chapter 22: Introduction to Storage and Storage Networking

Chapter 23: Advanced Data Center Storage

Part V Review

This chapter covers the following exam topics:

CHAPTER 22

Introduction to Storage and Storage Networking

Every day, thousands of devices are newly connected to the Internet. Devices previously only plugged into a power outlet are connected to the Internet and are sending and receiving tons of data. Powerful technology trends include the dramatic increase in processing power, storage, and bandwidth at ever-lower costs; the rapid growth of cloud, social media, and mobile computing; the ability to analyze Big Data and turn it into actionable information; and an improved ability to combine technologies (both hardware and software) in more powerful ways.

Companies are searching for more ways to efficiently manage expanding volumes of data, and to make that data accessible throughout the enterprise data centers. This demand is pushing the move of storage into the network. Storage area networks (SANs) are the leading storage infrastructure of today. SANs offer simplified storage management, scalability, flexibility, and availability, as well as improved data access, movement, and backup.

This chapter discusses the function and operation of the data center storage-networking technologies. It compares Small Computer System Interface (SCSI), Fibre Channel, and network-attached storage (NAS) connectivity for remote server storage. It covers Fibre Channel protocol and operations. This chapter goes directly into the edge/core layers of the SAN design and discusses topics relevant to the Introducing Cisco Data Center DCICN 200-150 certification.

"Do I Know This Already?" Quiz

The "Do I Know This Already?" quiz allows you to assess whether you should read this entire chapter thoroughly or jump to the "Exam Preparation Tasks" section. If you are in doubt about your answers to these questions or your own assessment of your knowledge of the topics, read the entire chapter. Table 22-1 lists the major headings in this chapter and their corresponding "Do I Know This Already?" quiz questions. You can find the answers in Appendix A, "Answers to the 'Do I Know This Already?' Quizzes."

Table 22-1   "Do I Know This Already?" Section-to-Question Mapping

Foundation Topics Section	Questions
What Is a Storage Device?	1
What Is a Storage Area Network?	2
How to Access a Storage Device	3
Storage Architectures	4
SAN Design	5
Fibre Channel	6–8
Virtual Storage Area Network	9
iSCSI	10

Caution   The goal of self-assessment is to gauge your mastery of the topics in this chapter. If you do not know the answer to a question or are only partially sure of the answer, you should mark that question as wrong for purposes of the self-assessment. Giving yourself credit for an answer you correctly guess skews your self-assessment results and might provide you with a false sense of security.

1. Which of the following options describe advantages of block-level storage systems? (Choose all the correct answers.)

    a. Block-level storage systems are very popular with storage area networks.

    b. They can support external boot of the systems connected to them.

    c. Block-level storage systems are generally inexpensive when compared to file-level storage systems.

    d. Each block or storage volume can be treated as an independent disk drive and is controlled by an external server OS.

    e. Block-level storage systems are well suited for bulk file storage.

2. Which of the following options describe advantages of storage-area network (SAN)? (Choose all the correct answers.)

    a. Consolidation

    b. Storage virtualization

    c. Business continuity

    d. Secure access to all hosts

    e. None

3. Which of the following protocols are file based? (Choose all the correct answers.)

    a. CIFS

    b. Fibre Channel

    c. SCSI

    d. NFS

4. Which options describe the characteristics of Tier 1 storage? (Choose all the correct answers.)

    a. Integrated large scale disk array.

    b. Centralized controller and cache system.

    c. It is used for mission-critical applications.

    d. Backup storage product.

5. Which of the following options should be taken into consideration during SAN design? (Choose all the correct answers.)

    a. Port density and topology requirements

    b. Device performance and oversubscription ratios

    c. Traffic management

    d. Low latency

6. Which of the following options are correct for Fibre Channel addressing? (Choose all the correct answers.)

    a. A dual-ported HBA has three WWNs: one nWWN, and one pWWN for each port.

    b. Every HBA, array controller, switch, gateway, and Fibre Channel disk drive has a single unique nWWN.

    c. The domain ID is an 8-bit field, and only 239 domains are available to the fabric.

    d. The arbitrated loop physical address (AL-PA) is a 16-bit address.

7. Which process allows an N Port to exchange information about ULP support with its target N Port to ensure that the initiator and target process can communicate?

    a. FLOGI

    b. PLOGI

    c. PRLI

    d. PRLO

8. Which type of port is used to create an ISL on a Fibre Channel SAN?

    a. E

    b. F

    c. TN

    d. NP

9. Which of the following options are correct for VSANs? (Choose all the correct answers)

    a. An HBA or a storage device can belong to only a single VSAN—the VSAN associated with the Fx port.

    b. An HBA or storage device can belong to multiple VSANs.

    c. Membership is typically defined using the VSAN ID to Fx ports.

    d. On a Cisco MDS switch, one can define 4096 VSANs.

10. Which of the following options are correct for iSCSI?

    a. Uses TCP port 3225

    b. Uses TCP port 3260

    c. Uses UDP port 3225

    d. Uses UDP port 3260

    e. Uses both UDP and TCP

22

Foundation Topics

What Is a Storage Device?

Data is stored on hard disk drives that can be both read and written on. A hard disk drive (HDD) is a data storage device used for storing and retrieving digital information using rapidly rotating disks (platters) coated with magnetic material. An HDD retains its data even when powered off. Data is read in a random-access manner, meaning individual blocks of data can be stored or retrieved in any order rather than sequentially. Depending on the methods that are used to run those tasks, and the HDD technology on which they were built, the read and write function can be faster or slower.

IBM introduced the first HDD in 1956; HDDs became the dominant secondary storage device for general-purpose computers by the early 1960s. Continuously improved, HDDs have maintained this position into the modern era of servers and personal computers. More than 200 companies have produced HDD units. Most current units are manufactured by Seagate, Toshiba, and Western Digital.

The primary characteristics of an HDD are its capacity and performance. Capacity is specified in unit prefixes corresponding to powers of 1000: a 1-terabyte (TB) drive has a capacity of 1000 gigabytes (GB; where 1 gigabyte = 1 billion bytes). HDDs are accessed over one of a number of bus types, including (as of 2011) parallel ATA (PATA, also called IDE or EIDE; described before the introduction of SATA as ATA), Serial ATA (SATA), SCSI, Serial Attached SCSI (SAS), and Fibre Channel.

As of 2014, the primary competing technology for secondary storage is flash memory in the form of solid-state drives (SSDs). HDDs are expected to remain the dominant medium for secondary storage due to predicted continuing advantages in recording capacity, price per unit of storage, write latency, and product lifetime. SSDs are replacing HDDs where speed, power consumption, and durability are more important considerations.

The basic interface for all modern drives is straightforward. The drive consists of a large number of sectors (512-byte blocks), each of which can be read or written. The sectors are numbered from 0 to $n - 1$ on a disk with n sectors. Thus, we can view the disk as an array of sectors; 0 to $n - 1$ is therefore the address space of the drive. Multisector operations are possible; indeed, many file systems will read or write 4 KB at a time (or more). A platter is a circular hard surface on which data is stored persistently by inducing magnetic changes to it. A disk may have one or more platters; each platter has two sides, each of which is called a surface. These platters are usually made of some hard material (such as aluminum) and then coated with a thin magnetic layer that enables the drive to persistently store bits even when the drive is powered off.

The platters are all bound together around the spindle, which is connected to a motor that spins the platters around (while the drive is powered on) at a constant (fixed) rate. The rate of rotation is often measured in rotations per minute (RPM), and typical modern values are in the 7200 RPM to 15,000 RPM range. Note that we will often be interested in the time of a single rotation; for example, a drive that rotates at 10,000 RPM means that a single rotation takes about 6 milliseconds (6 ms).

Data is encoded on each surface in concentric circles of sectors; we call one such concentric circle a track. There are usually 1024 tracks on a single disk, and all corresponding tracks from all disks define a cylinder (see Figure 22-1).

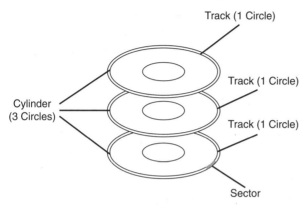

Figure 22-1   *Components of Hard Disk Drive*

A specific sector must be referenced through a three-part address composed of cylinder/head/sector information. And cache is just some small amount of memory (usually around 8 or 16 MB) that the drive can use to hold data read from or written to the disk. For example, when reading a sector from the disk, the drive might decide to read in all of the sectors on that track and cache them in its memory; doing so allows the drive to quickly respond to any subsequent requests to the same track. Although the internal system of cylinders, tracks, and sectors is interesting, it is also not used much anymore by the systems and subsystems that use disk drives. Cylinder, track, and sector addresses have been replaced by a method called logical block addressing (LBA), which makes disks much easier to work with by presenting a single flat address space. To a large degree, logical block addressing facilitates the flexibility of storage networks by allowing many types of disk drives to be integrated more easily into a large heterogeneous storage environment.

The most widespread standard for configuring multiple hard drives is RAID (Redundant Array of Inexpensive/Independent Disks), which comes in a number of standard configurations and nonstandard configurations. Data is distributed across the drives in one of several ways, referred to as RAID levels, depending on the specific level of redundancy and performance required. The different schemes or architectures are named by the word RAID followed by a number (RAID 0, RAID 1, and so on). Each scheme provides a different balance between the key goals: reliability, availability, performance, and capacity. RAID levels greater than RAID 0 provide protection against unrecoverable (sector) read errors as well as whole disk failure. JBOD (derived from "just a bunch of disks") is an architecture involving multiple hard drives, making them accessible either as independent hard drives or as a combined (spanned) single logical volume with no actual RAID functionality. Hard drives may be handled independently as separate logical volumes, or they may be combined into a single logical volume using a volume manager.

Typically, a disk array provides increased availability, resiliency, and maintainability by using existing components (controllers, power supplies, fans, disk enclosures, access ports, cache, and so on), often up to the point where all single points of failure (SPOFs) are elimi-nated from the design. Additionally, disk array components are often hot swappable. Disk arrays are divided into the following categories:

- Network-attached storage (NAS) arrays are based on file-level storage. In this type of storage, the storage disk is configured with a particular protocol (such as NFS, CIFS, and so on) and files are stored and accessed from it as such, in bulk.

   Advantages of file-level storage systems are the following:

   - File-level storage systems are simple to implement and simple to use.

   - They store files and folders and are visible as such to both the systems storing the files and the systems accessing them.

   - File-level storage systems are generally inexpensive when compared to block-level stor-age systems.

   - File-level storage systems are more popular with NAS-based storage systems.

   - They can be configured with common file-level protocols such as NTFS (Windows), NFS (Linux), and so on.

   - File-level storage systems are well suited for bulk file storage.

   The file-level storage device itself can generally handle operations such as access control, integration with corporate directories, and the like.

- Storage-area network (SAN) arrays are based on block-level storage. The raw blocks (storage volumes) are created, and each block can be controlled like an individual hard drive. Generally, these blocks are controlled by the server-based operating systems. Each block or storage volume can be individually formatted with the required file system.

   Advantages of block level storage systems are the following:

   - Block-level storage systems offer better performance and speed than file-level storage systems.

   - Each block or storage volume can be treated as an independent disk drive and is con-trolled by the external server OS.

   - Each block or storage volume can be formatted with the file system required by the application (NFS/NTFS/SMB).

   - Block-level storage systems are very popular with SANs.

   - Block-level storage systems are more reliable, and their transport systems are very efficient.

   - Block-level storage can be used to store files and also provide the storage required for spe-cial applications such as databases, Virtual Machine File Systems (VMFSs), and the like.

   - They can support external boot of the systems connected to them.

Primary vendors of storage systems include EMC Corporation, Hitachi Data Systems, NetApp, IBM, Hewlett-Packard, Oracle Corporation, Dell, Infortrend, and other companies that often act as OEMs for the previously mentioned vendors and do not themselves market the storage components they manufacture.

Servers are connected to the connection port of the disk subsystem using standard I/O techniques such as Small Computer System Interface (SCSI), Fibre Channel, and Internet SCSI (iSCSI) and can thus use the storage capacity that the disk subsystem provides (see Figure 22-2). The internal structure of the disk subsystem is completely hidden from the server, which sees only the hard disks that the disk subsystem provides to the server.

Direct-attached storage (DAS) is often implemented within a parallel SCSI implementation. DAS is commonly described as captive storage. Devices in a captive storage topology do not have direct access to the storage network and do not support efficient sharing of storage. To access data with DAS, a user must go through some sort of front-end network. DAS devices provide little or no mobility to other servers and little scalability. DAS devices limit file sharing and can be complex to implement and manage. For example, to support data backups, DAS devices require resources on the host and spare disk systems that cannot be used on other systems.

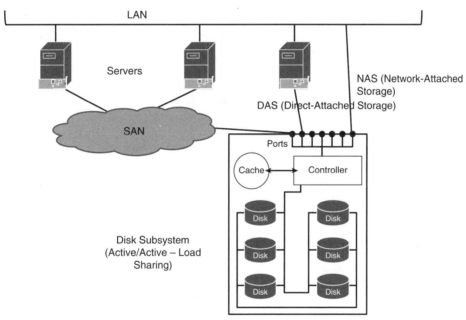

Figure 22-2 *Servers Connected to a Disk Subsystem Using Different I/O Techniques*

The controller of the disk subsystem must ultimately store all data on physical hard disks. Standard I/O techniques such as SCSI, Fibre Channel, and increasingly Serial ATA (SATA), Serial Attached SCSI (SAS), and Serial Storage Architecture (SSA) are being used for internal I/O channels between connection ports and the controller as well as between the controller and internal hard disks. Sometimes, however, proprietary—that is, manufacturer-specific—I/O techniques are used. The I/O channels can be designed with built-in redundancy to increase the fault-tolerance of a disk subsystem. There are four main I/O channel designs:

■ **Active:** In active cabling, the individual physical hard disks are connected via only one I/O channel; if this access path fails, it is no longer possible to access the data.

- **Active/passive:** In active/passive cabling, the individual hard disks are connected via two I/O channels; in normal operation the controller communicates with the hard disks via the first I/O channel, and the second I/O channel is not used. In the event of the failure of the first I/O channel, the disk subsystem switches from the first to the second I/O channel.

- **Active/active (no load sharing):** In this cabling method, the controller uses both I/O channels in normal operation. The hard disks are divided into two groups: in normal operation the first group is addressed via the first I/O channel and the second via the second I/O channel. If one I/O channel fails, both groups are addressed via the other I/O channel.

- **Active/active (load sharing):** In this approach, all hard disks are addressed via both I/O channels; in normal operation, the controller divides the load dynamically between the two I/O channels so that the available hardware can be optimally utilized. If one I/O channel fails, the communication goes through the other channel only.

A tape drive is a data storage device that reads and writes data on a magnetic tape. Magnetic tape data storage is typically used for offline, archival data storage. A tape drive provides sequential access storage, unlike a disk drive, which provides random access storage. A disk drive can move to any position on the disk in a few milliseconds, but a tape drive must physically wind tape between reels to read any one particular piece of data. As a result, tape drives have very slow average seek times for sequential access after the tape is positioned. However, tape drives can stream data very quickly. For example, as of 2010, Linear Tape-Open (LTO) supported continuous data transfer rates of up to 140 MBps, comparable to hard disk drives. A tape library, sometimes called a tape silo, tape robot, or tape jukebox, is a storage device that contains one or more tape drives, a number of slots to hold tape cartridges, a bar-code reader to identify tape cartridges, and an automated method for loading tapes (a robot). These devices can store immense amounts of data, currently ranging from 20 TB up to 2.1 EB (exabytes) of data or multiple thousand times the capacity of a typical hard drive and well in excess of capacities achievable with network-attached storage.

We talked about block-level and file-level storage. Now it is time to extend your knowledge to object storage. Object storage is not directly accessed by the operating system. It is not seen as a local or a remote file system. Instead, interaction occurs at the application level via an API. Block-level storage and file-level storage are designed to be consumed by the operating system; object storage is designed to be consumed by the application. Object storage devices offer the ability to aggregate storage into disparate grid storage structures that undertake work traditionally performed by single subsystems while providing load distribution capabilities and resilience far in excess of that available in a traditional SAN environment. Object storage devices operate as modular units that can become components of a larger storage pool and can be aggregated across locations. The advantages of this are considerable because distributed storage nodes can provide options to increase data resilience and enable disaster recovery strategies.

To better understand the object structure, think of the objects as the cells in a beehive. Each cell is a self-contained repository for an object ID number, metadata, data attributes, and the stored data itself. Each cell is also a separate object within the usable disk space pool.

Physically, object-based storage arrays are composed of stackable, self-contained disk units like any other SAN. Unlike traditional storage arrays, object-based systems are accessed via HTTP. That access method plus their ability to scale to petabytes of data make object-based systems a good choice for public cloud storage. An entire object storage cluster of disparate nodes can be easily combined to become an online, scalable file repository. Object storage works very well for unstructured data sets where data is generally read but not written to. Static web content, data backups and archival images, and multimedia (videos, pictures, or music) files are best stored as objects. Databases in an object storage environment ideally have data sets that are unstructured, where the use cases suggest the data will not require a large number of writes or incremental updates. Object storage is used for diverse purposes such as storing photos on Facebook, songs on Spotify, or files in online collaboration services such as Dropbox.

In the rapidly evolving landscape of enterprise data storage, one thing is clear: We need to store more data, more simply, more efficiently, and for a lower overall cost. Object storage addresses these issues without expensive custom hardware that will need to be replaced every few years. As we enter an age of zettabytes of data, more and more enterprises are turning to object storage as their go-to storage solution.

What Is Storage Area Network?

The Storage Networking Industry Association (SNIA) defines the storage-area network (SAN) as a network whose primary purpose is the transfer of data between computer systems and storage elements and among storage elements. A SAN consists of a communication infrastructure, which provides physical connections and a management layer. This layer organizes the connections, storage elements, and computer systems so that data transfer is secure and robust. The term SAN is usually (but not necessarily) identified with block I/O services rather than file-access services. A SAN is a specialized, high-speed network that attaches servers and storage devices. A SAN allows an any-to-any connection across the network by using interconnect elements such as switches and directors. It eliminates the traditional dedicated connection between a server and storage, and the concept that the server effectively owns and manages the storage devices. It also eliminates any restriction to the amount of data that a server can access, currently limited by the number of storage devices attached to the individual server. Instead, a SAN introduces the flexibility of networking to enable one server or many heterogeneous servers to share a common storage utility. A network might include many storage devices, including disk, tape, and optical storage. Additionally, the storage utility might be located far from the servers that it uses. Figure 22-3 portrays a sample SAN topology.

22

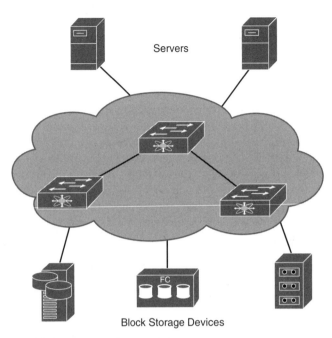

Figure 22-3 *Storage Connectivity*

The key benefits that a storage area network (SAN) might bring to a highly data-dependent business infrastructure can be summarized into three concepts: simplification of the infrastructure, information life-cycle management (ILS), and business continuity.

The simplification of the infrastructure consists of six main areas:

- **Consolidation:** Involves concentrating the systems and resources into locations with fewer, but more powerful, servers and storage pools that can help increase IT efficiency and simplify the infrastructure. In addition, centralized storage management tools can help improve scalability, availability, and disaster tolerance.

- **Storage virtualization:** Helps in making complexity nearly transparent and can offer a composite view of storage assets. We will be talking about storage virtualization in detail in Chapter 23, "Advanced Data Center Storage."

- **Automation:** Involves choosing storage components with autonomic capabilities, which can improve availability and responsiveness and can help protect data as storage needs grow. As soon as day-to-day tasks are automated, storage administrators might be able to spend more time on critical, higher-level tasks that arc unique to the company's business mission.

- **Integrated storage environments:** Simplify system management tasks and improve security. When all servers have secure access to all data, your infrastructure might be better able to respond to the information needs of your users.

- **Information life-cycle management (ILM):** A process for managing information through its life cycle, from conception until intentional disposal. The ILM process manages this information in a manner that optimizes storage and maintains a high level of access at the lowest cost. A SAN implementation makes it easier to manage the information life cycle because it integrates applications and data into a single-view system in which the information resides.

- **Business continuity (BC):** Involves building and improving resilience in your business; it's about identifying your key products and services and the most urgent activities that underpin them; then, after that analysis is complete, it is about devising plans and strategies that will enable you to continue your business operations and enable you to recover quickly and effectively from any type of disruption, whatever its size or cause. It gives you a solid framework to lean on in times of crisis and provides stability and security. In fact, embedding BC into your business is proven to bring business benefits. SANs play a key role in the business continuity. By deploying a consistent and safe infrastructure, SANs make it possible to meet any availability requirements.

Fibre Channel is a serial I/O interconnect that is capable of supporting multiple protocols, including access to open system storage (FCP), access to mainframe storage (FICON), and networking (TCP/IP). Fibre Channel supports point-to-point, arbitrated loop, and switched topologies with various copper and optical links that are running at speeds from 1 Gbps to 16 Gbps. The committee that is standardizing Fibre Channel is the INCITS Fibre Channel (T11) Technical Committee.

A storage system consists of storage elements, storage devices, computer systems, and appliances, plus all control software that communicates over a network. Storage subsystems, storage devices, and server systems can be attached to a Fibre Channel SAN. Depending on the implementation, several components can be used to build a SAN. It is, as the name suggests, a network, so any combination of devices that is able to interoperate is likely to be used. Given this definition, a Fibre Channel network might be composed of many types of interconnect entities, including directors, switches, hubs, routers, gateways, and bridges. It is the deployment of these different types of interconnect entities that allows Fibre Channel networks of varying scales to be built. In smaller SAN environments you can deploy hubs for Fibre Channel arbitrated loop topologies, or switches and directors for Fibre Channel switched fabric topologies. As SANs increase in size and complexity, Fibre Channel directors can be introduced to facilitate a more flexible and fault-tolerant configuration. Each of the components that compose a Fibre Channel SAN provides an individual management capability and participates in an often-complex end-to-end management environment.

22

How to Access a Storage Device

Each new storage technology introduced a new physical interface, electrical interface, and storage protocol. The intelligent interface model abstracts device-specific details from the storage protocol and decouples the storage protocol from the physical and electrical interfaces. This allows multiple storage technologies to use a common storage protocol. In this chapter, we will be categorizing them in three major groups:

- **Blocks:** Sometimes called a physical record, a block is a sequence of bytes or bits, usually containing some whole number of records having a maximum length (a block size). This type of structured data is called "blocked." Most file systems are based on a block device, which is a level of abstraction for the hardware responsible for storing and retrieving specified blocks of data, although the block size in file systems may be a multiple of the physical block size.

- **Files:** Files are granular containers of data created by the system or an application. By separating the data into individual pieces and giving each piece a name, the information is easily separated and identified. The structure and logic rule used to manage the groups of information and their names is called a "file system." Some file systems are used on local data storage devices; others provide file access via a network protocol.

- **Records:** Records are similar to the file system. There are several record formats; the details vary depending on the particular system. In general, the formats can be fixed length or variable length, with different physical organizations or padding mechanisms; metadata may be associated with the file records to define the record length, or the data may be part of the record. Different methods to access records may be provided—for example, sequential, by key, or by record number.

Block-Level Protocols

Block-oriented protocols (also known as block-level protocols) read and write individual fixed-length blocks of data. Small Computer Systems Interface (SCSI) is a block-level I/O protocol for writing and reading data blocks to and from a storage device. Data transfer is also governed by standards. SCSI is an American National Standards Institute (ANSI) standard that is one of the leading I/O buses in the computer industry. The SCSI bus is a parallel bus, which comes in a number of variants, as shown in Table 22-2. The first version of the SCSI standard was released in 1986. Since then, SCSI has been continuously developed.

The International Committee for Information Technology Standards (INCITS) is the forum of choice for information technology developers, producers, and users for the creation and maintenance of formal daily IT standards. INCITS is accredited by and operates under rules approved by the American National Standards Institute (ANSI). These rules are designed to ensure that voluntary standards are developed by the consensus of directly and materially affected interests. The Information Technology Industry Council (ITI) sponsors INCITS (see Figure 22-4). The standard process is that a technical committee (T10, T11, T13) prepares drafts. Drafts are sent to INCITS for approval. After the drafts are approved by INCITS, they become standards and are published by ANSI. ANSI promotes American National Standards to ISO as a joint technical committee member (JTC-1).

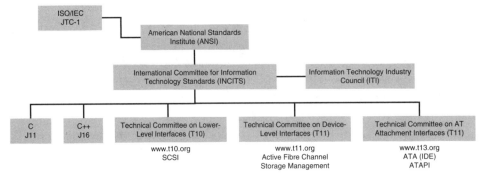

Figure 22-4 *Standard Groups: Storage*

As a medium, SCSI defines a parallel bus for the transmission of data with additional lines for the control of communication. The bus can be realized in the form of printed conductors on the circuit board or as a cable. Over time, numerous cable and plug types have been defined that are not directly compatible with one another (see Table 22-2). A so-called "daisy chain" can connect up to 16 devices together.

Table 22-2 SCSI Standards Comparison

SCSI Standard	Speed (MBps)	Cable Length	Devices Supported
SCSI-1	5	6	8
SCSI-2	5 to 10	6	8 or 16
Fast SCSI-2	10 to 20	3	8
Wide SCSI-2	20	3	16
Fast Wide SCSI-2	20	3	16
Ultra SCSI-3, 8-bit	20	1.5	8
Ultra SCSI-2, 16-bit	40	1.5	16
Ultra-2 SCSI	40	12	8
Wide Ultra-2 SCSI	80	12	16
Ultra-3 (Ultra 160/m)	160	12	16

All SCSI devices are intelligent, but SCSI operates as a master/slave model. One SCSI device (the initiator) initiates communication with another SCSI device (the target) by issuing a command, to which a response is expected. Thus, the SCSI protocol is half-duplex by design and is considered a command/response protocol.

The initiating device is usually a SCSI controller, so SCSI controllers typically are called initiators. SCSI storage devices typically are called targets (see Figure 22-5). A SCSI controller in a modern storage array acts as a target externally and acts as an initiator internally. Also note that array-based replication software requires a storage controller in the initiating storage array to act as initiator both externally and internally. SCSI targets have logical units that provide the processing context for SCSI commands. Essentially, a logical unit is a virtual machine (or virtual controller) that handles SCSI communications on behalf of real or virtual storage devices in a target. Commands received by targets are directed to the appropriate logical unit by a task router in the target controller.

22

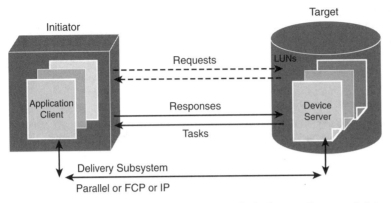

Figure 22-5   *SCSI Commands, Status, and Block Data Between Initiators and Targets*

The logical unit number (LUN) identifies a specific logical unit (virtual controller) in a target. Although we tend to use the term LUN to refer to a real or virtual storage device, a LUN is an access point for exchanging commands and status information between initiators and targets. A logical unit can be thought of as a "black box" processor, and the LUN is a way to identify SCSI black boxes. Logical units are architecturally independent of target ports and can be accessed through any of the target's ports, via a LUN. A target must have at least one LUN, LUN 0, and might optionally support additional LUNs. For instance, a disk drive might use a single LUN, whereas a subsystem might allow hundreds of LUNs to be defined.

The process of provisioning storage in a SAN storage subsystem involves defining a LUN on a particular target port and then assigning that particular target/LUN pair to a specific logical unit. An individual logical unit can be represented by multiple LUNs on different ports. For instance, a logical unit could be accessed through LUN 1 on Port 0 of a target and also accessed as LUN 8 on port 1 of the same target.

The bus, target, and LUN triad is defined from parallel SCSI technology. The bus represents one of several potential SCSI interfaces that are installed in the host, each supporting a separate string of disks. The target represents a single disk controller on the string. Depending on the version of the SCSI standard, a maximum of 8 or 16 IDs are permitted per SCSI bus. A server can be equipped with several SCSI controllers. Therefore, the operating system must note three things for the differentiation of devices: controller ID, SCSI ID, and LUN. The SCSI protocol permitted only eight IDs, with ID 7 having the highest priority. More recent versions of the SCSI protocol permit 16 different IDs. For reasons of compatibility, IDs 7 to 0 should retain the highest priority so that IDs 15 to 8 have a lower priority (see Figure 22-6).

Devices (servers and storage devices) must reserve the SCSI bus (arbitrate) before they may send data through it. During the arbitration of the bus, the device that has the highest priority SCSI ID always wins. In the event that the bus is heavily loaded, this can lead to devices with lower priorities never being allowed to send data. The SCSI arbitration procedure is therefore "unfair."

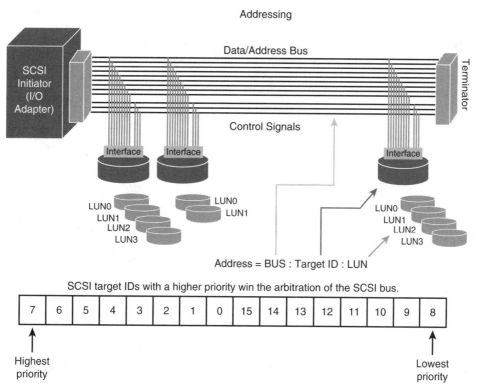

Figure 22-6 *SCSI Addressing*

The SCSI protocol layer sits between the operating system and the peripheral resources, so it has different functional components (see Figure 22-7). Applications typically access data as files or records. Although this information might be stored on disk or tape media in the form of data blocks, retrieval of the file requires a hierarchy of functions. These functions assemble raw data blocks into a coherent file that an application can manipulate.

It is important to understand that whereas SCSI-1 and SCSI-2 represent actual standards that completely define SCSI (connectors, cables, signals, and command protocol), SCSI-3 is an all-encompassing term that refers to a collection of standards that were written as a result of breaking SCSI-2 into smaller, hierarchical modules that fit within a general framework called SCSI Architecture Model (SAM).

The SCSI version 3 (SCSI-3) application client resides in the host and represents the upper layer application, file system, and operating system I/O requests. The SCSI-3 device server sits in the target device, responding to requests. It is often also assumed that SCSI provides in-order delivery to maintain data integrity. In-order delivery was traditionally provided by the SCSI bus and, therefore, was not needed by the SCSI protocol layer. In SCSI-3, the SCSI protocol assumes that proper ordering is provided by the underlying connection technology. In other words, the SCSI protocol does not provide its own reordering mechanism, and the network is responsible for the reordering of transmission frames that are received out of order. This is the main reason why TCP was considered essential for the iSCSI protocol that transports SCSI commands and data transfers over IP networking equipment: TCP provided ordering while other upper-layer protocols, such as UDP, did not. In SCSI-3, even faster bus types are introduced, along with serial SCSI buses that reduce the cabling overhead and allow a higher maximum bus length. It is at this point where the Fibre Channel model is introduced. As always, the demands and needs of the market push for new technologies. In particular, there is always a push for faster communications without limitations on distance or on the number of connected devices.

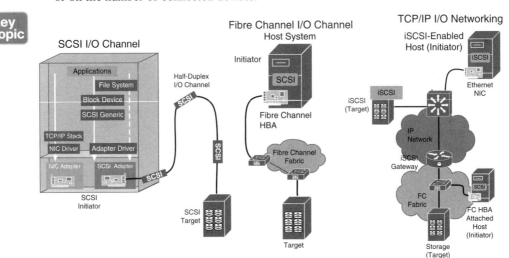

Figure 22-7 *SCSI I/O Channel, Fibre Channel I/O Channel, and TCP/IP I/O Networking*

The SCSI protocol is suitable for block-based, structured applications such as database applications that require many I/O operations per second (IOPS) to achieve high performance. IOPS (input/output operations per second, pronounced *eye-ops*) is a common performance measurement used to benchmark computer storage devices like hard disk drives (HDDs), solid-state drives (SSDs), and storage-area networks (SANs). The specific number of IOPS possible in any system configuration will vary greatly, depending on the variables the tester enters into the program, including the balance of read and write operations, the mix of sequential and random-access patterns, the number of worker threads and queue depth, as well as the data block sizes.

For HDDs and similar electromechanical storage devices, the random IOPS numbers are primarily dependent on the storage device's random seek time, whereas for SSDs and similar solid-state storage devices, the random IOPS numbers are primarily dependent on the storage device's internal controller and memory interface speeds. On both types of storage devices, the sequential IOPS numbers (especially when using a large block size) typically indicate the maximum sustained bandwidth that the storage device can handle. Often, sequential IOPS are reported as a simple MBps number, as follows:

IOPS x TransferSizeInBytes = BytesPerSec (and typically this is converted to megabytes per second)

SCSI messages and data can be transported in several ways:

- **Parallel SCSI cable:** This transport is mainly used in traditional deployments. Latency is low, but distance is limited to 25 m and is half-duplex, so data can flow in only one direction at a time.

- **iSCSI is SCSI over TCP/IP:** Internet Small Computer System Interface (iSCSI) is a transport protocol that carries SCSI commands from an initiator to a target. It is a data storage networking protocol that transports standard SCSI requests over the standard Transmission Control Protocol/Internet Protocol (TCP/IP) networking technology. iSCSI enables the implementation of IP-based SANs, enabling clients to use the same networking technologies for both storage and data networks. Because it uses TCP/IP, iSCSI is also suited to run over almost any physical network. By eliminating the need for a second network technology just for storage, iSCSI has the potential to lower the costs of deploying networked storage.

- **Fibre Channel cable:** This transport is the basis for a traditional SAN deployment. Latency is low and bandwidth is high (16 GBps). SCSI is carried in the payload of a Fibre Channel frame between Fibre Channel ports. Fibre Channel has a lossless delivery mechanism by using buffer-to-buffer credits (BB_Credits), which we explain in detail later in this chapter.

- **Fibre Channel connection (FICON):** This architecture is an enhancement of, rather than a replacement for, the traditional IBM Enterprise Systems Connection (ESCON) architecture. A SAN is Fibre Channel based (FC based). Therefore, FICON is a prerequisite for IBM z/OS systems to fully participate in a heterogeneous SAN, where the SAN switch devices allow the mixture of open systems and mainframe traffic. FICON is a protocol that uses Fibre Channel as its physical medium. FICON channels can achieve data rates up to 850 MBps and extend the channel distance (up to 100 km). At the time of writing this book, FICON can also increase the number of control unit images per link and the number of device addresses per control unit link. The protocol can also retain the topology and switch management characteristics of ESCON.

- **Fibre Channel over IP (FCIP):** Also known as Fibre Channel tunneling or storage tunneling. It is a method to allow the transmission of Fibre Channel information to be tunneled through the IP network. Because most organizations already have an existing IP infrastructure, the attraction of being able to link geographically dispersed SANs, at a relatively low cost, is enormous.

  FCIP encapsulates Fibre Channel block data and then transports it over a TCP socket. TCP/IP services are used to establish connectivity between remote SANs. Any congestion control and management and data error and data loss recovery is handled by TCP/IP services and does not affect Fibre Channel fabric services.

  The major consideration with FCIP is that it does not replace Fibre Channel with IP; it allows deployments of Fibre Channel fabrics by using IP tunneling. The assumption that this might lead to is that the industry decided that Fibre Channel–based SANs are more than appropriate. Another possible assumption is that the only need for the IP connection is to facilitate any distance requirement that is beyond the current scope of an FCP SAN.

- **Fibre Channel over Ethernet (FCoE):** This transport replaces the Fibre Channel cabling with 10 Gigabit Ethernet cables and provides lossless delivery over converged I/O. FCoE will be discussed in detail in Chapter 23.

22

Figure 22-8 portrays a networking stack comparison for all block I/O protocols.

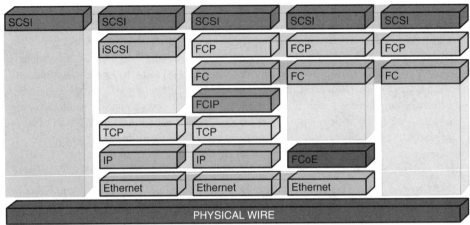

Figure 22-8 *Networking Stack Comparison for All Block I/O Protocols*

Fibre Channel provides high-speed transport for SCSI payload via a host bus adapter (HBA), as shown in Figure 22-9. HBAs are I/O adapters that are designed to maximize performance by performing protocol-processing functions in silicon. HBAs are roughly analogous to network interface cards (NICs), but HBAs are optimized for SANs and provide features that are specific to storage. Fibre Channel overcomes many shortcomings of Parallel I/O, including addressing for up to 16 million nodes, loop (shared) and fabric (switched) transport, host speeds of 100 to 1600 MBps (1–16 Gbps), support for multiple protocols, and combines the best attributes of a channel and a network together.

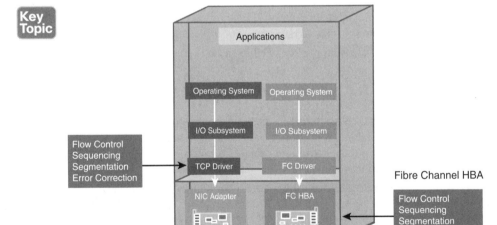

Figure 22-9 *Comparison Between Fibre Channel HBA and Ethernet NIC*

With NICs, software drivers perform protocol-processing functions such as flow control, sequencing, segmentation and reassembly, and error correction. The HBA offloads these protocol-processing functions onto the HBA hardware with some combination of an ASIC and firmware. Offloading these functions is necessary to provide the performance that storage networks require.

Fibre Channel Protocol (FCP) has an ANSI-based layered architecture that can be considered a general transport vehicle for upper layer protocols (ULPs) such as SCSI command sets, HIPPI data framing, IP, and others. Figure 22-10 shows an overview of the Fibre Channel model. The diagram shows the Fibre Channel, which is divided into four lower layers (FC-0, FC-1, FC-2, and FC-3) and one upper layer (FC-4). FC-4 is where the upper-level protocols are used, such as SCSI-3, Internet Protocol (IP), and Fibre Channel connection (FICON).

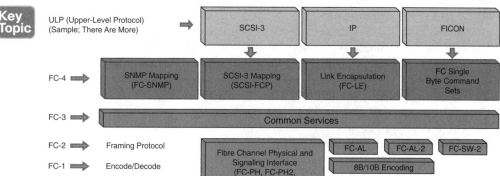

Figure 22-10 *Portrays Fibre Channel Protocol Architecture*

Here are the main functions of each Fibre Channel layer:

- **FC-4 upper-layer protocol (ULP) mapping:** Provides protocol mapping to identify the upper-level protocol (ULP) that is encapsulated into a protocol data unit (PDU) for delivery to the FC-2 layer.

- **FC-3 generic services:** Provides the Fibre Channel Generic Services (FC-GS) that are required for fabric management. Specifications exist here but are rarely implemented.

- **FC-2 framing and flow control:** Provides the framing and flow control that are required to transport the ULP over Fibre Channel. FC-2 functions include several classes of service, frame format definition, sequence disassembly and reassembly, exchange management, address assignment, alias address definition, protocols for hunt group, and multicast management and stacked connect requests.

- **FC-1 encoding:** Defines the transmission protocol that includes the serial encoding, decoding, and error control.

- **FC-0 physical interface:** Provides physical connectivity, including cabling, connectors, and so on.

Table 22-3 shows the evolution of Fibre Channel speeds. Fibre Channel is described in greater depth throughout this chapter. FCP is the FC-4 mapping of SCSI-3 onto FC. Fibre Channel throughput is commonly expressed in bytes per second rather than bits per second. In the initial FC specification, rates of 12.5 MBps, 25 MBps, 50 MBps, and 100 MBps were introduced on several different copper and fiber media. Additional rates were subsequently introduced, including 200 MBps and 400 MBps. 100 MBps FC is also known as 1Gbps FC, 200 MBps as 2Gbps FC, and 400 MBps as 4Gbps FC. The FC-PH specification defines baud rate as the encoded bit rate per second, which means the baud rate and raw bit rate are equal. The FC-PI specification redefines baud rate more accurately and states explicitly that FC encodes 1 bit per baud. FC-1 variants up to and including 8 Gbps use the same encoding scheme (8B/10B) as GE fiber-optic variants. 1Gbps FC operates at 1.0625 GBaud, provides a raw bit rate of 1.0625 Gbps, and provides a data bit rate of 850 Mbps. 2Gbps FC operates at 2.125 GBaud, provides a raw bit rate of 2.125 Gbps, and provides a data bit rate of 1.7 Gbps. 4Gbps FC operates at 4.25 GBaud, provides a raw bit rate of 4.25 Gbps, and provides a data bit rate of 3.4 Gbps. To derive ULP throughput, the FC-2 header and interframe spacing overhead must be subtracted. Note that FCP does not define its own header. Instead, fields within the FC-2 header are used by FCP. The basic FC-2 header adds 36 bytes of overhead. Inter-frame spacing adds another 24 bytes. Assuming the maximum payload (2112 bytes) and no optional FC-2 headers, the ULP throughput rate is 826.519 Mbps, 1.65304 Gbps, and 3.30608 Gbps for 1Gbps FC, 2Gbps FC, and 4Gbps FC, respectively. These ULP throughput rates are available directly to SCSI. The 1Gbps FC, 2Gbps FC, 4Gbps FC, and 8Gbps FC designs all use 8b/10b encoding, and the 10G and 16G FC standards use 64b/66b encoding. Unlike the 10Gbps FC standards, 16Gbps FC provides backward compatibility with 4Gbps FC and 8Gbps FC.

Table 22-3   Evolution of Fibre Channel Speeds

FC Speed	Baud Rate (Line-rate)	Data Rate Gbps	Data Rate (MBps)	Encoding	Available in the Market Since
1G FC	1.0625 GBaud	0.825	106	8b/10b	1997
2G FC	2.125 GBaud	1.65	212	8b/10b	2001
4G FC	4.25 GBaud	3.4	425	8b/10b	2005
8G FC	8.5 GBaud	6.8	850	8b/10b	2008
10G FC Serial	10.51875 GBaud	10.2	1275	64b/66b	2004
16G FC	14.1667 GBaud	13.6	1700	64b/66b	2011
32G FC	28.05 GBaud	27.2	3400	64b/66b	2016 (projected)

File-Level Protocols

File-oriented protocols (also known as file-level protocols) read and write variable-length files. Files are segmented into blocks before being stored on disk or tape. Common Internet File System (CIFS) and Network File System (NFS) are file-based protocols that are used for reading and writing files across a network. CIFS is found primarily on Microsoft Windows servers (a Samba service implements CIFS on UNIX systems), and NFS is found primarily on UNIX and Linux servers.

The theory of client/server architecture is based on the concept that one computer has the resources that another computer requires. These resources can be made available through NFS. The system with the resources is called the server, and the system that requires the resources is called the client. Examples of resources are email, database, and files. The client and the server communicate with each other through established protocols.

A distributed (client/server) network might contain multiple servers and multiple clients, or multiple clients and one server. The configuration of the network depends on the resource requirement of the environment.

The benefits of client/server architecture include cost reduction because of hardware and space requirements. The local workstations do not need as much disk space because commonly used data can be stored on the server. Other benefits include centralized support (backups and maintenance) that is performed on the server.

NFS is a widely used protocol for sharing files across networks. NFS is stateless, to allow for easy recovery in the event of server failure. In Figure 22-11, the server in the network is a network appliance storage system, and the client can be one of many versions of the UNIX or Linux operating system.

The storage system provides services to the client. These services include mount daemon (mounted), Network Lock Manager (nlm_main), NFS daemon (nfsd), Status Monitor (sm_1_main), quota daemon (rquot_1_main), and portmap (also known as rpcbind). Each service is required for successful operation of an NFS process. For example, a client cannot mount a resource if mountd is not running on the server. Similarly, if rpcbind is not running on the server, NFS communication cannot be established between the client and the server. Because CIFS and NFS are transported over TCP/IP, latency is high. CIFS and NFS are verbose protocols that send thousands of messages between the servers and NAS devices when reading and writing files.

These file-based protocols are suitable for file-based applications: Microsoft Office, Microsoft SharePoint, and File and Print services. One benefit of NAS storage is that files can be shared easily between users within a workgroup. Block I/O and file I/O are complementary solutions for reading and writing data to and from storage devices. Block I/O uses the SCSI protocol to transfer data in 512-byte blocks. SCSI is an efficient protocol and is the accepted standard within the industry. SCSI may be transported over many physical media. SCSI is mostly used in Fibre Channel SANs to transfer blocks of data between servers and storage arrays in a high-bandwidth, low-latency redundant SAN. Block I/O protocols are suitable for well-structured applications, such as databases that transfer small blocks of data when updating fields, records, and tables.

In the scenario portrayed in Figure 22-11, file-level data access applies to IP front-end networks, and block-level data access applies to Fibre Channel (FC) back-end networks. Front-end data communications are considered host-to-host or client/server. Back-end data communication is "host to storage" or "program to device."

22

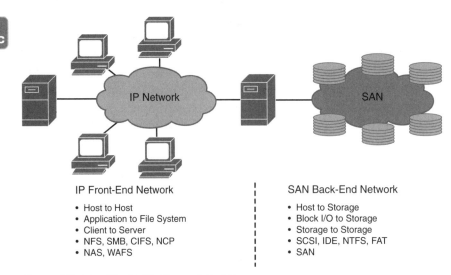

Figure 22-11 *Block I/O Versus File I/O*

Front-end protocols include FTP, NFS, SMB (Server Message Block—Microsoft NT), CIFS (Common Internet File System), and NCP (Netware Core protocol—Novell). Back-end protocols include SCSI and IDE, along with file system formatting standards such as FAT and NTFS. Network-attached storage (NAS) appliances reside on the front end. Storage-area networks (SANs) include the back-end along with front-end components.

Putting It All Together

Fibre Channel SAN, FCoE SAN, iSCSI SAN, and NAS are four techniques with which storage networks can be realized (see Figure 22-12). In contrast to NAS, in Fibre Channel, FCoE, and iSCSI the data exchange between servers and storage devices takes place in a block-based fashion. Storage networks are more difficult to configure. On the other hand, Fibre Channel supplies optimal performance for the data exchange between server and storage device. NAS servers are turnkey file servers. NAS servers have only limited suitability as data storage for databases due to lack of performance. Storage networks can be realized with a NAS server by installing an additional LAN between the NAS server and the application servers. In contrast to Fibre Channel, FCoE, and iSCSI, NAS transfers files or file fragments.

At this stage, you already figured out why Fibre Channel was introduced. SCSI is limited by distance, speed, number of storage devices per chain, resiliency, lack of device sharing, and management flexibility. Therefore, Fibre Channel was introduced to overcome these limitations. Fibre Channel offers a greater sustained data rate (1G FC–16G FC at the time of writing this book), loop or switched networks for device sharing and low latency, distances of hundreds of kilometers or greater with extension devices, virtually unlimited devices in a fabric, nondisruptive device addition, and centralized management with local or remote access.

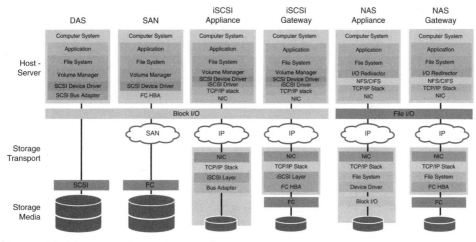

Figure 22-12   *DAS, SAN, iSCSI, and NAS Comparison*

Storage Architectures

Storage systems are designed in a way that customers can purchase some amount of capacity initially with the option of adding more as the existing capacity fills up with data. Increasing storage capacity is an important task for keeping up with data growth. Scaling architectures determine how much capacity can be added, how quickly it can be added, the impact on application availability, and how much work and planning are involved.

Scale-up and Scale-out Storage

Storage systems increase their capacity in one of two ways: by adding storage components to an existing system or by adding storage systems to an existing group of systems. An architecture that adds capacity by adding storage components to an existing system is called a scale-up architecture, and products designed with it are generally classified as monolithic storage. An architecture that adds capacity by adding individual storage systems, or nodes, to a group of systems is called a scale-out architecture. Products designed with this architecture are often classified as distributed. A scale-up solution is a way to increase only the capacity, but not the number of the storage controllers. A scale-out solution is like a set of multiple arrays with a single logical view.

Scale-up storage systems tend to be the least flexible and involve the most planning and longest service interruptions when adding capacity. The cost of the added capacity depends on the price of the devices, which can be relatively high with some storage systems. High availability with scale-up storage is achieved through component redundancy that eliminates single points of failure, and by software upgrades processes that take several steps to complete, allowing system updates to be rolled back, if necessary.

Scale-up and scale-out storage architectures have hardware, facilities, and maintenance costs. In addition, the lifespan of storage products built on these architectures is typically four years or less. This is the reason IT organizations tend to spend such a high percentage of their budget on storage every year.

22

Tiered Storage

Many storage environments support a diversity of needs and use disparate technologies that cause storage sprawl. In a large-scale storage infrastructure, this environment yields a sub-optimal storage design that can be improved only with a focus on data access characteristics analysis and management to provide optimum performance.

The Storage Networking Industry Association (SNIA) standards group defines tiered storage as "storage that is physically partitioned into multiple distinct classes based on price, performance, or other attributes. Data may be dynamically moved among classes in a tiered storage implementation based on access activity or other considerations."

Tiered storage is a mix of high-performing/high-cost storage with low-performing/low-cost storage and placing data based on specific characteristics, such as the performance needs, age, and importance of data availability. In Figure 22-13, you can see the concept and a cost-versus-performance relationship of a tiered storage environment.

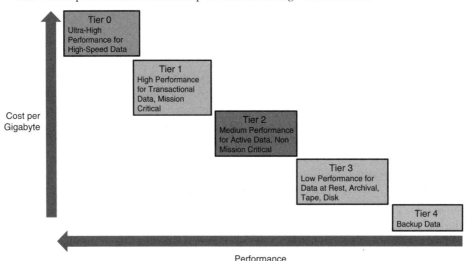

Figure 22-13 *Cost Versus Performance in a Tiered Storage Environment*

Typically, an optimal design keeps the active operational data in Tier 0 and Tier 1 and uses the benefits associated with a tiered storage approach mostly related to cost. By introducing solid-state drive (SSD) storage as Tier 0, you might more efficiently address the highest performance needs while reducing the enterprise-class storage, system footprint, and energy costs. A tiered storage approach can provide the performance you need and save significant costs associated with storage, because lower-tier storage is less expensive. Environmental savings, such as energy, footprint, and cooling reductions, are possible. However, the overall management effort increases when managing storage capacity and storage performance needs across multiple storage classes. Table 22-4 lists the different storage tier levels.

Table 22-4   Comparison of Storage Tier Levels

Tier	Characteristics	Use Case	Connectivity
Tier 0	Solid-state disk SLC/MLC, DRAM, or a mixture Low density—100s of gigabytes to 10s of terabytes 100+K IOPS	High-speed data (currency trading) Data caching Database logs and indexes	SAN (FC, FCoE), PCIe, iSCSI, SAS
Tier 1	Integrated large-scale disk array Centralized controller and cache system Ability to replicate between one or more devices 10+K IOPS Primarily structured data	Transactional data (online retail) Database Transaction processing Mission-critical application	SAN (FC, FCoE)
Tier 2	Higher capacity (100s of terabytes) High-speed drives (15K to 10K RPM drives) Sequential performance Scale-out design Both structured and unstructured data	Active data Application data (e.g., email to ERP) Transformation and transactional data	SAN (FC, FCoE), iSCSI, NAS
Tier 3	Mixture of disk, tape, and software Hierarchical storage manager Transparent to application or end user of data locality Primarily unstructured data Predictable latency between data request to data received	Data at rest Trend analysis Master file storage, collation storage	SAN (FC, FCoE), NAS
Tier 4	Mixture of disk, tape, and software Backup storage product Administrator assistance required for data recall	Backup data Compliance requirements (e.g., courts requesting data)	SAN (FC), server agents

22

SAN Design

SAN design doesn't have to be rocket science. Modern SAN design is about deploying ports and switches in a configuration that provides flexibility and scalability. It is also about making sure the network design and topology look as clean and functional one, two, or five years later as the day they were first deployed. In the traditional FC SAN design, each host and storage device is dual-attached to the network. This is primarily motivated by a desire to achieve 99.999% availability. To achieve 99.999% availability, the network should be built with redundant switches that are not interconnected. The FC network is built on two separate networks (commonly called path A and path B), and each end node (host or storage) is connected to both networks. Some companies take the same approach with their traditional IP/Ethernet networks, but most do not for reasons of cost. Because the traditional FC SAN design doubles the cost of network implementation, many companies are actively seeking alternatives. Some companies are looking to iSCSI and FCoE as the answer, and others are considering single-path FC SANs. Figure 22-14 illustrates a typical dual-path FC-SAN design.

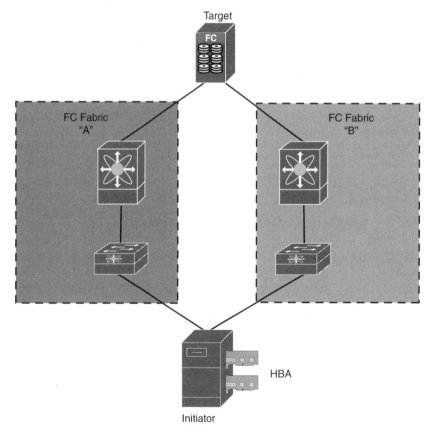

Figure 22-14   *SAN A and SAN B FC Networks*

Infrastructures for data access necessarily include options for redundant server systems. Although server systems might not necessarily be thought of as storage elements, they are clearly key pieces of data-access infrastructures. From a storage I/O perspective, servers are the starting point for most data access. Server filing systems are clearly in the domain of storage. Redundant server systems and filing systems are created through one of two approaches: clustered systems or server farms. Farms are loosely coupled individual systems that have common access to shared data, and clusters are tightly coupled systems that function as a single, fault-tolerant system. Multipathing software depends on having redundant I/O paths between systems and storage. In general, changing an I/O path involves changing the initiator used for I/O transmissions and, by extension, all downstream connections. This includes switches and network cables that are being used to transfer I/O data between a computer and its storage. *Multipathing* establishes two or more SCSI communication connections between a host system and the storage it uses. If one of these communication connections fails, another SCSI communication connection is used in its place. Figure 22-15 portrays two types of multipathing:

- **Active/Active:** Balanced I/O over both paths (implementation specific).
- **Active/Passive:** I/O over the primary path; switches to standby path upon failure.

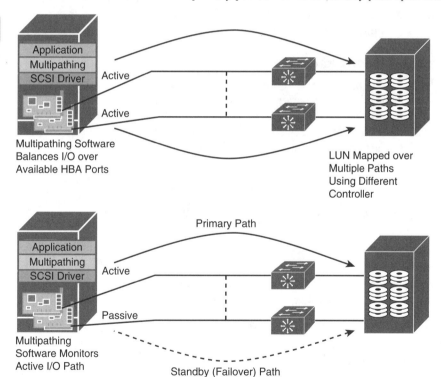

Figure 22-15 *Storage Multipathing Failover*

A single multiport HBA can have two or more ports connecting to the SAN that can be used by multipathing software. However, although multiport HBAs provide path redundancy, most current multipathing implementations use dual HBAs to provide redundancy for the

HBA adapter. Multipathing is not the only automated way to recover from a network problem in a SAN. SAN switches use the Fabric Shortest Path First (FSPF) routing protocol to converge new routes through the network following a change to the network configuration, including link or switch failures.

FSPF is the standard routing protocol used in Fibre Channel fabrics. FSPF automatically calculates the best path between any two devices in a fabric through dynamically computing routes, establishing the shortest and quickest path between any two devices. It also selects an alternative path in the event of failure of the primary path. Although FSPF itself provides for optimal routing between nodes, the Dijkstra algorithm on which it is commonly based has a worst-case running time that is the square of the number of nodes in the fabric.

Multipathing software in a host system can use new network routes that have been created in the SAN by switch-routing algorithms. This depends on switches in the network recognizing a change to the network and completing their route-convergence process prior to the I/O operation timing out in the multipathing software. As long as the new network route allows the storage path's initiator and LUN to communicate, the storage process uses the route. Considering this, it could be advantageous to implement multipathing so that the timeout values for storage paths exceed the times needed to converge new network routes.

SAN Design Considerations

The underlying principles of SAN design are relatively straightforward: plan a network topology that can handle the number of ports necessary now and into the future; design a network topology with a given end-to-end performance and throughput level in mind, taking into account any physical requirements of a design; and provide the necessary connectivity with remote data centers to handle the business requirements of business continuity and disaster recovery.

These underlying principles fall into five general categories:

- **Port density and topology requirements:** Number of ports required now and in the future
- **Device performance and oversubscription ratios:** Determination of what is acceptable and what is unavoidable
- **Traffic management:** Preferential routing or resource allocation
- **Fault isolation:** Consolidation while maintaining isolation
- **Control plane scalability:** Reduced routing complexity

Port Density and Topology Requirements

The single most important factor in determining the most suitable SAN design is determining the number of end ports for now and over the anticipated lifespan of the design. As an example, the design for a SAN that will handle a network with 100 end ports will be very different from the design for a SAN that has to handle a network with 1500 end ports.

From a design standpoint, it is typically better to overestimate the port count requirements than to underestimate them. Designing for a 1500-port SAN does not necessarily imply that 1500 ports need to be purchased initially, or even at all. It is about helping ensure that a design remains functional if that number of ports is attained, rather than later finding the design is unworkable. As a minimum, the lifespan for any design should encompass the depreciation schedule for equipment, typically three years or more. Preferably, a design should last longer than this, because redesigning and reengineering a network topology become both more time-consuming and more difficult as the number of devices on a SAN expands.

Where existing SAN infrastructure is present, determining the approximate port count requirements is not difficult. You can use the current number of end-port devices and the increase in number of devices during the previous 6, 12, and 18 months as rough guidelines for the projected growth in number of end-port devices in the future. Figure 22-16 portrays the SAN major design factors.

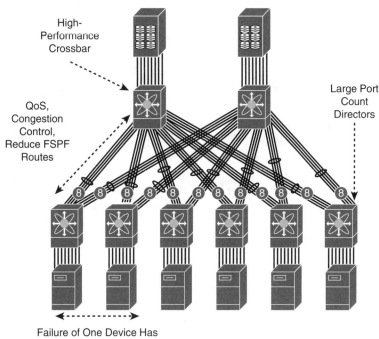

Figure 22-16 *SAN Major Design Factors*

For new environments, it is more difficult to determine future port-count growth requirements, but once again, it is not difficult to plan based on an estimate of the immediate server connectivity requirements, coupled with an estimated growth rate of 30% per year.

A design should also consider physical space requirements. For example, is the data center all on one floor? Is it all in one building? Is there a desire to use lower-cost connectivity options such as iSCSI for servers with minimal I/O requirements? Do you want to use IP SAN extension for disaster recovery connectivity? Any design should also consider increases in future port speeds, protocols, and densities. Although it is difficult to predict future requirements and capabilities, unused module slots in switches that have a proven investment protection record open the possibility to future expansion.

Device Performance and Oversubscription Ratios

Oversubscription, in a SAN switching environment, is the practice of connecting multiple devices to the same switch port to optimize switch use. SAN switch ports are rarely run at their maximum speed for a prolonged period, and multiple slower devices may fan in to a single port to take advantage of unused capacity. Oversubscription is a necessity of any networked infrastructure and directly relates to the major benefit of a network—to share common resources among numerous clients. The higher the rate of oversubscription, the lower the cost of the underlying network infrastructure and shared resources. Because storage subsystem I/O resources are not commonly consumed at 100% all the time by a single client, a fan-out ratio of storage subsystem ports can be achieved based on the I/O demands of various applications and server platforms. Most major disk subsystem vendors provide guidelines as to the recommended fan-out ratio of subsystem client-side ports to server connections. These recommendations are often in the range of 7:1 to 15:1.

> **Note**   A *fan-out ratio* is the relationship in quantity between a single port on a storage device and the number of servers that are attached to it. It is important to know the fan-out ratio in a storage area network (SAN) design so that each server gets optimal access to storage resources. When the fan-out ratio is high and the storage array becomes overloaded, application performance will be affected negatively. Too low a fan-out ratio, however, results in an uneconomic use of storage. Key factors in deciding the optimum fan-out ratio are server host bus adapter (HBA) queue depth, storage device input/output (IOPS), and port throughput. Fan-in is how many storage ports can be served from a single host channel.

When all the performance characteristics of the SAN infrastructure and the servers and storage devices are being considered, two oversubscription metrics must be managed: IOPS and the network bandwidth capacity of the SAN. The two metrics are closely related, although they pertain to different elements of the SAN. IOPS performance relates only to the servers and storage devices and their ability to handle high numbers of I/O operations, whereas bandwidth capacity relates to all devices in the SAN, including the SAN infrastructure itself. On the server side, the required bandwidth is strictly derived from the I/O load, which is derived from factors including I/O size, percentage of reads versus writes, CPU capacity, application I/O requests, and I/O service time from the target device. On the storage side, the supported bandwidth is again strictly derived from the IOPS capacity of the disk subsystem itself, including the system architecture, cache, disk controllers, and actual disks. Figure 22-17 portrays the major SAN oversubscription factors.

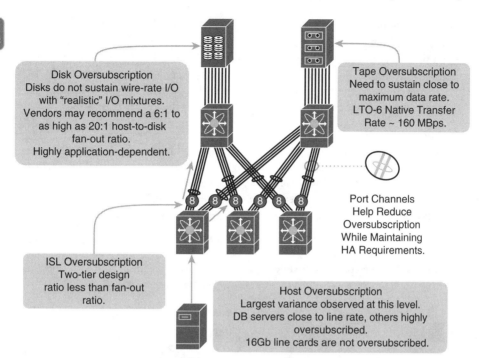

Disk Oversubscription
Disks do not sustain wire-rate I/O with "realistic" I/O mixtures. Vendors may recommend a 6:1 to as high as 20:1 host-to-disk fan-out ratio. Highly application-dependent.

Tape Oversubscription
Need to sustain close to maximum data rate. LTO-6 Native Transfer Rate ~ 160 MBps.

Port Channels Help Reduce Oversubscription While Maintaining HA Requirements.

ISL Oversubscription
Two-tier design ratio less than fan-out ratio.

Host Oversubscription
Largest variance observed at this level. DB servers close to line rate, others highly oversubscribed. 16Gb line cards are not oversubscribed.

Figure 22-17 *SAN Oversubscription Design Considerations*

In most cases, neither application server host bus adapters (HBAs) nor disk subsystem client-side controllers are able to handle full wire-rate sustained bandwidth. Although ideal scenario tests can be contrived using larger I/Os, large CPUs, and sequential I/O operations to show wire-rate performance, this is far from a practical real-world implementation. In more common scenarios, I/O composition, server-side resources, and application I/O patterns do not result in sustained full-bandwidth utilization. Because of this fact, oversubscription can be safely factored into SAN design. However, you must account for burst I/O traffic, which might temporarily require high-rate I/O service. The general principle in optimizing design oversubscription is to group applications or servers that burst high I/O rates at different time slots within the daily production cycle. This grouping can examine either complementary application I/O profiles or careful scheduling of I/O-intensive activities such as backups and batch jobs. In this case, peak time I/O traffic contention is minimized, and the SAN design oversubscription has little effect on I/O contention.

Best practice would be to build a SAN design using a topology that derives a relatively conservative oversubscription ratio (for example, 8:1) coupled with monitoring of the traffic on the switch ports connected to storage arrays and inter-switch links (ISLs) to see if bandwidth is a limiting factor. If bandwidth is not the limiting factor, application server performance is acceptable, and application performance can be monitored closely, the oversubscription ratio can be increased gradually to a level that both maximizes performance and minimizes cost.

Traffic Management

Are there any differing performance requirements for different application servers? Should bandwidth be reserved or preference be given to traffic in the case of congestion? Given two alternate traffic paths between data centers with differing distances, should traffic use one path in preference to the other? For some SAN designs, it makes sense to implement traffic management policies that influence traffic flow and relative traffic priorities.

Fault Isolation

Consolidating multiple areas of storage into a single physical fabric both increases storage utilization and reduces the administrative overhead associated with centralized storage management. The major drawback is that faults are no longer isolated within individual storage areas. Many organizations would like to consolidate their storage infrastructure into a single physical fabric, but both technical and business challenges make this difficult.

Technology such as virtual SANs (VSANs, see Figure 22-18) enables this consolidation while increasing the security and stability of Fibre Channel fabrics by logically isolating devices that are physically connected to the same set of switches. Faults within one fabric are contained within a single fabric (VSAN) and are not propagated to other fabrics.

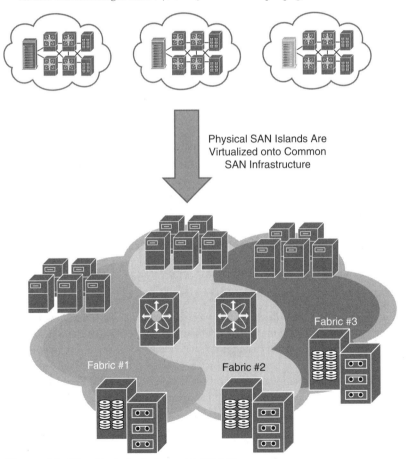

Physical SAN Islands Are Virtualized onto Common SAN Infrastructure

Fabric #3

Fabric #1

Fabric #2

Figure 22-18 *Fault Isolation with VSANs*

Control Plane Scalability

A SAN switch can be logically divided into two parts: a data plane, which handles the forwarding of data frames within the SAN; and a control plane, which handles switch management functions, routing protocols, Fibre Channel frames destined for the switch itself, such as Fabric Shortest Path First (FSPF), routing updates and keep-alives, name server and domain-controller queries, and other Fibre Channel fabric services.

Control plane scalability is the primary reason storage vendors set limits on the number of switches and devices they have certified and qualified for operation in a single fabric. Because the control plane is critical to network operations, any service disruption to the control plane can result in business impacting network outages. Control plane service disruptions (perpetrated either inadvertently or maliciously) are possible, typically through a high rate of traffic destined to the switch itself. These result in excessive CPU utilization and/or deprive the switch of CPU resources for normal processing. Control plane CPU deprivation can also occur when there is insufficient control plane CPU relative to the size of the network topology and a network-wide event (for example, loss of a major switch or significant change in topology) occurs.

FSPF is the standard routing protocol used in Fibre Channel fabrics. Although FSPF itself provides for optimal routing between nodes, the Dijkstra algorithm on which it is commonly based has a worst-case running time that is the square of the number of nodes in the fabric. That is, doubling the number of devices in a SAN can result in a quadrupling of the CPU processing required to maintain that routing.

A goal of SAN design should be to try to minimize the processing required with a given SAN topology. Attention should be paid to the CPU and memory resources available for control plane functionality and to port aggregation features such as Cisco Port Channels, which provide all the benefits of multiple parallel ISLs between switches (higher throughput and resiliency) but only appear in the topology as a single logical link rather than multiple parallel links.

22

SAN Topologies

The Fibre Channel standard defines three different topologies: fabric, arbitrated loop, and point-to-point (see Figure 22-19). Point-to-point defines a bidirectional connection between two devices. Arbitrated loop defines a unidirectional ring in which only two devices can ever exchange data with one another at any one time. Finally, fabric defines a network in which several devices can exchange data simultaneously at full bandwidth. A fabric basically requires one or more Fibre Channel switches connected together to form a control center between the end devices. Furthermore, the standard permits the connection of one or more arbitrated loops to a fabric. The fabric topology is the most frequently used of all topologies, and this is why more emphasis is placed upon the fabric topology than on the two other topologies in this chapter.

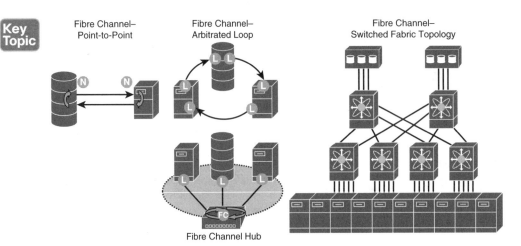

Figure 22-19 *Fibre Channel Topologies*

Common to all topologies is that devices (servers, storage devices, and switches) must be equipped with one or more Fibre Channel ports. In servers, the port is generally realized by means of so-called HBAs. A port always consists of two channels: one input and one output channel.

The connection between two ports is called a link. In the point-to-point topology and in the fabric topology, the links are always bidirectional: In this case, the input channel and the output channel of the two ports involved in the link are connected by a cross, so that every output channel is connected to an input channel. On the other hand, the links of the arbitrated loop topology are unidirectional: Each output channel is connected to the input channel of the next port until the circle is closed. The cabling of an arbitrated loop can be simplified with the aid of a hub. In this configuration, the end devices are bidirectionally connected to the hub; the wiring within the hub ensures that the unidirectional data flow within the arbitrated loop is maintained. Bandwidth is shared equally among all connected devices, of which there is a limit of 126. The more active devices connected, the less available bandwidth will be available. Switched fabrics have a theoretical address support for over 16 million connections, compared to arbitrated-loop at 126, but that exceeds the practical and physical limitation of the switches that make up a fabric. A switched fabric topology allows dynamic interconnections between nodes through ports connected to a fabric. It is possible for any port in a node to communicate with any port in another node connected to the same fabric. Adding a new device increases aggregate bandwidth; therefore, any port can communicate with another cut-through or store-and-forward switching. Also, switched FC fabrics are aware of arbitrated loop devices when attached.

Like Ethernet, FC switches can be interconnected in any manner. Unlike Ethernet, there is a limit to the number of FC switches that can be interconnected. Address space constraints limit FC-SANs to a maximum of 239 switches. Cisco's virtual SAN (VSAN) technology increases the number of switches that can be physically interconnected by reusing the entire FC address space within each VSAN. FC switches employ a routing protocol called Fabric Shortest Path First (FSPF) based on a link-state algorithm. FSPF reduces all physical topologies to a logical tree topology. Most FC SANs are deployed in one of two designs commonly known as the two-tier topology (core-edge-only) and three-tier topology (edge-core-edge) designs. The core-only is a star topology. Host-to-storage FC connections are generally redundant. However, single host-to-storage FC connections are common in cluster and grid environments because host-based failover mechanisms are inherent to such environments. In both the core-only and core-edge designs, the redundant paths are usually not interconnected. The edge switches in the core-edge design may be connected to both core switches, but this creates one physical network and compromises resilience against network-wide disruptions (for example, FSPF convergence). The complexity and the size of the FC SANs increase when the number of connections increases. Figure 22-20 illustrates the typical FC SAN topologies.

The Top-of-Rack (ToR) and End-of-Row (EoR) designs represent how access switches and servers are connected to each other. Both have a direct impact over a major part of the entire data center cabling system. ToR designs are based on intra-rack cabling between servers and smaller switches, which can be installed on the same racks as the servers. Although these designs reduce the amount of cabling and optimize the space used by network equipment, they offer the storage team the challenge to manage a higher number of devices. On the other hand, EoR designs are based on inter-rack cabling between servers and high-density switches installed on the same row as the server racks. EoR designs reduce the number of network devices and optimize port utilization on the network devices. But EoR flexibility taxes data centers with a great quantity of horizontal cabling running under the raised floor. The best design choice leans on the number of servers per rack, the data rate for the connections, the budget, and the operational complexity.

Typically, in a SAN design, the number of end devices determines the number of fabric logins needed. The increase in blade server deployments and the consolidation of servers through the use of server virtualization technologies affect the design of the network. With the use of features such as N-Port ID Virtualization (NPIV) and Cisco N-Port Virtualization (NPV), the number of fabric logins needed has increased even more. The proliferation of NPIV-capable end devices such as host bus adaptors (HBAs) and Cisco NPV-mode switches makes the number of fabric logins needed on a per-port, per-line-card, per-switch, and per-physical-fabric basis a critical consideration. The fabric login limits determine the design of the current SAN as well as its potential for future growth. The total number of hosts and NPV switches determines the number of fabric logins required on the core switch.

22

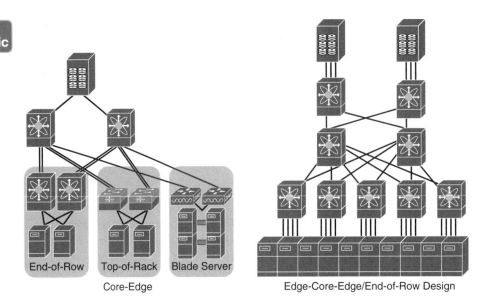

Figure 22-20   *Sample FC SAN Topologies*

SAN designs that can be built using a single physical switch are commonly referred to as collapsed core designs (see Figure 22-21). This terminology refers to the fact that a design is conceptually a core/edge design, making use of core ports (non-oversubscribed) and edge ports (oversubscribed), but that it has been collapsed into a single physical switch. Traditionally, a collapsed core design on Cisco MDS 9000 family switches would utilize both non-oversubscribed (storage) and oversubscribed (host-optimized) line cards.

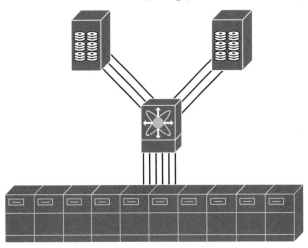

Figure 22-21   *Sample Collapsed Core FC SAN Design*

SAN designs should always use two isolated fabrics for high availability, with both hosts and storage connecting to both fabrics. Multipathing software should be deployed on the hosts to manage connectivity between the host and storage so that I/O uses both paths, and there is nondisruptive failover between fabrics in the event of a problem in one fabric. Fabric isolation can be achieved using either VSANs or dual physical switches. Both provide separation of fabric services, although it could be argued that multiple physical fabrics provide increased physical protection (for example, protection against a sprinkler head failing above a switch) and protection against equipment failure.

Fibre Channel

Fibre Channel (FC) is the predominant architecture upon which SAN implementations are built. Fibre Channel is a technology standard that allows data to be transferred at extremely high speeds. Current implementations support data transfers at up to 16 Gbps or even more. Many standards bodies, technical associations, vendors, and industry-wide consortiums accredit the Fibre Channel standard. There are many products on the market that take advantage of the high-speed and high-availability characteristics of the Fibre Channel architecture. Fibre Channel was developed through industry cooperation, unlike Small Computer System Interface (SCSI), which was developed by a vendor and submitted for standardization afterward.

> **Note**   Is it Fibre or Fiber? Fibre Channel was originally designed to support fiber-optic cabling only. When copper support was added, the committee decided to keep the name in principle, but to use the UK English spelling (Fibre) when referring to the standard. The U.S. English spelling (Fiber) is retained when referring generically to fiber optics and cabling.

Fibre Channel is an open, technical standard for networking that incorporates the channel transport characteristics of an I/O bus, with the flexible connectivity and distance characteristics of a traditional network. Because of its channel-like qualities, hosts and applications see storage devices that are attached to the SAN as though they are locally attached storage. Because of its network characteristics, it can support multiple protocols and a broad range of devices, and it can be managed as a network.

Fibre Channel is structured by a lengthy list of standards. Figure 22-22 portrays just few of them. Detailed information on all FC Standards can be downloaded from T11 at www.t11.org.

22

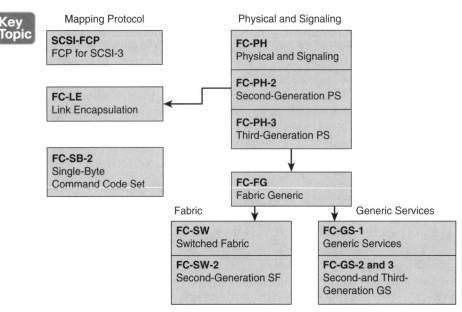

Figure 22-22   *Fibre Channel Standards*

The Fibre Channel protocol stack is subdivided into five layers (see Figure 22-10 in the "Block-Level Protocols" section). The lower four layers, FC-0 to FC-3, define the fundamental communication techniques; that is, the physical levels, the transmission, and the addressing. The upper layer, FC-4, defines how application protocols (upper-layer protocols, ULPs) are mapped on the underlying Fibre Channel network. The use of the various ULPs decides, for example, whether a real Fibre Channel network is used as an IP network, a Fibre Channel SAN (as a storage network), or both at the same time. The link services and fabric services are located quasi-adjacent to the Fibre Channel protocol stack. These services will be required to administer and operate a Fibre Channel network.

FC-0: Physical Interface

FC-0 defines the physical transmission medium (cable, plug) and specifies which physical signals are used to transmit the bits 0 and 1. In contrast to the SCSI bus, in which each bit has its own data line plus additional control lines, Fibre Channel transmits the bits sequentially via a single line. Fibre Channel can use either optical fiber (for distance) or copper cable links (for short distance at low cost). Fiber-optic cables have a major advantage in noise immunity. Overall, optical fibers provide a high-performance transmission medium, which was refined and proven over many years.

Mixing fiber optical and copper components in the same environment is supported, although not all products provide that flexibility. Product flexibility needs to be considered when you plan a SAN. Copper cables tend to be used for short distances, up to 30 meters (98 feet), and can be identified by their DB-9 nine-pin connector. Normally, fiber optic cabling is referred to by mode or the frequencies of light waves that are carried by a particular cable type:

■ **Multimode fiber:** For shorter distances. Multimode cabling is used with shortwave laser light and has either a 50-micron or a 62.5-micron core with a cladding of 125 micron.

The 50-micron or 562.5-micron diameter is sufficiently large for injected light waves to be reflected off the core interior. Multimode fiber (MMF) allows more than one mode of light. Common multimode core sizes are 50 micron and 62.5 micron. MMF fiber is better suited for shorter distance applications. Where costly electronics are heavily concentrated, the primary cost of the system does not lie with the cable. In such a case, MMF is more economical because it can be used with inexpensive connectors and laser devices, which reduces the total system cost.

■ **Single-mode fiber:** For longer distances. Single-mode fiber (SMF) allows only one pathway, or mode, of light to travel within the fiber. The core size is typically 8.3 micron. SMFs are used in applications where low signal loss and high data rates are required. An example of this type of application is on long spans between two system or network devices, where repeater and amplifier spacing needs to be maximized.

Fibre Channel architecture supports both short wave and long wave optical transmitter technologies in the following ways:

■ **Short wave laser:** This technology uses a wavelength of 780 nanometers and is compatible only with MMF.

■ **Long wave laser:** This technology uses a wavelength of 1300 nanometers. It is compatible with both SMF and MMF.

To connect one optical device to another, some form of fiber-optic link is required. If the distance is short, a standard fiber cable suffices. Over a slightly longer distance—for example, from one building to the next—a fiber link might need to be laid. This fiber might need to be laid underground or through a conduit, but it is not as simple as connecting two switches together in a single rack. If the two units that need to be connected are in different cities, the problem is much larger. Larger, in this case, is typically associated with more expensive. Because most businesses are not in the business of laying cable, they lease fiber-optic cables to meet their needs. When a company leases equipment, the fiber-optic cable that they lease is known as *dark fiber*, which generically refers to a long, dedicated fiber-optic link that can be used without the need for any additional equipment.

22

FC-1: Encode/Decode

FC-1 defines how data is encoded before it is transmitted via a Fibre Channel cable (8b/10b data transmission code scheme patented by IBM). FC-1 also describes certain transmission words (ordered sets) that are required for the administration of a Fibre Channel connection (link control protocol).

Encoding and Decoding

To transfer data over a high-speed serial interface, the data is encoded before transmission and decoded upon reception. The encoding process ensures that sufficient clock information is present in the serial data stream. This information allows the receiver to synchronize to the embedded clock information and successfully recover the data at the required error rate. This 8b/10b encoding finds errors that a parity check cannot. A parity check does not find the even-numbered bit errors, only the odd numbers. The 8b/10b encoding logic finds almost all errors. The 8b/10b encoding process converts each 8-bit byte into two possible 10-bit characters. This scheme is called 8b/10b encoding because it refers to the number of data bits input to the encoder and the number of bits output from the encoder.

The information sent on a link consists of transmission words containing four transmission characters each. There are two categories of transmission words: data words and ordered sets. Data words occur between the start-of-frame (SOF) and end-of-frame (EOF) delimiters. Ordered sets delimit frame boundaries and occur outside of frames. Ordered sets begin with a special transmission character (K28.5), which is outside the normal data space. A transmission word consists of four continuous transmission characters treated as a unit. They are 40 bits long, aligned on a word boundary.

The format of the 8b/10b character is of the format D/Kxx.y:

- **D or K**: D = data, K = special character
- **"xx"**: Decimal value of the five least significant bits
- **"y"**: Decimal value of the three most significant bits

Communications of 10 and 16 Gbps use 64/66b encoding. Sixty-four bits of data are transmitted as a 66-bit entity. The 66-bit entity is made by prefixing one of two possible 2-bit preambles to the 64 bits to be transmitted. If the preamble is 01, the 64 bits are entirely data. If the preamble is 10, an 8-bit type field follows, plus 56 bits of control information and data. The preambles 00 and 11 are not used, and they generate an error if seen. The use of the 01 and 10 preambles guarantees a bit transmission every 66 bits, which means that a continuous stream of zeros or ones cannot be valid data. It also allows easier clock and timer synchronization because a transmission must be seen every 66 bits. The overhead of the 64B/66B encoding is considerably less than the more common 8b/10b encoding scheme.

Ordered Sets

Fibre Channel uses a command syntax, which is known as an ordered set, to move the data across the network. The ordered sets are 4-byte transmission words that contain data and special characters, which have a special meaning. Ordered sets provide the availability to obtain bit and word synchronization, which also establishes word boundary alignment. An ordered set always begins with the special character K28.5. Three major types of ordered sets are defined by the signaling protocol.

The frame delimiters, the start-of-frame (SOF) and end-of-frame (EOF) ordered sets, establish the boundaries of a frame. They immediately precede or follow the contents of a frame. There are 11 types of SOF and eight types of EOF delimiters that are defined for the fabric and N_Port sequence control.

The two primitive signals, idle and receiver ready (R_RDY), are ordered sets that are designated by the standard to have a special meaning. An idle is a primitive signal that is transmitted on the link to indicate that an operational port facility is ready for frame transmission and reception. The R_RDY primitive signal indicates that the interface buffer is available for receiving further frames.

A primitive sequence is an ordered set that is transmitted and repeated continuously to indicate specific conditions within a port. Or the set might indicate conditions that are encountered by the receiver logic of a port. When a primitive sequence is received and recognized, a corresponding primitive sequence or idle is transmitted in response. Recognition of a primitive sequence requires consecutive detection of three instances of the same ordered set. The primitive sequences that are supported by the standard are illustrated in Table 22-5.

Table 22-5   Fibre Channel Primitive Sequences

Offline state (OLS)	A port to indicate one of the following conditions transmits the offline primitive sequence: The port is beginning the link initialization protocol, the port received and recognized the NOS protocol, or the port is entering the offline status.
Not operational (NOS)	A port in a point-to-point or fabric environment to indicate that the transmitting port detected a link failure transmits the "not operational" primitive sequence. Or, the NOS might indicate an offline condition, waiting for the OLS sequence to be received.
Link reset (LR)	The link reset primitive sequence is used to initiate a link reset.
Link reset response (LRR)	A port to indicate that it recognizes a link reset sequence and performed the appropriate link reset transmits to the link reset response.

FC-2: Framing Protocol

FC-2 is the most comprehensive layer in the Fibre Channel protocol stack. It determines how larger data units (for example, a file) are transmitted via the Fibre Channel network. It regulates the flow control that ensures that the transmitter sends the data only at a speed that the receiver can process it. And it defines various service classes that are tailored to the requirements of various applications:

- Multiple exchanges are initiated between initiators (hosts) and targets (disks).
- Each exchange consists of one or more bidirectional sequences (see Figure 22-23).
- Each sequence consists of one or more frames.
- For the SCSI3 ULP, each exchange maps to a SCSI command.

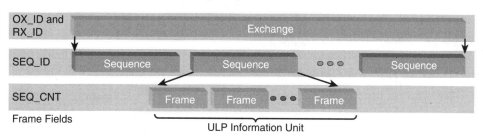

Figure 22-23   *Fibre Channel FC-2 Hierarchy*

A sequence is a larger data unit that is transferred from a transmitter to a receiver. Only one sequence can be transferred after another within an exchange. FC-2 guarantees that sequences are delivered to the receiver in the same order they were sent from the transmitter—hence the name "sequence." Furthermore, sequences are only delivered to the next protocol layer up when all frames of the sequence have arrived at the receiver. A sequence could be representing an individual database transaction.

A Fibre Channel network transmits control frames and data frames. Control frames contain no useful data; they signal events such as the successful delivery of a data frame. Data frames transmit up to 2112 bytes of useful data. Larger sequences, therefore, have to be broken down into several frames.

A Fibre Channel frame consists of a header, useful data (payload), and a Cyclic Redundancy Checksum (CRC), as shown in Figure 22-24. The frame is bracketed by a start-of-frame (SOF) delimiter and an end-of-frame (EOF) delimiter. Finally, six filling words must be transmitted by means of a link between two frames. In contrast to Ethernet and TCP/IP, Fibre Channel is an integrated whole: The layers of the Fibre Channel protocol stack are so well harmonized with one another that the ratio of payload-to-protocol overhead is very efficient, at up to 98%. The CRC checking procedure is designed to recognize all transmission errors if the underlying medium does not exceed the specified error rate of 10^{-12}.

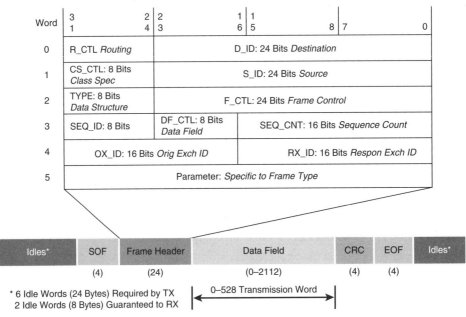

Figure 22-24 *Fibre Channel Frame Format*

Fibre Channel Service Classes

The Fibre Channel standard defines six service classes for exchange of data between end devices. Three of these defined classes (Class 1, Class 2, and Class 3) are realized in products available on the market, with hardly any products providing the connection-oriented Class 1. Almost all new Fibre Channel products (HBAs, switches, storage devices) support the service classes Class 2 and Class 3, which realize a packet-oriented service (datagram service). In addition, Class F serves for the data exchange between the switches within a fabric. Class 1 defines a connection-oriented communication connection between two node ports: a Class 1 connection is opened before the transmission of frames. Class 2 and Class 3, on the other hand, are packet-oriented services: no dedicated connection is built up. Instead, the frames are individually routed through the Fibre Channel network. A port can thus maintain several connections at the same time. Several Class 2 and Class 3 connections can thus share the bandwidth. Class 2 uses end-to-end flow control and link flow control. In Class 2, the receiver acknowledges each received frame. Class 3 achieves less than Class 2: frames are not acknowledged. This means that only link flow control takes place, not end-to-end flow control. In addition, the higher protocol layers must notice for themselves whether a frame has been lost. In Fibre Channel SAN implementations, the end devices themselves negotiate whether they communicate by Class 2 or Class 3. Table 22-6 lists the different Fibre Channel classes of service.

Table 22-6   Fibre Channel Classes of Service

Class Type	Delivery	Type of Service
Class 1	Acknowledged	Connection oriented, full bandwidth
Class 2	Acknowledged	Connectionless service
Class 3	Unacknowledged	Connectionless service
Class 4	Acknowledged	Connection-oriented, partial bandwidth service
Class 6	Acknowledged	Connection-oriented, full bandwidth, multicast service
Class F	Acknowledged	Connectionless service

Fibre Channel Flow Control

Flow control ensures that the transmitter sends data only at a speed that the receiver can receive it. Fibre Channel uses credit model. Each credit represents the capacity of the receiver to receive a Fibre Channel frame. If the receiver awards the transmitter a credit of 3, the transmitter may only send the receiver three frames. The transmitter may not send further frames until the receiver has acknowledged the receipt of at least some of the transmitted frames.

FC-2 defines two mechanisms for flow control: end-to-end flow control and link flow control (see Figure 22-25). In end-to-end flow control, two end devices negotiate the end-to-end credit before the exchange of data. The end-to-end flow control is realized on the HBA cards of the end devices. The link flow control takes place at each physical connection. Two communicating ports negotiating the buffer-to-buffer credits achieve this. This means that the link flow control also takes place at the Fibre Channel switches. Buffer-to-buffer credits are used in Class 2 and Class 3 services between a node and a switch. Initial credit levels are established with the fabric at login and then replenished upon receipt of receiver-ready (R_RDYY) from the target. The sender decrements one BB_Credit for each frame sent and increments one for each R_RDY received. BB_Credits are the more practical application and are very important for switches that are communicating across an extension (E_Port) because of the inherent delays present with transport over LAN/WAN/MAN.

End-to-end credits are used in Class 1 and Class 2 services between two end nodes, regardless of the number of switches in the network. After the initial credit level is set, the sender decrements one EE_Credit for each frame sent and increments one when an acknowledgement (ACK) is received.

22

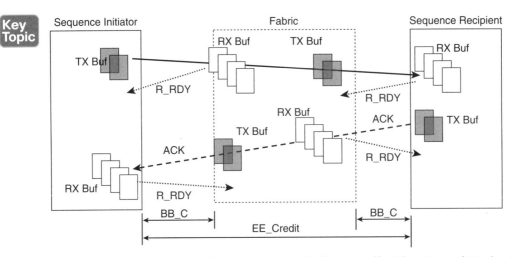

Figure 22-25   *Fibre Channel End-to-End and Buffer-to-Buffer Flow Control Mechanism*

FC flow control is critical to the efficiency of the SAN fabric. Flow control management occurs between two connected Fibre Channel ports to prevent a target device from being overwhelmed with frames from the initiator device. Buffer-to-buffer credits (BB_Credit) are negotiated between each device in an FC fabric; no concept of end-to-end buffering exists. One buffer is used per FC frame, regardless of its frame size; a small FC frame uses the same buffer as a large FC frame. FC frames are buffered and queued in intermediate switches. Hop-by-hop traffic flow is paced by return of Receiver Ready (R_RDY) frames and can only transmit up to the number of BB_Credits before traffic is throttled. Figure 22-26 portrays the Fibre Channel Frame buffering on an FC switched fabric. As distance increases or frame size decreases, the number of available BB_Credits required increases as well. Insufficient BB_Credits will throttle performance—no data will be transmitted until R_RDY is returned.

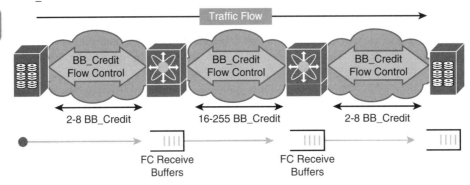

Figure 22-26   *Fibre Channel Frame Buffering*

The optimal buffer credit value can be calculated by determining the transmit time per FC frame and dividing that into the total round-trip time per frame. This helps keep the fiber-optic link full, and without running out of BB_Credits. The speed of light over a fiber-optic link is ~ 5 μsec per km. A Fibre Channel frame size is ~2 Kb (2148 bytes maximum). For a

10km link, the time it takes for a frame to travel from a sender to receiver and response to the sender is 100 μsec. (Speed of light over fiber-optic links ~5 μsec/km, 50 μsec x 2 =100 μsec). If the sender waits for a response before sending the next frame, the maximum number of frames in a second is 10,000 (1sec / 0. 0001 = 10,000). This implies that the effective data rate is ~ 20 MBps (2,000 bytes * 10,000 frames per sec). The transmit time for 2000m characters (2KB frame) is approximately 20 μsec (2000 /1 Gbps or 100 MBps FC data rate). If the round-trip time is 100 μsec, then BB_Credit >= 5 (100 μsec / 2 μsec =5). Table 22-7 illustrates the required BB_Credits for a specific FC frame size with specific link speeds.

Table 22-7   Fibre Channel BB_Credits

Frame Size	1 Gbps	2 Gbps	4 Gbps	8 Gbps	10 Gbps	16 Gbps
512 bytes	2 BB/km	4 BB/km	8 BB/km	16 BB/km	24 BB/km	32 BB/km
1024 bytes	1 BB/km	2 BB/km	4 BB/km	8 BB/km	12 BB/km	16 BB/km
2112 bytes	.5 BB/km	1 BB/km	2 BB/km	4 BB/km	6 BB/km	8 BB/km

FC-3: Common Services

FC-3 has been in its conceptual phase since 1988; in currently available products, FC-3 is empty. The following functions are being discussed for FC-3:

- Striping manages several paths between multiport end devices. Striping could distribute the frames of an exchange over several ports and thus increase the throughput between the two devices.

- Multipathing combines several paths between two multiport end devices to form a logical path group. Failure or overloading of a path can be hidden from the higher protocol layers.

- Compressing and encryption of the data to be transmitted preferably realized in the hardware on the HBA.

Fibre Channel Addressing

Fibre Channel uses World Wide Names (WWNs) and Fibre Channel IDs (FCIDs). WWNs are unique identifiers that are hardcoded into Fibre Channel devices. FCIDs are dynamically acquired addresses that are routable in a switch fabric. Fibre Channel ports are intelligent interface points on the Fibre Channel SAN. They are found embedded in various devices, such as an I/O adapter, array or tape controller, and switched fabric. Each Fibre Channel port has at least one WWN. Vendors buy blocks of WWNs from the IEEE and allocate them to devices in the factory.

WWNs are important for enabling Cisco Fabric Services because they have these characteristics: They are guaranteed to be globally unique and are permanently associated with devices.

These characteristics ensure that the fabric can reliably identify and locate devices. This capability is an important consideration for Cisco Fabric Services. When a management service or application needs to quickly locate a specific device, the following occurs:

1. The service or application queries the switch name server service with the WWN of the target device.

2. The name server looks up and returns the current port address that is associated with the target WWN.

3. The service or application communicates with the target device, using the port address.

The two types of WWNs are node WWNs (nWWNs) and port WWNs (pWWNs):

■ The nWWNs uniquely identify devices. Every HBA, array controller, switch, gateway, and Fibre Channel disk drive has a single unique nWWN.

■ The pWWNs uniquely identify each port in a device. A dual-ported HBA has three WWNs: one nWWN and one pWWN for each port.

The nWWNs and pWWNs are both needed because devices can have multiple ports. On a single-port device, the nWWN and pWWN may be the same. On multiport devices, the pWWN is used to uniquely identify each port. Ports must be uniquely identifiable because each port participates in a unique data path. The nWWNs are required because the node itself must sometimes be uniquely identified. For example, path failover and multiplexing software can detect redundant paths to a device by observing that the same nWWN is associated with multiple pWWNs. Figure 22-27 portrays Fibre Channel addressing on an FC fabric.

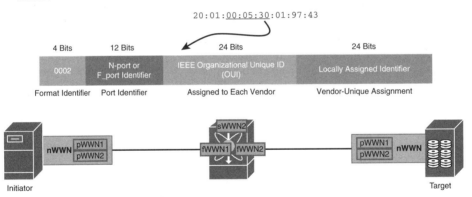

Figure 22-27 *Fibre Channel Naming on FC Fabric*

The Fibre Channel point-to-point topology uses a 1-bit addressing scheme. One port assigns itself an address of 0x000000 and then assigns the other port an address of 0x000001. Figure 22-28 portrays FCID addressing.

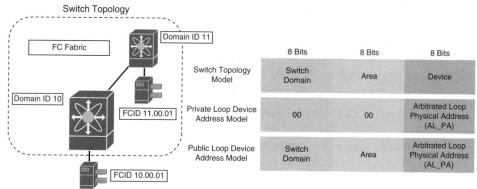

Figure 22-28 *FC ID Addressing*

The FC-AL topology uses an 8-bit addressing scheme:

- The arbitrated loop physical address (AL-PA) is an 8-bit address, which provides 256 potential addresses. However, only a subset of 127 addresses is available because of the 8B/10B encoding requirements.
- One address is reserved for an FL port, so 126 addresses are available for nodes.
- Addresses are cooperatively chosen during loop initialization.

Switched Fabric Address Space

The 24-bit Fibre Channel address consists of three 8-bit elements:

- The domain ID is used to define a switch. Each switch receives a unique domain ID.
- The area ID is used to identify groups of ports within a domain. Areas can be used to group ports within a switch. Areas are also used to uniquely identify fabric-attached arbitrated loops. Each fabric-attached loop receives a unique area ID.

Although the domain ID is an 8-bit field, only 239 domains are available to the fabric:

- Domains 01 through EF are available.
- Domains 00 and F0 through FF are reserved for use by switch services.

Each switch must have a unique domain ID, so there can be no more than 239 switches in a fabric. In practice, the number of switches in a fabric is far smaller because of storage-vendor qualifications.

Fibre Channel Link Services

Link services provide a number of architected functions that are available to the users of the Fibre Channel port. There are three types of link services defined, depending upon the type of function provided and whether the frame contains a payload. They are basic link services, extended link services, and FC-4 link services (generic services).

Basic link service commands support low-level functions such as aborting a sequence (ABTS) and passing control bit information. Extended link services (ELS) are performed in a single exchange. Most of the ELSs are performed as a two-sequence exchange: a request from the originator and a response from the responder. ELS service requests are not permitted prior to a port login except the fabric login. Following are ELS command examples: N_Port Login (PLOGI), F_Port Login (FLOGI), Logout (LOGO), Process Login (PRLI), Process Logout (PRLO), State Change Notification (SCN), Registered State Change Notification (RSCN), State Change Registration (SCR), and Loop Initialize (LINIT).

Generic services include the following: Directory Service, Management Services, Alias Services, Time Services, and Key Distribution Services. FC-CT (Fibre Channel Common Transport) protocol is used as a transport media for these services. FC-GS shares a Common Transport (CT) at the FC-4 level and the CT provides access to the services. Port login is required for generic services.

Fabric Login (FLOGI) is used by the N_Port to discover if a fabric is present. If a fabric is present, it provides operating characteristics associated with the fabric (service parameters such as max frame size). The fabric also assigns or confirms (if trying to reuse an old ID) the N_port identifier of the port initiating the BB_Credit value. N_Ports perform fabric login by transmitting the FLOGI extended link service command to the well-known address of 0xFFFFFE of the Fabric F_Port and exchanges service parameters, such as BB Credit, maximum payload size, and class of service supported. A new N Port Fabric Login source address is 0x000000 and destination address is 0xFFFFFE. Figure 22-29 portrays FC fabric, port login/logout, and FC query to the switch process.

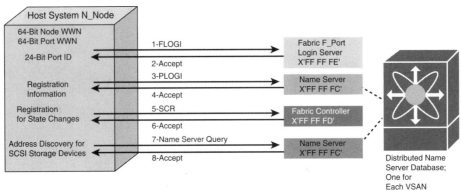

Figure 22-29 *Fibre Channel Fabric, Port Login, and State Change Registration*

Fibre Channel device login processes are:

1. **FLOGI Extended Link Service (ELS)**—Initiator/target to login server (0xFFFFFE) for switch fabric login.

2. **ACCEPT (ELS reply)**—Login server to initiator/target for fabric login acceptance. Fibre Channel ID (Port_Identifier) is assigned by login server to initiator/target.

3. **PLOGI (ELS)**—Initiator/target to name server (0xFFFFFC) for port login and establish a Fibre Channel session.

4. **ACCEPT (ELS reply)**—Name server to initiator/target using Port_Identifier as D_ID for port login acceptance.

5. **SCR (ELS)**—Initiator/target issues State Change Registration Command (SCRC) to the fabric controller (0xFFFFFD) for notification when a change in the switch fabric occurs.

6. **ACCEPT (ELS reply)**—Fabric controller to initiator/target acknowledging registration command.

7. **GA_NXT (Name Server Query)**—Initiator to name server (0xFFFFFC) requesting attributes about a specific port.

8. **ACCEPT (Query reply)**—Name server to initiator with list of attributes of the requested port.

9. **PLOGI (ELS)**—Initiator to target to establish an end-to-end Fibre Channel session (see Figure 22-30).

10. **ACCEPT (ELS reply)**—Target to initiator acknowledging initiator's port login and Fibre Channel session.

11. **PRLI (ELS)**—Initiator to target process login requesting an FC-4 session.

12. **ACCEPT (ELS reply)**—Target to initiator acknowledging session establishment. Initiator may now issue SCSI commands to the target.

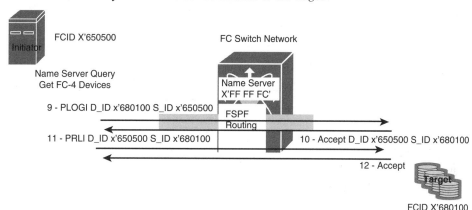

Figure 22-30 *Fibre Channel Port/Process Login to Target*

Fibre Channel Fabric Services

In a Fibre Channel topology, the switches manage a range of information that operates the fabric. This information is managed by fabric services. All FC services have in common that they are addressed via FC-2 frames and they can be reached by well-defined addresses. The fabric login server processes incoming fabric login requests with the address "0xFF FF FE." The fabric controller manages changes to the fabric under the address "0xFF FF FD." N-Ports can register for state changes in the fabric controller (State Change Registration, or SCR). The fabric controller then informs registered N-Ports of changes to the fabric (Registered State Change Notification, RSCN). Servers can use this service to monitor their storage devices.

The name server administers a database on N-Ports under the address 0xFF FF FC. It stores information such as port WWN, node WWN, port address, supported service classes, supported FC-4 protocols, and so on. N-Ports can register their own properties with the name server and request information on other N-Ports. Like all services, the name server appears as an N-Port to the other ports. N-Ports must log on with the name server by means of port login before they can use its services. Table 22-8 lists the reserved Fibre Channel addresses.

Table 22-8   FC-PH Has Defined a Block of Addresses for Special Functions (Reserved Addresses)

Address	Description
0xFF FF FF	Broadcast addresses
0xFF FF FE	Fabric login server
0xFF FF FD	Fabric controller
0xFF FF FC	Name server
0xFF FF FB	Time server
0xFF FF FA	Management server
0xFF FF F9	Quality of service facilitator
0xFF FF F8	Alias server
0xFF FF F7	Security key distribution server
0xFF FF F6	Clock synchronization server
0xFF FF F5	Multicast server
0xFF FF F0 – 0xFF FF F4	Reserved

FC-4: ULPs—Application Protocols

The layers FC-0 to FC-3 serve to connect end devices together by means of a Fibre Channel network. However, the type of data that end devices exchange via Fibre Channel connections remains open. This is where the application protocols (upper-layer protocols, or ULPs) come into play. A specific Fibre Channel network can serve as a medium for several application protocols—for example, SCSI and IP.

The task of the FC-4 protocol mappings is to map the application protocols onto the underlying Fibre Channel network. This means that the FC-4 protocol mappings support the application programming interface (API) of existing protocols upward in the direction of the operating system and realize these downward in the direction of the medium via the Fibre Channel network. The protocol mappings determine how the mechanisms of Fibre Channel are used in order to realize the application protocol by means of Fibre Channel. For example, they specify which service classes will be used and how the data flow in the application protocol will be projected onto the exchange sequence frame mechanism of Fibre Channel. This mapping of existing protocols aims to ease the transition to Fibre Channel networks: Ideally, no further modifications are necessary to the operating system except for the installation of a new device driver.

The application protocol for SCSI is called Fibre Channel Protocol (FCP), as shown in Figure 22-31. FCP maps the SCSI protocol onto the underlying Fibre Channel network. For the connection of storage devices to servers, the SCSI cable is therefore replaced by a Fibre Channel network. The idea of the FCP protocol is that the system administrator merely installs a new device driver on the server, and this realizes the FCP protocol. The operating system recognizes storage devices connected via Fibre Channel as SCSI devices, which it addresses like "normal" SCSI devices. This emulation of traditional SCSI devices should make it possible for Fibre Channel SANs to be simply and painlessly integrated into existing hardware and software.

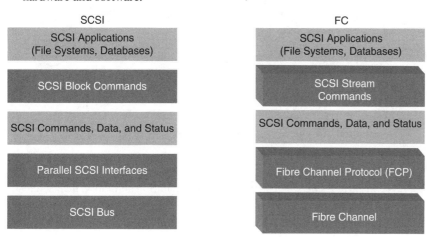

Figure 22-31   *FCP Protocol Stack*

A further application protocol is IPFC, which uses a Fibre Channel connection between two servers as a medium for IP data traffic. IPFC defines how IP packets will be transferred via a Fibre Channel network.

Fibre Connection (FICON) is a further important application protocol. FICON maps the ESCON protocol (Enterprise System Connection) used in the world of mainframes onto Fibre Channel networks. Using ESCON, it has been possible to realize storage networks in the world of mainframes since the 1990s. Fibre Channel is therefore taking the old familiar storage networks from the world of mainframes into the Open System world (UNIX, Windows, OS/400, Novell, and Mac OS).

Fibre Channel—Standard Port Types

Fibre Channel ports are intelligent interface points on the Fibre Channel SAN. They are found embedded in various devices, such as an I/O adapter, array or tape controller, and switched fabric.

When a server or storage device communicates, the interface point acts as the initiator or target for the connection. The server or storage device issues SCSI commands, which the interface point formats to be sent to the target device. These ports understand Fibre Channel. The Fibre Channel switch recognizes which type of device is attaching to the SAN and configures the ports accordingly. Figure 22-32 portrays the various Fibre Channel port types. These port types are detailed in the following list:

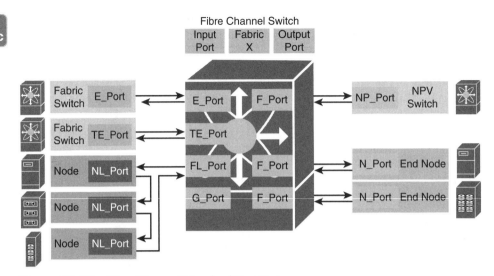

Figure 22-32 *Fibre Channel Standard Port Types*

- **Expansion port (E Port):** In E Port mode, an interface functions as a fabric expansion port. This port connects to another E Port to create an interswitch link (ISL) between two switches. E Ports carry frames between switches for configuration and fabric management. They also serve as a conduit between switches for frames that are destined to remote node ports (N Ports) and node loop ports (NL Ports). E Ports support Class 2, Class 3, and Class F service.

- **Fabric port (F Port):** In F Port mode, an interface functions as a fabric port. This port connects to a peripheral device (such as a host or disk) that operates as an N Port. An F Port can be attached to only one N Port. F Ports support Class 2 and Class 3 service.

- **Fabric loop port (FL Port):** In FL Port mode, an interface functions as a fabric loop port. This port connects to one or more NL Ports (including FL Ports in other switches) to form a public FC-AL. If more than one FL Port is detected on the FC-AL during initialization, only one FL Port becomes operational; the other FL Ports enter nonparticipating mode. FL Ports support Class 2 and Class 3 service.

- **Trunking expansion port (TE Port):** In TE Port mode, an interface functions as a trunking expansion port. This port connects to another TE Port to create an extended ISL (EISL) between two switches. TE Ports are specific to Cisco MDS 9000 Series switches and expand the functionality of E Ports to support virtual SAN (VSAN) trunking, transport quality of service (QoS) parameters, and the Fibre Channel Traceroute (fctrace) feature. When an interface is in TE Port mode, all frames that are transmitted are in the EISL frame format, which contains VSAN information. Interconnected switches use the VSAN ID to multiplex traffic from one or more VSANs across the same physical link.

- **Node-proxy port (NP Port):** An NP Port is a port on a device that is in N-Port Virtualization (NPV) mode and connects to the core switch via an F Port. NP Ports function like node ports (N Ports) but in addition to providing N Port operations, they also function as proxies for multiple physical N Ports.

- **Trunking fabric port (TF Port):** In TF Port mode, an interface functions as a trunking expansion port. This interface connects to another trunking node port (TN Port) or trunking node-proxy port (TNP Port) to create a link between a core switch and an NPV switch or a host bus adapter (HBA) to carry tagged frames. TF Ports are specific to Cisco MDS 9000 Series switches and expand the functionality of F Ports to support VSAN trunking. In TF Port mode, all frames are transmitted in the EISL frame format, which contains VSAN information.

- **TNP Port:** In TNP Port mode, an interface functions as a trunking expansion port. This interface connects to a TF Port to create a link to a core N-Port ID Virtualization (NPIV) switch from an NPV switch to carry tagged frames.

- **Switched Port Analyzer (SPAN) destination port (SD Port):** In SD Port mode, an interface functions as a SPAN. The SPAN feature is specific to Cisco MDS 9000 Series switches. An SD Port monitors network traffic that passes through a Fibre Channel interface. Monitoring is performed using a standard Fibre Channel analyzer (or a similar switch probe) that is attached to the SD Port. SD Ports cannot receive frames and transmit only a copy of the source traffic. This feature is nonintrusive and does not affect switching of network traffic for any SPAN source port.

- **SPAN tunnel port (ST Port):** In ST Port mode, an interface functions as an entry-point port in the source switch for the Remote SPAN (RSPAN) Fibre Channel tunnel. ST Port mode and the RSPAN feature are specific to Cisco MDS 9000 Series switches. When a port is configured as an ST Port, it cannot be attached to any device and therefore cannot be used for normal Fibre Channel traffic.

- **Fx Port:** An interface that is configured as an Fx Port can operate in either F or FL Port mode. Fx Port mode is determined during interface initialization, depending on the attached N or NL Port.

- **Bridge port (B Port):** Whereas E Ports typically interconnect Fibre Channel switches, some SAN extender devices implement a B Port model to connect geographically dispersed fabrics. This model uses B Ports that are as described in the T11 Standard Fibre Channel Backbone 2 (FC-BB-2).

- **G-Port (Generic_Port):** Modern Fibre Channel switches configure their ports automatically. Such ports are called G-Ports. If, for example, a Fibre Channel switch is connected to a further Fibre Channel switch via a G-Port, the G-Port configures itself as an E-Port.

- **Auto mode:** An interface that is configured in auto mode can operate in one of the following modes: F Port, FL Port, E Port, TE Port, or TF Port, with the port mode being determined during interface initialization.

Virtual Storage Area Network

A VSAN is a virtual storage area network (SAN). A SAN is a dedicated network that interconnects hosts and storage devices primarily to exchange SCSI traffic. In SANs, you use the physical links to make these interconnections. A set of protocols runs over the SAN to handle routing, naming, and zoning. You can design multiple SANs with different topologies.

22

A SAN island refers to a completely physically isolated switch or group of switches used to connect hosts to storage devices. The reasons for building SAN islands include to isolate different applications into their own fabric or to raise availability by minimizing the impact of fabric-wide disruptive events. Figure 22-33 portrays a VSAN topology and a representation of VSANs on an MDS 9700 Director switch by per-port allocation.

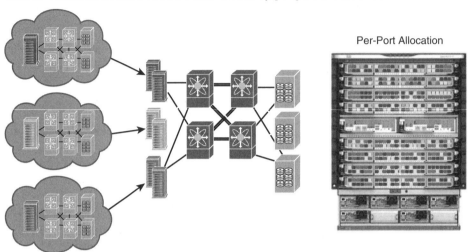

Figure 22-33 *VSANs*

Physically separate SAN islands offer a higher degree of security because each physical infrastructure contains a separate set of Cisco Fabric Services and management access. Unfortunately, in practice this situation can become costly and wasteful in terms of fabric ports and resources.

VSANs increase the efficiency of a SAN fabric by alleviating the need to build multiple physically isolated fabrics to meet organizational or application needs. Instead, fewer less-costly redundant fabrics can be built, each housing multiple applications and still providing island-like isolation.

Spare ports within the fabric can be quickly and nondisruptively assigned to existing VSANs, providing a clean method of virtually growing application-specific SAN islands.

VSANs provide not only a hardware-based isolation, but also a complete replicated set of Fibre Channel services for each VSAN. Therefore, when a VSAN is created, a completely separate set of Cisco Fabric Services, configuration management capabilities, and policies are created within the new VSAN.

With the introduction of VSANs, the network administrator can build a single topology containing switches, links, and one or more VSANs. Each VSAN in this topology has the same behavior and properties of a SAN. A VSAN has the following additional features:

- Multiple VSANs can share the same physical topology.
- The same Fibre Channel IDs (FC IDs) can be assigned to a host in another VSAN, thus increasing VSAN scalability.

- Every instance of a VSAN runs all required protocols, such as FSPF, domain manager, and zoning.
- Fabric-related configurations in one VSAN do not affect the associated traffic in another VSAN.
- Events causing traffic disruptions in one VSAN are contained within that VSAN and are not propagated to other VSANs.

Using a hardware-based frame tagging mechanism on VSAN member ports and EISL links isolates each separate virtual fabric. The EISL link type has been created and includes added tagging information for each frame within the fabric. The EISL link is supported between Cisco MDS and Nexus switch products. Membership to a VSAN is based on physical ports, and no physical port may belong to more than one VSAN.

VSANs offer the following advantages:

- **Traffic isolation:** Traffic is contained within VSAN boundaries, and devices reside in only one VSAN, ensuring absolute separation between user groups, if desired.
- **Scalability:** VSANs are overlaid on top of a single physical fabric. The ability to create several logical VSAN layers increases the scalability of the SAN.
- **Per VSAN fabric services:** Replication of fabric services on a per-VSAN basis provides increased scalability and availability.
- **Redundancy:** Several VSANs created on the same physical SAN ensure redundancy. If one VSAN fails, redundant protection (to another VSAN in the same physical SAN) is configured using a backup path between the host and the device.
- **Ease of configuration:** Users can be added, moved, or changed between VSANs without changing the physical structure of a SAN. Moving a device from one VSAN to another only requires configuration at the port level, not at a physical level.

Up to 256 VSANs can be configured in a switch. Of these, one is a default VSAN (VSAN 1) and another is an isolated VSAN (VSAN 4094). User-specified VSAN IDs range from 2 to 4093. Different characteristics of a VSAN can be summarized as below:

- VSANs equal SANs with routing, naming, and zoning protocols.
- VSANs limit unicast, multicast, and broadcast traffic.
- Membership is typically defined using the VSAN ID to Fx ports.
- An HBA or a storage device can belong only to a single VSAN—the VSAN associated with the Fx port.
- VSANs enforce membership at each E port, source port, and destination port.
- VSANs are defined for larger environments (storage service providers).
- VSANs encompass the entire fabric.
- VSANs equal SANs with routing, naming, and zoning protocols. Dynamic Port VSAN Membership (DPVM).

22

Port VSAN membership on the switch is assigned on a port-by-port basis. By default, each port belongs to the default VSAN. You can dynamically assign VSAN membership to ports by assigning VSANs based on the device WWN. This method is referred to as Dynamic Port VSAN Membership (DPVM). DPVM offers flexibility and eliminates the need to reconfigure the port VSAN membership to maintain fabric topology when a host or storage device connection is moved between two Cisco MDS switches or two ports within a switch. It retains the configured VSAN regardless of where a device is connected or moved.

DPVM configurations are based on port World Wide Name (pWWN) and node World Wide Name (nWWN) assignments. A DPVM database contains mapping information for each device pWWN/nWWN assignment and the corresponding VSAN. The Cisco NX-OS software checks the database during a device FLOGI and obtains the required VSAN details.

The pWWN identifies the host or device, and the nWWN identifies a node consisting of multiple devices. You can assign any one of these identifiers or any combination of these identifiers to configure DPVM mapping. If you assign a combination, preference is given to the pWWN. DPVM uses the Cisco Fabric Services (CFS) infrastructure to allow efficient database management and distribution.

Inter-VSAN Routing (IVR)

Virtual SANs (VSANs) improve storage area network (SAN) scalability, availability, and security by allowing multiple Fibre Channel SANs to share a common physical infrastructure of switches and ISLs. These benefits are derived from the separation of Fibre Channel services in each VSAN and the isolation of traffic between VSANs (see Figure 22-34). Data traffic isolation between the VSANs also inherently prevents sharing of resources attached to a VSAN, such as robotic tape libraries. Using IVR, you can access resources across VSANs without compromising other VSAN benefits. IVR transports data traffic between specific initiators and targets on different VSANs without merging VSANs into a single logical fabric. It establishes proper interconnected routes that traverse one or more VSANs across multiple switches. IVR is not limited to VSANs present on a common switch. Fibre Channel traffic does not flow between VSANs, nor can initiators access resources across VSANs other than the designated VSAN. It provides efficient business continuity or disaster recovery solutions when used in conjunction with Fibre Channel over IP (FCIP).

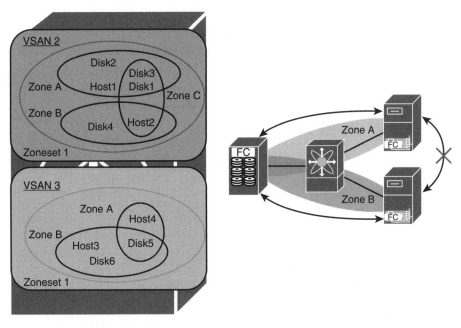

Figure 22-34 *Inter-VSAN Topology*

Internet Small Computer System Interface (iSCSI)

IP and Small Computer System Interface over IP (iSCSI) storage refer to the block access of storage disks across devices connected using traditional Ethernet and TCP/IP networks. iSCSI is an IP-based storage networking standard for linking data storage facilities.

The iSCSI protocol enables transport of SCSI commands over TCP/IP networks. By transmitting SCSI commands over IP networks, iSCSI can facilitate block-level transfers over an intranet and the Internet. The iSCSI architecture is similar to a client-server architecture in which the client initiates an I/O request to the storage target. The TCP payload of an iSCSI packet contains iSCSI protocol data units (PDUs), all of which begin with one or more header segments followed by zero or more data segments. iSCSI uses TCP (typically TCP ports 860 and 3260) for the protocols itself, with higher-level names used to address the objects within the protocol.

22

iSCSI Terminology

An iSCSI network consists of multiple devices such as iSCSI initiators and iSCSI targets. Each device has various components associated with it. Some of the iSCSI components that make up an iSCSI storage network are listed here:

- **iSCSI name:** The iSCSI name is a unique World Wide Name (WWN) by which the iSCSI node is known. The iSCSI name uses one of the following formats:
    - **iSCSI qualified name (IQN):** For example,
      iqn.1987-05.com.Cisco.00.9f9ccf185aa3508c.taget2

        Format: The iSCSI qualified name is documented in RFC 3720, with further examples of names in RFC 3721. Briefly, the fields are as follows:

        Literal iqn (iSCSI qualified name)

        Date (yyyy-mm) that the naming authority took ownership of the domain

        Reversed domain name of the authority

        Optional ":" prefixing a storage target name specified by the naming authority.

    - **Extended unique identifier (EUI-64 bit addressing):** Format: eui.02004565A425678D.

    - **T11 Network Address Authority (NAA):** IQN format addresses occur most commonly. They are qualified by a date (yyyy-mm) because domain names can expire or be acquired by another entity. Format: naa.{NAA 64 or 128 bit identifier} (for example, naa.52004567BA64678D).

- **iSCSI node:** The iSCSI node represents a single iSCSI initiator or iSCSI target.

- **Network entity:** The network entity represents a device or gateway that is accessible from the IP network (for example, a host or storage array).

- **Network portal:** The network portal is a component of a network entity that has a TCP/IP network address that is used by an iSCSI node. A network portal in an initiator is identified by its IP address, and a target is identified by its IP address and its listening TCP port.

A network entity contains one or more iSCSI nodes. The iSCSI node is accessible through one or more network portals. An iSCSI node is identified by its iSCSI name. Figure 22-35 shows the components of an iSCSI network.

An initiator functions as an iSCSI client. An initiator typically serves the same purpose to a computer as a SCSI bus adapter would, except that, instead of physically cabling SCSI devices (such as hard drives and tape changers), an iSCSI initiator sends SCSI commands over an IP network. An initiator falls into two broad types: a software initiator and hardware initiator.

A software initiator uses code to implement iSCSI. Typically, this happens in a kernel-resident device driver that uses the existing network card (NIC) and network stack to emulate SCSI devices for a computer by speaking the iSCSI protocol. Software initiators are available for most popular operating systems and are the most common method of deploying iSCSI.

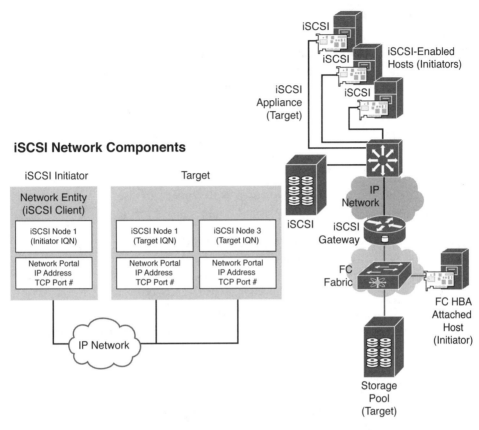

Figure 22-35 *iSCSI Network Components*

A hardware initiator uses dedicated hardware, typically in combination with firmware running on that hardware, to implement iSCSI. A hardware initiator mitigates the overhead of iSCSI and TCP processing and Ethernet interrupts, and thus may improve the performance of servers that use iSCSI. An iSCSI host bus adapter (HBA) implements a hardware initiator. A typical HBA is packaged as a combination of a Gigabit (or 10 Gigabit) Ethernet network interface controller, some kind of TCP/IP offload engine (TOE) technology, and a SCSI bus adapter, which is how it appears to the operating system. An iSCSI HBA can include PCI option ROM to allow booting from an iSCSI SAN.

An iSCSI offload engine, or iSOE card, offers an alternative to a full iSCSI HBA. An iSOE "offloads" the iSCSI initiator operations for this particular network interface from the host processor, freeing up CPU cycles for the main host applications. iSCSI HBAs or iSOEs are used when the additional performance enhancement justifies the additional expense of using an HBA for iSCSI, rather than using a software-based iSCSI client (initiator). iSOE may be implemented with additional services such as TCP offload engine (TOE) to further reduce host server CPU usage.

The iSCSI specification refers to a storage resource located on an iSCSI server (more generally, one of potentially many instances of iSCSI storage nodes running on that server) as a target.

The term "iSCSI target" should not be confused with the term "iSCSI," because the latter is a protocol and not a storage server instance.

An iSCSI target is often a dedicated network-connected hard disk storage device, but may also be a general-purpose computer, because as with initiators, software to provide an iSCSI target is available for most mainstream operating systems.

iSCSI Session

The highest level target available for most mainstream operating systems of an iSCSI communications path is a session that is formed between an iSCSI initiator and an iSCSI target. Two types of sessions are defined in iSCSI:

- An iSCSI discovery and login session used by the initiator to discover available targets
- A general iSCSI session to transfer SCSI data and commands after the login

A session is identified by a session ID (SSID), which consists of initiator (ISID) and target (TSID) components. TCP connections can be added and removed within a session; however, all connections are between the same unique initiator and target iSCSI nodes. Each connection within a session has a unique connection ID (CID).

An iSCSI session is established through the iSCSI login process. This session is used to identify all TCP connections associated with a particular SCSI initiator and target pair. One session can contain one or more TCP connections. The login process is started when the initiator establishes a TCP connection to the desired target either through the well-known port (3260) or a specified target port. The initiator and target can authenticate each other and negotiate a security protocol. During the login phase, numerous attributes are negotiated between the iSCSI initiator and target. Upon successful completion of the login phase, the session enters the full-featured phase.

Reference List

Storage Network Industry Association (SNIA)—http://www.snia.org

Internet Engineering Task Force – IP Storage— https://datatracker.ietf.org/wg/ips/documents/

ANSI T11 – Fibre Channel—http://www.t11.org/index.html

ANSI T10 Technical Committee—www.T10.org

IEEE Standards site—http://standards.ieee.org

SNIA dictionary—http://www.snia.org/education/dictionary

Farley, Marc. *Rethinking Enterprise Storage: A Hybrid Cloud Mode*. Microsoft Press, 2013

Kembel, Robert W. *Fibre Channel: A Comprehensive Introduction.* Northwest Learning Associates, Inc., 2000

Exam Preparation Tasks

Review All Key Topics

Review the most important topics in the chapter, noted with the key topics icon in the outer margin of the page. Table 22-10 lists a reference for these key topics and the page numbers on which each is found.

Table 22-10 Key Topics for Chapter 22

Key Topic Element	Description	Page
Section	Description of a storage device	568
Section	Description of RAID and JBOD	569
List	Description of NAS arrays	570
List	Description of SAN arrays	570
List	Description of I/O channel designs	571
List	Summarizes the key benefits of SAN	574
List	Description of common storage protocols	575
Section	Block-level protocols	576
Figure 22-4	Standard groups: storage	576
Section	Description of LUN	578
Figure 22-6	SCSI addressing	579
Figure 22-7	SCSI I/O channel, Fibre Channel I/O channel, and TCP/IP I/O networking	580
List	Summary of transportation of SCSI messages	580
Figure 22-8	Networking stack comparison for all block I/O protocols	582
Figure 22-9	Comparison between Fibre Channel HBA and Ethernet NIC	582
Figure 22-10	Fibre Channel Protocol architecture	583
Table 22-3	The evolution of Fibre Channel speeds	584
Figure 22-11	Comparison of block I/O versus file I/O	586
Figure 22-12	DAS, SAN, iSCSI, and NAS comparison	587
Section	Description of scale-up and scale-out storage	588
Section	Description of tiered storage	588
Figure 22-13	Cost versus performance in a tiered storage environment	588
Table 22-4	Comparison of storage tier levels	589
Figure 22-15	Storage multipathing failover	591

22

Key Topic Element	Description	Page
List	Summary of advantages of VSAN	619
List	VSAN characteristics	619
List	iSCSI terminology	622

Complete Tables and Lists from Memory

Print a copy of Appendix C, "Memory Tables," or at least the section for this chapter, and complete the tables and lists from memory. Appendix D, "Memory Tables Answer Key," includes completed tables and lists to check your work.

Define Key Terms

Define the following key terms from this chapter, and check your answers in the glossary:

virtual storage-area network (VSAN), zoning, fan-out ratio, fan-in ratio, logical unit number (LUN) masking, LUN mapping, Extended Link Services (ELS), multipathing, Big Data, IoE, N_Port Login (PLOGI), F_Port Login (FLOGI), logout (LOGO), process login (PRLI), process logout (PRLO), state change notification (SCN), registered state change notification (RSCN), state change registration (SCR), inter-VSAN routing (IVR), Fibre Channel Generic Services (FC-GS), hard disk drive (HDD), solid-state drive (SSD), Small Computer System Interface (SCSI), initiator, target, American National Standards Institute (ANSI), International Committee for Information Technology Standards (INCITS), Fibre Connection (FICON), T11, Input/output Operations per Second (IOPS), Common Internet File System (CIFS), Network File System (NFS), Cisco Fabric Services (CFS), Top-of-Rack (ToR), End-of-Row (EoR), Dynamic Port VSAN Membership (DPVM), inter-VSAN routing (IVR)

22

This chapter covers the following exam topics:

5.0. Advanced Data Center Storage

5.1. Describe FCoE concepts and operations

5.1.a. Encapsulation

5.1.b. DCB

5.1.c. vFC

5.1.d. Topologies

5.1.d.1. Single hop

5.1.d.2. Multihop

5.1.d.3. Dynamic

5.2. Describe node port virtualization

5.3. Describe zone types and their uses

5.4. Verify the communication between the initiator and target

5.4.a. FLOGI

5.4.b. FCNS

5.4.c. Active zone set

CHAPTER 23

Advanced Data Center Storage

In computing, *virtualization* means to create a virtual version of a device or resource, such as a server, storage device, or network, where the framework divides the resource into one or more execution environments. Devices, applications, and human users are able to interact with the virtual resource as if it were a real single logical resource. A number of computing technologies benefit from virtualization, including the following:

- **Storage virtualization:** Combining multiple network storage devices into what appears to be a single storage unit.
- **Server virtualization:** Partitioning a physical server into smaller virtual servers.
- **Network virtualization:** Using network resources through a logical segmentation of a single physical network.
- **Application virtualization:** Decoupling the application and its data from the operating system.

The first couple of pages of this chapter guide you through storage virtualization concepts, answering basic what, why, and how questions. The storage virtualization will help you to understand advanced data center storage concepts.

The foundation of the data center network is the network software that runs the network's switches. Cisco NX-OS software is the network software for Cisco MDS 9000 family and Cisco Nexus family data center switching products. It is based on a secure, stable, and standard Linux core, providing a modular and sustainable base for the long term. Formerly known as Cisco SAN-OS, starting from release 4.1 it has been rebranded as Cisco MDS 9000 NX-OS software. In Chapter 22, "Introduction to Storage and Storage Networking," we discussed basic storage area network concepts and key Cisco MDS 9000 Software features. In this chapter, we build our storage area network, starting from the initial setup configuration on Cisco MDS 9000 switches.

A classic data center design features a dedicated Ethernet LAN and a separate, dedicated Fibre Channel (FC) SAN. With Fibre Channel over Ethernet (FCoE), it is possible to run a single, converged network. As a standards-based protocol that allows Fibre Channel frames to be carried over Ethernet links, FCoE obviates the need to run separate LAN and SAN networks. FCoE allows an evolutionary approach to I/O consolidation by preserving all Fibre Channel constructs, maintaining the latency, security, and traffic management attributes of Fibre Channel while preserving investments in Fibre Channel tools, training, and SANs. Based on lossless, reliable Ethernet, FCoE networks combine LAN and multiple storage protocols on a converged network.

Now, multihop FCoE technology can be used to extend convergence beyond the access layer. The higher, more efficient speeds, such as 40 Gigabit Ethernet FCoE today, or the 100 Gigabit Ethernet FCoE in the future, help enable fewer and higher-speed Inter-Switch

Links (ISLs) in the network core. The converged architecture means you can wire once and deploy anywhere to support any storage protocol, including iSCSI or NFS. This consolidated infrastructure also helps to simplify management and significantly reduce total cost of ownership (TCO).

FCoE is one of the core components of the Cisco Converged Data Center, which helps enable multiprotocol networking through Cisco Unified Computing System (UCS), Cisco Nexus platforms, and Cisco MDS platforms. In this chapter, we discuss all the standards required to support FCoE protocol and the FCoE topologies.

This chapter discusses how to configure Cisco MDS 9000 Series multilayer switches as well as storage virtualization and FCoE concepts. It also describes how to verify virtual storage area networks (VSANs), zoning, the fabric login, and the fabric domain using command-line interface. This chapter goes directly into the practical configuration steps of the Cisco MDS product family and discusses topics relevant to Introducing Cisco Data Center Networking (DCICN) certification.

"Do I Know This Already?" Quiz

The "Do I Know This Already?" quiz allows you to assess whether you should read this entire chapter thoroughly or jump to the "Exam Preparation Tasks" section. If you are in doubt about your answers to these questions or your own assessment of your knowledge of the topics, read the entire chapter. Table 23-1 lists the major headings in this chapter and their corresponding "Do I Know This Already?" quiz questions. You can find the answers in Appendix A, "Answers to the 'Do I Know This Already?' Quizzes."

Table 23-1 "Do I Know This Already?" Section-to-Question Mapping

Foundation Topics Section	Questions
Where Do I Start Configuration?	1
The Cisco MDS NX-OS Setup Utility—Back to Basics	2, 3
The Power On Auto Provisioning	4
Licensing Cisco MDS 9000 Family NX-OS Software Features	5
Cisco MDS 9000 NX-OS Software Upgrade and Downgrade	6
Configuring Interfaces	7
Fibre Channel Zoning	8
VSAN Trunking and Setting Up ISL Port	9
What Is Storage Virtualization?	10
What Is Being Virtualized?	11, 12, 13, 14
Where Does the Storage Virtualization Occur?	15, 16, 17
IEEE Data Center Bridging	18, 19
Fibre Channel over Ethernet	20

CAUTION   The goal of self-assessment is to gauge your mastery of the topics in this chapter. If you do not know the answer to a question or are only partially sure of the answer, you should mark that question as wrong for purposes of the self-assessment. Giving yourself credit for an answer you correctly guess skews your self-assessment results and might provide you with a false sense of security.

1. Which of the following switches support Console port, COM1, and MGMT interface? (Choose all the correct answers.)

    a. MDS 9710

    b. MDS 9508

    c. MDS 9513

    d. MDS 9148S

    e. MDS 9706

2. During the initial setup script of MDS 9500, which interfaces can be configured with the IPv6 address?

    a. MGMT 0 interface

    b. All FC interfaces

    c. VSAN interface

    d. Out-of-band management interface

    e. None

3. During the initial setup script of MDS 9706, how can you configure in-band management?

    a. Via answering yes to Configure Advanced IP Options.

    b. Via enabling SSH service.

    c. There is no configuration option for in-band management on MDS family switches.

    d. MDS 9706 family director switch does not support in-band management.

4. Which MDS switch models support Power On Auto Provisioning with NX-OS 6.2(9)?

    a. MDS 9250i

    b. MDS 9148

    c. MDS 9148S

    d. MDS 9706

5. How does the On-Demand Port Activation license work on the Cisco MDS 9148S 16G FC switch?

    a. The base configuration of 20 ports of 16Gbps Fibre Channel, two ports of 10 Gigabit Ethernet for FCIP and iSCSI storage services, and eight ports of 10 Gigabit Ethernet for FCoE connectivity.

    b. The base switch model comes with 12 ports enabled and can be upgraded as needed with the 12-port activation license to support 24, 36, or 48 ports.

23

   c. The base switch model comes with eight ports and can be upgraded to models of 16, 32, or 48 ports.

   d. The base switch model comes with 24 ports enabled and can be upgraded as needed with a 12-port activation license to support 36 or 48 ports.

6. Which is the correct option for the boot sequence?

   a. System—Kickstart—BIOS—Loader

   b. BIOS—Loader—Kickstart—System

   c. System—BIOS—Loader—Kickstart

   d. BIOS—Loader—System—Kickstart

7. Which of the following options is the correct configuration for in-band management of MDS 9250i?

   a.
```
switch(config)# interface mgmt0
switch(config-if)# ip address 10.22.2.2 255.255.255.0
switch(config-if)# no shutdown
switch(config-if)# exit
switch(config)# ip default-gateway 10.22.2.1
```

   b.
```
switch(config)# interface mgmt0
switch(config-if)# ipv6 enable
switch(config-if)# ipv6 address ipv6 address 2001:0db8:800:200c::417a/64
switch(config-if)# no shutdown
```

   c.
```
switch(config)# interface vsan 1
switch(config-if)# ip address 10.22.2.3 255.255.255.0
switch(config-if)# no shutdown
```

   d.
```
switch(config-if)# (no) switchport mode F
switch(config-if)# (no) switchport mode auto
```

   e. None

8. Which of the following options are valid member types for a zone configuration on an MDS 9222i switch? (Choose all the correct answers.)

   a. pWWN

   b. IPv6 address

   c. Mac address of the MGMT 0 interface

   d. FCID

9. In which of the following trunk mode configurations between two MDS switches we can achieve trunking states are ISL and port modes are E port?

   a. Switch 1: Switchport mode E, trunk mode off; Switch 2: Switchport mode E, trunk mode off.

   b. Switch 1: Switchport mode E, trunk mode on; Switch 2: Switchport mode E, trunk mode on.

   c. Switch 1: Switchport mode E, trunk mode off; Switch 2: Switchport mode F, trunk mode auto.

   d. Switch 1: Switchport mode E, trunk mode auto; Switch 2: Switchport mode E, trunk mode auto.

   e. No correct answer exists.

10. Which of the following organizations defines the storage virtualization standards?

   a. INCITS (International Committee for Information Technology Standards).

   b. IETF (Internet Engineering Task Force).

   c. SNIA (Storage Networking Industry Association).

   d. Storage virtualization has no standard measure defined by a reputable organization.

11. Which of the following options can be virtualized according to SNIA storage virtualization taxonomy? (Choose all the correct answers.)

   a. Disks

   b. Blocks

   c. Tape systems

   d. File systems

   e. Switches

12. Which of the following options explains RAID 1+0?

   a. It is an exact copy (or mirror) of a set of data on two disks.

   b. It comprises block-level striping with distributed parity.

   c. It comprises block-level striping with double distributed parity.

   d. It creates a striped set from a series of mirrored drives.

13. Which of the following options explains RAID 6?

   a. It is an exact copy (or mirror) of a set of data on two disks.

   b. It comprises block-level striping with distributed parity.

   c. It creates a striped set from a series of mirrored drives.

   d. It comprises block-level striping with double distributed parity.

14. Which of the following options explain LUN masking? (Choose all the correct answers.)

   a. It is a feature of Fibre Channel HBA.

   b. It is a feature of storage arrays.

   c. It provides basic LUN-level security by allowing LUNs to be seen by selected servers.

   d. It is a proprietary technique that Cisco MDS switches offer.

   e. It should be configured on HBAs.

15. Which of the following options explain the Logical Volume Manager (LVM)? (Choose all the correct answers.)

   a. The LVM manipulates LUN representation to create virtualized storage to the file system.

   b. The LVM is a collection of ports from a set of connected Fibre Channel switches.

   c. LVM combines multiple hard disk drive components into a logical unit to provide data redundancy.

   d. LVMs can be used to divide large physical disk arrays into more manageable virtual disks.

23

16. Select the correct order of operations for completing asynchronous array-based replication.

  I.   The write operation is received by the primary storage array from the host.

  II. An acknowledgement is sent to the primary storage array by a secondary storage array after the data is stored on the secondary storage array.

  III. The write operation to the primary array is acknowledged locally; the primary storage array does not require a confirmation from the secondary storage array to acknowledge the write operation to the server.

  IV. The primary storage array maintains new data queued to be copied to the secondary storage array at a later time. It initiates a write to the secondary storage array.

  a. I, II, III, IV.

  b. I, III, IV, II.

  c. III, I, II, VI.

  d. I, III, II, IV.

  e. Asynchronous mirroring operation was not explained correctly.

17. Which of the following options are the advantages of host-based storage virtualization? (Choose all the correct answers.)

  a. It is close to the file system.

  b. It uses the operating system's built-in tools.

  c. It is licensed and managed per host.

  d. It uses the array controller's CPU cycles.

  e. It is independent of SAN transport.

18. Which of the following specifications of IEEE 802.1 are related to lossless Ethernet? (Choose all the correct answers.)

  a. PFC

  b. ETS

  c. FCF

  d. BBC

  e. QCN

19. Which option best defines the need for data center bridging (DCB)?

  a. A set of standards designed to replace the existing Ethernet and IP protocol stack with a goal of enhancing existing transmissions for delay-sensitive applications.

  b. A set of standards designed to transparently enhance Ethernet and IP traffic and provide special treatment and features for certain traffic types such as FCoE and HPC.

  c. An emerging LAN standard for future delay-sensitive device communication.

  d. A single protocol that is designed to transparently enhance Ethernet and IP traffic and provide special treatment and features for certain traffic types such as FCoE and HPC.

20. Which of the following options are correct for FIP and FCoE Ethertypes?

  a. FCoE 0x8906, FIP 0x8914

  b. FCoE 0x8907, FIP 0x8941

  c. FCoE 0x8908, FIP 0x8918

  d. FCoE 0x8902, FIP 0x8914

  e. FCoE 0x8909, FIP 0x8916

Foundation Topics

What Is Storage Virtualization?

Storage virtualization is a way to logically combine storage capacity and resources from various heterogeneous, external storage systems into one virtual pool of storage. This virtual pool can then be more easily managed and provisioned as needed. A single set of tools and processes performs everything from online any-to-any data migrations to heterogeneous replication. Unlike previous new protocols or architectures, however, storage virtualization has no standard measure defined by a reputable organization such as the INCITS (International Committee for Information Technology Standards) or the IETF (Internet Engineering Task Force). The closest vendor-neutral attempt to make storage virtualization concepts comprehensible has been the work of the Storage Networking Industry Association (SNIA), which has produced useful tutorial content on the various flavors of virtualization technology. According to the SNIA dictionary, storage virtualization is the act of abstracting, hiding, or isolating the internal function of a storage (sub) system or service from applications, computer servers, or general network resources for the purpose of enabling application- and network-independent management of storage or data.

The beginning of virtualization goes a long way back. Virtual memory operating systems evolved during the 1960s. One decade later, virtualization began to move into storage and some disk subsystems. The original mass storage device used a tape cartridge, which was a helical-scan cartridge that looked like a disk. The late 1970s witnessed the introduction of the first solid-state disk, which was a box full of DRAM chips that appeared to be rotating magnetic disks. Virtualization achieved a new level when the first Redundant Array of Inexpensive Disks (RAID) virtual disk array was announced in 1992 for mainframe systems. The first virtual tape systems appeared in 1997 for mainframe systems. Much of the pioneering work in virtualization began on mainframes and has since moved into the non-mainframe, open-system world. Virtualization gained momentum in the late 1990s as a result of virtualizing SANs and storage networks in an effort to tie together all the computing platforms from the 1980s. In 2003, virtual tape architectures moved away from the mainframe and entered new markets, increasing the demand for virtual tape. In 2005, virtual tape was the most popular storage initiative in many storage management pools.

Software-defined storage (SDS) was proposed in 2013 as a new category of storage software products. The term *software-defined storage* is a follow-up of the technology trend software-defined networking, which was first used to describe an approach in network technology that abstracts various elements of networking and creates an abstraction or virtualized layer in software. In networking, the control plane and the data plane have been intertwined within the traditional switches that are deployed today, making abstraction and virtualization more difficult to manage in complex virtual environments. SDS refers to the abstraction of the physical elements, similar to server virtualization. SDS delivers automated, policy-driven, application-aware storage services through orchestration of the underlining storage infrastructure in support of an overall software-defined environment. SDS represents a new evolution for the storage industry for how storage will be managed and deployed in the future.

23

How Storage Virtualization Works

Storage virtualization works through mapping. The storage virtualization layer creates a mapping from the logical storage address space (used by the hosts) to the physical address of the storage device. Such mapping information, also referred to as *metadata*, is stored in huge mapping tables. When a host requests I/O, the virtualization layer looks at the logical address in that I/O request and, using the mapping table, translates the logical address into the address of a physical storage device. The virtualization layer then performs I/O with the underlying storage device using the physical address; when it receives the data back from the physical device, it returns that data to the application as if it had come from the logical address. The application is unaware of the mapping that happens beneath the covers. Figure 23-1 illustrates this virtual storage layer that sits between the applications and the physical storage devices.

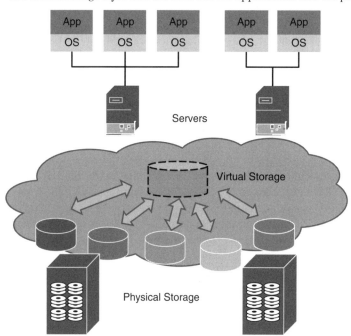

Figure 23-1 *Storage Virtualization Mapping Heterogeneous Physical Storage to Virtual Storage*

Why Storage Virtualization?

The business drivers for storage virtualization are much the same as those for server virtualization. CIOs and IT managers must cope with shrinking IT budgets and growing client demands. They must simultaneously improve asset utilization, use IT resources more efficiently, ensure business continuity, and become more agile. In addition, they are faced with ever-increasing constraints on power, cooling, and space. The major economic driver is to reduce costs without sacrificing data integrity or performance. Organizations can use the technology to resolve the issue and create a more adaptive, flexible service-based infrastructure to reflect ongoing changes in business requirements. The top seven reasons to use storage virtualizations are

- Exponential data growth and disruptive storage upgrades
- Low utilization of existing assets
- Growing management complexity with flat or decreasing budgets for IT staff head count
- Increasing hard costs and environmental costs to acquire, run, and manage storage
- Ensuring rapid, high-quality storage service delivery to application and business owners
- Achieving cost-effective business continuity and data protection
- Power and cooling consumption in the data center

What Is Being Virtualized?

The Storage Networking Industry Association (SNIA) taxonomy for storage virtualization is divided into three basic categories: what is being virtualized, where the virtualization occurs, and how it is implemented. This is illustrated in Figure 23-2.

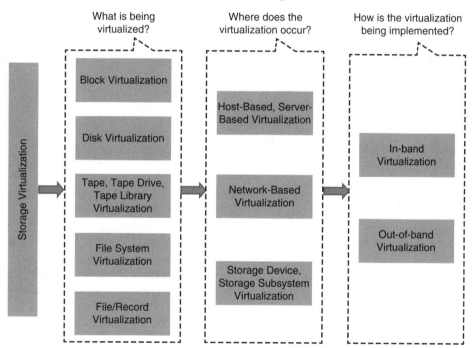

Figure 23-2   *SNIA Storage Virtualization Taxonomy Separates Objects of Virtualization from Location and Means of Execution*

What is being virtualized may include blocks, disks, tape systems, file systems, and file or record virtualization. Where virtualization occurs may be on the host, in storage arrays, or in the network via intelligent fabric switches or SAN-attached appliances. How the virtualization occurs may be via in-band or out-of-band separation of control and data paths. Storage virtualization provides the means to build higher-level storage services that mask the complexity of all underlying components and enable automation of data storage operations.

The most important reasons for storage virtualization were covered in the "Why Storage Virtualization?" section. The ultimate goal of storage virtualization should be to simplify storage administration. This can be achieved via a layered approach, binding multiple levels of technologies on a foundation of logical abstraction.

The abstraction layer that masks physical from logical storage may reside on host systems such as servers, within the storage network in the form of a virtualization appliance, within SAN switches, or on a storage array or tape subsystem targets. In common usage, these alternatives are referred to as host-based, network-based, or array-based virtualization. Figure 23-3 illustrates all components of an intelligent SAN.

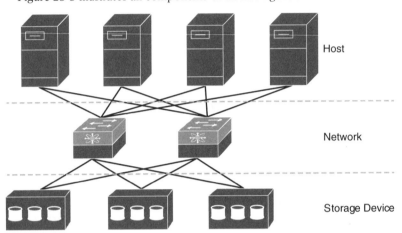

Figure 23-3   *Possible Alternatives Where the Storage Virtualization May Occur*

In addition to differences between where storage virtualization is located, vendors have different methods for implementing virtualized storage transport. The in-band method places the virtualization engine directly in the data path so that both block data and the control information that govern its virtual appearance transit the same link. The out-of-band method provides separate paths for data and control, presenting an image of virtual storage to the host by one link and allowing the host to directly retrieve data blocks from physical storage on another. In-band and out-of-band virtualization techniques are sometimes referred to as symmetrical and asymmetrical, respectively. In the in-band method, the appliance acts as an I/O target to the hosts and acts as an I/O initiator to the storage. It has the opportunity to work as a bridge. For example, it can present an iSCSI target to the host while using standard FC-attached arrays for the storage. This capability enables end users to preserve investment in storage resources while benefiting from the latest host connection mechanisms such as Fibre Channel over Ethernet (FCoE).

Block Virtualization—RAID

RAID is another data storage virtualization technology that combines multiple hard disk drive components into a logical unit to provide data redundancy and improve performance or capacity. Originally, in 1988, it was defined as Redundant Arrays of Inexpensive Disks (RAID) on a paper written by David A. Patterson, Gary A. Gibson, and Randy Katz, from the University of California. Now it is commonly used as Redundant Array of *Independent* Disks (RAID).

Data is distributed across the hard disk drives in one of several ways, depending on the specific level of redundancy and performance required, referred to as RAID levels. The different schemes or architectures are named by the word RAID followed by a number (for example, RAID 0, RAID 1). Each scheme provides a different balance between the key goals: reliability and availability, performance, and capacity. Originally, there were five RAID levels, but many variations have evolved—notably, several nested levels and many nonstandard levels (mostly proprietary). The Storage Networking Industry Association (SNIA) standardizes RAID levels and their associated data formats in the common RAID Disk Drive Format (DDF) standard.

Today, RAID is a staple in most storage products. It can be found in disk subsystems, host bus adapters, system motherboards, volume management software, device driver software, and virtually any processor along the I/O path. Because RAID works with storage address spaces and not necessarily storage devices, it can be used on multiple levels recursively. Host volume management software typically has several RAID variations and, in some cases, offers many sophisticated configuration options. Running RAID in a volume manager opens the potential for integrating file system and volume management products for management and performance-tuning purposes. RAID has been implemented in adapters/controllers for many years, starting with SCSI and including Advanced Technology Attachment (ATA) and serial ATA. Disk subsystems have been the most popular product for RAID implementations and probably will continue to be for many years to come. An enormous range of capabilities is offered in disk subsystems across a wide range of prices.

RAID levels greater than RAID 0 provide protection against unrecoverable (sector) read errors, as well as whole disk failure. Many RAID levels employ an error protection scheme called "parity," a widely used method in information technology to provide fault tolerance in a given set of data. Most of the RAID levels use simple XOR, but RAID 6 uses two separate parities based, respectively, on addition and multiplication in a particular Galois Field or Reed-Solomon error correction that we will not be covering in this chapter. The most common RAID levels used today are RAID 0 (striping), RAID 1 and variants (mirroring), RAID 5 (distributed parity), and RAID 6 (dual parity).

A RAID 0 array (also known as a stripe set or striped volume) splits data evenly across two or more disks (striped), without parity information. RAID 0 is normally used to increase performance, although it can also be used as a way to create a large logical disk out of two or more physical ones. It provides no data redundancy. A RAID 0 array can be created with disks of different sizes, but the storage space added to the array by each disk is limited to the size of the smallest disk. For example, if an 800GB disk is striped together with a 500GB disk, the size of the array will be 1TB (500GB x 2).

A RAID 1 array is an exact copy (or mirror) of a set of data on two disks. This is useful when read performance or reliability is more important than data storage capacity. Such an array can only be as big as the smallest member disk. A classic RAID 1 mirrored pair contains two disks. For example, if a 500GB disk is mirrored together with a 400GB disk, the size of the array will be 400GB.

A RAID 5 array comprises block-level striping with distributed parity. It requires that all drives but one be present to operate. Upon failure of a single drive, subsequent reads can be calculated from the distributed parity so that no data is lost. RAID 5 requires a minimum of three disks.

A RAID 6 array comprises block-level striping with double distributed parity. Double parity provides fault tolerance up to two failed drives. This makes larger RAID groups more practical, especially for high-availability systems, because large-capacity drives take longer to restore. As with RAID 5, a single drive failure results in reduced performance of the entire array until the failed drive has been replaced. With a RAID 6 array, using drives from multiple sources and manufacturers, it is possible to mitigate most of the problems associated with RAID 5. The larger the drive capacities and the larger the array size, the more important it becomes to choose RAID 6 instead of RAID 5.

Many storage controllers allow RAID levels to be nested (hybrid), and storage arrays are rarely nested more than one level deep. The final array of the RAID level is known as the top array. When the top array is RAID 0 (such as in RAID 1+0 and RAID 5+0), most vendors omit the "+", which yields RAID 10 and RAID 50, respectively. Here are the common examples of nested RAID levels:

- **RAID 0+1:** Creates a second striped set to mirror a primary striped set. The array continues to operate with one or more drives failed in the same mirror set, but if drives fail on both sides of the mirror, the data on the RAID system is lost.

- **RAID 1+0:** Creates a striped set from a series of mirrored drives. The array can sustain multiple drive losses as long as no mirror loses all its drives.

Table 23-2 provides an overview of the standard RAID levels.

Table 23-2   Overview of Standard RAID Levels

Level	Description	Minimum Number of Drives	Figure of the RAID Level
RAID 0	Block-level striping without parity or mirroring	2	Figure 23-4 shows how the data is distributed into Bx stripes to the disks. Accessing the stripes in the order B1, B2, B3, ... provides the illusion of a larger and faster drive. 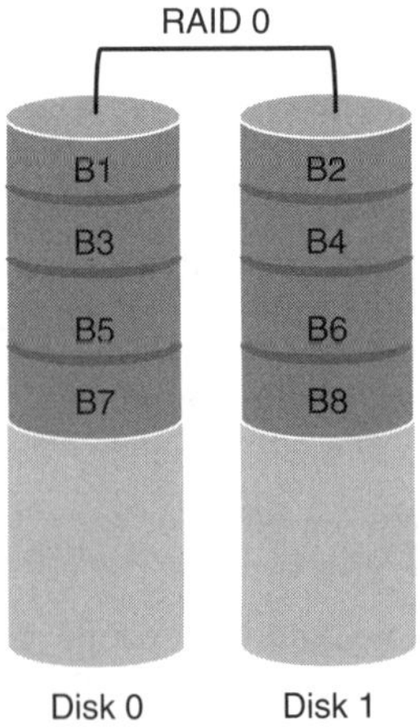

RAID 0

B1   B2

B3   B4

B5   B6

B7   B8

Disk 0   Disk 1

Figure 23-4

	Level	Description	Minimum Number of Drives	Figure of the RAID Level
Key Topic	RAID 1	Mirroring without parity or striping	2	Figure 23-5 is a RAID 1 setup. 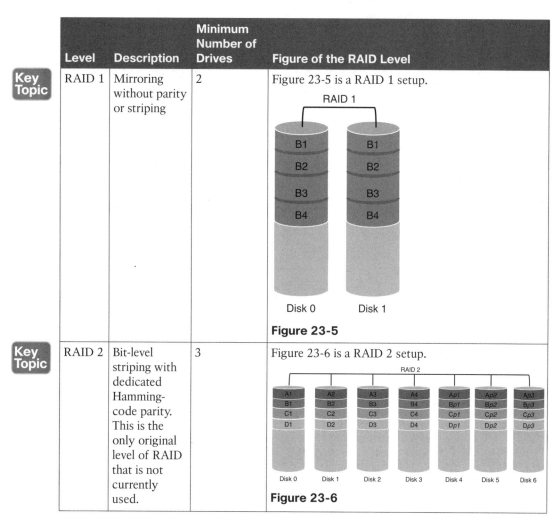
Key Topic	RAID 2	Bit-level striping with dedicated Hamming-code parity. This is the only original level of RAID that is not currently used.	3	Figure 23-6 is a RAID 2 setup.

	Level	Description	Minimum Number of Drives	Figure of the RAID Level
Key Topic	RAID 3	Byte-level striping with dedicated parity. RAID 3 is very rare in practice, usually implemented in hardware, and the performance impact is addressed by using large disk caches.	3	Figure 23-7 is a RAID 3 setup of 6-byte blocks and two parity bytes. Shown are two blocks of data in different colors. 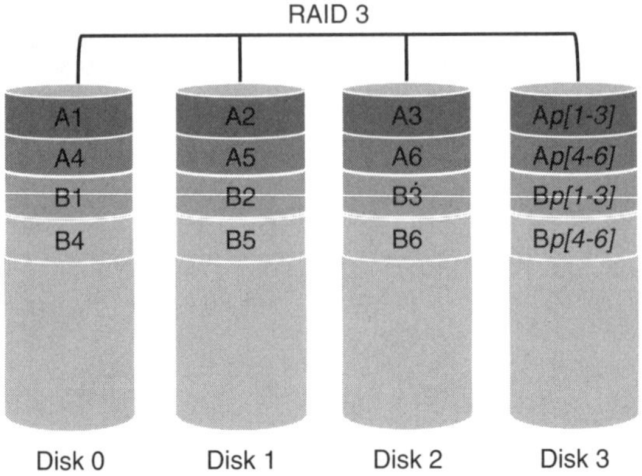 Figure 23-7
Key Topic	RAID 4	Block-level striping with dedicated parity. In the example on the right, a read request for block A1 would be serviced by disk 0. A simultaneous read request for block B1 would have to wait, but a read request for B2 could be serviced concurrently by disk 1.	3	Figure 23-8 is a RAID 4 setup with a dedicated parity disk, with each color representing the group of blocks in the respective parity block (a stripe). 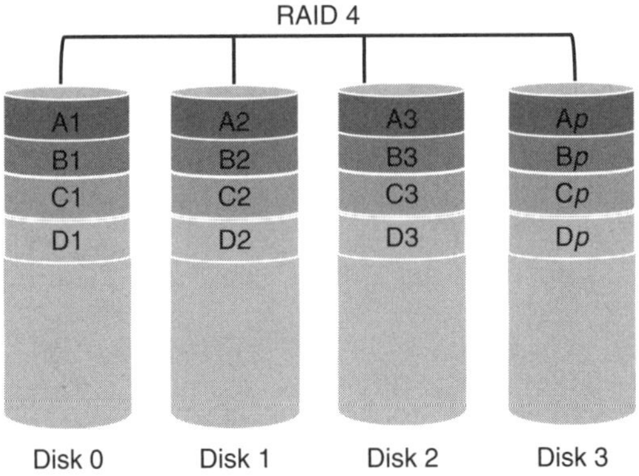 Figure 23-8

Figure 23-7 (RAID 3):
- Disk 0: A1, A4, B1, B4
- Disk 1: A2, A5, B2, B5
- Disk 2: A3, A6, B3, B6
- Disk 3: Ap[1-3], Ap[4-6], Bp[1-3], Bp[4-6]

Figure 23-8 (RAID 4):
- Disk 0: A1, B1, C1, D1
- Disk 1: A2, B2, C2, D2
- Disk 2: A3, B3, C3, D3
- Disk 3: Ap, Bp, Cp, Dp

	Level	Description	Minimum Number of Drives	Figure of the RAID Level
Key Topic	RAID 5	Block-level striping with distributed parity	3	Figure 23-9 is a RAID 5 setup with distributed parity, with each color representing the group of blocks in the respective parity block (a stripe). This figure shows the left asymmetric algorithm. 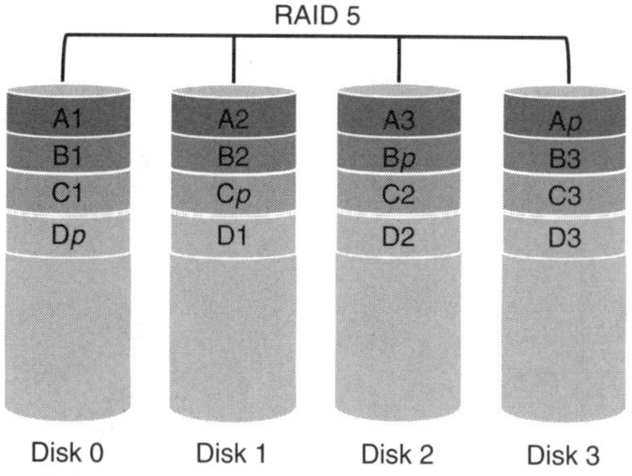 Figure 23-9
Key Topic	RAID 6	Block-level striping with double distributed parity	4	Figure 23-10 is a RAID 6 setup, which is identical to RAID 5 other than the addition of a second parity block. 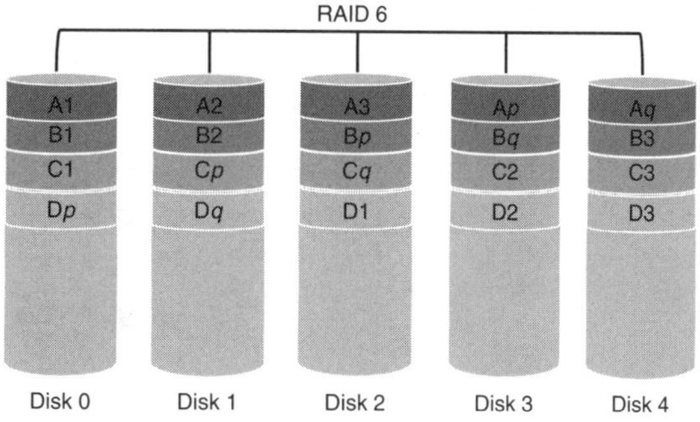 Figure 23-10

23

Level	Description	Minimum Number of Drives	Figure of the RAID Level
Key Topic RAID 1+0	Mirroring without parity, and block-level striping	4	Figure 23-11 is a RAID 1+0 setup. 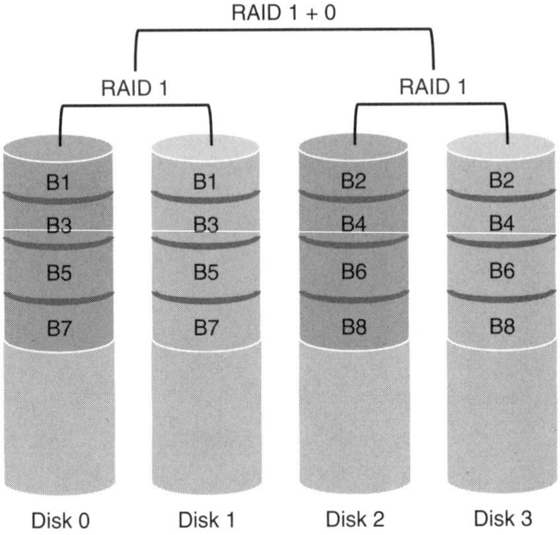 **Figure 23-11**
Key Topic RAID 0+1	Block-level striping and mirroring without parity	4	Figure 23-12 is a RAID 0+1 setup. 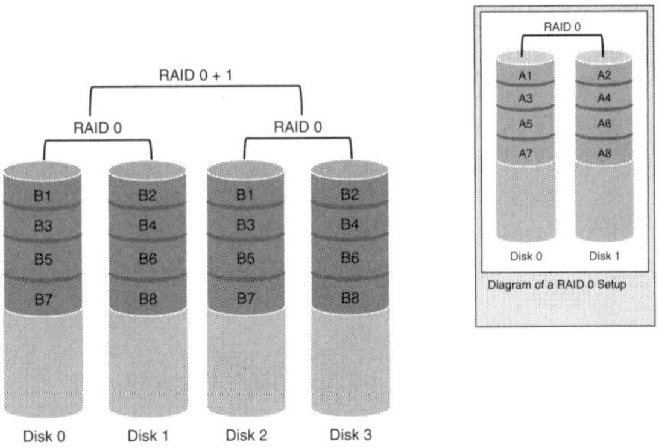 **Figure 23-12**

Virtualizing Logical Unit Numbers (LUNs)

Virtualization of storage helps to provide location independence by abstracting the physical location of the data. The user is presented with a logical space for data storage by the virtualization system, which manages the process of mapping that logical space to the physical location.

You can have multiple layers of virtualization or mapping by using the output of one layer as the input for a higher layer of virtualization. A logical unit number (LUN) is a unique identifier that designates individual hard disk devices or grouped devices for address by a protocol associated with an SCSI, iSCSI, Fibre Channel (FC), or similar interface. LUNs are central to the management of block storage arrays shared over a storage area network (SAN).

Virtualization maps the relationships between the back-end resources and front-end resources. A back-end resource refers to a LUN that is not presented to the computer or host system for direct use. A front-end LUN or volume is presented to the computer or host system for use. The mapping of the LUN performed depends on the implementation. Typically, one physical disk is broken down into smaller subsets in multiple megabytes or gigabytes of disk space. In a block-based storage environment, one block of information is addressed by using a LUN and an offset within that LUN, known as a logical block address (LBA).

In most SAN environments, each individual LUN must be discovered by only one server host bus adapter (HBA). Otherwise, the same volume will be accessed by more than one file system, leading to potential loss of data or security. There are three ways to prevent this multiple access:

- **LUN masking:** LUN masking, a feature of enterprise storage arrays, provides basic LUN-level security by allowing LUNs to be seen only by selected servers that are identified by their port World Wide Name (pWWN). Each storage array vendor has its own management and proprietary techniques for LUN masking in the array. In a heterogeneous environment with arrays from different vendors, LUN management becomes more difficult.

- **LUN mapping:** LUN mapping, a feature of Fibre Channel HBAs, allows the administrator to selectively map some LUNs that have been discovered by the HBA. LUN mapping must be configured on every HBA. In a large SAN, this mapping is a large management task. Most administrators configure the HBA to automatically map all LUNs that the HBA discovers. They then perform LUN management in the array (LUN masking) or in the network (LUN zoning).

- **LUN zoning:** LUN zoning, a proprietary technique that Cisco MDS switches offer, allows LUNs to be selectively zoned to their appropriate host port. LUN zoning can be used instead of, or in combination with, LUN masking in heterogeneous environments or where Just a Bunch of Disks (JBODs) are installed.

Figure 23-13 illustrates LUN masking, LUN mapping, and LUN zoning.

NOTE JBODs do not have a management function or a storage controller and therefore do not support LUN masking.

23

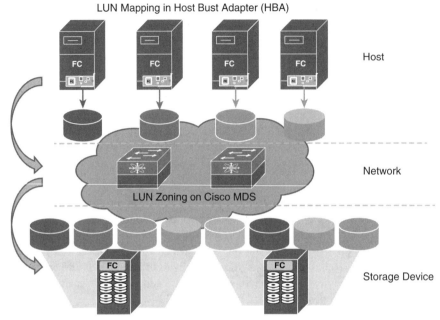

LUN Mapping in Host Bust Adapter (HBA)

Host

Network

LUN Zoning on Cisco MDS

Storage Device

RAID Configuration and LUN Masking in the Storage Arrays

Figure 23-13 *LUN Masking, LUN Mapping, and LUN Zoning on a Storage Area Network (SAN)*

In most LUN virtualization deployments, a virtualizer element is positioned between a host and its associated target disk array. This virtualizer generates a virtual LUN (vLUN) that proxies server I/O operations while hiding specialized data block processes that are occurring in the pool of disk arrays. The physical storage resources are aggregated into storage pools from which the logical storage is created. More storage systems, which may be heterogeneous in nature, can be added when needed, and the virtual storage space will scale up by the same amount. This process is fully transparent to the applications using the storage infrastructure. Thin-provisioning is a LUN virtualization feature that helps reduce the waste of block storage resources. When this technique is used, although a server can detect a vLUN with a "full" size, only blocks that are present in the vLUN are saved on the storage pool. This feature brings the concept of oversubscription to data storage, consequently demanding special attention to the ratio between "declared" and actually used resources. Utilizing vLUNs disk expansion and shrinking can be managed easily. More physical storage can be allocated by adding to the mapping table (assuming the using system can cope with online expansion). Similarly, disks can be reduced in size by removing some physical storage from the mapping (uses for this are limited because there is no guarantee of what resides on the areas removed). Each storage vendor has different LUN virtualization solutions and techniques. In this chapter we have briefly covered a subset of these features.

Tape Storage Virtualization

Tape storage virtualization can be divided into two categories: the tape media virtualization and the tape drive and library virtualization (VTL). Tape media virtualization resolves the problem of underutilized tape media; it saves tapes, tape libraries, and floor space. With tape media virtualization, the amount of mounts is reduced.

A virtual tape library (VTL) is used typically for backup and recovery purposes. A VTL presents a storage component (usually hard disk storage) as tape libraries or tape drives for use with existing backup software. Virtualizing the disk storage as tape allows integration of VTLs with existing backup software and existing backup and recovery processes and policies. The benefits of such virtualization include storage consolidation and faster data restore processes.

Most current VTL solutions use SAS or SATA disk arrays as the primary storage component because of their relatively low cost. The use of array enclosures increases the scalability of the solution by allowing the addition of more disk drives and enclosures to increase the storage capacity. The shift to VTL also eliminates streaming problems that often impair efficiency in tape drives, because disk technology does not rely on streaming and can write effectively regardless of data transfer speeds. By backing up data to disks instead of tapes, VTL often increases performance of both backup and recovery operations. Restore processes are found to be faster than backup regardless of implementations. In some cases, the data stored on the VTL's disk array is exported to other media, such as physical tapes, for disaster recovery purposes. (This scheme is called disk-to-disk-to-tape, or *D2D2T*).

Alternatively, most contemporary backup software products introduced direct usage of the file system storage (especially network-attached storage, accessed through NFS and CIFS protocols over IP networks). They also often offer a disk staging feature: moving the data from disk to a physical tape for long-term storage.

Virtualizing Storage Area Networks

A virtual storage area network (VSAN) is a collection of ports from a set of connected Fibre Channel switches that form a virtual fabric. Ports within a single switch can be partitioned into multiple VSANs, despite sharing hardware resources. Conversely, multiple switches can join a number of ports to form a single VSAN. VSANs were designed by Cisco, modeled after the virtual local area network (VLAN) concept in Ethernet networking, and applied to a SAN. In October 2004, the Technical Committee T11 of the International Committee for Information Technology Standards approved VSAN technology to become a standard of the American National Standards Institute (ANSI).

A VSAN, like each FC fabric, can offer different high-level protocols such as FCP, FCIP, FICON, and iSCSI. Each VSAN is a separate self-contained fabric using distinctive security policies, zones, events, memberships, and name services. The use of VSANs allows traffic to be isolated within specific portions of the network. If a problem occurs in one VSAN, that problem can be handled with a minimum of disruption to the rest of the network. VSANs can also be configured separately and independently. Figure 23-14 portrays three different SAN islands that are being virtualized onto a common SAN infrastructure on Cisco MDS switches. The geographic location of the switches and the attached devices are independent of their segmentation into logical VSANs.

23

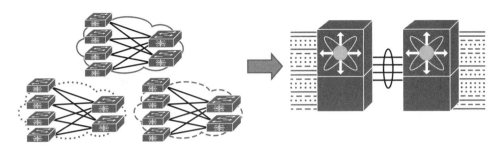

Figure 23-14 *Independent Physical SAN Islands Virtualized onto a Common SAN Infrastructure*

VSANs were not designed to be confined within a single switch. They can be extended to other switches, spreading a virtual Fibre Channel fabric over multiple devices. Although E_Ports can also be configured to extend a single VSAN, a *trunk* is usually the recommended extension between VSAN-enabled switches. By definition, a Trunk Expansion Port (TE_Port) can carry the traffic of several VSANs over a single *Enhanced Inter-Switch Link (EISL)*.

In an EISL, an 8-byte VSAN header is included between the Start of Frame (SOF) and the frame header. Figure 23-15 illustrates the VSAN EISL header. In the EISL header, the VSAN ID field occupies 12 bits and is used to mark the frame as part of a particular VSAN.

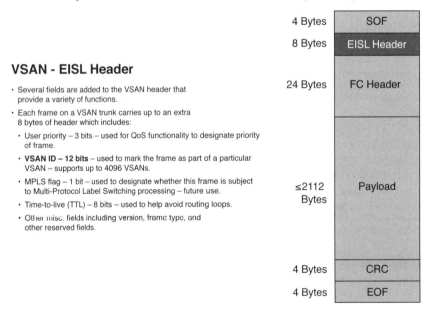

Figure 23-15 *VSAN Enhanced Inter-Switch Link (EISL) Header*

Since December 2002, Cisco has enabled multiple virtualization features within intelligent SANs. Several examples are Inter-VSAN routing (IVR), N-Port ID Virtualization (NPIV), and N-Port Virtualizer.

N-Port ID Virtualization (NPIV)

NPIV allows a Fibre Channel host connection or N-Port to be assigned multiple N-Port IDs or Fibre Channel IDs (FCIDs) over a single link. All FCIDs assigned can now be managed on a Fibre Channel fabric as unique entities on the same physical host. Different applications can be used in conjunction with NPIV. In a virtual machine environment where many host operating systems or applications are running on a physical host, each virtual machine can now be managed independently from zoning, aliasing, and security perspectives. Figure 23-16 illustrates an N-Port ID virtualization topology. NPIV must be globally enabled for all VSANs on the switch to allow the NPIV-enabled applications to use multiple N-Port identifiers.

NPIV - Control and Monitor VMs in the SAN

- NPIV gives Virtual Servers SAN identity. Allows multiple applications to share the same Fiber Channel adapter port.
  - Designed for virtual server environments.
- Allows SAN control of VMs.
  - Zoning and LUN Masking at VM level.
- Multiple applications on the same port can use different IDs.
  - Better utilization of the server connectivity.

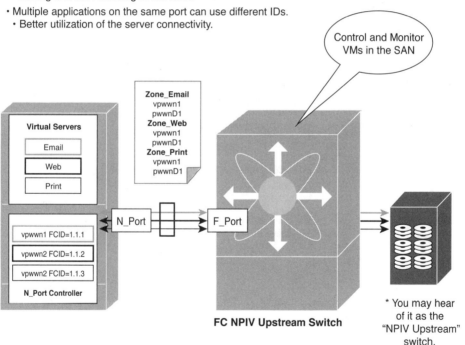

Figure 23-16 *NPIV—Control and Monitor VMs in the SAN*

Fibre Channel standards define that an FC HBA N-Port must be connected to one and only one F-Port on a Fibre Channel switch. When the device is connected to the switch, the link comes up and the FC HBA sends a FLOGI command containing its pWWN to the FC switch requesting a Fibre Channel ID. The switch responds with a unique FCID based on the domain ID of the switch, an area ID, and a port ID. This is fine for servers with a single operating environment but is restrictive for virtual servers, which may have several operating environments sharing the same FC HBA. Each virtual server requires its own FCID.

NPIV provides the ability to assign a separate FCID to each virtual server that requests one through its own FLOGI command.

N-Port Virtualizer (NPV)

An extension to NPIV is the N-Port Virtualizer feature. The N-Port Virtualizer feature allows the blade switch or top-of-rack fabric device to behave as an NPIV-based host bus adapter (HBA) to the core Fibre Channel director. The device aggregates the locally connected host ports or N-Ports into one or more uplinks (pseudo-interswitch links) to the core switches. Whereas NPIV is primarily a host-based solution, NPV is primarily a switch-based technology. It is designed to reduce switch management and overhead in larger SAN deployments. Consider that every Fibre Channel switch in a fabric needs a different domain ID, and that the total number of domain IDs in a fabric is limited. In some cases, this limit can be fairly low depending on the devices attached to the fabric. The problem, though, is that you often need to add Fibre Channel switches to scale the size of your fabric. There is, therefore, an inherent conflict between trying to reduce the overall number of switches to keep the domain ID count low while also needing to add switches to have a sufficiently high port count. NPV is intended to address this problem. NPV makes use of NPIV to get multiple FCIDs allocated from the core switch on the NP port. Figure 23-17 illustrates an NPV SAN topology.

What is NPV?

- N-Port Virtualizer (NPV) utilizes NPIV functionality to allow a "switch" to act like a server performing multiple logins through a single physical link.
- Physical servers connected to the NPV switch login to the upstream NPIV core switch.
  - Physical uplink from NPV switch to FC NPIV core switch does actual "FLOGI".
  - Subsequent logins are converted (proxy) to "FDISC" to log in to upstream FC switch.
- No local switching is done on an FC switch in NPV mode.
- FC edge switch in NPV mode does not take up a Domain ID, it is an extension of the Core Domain.
- Scalability will be dependent on FC "login" limitation.

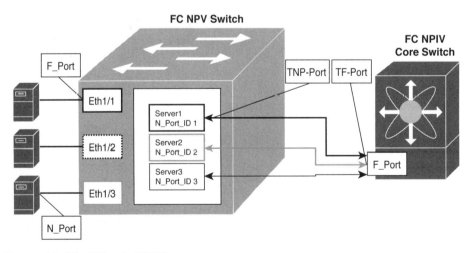

Figure 23-17 *What Is NPV?*

A switch is in NPV mode after a user has enabled NPV and the switch has successfully rebooted. NPV mode applies to an entire switch. All end devices connected to a switch that is in NPV mode must log in as an N-Port to use this feature (loop-attached devices are not supported). All links from the edge switches (in NPV mode) to the NPV core switches are established as NP ports (not E ports), which are used for typical interswitch links. NPIV is used by the switches in NPV mode to log in to multiple end devices that share a link to the NPV core switch. An NP port (proxy N port) is a port on a device that is in NPV mode and connected to the NPV core switch using an F port. NP ports behave like N ports except that in addition to providing N port behavior, they also function as proxies for multiple, physical N ports. An NP link is an NPIV uplink to a specific end device. NP links are established when the uplink to the NPV core switch comes up; the links are terminated when the uplink goes down. Once the uplink is established, the NPV switch performs an internal fabric login (FLOGI) to the NPV core switch, and then (if the FLOGI is successful) registers itself with the NPV core switch's name server.

Once the uplink is established, the NPV switch performs an internal fabric and sends a FLOGI request that includes the following parameters:

- The fWWN (fabric port WWN) of the NP port used as the pWWN in the internal login
- The VSAN-based sWWN (switch WWN) of the NPV device used as nWWN (node WWN) in the internal FLOGI

After completing its FLOGI request (if the FLOGI is successful), the NPV device registers itself with the fabric name server using the following additional parameters:

- The switch name and interface name (for example, fc1/4) of the NP port are embedded in the symbolic port name in the name server registration of the NPV device itself.
- The IP address of the NPV device is registered as the IP address in the name server registration of the NPV device.

Subsequent FLOGIs from end devices in this NP link are converted to fabric discoveries (FDISCs).

NPV devices use only IP as the transport medium. CFS uses multicast forwarding for CFS distribution. NPV devices do not have ISL connectivity and FC domain. To use CFS over IP, multicast forwarding has to be enabled on the Ethernet IP switches all along the network that physically connects the NPV switch. You can also manually configure the static IP peers for CFS distribution over IP on NPV-enabled switches.

In-order data delivery is not required in NPV mode because the exchange between two end devices always takes the same uplink to the core from the NPV device. For traffic beyond the NPV device, core switches will enforce in-order delivery if needed and/or configured. Three different types of traffic management exist for NPV:

- **Auto:** When a server interface is brought up, an external interface with the minimum load is selected from the available links. There is no manual selection on the server interfaces using the external links. Also, when a new external interface was brought up, the existing load was not distributed automatically to the newly available external interface. This newly brought up interface is used only by the server interfaces that come up after this interface.

23

■ **Traffic map:** This feature facilitates traffic engineering by providing dedicated external interfaces for the servers connected to NPV. It uses the shortest path by selecting external interfaces per server interface. It utilizes the persistent FCID feature by providing the same traffic path after a link break, or reboot of the NPV or core switch. It also balances the load by allowing the user to evenly distribute the load across external interfaces.

■ **Disruptive:** Disruptive load balance works independent of automatic selection of interfaces and a configured traffic map of external interfaces. This feature forces reinitialization of the server interfaces to achieve load balance when this feature is enabled and whenever a new external interface comes up. To avoid flapping the server interfaces too often, enable this feature once and then disable it whenever the needed load balance is achieved. If disruptive load balance is not enabled, you need to manually flap the server interface to move some of the load to a new external interface.

Figure 23-18 illustrates the NPV auto load balancing.

NPV Auto Load Balancing

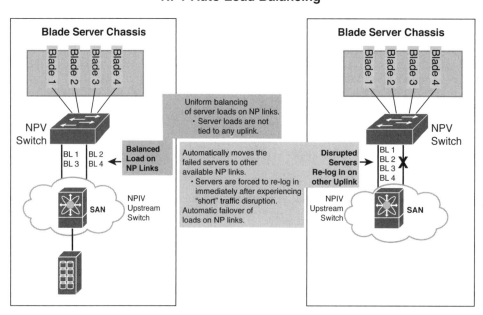

Figure 23-18 *NPV Auto Load Balancing*

An F port channel is a logical interface that combines a set of F ports connected to the same Fibre Channel node and operates as one link between the F ports and the NP ports. The F port channels support bandwidth utilization and availability like the E port channels. F port channels are mainly used to connect MDS core and NPV switches to provide optimal band-width utilization and transparent failover between the uplinks of a VSAN. An F port channel trunk combines the functionality and advantages of a TF port and an F port channel. F port channel trunks allow for the fabric logins from the NPV switch to be virtualized over the port channel. This provides nondisruptive redundancy should individual member links fail. The individual links by default are in rate-mode shared, but can be rate-mode dedicated as well. Figure 23-19 illustrates F port channel and F port channel trunking features.

F-Port Port Channel

```
feature npv

interface port-channel 1
channel mode active
  switchport mode NP
  switchport trunk mode off
  switchport rate-mode dedicated
  switchport trunk mode on

interface fc1/1
  switchport mode NP
  switchport trunk mode off
  port-license acquire
  channel-group 1 force
  no shutdown
```

```
feature fport-channel-trunk
feature npiv

interface port-channel 1
  channel mode active
  switchport mode F
  switchport trunk mode off
  switchport rate-mode dedicated

interface fc1/1
  switchport rate-mode dedicated
  switchport mode F
  switchport trunk mode off
  channel-group 1 force
  no shutdown
```

F-Port Trunking

```
feature npv

interface port-channel 1
  channel mode active
  switchport mode NP
  switchport trunk allowed vsan 1-3
  switchport rate-mode dedicated
  switchport trunk mode on

interface fc1/1
  switchport mode NP
  switchport trunk mode on
  port-license acquire
  channel-group 1 force
  no shutdown
```

```
feature fport-channel-trunk
feature npiv

interface port-channel 1
  channel mode active
  switchport mode F
  switchport trunk allowed vsan 1-3
  switchport rate-mode dedicated

interface fc1/1
  switchport rate-mode dedicated
  switchport mode F
  channel-group 1 force
  no shutdown
```

Figure 23-19   *F Port Channel and F Port Channel Trunking*

Virtualizing File Systems

A virtual file system is an abstraction layer that allows client applications using heteroge-neous file-sharing network protocols to access a unified pool of storage resources. These systems are based on a global file directory structure that is contained on dedicated file metadata servers. Whenever a file system client needs to access a file, it must retrieve infor-mation about the file from the metadata servers first (see Figure 23-20).

The purpose of a VFS is to allow client applications to access different types of concrete file systems in a uniform way. A VFS can, for example, be used to access local and network storage devices transparently without the client application noticing the difference. It can be used to bridge the differences in Windows, Mac OS, and Unix file systems so that applica-tions can access files on local file systems of those types without having to know what type of file system they are accessing.

23

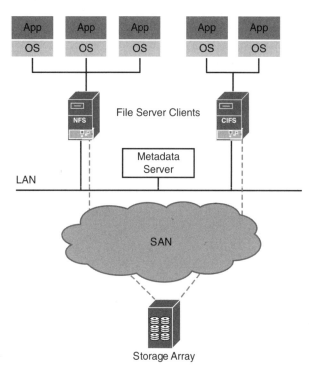

Figure 23-20   *File System Virtualization*

A VFS specifies an interface (or a "contract") between the kernel and a concrete file system. Therefore, it is easy to add support for new file system types to the kernel simply by fulfilling the contract. The terms of the contract might bring incompatibility from release to release, which would require that the concrete file system support be recompiled, and possibly modified before recompilation, to allow it to work with a new release of the operating system. Or the supplier of the operating system might make only backward-compatible changes to the contract so that concrete file system support built for a given release of the operating system would work with future versions of the operating system.

Sun Microsystems introduced one of the first VFSes on Unix-like systems. The VMware Virtual Machine File System (VMFS), NTFS, Linux's Global File System (GFS), and the Oracle Clustered File System (OCFS) are all examples of virtual file systems.

File/Record Virtualization

File virtualization unites multiple storage devices into a single logical pool of files. It is a vital part of both file area network (FAN) and network file management (NFM) concepts.

File virtualization is similar to Dynamic Name Service (DNS), which removes the requirement to know the IP address of a website; you simply type in the domain name. In a similar fashion, file virtualization eliminates the need to know exactly where a file is physically located. Users look to a single mount point that shows all their files. Data can be moved from a tier-one NAS to a tier-two or tier-three NAS or network file server automatically. In Chapter 22, we discussed different types of tiered storage, as you will remember. In a common scenario, the primary NAS could be a high-speed high performance system storing production data. Because these files are less frequently accessed, they can be moved to lower-cost, more-power-efficient systems that bring down capital and operational costs.

Two types of file virtualization methods are available today. The first is one that's built in to the storage system or the NAS itself, often called a "global" file system. There may be some advantage here because the file system itself is managing the metadata that contains the file locations, which could solve the file stub and manual look-up problems. The challenge, however, is that this metadata is unique to the users of that specific file system, meaning the same hardware must be used to expand these systems and is often available from only one manufacturer. This eliminates one of the key capabilities of a file virtualization system: the flexibility to mix hardware in a system. With this solution, you could lose the ability to store older data on a less expensive storage system, a situation equivalent to not being able to mix brands of servers in a server virtualization project. Often, global file systems are not granular to the file level.

The second file virtualization method uses a standalone virtualization engine—typically an appliance. These systems can either sit in the data path (in-band) or outside the data path (out-of-band) and can move files to alternate locations based on a variety of attribute-related policies. In-band solutions typically offer better performance, whereas out-of-band solutions are simpler to implement. Both offer file-level granularity, but most important, standalone file virtualization systems do not have to use all the same hardware.

Where Does the Storage Virtualization Occur?

Storage virtualization functionality, including aggregation (pooling), transparent data migration, heterogeneous replication, and device emulation, can be implemented at the host server in the data path on a network switch blade or on an appliance, as well as in a storage system. The best location to implement storage virtualization functionality depends in part on the preferences, existing technologies, and objectives for deploying storage virtualization.

Host-Based Virtualization

A host-based virtualization requires additional software running on the host as a privileged task or process. In some cases, volume management is built in to the operating system, and in other instances it is offered as a separate product. A physical device driver handles the volumes (LUN) presented to the host system. However, a software layer, the logical volume manager, residing above the disk device driver intercepts the I/O requests (see Figure 23-21) and provides the metadata lookup and I/O mapping.

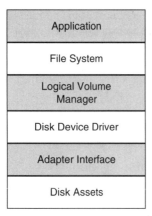

Figure 23-21   *Logical Volume Manager on a Server System*

The LVM manipulates LUN representation to create virtualized storage to the file system or database manager. So with host-based virtualization, heterogeneous storage systems can be used on a per-server basis. For smaller data centers, this may not be a significant issue, but manual administration of hundreds or thousands of servers in a large data center can be very costly. LVMs can be used to divide large physical disk arrays into more manageable virtual disks or to create large virtual disks from multiple physical disks. The logical volume manager treats any LUN as a vanilla resource for storage pooling; it will not differentiate the RAID levels. So the storage administrator must ensure that the appropriate classes of storage under LVM control are paired with individual application requirements.

Most modern operating systems have some form of logical volume management built in that performs virtualization tasks (in Linux, it's called Logical Volume Manager, or LVM; in Solaris and FreeBSD, it's ZFS's zpool layer; in Windows, it's Logical Disk Manager, or LDM). Host-based storage virtualization may require more CPU cycles. Use of host-resident virtualization must therefore be balanced against the processing requirements of the upper-layer applications so that overall performance expectations can be met. For higher perfor-mance requirements, logical volume management may be complemented by hardware-based virtualization. RAID controllers for internal DAS and JBOD external chassis are good exam-ples of hardware-based virtualization. RAID can be implemented without a special control-ler, but the software that performs the striping calculations often places a noticeable burden on the host CPU.

Network-Based (Fabric-Based) Virtualization

A network-based virtualization is a fabric-based switch infrastructure. The SAN fabric pro-vides connectivity to heterogeneous server platforms and heterogeneous storage arrays and tape subsystems. Fabric may be composed of multiple switches from different vendors; the virtualization capabilities require standardized protocols to ensure interoperability between fabric-hosted virtualization engines. Fabric-based storage virtualization dynamically interacts with virtualizers on arrays, servers, or appliances.

A host-based (server-based) virtualization provides independence from vendor-specific stor-age, and storage-based virtualization provides independence from vendor-specific servers and operating systems. Network-based virtualization provides independence from both.

Fabric-based virtualization requires processing power and memory on top of a hardware architecture that is providing processing power for fabric services, switching, and other tasks. The fabric-based virtualization engine can be hosted on an appliance, an application-specific integrated circuit (ASIC) blade, or auxiliary module. It can be either in-band or out-of-band, referring to whether the virtualization engine is in the data path. Out-of-band solutions typically run on the server or on an appliance in the network and essentially process the control traffic, routing I/O requests to the proper physical locations, but don't handle data traffic. This can result in less latency than in-band storage virtualization because the virtualization engine doesn't handle the data; it's also less disruptive if the virtualization engine goes down.

In-band solutions intercept I/O requests from hosts, map them to the physical storage locations, and regenerate those I/O requests to the storage systems on the back end. They do require that the virtualization engine handle both control traffic and data, which requires the processing power and internal bandwidth to ensure that they don't add too much latency to the I/O process for host servers.

Multivendor fabric-based virtualization provides high availability, and it initiated the fabric application interface standard (FAIS). FAIS is an open-systems project of the ANSI/INCITS T11.5 task group and defines a set of common application programming interfaces (APIs) to be implemented within fabrics. The APIs are a means to more easily integrate storage applications that were originally developed as host, array, or appliance-based utilities to now be supported within fabric switches and directors. FAIS development is thus being driven by the switch manufacturers and by companies that have developed storage virtualization software and virtualization hardware-assist components.

The FAIS initiative separates control information from the data path. There are two types of processors: the CPP and the DCP. The control path processor (CPP) includes some form of operating system, the FAIS application interface, and the storage virtualization application. The CPP is therefore a high-performance CPU with auxiliary memory, centralized within the switch architecture. Allocation of virtualized storage to individual servers and management of the storage metadata are the responsibility of the storage application running on the CPP.

The data path controller (DPC) may be implemented at the port level in the form of an application-specific integrated circuit (ASIC) or dedicated CPU. The DPC is optimized for low latency and high bandwidth to execute basic SCSI read/write transactions under the management of one or more CPPs. The FAIS specifications do not define a particular hardware design for CPP and DPC entities, so vendor implementation may be different. The FAIS initiative aims to provide fabric-based services, such as snapshots, mirroring, and data replication, while maintaining high-performance switching of storage data.

Network-based virtualization can be done with one of the following approaches:

- **Symmetric or in-band:** With an in-band approach, the virtualization device is sitting in the path of the I/O data flow. Hosts send I/O requests to the virtualization device, which perform I/O with the actual storage device on behalf of the host. Caching for improving performance and other storage management features such as replication and migration can be supported.

- **Asymmetric or out-of-band:** The virtualization device in this approach sits outside the data path between the host and storage device. What this means is that special software is needed on the host, which knows to first request the location of data from the virtualization device and then use that mapped physical address to perform the I/O.

■ **Hybrid split-path:** This method uses a combination of in-band and out-of-band approaches, taking advantage of intelligent SAN switches to perform I/O redirection and other virtualization tasks at wire speed. Specialized software running on a dedicated highly available appliance interacts with the intelligent switch ports to manage I/O traffic and map logical-to-physical storage resources at wire speed. Whereas in typical in-band solutions, the CPU is susceptible to being overwhelmed by I/O traffic, in the split-path approach the I/O-intensive work is offloaded to dedicated port-level ASICs on the SAN switch. These ASICs can look inside Fibre Channel frames and perform I/O mapping and reroute the frames without introducing any significant amount of latency. Figure 23-22 portrays the three architecture options for implementing network-based storage virtualization.

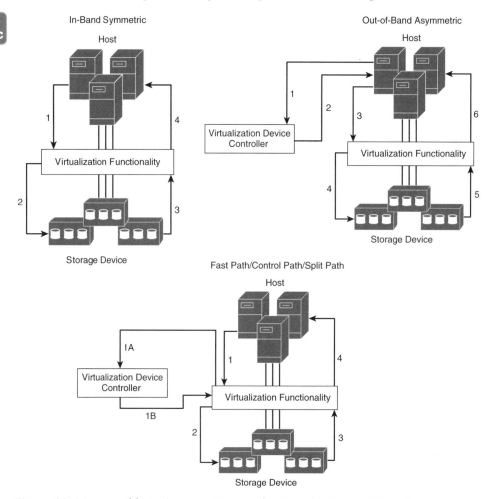

Figure 23-22 *Possible Architecture Options for How the Storage Virtualization Is Implemented*

There are many debates regarding the architecture advantages of in-band (in the data path) vs. out-of-band (out-of-data path with agent and metadata controller) or split path (hybrid of in-band and out-of-band). Some applications and their storage requirements are best suited for a combination of technologies to address specific needs and requirements.

Cisco SANTap is one of the Intelligent Storage Services features supported on the Storage Services Module (SSM), MDS 9222i Multiservice Modular Switch, and MDS 9000 18/4-Port Multiservice Module (MSM-18/4). Cisco SANTap is a good example of network-based virtualization. The Cisco MDS 9000 SANTap service enables customers to deploy third-party appliance-based storage applications without compromising the integrity, availability, or performance of a data path between the server and disk. The protocol-based interface that is offered by SANTap allows easy and rapid integration of the data storage service application because it delivers a loose connection between the application and an SSM, which reduces the effort needed to integrate applications with the core services being offered by the SSM. SANTap has a control path and a data path. The control path handles requests that create and manipulate replication sessions sent by an appliance. The control path is implemented using an SCSI-based protocol. An appliance sends requests to a Control Virtual Target (CVT), which the SANTap process creates and monitors. Responses are sent to the control logical unit number (LUN) on the appliance. SANTap also allows LUN mapping to Appliance Virtual Targets (AVTs).

Array-Based Virtualization

In the array-based approach, the virtualization layer resides inside a storage array controller, and multiple other storage devices from the same vendor or from a different vendor can be added behind it. That controller, called the primary storage array controller, is responsible for providing the mapping functionality. The primary storage array controller also provides replication, migration, and other storage management services across the storage devices that it is virtualizing. The communication between separate storage array controllers enables the disk resources of each system to be managed collectively, either through a distributed management scheme or through a hierarchal master/slave relationship. The communication protocol between storage subsystems may be proprietary or based on the SNIA SMI-S standard.

As one of the first forms of array-to-array virtualization, data replication requires that a storage system function as a target to its attached servers and as an initiator to a secondary array. This is commonly referred to as disk-to-disk (D2D) data replication.

Array-based data replication may be synchronous or asynchronous. In a synchronous replication operation, each write to a primary array must be completed on the secondary array before the SCSI transaction acknowledges completion. The SCSI I/O is therefore dependent on the speed at which both writes can be performed, and any latency between the two systems affects overall performance. For this reason, synchronous data replication is generally limited to metropolitan distances (~150 kilometers) to avoid performance degradation due to speed of light propagation delay. Figure 23-23 illustrates synchronous mirroring.

23

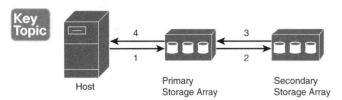

1. Write operation received by primary storage array.
2. Primary storage array delays the confirmation and initiates write to the secondary storage array.
3. Secondary storage array sends an acknowledgement to the primary storage array after the data is stored on the secondary.
4. A write complete confirmation is sent to the host (server).

Figure 23-23 *Synchronous Mirroring*

In asynchronous array-based replication, individual write operations to the primary array are acknowledged locally, while one or more write transactions may be queued to the secondary array. This solves the problem of local performance, but may result in loss of the most current write to the secondary array if the link between the two systems is lost. To minimize this risk, some implementations required the primary array to temporarily buffer each pending transaction to the secondary so that transient disruptions are recoverable. Figure 23-24 illustrates asynchronous mirroring.

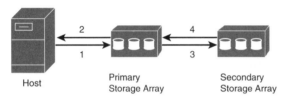

1. Write operation is received by primary storage array from the host.
2. Primary storage array does not require a confirmation from the secondary storage array to acknowledge the write operation to the server.
3. Primary storage array will maintain new data queued to be copied to the secondary storage array later. It initiates a write to the secondary storage array.
4. An acknowledgement is sent to the primary storage array by the secondary storage array after the data is stored on the secondary storage array.

Figure 23-24 *Asynchronous Mirroring*

Array-based virtualization services often include automated point-in-time copies or snapshots that may be implemented as a complement to data replication. Point-in-time copy is a technology that permits you to make the copies of large sets of data a common activity. Like photographic snapshots capture images of physical action, point-in-time copies (or snapshots) are virtual or physical copies of data that capture the state of data set contents at a single instant. Both virtual (copy-on-write) and physical (full-copy) snapshots protect against corruption of data content. Additionally, full-copy snapshots can protect against physical destruction. These copies can be used for a backup, a checkpoint to restore the state of an application, data mining, test data, and a kind of off-host processing.

Solutions need to be able to scale in terms of performance, connectivity, and ease of management, functionality, and resiliency without introducing instability. There are many approaches to implement and deploy storage virtualization functionality to meet various requirements.

The best solution is going to be the one that meets customers' specific requirements and may vary by customers' different tiers of storage and applications. Table 23-3 provides a basic comparison between various approaches based on SNIA's virtualization tutorial.

Table 23-3   Comparison of Storage Virtualization Levels

Virtualization Level	Advantages	Considerations
Host-based	Independent of storage subsystem Close to the file system Use operating system (OS) built-in tools No array controller cycles Independent of SAN transport Software solution	OS dependence HW dependence (maybe) Uses OS built-in-tools Uses host CPU cycles Licensed and managed per host
Network-based	Subsystem independence Host and OS independence No host CPU cycles Choice of band (in, out)	Switch dependence (maybe) Uses switch cycles Choice of band (in, out) Management cost
Array-based	Host and operating system (OS) independence Close to the devices No host CPU cycles High performance and scalable	Array dependence Far from the file system Uses controller cycles Specialized training (maybe)

Fibre Channel Zoning and LUN Masking

VSANs are used to segment the physical fabric into multiple logical fabrics. Zoning provides security within a single fabric, whether physical or logical, to restrict access between initiators and targets (see Figure 23-25). LUN masking is used to provide additional security to LUNs after an initiator has reached the target device.

The zoning service within a Fibre Channel fabric is designed to provide security between devices that share the same fabric. The primary goal is to prevent certain devices from accessing other devices within the fabric. With many types of servers and storage devices on the network, the need for security is crucial. For example, if a host were to access a disk that another host is using, potentially with a different operating system, the data on the disk could become corrupted. To avoid any compromise of crucial data within the SAN, zoning allows the user to overlay a security map. This process dictates which devices—namely hosts—can see which targets, thus reducing the risk of data loss.

Zoning and VSANs

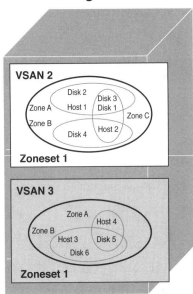

- First assign physical ports to VSANs.
- Then configure zones within each VSAN.
- Assign zones to active zoneset.
- Each VSAN has its own zoneset.
- A zone consists of multiple zone members.
- Members in a zone can access each other; members in different zones cannot access each other.
- Devices can belong to more than one zone.

Figure 23-25   *VSANs Versus Zoning*

Advanced zoning capabilities specified in the FC-GS-4 and FC-SW-3 standards are provided. You can use either the existing basic zoning capabilities or the advanced (enhanced), standards-compliant zoning capabilities.

There are two main methods of zoning: hard and soft. More recently, the differences between the two have blurred. All modern SAN switches then enforce soft zoning in hardware. The fabric name service allows each device to query the addresses of all other devices. Soft zoning restricts only the fabric name service, to show only an allowed subset of devices. Therefore, when a server looks at the content of the fabric, it will see only the devices it is allowed to see. However, any server can still attempt to contact any device on the network by address. In this way, soft zoning is similar to the computing concept of security through obscurity.

In contrast, hard zoning restricts actual communication across a fabric. This requires efficient hardware implementation (frame filtering) in the fabric switches, but is much more secure. That stated, modern switches would employ hard zoning when you implement soft. Cisco MDS 9000 and Cisco Nexus family switches implement hard zoning.

Zoning does have its limitations. Zoning was designed to do nothing more than prevent devices from communicating with other unauthorized devices. It is a distributed service that is common throughout the fabric. Any installed changes to a zoning configuration are therefore disruptive to the entire connected fabric. Zoning was also not designed to address availability or scalability of a Fibre Channel infrastructure.

Zoning has the following features:

- A zone consists of multiple zone members. Members in a zone can access each other; members in different zones cannot access each other. If zoning is not activated, all devices are members of the default zone. If zoning is activated, any device that is not in an active zone (a zone that is part of an active zone set) is a member of the default zone. Zones can vary in size. Devices can belong to more than one zone.

- A zone set consists of one or more zones. A zone set can be activated or deactivated as a single entity across all switches in the fabric. Only one zone set can be activated at any time. A zone can be a member of more than one zone set. A Cisco MDS switch can have a maximum of 500 zone sets.

- Zoning can be administered from any switch in the fabric. When you activate a zone (from any switch), all switches in the fabric receive the active zone set. Additionally, full zone sets are distributed to all switches in the fabric, if this feature is enabled in the source switch. If a new switch is added to an existing fabric, zone sets are acquired by the new switch.

- Zone changes can be configured nondisruptively. New zones and zone sets can be activated without interrupting traffic on unaffected ports or devices.

- Zone membership criteria is based mainly on WWNs or FCIDs.

  - **Port World Wide Name (pWWN):** Specifies the pWWN of an N port attached to the switch as a member of the zone.

  - **Fabric pWWN:** Specifies the WWN of the fabric port (switch port's WWN). This membership is also referred to as port-based zoning.

  - **FCID:** Specifies the FCID of an N port attached to the switch as a member of the zone.

  - **Interface and switch WWN (sWWN):** Specifies the interface of a switch identified by the sWWN. This membership is also referred to as interface-based zoning.

  - **Interface and domain ID:** Specifies the interface of a switch identified by the domain ID.

  - **Domain ID and port number:** Specifies the domain ID of an MDS domain and additionally specifies a port belonging to a non-Cisco switch.

  - **IPv4 address:** Specifies the IPv4 address (and optionally the subnet mask) of an attached device.

  - **IPv6 address:** The IPv6 address of an attached device in 128 bits in colon-separated hexadecimal format.

  - **Symbolic node name:** Specifies the member symbolic node name. The maximum length is 240 characters.

- Default zone membership includes all ports or WWNs that do not have a specific membership association. Access between default zone members is controlled by the default zone policy. Figure 23-26 illustrates zoning examples.

23

Zoning Examples

- Non-zoned devices are members of the default zone.

- A physical fabric can have a maximum of 16,000 zones (MDS 9700-only network).

- Attributes can include pWWN, FC alias, FCID, FWWN, Switch Interface fc x/y, Symbolic node name, Device alias.

```
zone name OZI_NetApp vsan 42
  member pwwn 20:03:00:25:b5:0a:00:06
  member pwwn 50:0a:09:84:9d:53:43:54
```

```
device-alias name OZ_Server
  pwwn 20:03:00:25:b5:0a:00:06
device-alias name NTAP
  member pwwn 50:0a:09:84:9d:53:43:54
zone name OZI_NetApp vsan 42
  member device-alias OZ_Server
  member device-alias NTAP
```

Figure 23-26   *Zoning Examples*

SAN administrators allow servers (initiators) and storage devices (targets) in a Fibre Channel SAN to talk to each other by adding them to the same zone. In the fabric, permissions defined in this way are converted to access control entries (ACEs), which are programmed into ternary content-addressable memory (TCAM) hardware in the switches. Traditionally, zones have members, and all members of a zone can talk to each other. Each pair of members consumes two ACEs in the TCAM: One ACE permits the first member to receive traffic from the second member, and the other ACE permits the second member to receive traffic from the first member. Mathematically, the number of ACEs consumed by a zone with n members would be $n \times (n - 1)$. Since hardware resources are finite, a moderate number of large zones can exceed the TCAM capacity of a switch (see Figure 23-27). The solution to this problem has been to use 1-1 zoning, where each zone consists of a single initiator and a single target. This solution solves the problem of excessive TCAM consumption, but it imposes a burden on the SAN administrator by requiring the creation and management of a large number of zones. More zones generate more work—and more possibilities for errors. In very large fabrics, this solution may even run up against system software limits on the size of the total zone database.

The Trouble with Sizable Zoning
All Zone Members are Created Equal

- Standard zoning model just has "members".
- Any member can talk to any other member.
- Recommendation: 1-1 zoning.
- Each pair consumes an ACL entry in Ternary content-addressable memory (TCAM).
- Result: $n \times (n-1)$ entries.
- Admin pays price for internal inefficiency.

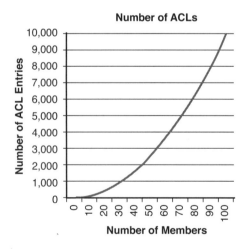

Figure 23-27   *The Trouble with Sizable Zoning*

Cisco Smart Zoning takes advantage of the fact that storage traffic is not symmetrical or egalitarian like LAN traffic, where any Ethernet or TCP/IP host may need to talk to any other host. Storage is asymmetrical: zone members are either initiators or targets, and in most cases, initiators do not talk to other initiators, and targets do not talk to other targets. There are exceptions to this generalization, such as array-to-array replication, and any solution must take those into account. Consider an example in which an application has eight servers, each with dual host bus adapters (HBAs) or converged network adapters (CNAs), talking to eight storage ports. These devices are split among two redundant, disjoint SAN fabrics, so each fabric has eight HBAs and four storage ports for this application. A total of 132 ACEs is created because each of the 12 members of the zone is provisioned with access to all 11 other members. With Smart Zoning, zones can now be defined as one-to-many, many-to-one, or many-to-many without incurring a penalty in switch resource consumption. Thus, administrators can now define zones to correspond to entities that actually are meaningful in their data center operations. For example, they can define a zone for an application, for an application cluster, or for a hypervisor cluster without compromising internal resource utilization. Consider a maximum VMware vSphere cluster of 32 servers that uses a total of eight storage ports. A single zone for this cluster has 40 members. With traditional zoning, it would consume $n \times (n - 1)$ ACL entries, which translates to $40 \times 39 = 1560$ ACL entries. With Smart Zoning, ACL consumption drops to $32 \times 8 \times 2 = 512$ ACL entries.

The following guidelines must be considered when creating zone members:

- Configuring only one initiator and one target for a zone provides the most efficient use of the switch resources.

- Configuring the same initiator to multiple targets is accepted.

- Configuring multiple initiators to multiple targets is not recommended.

The zoning feature complies with the FC-GS-4 and FC-SW-3 standards. Both standards support the basic zoning functionalities and the enhanced zoning functionalities.

LUN masking is the most common method of ensuring LUN security. Each SCSI host uses a number of primary SCSI commands to identify its target, discover LUNs, and obtain their size. The following are the commands:

- **Identify:** Which device are you?

- **Report LUNs:** How many LUNs are behind this storage array port?

- **Report capacity:** What is the capacity of each LUN?

- **Request sense:** Is a LUN online and available?

It is important to ensure that only one host accesses each LUN on the storage array at a time, unless the hosts are configured in a cluster. As the host mounts each LUN volume, it writes a signature at the start of the LUN to claim exclusive access. If a second host should discover and try to mount the same LUN volume, it overwrites the previous signature.

LUN masking ensures that only one host can access a LUN; all other hosts are masked out. LUN masking is essentially a mapping table inside the front-end array controllers. LUN masking determines which LUNs are to be advertised through which storage array ports, and which host is allowed to own which LUNs.

23

An alternative method of LUN security is LUN mapping. If LUN masking is unavailable in the storage array, LUN mapping can be used, although both methods can be used concurrently.

LUN mapping is configured in the HBA of each host, to ensure that only one host at a time can access each LUN. LUNs can be advertised on many storage ports and discovered by several hosts at the same time. Many LUNs are to be visible, but it is the responsibility of the administrator to configure each HBA so that each host has exclusive access to its LUNs. When there are many hosts, a mistake is more likely to be made and more than one host might access the same LUN by accident. Table 23-4 compares the characteristic differences between VSAN and Zone.

Table 23-4   VSAN and Zone Comparison

VSAN Characteristic	Zone Characteristic
VSANs equal SANs with routing, naming, and zoning protocols.	Routing, naming, and zoning protocols are not available on a per-zone basis.
—	Zones are always contained within a VSAN. Zones never span two VSANs.
VSANs limit unicast, multicast, and broadcast traffic.	Zones limit unicast traffic.
Membership is typically defined using the VSAN ID to Fx ports.	Membership is typically defined by the pWWN.
An HBA or a storage device can belong only to a single VSAN—the VSAN associated with the Fx port.	An HBA or storage device can belong to multiple zones.
VSANs enforce membership at each E port, source port, and destination port.	Zones enforce membership only at the source and destination ports.
VSANs are defined for larger environments (storage service providers).	Zones are defined for a set of initiators and targets not visible outside the zone.
VSANs encompass the entire fabric.	Zones are configured at the fabric edge.

Device Aliases Versus Zone-Based (FC) Aliases

When the port WWN (pWWN) of a device must be specified to configure different features (zoning, QoS, port security) in a Cisco MDS 9000 family switch, you must assign the correct device name each time you configure these features. An incorrect device name may cause unexpected results. You can avoid this problem if you define a user-friendly name for a port WWN and use this name in the entire configuration commands as required. These user-friendly names are referred to as device aliases.

Device aliases support two modes—basic and enhanced—as detailed here:

■ When you configure the basic mode using device aliases, the application immediately expands to pWWNs. This operation continues until the mode is changed to enhanced.

■ When a device alias runs in the enhanced mode, all applications accept the device alias configuration in the native format. The applications store the device alias name in the configuration and distribute it in the device alias format instead of expanding to pWWN. The applications track the device alias database changes and take actions to enforce it.

When a device alias mode is changed from basic mode to enhanced mode, the corresponding applications are informed about the change. The applications then start accepting the device alias–based configuration in the native format.

Device aliases have the following features:

- Device alias information is independent of your VSAN configuration.
- Device alias configuration and distribution is independent of the zone server and the zone server database.
- You can import legacy zone alias configurations without losing data.
- The device alias application uses the Cisco Fabric Services (CFS) infrastructure to enable efficient database management and distribution. Device aliases use the coordinated distribution mode and the fabric-wide distribution scope.
- When you configure zones, IVR zones, or QoS features using device aliases, and if you display these configurations, you will automatically see that the device aliases are displayed along with their respective pWWNs.

Device aliases have the following requirements:

- You can only assign device aliases to pWWNs.
- The mapping between the pWWN and the device alias to which it is mapped must have a one-to-one relationship. A pWWN can be mapped to only one device alias, and vice versa.
- A device alias name is restricted to 64 alphanumeric characters and may include one or more of the following characters:
  - a to z and A to Z
  - 1 to 9
  - - (hyphen) and _ (underscore)
  - $ (dollar sign) and ^ (up caret)

Table 23-5 compares the differences between zone and device aliases.

Table 23-5   Comparison Between Zone Aliases and Device Aliases

Zone-Based Aliases	Device Aliases
Aliases are limited to the specified VSAN.	You can define device aliases without specifying the VSAN number. You can also use the same definition in one or more VSANs without any restrictions.
Zone aliases are part of the zoning configuration. The alias mapping cannot be used to configure other features.	Device aliases can be used with any feature that uses the pWWN.

23

Zone-Based Aliases	Device Aliases
You can use any zone member type to specify the end devices.	Only pWWNs are supported along with new device aliases, such as IP addresses.
Configuration is contained within the Zone Server database and is not available to other features.	Device aliases are not restricted to zoning. Device alias configuration is available to the FCNS, zone, fcping, traceroute, and IVR applications.
FC aliases are not displayed with the associated WWNs in the **show** command outputs, such as **show zone set active**, **show flogi database**, and **show fcns database**.	Device aliases are displayed with the associated WWNs in the **show** command outputs such as **show zone set active**, **show flogi database**, and **show fcns database**.
FC aliases are not distributed as part of the active zone set and are distributed only as part of a full zone database as per the FC standards.	Device aliases are distributed through CFS.

Where Do I Start Configuration?

The Cisco MDS 9000 family of storage networking products support 1, 2, 4, 8, 10, and 16 Gbps Fibre Channel; 10 and 40 Gbps Fibre Channel over Ethernet (FCoE); 1 and 10 Gbps Fibre Channel over IP (FCIP); and Internet Small Computer Interface (iSCSI) on Gigabit Ethernet ports at the time of writing this book. The MDS multilayer directors have dual supervisor modules, and each of the supervisor modules have one management and one-console port. The MDS multiservice and multilayer switches have one management and one-console port as well.

Before any configuration is started, the equipment should be installed and mounted onto the racks. For each MDS product family switch there is a specific hardware installation guide that explains in detail how and where to install specific components of the MDS switches. This section starts with explaining what to do after the switch is installed and powered on following the hardware installation guide.

The Cisco MDS family switches provide the following types of ports:

- **Console port (supervisor modules):** The console port is available for all the MDS product family. The console port, labeled "Console," is an RS-232 port with an RJ-45 interface. It is an asynchronous (sync) serial port; any device connected to this port must be capable of asynchronous transmission. This port is used to create a local management connection to set the IP address and other initial configuration settings before connecting the switch to the network for the first time.

To connect the console port to a computer terminal, follow these steps:

Step 1.   Configure the terminal emulator program to match the following default port characteristics: 9600 baud, 8 data bits, 1 stop bit, no parity.

Step 2.   Connect the supplied RJ-45 to DB-9 female adapter or RJ-45 to DP-25 female adapter (depending on your computer) to the computer serial port. We recommend using the adapter and cable provided with the switch.

Step 3.   Connect the console cable (a rollover RJ-45 to RJ-45 cable) to the console port and to the RJ-45-to-DB-9 adapter or the RJ-45-to-DP-25 adapter (depending on your computer) at the computer serial port.

■ **COM1 port:** This is an RS-232 port that you can use to connect to an external serial communication device such as a modem. The COM1 port is available for all the MDS product family except MDS 9700 director switches. It is available on each supervisor module of MDS 9500 Series switches.

The COM1 port (labeled "COM1") is an RS-232 port with a DB-9 interface. You can use it to connect to an external serial communication device such as a modem. To connect the COM1 port to a modem, follow these steps:

Step 1.   Connect the modem to the COM1 port using the adapters and cables.

    a. Connect the DB-9 serial adapter to the COM1 port.

    b. Connect the RJ-45-to-DB-25 modem adapter to the modem.

    c. Connect the adapters using the RJ-45-to-RJ-45 rollover cable (or equivalent crossover cable).

Step 2.   The default COM1 settings are as follows:

line Aux: |Speed: 9600 bauds Databits: 8 bits per byte Stopbits: 1 bit(s) Parity: none Modem In: Enable Modem Init-String - default: ATE0Q1&D2&C1S0=1\015 Statistics: tx:17 rx:0 Register Bits:RTS|DTR

■ **MGMT 10/100/1000 Ethernet port (supervisor module):** This is an Ethernet port that you can use to access and manage the switch by IP address, such as through Cisco Data Center Network Manager (DCNM). MGMT Ethernet port is available for all the MDS product family. The supervisor modules support an autosensing MGMT 10/100/1000 Ethernet port (labeled "MGMT 10/100/1000") and have an RJ-45 interface. You can connect the MGMT 10/100/1000 Ethernet port to an external hub, switch, or router. You need to use a modular, RJ-45, straight-through UTP cable to connect the MGMT 10/100/1000 Ethernet port to an Ethernet switch port or hub or use a crossover cable to connect to a router interface.

23

NOTE   For high availability, connect the MGMT 10/100/1000 Ethernet port on the active supervisor module and on the standby supervisor module to the same network or VLAN. The active supervisor module owns the IP address used by both of these Ethernet connections. On a switchover, the newly activated supervisor module takes over this IP address. This process requires an Ethernet connection to the newly activated supervisor module.

■ **Fibre Channel ports (switching modules):** These are Fibre Channel (FC) ports that you can use to connect to the SAN or for in-band management. The Cisco MDS 9000 family supports both Fibre Channel and FCoE protocols for SFP+ transceivers. Each transceiver must match the transceiver on the other end of the cable, and the cable must not exceed the stipulated cable length for reliable communication.

- **Fibre Channel over Ethernet ports (switching modules):** These are Fibre Channel over Ethernet (FCoE) ports that 'you can use to connect to the SAN or for in-band management.

- **Gigabit Ethernet ports (IP storage ports):** These are IP Storage Services ports that are used for the FCIP or iSCSI connectivity.

- **USB drive/port:** This is a simple interface that allows you to connect to different devices supported by NX-OS. The USB drive is not available for MDS 9100 Series switches. The Cisco MDS 9700 Series switch has two USB drives (in each Supervisor-1 module). In the supervisor module, there are two USB drives: Slot 0 and LOG FLASH. The LOG FLASH and Slot 0 USB ports use different formats for their data.

Let's also review the transceivers before we continue with the configuration. You can use any combination of SFP or SFP+ transceivers that are supported by the switch. The only restrictions are that short wavelength (SWL) transceivers must be paired with SWL transceivers, and long wavelength (LWL) transceivers with LWL transceivers, and the cable must not exceed the stipulated cable length for reliable communications. The Cisco SFP, SFP+, and X2 devices are hot-swappable transceivers that plug in to Cisco MDS 9000 family director switching modules and fabric switch ports. They allow you to choose different cabling types and distances on a port-by-port basis. The most up-to-date information can be found for pluggable transceivers here: http://www.cisco.com/c/en/us/products/collateral/storage-networking/mds-9000-series-multilayer-switches/product_data_sheet09186a00801bc698.html.

The SFP hardware transmitters are identified by their acronyms when displayed in the **show interface brief** command. If the related SFP has a Cisco-assigned extended ID, the **show interface** and **show interface brief** commands display the ID instead of the transmitter type. The **show interface transceiver** command and the **show interface fc slot/port transceiver** command display both values for Cisco-supported SFPs.

What are the differences between SFP+, SFP, and XFP? SFP, SFP+, and XFP are all terms for a type of transceiver that plugs in to a special port on a switch or other network device to convert the port to a copper or fiber interface. SFP has the lowest cost among all three. SFP+ was replaced by the XFP 10 G modules and became the mainstream. An advantage of the SFP+ modules is that SFP+ has a more compact form factor package than X2 and XFP. It can connect with the same type of XFP, X2, and XENPAK directly. The cost of SFP+ is lower than XFP, X2, and XENPAK.

SFP and SFP+ specifications are developed by the MSA (Multiple Source Agreement) group. They both have the same size and appearance but they are based on different standards. SFP is based on the INF-8074i specification and SFP+ is based on the SFF-8431 specification.

XFP and SFP+ are 10G fiber optical modules and can connect with other type of 10G modules. The size of SFP+ is smaller than XFP; therefore, it moves some functions to the motherboard, including signal modulation function, MAC, CDR, and EDC. XFP is based on the standard of XFP MSA. SFP+ is in compliance with the protocol of IEEE802.3ae, SFF-8431, and SFF-8432 specifications. SFP+ is the mainstream design.

To get the most up-to-date technical specifications for fiber optics per the current standards and specs, maximum supportable distances, and attenuation for optical fiber applications by fiber type, check the Fiber Optic Association page (FOA) at http://www.thefoa.org/tech/Linkspec.htm.

The Cisco MDS product family uses the same operating system as NX-OS. The Nexus product line and MDS family switches use mostly the same management features. The Cisco MDS 9000 family switches can be accessed and configured in many ways, and they support standard management protocols. Figure 23-28 portrays the tools for configuring the Cisco NX-OS software.

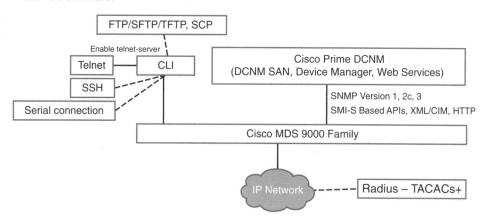

Figure 23-28 *Tools for Configuring Cisco NX-OS Software*

The different protocols that are supported in order to access, monitor, and configure the Cisco MDS 9000 family of switches are described in Table 23-6.

Table 23-6   Protocols to Access, Monitor, and Configure the Cisco MDS Family

Management Protocol	Purpose
Telnet/SSH	Provides remote access to the CLI for a Cisco MDS 9000 switch.
FTP/SFTP/TFTP, SCP	Copies configuration and software images between devices.
SNMPv1, v2c, and v3	Includes over 70 distinct management information bases (MIBs). Cisco MDS 9000 family switches support SNMP version 1, 2, and 3 as well as RMON V1 and V2. RMON provides advanced alarm and event management, including setting thresholds and sending notifications based on changes in device or network behavior. By default, the Cisco Prime DCNM communicates with Cisco MDS 9000 family switches using SNMPv3, which provides secure authentication using encrypted usernames and passwords. SNMPv3 also provides the option to encrypt all management traffic.
HTTP	HTTP is used only for the distribution and installation of the Cisco Fabric Manager software. It is not used for Cisco Prime DCNM installation. It is not used for communication between the Cisco Fabric Manager and Cisco MDS 9000 family switches.

23

Management Protocol	Purpose
ANSI T11 FC-GS3	Fibre Channel-Generic Services (FC-GS3) in the definition of the management servers defines the Fabric Configuration Server (FCS), which is a standard mechanism to collect information about platforms (end devices) and interconnecting elements (switches) building the fabric. The Cisco MDS 9000 uses the information provided by FCS on top of the information contained in the Name Server database and in the Fibre Channel Shortest Path First (FSPF) topology database to build a detailed topology view and collect information for all the devices building the fabric.
XML/CIM	CIM server support for designing storage area network management applications to run on Cisco MDS NX-OS.

The Cisco MDS NX-OS Setup Utility—Back to Basics

The Cisco MDS NX-OS setup utility is an interactive command-line interface (CLI) mode that guides you through a basic (also called a startup) configuration of the system. The setup utility allows you to configure only enough connectivity for system management. The setup utility allows you to build an initial configuration file using the System Configuration dialog. The setup starts automatically when a device has no configuration file in NVRAM. The dialog guides you through initial configuration. After the file is created, you can use the CLI to perform additional configuration.

You can press Ctrl+C at any prompt to skip the remaining configuration options and proceed with what you have configured up to that point, except for the administrator password. If you want to skip answers to any questions, press Enter. If a default answer is not available (for example, the device hostname), the device uses what was previously configured and skips to the next question. Figure 23-29 portrays the setup script flow.

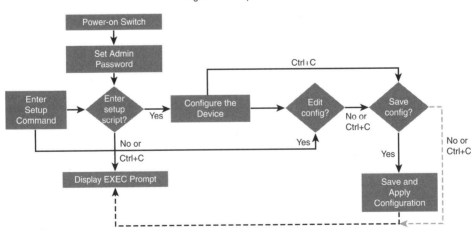

Figure 23-29 *Setup Script Flow*

You use the setup utility mainly for configuring the system initially, when no configuration is present. However, you can use the setup utility at any time for basic device configuration. The setup script only supports IPv4. The setup utility keeps the configured values when you skip steps in the script. For example, if you have already configured the mgmt0 interface, the setup utility does not change that configuration if you skip that step. However, if there is a default value for the step, the setup utility changes to the configuration using that default, not the configured value. Be sure to carefully check the configuration changes before you save the configuration.

> **NOTE**   Be sure to configure the IPv4 route, the default network IPv4 address, and the default gateway IPv4 address to enable SNMP access. If you enable IPv4 routing, the device uses the IPv4 route and the default network IPv4 address. If IPv4 routing is disabled, the device uses the default gateway IPv4 address.

Before starting the setup utility, you need to execute the following steps:

Step 1.   Have a password strategy for your network environment.

Step 2.   Connect the console port on the supervisor module to the network. If you have dual supervisor modules, connect the console ports on both supervisor modules to the network.

Step 3.   Connect the Ethernet management port on the supervisor module to the network. If you have dual supervisor modules, connect the Ethernet management ports on both supervisor modules to the network.

The first time you access a switch in the Cisco MDS 9000 family, it runs a setup program that prompts you for the IP address and other configuration information necessary for the switch to communicate over the supervisor module Ethernet interface. This information is required to configure and manage the switch. The IP address can only be configured from the CLI. When you power up the switch for the first time, assign the IP address. After you perform this step, the Cisco MDS 9000 Family Cisco Prime DCNM can reach the switch through the console port. There are two types of management through MDS NX-OS CLI. You can configure out-of-band management on the mgmt 0 interface. The in-band management logical interface is VSAN 1. This management interface uses the Fibre Channel infrastructure to transport IP traffic. An interface for VSAN 1 is created on every switch in the fabric. Each switch should have its VSAN 1 interface configured with either an IPv4 address or an IPv6 address in the same subnetwork. A default route that points to the switch providing access to the IP network should be configured on every switch in the Fibre Channel fabric. The following are the initial setup procedure steps for configuring out-of-band management on the mgmt0 interface:

Step 1.   Power on the switch. Switches in the Cisco MDS 9000 family boot automatically.

Step 2.   Enter **yes** (yes is the default) to enable a secure password standard.

```
Do you want to enforce secure password standard (yes/no) : yes
```

You can also enable a secure password standard using the **password strength-check** command. A secure password should contain characters from at least three of these classes: lowercase letters, uppercase letters, digits, and special characters.

Step 3.   Enter the password for the administrator.

```
Enter the password for admin: admin-password
Confirm the password for admin: admin-password
```

Step 4.   Enter **yes** to enter the setup mode.

This setup utility will guide you through the basic configuration of the system. Setup configures only enough connectivity for management of the system. Note that setup is mainly used for configuring the system initially, when no configuration is present. Therefore, setup always assumes system defaults and not the current system configuration values. Press Enter at any time to skip a dialog. Use Ctrl+C at any time to skip the remaining dialogs.

```
Would you like to enter the basic configuration dialog (yes/no): yes
```

The setup utility guides you through the basic configuration process. Press Ctrl+C at any prompt to end the configuration process.

Step 5.   Enter **yes** (no is the default) if you do not want to create additional accounts.

```
Create another login account (yes/no) [no]: yes
```

While configuring your initial setup, you can create an additional user account (in the network-admin role) besides the administrator's account.

```
Enter the user login ID: user_name
Enter the password for user_name: user-password
Confirm the password for user_name: user-password
Enter the user role [network-operator]: network-admin
```

By default, two roles exist in all switches:

- **Network operator (network-operator):** Has permission to view the configuration only. The operator cannot make any configuration changes.

- **Network administrator (network-admin):** Has permission to execute all commands and make configuration changes. The administrator can also create and customize up to 64 additional roles. One of these 64 additional roles can be configured during the initial setup process.

Step 6.   Configure the read-only or read-write SNMP community string.

a. Enter **yes** (no is the default) to avoid configuring the read-only SNMP community string.

```
Configure read-only SNMP community string (yes/no) [n]: yes
```

b. Enter the SNMP community string.

```
SNMP community string: snmp_community
```

Step 7.   Enter a name for the switch. The switch name is limited to 32 alphanumeric characters.

The default switch name is "switch."

```
Enter the switch name: switch_name
```

Step 8. Enter **yes** (yes is the default) at the configuration prompt to configure out-of-band management.

IP version 6 (IPv6) is supported in Cisco MDS NX-OS Release 4.1(x) and later. However, the setup script supports only IP version 4 (IPv4) for the management interface.

```
Continue with out-of-band (mgmt0) management configuration? [yes/no]: yes
```

Enter the mgmt0 IPv4 address.

```
Mgmt0 IPv4 address: ip_address
```

Enter the mgmt0 IPv4 subnet mask.

```
Mgmt0 IPv4 netmask: subnet_mask
```

Step 9. Enter **yes** (yes is the default) to configure the default gateway.

```
Configure the default-gateway: (yes/no) [y]: yes
Enter the default gateway IP address.
IP address of the default gateway: default_gateway
```

Step 10. Enter **yes** (no is the default) to configure advanced IP options such as in-band management static routes, default network, DNS, and domain name.

```
Configure Advanced IP options (yes/no)? [n]: yes
```

a. Enter **no** (no is the default) at the in-band management configuration prompt.

```
Continue with in-band (VSAN1) management configuration? (yes/no) [no]: no
```

b. Enter **yes** (yes is the default) to enable IPv4 routing capabilities.

```
Enable ip routing capabilities? (yes/no) [y]: yes
```

c. Enter **yes** (yes is the default) to configure a static route.

```
Configure static route: (yes/no) [y]: yes
```

Enter the destination prefix.

```
Destination prefix: dest_prefix
```

Enter the destination prefix mask.

```
Destination prefix mask: dest_mask
```

Enter the next hop IP address.

```
Next hop ip address: next_hop_address
```

d. Enter **yes** (yes is the default) to configure the default network.

```
Configure the default-network: (yes/no) [y]: yes
```

Enter the default network IPv4 address.

```
Default network IP address [dest_prefix]: dest_prefix
```

e. Enter **yes** (yes is the default) to configure the DNS IPv4 address.

```
Configure the DNS IP address? (yes/no) [y]: yes
```

Enter the DNS IP address.

```
DNS IP address: name_server
```

23

f. Enter **yes** (no is the default) to skip the default domain name configuration.

```
Configure the default domain name? (yes/no) [n]: yes
```

Enter the default domain name.

```
Default domain name: domain_name
```

Step 11. Enter **yes** (yes is the default) to enable the SSH service.

```
Enabled SSH service? (yes/no) [n]: yes
```

Enter the SSH key type.

```
Type the SSH key you would like to generate (dsa/rsa)? rsa
```

Enter the number of key bits within the specified range.

```
Enter the number of key bits? (768-2048) [1024]: 2048
```

Step 12. Enter **yes** (no is the default) to disable the Telnet service.

```
Enable the telnet service? (yes/no) [n]: yes
```

Step 13. Enter **yes** (yes is the default) to configure congestion or no_credit drop for FC interfaces.

```
Configure congestion or  no_credit drop for fc interfaces? (yes/no) [q/
quit] to quit [y]:yes
```

Step 14. Enter **con** (con is the default) to configure congestion or no_credit drop.

```
Enter the type of drop to configure congestion/no_credit drop? (con/no)
[c]:con
```

Step 15. Enter a value from 100 to 1000 (d is the default) to calculate the number of milliseconds for congestion or no_credit drop.

```
Enter number of milliseconds for congestion/no_credit drop[100 - 1000] or
[d/default] for default: 100
```

Step 16. Enter a mode for congestion or no_credit drop.

```
Enter mode for congestion/no_credit drop[E/F]:
```

Step 17. Enter **yes** (no is the default) to configure the NTP server.

```
Configure NTP server? (yes/no) [n]: yes
Enter the NTP server IPv4 address.
NTP server IP address: ntp_server_IP_address
```

Step 18. Enter **shut** (shut is the default) to configure the default switch port interface to the shut (disabled) state.

```
Configure default switchport interface state (shut/noshut) [shut]: shut
```

The management Ethernet interface is not shut down at this point. Only the Fibre Channel, iSCSI, FCIP, and Gigabit Ethernet interfaces are shut down.

Step 19. Enter **on** (off is the default) to configure the switch port trunk mode.

```
Configure default switchport trunk mode (on/off/auto) [off]: on
```

Step 20. Enter **yes** (yes is the default) to configure the switchport mode F.

```
Configure default switchport mode F (yes/no) [n]: y
```

Step 21. Enter **on** (off is the default) to configure the port-channel auto-create state.

```
Configure default port-channel auto-create state (on/off) [off]: on
```

Step 22. Enter **permit** (deny is the default) to deny a default zone policy configuration.

```
Configure default zone policy (permit/deny) [deny]: permit
```

This permits traffic flow to all members of the default zone.

Step 23. Enter **yes** (no is the default) to disable a full zone set distribution.

```
Enable full zoneset distribution (yes/no) [n]: yes
```

This overrides the switch-wide default for the full zone set distribution feature.

You see the new configuration. Review and edit the configuration that you have just entered.

Step 24. Enter **enhanced** (basic is the default) to configure default-zone mode as enhanced.

```
Configure default zone mode (basic/enhanced) [basic]: enhanced
```

This overrides the switch-wide default zone mode as enhanced.

Step 25. Enter **no** (no is the default) if you are satisfied with the configuration.

The following configuration will be applied:

```
username admin password admin_pass role network-admin
username user_name password user_pass role network-admin
snmp-server community snmp_community ro
switchname switch
interface mgmt0
  ip address ip_address subnet_mask
  no shutdown
ip routing
ip route dest_prefix dest_mask dest_address
ip default-network dest_prefix
ip default-gateway default_gateway
ip name-server name_server
ip domain-name domain_name
telnet server disable
ssh key rsa 2048 force
ssh server enable
ntp server ipaddr ntp_server
system default switchport shutdown
system default switchport trunk mode on
system default switchport mode F
system default port-channel auto-create
zone default-zone permit vsan 1-4093
zoneset distribute full vsan 1-4093
system default zone mode enhanced
Would you like to edit the configuration? (yes/no) [n]: n
```

23

Step 26.   Enter **yes** (yes is default) to use and save this configuration.

```
Use this configuration and save it? (yes/no) [y]: yes
```

If you do not save the configuration at this point, none of your changes are updated the next time the switch is rebooted. Type **yes** to save the new configuration. This ensures that the kickstart and system images are also automatically configured.

Step 27.   Log in to the switch using the new username and password.

Step 28.   Verify that the required licenses are installed in the switch using the **show license** command.

Step 29.   Verify that the switch is running Cisco NX-OS 6.2(x) software, depending on which you installed, issuing the **show version** command. Example 23-1 portrays show version display output.

Example 23-1   *Verifying NX-OS Version on an MDS 9710 Switch*

```
DS-9710-1# show version
Cisco Nexus Operating System (NX-OS) Software TAC support: http://www.cisco.com/tac
Documents: http://www.cisco.com/en/US/products/ps9372/tsd_products_support_series_
home.html
Copyright (c) 2002-2013, Cisco Systems, Inc. All rights reserved.
The copyrights to certain works contained in this software are
owned by other third parties and used and distributed under
license. Certain components of this software are licensed under
the GNU General Public License (GPL) version 2.0 or the GNU
Lesser General Public License (LGPL) Version 2.1. A copy of each
such license is available at
http://www.opensource.org/licenses/gpl-2.0.php and
http://www.opensource.org/licenses/lgpl-2.1.php
Software
  BIOS:      version 3.1.0
  kickstart: version 6.2(3)
  system:    version 6.2(3)
  BIOS compile time:       02/27/2013
  kickstart image file is: bootflash:///kickstart
  kickstart compile time:  7/10/2013 2:00:00 [07/31/2013 10:10:16]
  system image file is:    bootflash:///system
  system compile time:     7/10/2013 2:00:00 [07/31/2013 11:59:38]
Hardware
  cisco MDS 9710 (10 Slot) Chassis ("Supervisor Module-3")
  Intel(R) Xeon(R) CPU       with 8120784 kB of memory.
  Processor Board ID JAE171504KY
  Device name: MDS-9710-1
  bootflash:     3915776 kB
  slot0:               0 kB (expansion flash)
```

```
Kernel uptime is 0 day(s), 0 hour(s), 39 minute(s), 20 second(s)
Last reset
  Reason: Unknown
System version: 6.2(3)
  Service:
Plugin
  Core Plugin, Ethernet Plugin
```

Step 30.   Verify the status of the modules on the switch using the **show module** command (see Example 23-2).

Example 23-2   *Verifying Modules on an MDS 9710 Switch*

```
MDS-9710-1# show module
Mod  Ports  Module-Type                          Model               Status
---  -----  ------------------------------------ ------------------  ----------
1    48     2/4/8/10/16 Gbps Advanced FC Module  DS-X9448-768K9      ok
2    48     2/4/8/10/16 Gbps Advanced FC Module  DS-X9448-768K9      ok
5    0      Supervisor Module-3                  DS-X97-SF1-K9       active *
6    0      Supervisor Module-3                  DS-X97-SF1-K9       ha-standby
Mod  Sw             Hw
---  -------------- ------
1    6.2(3)         1.1
2    6.2(3)         1.1
5    6.2(3)         1.0
6    6.2(3)         1.0
Mod  MAC-Address(es)                       Serial-Num
---  ------------------------------------- ----------
1    1c-df-0f-78-cf-d8 to 1c-df-0f-78-cf-db JAE171308VQ
2    1c-df-0f-78-d8-50 to 1c-df-0f-78-d8-53 JAE1714019Y
5    1c-df-0f-78-df-05 to 1c-df-0f-78-df-17 JAE171504KY
6    1c-df-0f-78-df-2b to 1c-df-0f-78-df-3d JAE171504E6
Mod  Online Diag Status
---  ------------------
1    Pass
2    Pass
5    Pass
6    Pass
Xbar Ports  Module-Type                          Model               Status
---  -----  ------------------------------------ ------------------  ----------
1    0      Fabric Module 1                      DS-X9710-FAB1       ok
2    0      Fabric Module 1                      DS-X9710-FAB1       ok
3    0      Fabric Module 1                      DS-X9710-FAB1       ok
Xbar Sw             Hw
---  -------------- ------
1    NA             1.0
```

23

```
2    NA              1.0
3    NA              1.0
Xbar MAC-Address(es)                             Serial-Num
---  ------------------------------------        ----------
1    NA                                           JAE1710085T
2    NA                                           JAE1710087T
3    NA                                           JAE1709042X
```

The following are the initial setup procedure steps for configuring the in-band management logical interface on VSAN 1:

You can configure both in-band and out-of-band configuration together by entering **yes** in both step 10c and step 10d in the following procedure.

Step 10. Enter **yes** (no is the default) to configure advanced IP options such as in-band management, static routes, default network, DNS, and domain name.

```
Configure Advanced IP options (yes/no)? [n]: yes
```

   a. Enter **yes** (no is the default) at the in-band management configuration prompt.

```
Continue with in-band (VSAN1) management configuration? (yes/no) [no]:
yes
```

   Enter the VSAN 1 IPv4 address.

```
VSAN1 IPv4 address: ip_address
```

   Enter the IPv4 subnet mask.

```
VSAN1 IPv4 net mask: subnet_mask
```

   b. Enter **no** (yes is the default) to enable IPv4 routing capabilities.

```
Enable ip routing capabilities? (yes/no) [y]: no
```

   c. Enter **no** (yes is the default) to configure a static route.

```
Configure static route: (yes/no) [y]: no
```

   d. Enter **no** (yes is the default) to configure the default network.

```
Configure the default-network: (yes/no) [y]: no
```

   e. Enter **no** (yes is the default) to configure the DNS IPv4 address.

```
Configure the DNS IP address? (yes/no) [y]: no
```

   f. Enter **no** (no is the default) to skip the default domain name configuration.

```
Configure the default domain name? (yes/no) [n]: no
```

   In the final configuration, the following CLI commands will be added to the configuration:

```
interface vsan1
    ip address ip_address subnet_mask
    no shutdown
```

The Power On Auto Provisioning

POAP (Power On Auto Provisioning) automates the process of upgrading software images and installing configuration files on Cisco MDS and Nexus switches that are being deployed in the network. When a Cisco MDS switch with the POAP feature boots and does not find the startup configuration, the switch enters POAP mode, locates the DCNM DHCP server, and bootstraps itself with its interface IP address, gateway, and DCNM DNS server IP addresses. It also obtains the IP address of the DCNM server to download the configuration script that is run on the switch to download and install the appropriate software image and device configuration file.

Starting with NX-OS 6.2(9), the POAP capability is available on Cisco MDS 9148 and MDS 9148S multilayer fabric switches (at the time of writing this book).

When you power up a switch for the first time, it loads the software image that is installed at manufacturing and tries to find a configuration file from which to boot. When a configuration file is not found, POAP mode starts. During startup, a prompt appears, asking if you want to abort POAP and continue with a normal setup. You can choose to exit or continue with POAP. If you exit POAP mode, you enter the normal interactive setup script. If you continue in POAP mode, all the front-panel interfaces are set up in the default configuration. The USB device on MDS 9148 or on MDS 9148S does not contain the required installation files. The POAP setup requires the following network infrastructure: a DHCP server to bootstrap the interface IP address, gateway address, and DNS (Domain Name System) server.

A TFTP server that contains the configuration script is used to automate the software image installation and configuration process.

One or more servers can contain the desired software images and configuration files. Figure 23-30 portrays the network infrastructure for POAP.

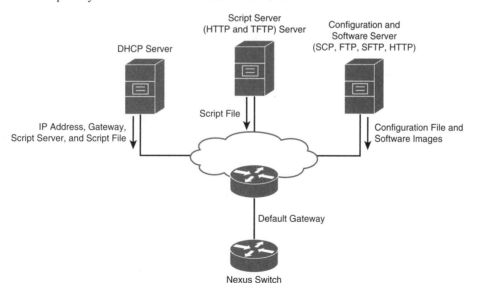

Figure 23-30   *POAP Network Infrastructure*

Here are the steps to set up the network environment using POAP:

Step 1. (Optional) Put the POAP configuration script and any other desired software image and switch configuration files on a USB device that is accessible to the switch.

Step 2. Deploy a DHCP server and configure it with the interface, gateway, and TFTP server IP addresses and a boot file with the path and name of the configuration script file. This information is provided to the switch when it first boots.

Step 3. Deploy a TFTP server to host the configuration script.

Step 4. Deploy one or more servers to host the software images and configuration files.

After you configure the network environment for POAP setup, follow these steps to configure the switch using POAP:

Step 1. Install the switch in the network.

Step 2. Power on the switch.

Step 3. (Optional) If you want to exit POAP mode and enter the normal interactive setup script, enter **y** (yes).

To verify the configuration after bootstrapping the device using POAP, use one of the following commands:

- **Show running config:** Displays the running configuration
- **Show startup config:** Displays the startup configuration

Licensing Cisco MDS 9000 Family NX-OS Software Features

Licenses are available for all switches in the Cisco MDS 9000 family. Licensing allows you to access specified premium features on the switch after you install the appropriate license for that feature. You can also obtain licenses to activate ports on the Cisco MDS 9124 Fabric Switch, the Cisco MDS 9134 Fabric Switch, the Cisco Fabric Switch for HP c-Class Blade System, and the Cisco Fabric Switch for IBM BladeCenter. Any feature not included in a license package is bundled with the Cisco MDS 9000 family switches.

The licensing model defined for the Cisco MDS product line has two options:

- **Feature-based licenses:** Allow features that are applicable to the entire switch. The cost varies based on a per-switch usage.
- **Module-based licenses:** Allow features that require additional hardware modules. The cost varies based on a per-module usage. An example is the IPS-8 or IPS-4 module using the FCIP feature.

Some features are logically grouped into add-on packages that must be licensed separately, such as the Cisco MDS 9000 Enterprise Package, SAN Extension over IP Package, Mainframe Package, DCNM Packages, DMM Package, IOA Package, and XRC

Acceleration Package. On-demand port activation licenses are also available for the Cisco MDS 9000 family blade switches and 4Gbps Cisco MDS 9100 Series multilayer fabric switches. Cisco license packages require a simple installation of an electronic license: No software installation or upgrade is required. Licenses can also be installed on the switch in the factory. Cisco MDS stores license keys on the chassis serial PROM (SPROM), so license keys are never lost even during a software reinstallation.

Cisco Data Center Network Manager for SAN includes a centralized license management console that provides a single interface for managing licenses across all Cisco MDS switches in the fabric. This single console reduces management overhead and prevents problems because of improperly maintained licensing. If an administrative error does occur with licensing, the switch provides a grace period before the unlicensed features are disabled. The grace period allows plenty of time to correct the licensing issue. All licensed features may be evaluated for up to 120 days before a license expires. Devices with dual supervisors have the following additional high-availability features:

- The license software runs on both supervisor modules and provides failover protection.
- The license key file is mirrored on both supervisor modules. Even if both supervisor modules fail, the license file continues to function from the version that is available on the chassis.

License Installation

You can either obtain a factory-installed license (only applies to new device orders) or per-form a manual installation of the license (applies to existing devices in your network).

- **Obtaining a factory-installed license:** You can obtain factory-installed licenses for a new Cisco NX-OS device. The first step is to contact the reseller or Cisco representative and request this service. The second step is to use the device and the licensed features.
- **Performing a manual installation:** If you have existing devices or if you want to install the licenses on your own, you must first obtain the license key file and then install that file in the device.

Obtaining the license key file consists of the following steps:

Step 1.   Obtain the serial number for your device by entering the **show license host-id** command. The host ID is also referred to as the device serial number.

```
mds9710-1# show licenser host-id
License hostid: VDH=JAF1710BBQH
```

Step 2.   Obtain your software license claim certificate document. If you cannot locate your software license claim certificate, contact Cisco Technical Support at this URL: http://www.cisco.com/c/en/us/support/web/tsd-cisco-worldwide-contacts.html.

Step 3.   Locate the product authorization key (PAK) from the software license claim certificate document.

Step 4.   Locate the website URL from the software license claim certificate document. You can access the Product License Registration website from the Software Download website at this URL: https://software.cisco.com/download/navigator.html.

Step 5.   Follow the instructions on the Product License Registration website to register the license for your device.

Step 6.   Use the **copy licenses** command to save your license file to either the bootflash: directory or a slot0: device.

Step 7.   You can use a file transfer service (tftp, ftp, sftp, sfp, or scp) or use the Cisco Fabric Manager License Wizard under Fabric Manager Tools to copy a license to the switch.

Installing the license key file consists of the following steps:

Step 1.   Log in to the device through the console port of the active supervisor.

Step 2.   You can use a file transfer service (tftp, ftp, sftp, sfp, or scp) or use the Cisco Fabric Manager License Wizard under Fabric Manager Tools to copy a license to the switch.

Step 3.   Perform the installation by using the **install license** command on the active supervisor module from the device console.

```
switch# install license bootflash:license_file.lic
Installing license ..done
```

Step 4.   (Optional) Back up the license key file.

Step 5.   Exit the device console and open a new terminal session to view all license files installed on the device using the **show license** command, as shown in Example 23-3.

Example 23-3   *Show License Output on MDS 9222i Switch*

```
MDS-9222i# show license
MDS20090713084124110.lic:
SERVER this_host ANY
VENDOR cisco
INCREMENT ENTERPRISE_PKG cisco 1.0 permanent uncounted \
        VENDOR_STRING=<LIC_SOURCE>MDS_SWIFT</LIC_SOURCE><SKU>M9200-ALL-LICENSES-
INTRL</SKU> \
        HOSTID=VDH=FOX1244H0U4 \
        NOTICE="<LicFileID>20090713084124110</LicFileID><LicLineID>1</LicLineID> \
        <PAK></PAK>" SIGN=D2ABC826DB70
INCREMENT STORAGE_SERVICES_ENABLER_PKG cisco 1.0 permanent 1 \
        VENDOR_STRING=<LIC_SOURCE>MDS_SWIFT</LIC_SOURCE><SKU>M9200-ALL-
LICENSES-INTRL</SKU> \
        HOSTID=VDH=FOX1244H0U4 \
        NOTICE="<LicFileID>20090713084124110</LicFileID><LicLineID>2</LicLineID> \
        <PAK></PAK>" SIGN=9287E36C708C
INCREMENT SAN_EXTN_OVER_IP cisco 1.0 permanent 1 \
        VENDOR_STRING=<LIC_SOURCE>MDS_SWIFT</LIC_SOURCE><SKU>M9200-ALL-LICENSES-
INTRL</SKU> \
        HOSTID=VDH=FOX1244H0U4 \
        NOTICE="<LicFileID>20090713084124110</LicFileID><LicLineID>3</LicLineID> \
        <PAK></PAK>" SIGN=C03E97505672
<snip> …
```

You can use the **show license brief** command to display a list of license files installed on the device (see Example 23-4).

Example 23-4   *Show License Brief Output on MDS 9222i Switch*

```
MDS-9222i#  show license brief
MDS20090713084124110.lic
MDS201308120931018680.lic
MDS-9222i# show license file MDS201308120931018680.lic
MDS201308120931018680.lic:
SERVER this_host ANY
VENDOR cisco
INCREMENT SAN_EXTN_OVER_IP_18_4 cisco 1.0 permanent 2 \
        VENDOR_STRING=<LIC_SOURCE>MDS_SWIFT</LIC_SOURCE><SKU>L-M92EXT1AK9=</SKU> \
        HOSTID=VDH=FOX1244H0U4 \
        NOTICE="<LicFileID>20130812093101868</LicFileID><LicLineID>1</LicLineID> \
        <PAK></PAK>" SIGN=DD075A320298
```

When you enable a Cisco NX-OS software feature, it can activate a license grace period:

```
switch# show license usage ENTERPRISE_PKG
Application
-----------
ivr
qos_manager
-----------
```

You can use the **show license usage** command to identify all the active features.

To uninstall the installed license file, you can use **clear license** *filename* **command**, where *filename* is the name of the installed license key file:

```
switch# clear license Enterprise.lic
Clearing license Enterprise.lic:
SERVER this_host
ANY VENDOR cisco
```

If the license is time bound, you must obtain and install an updated license. You need to contact technical support to request an updated license. After obtaining the license file, you can update the license file by using the **update license** *url* **command**, where *url* specifies the bootflash:, slot0:, usb1:, or usb2: location of the updated license file. You can enable the grace period feature by using the **license grace-period** command:

```
switch# configure terminal
switch(config)# license grace-period
```

Verifying the License Configuration

To display the license configuration, use one of the following commands:

- **show license:** Displays information for all installed license files
- **show license brief:** Displays summary information for all installed license files

23

- **show license file:** Displays information for a specific license file
- **show license host-id:** Displays the host ID for the physical device
- **show license usage:** Displays the usage information for installed licenses

On-Demand Port Activation Licensing

The Cisco MDS 9250i is available in a base configuration of 20 ports (upgradable to 40 through On-Demand Port Activation license) of 16Gbps Fibre Channel, two ports of 10 Gigabit Ethernet for FCIP and iSCSI storage services, and eight ports of 10 Gigabit Ethernet for FCoE connectivity.

On the Cisco MDS 9148, the On-Demand Port Activation license allows the addition of eight 8Gbps ports. Customers have the option of purchasing preconfigured models of 16, 32, or 48 ports and upgrading the 16- and 32-port models onsite all the way to 48 ports by adding these licenses.

The Cisco MDS 9148S 16G Multilayer Fabric Switch compact one rack-unit (1RU) switch scales from 12 to 48 line-rate 16Gbps Fibre Channel ports. The base switch model comes with 12 ports enabled and can be upgraded as needed with the 12-port Cisco MDS 9148S On-Demand Port Activation license to support configurations of 24, 36, or 48 enabled ports.

You can use the **show license usage** command (see Example 23-5) to view any licenses assigned to a switch. If a license is in use, the status displayed is **In use**. If a license is installed but no ports have acquired a license, the status displayed is **Unused**. The PORT_ACTIVATION_PKG does not appear as installed if you have only the default license installed.

Example 23-5   *Verifying License Usage on an MDS 9148 Switch*

```
MDS-9148# show license usage
Feature                  Ins  Lic   Status Expiry Date Comments
                              Count
--------------------------------------------------------------------------
FM_SERVER_PKG            No   -     Unused                 -
ENTERPRISE_PKG           No   -     Unused              Grace expired
PORT_ACTIVATION_PKG      No   16    In use never           -
```

Example 23-6 shows the default port license configuration for the Cisco MDS 9148 switch.

Example 23-6   *Verifying Port-License Usage on an MDS 9148 Switch*

```
bdc-mds9148-2# show port-license
Available port activation licenses are 0
-----------------------------------------------
  Interface    Cookie    Port Activation License
-----------------------------------------------
  fc1/1       16777216       acquired
  fc1/2       16781312       acquired
  fc1/3       16785408       acquired
  fc1/4       16789504       acquired
  fc1/5       16793600       acquired
  fc1/6       16797696       acquired
  fc1/7       16801792       acquired
  fc1/8       16805888       acquired
  fc1/9       16809984       acquired
  fc1/10      16814080       acquired
  fc1/11      16818176       acquired
  fc1/12      16822272       acquired
  fc1/13      16826368       acquired
  fc1/14      16830464       acquired
  fc1/15      16834560       acquired
  fc1/16      16838656       acquired
  fc1/17      16842752       eligible
<snip>
  fc1/46      16961536       eligible
  fc1/47      16965632       eligible
  fc1/48      16969728       eligible
```

The three different statuses for port licenses are described in Table 23-7.

Table 23-7   Port Activation License Status Definitions

Port Activation License Status	Definition
acquired	The port is licensed and active.
eligible	The port is eligible to receive a license but does not yet have one.
ineligible	The port is not allowed to receive a license.

Making a Port Eligible for a License

By default, all ports are eligible to receive a license. However, if a port has already been made ineligible and you prefer to activate it, you must make that port eligible by using the **port-license** command. Here are the steps to follow:

Step 1.   Configure terminal.

Step 2.   interface fc slot/port

Step 3.   [no] port-license

Step 4.   Exit.

Step 5.   (Optional) show port-license

Step 6.   (Optional) copy running-config startup-config

Acquiring a License for a Port

If you prefer not to accept the default on-demand port license assignments, you will need to first acquire licenses for ports to which you want to move the license.

Step 1.   Configure terminal.

Step 2.   interface fc slot/port

Step 3.   [no] port-license acquire

Step 4.   Exit.

Step 5.   (Optional) show port-license

Step 6.   (Optional) copy running-config startup-config

Moving Licenses Among Ports

You can move a license from a port (or range of ports) at any time. If you attempt to move a license to a port and no license is available, the switch returns the message "port activation license not available."

Step 1.   Configure terminal.

Step 2.   interface fc slot/port

Step 3.   Shut down.

Step 4.   no port-license

Step 5.   Exit.

Step 6.   interface fc slot/port

Step 7.   Shut down.

Step 8.   port-license acquire

Step 9.   No shutdown.

Step 10. Exit.

Step 11. (Optional) show port-license

Step 12. (Optional) copy running-config startup-config

Cisco MDS 9000 NX-OS Software Upgrade and Downgrade

Each switch is shipped with the Cisco MDS NX-OS operating system for Cisco MDS 9000 family switches. The Cisco MDS NX-OS software consists of two images: the kickstart image and the system image. The images and variables are important factors in any install procedure. You must specify the variable and the respective image to upgrade or downgrade your switch. Both images are not always required for each install.

- To select the kickstart image, use the KICKSTART variable.

- To select the system image, use the SYSTEM variable.

The software image install procedure is dependent on the following factors:

- **Software images:** The kickstart and system image files reside in directories or folders that can be accessed from the Cisco MDS 9000 family switch prompt.

- **Image version:** Each image file has a version.

- **Flash disks on the switch:** The bootflash: directory resides on the supervisor module and the Compact Flash disk is inserted into the slot0: device.

- **Supervisor modules:** There are single and dual supervisor modules. On switches with dual supervisor modules, both supervisor modules must have Ethernet connections on the management interfaces (mgmt 0) to maintain connectivity when switchovers occur during upgrades and downgrades.

Before starting any software upgrade or downgrade, the user should review NX-OS Release Notes. In the Release Notes, there are specific sections that explain compatibility between different software versions and hardware modules. In some cases, the user may need to take a specific path to perform nondisruptive software upgrades or downgrades.

NOTE   What is a nondisruptive NX-OS upgrade or downgrade? Nondisruptive upgrades on the Cisco MDS fabric switches take down the control plane for not more than 80 seconds. In some cases, when the upgrade has progressed past the point at which it cannot be stopped gracefully, or if a failure occurs, the software upgrade may be disruptive. During the upgrade, the control plane is down, but the data plane remains up. So new devices will be unable to log in to the fabric via the control plane, but existing devices will not experience any disruption of traffic via the data plane.

If the running image and the image you want to install are incompatible, the software reports the incompatibility. In some cases, you may decide to proceed with this installation. If the active and the standby supervisor modules run different versions of the image, both images may be high availability (HA) compatible in some cases and incompatible in others.

Compatibility is established based on the image and configuration:

- **Image incompatibility:** The running image and the image to be installed are not compatible.

- **Configuration incompatibility:** There is a possible incompatibility if certain features in the running image are turned off, because they are not supported in the image to be installed. The image to be installed is considered incompatible with the running image if one of the following statements is true:

■ An incompatible feature is enabled in the image to be installed and it is not available in the running image and may cause the switch to move into an inconsistent state. In this case, the incompatibility is strict.

■ An incompatible feature is enabled in the image to be installed and it is not available in the running image and does not cause the switch to move into an inconsistent state. In this case, the incompatibility is loose.

To view the results of a dynamic compatibility check, issue the **show incompatibility system bootflash:***filename* command. Use this command to obtain further information when the **install all** command returns the following message:

```
Warning: The startup config contains commands not supported by
the standby supervisor; as a result, some resources might become
unavailable after a switchover.
Do you wish to continue? (y/ n) [y]: n
```

You can upgrade any switch in the Cisco MDS 9000 family using one of the following methods:

■ **Automated, one-step upgrades using the "install all" command:** This upgrade is nondisruptive for director switches. The **install all** command compares and presents the results of the compatibility before proceeding with the installation. You can exit if you do not want to proceed with these changes.

■ **Quick, one-step upgrade using the "reload" command:** This upgrade is disruptive. Before running the **reload** command, copy the correct kickstart and system images to the correct location and change the **boot** commands in your configuration.

When the Cisco MDS 9000 Series multilayer switch is first switched on or during reboot, the system BIOS on the supervisor module first runs power-on self-test (POST) diagnostics. The BIOS then runs the loader bootstrap function.

The boot parameters are held in NVRAM and point to the location and name of both the kickstart and system images. The loader obtains the location of the kickstart file, usually on bootflash, and verifies the kickstart image before loading it.

The kickstart loads the Linux kernel and device drivers and then needs to load the system image. Again, the boot parameters in NVRAM should point to the location and name of the system image, usually on bootflash. The kickstart then verifies and loads the system image.

Finally, the system image loads the Cisco NX-OS Software, checks the file systems, and proceeds to load the startup configuration that contains the switch configuration from NVRAM.

If the boot parameters are missing or have an incorrect name or location, the boot process fails at the last stage. If this error happens, the administrator must recover from the error and reload the switch. The **install all** command launches a script that greatly simplifies the boot procedure and checks for errors and the upgrade impact before proceeding. Figure 23-31 portrays the boot sequence.

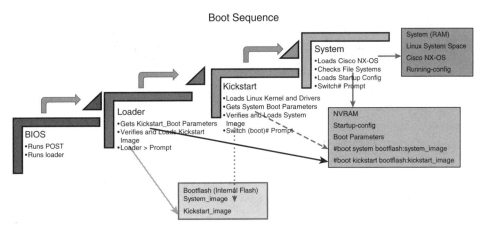

Figure 23-31 *Boot Sequence*

For the MDS Director switches with dual supervisor modules, the boot sequence steps are as follows:

1. Upgrade the BIOS on the active and standby supervisor modules and the data modules.

2. Bring up the standby supervisor module with the new kickstart and system images.

3. Switch over from the active supervisor module to the upgraded supervisor module.

4. Bring up the old active supervisor module with the new kickstart and system images.

5. Perform a nondisruptive image upgrade for each data module (one at a time).

6. Upgrade complete.

Upgrading to Cisco NX-OS on an MDS 9000 Series Switch

During any firmware upgrade, use the console connection. Be aware that if you are upgrading through the management interface, you must have a working connection to both supervisors, because this process causes a switchover and the current standby supervisor will be active after the upgrade. In this section, we discuss firmware upgrade steps for a director switch with dual supervisor modules. For MDS switches with only one supervisor module, steps 7 and 8 will not be executed.

To upgrade the switch, use the latest Cisco MDS NX-OS Software on the Cisco MDS 9000 Director Series switch and then follow these steps:

Step 1. Verify the following physical connections for the new Cisco MDS 9500 family switch:

■ The console port is physically connected to a computer terminal (or terminal server).

■ The management 10/100 Ethernet port (mgmt0) is connected to an external hub, switch, or router.

23

Step 2. Issue the **copy running-config startup-config** command to store your current running configuration. You can also create a backup of your existing configuration to a file by issuing the **copy running-config bootflash:backup_config.txt** command.

Step 3. Install licenses (if necessary) to ensure that the required features are available on the switch.

Step 4. Ensure that the required space is available in the bootflash: directory for the image file(s) to be copied using the **dir bootflash:** command. Use the **delete bootflash:** filename command to remove unnecessary files.

Step 5. If you need more space on the active supervisor module bootflash, delete unnecessary files to make space available.

```
switch# del m9500-sf2ek9-kickstart-mz.6.2.6.27.bin
switch# del m9500-sf2ek9-mz-npe.6.2.5.bin
```

Step 6. Verify that space is available on the standby supervisor module bootflash on a Cisco MDS 9500 Series switch.

```
switch# attach mod x (where x is the module number of the standby
supervisor)
switch(standby)s# dir bootflash:
12288 Aug 26 19:06:14 2011 lost+found/
16206848 Jul 01 10:54:49 2011 m9500-sf2ek9-kickstart-mz.6.2.5.bin
16604160 Jul 01 10:20:07 2011 m9500-sf2ek9-kickstart-mz.6.2.5c.bin
Usage for bootflash://sup-local
122811392 bytes used
61748224 bytes free
184559616 bytes total
switch(standby)# exit ( to return to the active supervisor )
```

Step 7. If you need more space on the standby supervisor module bootflash on a Cisco MDS 9500 Series switch, delete unnecessary files to make space available.

```
switch(standby)# del bootflash: m9500-sf2ek9-kickstart-mz.6.2.5.bin
switch(standby)# del bootflash: m9500-sf2ek9-mz.6.2.5.bin
```

Step 8. Access the Software Download Center and select the required Cisco MDS NX-OS Release 6.2(x) image file, depending on which one you are installing.

Step 9. Download the files to an FTP or TFTP server.

Step 10. Copy the Cisco MDS NX-OS kickstart and system images to the active supervisor module bootflash using FTP or TFTP.

```
switch# copy tftp://tftpserver.cisco.com/MDS/m9500-sf2ek9-kickstart-
mz.6.2.x.bin bootflash:m9500-sf2ek9-kickstart-mz.6.2.x.bin
switch# copy tftp://tftpserver.cisco.com/MDS/m9500-sf2ek9-mz.6.2.x.bin
bootflash:m9500-sf2ek9-mz.6.2.x.bin
```

Step 11. Verify that the switch is running the required software version by issuing the **show version** command.

Step 12.   Verify that your switch is running compatible hardware by checking the Release Notes.

Step 13.   Perform the upgrade by issuing the **install all** command.

```
switch# install all kickstart m9500-sf2ek9-kickstart-mz.6.2.9.bin
system m9500-sf2ek9-mz.6.2.9.bin ssi m9000-ek9-ssi-mz.6.2.9.bin
```

The **install all** process verifies all the images before installation and detects incompatibilities. The process checks configuration compatibility. After information is provided about the impact of the upgrade before it takes place, the script will check whether you want to continue with the upgrade.

```
Do you want to continue with the installation (y/n)? [n] y
```

If the input is entered as **y**, the install will continue.

You can display the status of a nondisruptive upgrade by using the **show install all status** command. The output displays the status only after the switch has rebooted with the new image. All actions preceding the reboot are not captured in this output because when you enter the **install all** command using a Telnet session, the session is disconnected when the switch reboots. When you can reconnect to the switch through a Telnet session, the upgrade might already be complete, in which case the output will display the status of the upgrade.

Downgrading Cisco NX-OS Release on an MDS 9500 Series Switch

During any firmware upgrade, use the console connection. Be aware that if you are downgrading through the management interface, you must have a working connection to both supervisors, because this process causes a switchover and the current standby supervisor will be active after the downgrade. In this section, we discuss firmware upgrade steps for an MDS director switch with dual supervisor modules. For MDS switches with only one supervisor module, steps 7 and 8 will not be executed.

You should first read the Release Notes and follow the steps for specific NX-OS downgrade instructions. Use the **install all** command to downgrade the switch and handle configuration conversions. When downgrading any switch in the Cisco MDS 9000 family, avoid using the **reload** command. Here we outline the major steps for the downgrade:

Step 1.   Verify that the system image files for the downgrade are present on the active supervisor module bootflash with the **dir bootflash** command.

Step 2.   If the software image file is not present, download it from an FTP or TFTP server to the active supervisor module bootflash. If you need more space on the active supervisor module bootflash: directory, use the **delete** command to remove unnecessary files and ensure that the required space is available on the active supervisor. (Refer to step 5 in the upgrade section.) If you need more space on the standby supervisor module bootflash: directory, delete unnecessary files to make space available. (Refer to steps 6 and 7 in the upgrade section.)

```
switch# copy tftp://tftpserver.cisco.com/MDS/m9700-sf3ek9-mz.6.2.5.bin
bootflash:m9700-sf3ek9-kickstart-mz.6.2.5.bin
switch# copy tftp://tftpserver.cisco.com/MDS/m9700-sf3ek9-mz.6.2.5.bin
bootflash:m9700-sf3ek9-mz.6.2.5.bin
```

23

Step 3. Ensure that the required space is available on the active supervisor.

```
switch# dir bootflash:
```

Step 4. Issue the **show incompatibility system** command (see Example 23-7) to determine if you need to disable any features not supported by the earlier release.

Example 23-7 *Show Incompatibility System Output on MDS 9500 Switch*

```
switch# show incompatibility system bootflash:m9500-sf2ek9-mz.5.2.1.bin
The following configurations on active are incompatible with the system image
1) Service : port-channel , Capability : CAP_FEATURE_AUTO_CREATED_41_PORT_CHANNEL
Description : auto create enabled ports or auto created port-channels are present
Capability requirement : STRICT
Disable command :
1.Disable autocreate on interfaces (no channel-group auto).
2.Convert autocreated port channels to be persistent (port-channel 1 persistent)
...
```

Step 5. Disable any features that are incompatible with the downgrade system image.

```
switch# configure terminal
Enter configuration commands, one per line. End with CNTL/Z.
switch(config)# interface fcip 31
switch(config-if)# no channel-group auto
switch(config-if)# end
switch# port-channel 127 persistent
switch#
```

Step 6. Save the configuration using the **copy running-config startup-config** command.

```
switch# copy running-config startup-config
```

Step 7. Issue the **install all** command to downgrade the software.

```
switch# install all kickstart bootflash:m9500-sf2ek9-kickstart-
mz.5.2.1.bin.S74 system bootflash:m9500-sf2ek9-mz.5.2.1.bin.S74
```

Step 8. Verify the status of the modules on the switch using the **show module** command.

Configuring Interfaces

The main function of a switch is to relay frames from one data link to another. To relay the frames, the characteristics of the interfaces through which the frames are received and sent must be defined. The configured interfaces can be Fibre Channel interfaces, Gigabit Ethernet interfaces, the management interface (mgmt0), or VSAN interfaces. Each physical Fibre Channel interface in a switch may operate in one of several port modes: E port,

F port, FL port, TL port, TE port, SD port, ST port, and B port (see Figure 23-32). Besides these modes, each interface may be configured in auto or Fx port modes. These two modes determine the port type during interface initialization. Interfaces are created in VSAN 1 by default. When a module is removed and replaced with the same type of module, the configuration is retained. If a different type of module is inserted, the original configuration is no longer retained. In Chapter 22, we discussed the different Fibre Channel port types.

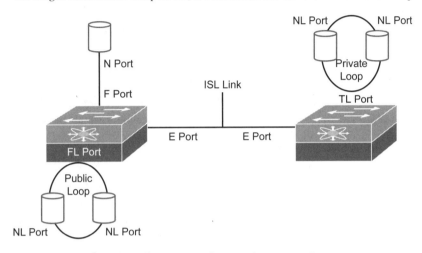

Figure 23-32   *Cisco MDS 9000 Family Switch Port Modes*

The interface state depends on the administrative configuration of the interface and the dynamic state of the physical link. Table 23-8 summarizes the interface states.

Table 23-8   Interface States

Administrative States	Up	Interface is enabled.
	Down	Interface is disabled. If the interface is administratively disabled, the physical link layer state change is ignored.
Operational States	Up	Interface is transmitting or receiving traffic as desired. To be in this state, an interface must be administratively up, the interface link layer state must be up, and the interface initialization must be completed.
	Down	Interface cannot transmit or receive (data) traffic.
	Trunking	Interface is operational in TE or TF mode.

Graceful Shutdown

Interfaces on a port are shut down by default (unless you modified the initial configuration). The Cisco NX-OS software implicitly performs a graceful shutdown in response to either of the following actions for interfaces operating in the E port mode:

■ If you shut down an interface.

■ If a Cisco NX-OS software application executes a port shutdown as part of its function.

A graceful shutdown ensures that no frames are lost when the interface is shutting down. When a shutdown is triggered either by you or the Cisco NX-OS software, the switches connected to the shutdown link coordinate with each other to ensure that all frames in the ports are safely sent through the link before shutting down. This enhancement reduces the chance of frame loss.

Port Administrative Speeds

By default, the port administrative speed for an interface is automatically calculated by the switch.

Autosensing speed is enabled on all 4Gbps and 8Gbps switching module interfaces by default. This configuration enables the interfaces to operate at speeds of 1 Gbps, 2 Gbps, or 4 Gbps on the 4Gbps switching modules, and 8 Gbps on the 8Gbps switching modules. When autosensing is enabled for an interface operating in dedicated rate mode, 4 Gbps of bandwidth is reserved, even if the port negotiates at an operating speed of 1 Gbps or 2 Gbps.

Frame Encapsulation

The **switchport encap eisl** command applies only to SD (SPAN destination) port interfaces. This command determines the frame format for all frames transmitted by the interface in SD port mode. If the encapsulation is set to EISL, all outgoing frames are transmitted in the EISL frame format, regardless of the SPAN sources. In SD port mode, where an interface functions as a SPAN, an SD port monitors network traffic that passes through a Fibre Channel interface. Monitoring is performed using a standard Fibre Channel analyzer (or a similar Switch Probe) that is attached to the SD port.

Bit Error Thresholds

The bit error rate threshold is used by the switch to detect an increased error rate before performance degradation seriously affects traffic. The bit errors can occur for the following reasons:

- Faulty or bad cable.
- Faulty or bad GBIC or SFP.
- GBIC or SFP is specified to operate at 1 Gbps but is used at 2 Gbps.
- GBIC or SFP is specified to operate at 2 Gbps but is used at 4 Gbps.
- Short-haul cable is used for a long haul or long-haul cable is used for a short haul.
- Momentary sync loss.
- Loose cable connection at one or both ends.
- Improper GBIC or SFP connection at one or both ends.

A bit error rate threshold is detected when 15 error bursts occur in a 5-minute period. By default, the switch disables the interface when the threshold is reached. You can enter a **shutdown** or **no shutdown** command sequence to reenable the interface.

Local Switching

Local switching can be enabled in Generation 4 modules, which allows traffic to be switched directly with a local crossbar when the traffic is directed from one port to another on the same line card. Because local switching is used, an extra switching step is avoided, which decreases the latency. When using local switching, note the following guidelines:

- All ports need to be in shared mode, which usually is the default state. To place a port in shared mode, enter the **switchport rate-mode shared** command.
- E ports are not allowed in the module because they must be in dedicated mode.

NOTE   Local switching is not supported on the Cisco MDS 9710 switch.

Dedicated and Shared Rate Modes

Ports on Cisco MDS 9000 family line cards are placed into port groups that have a fixed amount of bandwidth per port group (see Table 23-9). The Cisco MDS 9000 family allows for the bandwidth of ports in a port group to be allocated based on the requirements of individual ports. When you're planning port bandwidth requirements, allocation of the bandwidth within the port group is important. Ports in the port group can have bandwidth dedicated to them, or ports can share a pool of bandwidth. For ports that require high-sustained bandwidth, such as ISL ports, storage and tape array ports, and ports on high-bandwidth servers, you can have bandwidth dedicated to them in a port group by using the **switchport rate-mode dedicated** command. For other ports, typically servers that access shared storage-array ports (that is, storage ports that have higher fan-out ratios), you can share the bandwidth in a port group by using the **switchport rate-mode shared** command. When configuring the ports, be sure not to exceed the available bandwidth in a port group.

Table 23-9   Bandwidth and Port Group Configurations for Fibre Channel Modules

Cisco Part Number	Description	Number of Port Groups	Number of Ports per Port Group	Bandwidth per Port Group (Gbps)	
DS-X9248-256K9	48-port 8Gbps Advanced Fibre Channel module	8	6	32.4[1]	12.8[2]
DS-X9232-256K9	32-port 8Gbps Advanced Fibre Channel module	8	4	32.4[1]	12.8[2]
DS-X9248-96K9	48-port 8Gbps Fibre Channel module	8	6	12.8[3]	
DS-X9224-96K9	24-port 8Gbps Fibre Channel module	8	3	12.8[3]	
DS-X9448-768K9	48-port 16Gbps module	12	4	64[4]	

1 Cisco MDS 9513 Multilayer Director with Fabric 3 module installed
2 Cisco MDS 9506 (all) and 9509 (all) or 9513 Multilayer Director with Fabric 2 module installed
3 Cisco MDS 9506 (all), 9509 (all), or 9513 (all)
4 Cisco MDS 9710 Multilayer Director (all)

For example, a Cisco MDS 9513 Multilayer Director with a Fabric 3 module installed, using a 48-port 8Gbps Advanced Fibre Channel module, has eight port groups of six ports each. Each port group has 32.4 Gbps of bandwidth available. You cannot configure all six ports of a port group at the 8Gbps dedicated rates because that would require 48 Gbps of bandwidth, and the port group has only 32.4 Gbps of bandwidth. You can, however, configure all six ports in shared rate mode, so that the ports run at 8 Gbps and are oversubscribed at a rate of 1.48:1 (6 ports x 8 Gbps = 48 Gbps/32.4 Gbps). This oversubscription rate is well below the oversubscription rate of the typical storage array port (fan-out ratio) and does not affect performance. Most major disk subsystem vendors provide guidelines as to the recommended fan-out ratio of subsystem client-side ports to server connections. These recommendations are often in the range of 7:1 to 15:1. In Chapter 22, we discussed the fan-out ratio. You can also mix dedicated and shared rate ports in a port group.

Slow Drain Device Detection and Congestion Avoidance

This feature provides various enhancements to detect slow drain devices that are causing congestion in the network and also provides a congestion avoidance function. It is focused mainly on the edge ports that are connected to slow drain devices. The goal is to avoid or minimize the frames being stuck in the edge ports due to slow drain devices that are causing ISL blockage. To avoid or minimize the stuck condition, configure a lesser frame timeout for the ports. No-credit timeout drops all packets after the slow drain is detected using the configured thresholds. The lesser frame timeout value helps to alleviate the slow drain condition that affects the fabric by dropping the packets on the edge ports sooner than the time they actually get timed out (500 mms). This function frees the buffer space in ISL, which can be used by other unrelated flows that do not experience the slow drain condition.

A slow drain device is a device that does not accept frames at a rate generated by the source. In the presence of slow drain devices, Fibre Channel networks are likely to lack frame buffers, resulting in switch port buffer starvation and potentially choking ISLs. The impact of choked ISLs is observed on other devices that are not slow drain devices but share the same switches and ISLs. As the size of the fabric grows, more and more ports are impacted by a slow drain situation. Because the impact is seen across a large number of ports, it becomes extremely important to detect, troubleshoot, and immediately recover from the situation. Traffic flow is severely impacted due to which applications face latency issues or stop responding completely until recovery is made or if the slow drain device is disconnected from the fabric.

Following are reasons for slow drain on edge devices and ISLs.

Edge Devices

- Server performance problems: applications or the OS.
- Host bus adapter (HBA) problems: driver or physical failure.
- Speed mismatches: one fast device and one slow device.
- Virtual machines which were not gracefully shutdown, resulting in frames held in HBA buffers.
- Storage subsystem performance problems, including overload.
- Poorly performing tape drives.

ISLs

- Lack of B2B credits for the distance the ISL is traversing
- The existence of slow drain edge devices.

Any device exhibiting such behavior is called a *slow drain device*.

All data traffic between end devices in a SAN fabric is carried by Fibre Channel Class 3. In some cases, the traffic is carried by Class 2 services that use link-level, per-hop-based, and buffer-to-buffer flow control. These classes of service do not support end-to-end flow control. When slow devices are attached to the fabric, the end devices do not accept the frames at the configured or negotiated rate. The slow devices lead to ISL credit shortage in the traffic destined for these devices, and they congest the links. The credit shortage affects the unrelated flows in the fabric that use the same ISL link, even though destination devices do not experience slow drain.

Cisco has taken a holistic approach by providing features to detect, troubleshoot, and automatically recover from slow drain situations. Detecting a slow drain device is the first step, followed by troubleshooting, which enables SAN administrators to take the manual action of disconnecting an offending device. However, manual actions are cumbersome and involve delay. To alleviate this limitation, Cisco MDS 9000 family switches have intelligence to constantly monitor the network for symptoms of slow drain and send alerts or take automatic recovery actions such as the following:

- Drop all frames queued to a slow drain device.
- Drop new frames destined to a slow drain device at line rate.
- Perform link reset on the affected port.
- Flap the affected port.
- Error disable the port.

All the 16Gbps MDS platforms (MDS 9700, MDS 9396S, MDS 9148S, and MDS 9250i) provide hardware-enhanced slow drain features. These enhanced features are a direct benefit of advanced capabilities of port ASIC. Following is a summary of advantages of hardware-enhanced slow drain features:

- Detection granularity in microseconds (μs) using port ASIC hardware counters.
- A new feature called slow port-monitor maintains a history of transmit credit unavailability duration on all the ports at as low as 1 millisecond (ms).
- Graphical display of credit unavailability duration on all the ports on a switch over last 60 seconds, 60 minutes, and 72 hours.
- Immediate automatic recovery from a slow drain situation without any software delay.

In addition to the hardware-enhanced slow drain features on Cisco MDS 9000 family switches, Cisco DCNM provides slow drain diagnostics from Release 7.1(1) and later. DCNM automates the monitoring of thousands of ports in a fabric in a single pane of glass and provides visual representation in the form of graphs showing fluctuation in counters. This feature leads to faster detection of slow drain devices, reduced false positives, and reduced troubleshooting time from weeks to minutes.

23

> **NOTE**   This feature is used mainly for edge ports that are connected to slow edge devices. Even though this feature can be applied to ISLs as well, we recommend that you apply this feature only for edge F ports and retain the default configuration for ISLs as E and TE ports.

Management Interfaces

You can remotely configure the switch through the management interface (mgmt0). To configure a connection on the mgmt0 interface, you must configure either the IP version 4 (IPv4) parameters (IP address, subnet mask, and default gateway) or the IP version 6 (IPv6) parameters so that the switch is reachable.

The management port (mgmt0) is autosensing and operates in full-duplex mode at a speed of 10/100/1000 Mbps. Autosensing supports both the speed and the duplex mode. On a Supervisor-1 module, the default speed is 100 Mbps and the default duplex mode is auto. On a Supervisor-2 module, the default speed is auto and the default duplex mode is auto.

VSAN Interfaces

VSANs apply to Fibre Channel fabrics and enable you to configure multiple isolated SAN topologies within the same physical infrastructure. You can create an IP interface on top of a VSAN and then use this interface to send frames to this VSAN. To use this feature, you must configure the IP address for this VSAN. VSAN interfaces cannot be created for non-existing VSANs. Here are the guidelines when creating or deleting a VSAN interface: Create a VSAN before creating the interface for that VSAN. If a VSAN does not exist, the interface cannot be created. Create the interface VSAN; it is not created automatically. If you delete the VSAN, the attached interface is automatically deleted. Configure each interface only in one VSAN. All the NX-OS CLI commands for interface configuration and verification are summarized in Table 23-10.

Table 23-10   Summary of NX-OS CLI Commands for Interface Configuration and Verification

Command	Purpose
switch#config t	Enter configuration mode.
switch(config)# **interface fc1/1** switch(config-if)# **shutdown**	When a Fibre Channel interface is configured, it is automatically assigned a unique World Wide Name (WWN). If the interface's operational state is up, it is also assigned a Fibre Channel ID (FCID).
switch(config-if)# (no) **switchport mode F** switch(config-if)# (no) **switchport mode auto**	Configures the administrative mode of the port. You can set the operational state to auto, E, F, FL, Fx, TL, NP, or SD port mode.

Command	Purpose
switch(config)# (no) **system default switchport mode F**	Sets the administrative mode of Fibre Channel ports to mode F.
switch(config)# (no) **system default switchport trunk mode auto**	Sets the default trunk mode auto.
switch(config)# (no) **system default switchport shutdown**	Sets the default switchport shut.
switch(config)# (no) switchport **rate-mode dedicated**	Sets the bandwidth dedicated to a specified port.
switch(config)# (no) **switchport rate-mode shared**	Sets the bandwidth shared between ports within a port group.
switch(config-if)# (no) **switchport speed 10000**	Configures the port speed of the interface to 10,000 Mbps.
switch(config-if)# (no) **switchport speed 8000**	
switch(config-if)# (no) **switchport speed auto max 4000**	Configures the port speed of the interface to 8000 Mbps.
	Configures maximum speed as 4000 Mbps.
switch(config-if)# (no) **switchport description WIN-HBA2**	Configures the description of the interface.
switch(config-if)# (no) **switchport beacon**	Enables the beacon mode for the interface.
switch(config-if)#(no) **switchport ignore bit-errors**	Prevents the detection of bit error threshold events from enabling the interface.
switch(config)# **interface mgmt0**	Selects the management Ethernet interface on the switch.
switch(config-if)# **ip address 10.22.2.2 255.255.255.0**	Configures the IPv4 address and IPv4 subnet mask.
switch(config-if)# **no shutdown**	Enables the interface.
switch(config-if)# **exit**	Returns to configuration mode.
switch(config)# **ip default-gateway 10.22.2.1**	Configures the default gateway IPv4 address.
switch(config)# **interface mgmt0**	Selects the management Ethernet interface on the switch.
switch(config-if)# **ipv6 enable**	
switch(config-if)# **ipv6 address ipv6 address 2001:0db8:800:200c::417a/64**	Enables IPv6 and assigns a link-local address on the interface.
switch(config-if)# **no shutdown**	Specifies an IPv6 unicast address and prefix length on the interface.
	Enables the interface.
switch(config)# **interface vsan 2**	Configures a VSAN with the ID 2.
switch(config-if)# **no shutdown**	Enables the interface.

23

Command	Purpose
switch(config)# **interface fc1/1**	Selects the fc interface 1/1.
switch(config-if)# **errdisable detect cause link-down** [**num-times** *number* **duration** *seconds*] switch(config-if)# **errdisable detect cause** { **trustsec-violation** | **bit-errors** | **credit-loss** | **link-reset** | **signal-loss** | **sync-loss** } [**num-times** *number* **duration** *seconds*]	Enables the port guard configuration for the interface. Brings the port to a down state if the link flaps for the *number* of instances within the specified *seconds*.
switch(config) # **system default interface congestion timeout milliseconds mode** {**core** | **edge**}	Configures a new congestion frame timeout value in milliseconds and the port mode for the device.
switch(config)# **system timeout congestion-drop** *seconds* **mode E|F**	Specifies the stuck frame timeout value in ms and the port mode for the switch.
switch(config)# **system timeout no-credit-drop milli** *seconds* **mode F**	Specifies the no-credit timeout value for F port mode for the switch.
switch(config)# **system timeout slow-port-monitor milliseconds mode E/F**	Specifies the slow port monitor timeout value for E or F port mode for the switch.

Command	Purpose
switch# **show port internal info interface fc ½**	Shows the internal information about a port.
switch# **show interface fc 1/2 , fc 3/6**	
switch# **show interface description**	Displays a specific fc interface.
switch# **show interface brief**	Displays a description of an interface.
switch# **show interface counters**	Displays brief information for all the interfaces.
switch# **show interface counters brief**	Displays interface counters.
switch# **show interface transceiver**	Displays interface counters briefly.
switch# **show running-config interface fc1/1**	Displays Cisco-supported SFPs.
switch# **show port-monitor slowdrain**	Displays a running configuration of interface fc 1/1.
switch# **show interface mgmt 0**	
switch# **show port-monitor**	Displays port monitor status and policies.
switch# **show interface vsan 2**	Displays the management interface configuration.
switch# **show module**	Displays port monitor status and policies.
switch# **show port-resources module 8**	Displays VSAN interface information.
switch# **show process creditmon slowport-monitor-events**	Displays status of all the modules.
switch# **show logging onboard flow-control request-timeout**	Displays resource availability for a specific module.
	Displays slow port monitor events.
switch# **show interface fc2/31 bbcredit**	Displays the request timeout for a source-destination pair per module with the timestamp information.
	Displays the BB_credit configuration for the specific interface.

Verify Initiator and Target Fabric Login

In Chapter 22, we discussed a theoretical explanation of virtual SANs (VSANs), zoning, Fibre Channel services, Fibre Channel concepts, and SAN topologies. In this section, we discuss the configuration and verification steps to build a Fibre Channel SAN topology. In this chapter, we build up the following sample SAN topology together to practice what you have learned so far (see Figure 23-33).

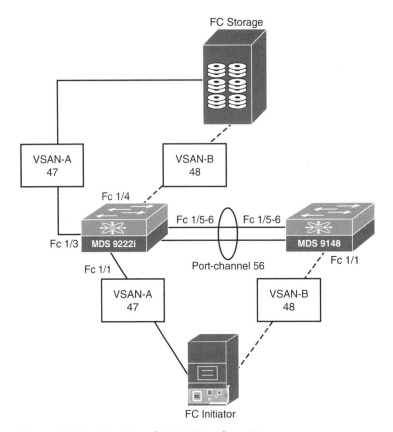

Figure 23-33 *Our Sample SAN Topology Diagram*

VSAN Configuration

You can achieve higher security and greater stability in Fibre Channel fabrics by using virtual SANs (VSANs) on Cisco MDS 9000 family switches and Cisco Nexus 5000, Nexus 6000, Nexus 7000, and Nexus 9000 Series switches, and UCS Fabric Interconnect. VSANs provide isolation among devices that are physically connected to the same fabric. With VSANs, you can create multiple logical SANs over a common physical infrastructure. Each VSAN can contain up to 239 switches and has an independent address space that allows identical Fibre Channel IDs (FCIDs) to be used simultaneously in different VSANs.

VSANs have the following attributes:

- **VSAN ID:** The VSAN ID identifies the VSAN as the *default* VSAN (VSAN 1), user-defined VSANs (VSAN 2 to 4093), or the *isolated* VSAN (VSAN 4094). A VSAN is in the operational state if the VSAN is active and at least one port is up. This state indicates that traffic can pass through this VSAN. This state cannot be configured.

- **State:** The administrative state of a VSAN can be configured to an *active* (default) or *suspended* state. After VSANs are created, they may exist in various conditions or states.

The active state of a VSAN indicates that the VSAN is configured and enabled. By enabling a VSAN, you activate the services for that VSAN.

The suspended state of a VSAN indicates that the VSAN is configured but not enabled. If a port is configured in this VSAN, it is disabled. Use this state to deactivate a VSAN without losing the VSAN's configuration. All ports in a suspended VSAN are disabled. By suspending a VSAN, you can preconfigure all the VSAN parameters for the whole fabric and activate the VSAN immediately.

- **VSAN name:** This text string identifies the VSAN for management purposes. The name can be from 1 to 32 characters long and it must be unique across all VSANs. By default, the VSAN name is a concatenation of "VSAN" and a four-digit string representing the VSAN ID. For example, the default name for VSAN 3 is VSAN0003.

- **Load balancing attributes:** These attributes indicate the use of the source-destination ID (src-dst-id) or the originator exchange OX ID (src-dst-ox-id, the default) for load balancing path selection.

- **Interop mode:** Interoperability enables the products of multiple vendors to interact with each other. Fibre Channel standards guide vendors toward common external Fibre Channel interfaces.

  Each vendor has a regular mode and an equivalent interoperability mode that specifically turns off advanced or proprietary features and provides the product with a more amiable standards-compliant implementation. Cisco NX-OS software supports the following four interop modes:

  - **Mode 1:** Standards-based interop mode that requires all other vendors in the fabric to be in interop mode
  - **Mode 2:** Brocade native mode (Core PID 0)
  - **Mode 3:** Brocade native mode (Core PID 1)
  - **Mode 4:** McData native mode

Port VSAN Membership

Port VSAN membership on the switch is assigned on a port-by-port basis. By default, each port belongs to the default VSAN. You can assign VSAN membership to ports using one of two methods:

- **Statically:** By assigning VSANs to ports.
- **Dynamically:** By assigning VSANs based on the device WWN. This method is referred to as dynamic port VSAN membership (DPVM), which is explained in Chapter 22.

In Example 23-8, we begin configuring and verifying VSANs on our sample topology shown in Figure 23-33.

Example 23-8 *VSAN Creation and Verification on MDS-9222i Switch*

```
!Initial Configuration and entering the VSAN configuration database
MDS-9222i# conf t
Enter configuration commands, one per line.  End with CNTL/Z.
MDS-9222i(config)# vsan database
! Creating VSAN 47
```

23

```
MDS-9222i(config-vsan-db)# vsan 47 ?
MDS-9222i(config-vsan-db)# vsan 47 name VSAN-A
! Configuring VSAN name for VSAN 47
MDS-9222i(config-vsan-db)# vsan 47 name VSAN-A ?
  <CR>
  interop        Interoperability mode value
  loadbalancing  Configure loadbalancing scheme
suspend          Suspend vsan
! Other attributes of a VSAN configuration can be displayed with a question mark after
VSAN name.
MDS-9222i(config-vsan-db)# vsan 47 name VSAN-A interop loadbalanci ?
  src-dst-id     Src-id/dst-id for loadbalancing
  src-dst-ox-id  Ox-id/src-id/dst-id for loadbalancing(Default)
! Load balancing attributes of a VSAN
! To exit configuration mode issue command end
MDS-9222i(config-vsan-db)# end
! Verifying the VSAN state, the operational state is down since no FC port is up
MDS-9222i# show vsan 47
vsan 47 information
         name:VSAN-A  state:active
         interoperability mode:default
         loadbalancing:src-id/dst-id/oxid
         operational state:down
MDS-9222i(config)# vsan database
! Interface fc1/1 and fc 1/3 are included in VSAN 47
MDS-9222i(config-vsan-db)# vsan 47 interface fc1/1,fc1/3
MDS-9222i(config-vsan-db)# interface fc1/1, fc1/3
! Change the state of the fc interfaces
MDS-9222i(config-if)# no shut
! Verifying status of the interfaces
MDS-9222i(config-if)# show int fc 1/1, fc1/3 brief
-------------------------------------------------------------------------------
Interface  Vsan  Admin  Admin  Status      SFP   Oper  Oper   Port
                 Mode   Trunk                     Mode  Speed  Channel
                        Mode                             (Gbps)
fc1/1      47    FX     on     up          swl   F     2      --
fc1/3      47    FX     on     up          swl   FL    4      --
```

Note, as highlighted, that the Admin Mode is FX (the default), which allows the port to come up in either F mode or FL mode:

- **F mode:** Point-to-point mode for server connections and most storage connections (storage ports in F mode have only one target logging in to that port, associated with the storage array port).

- **FL mode:** Arbitrated loop mode—storage connections that allow multiple storage targets to log in to a single switch port. We have done this just so that you can see multiple storage targets for zoning.

The last steps for the VSAN configuration will be verifying the VSAN membership and usage (see Example 23-9).

Example 23-9 *The Verification Steps for VSAN Membership and Usage*

```
! Verifying the VSAN membership
MDS-9222i# show vsan membership
vsan 1 interfaces:
    fc1/1            fc1/2            fc1/3            fc1/4
    fc1/5            fc1/6            fc1/7            fc1/8
    fc1/9            fc1/10           fc1/11           fc1/12
    fc1/13           fc1/14           fc1/15           fc1/16
    fc1/17           fc1/18
vsan 47 interfaces:
    fc1/1            fc1/3
vsan 4079(evfp_isolated_vsan) interfaces:
vsan 4094(isolated_vsan) interfaces:
! Verifying VSAN usage
MDS-9222i# show vsan usage
1 vsan configured
configured vsans: 1, 47
vsans available for configuration: 2-46,48-4093
```

In a Fibre Channel fabric, each host or disk requires a Fibre Channel ID. Use the **show flogi** command to verify if a storage device is displayed in the FLOGI table, as in the next section. If the required device is displayed in the FLOGI table, the fabric login is successful. Examine the FLOGI database on a switch that is directly connected to the host HBA and connected ports.

The name server functionality maintains a database containing the attributes for all hosts and storage devices in each VSAN. Name servers allow a database entry to be modified by a device that originally registered the information. The name server stores name entries for all hosts in the FCNS database. The name server permits an Nx port to register attributes during a PLOGI (to the name server) to obtain attributes of other hosts. These attributes are deregistered when the Nx port logs out either explicitly or implicitly.

In a multiswitch fabric configuration, the name server instances running on each switch share information in a distributed database. One instance of the name server process runs on each switch. In Example 23-10, we continue verifying FCNS and FLOGI databases on our sample SAN topology.

Example 23-10   Verifying FCNS and FLOGI Databases on MDS-9222i Switch

```
! Verifying fc interface status
MDS-9222i(config-if)# show interface fc 1/1
fc1/1 is up
    Hardware is Fibre Channel, SFP is short wave laser w/o OFC (SN)
    Port WWN is 20:01:00:05:9b:77:0d:c0
    Admin port mode is FX, trunk mode is on
```

23

```
      snmp link state traps are enabled
      Port mode is F, FCID is 0x410100
      Port vsan is 47
      Speed is 2 Gbps
      Rate mode is shared
      Transmit B2B Credit is 3
      Receive B2B Credit is 16
      Receive data field Size is 2112
      Beacon is turned off
      5 minutes input rate 88 bits/sec, 11 bytes/sec, 0 frames/sec
      5 minutes output rate 32 bits/sec, 4 bytes/sec, 0 frames/sec
        18 frames input, 3632 bytes
          0 discards, 0 errors
          0 CRC,  0 unknown class
          0 too long, 0 too short
        18 frames output, 1396 bytes
          0 discards, 0 errors
        0 input OLS, 0 LRR, 0 NOS, 2 loop inits
        1 output OLS, 1 LRR, 0 NOS, 1 loop inits
        16 receive B2B credit remaining
        3 transmit B2B credit remaining
        3 low priority transmit B2B credit remaining
      Interface last changed at Mon Sep 22 09:55:15 2014


! The port mode is F mode and there is automatically FCID is assigned to the FC
Initiator,
which is attached to fc 1/1. The buffer-to-buffer credits are negotiated during the
port login.
! Verifying flogi database , the initiator is connected to fc 1/1 the domain id is x41
MDS-9222i(config-if)# show flogi database
--------------------------------------------------------------------------------
INTERFACE       VSAN    FCID        PORT NAME              NODE NAME
--------------------------------------------------------------------------------
fc1/1           47      0x410100    21:00:00:e0:8b:0a:f0:54 20:00:00:e0:8b:0a:f0:54
! JBOD FC target contains 2 NL_Ports (disks) and is connected to domain x041
! FC Initiator with the pWWN 21:00:00:e0:8b:0a:f0:54 is attached to fc interface 1/1,
the VSAN domain manager 47 has assigned FCID 0x410100 to the device during FLOGI.
fc1/3           47      0x4100e8    c5:9a:00:06:2b:04:fa:ce c5:9a:00:06:2b:01:00:04
fc1/3           47      0x4100ef    c5:9a:00:06:2b:01:01:04 c5:9a:00:06:2b:01:00:04
Total number of flogi = 3.
! Verifying name server database
! The assigned FCID 0x410100 and device WWN information are registered in the FCNS
and attain fabric-wide visibility.
MDS-9222i(config-if)# show fcns database
VSAN 47:
--------------------------------------------------------------------------------
```

```
FCID          TYPE  PWWN                          (VENDOR)      FC4-TYPE:FEATURE
-------------------------------------------------------------------------
0x4100e8      NL    c5:9a:00:06:2b:04:fa:ce                     scsi-fcp:target
0x4100ef      NL    c5:9a:00:06:2b:01:01:04                     scsi-fcp:target
0x410100      N     21:00:00:e0:8b:0a:f0:54 (Qlogic)            scsi-fcp:init
Total number of entries = 3
MDS-9222i(config-if)# show fcns database detail
-----------------------
VSAN:47    FCID:0x4100e8
-----------------------
port-wwn (vendor)            :c5:9a:00:06:2b:04:fa:ce
node-wwn                     :c5:9a:00:06:2b:01:00:04
class                        :3
node-ip-addr                 :0.0.0.0
ipa                          :ff ff ff ff ff ff ff ff
fc4-types:fc4_features       :scsi-fcp:target
symbolic-port-name           :SANBlaze V4.0 Port
symbolic-node-name           :
port-type                    :NL
port-ip-addr                 :0.0.0.0
fabric-port-wwn              :20:03:00:05:9b:77:0d:c0
hard-addr                    :0x000000
permanent-port-wwn (vendor)  :00:00:00:00:00:00:00:00
connected interface          :fc1/3
switch name (IP address)     :MDS-9222i (10.2.8.44)
-----------------------
VSAN:47    FCID:0x4100ef
-----------------------
port-wwn (vendor)            :c5:9a:00:06:2b:01:01:04
node-wwn                     :c5:9a:00:06:2b:01:00:04
class                        :3
node-ip-addr                 :0.0.0.0
ipa                          :ff ff ff ff ff ff ff ff
fc4-types:fc4_features       :scsi-fcp:target
symbolic-port-name           :SANBlaze V4.0 Port
symbolic-node-name           :
port-type                    :NL
port-ip-addr                 :0.0.0.0
fabric-port-wwn              :20:03:00:05:9b:77:0d:c0
hard-addr                    :0x000000
permanent-port-wwn (vendor)  :00:00:00:00:00:00:00:00
connected interface          :fc1/3
switch name (IP address)     :MDS-9222i (10.2.8.44)
-----------------------
VSAN:47    FCID:0x410100 ! Initiator connected to fc 1/1
! The vendor of the host bus adapter (HBA) is Qlogic where we can see in the vendor
```

```
pWWN
-----------------------
port-wwn (vendor)           :21:00:00:e0:8b:0a:f0:54 (Qlogic)
node-wwn                    :20:00:00:e0:8b:0a:f0:54
class                       :3
node-ip-addr                :0.0.0.0
ipa                         :ff ff ff ff ff ff ff ff
fc4-types:fc4_features      :scsi-fcp:init
symbolic-port-name          :
symbolic-node-name          :QLA2342 FW:v3.03.25 DVR:v9.1.8.6
port-type                   :N
port-ip-addr                :0.0.0.0
fabric-port-wwn             :20:01:00:05:9b:77:0d:c0
hard-addr                   :0x000000
permanent-port-wwn (vendor) :21:00:00:e0:8b:0a:f0:54 (Qlogic)
connected interface         :fc1/1
switch name (IP address)    :MDS-9222i (10.2.8.44)
Total number of entries = 3
```

The DCNM Device Manager for MDS 9222i will display the ports in two tabs: the Summary tab and the Device tab, which is a GUI display of the physical ports (see Figure 23-34).

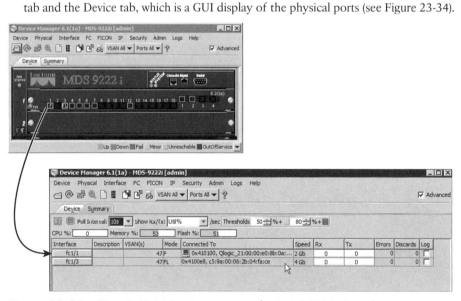

Figure 23-34   *Cisco DCNM Device Manager for MDS 9222i Switch*

In Table 23-11, we summarize the NX-OS CLI commands that are related to VSAN configuration and verification.

Table 23-11   Summary of NX-OS CLI Commands for VSAN Configuration and Verification

Command	Purpose
switch# config t	Enters configuration mode.
switch(config)# **vsan database**	Configures the database for a VSAN.
switch(config-vsan-db)# (no) **vsan 2**	Creates a VSAN with the specified ID (2).
switch(config-vsan-db)# **vsan 2 name VSAN-A**	Updates the VSAN with the assigned name.
switch(config-vsan-db)# (no) **vsan 2 suspend**	Suspends the selected VSAN.
switch(config-vsan-db)# (no) **vsan 1 interop [1-4]**	Enables interop mode for a specified VSAN.
switch(config-vsan-db)# (no) **vsan 2 loadbalancing src-dst-id**	Enables the load-balancing guarantee for the selected VSAN. It directs the switch to use the source and destination ID for its path selection process or the source ID, the destination ID, and the OX ID (default) algorithm.
switch(config-vsan-db)# (no) **vsan 2 loadbalancing src-dst-ox-id**	
switch(config-vsan-db)# end	
switch#	
switch(config)# **vsan database**	Enters VSAN database configuration submode.
switch(config-vsan-db)# **vsan 2 interface fc1/8**	Assigns the membership of the fc1/8 interface to the specified VSAN (VSAN 2).
switch# **show vsan**	Displays information about configured VSANs.
switch# **show vsan 100**	Displays the configuration for a specific VSAN.
switch# **show vsan usage**	Displays the VSAN usage.
switch # **show vsan 1 membership**	Displays membership information for a specific VSAN.
switch # **show vsan membership**	Displays membership information for all interfaces.
switch # **show vsan membership interface fc1/1**	Displays membership information for a specific interface.
switch# **show fabric switch information vsan 100**	Displays information about all the switches in the fabric.
switch# **show fcns database**	Displays FC Name Service database for all the devices.
switch# **show fcns database detail**	Displays FC Name Service database details for all devices.
switch# **show flogi database**	Displays fabric login database for all devices.

23

Fibre Channel Zoning

Zoning is used to provide security and to restrict access between initiators and targets on the SAN fabric. With many types of servers and storage devices on the network, security is crucial. For example, if a host were to gain access to a disk that was being used by another host, potentially with a different operating system, the data on this disk could become corrupted. To avoid any compromise of crucial data within the SAN, zoning allows the user to overlay a security map. This map dictates which devices (namely hosts) can see which targets, thus reducing the risk of data loss. In addition, the NX-OS software provides support for Smart Zoning, which dramatically reduces operational complexity while consuming fewer resources on the switch. Smart Zoning enables customers to intuitively create fewer multimember zones at an application level, a physical cluster level, or a virtualized cluster level without sacrificing switch resources, instead of creating multiple two-member zones.

Cisco MDS 9000 NX-OS supports the following types of zoning:

- **N-port zoning:** Defines zone members based on the end-device (host and storage) port:
  - WWN
  - Fibre Channel identifier (FCID)
- **Fx-port zoning:** Defines zone members based on the switch port:
  - WWN
  - WWN plus interface index, or domain ID plus interface index
  - Domain ID plus port number (for Brocade interoperability)
  - Fabric port WWN
  - Interface plus domain ID, or plus switch WWN of the interface
- **iSCSI zoning:** Defines zone members based on the host zone:
  - iSCSI name
  - IP address

To provide strict network security, zoning is always enforced per frame using access control lists (ACLs) that are applied at the ingress switch. All zoning policies are enforced in hardware, and none of them cause performance degradation. The zoning feature complies with the FC-GS-4 and FC-SW-3 standards. Both standards support the basic and enhanced zoning functionalities. Enhanced zoning session-management capabilities further enhance security by allowing only one user at a time to modify zones.

A zone set consists of one or more zones:

- A zone set can be activated or deactivated as a single entity across all switches in the fabric.
- Only one zone set can be activated at any time.
- A zone can be a member of more than one zone set.
- A zone consists of multiple zone members. Members in a zone can access one another. Members in different zones cannot access one another.

Zone set distribution—You can distribute full zone sets using one of two methods: one-time distribution or full zone set distribution.

Zone set duplication—You can make a copy of a zone set and then edit it without altering the original zone set. You can copy an active zone set from the bootflash: directory, volatile: directory, or slot0, to one of the following areas:

- To the full zone set
- To a remote location (using FTP, SCP, SFTP, or TFTP)

The active zone set is not part of the full zone set. You cannot make changes to an existing zone set and activate it if the full zone set is lost or is not propagated.

In Example 23-11, we continue building our sample topology with zoning configuration.

Example 23-11   Configuring Zoning on MDS-9222i Switch

```
! Creating zone in VSAN 47
MDS-9222i(config-if)# zone name zoneA vsan 47
MDS-9222i(config-zone)# member ?
! zone member can be configured with one of the below options
  device-alias        Add device-alias member to zone
  domain-id           Add member based on domain-id,port-number
  fcalias             Add fcalias to zone
  fcid                Add FCID member to zone
  fwwn                Add Fabric Port WWN member to zone
  interface           Add member based on interface
  ip-address          Add IP address member to zone
  pwwn                Add Port WWN member to zone
  symbolic-nodename   Add Symbolic Node Name member to zone
! Inserting a disk (FC target) into zoneA
MDS-9222i(config-zone)# member pwwn c5:9a:00:06:2b:01:01:04
! Inserting pWWN of an initiator which is connected to fc 1/1 into zoneA
MDS-9222i(config-zone)# member pwwn 21:00:00:e0:8b:0a:f0:54
! Verifying zone zoneA if the correct members are configured or not
MDS-9222i(config-zone)# show zone name zoneA
zone name zoneA vsan 47
  pwwn c5:9a:00:06:2b:01:01:04
  pwwn 21:00:00:e0:8b:0a:f0:54
! Creating zone set in VSAN 47
MDS-9222i(config-zone)# zoneset name zonesetA vsan 47
MDS-9222i(config-zoneset)# member zoneA
MDS-9222i(config-zoneset)# exit
! Inserting a disk (FC target) into zoneA
MDS-9222i(config)# zoneset activate name zonesetA vsan 47
Zoneset activation initiated. check zone status
! Verifying the active zone set status in VSAN 47
MDS-9222i(config)# show zoneset active
zoneset name zonesetA vsan 47
  zone name zoneA vsan 47
```

23

```
     * fcid 0x4100ef [pwwn c5:9a:00:06:2b:01:01:04]
   * fcid 0x410100 [pwwn 21:00:00:e0:8b:0a:f0:54]
   The asterisks (*) indicate that a device is currently logged into the fabric (online).
   A missing asterisk may indicate an offline device or an incorrectly configured zone,
   possibly a mistyped pWWN.
   MDS-9222i(config)# show zoneset brief
   zoneset name zonesetA vsan 47
     zone zoneA
```

Setting up multiple switches independently and then connecting them into one fabric *can* be done in DCNM. However, DCNM is really best at viewing and operating on *existing* fabrics (that is, just about everything except making initial connections of multiple switches into one fabric). In this chapter, we just use the CLI versions of these commands.

About Smart Zoning

Smart Zoning implements hard zoning of large zones with fewer hardware resources than was previously required. The traditional zoning method allows each device in a zone to communicate with every other device in the zone. The administrator is required to manage the individual zones according to the zone configuration guidelines. Smart Zoning eliminates the need to create a single initiator to single target zones. By analyzing device-type information in the FCNS, the Cisco MDS NX-OS software can implement useful combinations at the hardware level, and the combinations that are not used are ignored. For example, initiator-target pairs are configured, but not initiator-initiator pairs.

The device type information of each device in a smart zone is automatically populated from the Fibre Channel Name Server (FCNS) database as host, target, or both. This information allows more efficient utilization of switch hardware by identifying initiator-target pairs and configuring those only in hardware. In the event of a special situation, such as a disk controller that needs to communicate with another disk controller, Smart Zoning defaults can be overridden by the administrator to allow complete control. Smart Zoning can be enabled at the VSAN level but can also be disabled at the zone level.

About LUN Zoning and Assigning LUNs to Storage Subsystems

Logical unit number (LUN) zoning is a feature specific to switches in the Cisco MDS 9000 family. A storage device can have multiple LUNs behind it. If the device port is part of a zone, a member of the zone can access any LUN in the device. When LUN 0 is not included within a zone, then, as per standards requirements, control traffic to LUN 0 (for example, REPORT_LUNS, INQUIRY) is supported, but data traffic to LUN 0 (for example, READ, WRITE) is denied. With LUN zoning, you can restrict access to specific LUNs associated with a device. LUN masking and mapping restricts server access to specific LUNs. If LUN masking is enabled on a storage subsystem, and if you want to perform additional LUN zoning in a Cisco MDS 9000 family switch, the LUN number for each host bus adapter (HBA) from the storage subsystem should be configured with the LUN-based zone procedure.

About Enhanced Zoning

The zoning feature complies with the FC-GS-4 and FC-SW-3 standards. Both standards support the basic zoning functionalities explained in Chapter 22 and the enhanced zoning functionalities described in this section. The default zoning mode can be selected during the initial setup. By default, the enhanced zoning feature is disabled in all switches in the Cisco MDS 9000 family. The default zoning is basic mode. Enhanced zoning can be turned on per VSAN as long as each switch within that VSAN is enhanced zoning capable. Enhanced zoning needs to be enabled on only one switch within the VSAN in the existing SAN topology. At the time enhanced zoning is enabled, the command will be propagated to the other switches within the VSAN automatically.

Enhanced zoning uses the same techniques and tools as basic zoning, with a few added commands. The flow of enhanced zoning, however, differs from that of basic zoning. For one thing, a VSAN-wide lock, if available, is implicitly obtained for enhanced zoning. Second, all zone and zone set modifications for enhanced zoning include activation. Last, changes are either committed or aborted with enhanced zoning.

To enable enhanced zoning in a VSAN, follow these steps:

Step 1. Enter configuration mode.

```
switch# config t
```

Step 2. Change the zoning mode to enhanced for VSAN 200. You need to check the zone status to verify the status.

```
switch(config)# zone mode enhanced vsan 222
```

The following command disables the enhanced zoning mode for a specific VSAN:

```
switch(config)# no zone mode enhanced vsan 222
```

Step 3. The zone status can be verified with the **show zone status** command. The zone mode will display enhanced for enhanced mode, and the default zone distribution policy is full for enhanced mode. In basic zone mode, the default zone distribution policy is active.

```
switch# show zone status vsan 222
VSAN: 222 default-zone: deny distribute: full Interop: default
    mode: enhanced merge-control: allow
    session: none
    hard-zoning: enabled broadcast: enabled
    smart-zoning: disabled
    rscn-format: fabric-address
Default zone:
    qos: none broadcast: disabled ronly: disabled
Full Zoning Database :
    DB size: 44 bytes
    Zonesets:0  Zones:0 Aliases: 0 Attribute-groups: 1
Active Zoning Database :
    Database Not Available
```

23

The rules for enabling enhanced zoning are as follows:

■ Enhanced zoning needs to be enabled on only one switch in the VSAN of an existing converged SAN fabric. Enabling it on multiple switches within the same VSAN can result in failure to activate properly.

■ Enabling enhanced zoning does not perform a zone set activation.

■ The switch that is chosen to initiate the migration to enhanced zoning will distribute its full zone database to the other switches in the VSAN, thereby overwriting the destination switches' full zone set database.

Table 23-12 details the advantages of using enhanced zoning.

Table 23-12 Advantages of Enhanced Zoning

Basic Zoning	Enhanced Zoning	Enhanced Zoning Advantages
Administrators can make simultaneous configuration changes.	Performs all configurations within a single configuration session. When you begin a session, the switch locks the entire fabric to implement the change.	One configuration session for the entire fabric ensures consistency within the fabric.
If a zone is part of multiple zone sets, you create an instance of this zone in each zone set.	References to the zone are used by the zone sets as required after you define the zone.	Reduced payload size as the zone is referenced.
The default zone policy is defined per switch. To ensure smooth fabric operation, all switches in the fabric must have the same default zone setting.	Enforces and exchanges the default zone setting throughout the fabric.	Fabric-wide policy enforcement reduces troubleshooting time.
To retrieve the results of the activation on a per-switch basis, the managing switch provides a combined status about the activation. It does not identify the failure switch.	Retrieves the activation results and the nature of the problem from each remote switch.	Enhanced error reporting eases the troubleshooting process.
To distribute the zoning database, you must reactivate the same zone set. The reactivation may affect hardware changes for hard zoning on the local switch and on remote switches.	Implements changes to the zoning database and distributes it without reactivation.	Distribution of zone sets without activation avoids hardware changes for hard zoning in the switches.
The MDS-specific zone member types are IPv4 address, IPv6 address, symbolic node name, and other types. During a merge, the non-Cisco switches can misunderstand the MDS-specific types.	Provides a vendor ID along with a vendor-specific type value to uniquely identify a member type.	Unique vendor type.

Basic Zoning	Enhanced Zoning	Enhanced Zoning Advantages
The fWWN-based zone membership is supported only in Cisco interop mode.	Supports fWWN-based membership in the standard interop mode (interop mode 1).	The fWWN-based member type is standardized.

Let's return to our sample SAN topology (see Figure 23-35). So far we managed to build only separate SAN islands.

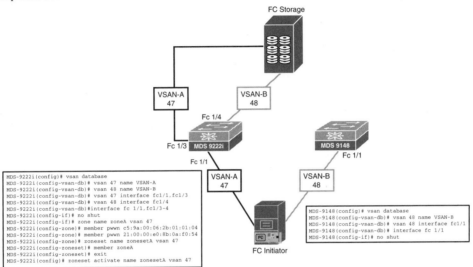

Figure 23-35 *SAN Topology with CLI Configuration*

On MDS 9222i, we configured two VSANs: VSAN 47 and VSAN 48. Both VSANs are active and their operational states are up (see Example 23-12).

Example 23-12 *Verifying Initiator and Target Logins*

```
MDS-9222i(config-if)# show interface fc1/1,fc1/3,fc1/4,fc1/12 brief

--------------------------------------------------------------------------------

Interface  Vsan   Admin   Admin   Status        SFP    Oper  Oper    Port
                  Mode    Trunk                         Mode  Speed   Channel
                          Mode                                (Gbps)

--------------------------------------------------------------------------------

fc1/1      47     FX      on      up             swl    F     2       --

fc1/3      47     FX      on      up             swl    FL    4       --

fc1/4      48     FX      on      up             swl    FL    4       --


MDS-9222i(config-if)# show fcns database

VSAN 47:

--------------------------------------------------------------------------------

FCID       TYPE   PWWN                     (VENDOR)       FC4-TYPE:FEATURE
```

23

```
-------------------------------------------------------------------------
0x4100e8    NL    c5:9a:00:06:2b:04:fa:ce                    scsi-fcp:target
0x4100ef    NL    c5:9a:00:06:2b:01:01:04                    scsi-fcp:target
0x410100    N     21:00:00:e0:8b:0a:f0:54 (Qlogic)           scsi-fcp:init
Total number of entries = 3
VSAN 48:

-------------------------------------------------------------------------
FCID        TYPE  PWWN                      (VENDOR)         FC4-TYPE:FEATURE
-------------------------------------------------------------------------
0x4100e8    NL    c5:9b:00:06:2b:14:fa:ce                    scsi-fcp:target
0x4100ef    NL    c5:9b:00:06:2b:02:01:04                    scsi-fcp:target
Total number of entries = 2
MDS-9148(config-if)# show flogi database
-------------------------------------------------------------------------
INTERFACE       VSAN    FCID     PORT NAME            NODE NAME
-------------------------------------------------------------------------
fc1/1           48     0x420000 21:01:00:e0:8b:2a:f0:54 20:01:00:e0:8b:2a:f0:54
Total number of flogi = 1.


MDS-9148(config-if)# show fcns database
VSAN 48:
-------------------------------------------------------------------------
FCID        TYPE  PWWN                      (VENDOR)         FC4-TYPE:FEATURE
-------------------------------------------------------------------------
0x420000    N     21:01:00:e0:8b:2a:f0:54 (Qlogic)           scsi-fcp:init
Total number of entries = 1
```

Table 23-13 summarizes the NX-OS CLI commands for zone configuration and verification. The zoning features, which require the Enterprise package license, are LUN zoning, read-only zones, zone-based traffic prioritizing, and zone-based FC QoS.

Table 23-13 Summary of NX-OS CLI Commands for Zone Configuration and Verification

Command	Purpose
switch# config t	Enters configuration mode.
switch(config)# **zone name Zone1 vsan 3**	Configures a zone called Zone1 VSAN 3.
pWWN example:	
switch(config-zone)# **member pwwn 10:00:00:23:45:67:89:aa**	Configures a member for the specified zone (Zone1) based on the type (pWWN, fabric pWWN, FCID, fcalias, domain ID, IPv4 address, IPv6 address, or interface) and value specified.
Fabric pWWN example:	
switch(config-zone)# **member fwwn 10:01:10:01:10:ab:cd:ee**	
FCID example:	
switch(config-zone)# **member fcid 0xce00d2**	
FC alias example:	
switch(config-zone)# **member fcalias Payroll**	
Domain ID example:	
switch(config-zone)# **member domain-id 2 portnumber 24**	
IPv4 address example:	
switch(config-zone)# **member ip-address 10.16.0.0 255.255.0.0**	
IPv6 address example:	
switch(config-zone)# **member ipv6-address 2001::db8:800:200c:417a/64**	
Local sWWN interface example:	
switch(config-zone)# **member interface fc 2/1**	
Remote sWWN interface example:	
{ Use the **show wwn switch** command to retrieve the sWWN. If you do not provide an sWWN, the software automatically uses the local sWWN.}	
switch(config-zone)# **member interface fc2/1 swwn 20:00:00:05:30:00:4a:aa**	
Domain ID interface example:	
switch(config-zone)# **member interface fc2/1 domain-id 24**	
switch(config-zone)# **member symbolic-nodename iqn.test**	

23

Command	Purpose
switch(config)# **zone set name Zoneset1 vsan 3** switch(config-zoneset)# **member Zone1** switch(config-zoneset)# **zone name InlineZone1** switch(config-zoneset-zone)# **member fcid 0x111122**	Configures a zone set called Zoneset1. Adds Zone1 as a member of the specified zone set. Adds a zone (InlineZone1) to the specified zone set. Adds a new member (FCID 0x111122).
switch(config)# (no) **zoneset activate name Zoneset1 vsan 3**	Activates the zone set and updates the new zone name in the active zone set.
switch(config)# (no) **zone default-zone permit vsan 1**	Permits traffic flow to default zone members.
switch(config)# **zoneset distribute full vsan 22** switch# **zoneset distribute vsan 2-4**	Enables sending a full zone set along with an active zone set.
switch# **zoneset import interface fc1/3 vsan 2-4** switch# **zoneset export vsan 6-8** switch# **zone copy active-zoneset full-zoneset vsan 2** Please enter yes to proceed.(y/n) [n]? y switch# **zone copy vsan 2 active-zoneset scp:// guest@server/tmp/active_zoneset.txt**	Imports the zone set from the adjacent switch. Exports the zone set to the adjacent switch. Makes a copy of the active zone set in VSAN 2 to the full zone set. Copies the active zone in VSAN 2 to a remote location using SCP.
switch(config)# **zoneset rename oldname newname vsan 2** switch(config)# **fcalias rename oldname newname vsan 2** switch(config)# **zone-attribute-group rename oldname newname vsan 2** switch(config)# **zoneset clone oldname newname vsan 2** switch(config)# **fcalias clone oldname newname vsan 2** switch(config)# **zone-attribute-group clone oldname newname vsan 2**	Renames a zone set in the specified VSAN. Renames an fcalias in the specified VSAN. Renames a zone attribute group in the specified VSAN. Clones a zone set in the specified VSAN. Clones an fcalias in the specified VSAN. Clones a zone attribute group.

Command	Purpose
switch(config)# **zone-attribute-group name SampleAttributeGroup vsan 2**	In enhanced mode, creates an attribute group.
switch(config-attribute-group)# **readonly**	
switch(config-attribute-group)# **broadcast**	Read-only attribute.
switch(config-attribute-group)# **qos priority medium**	Broadcast attribute.
	Qos priority medium.
! Readonly and broadcast commands are not supported from NX-OS 5.2 release onwards.	
switch(config)# **zone name Zone1 vsan 2**	
switch(config-zone)# **attribute-group SampleAttributeGroup**	Configures a zone called Zone1 for VSAN 2.
	Includes attribute-group to Zone1.
switch(config-zone)# exit	

23

Command	Purpose
switch(config)# (no) **zone smart-zoning enable vsan 1**	Enables Smart Zoning on a VSAN.
switch(config)# (no) **system default zone smart-zone enable**	Enables Smart Zoning on a specified default value.
switch(config)# **zone convert smart-zoning fcalias name <alias-name> vsan <vsan no>**	Fetches the device type information from the name server for the fcalias members.
switch(config)# **zone convert smart-zoning zone name <zone name> vsan <vsan no>**	Fetches the device type information from the name server for the zone members.
switch(config)# **zone convert smart-zoning zoneset name <zoneset name> vsan <vsan no>**	
switch(config)# **zone convert smart-zoning vsan <vsan no>**	Fetches the device type information from the name server for all the zones and fcalias members for all the zone sets present in the VSAN.
switch(config-zoneset-zone)# **member device-alias <name> both**	
switch(config-zoneset-zone)# **member pwwn <number> target**	Removes the device type configuration for all the members of the specified zone.
switch(config-zoneset-zone)# **member fcid <number>**	
switch(config)# **clear zone smart-zoning fcalias name <alias-name> vsan <vsan no>**	
switch(config)# **clear zone smart-zoning zone name <zone name> vsan <vsan no>**	Smart zoning is disabled for the selected zone.
switch(config)# **clear zone smart-zoning zoneset name <zoneset name> vsan <vsan no>**	
switch(config)# **clear zone smart-zoning vsan <vsan no>**	
switch(config)# **zone name zone1 vsan 1**	
switch(config-zone)# **no attribute disable-smart-zoning**	

Command	Purpose
switch(config)# (no) **zone mode enhanced vsan 2000**	Enables enhanced zoning in the specified VSAN.
switch(config)# (no) **zone commit vsan 2 force**	Forcefully applies the changes to the enhanced zone database and closes the session created by another user.
switch(config)# (no) **zone commit vsan 2**	
No pending info found	Enables the **confirm-commit** option for zone database for a given VSAN.
switch(config)# (no) **zone confirm-commit enable vsan vsan-id**	
switch(config-zone)# **zone commit vsan 12**	If the **zone confirm-commit** command is enabled for a VSAN, on committing the pending database, the **pending-diff** is displayed on the console and the user is prompted for Yes or No. If the **zone confirm-commit** command is disabled, the **pending-diff** is not displayed and the user is not prompted for Yes or No.
The following zoning changes are about to be committed	
+zone name zone-1 vsan 12	
Do you want to continue? (y/n) [n]	
switch# config t	
switch(config)# **no zone commit vsan 2**	If session locks remain on remote switches after using the **no zone commit vsan** command, you can use the **clear zone lock vsan** command on the remote switches.
switch# **clear zone lock vsan 2**	
switch(config)# **zone name Lun1 vsan 2**	Configures a zone member based on the specified pWWN and LUN values. The CLI interprets the LUN identifier value as a hexadecimal value whether or not the 0x prefix is included. LUN 0x64 in hex format corresponds to 100 in decimal format.
switch(config-zone)# **member pwwn 10:00:00:23:45:67:89:ab lun 0x64**	
switch(config-zone)# **member fcid 0x12465 lun 0x64**	
switch(config-zone)# (no) **attribute read-only**	

23

Command	Purpose
switch# **show zone**	Display zone information for all VSANs.
switch# **show zone status vsan 9**	Displays zone status.
switch# **show zone vsan 1**	Displays the zone for the specified VSAN.
switch# **show zoneset vsan 1**	Displays the zone set for the specified VSAN.
switch# **show zone name Zone1**	
switch# **show fcalias vsan 1**	Displays members of a specific zone.
switch# **show zone member pwwn 21:00:00:20:37:9c:48:e5**	Displays fcalias configuration.
	Displays membership status.
switch# **show zone statistics**	Displays zone statistics.
switch# **show zone statistics lun-zoning**	Displays LUN zone statistics.
switch# **show zone statistics read-only-zoning**	Displays read-only zone statistics.
switch# **show zone active**	Displays the active zone.
switch# **show zoneset brief**	Displays the zone set brief.
switch# **show zoneset active**	Displays the local interface active zone details.
switch# **show running**	
switch# **show zone policy vsan 1**	Displays the running configuration.
config# **zone convert smart-zoning vsan 1**	Displays the zone policy for the specified VSAN.
	Fetches the device type information from the name server for all the zones and fcalias members for all the zone sets present in the VSAN.

VSAN Trunking and Setting Up ISL Port

VSAN trunking is a feature specific to switches in the Cisco MDS 9000 family. Trunking enables interconnect ports to transmit and receive frames in more than one VSAN, over the same physical link. Trunking is supported on E ports and F ports. Figure 23-36 represents the possible trunking scenarios in a SAN with MDS core switches, NPV switches, third-party core switches, and HBAs.

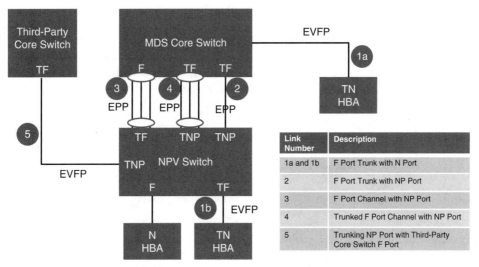

Figure 23-36   *Trunking F Ports*

The trunking feature includes the following key concepts:

■ **TE port:** If trunk mode is enabled in an E port and that port becomes operational as a trunking E port, it is referred to as a TE port.

■ **TF port:** If trunk mode is enabled in an F port (see link 2 in Figure 23-36) and that port becomes operational as a trunking F port, it is referred to as a TF port.

■ **TN port:** If trunk mode is enabled (not currently supported) in an N port (see link 1b in Figure 23-36) and that port becomes operational as a trunking N port, it is referred to as a TN port.

■ **TNP port:** If trunk mode is enabled in an NP port (see link 2 in Figure 23-36) and that port becomes operational as a trunking NP port, it is referred to as a TNP port.

■ **TF PortChannel:** If trunk mode is enabled in an F port channel (see link 4 in Figure 23-36) and that port channel becomes operational as a trunking F port channel, it is referred to as TF port channel. Cisco Port Trunking Protocol (PTP) is used to carry tagged frames.

■ **TF-TN port link:** A single link can be established to connect an F port to an HBA to carry tagged frames (see links 1a and 1b in Figure 23-36) using Exchange Virtual Fabrics Protocol (EVFP). A server can reach multiple VSANs through a TF port without inter-VSAN routing (IVR).

■ **TF-TNP port link:** A single link can be established to connect a TF port to a TNP port using the PTP protocol to carry tagged frames (see link 2 in Figure 23-36). PTP is used because PTP also supports trunking port channels.

■ A Fibre Channel VSAN is called Virtual Fabric and uses a VF_ID in place of the VSAN ID. By default, the VF_ID is 1 for all ports. When an N port supports trunking, a pWWN is defined for each VSAN and called a logical pWWN. In the case of MDS core switches, the pWWNs for which the N port requests additional FCIDs are called virtual pWWNs.

23

Table 23-14 summarizes the supported trunking protocols.

Table 23-14   Supported Trunking Protocols

Trunk Link	Default Protocol
E-TE port link	Cisco EPP (PTP)
TF-TN port link	FC-LS Rev 1.62 EVFP
TF-TNP port link	Cisco EPP (PTP)
E or F port channel	Cisco EPP (PCP)
TF port channel	Cisco EPP (PTP and PCP)
Third-party TF-TNP port link	FC-LS Rev 1.62 EVFP

By default, the trunking protocol is enabled on E ports and disabled on F ports. If the trunking protocol is disabled on a switch, no port on that switch can apply new trunk configurations. Existing trunk configurations are not affected. The TE port continues to function in trunk mode, but only supports traffic in VSANs that it negotiated with previously (when the trunking protocol was enabled). Also, other switches that are directly connected to this switch are similarly affected on the connected interfaces. In some cases, you may need to merge traffic from different port VSANs across a nontrunking ISL. If so, disable the trunking protocol.

Trunk Modes

By default, trunk mode is enabled on all Fibre Channel interfaces (Mode: E, F, FL, Fx, ST, and SD) on non-NPV switches. On NPV switches, by default, trunk mode is disabled. You can configure trunk mode as on (enabled), off (disabled), or auto (automatic). The trunk mode configuration at the two ends of an ISL, between two switches, determines the trunking state of the link and the port modes at both ends. The preferred configuration on the Cisco MDS 9000 family switches is one side of the trunk set to auto and the other side set to on. Table 23-15 summarizes the trunk mode status between switches. When connected to a third-party switch, the trunk mode configuration on E ports has no effect. The ISL is always in a trunking disabled state. In the case of F ports, if the third-party core switches accept (ACC) physical FLOGI with the EVFP bit configured, then the EVFP protocol enables trunking on the link.

Each Fibre Channel interface has an associated trunk-allowed VSAN list. In TE-port mode, frames are transmitted and received in one or more VSANs specified in this list. By default, the VSAN range (1 through 4093) is included in the trunk-allowed list.

There are a couple of important guidelines and limitations for the trunking feature:

- F ports support trunking in Fx mode.
- The trunk-allowed VSANs configured for TE, TF, and TNP links are used by the trunking protocol to determine the allowed active VSANs in which frames can be received or transmitted.
- If a trunking-enabled E port is connected to a third-party switch, the trunking protocol ensures seamless operation as an E port.
- MDS does not enforce the uniqueness of logical pWWNs across VSANs.

Table 23-15   Trunk Mode Status Between Switches

Trunk Mode Configuration			State and Port Mode	
Port Type	**Switch 1**	**Switch 2**	**Trunking State**	**Port Mode**
E ports	On	Auto or on	Trunking (EISL)	TE port
	Off	Auto, on, or off	No trunking (ISL)	E port
	Auto	Auto	No trunking (ISL)	E port
Port Type	**Core Switch**	**NPV Switch**	**Trunking State**	**Link Mode**
F and NP ports	On	Auto or on	Trunking	TF-TNP link
	Auto	On	Trunking	TF-TNP link
	Off	Auto, on, or off	No trunking	F-NP link

Port channels aggregate multiple physical ISLs into one logical link with higher bandwidth and port resiliency for both Fibre Channel and FICON traffic. With this feature, up to 16 expansion ports (E ports) or trunking E ports (TE ports) can be bundled into a port channel. ISL ports can reside on any switching module, and they do not need a designated master port. If a port or a switching module fails, the port channel continues to function properly without requiring fabric reconfiguration.

Port Channel Modes

You can configure each port channel with a channel group mode parameter to determine the port channel protocol behavior for all member ports in this channel group. The possible values for a channel group mode are as follows:

■ **ON (default):** The member ports only operate as part of a port channel or remain inactive. In this mode, the port channel protocol is not initiated. However, if a port channel protocol frame is received from a peer port, the software indicates its nonnegotiable status.

■ **ACTIVE:** The member ports initiate port channel protocol negotiation with the peer port(s) regardless of the channel group mode of the peer port. If the peer port, while configured in a channel group, does not support the port channel protocol, or responds with a nonnegotiable status, it will default to the ON mode behavior. The ACTIVE port channel mode allows automatic recovery without explicitly enabling and disabling the port channel member ports at either end.

In our sample SAN topology, we will connect two SAN islands by creating a port channel using ports 5 and 6 on both MDS switches. Ports in auto mode will automatically come up as ISL (E ports) after they are connected to another switch. Ports are also in trunk mode, so when ISL comes up it will automatically carry all VSANs in common between switches. Figure 23-37 portrays the minimum required configuration steps to set up ISL port channel with mode active between two MDS switches.

23

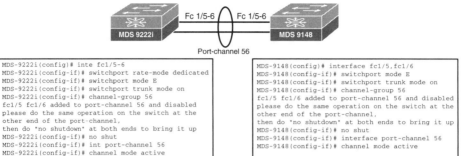

```
MDS-9222i(config)# inte fc1/5-6
MDS-9222i(config-if)# switchport rate-mode dedicated        MDS-9148(config)# interface fc1/5,fc1/6
MDS-9222i(config-if)# switchport mode E                      MDS-9148(config-if)# switchport mode E
MDS-9222i(config-if)# switchport trunk mode on               MDS-9148(config-if)# switchport trunk mode on
MDS-9222i(config-if)# channel-group 56                       MDS-9148(config-if)# channel-group 56
fc1/5 fc1/6 added to port-channel 56 and disabled            fc1/5 fc1/6 added to port-channel 56 and disabled
please do the same operation on the switch at the            please do the same operation on the switch at the
other end of the port-channel,                               other end of the port-channel,
then do "no shutdown" at both ends to bring it up            then do "no shutdown" at both ends to bring it up
MDS-9222i(config-if)# no shut                                MDS-9148(config-if)# no shut
MDS-9222i(config-if)# int port-channel 56                    MDS-9148(config-if)# interface port-channel 56
MDS-9222i(config-if)# channel mode active                    MDS-9148(config-if)# channel mode active
```

Figure 23-37 *Setting Up ISL Port on Sample SAN Topology*

On 9222i, ports need to be put into dedicated rate mode to be ISLs (or be set to mode auto). Groups of six ports have a total of 12.8 Gbps of bandwidth. When we set these two ports to dedicated mode, they will reserve a dedicated 4 Gb of bandwidth (leaving 4.8 Gb shared between the other group members). Example 23-13 shows the verification and configuration steps on the NX-OS CLI for port channel configuration on our sample SAN topology.

Example 23-13   Verifying Port Channel on Our Sample SAN Topology

```
! Before changing the ports to dedicated mode , the interface Admin Mode is FX
MDS-9222i# show interface fc1/5,fc1/6 brief
--------------------------------------------------------------------------------

Interface  Vsan   Admin  Admin   Status       SFP     Oper  Oper   Port
                  Mode   Trunk                        Mode  Speed  Channel
                         Mode                                (Gbps)
--------------------------------------------------------------------------------

fc1/5      1      FX     on      down         swl     --           --
fc1/6      1      FX     on      down         swl     --           --
! On 9222i ports need to be put into dedicated rate mode in order to be configured as
ISL (or be set to mode auto).On MDS 9222i there are three port-groups ! available and
each port-group consists of six Fibre Channel ports. Show port-resources module com-
mand will show the default and configured interface !rate mode, buffer-to-buffer
credits, and bandwidth.
MDS-9222i(config)# show port-resources module 1
Module 1
  Available dedicated buffers are 3987
 Port-Group 1
  Total bandwidth is 12.8 Gbps
  Total shared bandwidth is 12.8 Gbps
  Allocated dedicated bandwidth is 0.0 Gbps
  ------------------------------------------------------------------
  Interfaces in the Port-Group      B2B Credit  Bandwidth  Rate Mode
                                    Buffers     (Gbps)
  ------------------------------------------------------------------
  fc1/1                             16          4.0        shared
  fc1/2                             16          4.0        shared
```

```
    fc1/3                                   16      4.0   shared
    fc1/4                                   16      4.0   shared
    fc1/5                                   16      4.0   shared
    fc1/6                                   16      4.0   shared
   <snip>
```

! Changing the rate-mode to dedicated

```
MDS-9222i(config)# inte fc1/5-6
MDS-9222i(config-if)# switchport rate-mode dedicated
MDS-9222i(config-if)# switchport mode auto
MDS-9222i(config-if)# sh interface fc1/5-6 brief
--------------------------------------------------------------------------

Interface  Vsan   Admin   Admin   Status       SFP    Oper  Oper    Port
                  Mode    Trunk                        Mode  Speed   Channel
                          Mode                                (Gbps)

--------------------------------------------------------------------------
fc1/5      1      auto    on      down          swl    --            --
fc1/6      1      auto    on      down          swl    --            --
```

! Interface fc 1/5-6 are configured for dedicated rate mode

```
MDS-9222i(config-if)# show port-resources module 1
Module 1
  Available dedicated buffers are 3543
 Port-Group 1
  Total bandwidth is 12.8 Gbps
  Total shared bandwidth is 4.8 Gbps
  Allocated dedicated bandwidth is 8.0 Gbps
  ------------------------------------------------------------------
  Interfaces in the Port-Group      B2B Credit  Bandwidth  Rate Mode
                                    Buffers     (Gbps)
  ------------------------------------------------------------------
    fc1/1                                  16      4.0   shared
    fc1/2                                  16      4.0   shared
    fc1/3                                  16      4.0   shared
    fc1/4                                  16      4.0   shared
    fc1/5                                 250      4.0   dedicated
    fc1/6                                 250      4.0   dedicated
<snip>
```

! Configuring port-channel interface

```
MDS-9222i(config-if)# channel-group 56
fc1/5 fc1/6 added to port-channel 56 and disabled
please do the same operation on the switch at the other end of the port-channel,
then do "no shutdown" at both ends to bring it up
MDS-9222i(config-if)# no shut
MDS-9222i(config-if)# int port-channel 56
MDS-9222i(config-if)# channel mode active
MDS-9222i(config-if)# sh interface fc1/5-6 brief
--------------------------------------------------------------------------
```

23

```
Interface  Vsan   Admin  Admin  Status         SFP   Oper  Oper   Port
                  Mode   Trunk                       Mode  Speed  Channel
                         Mode                              (Gbps)
------------------------------------------------------------------------------
fc1/5      1      auto   on     trunking       swl   TE    4      56
fc1/6      1      auto   on     trunking       swl   TE    4      56
```
! Verifying the portchannel interface, VSAN 1 and VSAN 48 are up but VSAN 47 is in
isolated status because VSAN 47 is not configured
! on MDS 9148 switch MDS 9148 is only carrying SAN-B traffic.
```
MDS-9222i(config-if)# show int port-channel 56
port-channel 56 is trunking
    Hardware is Fibre Channel
    Port WWN is 24:38:00:05:9b:77:0d:c0
    Admin port mode is auto, trunk mode is on
    snmp link state traps are enabled
    Port mode is TE
    Port vsan is 1
    Speed is 8 Gbps
    Trunk vsans (admin allowed and active) (1,47-48)
    Trunk vsans (up)                       (1,48)
    Trunk vsans (isolated)                 (47)
    Trunk vsans (initializing)             ()
    5 minutes input rate 1024 bits/sec, 128 bytes/sec, 1 frames/sec
    5 minutes output rate 856 bits/sec, 107 bytes/sec, 1 frames/sec
      363 frames input, 36000 bytes
        0 discards, 0 errors
        0 CRC,  0 unknown class
        0 too long, 0 too short
      361 frames output, 29776 bytes
        0 discards, 0 errors
      2 input OLS, 4 LRR, 0 NOS, 22 loop inits
      2 output OLS, 0 LRR, 2 NOS, 2 loop inits
    Member[1] : fc1/5
    Member[2] : fc1/6
```
! During ISL bring up there will be principal switch election, for VSAN 1 the one with
the lowest priority won the election which is MDS
! 9222i in our sample SAN topology.
```
MDS-9222i# show fcdomain vsan 1
The local switch is the Principal Switch.
Local switch run time information:
        State: Stable
        Local switch WWN:    20:01:00:05:9b:77:0d:c1
        Running fabric name: 20:01:00:05:9b:77:0d:c1
        Running priority: 2
        Current domain ID: 0x51(81)
Local switch configuration information:
```

```
        State: Enabled
        FCID persistence: Enabled
        Auto-reconfiguration: Disabled
        Contiguous-allocation: Disabled
        Configured fabric name: 20:01:00:05:30:00:28:df
        Optimize Mode: Disabled
        Configured priority: 128
        Configured domain ID: 0x00(0) (preferred)
Principal switch run time information:
        Running priority: 2
Interface              Role            RCF-reject
----------------    -------------    ------------
port-channel 56     Downstream       Disabled
----------------    -------------    ------------
MDS-9148(config-if)# show fcdomain vsan 1
The local switch is a Subordinated Switch.
Local switch run time information:
        State: Stable
        Local switch WWN:    20:01:54:7f:ee:05:07:89
        Running fabric name: 20:01:00:05:9b:77:0d:c1
        Running priority: 128
        Current domain ID: 0x52(82)
Local switch configuration information:
        State: Enabled
        FCID persistence: Enabled
        Auto-reconfiguration: Disabled
        Contiguous-allocation: Disabled
        Configured fabric name: 20:01:00:05:30:00:28:df
        Optimize Mode: Disabled
        Configured priority: 128
        Configured domain ID: 0x00(0) (preferred)
Principal switch run time information:
        Running priority: 2
Interface              Role            RCF-reject
----------------    -------------    ------------
port-channel 56     Upstream         Disabled
----------------    -------------    ------------
MDS-9222i# show port-channel database
port-channel 56
    Administrative channel mode is active
    Operational channel mode is active
    Last membership update succeeded
    First operational port is fc1/6
    2 ports in total, 2 ports up
    Ports:   fc1/5    [up]
             fc1/6    [up] *
```

23

```
! The asterisks (*) indicate which interface became online first.
MDS-9148(config-if)# show port-channel database
port-channel 56
    Administrative channel mode is active
    Operational channel mode is active
    Last membership update succeeded
    First operational port is fc1/6
    2 ports in total, 2 ports up
    Ports:   fc1/5    [up]
             fc1/6    [up] *
```

To bring up the rest of our sample SAN topology, we need to provide access to our initiator, which is connected to fc 1/1 of MDS 9148 via VSAN 48 to a LUN that resides on a storage array connected to fc 1/14 of MDS 9222i (VSAN 48). Figure 23-38 portrays the necessary zoning configuration. Zoning through the switches allows traffic on the switches to connect only chosen sets of servers and storage end devices on a particular VSAN. (Zoning on separate VSANs is completely independent.) Usually members of a zone are identified using the end device's World Wide Port Number (WWPN), although they could be identified using switch physical port numbers.

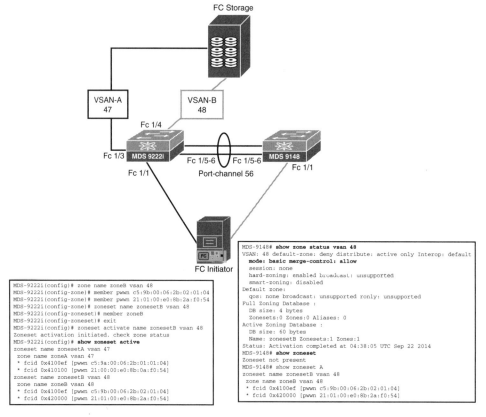

Figure 23-38 *Zoning Configuration on Our Sample SAN Topology*

Our sample SAN topology is up with the preceding zone configuration. The FC initiator via a dual host bus adapter (HBA) can access the same LUNs from SAN A (VSAN 47) and SAN B (VSAN 48).

Table 23-16 summarizes the NX-OS CLI commands for trunking and port channels.

Table 23-16   Summary of NX-OS CLI Commands for Trunking and Port Channels

Command	Status
switch# **config t**	Enters configuration mode
switch(config)# (no) **trunk protocol enable**	Enables the Cisco PTP trunking protocol (default)
switch(config)# (no) **feature fport-channel-trunk**	Enables the F port trunking and channeling protocol
switch(config)# **interface fc1/1**	Configures the specified interface
switch(config-if)# **switchport trunk mode on**	Enables (default) the trunk mode for the specified interface
switch(config-if)# **switchport trunk mode off**	Disables the trunk mode for the specified interface
switch(config-if)# **switchport trunk mode auto**	Configures the trunk mode to **auto** mode
switch(config-if)# (no) **switchport trunk allowed vsan 2-4**	Changes the allowed list for the specified VSANs
switch(config-if)# **(no) switchport trunk allowed vsan add 5** updated trunking membership	Expands the specified VSAN (5) to the new allowed list
switch# **config t**	Enters configuration mode
switch(config)# (no) **interface port-channel 1**	Configures the specified port channel using the default ON mode
switch(config-if)# **(no) channel mode active**	Configures the ACTIVE mode
switch(config)# **interface fc1/15**	Configures the specified port interface (fc1/15)
switch(config-if)# **channel-group 15**	Adds physical Fibre Channel port 1/15 to channel group 15
switch(config- if)# **channel-group auto**	Automatically creates the channel group for the selected interface(s)
switch# **show interface fc1/13**	Displays interface details for fc1/13
switch# **show trunk protocol**	Displays whether the trunk protocol is enabled
switch# **show interface trunk vsan 1-1000**	Displays whether the interface is trunking, and the allowed VSAN list for each trunking interface

23

Command	Status
switch# **show port-channel summary**	Displays a summary of port channels within the switch
switch# **show port-channel database**	
switch# **show port-channel consistency**	Displays the port channel configured in the default ON mode and ACTIVE mode
switch# **show port-channel consistency detail**	Displays the consistency status
switch# **show port-channel usage**	Displays the port channel usage
switch# **show port-channel compatibility-parameters**	Displays the port channel compatibility
	Displays the specified port channel interface
switch# **show port-channel database interface port-channel 128**	Displays FC domain information for VSAN 1
switch# **show fcdomain vsan 1**	Displays resource availability for a specific module
switch# **show port-resources module 1**	

What Is Cisco Unified Fabric?

Cisco Unified Fabric is the networking foundation that enables the network of today and tomorrow. It is also an enabler for IT departments to achieve their goals.

IT is the strategic business enabler that must evolve as the business evolves. To do this, IT must be ahead of emerging trends, and to be a real partner to the business, the IT department needs to increase the speed at which projects are rolled out. To meet business goals, deployment times that range from 6 to 36 months are unacceptable. In the past, CIOs could increase staff to meet business needs, but today's budget constraints make that solution no longer feasible. The real solution is to shift the activity of the current IT staff from the current maintenance of ongoing operations to more business-oriented projects without endangering the current operations.

Evolution in the data center can help transform IT departments and break organizational silos and reduce technological complexity. Private clouds and private/public cloud hybrids and other strategies can automate the data center and enable self-service for both IT and the business units. However, making the transition to any of these models is not a simple task, but a journey that requires multiple steps. Every data center has different requirements to serve the business. Most IT departments have started on server virtualization and consolidation projects, which constitute the first steps. 10 Gigabit Ethernet and the evolution of the data center network into a virtualization-enabling environment are also part of it. The next step is to prepare the network for the journey to the cloud, whether a private or a private/public hybrid environment.

A key building block for general-purpose, virtualized, cloud-based data centers, Cisco Unified Fabric provides the foundational connectivity and unifies storage, data networking, and network services delivering architectural flexibility and consistent networking across physical, virtual, and cloud environments. Cisco Unified Fabric enables CIOs to address the challenges of the data center in a comprehensive and complete manner. Cisco Unified

Fabric creates a true multiprotocol environment on a single network that enables efficient communication between data center resources. Unified Fabric provides the architectural flexibility needed for companies to match their data centers to business needs and change as technology and the business changes. The functions of the data center are becoming more automated, shifting the focus from the maintenance of infrastructure to the servicing of business needs. Operating costs for the data center, including energy (both electrical costs and HVAC [heating, ventilation, and air conditioning] costs), need to be reduced—or at least not increase as energy prices increase. For IT to meet these goals, it needs a strong and flexible foundation to run on, and Cisco Unified Fabric provides the architectural flexibility necessary. Cisco Unified Fabric provides the networking foundation for the Cisco Unified Data Center on which you can build the data center architecture, whether you run a traditional data center or are on the journey to full private cloud computing or hybrid private/public cloud computing.

Cisco Unified Fabric is built on three main pillars: convergence, scalability, and intelligence. This brings solutions when you need them, enabling optimized resources, faster application rollout, greater application performance as well as lower operating costs. Cisco Unified Fabric can help you reduce costs, migrate to the next-generation data center, and bring value to your business.

- **Convergence:** The convergence of the data center network is the melding of the storage network (SAN) with the general data network (LAN). The traditionally separate LAN and SAN fabrics evolve into a converged, unified storage network through normal refresh cycles that replace old servers containing host bus adapters (HBAs) with new ones containing converged network adapters (CNAs); storage devices undergo a similar refresh process. Customer investments are protected throughout their service and financial life; transitions are gradual and managed. One concern about the converged network is that Ethernet networks are not reliable enough to handle sensitive storage traffic: storage traffic needs to arrive with dependable regularity, and in order and without any frames being dropped. However, with fully standardized IEEE Data Center Bridging (DCB), Cisco provides lossless, in-order reliability for data center environments in conjunction with Cisco's work with INCITS on Fibre Channel over Ethernet (FCoE). Cisco customers can deploy an Ethernet network for the data center that conforms to the needs of storage traffic, with a lossless, in-order, highly reliable network for the data center. Cisco Unified Fabric integrates with the existing infrastructure, preserving the customer's investment in current SAN technology. Both the Cisco MDS 9000 family and the Cisco Nexus product family have features that facilitate network convergence. For instance, the Cisco MDS 9000 family can provide full, bidirectional bridging for FCoE traffic to older Fibre Channel–only storage arrays and SANs. Similarly, servers attached through HBAs can access newer storage devices connected through FCoE ports. The Cisco Nexus 5548UP, Nexus 5596UP, and Nexus 5672UP switches have unified ports at the time of writing this book. These ports can support 10 Gigabit Ethernet (including FCoE) or Fibre Channel. Cisco Nexus models now connect to traditional systems with HBAs and convert to FCoE or other Ethernet- and IP-based storage protocols such as Small Computer System Interface over IP (iSCSI) or network-attached storage (NAS) as those servers are refreshed. Figure 23-29 illustrates SAN and LAN protocols that are commonly used in the data centers.

23

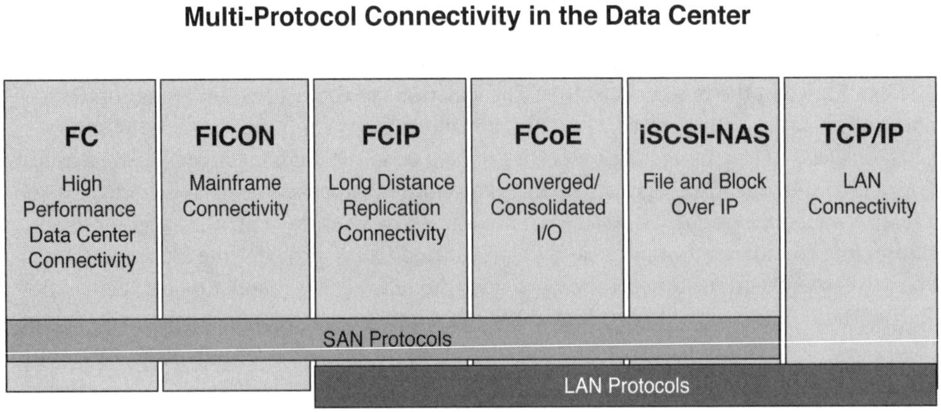

Multi-Protocol Connectivity in the Data Center

Figure 23-39 *Multiprotocol Connectivity in the Data Center*

Consolidation of the general data and storage network can save customers money. A standard server requires at least four networking cables—two for the SAN and two for the LAN—with current 10 Gigabit Ethernet and Fibre Channel technology. Often, more 10 Gigabit Ethernet ports are needed to meet bandwidth requirements and to provide additional connections for server management and for a private connection for server clusters. Two 10 Gigabit Ethernet converged ports can replace all these ports, providing a cable savings of at least 2:1. From a larger data center perspective, this cable reduction means fewer ports and the capability to decrease the number of switches and layers in the data center, correspondingly reducing the amount of network oversubscription. Reducing cabling saves both acquisition cost and the cost of running the cables, and it reduces cooling costs by improving airflow.

■ **Scalability:** This is the ability to grow as needs change, often described by the number of nodes that a given architecture can ultimately support. Cisco Unified Fabric offers multi-dimensional scalability, encompassing device performance, fabric and system scalability, and geographic span. Scalability begins with 10 Gigabit Ethernet. 10 Gigabit Ethernet allows customers to consolidate their networks, which means fewer tiers to the network and fewer overall ports while providing exponentially more usable bandwidth for servers and storage. By moving to 10, 40, and 100 Gigabit Ethernet technologies, you are able to consolidate the number of ports and cables dedicated to servers as well as the over-all number of switches under management in the data center. The reduction of devices reduces management overhead and comes with a concomitant reduction in rack space use, power, and cooling. In many cases, the consolidation of the network is in concert with or directly follows server consolidation through server virtualization. The capability to grow the network is a crucial aspect of scalability. Growth of the network depends on two factors: the capability to upgrade hardware and the capability to support new protocols as they arise. The Cisco Nexus and Cisco MDS 9000 families both use Cisco NX-OS, a modern modular operating system that facilitates easy upgrades to the latest features and protocols as they become available.

■ **Intelligence:** The intelligence in Cisco Unified Fabric is implemented with policy-based network services. By using policy, data center managers can achieve several advantages.

After a policy is set, it can be applied the same way to any workload. This feature is particularly advantageous in a virtualized environment, where workloads tend to proliferate, particularly in the application development area. Security is one area in which policy-based network services can enable operations. With consistent policy, every workload can have the proper security settings for its security class.

Security audits are much simpler to perform, and overall security of the data center environment is significantly increased. Security of stored data can be protected using Cisco Storage Media Encryption (SME) for the Cisco MDS 9000 family so that organizations no longer have to worry about data loss if backup tapes are lost or failing disk drives are replaced. Cisco Data Mobility Manager improves application availability by allowing applications to continue to run while data is migrated from one storage array to another. Cisco Unified Fabric contains a complete portfolio of security and Layer 4 through 7 application-networking services that are completely virtualization aware. These services run as virtual workloads to provide the scalable, cloud-ready services that your critical applications demand. The use of policy also enables faster deployment of applications. In the past, deploying an application required considerable effort to configure the overall physical infrastructure. With Cisco Unified Fabric, policy can be set with standard availability, security, and performance characteristics while maintaining the capability to tune those features to the needs of a specialized application if necessary. In that case, policies for that application can be built using the standard policies, with the policies retained, making reinstallation or expansion of even a specialized application easy. In addition, with policies, if the performance characteristics of the network change, rolling the change to every workload is as simple as changing the policy and applying it. With consistent policies, application uptime is significantly increased. The potential for human error is essentially eliminated.

Management of the network is the core of the network's intelligence. With Cisco Prime DCNM, Cisco Nexus and Cisco MDS 9000 family products can be managed from a single pane. Cisco Prime DCNM can be used to set policy and to automatically provision that policy in converged LAN and SAN environments. Cisco Prime DCNM also proactively monitors performance and can perform path analytics for both physical and virtual machine environments. The features provided by Cisco NX-OS can all be deployed with Cisco Prime DCNM, and it provides multiple dashboards for ease of use. These dashboards include operational features and can also include network topological views. Cisco Prime DCNM allows customers to analyze the network from end to end, including virtualized elements, and record historical performance and capacity trends. Cisco DCNM has been updated to include FCoE, handling provisioning and monitoring of FCoE deployments, including paths containing a mix of Fibre Channel and FCoE.

Cisco Unified Fabric supports numerous IT trends, including server virtualization, network consolidation, private cloud, and data center consolidation. In many cases, the Unified Fabric functions as the basis for the trend, providing the bandwidth, automation, and intelligence required to implement the trend in the organization. These trends require a network that is not merely good enough, but one that is data center class and ready for more change in the future as technology and trends continue to evolve.

23

Growth in the data center, particularly the increase in overall use of bandwidth, has been a challenge for as long as there have been data center networks. With the continued exponential growth of data, and with ever more devices accessing the network in the data center (virtual machines) and in the access layer (tablets, smartphones, and laptops), data growth is unlikely to abate. Everybody now expects to have the world at their fingertips, and slow response times are unacceptable to people who have become accustomed to nearly universal access.

Data center networks have been rapidly evolving in recent years as the nature of their workloads have evolved. Traffic in the data center generally flows in three directions. "North-South" traffic is limited to traffic that enters and exits the data center. "East-West" traffic, on the other hand, flows between data center devices and applications and never leaves the data center. Finally, there is "Inter-DC" traffic, which flows between multiple data centers, and between data centers and the private and public cloud. Unlike traditional enterprise client-server workloads, the modern data center's workload is dominated by server-to-server traffic. This new workload requires intensive communication across the data center network between tens to hundreds and even thousands of servers, often on a per-job basis. Hence, network latency and throughput are extremely important for application performance, while packet loss can be unacceptably detrimental. Accordingly, data center networks no longer employ the traditional access, aggregation, and core architecture of the large enterprise. Instead, commercially available switches are used to build the network in multirooted Clos or Fat-Tree topologies. Generally, architects are choosing smaller, dense, top-of-rack switches at the leaf for server connectivity connected to larger, modular switches in the spine, creating very flat, densely connected networks. Liberal use of multipathing is used to scale bandwidth. This Spine-Leaf architecture (shown in Figure 23-40) is designed to provide very scalable throughput in a uniform and predictable manner across thousands to hundreds of thousands of ports. In effect, it approximates the ideal network—a very large, nonblocking switch where all servers are directly connected.

In traditional data center designs, a three-tier strategy yielded the most benefits for companies, and many companies adopted this design. In today's modern, fully virtualized or private cloud data center, three-tier designs may not be the most efficient. For some companies, that will mean a single-tier design; for other companies, it will mean a two- or three-tier design.

Cisco Unified Fabric provides the foundational connectivity and unifies storage, data networking, and network services delivering architectural flexibility and consistent networking across physical, virtual, and cloud environments.

Three-Tier Architecture

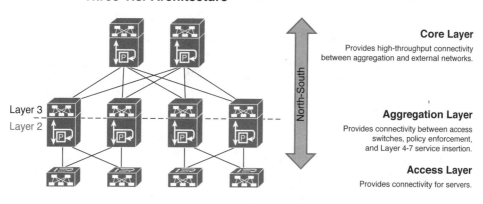

Core Layer
Provides high-throughput connectivity between aggregation and external networks.

Aggregation Layer
Provides connectivity between access switches, policy enforcement, and Layer 4-7 service insertion.

Access Layer
Provides connectivity for servers.

Layer 3
Layer 2

North-South

CLOS Spine-Leaf Architecture

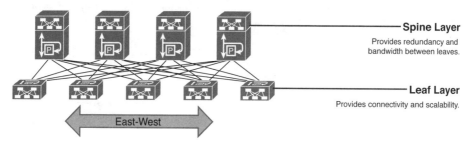

Spine Layer
Provides redundancy and bandwidth between leaves.

Leaf Layer
Provides connectivity and scalability.

East-West

Figure 23-40   *Three-tier and Spine-Leaf Network Architecture*

A classic data center design features a dedicated Ethernet network for LAN and a separate, dedicated Fibre Channel (FC) network for storage area network (SAN) traffic. The increased adoption of 10 Gigabit Ethernet (10GbE) in the data center, combined with the availability of Fibre Channel over Ethernet (FCoE) and new lossless 10GbE technologies, makes it possible to consolidate FC data flows with LAN and IP data traffic on the same Ethernet infrastructure. Network convergence enables you to preserve your existing investments in FC storage, reduce data center costs and complexity, and simplify network management. With FCoE, it is possible to run a single, converged network. As a standards-based protocol that allows Fibre Channel frames to be carried over Ethernet links, FCoE obviates the need to run separate LAN and SAN networks. In the first phase of data center architecture evolution, shown in Figure 23-41, unified access is delivered by Cisco Nexus switches. Unified Fabric drastically reduces the number of I/O adapters, cables, and switches in the data center, when deployed as an access layer convergence solution. In the second phase, multihop FCoE technology can be used to extend convergence beyond the access layer. The higher, more efficient speeds, such as 40 Gigabit Ethernet FCoE today, or the 100 Gigabit Ethernet FCoE in the future, help enable fewer and higher-speed Inter-Switch Links (ISLs) in the network core. The converged architecture means you can wire once and deploy anywhere to support any storage protocol, including iSCSI or NFS. This consolidated infrastructure also helps to simplify management and significantly reduce total cost of ownership (TCO).

23

Evolving the Data Center in Phases

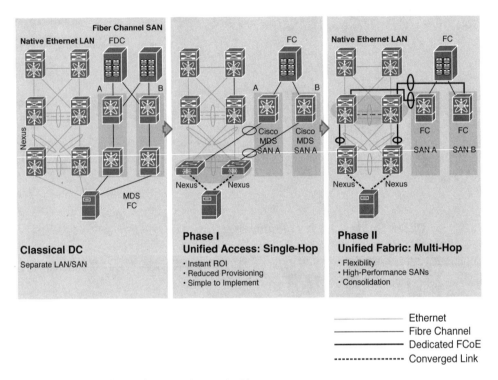

Figure 23-41 *Evolving the Data Center in Phases*

FCoE is one of the core components of the Cisco Unified Data Center, which helps enable multiprotocol networking through Cisco Unified Computing System (UCS), Cisco Nexus platforms, and Cisco MDS platforms.

Packet drops have unique effects on different protocols, with applications responding in different ways: Some applications can tolerate and recover from drops with resends. Ethernet supports these cases, but other applications cannot tolerate any packet loss, requiring some guarantee of end-to-end transmission with no drops. Fibre Channel traffic carried over Ethernet is one example of an application requirement for no-drop service. For Ethernet networks to support applications with no-packet-drop requirements, a method for providing a lossless service class over Ethernet needs to be established. IEEE Data Center Bridging extensions for traffic management provide the enhancements required to implement Unified Fabric.

IEEE Data Center Bridging

IEEE Data Center Bridging has been well thought out to take advantage of classical Ethernet's strengths, add several crucial extensions to provide the next-generation infrastructure for data center networks, and deliver the Unified Fabric architecture. This section outlines IEEE Data Center Bridging (DCB) and describes how each of the main components of the architecture contributes to a robust Ethernet network capable of meeting today's growing application requirements and responding to future data center network needs.

To transport Fibre Channel storage traffic or any other application that requires lossless service over an Ethernet network and achieve a unified fabric, a lossless service class is required. Fibre Channel storage traffic requires no-drop capability. A no-drop traffic class can be created using IEEE Data Center Bridging and a lossless Ethernet switch fabric.

The FCoE protocol maps native Fibre Channel frames over Ethernet, independent of the native Ethernet forwarding scheme. It allows an evolutionary approach to I/O consolidation by preserving all Fibre Channel constructs. INCITS T11 is writing the standard for FCoE. This group will mandate that a lossless Ethernet network is required to support FCoE.

DCB aims, for selected traffic, to eliminate loss due to queue overflow (lossless Ethernet) and to be able to allocate bandwidth on links. Essentially, DCB enables, to some extent, the treatment of different priorities as if they were different pipes. To meet these goals, standards have been developed that either extend the existing set of Ethernet protocols or emulate the connectivity offered by Ethernet protocols. They have been developed respectively by two separate standards bodies:

- The Institute of Electrical and Electronics Engineers (IEEE) Data Center Bridging Task Group of the IEEE 802.1 Working Group.
- Internet Engineering Task Force (IETF).

Fibre Channel and Fibre Channel over Ethernet (FCoE) are structured by a lengthy list of standards. Figure 23-42 illustrates FC and FCoE standard groups and protocols. In Chapter 22, we discussed storage standard groups. Detailed information on all FC and FCoE standards can be downloaded from T11 at www.t11.org.

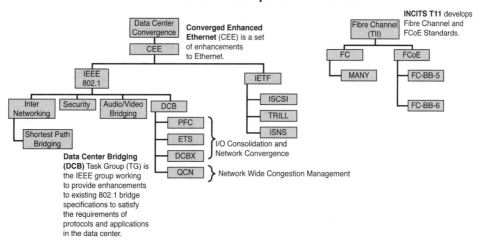

Figure 23-42 *Standard Groups and Protocols*

Different terms have been used to market products based on data center bridging standards:

- **Data Center Ethernet** (DCE) was a term trademarked by Brocade Communications Systems in 2007 but abandoned by request in 2008. DCE referred to Ethernet enhancements for the Data Center Bridging standards, and also including a Layer 2 multipathing implementation based on the IETF's Transparent Interconnection of Lots of Links (TRILL) standard.

- **Convergence Enhanced Ethernet** or **Converged Enhanced Ethernet (CEE)** was defined from 2008 through January 2009 by a group including Broadcom, Brocade Communications Systems, Cisco Systems, Emulex, HP, IBM, Juniper Networks, and QLogic. The ad-hoc group formed to create proposals for enhancements that enable networking protocol convergence over Ethernet, especially Fibre Channel. Proposed specifications to IEEE 802.1 working groups initially included the following:

  - The Priority-based Flow Control (PFC) Specification was submitted for use in the IEEE 802.1Qbb project, under the DCB task group of the IEEE 802.1 working group.

  - The Enhanced Transmission Selection (ETS) Specification was submitted for use in the IEEE 802.1Qaz project, under the DCB task group of the IEEE 802.1 working group.

  - The Data Center Bridging eXchange (DCBX) Specification was submitted for use in the IEEE 802.1Qaz project.

The following have been adopted as IEEE standards:

- **Priority-based Flow Control (PFC):** IEEE 802.1Qbb provides a link-level flow control mechanism that can be controlled independently for each frame priority. The goal of this mechanism is to ensure zero loss under congestion in DCB networks.

- **Enhanced Transmission Selection (ETS):** IEEE 802.1Qaz provides a common management framework for assignment of bandwidth to frame priorities.

- **Congestion Notification:** IEEE 802.1Qau provides end-to-end congestion management for protocols that are capable of transmission rate limiting to avoid frame loss. It is expected to benefit protocols such as TCP that do have native congestion management because it reacts to congestion in a timely manner.

- **Data Center Bridging Capabilities Exchange Protocol (DCBX):** A discovery and capability exchange protocol that is used for conveying capabilities and configuration of the preceding features between neighbors to ensure consistent configuration across the network. This protocol leverages functionality provided by IEEE 802.1AB (LLDP). It is actually included in the 802.1az standard.

Priority-based Flow Control: IEEE 802.1Qbb

Link sharing is critical to I/O consolidation. For link sharing to succeed, large bursts from one traffic type must not affect other traffic types, large queues of traffic from one traffic type must not starve other traffic types' resources, and optimization for one traffic type must not create large latency for small messages of other traffic types. The Ethernet pause mechanism can be used to control the effects of one traffic type on another. Priority-based Flow Control (PFC), shown in Figure 23-43, is an enhancement to the pause mechanism.

IEEE 802.1Qbb Priority Flow Control (PFC)

Flow Control

• VLAN Tag enables 8 priorities for Ethernet traffic.

• Enables lossless Ethernet using PAUSE based on a COS as defined in 802.1p.

• When link is congested, CoS assigned to "no-drop" will be PAUSED.

• Receiving device/switch sends Pause frame when receiving buffer passes threshold.
  Distance support is determined by how much buffer is available to absorb data in flight.

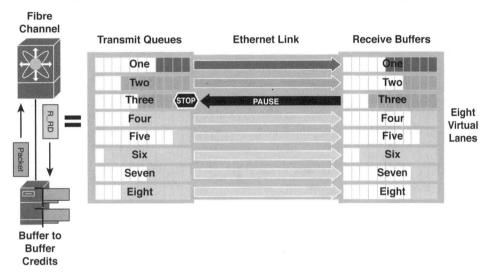

Figure 23-43 *IEEE 802.1 Qbb Priority Flow Control*

The current Ethernet pause option stops all traffic on a link; essentially it is a link pause for the entire link. PFC creates eight separate virtual links on the physical link and allows any of these links to be paused and restarted independently. This approach enables the network to create a no-drop class of service for an individual virtual link that can coexist with other traffic types on the same interface. PFC allows differentiated Quality of Service (QoS) policies for the eight unique virtual links. PFC also plays a primary role when used with an arbiter for intra-switch fabrics, linking ingress ports to egress port resources. The capability to invoke pause for differentiated traffic types enables the traffic to be consolidated over a single interface.

Although not defined within IEEE Data Center Bridging, a data center switch must provide a lossless architecture to ensure that the lossless transmission service class will not drop a frame. To support FCoE, a lossless fabric is mandatory to help ensure that storage traffic has no-drop service. To create a lossless Ethernet fabric with multiprotocol support, two elements are required: a priority-based pause mechanism (PFC) and an intelligent switch fabric arbitration mechanism that ties ingress port traffic to egress port resources to honor any pause requirements.

PFC provides a no-drop option on each logical link with its capability to halt independent logical traffic types. PFC (as well as the standard pause mechanism) makes a link lossless, but that is not enough to make a network a lossless fabric. In addition to no-drop service on the link, a way to tie the ingress port pause behavior to the egress port resources is required across the intra-switch fabric using PFC. To make the network lossless, each switch needs to associate the resources of the ingress links with the resources of the egress links. Logically tying egress port resource availability to the ingress port traffic allows arbitration to occur to help ensure that no packets are dropped—which is the definition of a lossless switch fabric architecture. This lossless Ethernet intra-switch fabric behavior provides the required no-drop service that emulates the buffer credit management system seen in Fibre Channel switches today.

On Cisco Nexus and MDS switches, system-defined class maps for **class-fcoe** and **class-default** are enabled. These two classes cannot be deleted. The **class-fcoe** is defined as no-drop (pause-enabled) and has a maximum transmission unit (MTU) configuration of 2158 bytes on the Cisco Nexus 6000. On the Cisco Nexus 7000 and MDS, the MTU is set to 2112. This MTU helps to ensure the Ethernet frame will encapsulate the largest FC frame and associated FCoE headers. All other traffic falls under **class-default** and may be dropped. The MTU for **class-default** is set to 1500 bytes, but it is recommended to be changed to 9216 bytes. Here is the policy with **show policy-map system**:

```
N6K# show policy-map system type network-qos
Type network-qos policy-maps
================================
policy-map type network-qos fcoe-default-nq-policy
class type network-qos class-fcoe
match qos-group 1
pause no-drop
mtu 2158
class type network-qos class-default
match qos-group 0
mtu 1500
```

Note that **class-fcoe** is assigned to **qos-group 1** while **class-default** is assigned to **qos-group 0**. The following output is for the Cisco Nexus 7000:

```
N7K-storage# show policy-map system type network-qos
Type network-qos policy-maps
=============================
policy-map type network-qos default-nq-7e-policy
class type network-qos c-nq-7e-drop
match cos 0-2,4-7
congestion-control tail-drop
mtu 1500
class type network-qos c-nq-7e-ndrop-fcoe
match cos 3
match protocol fcoe
pause
mtu 2112
```

Here is the output for Cisco MDS switches:

```
MDS9513-A# show policy-map type network-qos default-nq-7e-policy
Type network-qos policy-maps
============================
policy-map type network-qos default-nq-7e-policy template 7e
class type network-qos c-nq-7e-drop
congestion-control tail-drop
mtu 1500
class type network-qos c-nq-7e-ndrop-fcoe
pause
mtu 2112
```

By default, PFC is enabled on all interfaces with a setting of **auto**. To check the PFC status on interfaces, run the **show interface priority-flow-control** command. PFC is the enabling feature that allows a receiver to issue a Pause frame to a transmitter, thus allowing for lossless (no-drop) traffic.

When **class-fcoe** is not included in the Quality of Service (QoS) policies, virtual Fiber Channel interfaces do not come up and increased drops occur. Specifically, the VFC VSAN will stay in an initializing state.

Enhanced Transmission Selection: IEEE 802.1Qaz

Priority-based flow control can create eight distinct virtual link types on a physical link, and it can be advantageous to have different traffic classes defined within each virtual link. Traffic within the same PFC IEEE 802.1p class can be grouped together and yet treated differently within each group. Enhanced Transmission Selection (ETS) provides prioritized processing based on bandwidth allocation, low latency, or best effort, resulting in per-group traffic class allocation. Extending the virtual link concept, the network interface controller (NIC) provides virtual interface queues: one for each traffic class. Each virtual interface queue is accountable for managing its allotted bandwidth for its traffic group, but has flexibility within the group to dynamically manage the traffic. For example, virtual link 3 for the IP class of traffic may have a high-priority designation and a best effort within that same class, with the virtual link 3 class sharing a percentage of the overall link with other traffic classes. ETS allows differentiation among traffic of the same priority class, thus creating priority groups (as shown in Figure 23-44).

Today's IEEE 802.1p implementation specifies a strict scheduling of queues based on priority. With ETS, a flexible, drop-free scheduler for the queues can prioritize traffic according to the IEEE 802.1p traffic classes and the traffic treatment hierarchy designated within each priority group. The capability to apply differentiated treatment to different traffic within the same priority class is enabled by implementing ETS.

23

IEEE 802.1Qaz Enhanced Transmission Selection (ETS)
Bandwidth Management

• Prevents a single traffic class of "hogging" all the bandwidth and starving other classes.
• When a given load doesn't fully utilize its allocated bandwidth, it is available to other classes.
• Helps accommodate for classes of a "bursty" nature.

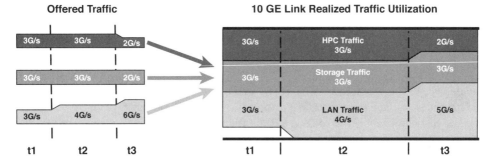

Figure 23-44 *Enhanced Transmission Selection*

Default bandwidth allocations for ETS are also configured through maps. Of the eight possible classes of service, FCoE is assigned to CoS 3. The default bandwidth percentage assigned to CoS 3 is 50%. This allocates 50% of the link bandwidth to FCoE traffic during periods of congestion. During periods of noncongestion, other classes can use this bandwidth if FCoE is not. Although not normally required, the following example shows how to change the allocated bandwidth in different classes:

```
nx5k-1(config)# policy-map type queuing class-fcoe
nx5k-1(config-pmap-que)# class type queuing class-fcoe
nx5k-1(config-pmap-c-que)# bandwidth percent 60
nx5k-1(config-pmap-c-que)# class type queuing class-default
nx5k-1(config-pmap-c-que)# bandwidth percent 40
```

On the Cisco Nexus 7000, you will need to apply the **network-qos** type "**default-nq-7e-policy**" under system qos. To see the queueing policy map, enter the **show policy-map system** command:

```
n7k# show policy-map system type queuing
Service-policy (queuing) input: default-in-policy
policy statistics status: disabled
Class-map (queuing): class-fcoe (match-any)
Match: qos-group 1
bandwidth percent 50
Class-map (queuing): class-default (match-any)
Match: qos-group 0
bandwidth percent 50
Service-policy (queuing) output: default-out-policy
policy statistics status: disabled
```

```
Class-map (queuing): class-fcoe (match-any)
Match: qos-group 1
bandwidth percent 50
Class-map (queuing): class-default (match-any)
Match: qos-group 0
bandwidth percent 50
```

In the previous example, **qos-group 0** and **1** are both assigned 50% of the I/O bandwidth.

Cisco Nexus 7000 shows queuing interface output:

```
show queuing interface ethernet 1/1
slot 1
=======
Egress Queuing for Ethernet1/1 [System]
-----------------------------------------
Template: 8Q7E
-----------------------------------
Group Bandwidth% PrioLevel Shape%
-----------------------------------
0 50 - -
1 50 - -
```

Data Center Bridging Exchange Protocol: IEEE 802.1Qaz

Data Center Bridging Exchange (DCBX) Protocol is a discovery and capability exchange protocol developed by Cisco, Nuova, and Intel that is used by IEEE Data Center Bridges to discover peers and exchange configuration information between DCB-compliant devices (as shown in Figure 23-45). DCBX is implemented on top of the Link Layer Discovery Protocol (IEEE 802.1AB) by using some additional type-length-values (TLVs). The following parameters of the IEEE Data Center Bridge can be exchanged with DCBX:

- Priority groups in ETS
- PFC
- Congestion Notification
- Applications
- Logical link-down
- Network interface virtualization

23

IEEE 802.1Qaz DCBX: Data Center Bridging eXchange

Control Protocol—the "Handshake"

- Allows network devices to advertise their identities and capabilities over the network.
  - Enables hosts to pick up proper configuration from the network.
  - Enables switches to verify proper configuration.

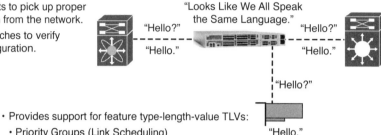

- Provides support for feature type-length-value TLVs:
  - Priority Groups (Link Scheduling)
  - Priority-Based Flow Control
  - Congestion Management (Backwards Congestion Notification)
  - Application (Frame Priority Usage)
  - Logical Link Down

Figure 23-45 *Data Center Bridging Exchange Protocol*

DCBXP is enabled by default when you enable LLDP. When LLDP is enabled, DCBXP can be enabled or disabled using the [no] lldp tlv-select dcbxp command. DCBXP is disabled on ports where LLDP transmit or receive is disabled.

You can enable LLDP on each FCoE switch by issuing the **feature lldp** command. On the Cisco Nexus 7000, LLDP is enabled when the FCoE feature set is installed (in the storage VDC). You cannot disable LLDP while the FCoE feature is installed.

```
N6K# show feature | include lldp
lldp 1 enabled
```

Verify that the FCoE-designated Ethernet interface is configured properly using the following command (the default and correct values are used in this example):

```
N6K# show run interface eth101/1/1 all | include "lldp|priority-flow"
priority-flow-control mode auto
lldp transmit
lldp receive
```

Congestion Notification: IEEE 802.1Qau

Congestion Notification is traffic management that pushes congestion to the edge of the network by instructing rate limiters to shape the traffic causing the congestion. The IEEE 802.1Qau working group accepted the Cisco proposal for Congestion Notification, which defines an architecture for actively managing traffic flows to avoid traffic jams. As of July 2007, the IEEE 802.1Qau working group unanimously approved a baseline proposal that accepts the Cisco Quantized Congestion Notification (QCN) proposal. This model defines a two-point architecture with a congestion point and a reaction point. In this architecture, congestion is measured at the congestion point, and rate limiting, or back pressure, is imposed on the reaction point to shape traffic and reduce the impact of congestion.

In this architecture, an aggregation-level switch can send control frames to two access-level switches, asking them to throttle back their traffic (as shown in Figure 23-46). This approach maintains the integrity of the network's core and affects only the parts of the network causing the congestion, close to the source.

IEEE 802.1Qau Congestion Management:
BCN and QCN

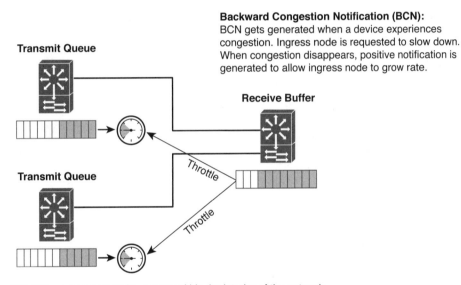

Backward Congestion Notification (BCN):
BCN gets generated when a device experiences congestion. Ingress node is requested to slow down. When congestion disappears, positive notification is generated to allow ingress node to grow rate.

802.1Qau, when congestion occurs within the interior of the network,
traffic sources at the edges are instructed to throttle transmission, thus reducing congestion.

Figure 23-46   *Congestion Notification*

Fibre Channel over Ethernet

I/O consolidation is the ability to carry different types of traffic with different traffic characteristics and handling requirements over the same physical media. The most difficult challenge of I/O consolidation is to satisfy the requirements of different traffic classes within a single network. The goal of FCoE is to provide I/O consolidation over Ethernet, allowing Fibre Channel and Ethernet networks to share a single, integrated infrastructure, thereby reducing network complexities in the data center. FCoE consolidates both SANs and Ethernet traffic onto one converged network adapter (CNA), eliminating the need for using separate host bus adapters (HBAs) and network interface cards (NICs).

SAN A and SAN B separation in traditional Fibre Channel SANs makes sure that the design is highly available even when one of the fabrics goes down. In end-to-end FCoE designs,

23

SAN A and SAN B separation can be achieved physically or logically by separating the FCoE VLANs that are carried across the LAN. The FCoE VLANs synonymous with VLANs in traditional LANs can be used as a mechanism to separate the SAN fabrics from each other. Many data center architectures allow this fabric separation by not using the same VLAN across the switches carrying FCoE traffic.

The FC-BB-5 working group of the INCITS Technical Committee T11 developed the FCoE standard (shown in Figure 23-47). It leverages the same fundamental characteristics of the traditional Fibre Channel protocol, while allowing the flexibility of running it on top of the ever-increasing high-speed Ethernet fabric. FCoE is one of the options available for storage traffic transport. The IEEE 802.1 organization facilitates FCoE by defining enhancements to Ethernet. These enhancements fall under the DCB umbrella—specifically, three enabling standards for Ethernet to support FCoE:

- Priority-based Flow Control (PFC)

- Enhanced Transmission Selection (ETS)

- Data Center Bridging Exchange (DCBX)

Standards for FCoE
FCoE is defined in FC-BB-5 and FC-BB-6 standards.

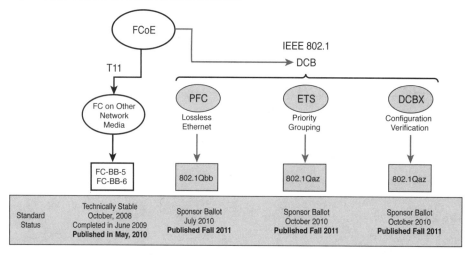

Figure 23-47 *Standards for FCoE*

From the perspective of Ethernet, FCoE is just another upper layer protocol, such as IP, identified by a specific Ethertype (0x8906). Figure 23-48 illustrates FCoE protocols. The FCoE standard also includes an FCoE Initialization Protocol (FIP). FIP is an Ethernet protocol, with a dedicated Ethertype (0x8914) that is different from FCoE Ethertype (0x8906). The specification for FCoE defines two types of Ethernet frames: the FCoE type Ethernet frame that carries a normal FC packet, and the FIP (FCoE Initialization Protocol) packet that is used for discovery, link establishment, link maintenance, and link disconnect (login/logout and so on).

Fiber Channel over Ethernet
Data and Control Plane—Two Different Protocols

FCoE Itself
- It is the data plane protocol.
- It is used to carry most of the FC frames and all the SCSI traffic.
- It uses Ethertype 0x8906.

FIP (FCoE Initialization Protocol)
- It is the control plane protocol.
- It is used to discover the FC entities connected to an Ethernet cloud.
- It is also used to log in to and log out from the FC fabric.
- It uses Ethertype 0x8914.

Both Protocols Have...
- Two different Ethertypes FIP 0x8914, FCoE 0x8906.
- Two different frame formats.
- Both are defined in FC-BB-5.

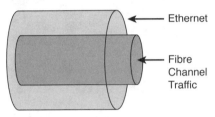

Ethernet

Fibre Channel Traffic

Figure 23-48 *FCoE Protocols*

An entire unmodified FC frame is included in a single Ethernet frame; there is no fragmentation. As a result, jumbo frames are required on links supporting FCoE because the FC payload can go up to 2180 bytes. Fields such as the start-of-frame (SOF) and end-of-frame (EOF) use symbols specific to FC lower layers. They are re-encoded following the existing model used by FCIP and carried in the FCoE header enclosing the FC frame.

From the perspective of FC, FCoE is just a different way of implementing the lower layers of the FC stack. FCoE encapsulates a Fibre Channel frame within an Ethernet frame. Figure 23-49 represents the frame format as agreed to by the INCITS T11.3 standards body. The first 48 bits in the frame are used to specify the destination MAC address and the next 48 bits specify the source MAC addresses. The 32-bit IEEE 802.1Q tag provides the same function as it does for virtual LANs, allowing multiple virtual networks across a single physical infrastructure. FCoE has its own Ethertype as designated by the next 16 bits, followed by the 4-bit version field. The next 100 bits are reserved and are followed by the 8-bit start-of-frame and then the actual FC frame. The 8-bit end-of frame delimiter is followed by 24 reserved bits. The frame ends with the final 32 bits dedicated to the FCS function that provides error detection for the Ethernet frame. The encapsulated Fibre Channel frame consists of the original 24-byte FC header and the data being transported (including the Fibre Channel CRC). The CRC is a cyclical redundancy check used for error detection. The FC header is maintained so that when a traditional FC storage area network is connected to an FCoE-capable switch, the frame is de-encapsulated and handed off seamlessly. This capability enables FCoE to integrate with existing FC SANs without the need of a gateway. Frame size is also a factor in FCoE. A typical Fibre Channel data frame has a 2112-byte payload,

23

a header, and FCS. A classical Ethernet frame is typically 1.5 KB or less. To maintain good performance, FCoE must utilize jumbo frames (or the 2.5 KB "baby jumbo") to prevent a Fibre Channel frame from being split into two Ethernet frames.

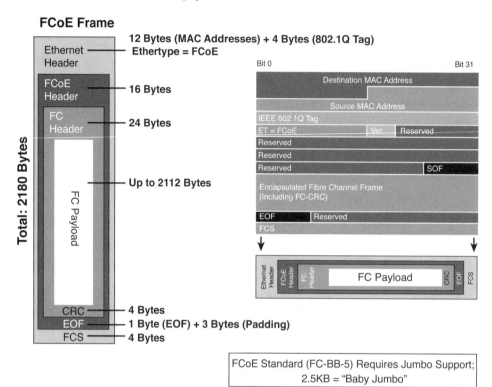

Figure 23-49 *FCoE Frame Format*

To highlight the changes introduced by FCoE, it is necessary to provide a high-level overview of the various layers in the FC protocol stack. With FCoE, the normal FC 0–4 layers have the lower 0, 1, 2P, and 2M layers replaced with an FCoE Mapping function along with the Lossless Ethernet (DCB) MAC and Physical layer.

The FCoE Mapping function is responsible for adding the Ethernet Encapsulation (or stripping off the Ethernet Encapsulation). The resultant FCoE frame is depicted with the Encapsulated FC packet. Figure 23-50 illustrates FC-to-FCoE protocol mapping.

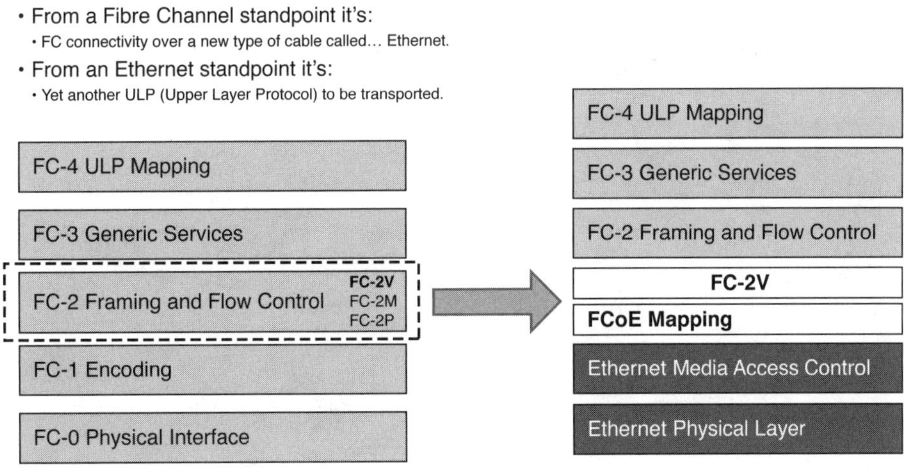

- From a Fibre Channel standpoint it's:
  - FC connectivity over a new type of cable called... Ethernet.
- From an Ethernet standpoint it's:
  - Yet another ULP (Upper Layer Protocol) to be transported.

Figure 23-50 *FC-to-FCoE Protocol Mapping*

The FC-2 level serves as the transport mechanism of the Fibre Channel. The transported data is transparent to FC-2 and visible to FC-3 and above. FC-2 contains three sublevels: FC-2P (that is, the FC-2 Physical sublevel), FC-2M (that is, the FC-2 Multiplexer sublevel), and FC-2V (that is, the FC-2 Virtual sublevel).

FC-2P specifies the rules and provides mechanisms that are used to transfer frames via a specific FC-1 level. FC-2P functions include frame transmission and reception, buffer-to-buffer flow control, and clock synchronization. In FCoE, this is replaced by the DCB NIC Ethernet handling. FC-2M specifies the addressing and functions used to route frames between a link control facility and a VN_Port (Virtual N_Port). This Multiplexer sublevel is not required by FCoE. FC-2V defines functions and facilities that a VN_Port may provide for use by an FC-4 level, regardless of the FC-1 that is used. FC-2V functions include frame content construction and analysis, sequence initiation, termination, disassembly and reassembly, exchange management, name identifiers, and frame sequence error detection.

T11 FC-BB-5 FCoE defines two types of endpoints for the Ethernet encapsulation of Fibre Channel frames: FCoE nodes (ENodes) and Fibre Channel Forwarders (FCFs). Figure 23-51 shows the FCoE and FC node types. ENodes are the combination of FCoE termination functions and Fibre Channel stack on the CNAs, and in that sense they are equivalent to host bus adapters (HBAs) in native Fibre Channel networks. FCFs are the combination of FCoE termination functions and Fibre Channel stack on Ethernet switches (dual-stack switches) and are therefore equivalent to Fibre Channel switches in native Fibre Channel networks.

23

FCoE and FC Node Types

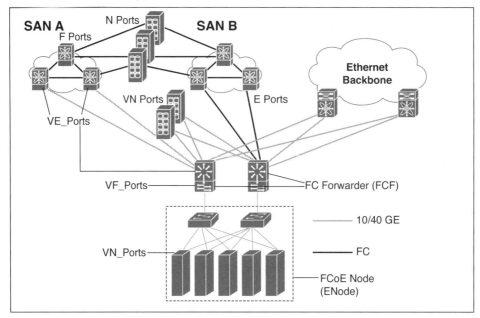

Figure 23-51 *FCoE and FC Node Types*

ENodes present virtual FC interfaces in the form of VN_Ports, which can establish FCoE virtual links with FCFs' VF_Ports. FCFs present virtual FC interfaces in the forms of VF_Ports or VE_Ports; a VF_Port establishes FCoE virtual links with a CNA's VN_Port, and VE_Ports enable FCFs to establish FCoE virtual links with one another. These interface types have their equivalents in native Fibre Channel's N_Ports, F_Ports, and E_Ports. A virtual fabric (VF) port in an FCoE network acts as a fabric port that connects to a peripheral device (host or disk) operating as an N_port. A VF_port can be attached to only one N_port. A virtual expansion (VE) port acts as an expansion port in an FCoE network. VE ports can connect multiple FCoE switches together in the network. A virtual expansion (VE) port can be bound to a physical Ethernet port or a port channel. Traffic is load balanced across equal-cost E_Ports and VE_Ports based on SID, DID, and OXID. Traffic across members of a port channel that a VE_Port is bound to is load balanced based on SID, DID, and OXID. Connectivity from an FCoE NPV bridge to the FCF is supported only over point-to-point links. For each FCF connected to an Ethernet interface, a vFC interface must be created and bound to it. These vFC interfaces must be configured as VNP ports. On the VNP port, the FCoE NPV bridge emulates an FCoE-capable host with multiple ENodes, each with a unique ENode MAC address. Later in this chapter, we talk about FCoE NPV. Figure 23-52 illustrates all the FC and FCoE node types.

FCoE virtual links replace the physical Fibre Channel links by encapsulating Fibre Channel frames in Ethernet frames, and an FCoE virtual link is identified by the MAC addresses of the two FCoE endpoints. T11 FC-BB-5 FCoE mandates lossless characteristics for the Ethernet segments traversed by encapsulated Fibre Channel frames, and although it does not specify the exact means to obtain such QoS, IEEE 802.1 Data Center Bridging (DCB), and specifically 802.1Qbb, is assumed for this purpose on the Ethernet segments.

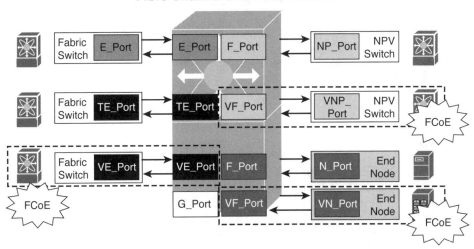

Figure 23-52 *FCoE and FC Node Types*

Communication from one endpoint to the other in an FCoE virtual link uses Ethernet forwarding semantics, augmented by IEEE 802.1 DCB functions. Obviously, if no FCoE passthrough switches exist in the path between the two FCoE endpoints (FCoE direct attach), no Ethernet switching is required, but IEEE 802.1 DCB semantics still apply on the physical Ethernet link. Switching from an ingress to egress virtual interface of an FCF requires Fibre Channel forwarding semantics.

A Fibre Channel virtual link between two FCoE devices, A and B, is uniquely identified by this triplet:

[MAC address of FCoE device A, MAC address of FCoE device B, FCoE VLAN ID]

Given a physical Ethernet interface on an FCoE device (or, more accurately, what FC-BB-5 calls an FCoE controller behind that interface), the FCoE device must establish all the virtual links for which that physical interface is configured. Typically, the configuration is represented in the form of one or more virtual FC interfaces (what FC-BB-5 calls FCoE logical endpoints [FCoE-LEPs]) mapped on top of the physical Ethernet interface.

The information for the triplets that characterize the virtual links can be statically configured on the FCoE device, but FC-BB-5 defines FIP to dynamically discover all the information required. In other words, for every virtual FC interface configured on top of a physical Ethernet interface, FIP is responsible for discovering a pairing virtual FC interface somewhere else in the Ethernet network and establishing a virtual link between the two virtual interfaces in a specific FCoE VLAN.

Figure 23-53 illustrates a functional diagram of an FCoE-capable switch as depicted by the larger, grey field. Inside this device is an Ethernet switch function as well as a Fibre Channel switch function. Note the Fibre Channel over Ethernet entity within the FC switch. This entity encapsulates FC frames into FCoE frames and de-encapsulates FCoE frames back to FC frames. FC traffic flows into one end of the FCoE entity, and FCoE traffic flows out

23

the other end. The FCoE entity has an Ethernet MAC address that will be used as a source or destination address when FCoE frames are transmitted through an Ethernet fabric.

FCoE Forwarding

- FCF (Fibre Channel Forwarder) is a logical FC switch inside an FCoE switch.
  - Fibre Channel login happens at the FC.
  - Contains an FCF-MAC address.
  - Consumes a Domain ID.
- FCoE encapsulation/de-capsulation happens within the FCF.

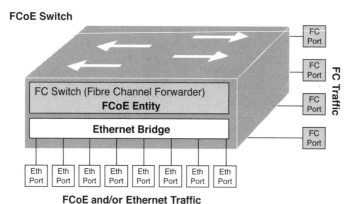

Figure 23-53   *Functional Diagram of an FCoE Switch*

The FC frame enters from the green FC ports to the right and into the FC switch where the entity encapsulates the Fibre Channel frame into an FCoE frame. The FCoE frame is sent to an Ethernet bridge where it is distributed to the appropriate Ethernet port on the bottom of the diagram. The reverse is also true; FCoE traffic will flow from the blue ports, through the Ethernet Bridge, until it is de-encapsulated inside of the FCoE Entity, where it passes through the FC switch to the appropriate FC port.

A Fibre Channel Bridge connects an FCoE network to a Fibre Channel network. A Fibre Channel Bridge de-encapsulates an FCoE frame and sends the Fibre Channel frame to the Fibre Channel network. A Fibre Channel Bridge also encapsulates FC frames from a Fibre Channel network and forwards them to the FCoE network. Cisco MDS 9700 switches, Cisco MDS 9500 switches, and MDS 9250i switches support Fibre Channel Bridge functions.

FC and FCoE Address Mapping

Traditional Fibre Channel fabric switches maintain forwarding tables FCIDs. FC switches use these forwarding tables to select the best link available for a frame so the frame reaches its destination port. Fibre Channel links are typically point-to-point and do not need an address at the link layer. An Ethernet network is different because it does not form an end-point-to-endpoint connection in the manner of FC. This requires FCoE to rely on Ethernet MAC addresses to direct a frame to its correct Ethernet destination (the first two fields of the FCoE frame are MAC addresses, as outlined previously in Figure 23-49).

Figure 23-54 illustrates how traditional FC addresses align with MAC addresses in an FCoE network. On the left is a storage array attached to a Fibre Channel switch labeled FC Domain 2. This storage array is in a traditional SAN and stores information for a Human Resources (HR) host on an FCoE-enabled fabric. The HR host has both an FCID of 1.1.1 and an FC MAC address.

FCoE Addressing and Forwarding

Fibre Channel Forwarder (FCF)

- FCoE frames have:
  - MAC Addresses (Hop-By-Hop)
  - FC Addresses (End-to-End)

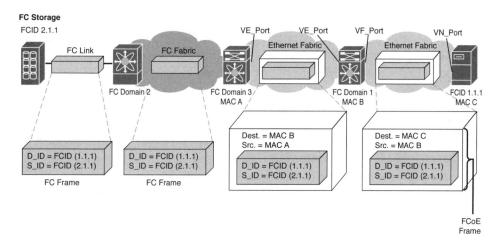

Figure 23-54 *FCoE Addressing and Forwarding*

The FCoE forwarding in Figure 23-54 can be summarized in the following steps:

1. The Fibre Channel N_port on the storage array sends out the FC frame, which includes the Destination FCID (D_ID = 1.1.1) and the Source FCID (S_ID = 2.1.1) in the header. For simplicity, only the header information is displayed in the figure.

2. The Fibre Channel switch with Domain ID 2 receives the frame. Since the destination ID (D_ID) is not in this FC domain (2), the switch looks up the destination domain ID in its forwarding table and transmits the frame on the port associated with the shortest path, as determined by the Fabric Shortest Path First (FSPF) algorithm.

3. The switch with the FC Domain ID 3 receives the frame and determines that the destination ID (D_ID) is not in Domain 3 and repeats the lookup process in step 2. However, in this case the FC frame will be transmitted across an FCoE-enabled Ethernet fabric. This requires the frame to be encapsulated by an FCoE entity in the switch and then transmitted on the port associated with the shortest path. Although the original FC source and destination IDs are maintained in the encapsulated FC frame, the FCoE entity will populate a new destination and source MAC address located in the Ethernet header. As mentioned before, the entity has its own MAC address. In this case, the destination is MAC address B (the MAC address of the

FCoE entity in the receiving switch) and source MAC address A (the MAC address of the FCoE entity in the transmitting switch).

4. When the FCoE frame arrives at the FCoE entity with MAC address B, the frame is de-encapsulated and the switch determines that the FC frame destination is within its domain (Domain 1). The FC frame is reencapsulated with the new destination MAC address C (which corresponds to the FC D_ID 1.1.1) and the new source MAC address B. Then the frame is transmitted out the appropriate port to the FCoE host with MAC address C.

5. When the frame is received by the FCoE host bus adapter with MAC address C, the FCoE frame is de-encapsulated and the FC frame accepted by the HR host with FCID 1.1.1.

FCoE VLANs

FCoE packets must be exchanged in a VLAN. For FCFs with a Fibre Channel stack that includes multi-VSAN capabilities like the Cisco MDS and Nexus Series switches, the FCoE traffic belonging to different VSANs must remain separated by different VLANs on the Ethernet plane. This choice simplifies the implementation, because it removes the necessity to include both a VLAN and a VSAN header in each FCoE packet: The VLAN is assumed to be a proxy for a VSAN.

For this reason, in NX-OS software, there is a concept of a mapping table between FCoE VLANs and Fibre Channel VSANs. For each Fibre Channel VSAN used in the Fibre Channel fabric, the administrator associates one and only one unique FCoE VLAN; all FCoE packets tagged with that VLAN ID are then assumed for Fibre Channel control plane and forwarding purposes to belong to the corresponding Fibre Channel VSAN.

On the Cisco Nexus 5000, Nexus 6000, MDS 9000, Nexus 7000, and Nexus 9000 platforms, you must associate the VSAN to an FCoE-designated VLAN. This is the VLAN that will be used for the FIP control plane and FCoE data plane. On the Cisco Nexus 7000, all VSAN and FC-related commands are configured in the storage VDC. First, create the VSAN and then map it to the FCoE VLAN with the following commands:

```
N6K# configure terminal
N6K(config)# vsan database
N6K#(config-vsan-db) vsan 101
N6K#(config-vsan-db) exit
N6K(config)# vlan 101
N6K(config-vlan)# fcoe vsan 101
N6K(config-vlan)# end
N6K# show vlan fcoe
VLAN     VSAN     Status
-------- -------- --------
101      101      Operational
```

Before you ask whether disabling STP on the FCoE VLAN was a wise decision, you should remember that an FCF does not bridge an FCoE frame. In truth, an FCF must de-encapsulate and route the inner Fibre Channel frame through its FSPF-generated routes, exactly like a Fibre Channel switch. FCoE does not require full Spanning Tree Protocol (STP) because FCoE has no bridging functionality, which means that no STP loops are created in the network. STP Lite on FCoE interfaces ensures rapid convergence across the network by sending an agreement bridge protocol data unit (BPDU) whenever it receives a proposal BPDU. The FCoE link sends the identical agreement BPDU in response to either a Multiple Spanning Tree (MST) or a Per VLAN Rapid Spanning Tree Plus (PVRST+) proposal BPDU. Additionally, STP Lite suppresses the MAC address flushing function for FCoE VLANs.

STP Lite is enabled automatically by default across the entire device for FCoE VLANs as soon as the first FCoE VLAN comes up. At the same time, the system automatically converts all FCoE links as the STP-type normal ports. This feature runs only in FCoE VLANs.

When running multi-instance STP in an Ethernet environment, it is required that all switches in the same MST region have the identical mapping of VLANs to instances. This does not require that all VLANs be defined on all switches. When you're running FCoE over an environment using MST, it is recommended to have a dedicated MST instances for the FCoE VLANs belonging to SAN A and a dedicated MST instance for the FCoE VLANs belonging to SAN B. These instances should be separate from any instances that include regular Ethernet VLANs.

FCoE Initialization Protocol (FIP)

FCoE Initialization Protocol (FIP) is the FCoE control protocol responsible for establishing and maintaining Fibre Channel virtual links between pairs of FCoE devices (ENodes or FCFs). During the virtual link establishment phase, FIP first discovers FCoE VLANs and remote virtual FC interfaces; then it performs virtual link initialization functions (fabric login [FLOGI] and fabric discovery [FDISC], or exchange link parameters [ELP]) similar to their native Fibre Channel equivalents. After the virtual link is established, Fibre Channel payloads can be exchanged on the virtual link, and FIP remains in the background to perform virtual link maintenance functions; it continuously verifies reachability between the two virtual FC interfaces on the Ethernet network, and it offers primitives to delete the virtual link in response to administrative actions to that effect.

FIP aims to establish virtual FC links between VN_Ports and VF_Ports (ENode to FCF), as well as between pairs of VE_Ports (FCF to FCF), because these are the only legal combinations supported by native Fibre Channel fabrics.

Discovery and Virtual Link Establishment

FIP defines two discovery protocols as well as a protocol to establish virtual links between VN_Ports and VF_Ports. Figure 23-55 shows a typical FIP protocol exchange resulting in the establishment of a virtual link between an ENode's VN_Port and an FCF's VF_Port.

23

Fiber Channel over Ethernet Protocol
FCoE Initialization Protocol (FIP)

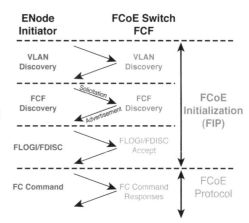

- Step 1: **FCoE VLAN Discovery**

  FIP sends out a multicast to ALL_FCF_MAC address looking for the **FCoE VLAN.**

  FIP frames use the native VLAN.

- Step 2: **FCF Discovery**

  FIP sends out a multicast to the ALL_FCF_MAC address on the **FCoE VLAN** to find the FCFs answering for that **FCoE VLAN.**

  FCFs respond back with their MAC address.

- Step 3: **Fabric Login**

  FIP sends a **FLOGI** request to the FCF_MAC found in Step 2.

  Establishes a virtual link between host and FCF.

** FIP does not carry any Fibre Channel frames.

Figure 23-55 *FCoE Initialization Protocol (FIP)*

All the protocols are usually initiated by ENodes, although FCFs can generate unsolicited FIP advertisements. Note that the FIP frames at the top and the FCoE frames at the bottom of Figure 23-55 use different Ethertypes and encapsulations, since the FCoE frames encapsulate native Fibre Channel payloads, whereas FIP frames describe a new set of protocols that have no reason to exist in native Fibre Channel definitions. Among the differences, note that ENodes use different source MAC addresses for FIP and FCoE encapsulation. FIP packets are built using a globally unique MAC address assigned to the CNA at manufacturing (called the ENode MAC address), whereas FCoE packets are encapsulated using a locally unique MAC address (that is, unique only within the boundaries of the local Ethernet subnet) dynamically assigned to the ENode by the FCF as part of the FIP virtual link establishment process (a fabric-provided MAC address [FPMA]). The definition of the FPMA is shown in Figure 23-56.

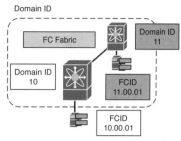

ENode MAC Address
Fibre Channel over Ethernet Addressing Scheme

• **ENode FCoE MAC** assigned for each FCID.
• **ENode FCoE MAC** composed of an **FC-MAP** and **FCID:**
  • **FC-MAP** is the upper 24 bits of the **ENode's FCoE MAC.**
  • **FCID** is the lower 24 bits of the **ENode's MAC.**

**Fibre Channel
FCID Addressing**

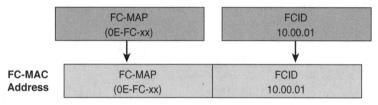

Figure 23-56 *Fabric-Provided MAC Address (FPMA)*

FPMAs use the 24-bit-wide Fibre Channel ID (FCID) assigned to the CNA during the FIP FLOGI and FDISC exchange, and therefore they are not available to the CNA before the fabric login has occurred. The FPMA is built by appending the FCID to a 24-bit quantity called the FCoE MAC address prefix (FC-MAP). FC-BB-5 defined a range of 256 FC-MAPs to facilitate FCoE deployments. Cisco has established very simple best practices (see "FCoE VLANs" earlier in this document) that make the manipulation of FC-MAPs unnecessary, and most users should find the default FC-MAP value 0E-FC-00 sufficient. The 256 different FC-MAPs make available to users up to 256 pools of locally unique MAC addresses. The pools are useful when the FCIDs are not unique on an Ethernet VLAN; for instance, when different Fibre Channel fabrics or different VSANs are encapsulated in the same Ethernet VLAN, the ranges of FCIDs assigned in each Fibre Channel fabric may overlap. Cisco strongly recommends that you never attempt to map multiple Fibre Channel fabrics onto the same Ethernet VLAN. Most users will not ever need to map multiple Fibre Channel fabrics onto the same physical Ethernet network, but if such a need arises, each Fibre Channel fabric should be encapsulated in a separate VLAN.

By default, when the **feature fcoe** command is used to enable FCoE on a Cisco Nexus Series switch, a default FC-MAP is assigned to the switch. The simplest way to ensure SAN A and SAN B isolation between FCoE-enabled switches in the Ethernet fabric is to change the FC-MAP value to something other than the default for all switches belonging to Fabric B. This will prohibit FCoE switches from joining the wrong fabric and will also provide the SAN isolation which is a requirement for FC and FCoE traffic.

Here's how to change the FC-MAP of a switch:

```
switch# configure terminal
switch(config)# fcoe fcmap 0e.fc.2a
```

FIP VLAN Discovery

FIP VLAN discovery discovers the FCoE VLAN that will be used by all other FIP protocols as well as by the FCoE encapsulation for Fibre Channel payloads on the established virtual link. One of the goals of FC-BB-5 was to be as nonintrusive as possible on initiators and targets, and therefore FIP VLAN discovery occurs in the native VLAN used by the initiator or target to exchange Ethernet traffic. The FIP VLAN discovery protocol is the only FIP protocol running on the native VLAN; all other FIP protocols run on the discovered FCoE VLANs.

The ENode sends a FIP VLAN discovery request to a multicast MAC address called All-FCF-MACs, which is a multicast MAC address to which all FCFs listen. All FCFs that can be reached in the native VLAN of the ENode are expected to respond on the same VLAN with a response that lists one or more FCoE VLANs that are available for the ENode's VN_Port login. This protocol has the sole purpose of allowing the ENode to discover all the available FCoE VLANs, and it does not cause the ENode to select an FCF.

FIP VLAN discovery is an optional protocol in FC-BB-5. An ENode implementation can choose to offer only manual configuration for FCoE VLANs, and therefore choose not to perform FIP VLAN discovery. It is commonly assumed that such implementation will default to VLAN 1002 for its FCoE VLAN. The Cisco Nexus Series switches support FIP VLAN discovery, and it will respond to any ENode that performs a query.

FIP FCF Discovery

FIP FCF discovery is the protocol used by ENodes to discover FCFs that can accept logins. FCFs periodically send FIP FCF discovery advertisement messages on each configured FCoE VLAN; these messages are destined for the multicast MAC address All-ENode-MACs, a multicast MAC address to which all ENodes listen. The FIP FCF discovery advertisement is used by the FCF to inform any potential ENode in the VLAN that FCF VF_Ports are available for virtual link establishment with ENodes' VN_Ports. The advertisement includes the MAC address of the FCF as well as other parameters useful for tuning the characteristics of the virtual link (FIP timeout values, FCF priority, etc.).

Given the periodic nature of the advertisements, new ENodes joining the network will typically not want to wait to collect multicast FIP FCF discovery advertisements from all FCFs, and therefore FC-BB-5 allows ENodes to solicit unicast advertisements by sending a FIP FCF discovery solicitation to the All-FCF-MACs multicast MAC address. FCFs receiving the solicitation can generate a unicast FIP FCF discovery advertisement addressed to the requesting ENode. Upon collection of these advertisements, the ENode can make the final decision as to which FCF to contact for the establishment of a virtual link with its VN_Port.

FIP FLOGI and FDISC

After the ENode has discovered all FCFs and selected one for login, the last step is to inform the selected FCF of the intention to create a virtual link with its VF_Port. After this step, Fibre Channel payloads (encapsulated in FCoE frames) can start being exchanged on the new virtual link just established. On any native Fibre Channel link between an N_Port and an F_Port, the first protocol exchange performed as part of activating the data-link layer is the fabric login, or FLOGI, which results in the assignment of an FCID to the N_Port. In designing FIP, the T11 committee decided to merge the logical step of FCF selection by an ENode in FIP with the native Fibre Channel fabric login exchange. The result of this optimization is a single FIP exchange that serves both purposes of FCF selection, as well as fabric login and FCID allocation. This optimization is not only convenient; it is a requirement for obtaining an appropriate FPMA for the ENode to use in the subsequent FCoE encapsulated frames.

FIP FLOGI and FDISC are unicast frames almost identical to the native Fibre Channel FLOGI and FDISC frames they replace. The VN_Port sends an FLOGI or an FDISC request, the FCF responds with accept payload to the corresponding FLOGI or FDISC. Completion of this exchange terminates the FIP virtual link establishment phase.

Virtual Fibre Channel Interfaces

The NX-OS software uses the virtual Fibre Channel interface construct to infer the number of VF_Ports that need to be exposed by FIP in each FCoE VLAN. Like any interface in Cisco NX-OS, virtual FC interfaces (called vfc in the CLI) are configurable objects with properties such as state and properties. A virtual FC interface getx assigned to a VSAN, and the combination of the vFC VSAN assignment and the global VLAN-to-VSAN mapping table enables the Cisco Nexus and MDS Series switches FIP implementation to choose the appropriate VLAN for a VF_Port. A virtual Fibre Channel (vFC) interface must be bound to an interface before it can be used. The binding is to a physical Ethernet interface when the converged network adapter (CNA) is directly connected to the switch or port channel when the CNA connects to the Fibre Channel Forwarder (FCF) over a virtual port channel (vPC). Virtual FC interfaces bound to a physical Ethernet interface on the Cisco Nexus Series switch expects the CNA to be at the other end of the physical Ethernet cable, and it accepts one FLOGI from that one CNA, regardless of its ENode MAC address; moving the CNA to a different physical Ethernet interface on the switch will cause the CNA to become subject to the configuration on the vfc attached to the other interface (if any). After the FLOGI, more FDISC operations can follow if N_port ID virtualization (NPIV) is enabled, with exactly the same semantics as native Fibre Channel interfaces. FIP VLAN discovery advertises only the FCoE VLAN that maps to the VSAN configured on the vFC.

Virtual FC interfaces bound to an ENode MAC address signal to the software that a remote-attach model is used to create a virtual link with that specific ENode. FIP FCF advertisements are exchanged on all physical Ethernet interfaces that are not subject to direct-attach bindings, and the ENode can create a virtual link through any of those interfaces. However, regardless of the ingress interface, it will always be subject to the vFC that is bound to its MAC address. It is important to understand the virtual interfaces that make up an FCoE implementation and how they map to physical Ethernet interfaces. FCoE interfaces are defined as port types, as identified in Table 23-17.

Table 23-17   Summary of NX-OS CLI Commands for Trunking and Port Channels

Port Type	FCoE Virtual Interface	Binds to	Example Interface
VF port or virtual fabric port	vfc1	Ethernet interface	Ethernet101/1/1
VE port or virtual expansion port (ISL)	vfc100	Ethernet interface or port-channel interface	Port-channel 100

23

Note that in the case of port channels, a virtual FCoE interface is created over a virtual port channel interface (virtual mapped to virtual mapped to physical). It is the port channel that is mapped to physical Ethernet ports. Virtual FCoE interfaces are bound to physical interfaces. This binding is a one-to-one mapping. A physical Ethernet interface can only have one VFC bound to it (also true when bound to a port channel). Once defined, the configuration of virtual interfaces is similar to physical interfaces—that is, virtual interfaces need to have **shutdown** or **no-shutdown** commands issued to them. You can check the status of virtual interfaces with the **show** command (for example, a **show interface vfc1 command**). It should be evident that a VFC interface cannot be in the up state until the physical interface to which it is bound is in the up state. In order for virtual interfaces to come to the up state, proper configuration is required in the network, specifically pertaining to the DCB enhancements to Ethernet. FC communication between end devices (for example, a host and storage port) cannot occur until

- Their associated physical port VFC interface is in the up state.
- The FIP process has taken place.
- The proper FC zoning is defined and active.

Creating VFC for Storage (Target):

A VFC port is bound to a specific Ethernet port. First, configure the Ethernet interface to which the VFC will be bound:

```
N6K# configure terminal
N6K(config)# interface Ethernet101/1/1
N6K(config-if)# description server101
N6K(config-if)# switchport mode trunk
N6K(config-if)# switchport trunk allowed vlan [data vlan and 101]
N6K(config-if)# spanning-tree port type edge trunk
N6K(config-if)# no shut
```

Now create the VFC and bind to the Ethernet interface with the following commands:

```
N6K# configure terminal
N6K(config)# interface vfc 1
N6K(config)# vsan database
N6K(config-vsan-db)# vsan 101 interface vfc1
N6K(config)# interface vfc 1
N6K(config-if)# switchport trunk allowed vsan 101
N6K(config-if)# bind interface Ethernet101/1/1
N6K(config-if)# no shut
```

Assuming the CNA on the host is configured properly, connectivity is good, and all switch configuration is proper, the physical and virtual interfaces should come up. An easy check can be done with the following command:

```
N6K# show interface Ethernet101/1/1 fcoe
Ethernet101/1/1 is FCoE UP
vfc1 is Up
FCID is 0x490100
PWWN is 21:00:00:1b:32:0a:e7:b8
MAC addr is 00:c0:dd:0e:5f:76
```

Below configuration steps illustrate another VFC interface creation for Storage (Target):

```
N7K# configure terminal
N7K(config)# interface Ethernet1/1
N7K(config-if)# description HDS_array01_01
N7K(config-if)# switchport trunk allowed vlan [data vlan and 101]
N7K(config-if)# switchport mode trunk
N7K(config-if)# spanning-tree port type edge trunk
N7K(config-if)# no shut
```

Now create the VFC and bind to the Ethernet interface with the following commands:

```
N7K# configure terminal
N7K(config)# interface vfc 1/1
N7K(config)# vsan database
N7K(config-vsan-db)# vsan 101 interface vfc1
N7K(config)# interface vfc 1/1
N7K(config-if)# switchport trunk allowed vsan 101
N7K(config-if)# bind interface Ethernet1/1
N7K(config-if)# no shut
```

Assuming the array port (CNA) is configured properly, connectivity is good, and all switch configurations are proper, the physical and virtual interfaces should come up. An easy check can be done with the following command:

```
N7K# show interface Ethernet1/1 fcoe
Ethernet1/1 is FCoE UP
vfc1/1 is Up
FCID is 0x100100
PWWN is 50:00:00:1b:32:0a:10:20
MAC addr is 00:c0:dd:0d:1a:b2
```

An output similar to the preceding example indicates the physical and VFC interfaces are up, and the FIP process completed successfully with the end device having performed a fabric login (FLOGI). The preceding command provides summary output to the more detailed, individual commands that follow. These commands and the resulting output are similar on both the Cisco Nexus 6000 and 7000.

To check the status of the VFC interface, run the following command:

```
N6K# show int vfc1
vfc1 is trunking
Bound interface is Ethernet101/1/1
Hardware is Ethernet
Port WWN is 20:00:00:2a:6a:35:a5:3f
Admin port mode is F, trunk mode is on
snmp link state traps are enabled
Port mode is TF
Port vsan is 101
Trunk vsans (admin allowed and active) (101)
```

```
Trunk vsans (up) (101)
Trunk vsans (isolated) ()
Trunk vsans (initializing) ()
```

...

To check the status of the FC FLOGI, enter the following command:

```
N6K# show flogi database interface vfc1
-------------------------------------------------------------------------

INTERFACE VSAN  FCID    PORT NAME                NODE NAME
-------------------------------------------------------------------------

vfc1     101   0xd10000 20:00:74:26:ac:17:2a:b1 10:00:74:26:ac:17:2a:b1
Total number of flogi = 1.
```

Converged Network Adapter and Unified Ports

A converged network adapter (CNA) is a single network interface card (NIC) that contains both a Fibre Channel (FC) host bus adapter (HBA) and a TCP/IP Ethernet NIC. It connects servers to FC-based storage area networks (SANs) and Ethernet-based local area networks (LANs). In networks without CNAs, servers have to have at least two adapters: one with an FC HBA to connect the server to the storage network, and another with a TCP/IP Ethernet NIC to connect the server to the LAN. Using a single CNA to connect servers to storage and networks reduces costs by requiring fewer adapter cards, cables, switch ports, and PCIe slots. Figure 23-57 illustrates SAN and LAN adapters.

In addition to supporting standard 10 Gigabit Ethernet network interface cards (NICs) on servers, the Cisco Nexus Series switches integrate with multifunction converged network adapters (CNAs) that combine the functions of Ethernet NICs and Fibre Channel host bus adapters (HBAs), making the transition to a single, unified network fabric transparent and consistent with existing practices, management software, and OS drivers. The switch series is compatible with integrated transceivers and Twinax cabling solutions that deliver cost-effective connectivity for 10 Gigabit Ethernet to servers at the rack level, eliminating the need for expensive optical transceivers. The Cisco Nexus Series switch portfolio also provides the flexibility to connect directly to servers using 10GBASE-T connections or fiber with Enhanced Small Form-Factor Pluggable (SFP+) transceivers.

Cisco Nexus unified ports allow you to configure a physical port on a Cisco Nexus device switch as a 1/10 Gigabit Ethernet, Fibre Channel over Ethernet (FCoE), or 2, 4, 8, 16 Gigabit native Fibre Channel port.

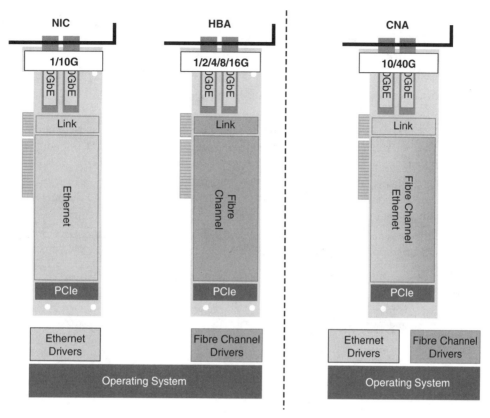

Figure 23-57   *Converged Network Adapter (CNA)*

Currently, most networks have two types of switches for different types of networks. For example, LAN switches carry Ethernet traffic up to Catalyst. Nexus switches carry FC traffic from servers to MDS switches. With unified port technology, you can deploy a unified platform, unified device, and unified wire approach. Unified ports allow users to move from an existing segregated platform approach, where they can choose LAN and SAN port options, and transition to a single, unified fabric that is transparent and consistent with existing practices and management software. A unified fabric includes the following:

- **Unified platform:** Uses the same hardware platform and the same software code level, and certifies it once for your LAN and SAN environments.

- **Unified device:** Runs LAN and SAN services on the same platform switch. The unified device allows you to connect your Ethernet and Fibre Channel cables to the same device.

- **Unified wire:** Converges LAN and SAN networks on a single converged network adapter (CNA) and connects them to your server.

Here are the guidelines and limitations for unified ports:

- On the Cisco Nexus 5548UP switch, the 32 ports of the main slot (slot1) are unified ports. The Ethernet ports start from port 1/1 to port 1/32. The Fibre Channel ports start from port 1/32 and go backward to port 1/1.

- On the Cisco Nexus 5596T switch, the last 16 ports (ports 33–48) are Fiber Channel and are configurable as unified ports. The first 32 ports (1–32) are 10GBase-T Ethernet ports only and cannot be configured as unified ports.

- On a Cisco Nexus 5672UP switch, the Fibre Channel port range is 33–48, but must end at port 48.

- On a Cisco Nexus 5672UP-16G switch, the Fibre Channel port range is 2/1–2/24 or 2/13–2/24.

- On a Cisco Nexus 56128P switch, only the expansion modules in slot 2 and 3 support the native FC type. On each module, the Fibre Channel port range is 1–24, but must start from port 1.

- On a Cisco Nexus 5696Q switch, only M20UP expansion modules support the native FC type. All 20 ports can be configured as native Fibre Channel ports, but the port range must either start with 1 or end at 20.

- At the time this book was written, Nexus 9300EX switches are hardware capable of supporting unified ports. The configuration capability is not available on Cisco NX-OS.

Figure 23-58 illustrates the CLI configuration for unified ports.

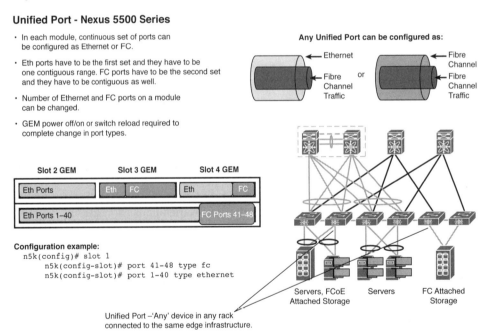

Figure 23-58 *Unified Port Support on Nexus 5500 Series Switches*

The Story of the Interface Speeds

Fibre Channel can leverage the raw speed and capacity of Ethernet for deployments that are looking to run multiprotocol traffic over a ubiquitous infrastructure inside their data center. Realistically, 10G Ethernet (10GbE) was the first technology that allowed administrators to efficiently use increasing capacity for multiprotocol traffic. It was the first time that we could

- Have enough bandwidth to accommodate storage requirements alongside traditional Ethernet traffic.

- Have lossless and lossy traffic running at the same time on the same wire.

- Independently manage design requirements for both nondeterministic LAN and deterministic SAN traffic at the same time on the same wire.

- Provide more efficient, dynamic allocation of bandwidth for that LAN and SAN traffic without them starving each other.

- Reduce or even eliminate bandwidth waste.

Consolidating that I/O with LAN traffic and creating policies for bandwidth usage can mean that you still have that FC throughput guaranteed but are also able to use additional bandwidth for LAN traffic as well. Moreover, if there is bandwidth left over, bursty FC traffic could use all the remaining additional bandwidth as well. Because LAN and SAN traffic is not constant or static, despite what benchmark tests might have us believe, this dynamic approach to running multiple types becomes even more compelling when the bandwidth increases beyond 10G to 40G, and even 100G. In order to understand just how much throughput we're talking about, you need to understand that it's more complex than just the "apparent" speed. Throughput is based on both the interface clocking (how fast the interface transmits) and how efficient it is (that is, how much overhead there is).

Figure 23-59 shows exactly how much the bandwidth threshold is being pushed with technologies that are either available today or just around the corner.

The Story of Interface Speeds

Protocol	Clocking Gbps	Endcoding Data/Sent	Data Gbps	Rate MB/s
8G FC	8.500	8b/10b	6.8	850
10G FC	10.51875	64b/66b	10.2	1,275
10G FCoE	10.3125	64b/66b	10.0	1,250
16G FC	14.025	64b/66b	13.6	1,700
32G FC	28.050	64b/66b	27.2	3,400
40G FCoE	41.250	64b/66b	40.0	5,000

- Comparing speeds is more complex than just the "apparent" speed.
- Data throughput is based on both the interface clocking (how fast the interface transmits) and how efficient the interface transmits (how much encoding overhead).

Figure 23-59   *Bandwidth Comparison for FC and FCoE*

Data centers can expand, and sometimes they even can shrink. One thing they do not do, however, is remain static over time. New servers, new ASICs, new software and hardware—all of these affect the growth patterns of the data center. When this happens, the network infrastructure is expected to be able to accommodate these changes. For this reason, we often see administrators "expect the unexpected" by over-preparing the data center's networking capacity, just in case. No one can be expected to predict the future, and yet this is what we ask of our storage and network architects every day. Because of this, even the most carefully designed data center can be taken by surprise. Equipment that was not expected to live beyond its projected time frame is being called upon to work overtime to accommodate capacity requirement increases. Meanwhile, equipment that was "absolutely necessary" remains underutilized because expected use cases didn't meet planned projections. Multiprotocol, higher-capacity networks solve both of these problems.

23

FCoE Topologies

High availability is a crucial requirement in any data center design. It is especially important in a converged network, an environment in which loss-intolerant storage traffic shares the network infrastructure with loss-tolerant Ethernet traffic. High availability is implemented at many different levels of the network: chassis level, link level, and process level. Cisco Nexus 7000 Series and Cisco MDS 9500 Series switches have hardware and software features that help network designers meet the high-availability requirements of their data centers and secure the uptime and integrity of the storage traffic in a consolidated environment.

Traditionally, SAN designers have used redundant network links and network equipment to create high availability in their networks. These designs provision and manage parallel, disparate SANs. These parallel, independent SANs are often referred to as SAN A and SAN B. Data center designers need to consider high-availability options when designing a consolidated network. Hardware requirements vary based on the platform used for FCoE connectivity. The data center design also depends on the application requirements. In this chapter, we discuss various network topologies synonymous with the traditional Fibre Channel SAN designs but running FCoE end to end. In a typical data center, a server is connected to two different and independent networks: a LAN to provide IP connectivity, and a Fibre Channel SAN to provide storage connectivity. The first logical step in reducing the number of host adapters and discrete switching platforms is to converge the access-layer LAN and SAN switches into a single set of host adapters and single switching platform. Access-layer convergence significantly reduces capital expenditures (CapEx) and operating expenses (OpEx), and extending convergence beyond the access layer increases those benefits. The capability to bridge converged access designs with Fibre Channel SANs preserves existing and continued investments made in the Fibre Channel SAN. This design also allows the IT operators to start their migration to convergence with director classes of service (CoS) offered by these switches (such as high availability, high port density, and intelligent SAN services). A phased approach to convergence enables data center operators to enhance their deployments as more advanced FCoE storage solutions become available and at the same time move toward a converged network that benefits from the economics of Ethernet.

Single-Hop FCoE Design

There are two possible single-hop solutions when deploying FCoE with a Cisco Nexus Series switch and Cisco Nexus 2000 Series Fabric Extender. The first solution is referred to as "direct connect," where a host is directly connected to the first-hop converged access switch. The second single-hop solution deploys an FEX between the server and the first-hop switch. Because the FEX acts as a remote line card to the parent switch and has no local switching capabilities, it is not considered a hop in the Ethernet and storage topologies. Figure 23-60 illustrates a single-hop FCoE design.

Single Hop FCoE Design

- Single Hop (Directly Connected) FCoE from the CNA to FCF, then broken out to Native FC.

- Trunking is not required on the host driver—all FCoE frames are tagged by the CNA.

- FCoE VLANs can be pruned from Ethernet links that are not designated for FCoE.

- Maintains isolated edge switches for SAN 'A' and 'B' and separate LAN switches for NIC 1 and NIC 2 (standard NIC teaming or Link Aggregation).

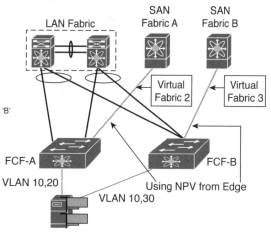

Figure 23-60 *Single-Hop FCoE*

Switch Mode and NPV Mode

The Cisco Nexus 5000 Series switch has two modes of operation relating to storage traffic forwarding: switch mode and N-Port Virtualizer (NPV) mode. This is the same as the modes of operation available on the Cisco Multiprotocol Director Series (MDS) Fibre Channel switches. On Cisco Nexus 9000, at the time of writing this book, we only have N-Port Virtualizer (NPV) mode. The default mode on Cisco Nexus 5000 and MDS 9000 platforms is "Fibre Channel switch" mode. In the following topologies, the Cisco Nexus 5000 Series switch can either be in switch or NPV mode. The only requirement for a Cisco Nexus 5000 Series switch in NPV mode is that the upstream device supports the standard N-Port ID Virtualization (NPIV) functionality.

When the Cisco Nexus 5000 Series switch is operating in switch mode, all fabric services (for example, FSPF, zoning, or DNS) are native on the access device. This means that all forwarding decisions are made by FSPF running on the switch. This mode also means that the switch consumes a domain ID within the Fibre Channel fabric. Limitations exist as to the number of domain IDs that are supported within a single fabric. Specific domain ID limitations are defined by the storage vendors and OSM partners.

NPV defines the ability for a Fibre Channel switch to act as a proxy for both FLOGIs and forwarding decisions and to pass those duties to an upstream device. This upstream device must be capable of running NPIV, which is an FC standard allowing multiple FCIDs to be handed out to a single FC port. The benefit of an NPV device in an FC network is the elimination of the domain ID and therefore the ability to add more FC switches to a fabric without exceeding the supported domain ID limitation.

The Cisco Nexus 5000, Nexus 9000, and MDS 9000 Series switches can operate in NPV mode. When NPV is enabled on the switch, no FC fabric services are run locally on the platform; instead, forwarding and zoning services are handled by the upstream NPIV device. To avoid interoperability challenges when connecting a switch to a non-Cisco SAN core switch, Cisco recommends that the switch be configured in NPV mode.

23

Enabling NPV on the switch is a disruptive process and should be done at the time of initial set up to avoid any disruption to the fabric. Because enabling NPV requires a switch reboot and erases the current running configuration, be sure to save the current running configuration to an external text file so that it can be reapplied after the reboot occurs if enabling NPV after the initial set up of the switch.

Changing between switch mode and NPV mode can be done using the **feature npv** command.

vPC and Active/Standby

Host-facing interfaces on the Nexus 5000 Series switch can provide connections to servers in a couple of different ways: single attached NICs for single attached hosts, active/standby NIC teaming for dual-homed servers, and vPC for dual-homed servers. This chapter focuses on the dual-homed server options because FC requires two independent paths to storage: Fabric A and Fabric B.

Active/standby connections refers to servers that are dual-homed to an Ethernet LAN but only actively forwarding out one link. The second link is used as a backup in case of a failure, but it does not actively forward traffic unless a failure occurs. vPC is a technology introduced by Cisco Nexus products that allows a dual-homed server to actively forward out both Ethernet links simultaneously. The benefits of vPC is that it gives servers access to twice as much bandwidth as in an active/standby configuration and also has the ability to converge faster than Spanning Tree in the event of a failure.

Based on the Ethernet high-availability requirement, LAN admins may choose to attach servers using active/standby connections or vPC connections. Regardless of the method used to dual-home a server, FCoE can coexist with both of these topologies. Although Ethernet traffic is dual-homed between an FEX and a switch pair in an enhanced vPC topology, FCoE traffic must be single-homed to maintain SAN isolation. Therefore, although enhanced vPC supports FCoE, a single-homed FEX topology can be a better choice when SAN isolation and high FCoE bandwidth are required. Option A in Figure 23-61 illustrates a single-homed FEX topology, and option B illustrates dual-homed FEX topology.

The single-homed FEX topology is well suited for servers with multiple NICs that support 802.3ad port channel. The dual-homed FEX topology is ideal for servers with one NIC, because the failure of one Cisco Nexus 5000 Series device does not bring down the FEX and does not cut the single NIC server out of the network. The dual-homed FEX topology can also be deployed for servers that have multiple NICs but do not support 802.3ad. Without an enhanced vPC server, you cannot connect port channels to FEXs when the FEXs are dual-homed to both Cisco Nexus 5000 Series devices.

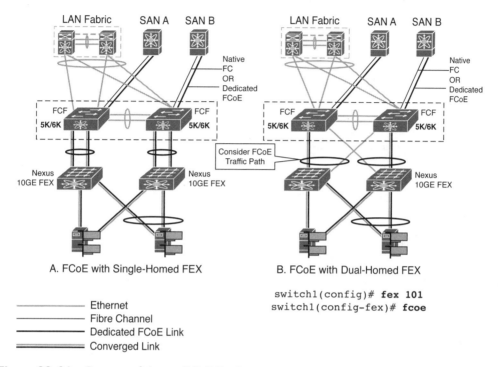

Figure 23-61 *Converged Access FCoE Designs*

Consider the following disadvantages of enhanced vPC for a single-homed topology:

- A typical SAN network maintains two fabrics—SAN A and SAN B—with traffic isolated between the two. In an enhanced vPC topology, each switch must be paired (single-homed) with an FEX to ensure that FCoE traffic from one FEX is sent to only one switch, whereas Ethernet traffic is dual-homed between each FEX and both switches. Because FCoE traffic from the FEX flows to only one switch while Ethernet traffic flows to both, the traffic load for the FEX uplinks is not evenly balanced.

- In an FEX with eight uplink ports, Ethernet traffic can use all eight ports, while the single-homed FCoE traffic is limited by this topology to using only four of those ports, restricting the maximum bandwidth available for FCoE. As a further restriction, the default QoS template for the shared link allocates only half the link bandwidth to FCoE traffic, with the other half allocated to Ethernet traffic.

- In an enhanced vPC topology with FCoE, the host vPC is limited to two ports, one to each FEX.

23

This example shows how to pair each FEX to a switch for FCoE traffic in dual-homed FEX:

```
nexus5000 sanA# configure terminal
nexus5000-sanA(config) # fex 101
nexus5000-sanA(config-fex) # fcoe
nexus5000-sanA(config-fex) # interface vfc 1
nexus5000-sanA(config-if) # bind interface ethernet 101/1/1
nexus5000-sanA(config-if) # no shutdown
nexus5000-sanA(config-if) # end

nexus5000-sanB# configure terminal
nexus5000-sanB(config) # fex 102
nexus5000-sanB(config-fex) # fcoe
nexus5000-sanB(config-fex) # interface vfc 1
nexus5000-sanB(config-if) # bind interface ethernet 102/1/1
nexus5000-sanB(config-if) # no shutdown
nexus5000-sanB(config-if) # end

nexus5500-sanA# configure terminal
nexus5500-sanA(config) # fex 101
nexus5500-sanA(config-fex) # fcoe
nexus5500-sanA(config-fex) # interface vfc 1
nexus5500-sanA(config-if) # bind interface ethernet 101/1/1
nexus5500-sanA(config-if) # no shutdown
nexus5500-sanA(config-if) # end

nexus5500-sanB# configure terminal
nexus5500-sanB(config) # fex 102
nexus5500-sanB(config-fex) # fcoe
nexus5500-sanB(config-fex) # interface vfc 1
nexus5500-sanB(config-if) # bind interface ethernet 102/1/1
nexus5500-sanB(config-if) # no shutdown
nexus5500-sanB(config-if) # end
```

Multihop FCoE

Multihop FCoE is achieved with the support of a virtual E ports (VE ports) connection to two FCFs. Like E_Ports in native FC, VE ports are used to expand the FCoE fabric. There are two options for connecting Nexus Series switches with the use of VE ports: using single links or over a port channel.

In order to maintain fabric isolation, the Cisco Nexus Series FCF switches in each fabric should be configured to have the same FC-MAP value. The FC-MAP values should be different between Fabric A and Fabric B. Cisco's multihop FCoE solution allows the use of a Cisco Nexus 7000 Series switch as a converged Ethernet aggregation and SAN core switch. This switch can then be connected to a Cisco MDS 9500 Series switch in a three-tier edge-core-edge SAN design. Use of dedicated links to connect the access layer to the aggregation layer in this scenario provides a separation for the storage traffic and isolates each fabric, which is a requirement for many SAN operators. Figure 23-62 illustrates a multihop FCoE design.

Multihop FCoE Design

- Leverage FC SAN to Ethernet DCB switches in Aggregation layer with Dedicated links.
- Maintain the A—B SAN Topology with Storage VDC and Dedicated links.
- Nexus 5K or 6K as Consolidated Access layer.
- Dedicated FCoE Ports between:
  - Access and Aggregation
  - FC SAN and Aggregation
- Zoning controlled by SAN A/B Core Switches.

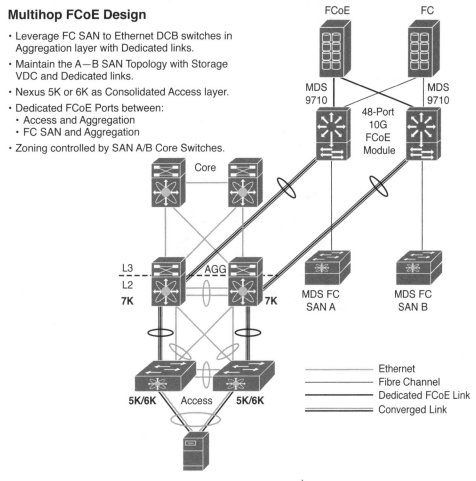

Figure 23-62 *Multihop FCoE Design*

The port density offered by the Cisco Nexus 7000 Series switches also enables the LAN and SAN designers to directly attach FCoE storage arrays to Cisco Nexus 7000 Series aggregation switches in their networks. SAN separation beyond the access layer still is achieved using dedicated FCoE links. The capability of the network designer to directly lay the FCoE network over the existing LAN increases the number of devices that can be enabled to access FCoE storage while maintaining the SAN isolation that may be required, through the use of virtual device contexts (VDCs) and dedicated Inter-Switch Links (ISLs). Directly attaching storage to aggregation switches creates a core-edge SAN topology and allows storage operators to take advantage of director-class services available on these core switches such as high availability, security, and port scalability. Figure 23-63 illustrates converged versus dedicated ISLs. The storage VDC can have two types of interfaces; dedicated and shared. Dedicated interfaces are FCoE only and are not used for host connectivity. Usually used for FCoE-only storage controllers and host CNAs dedicated to FCoE or FCoE only trunks to distribution switches (Nexus 5000 Series switches). Shared interfaces are typically used to connect hosts. The interface is shared between two VDCs, one being the storage VDC and the other being a data VDC. The storage VDC will handle the FCoE traffic and the data VDC will handle all the rest of the traffic. Prerequisite of shared interfaces is that they are in trunk mode and spanning-tree allows it to come up quickly.

Converged Versus Dedicated ISLs

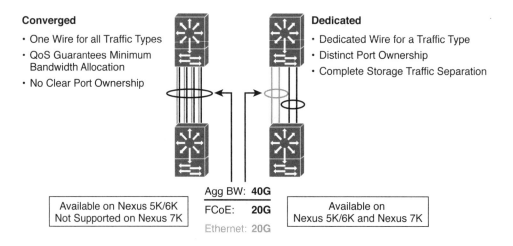

Figure 23-63   *Converged versus Dedicated ISLs*

Below, Nexus 7000 Series switch configuration covers steps for the shared interfaces in the storage VDC.

```
!Enable associated features and interface to share:
switch# configure terminal
switch(config)# feature lldp
switch(config)# feature lacp
switch(config)# system qos
switch(config-sys-qos)# service-policy type network-qos default-nq-7e-policy

switch(config-sys-qos)# interface ethernet 2/1
switch(config-if)# switchport mode trunk
switch(config-if)#  spanning-tree port type edge trunk
switch(config-if)# no shutdown
```

```
!Create Storage VDC and allocate resources:
switch(config-if)# install feature-set fcoe
switch(config)# vdc fcoe_vdc type storage
switch(config-if)# allocate fcoe-vlan-range 10-20 from vdc switch
switch(config-vdc)# allocate shared interface ethernet 2/1

!Switch to storage VDC and bring up the shared interface:
switch(config-vdc)# switchto vdc fcoe_vdc
switch-fcoe_vdc# configure terminal
switch-fcoe_vdc(config)# feature lldp
switch-fcoe_vdc(config)# interface ethernet 2/1
switch-fcoe_vdc(config-if)# no shutdown
```

FCoE NPV

Fiber Channel over Ethernet (FCoE) N-port Virtualization (NPV) is an enhanced form of FCoE Initialization Protocol (FIP) snooping that provides a secure method to connect FCoE-capable hosts to an FCoE-capable FCoE Forwarder (FCF) device.

Key Topic

FCoE NPV enables the following:

- The switch to act as an N-port Virtualizer (NPV) connected to the core switch (FCF).
- The core switch (FCF) to view the NPV switch as another host.
- The multiple hosts connected to the NPV switch are presented as virtualized N-ports.

FCoE NPV provides the following:

- FCoE NPV provides the advantages of NPV-to-FCoE deployments (such as preventing domain ID sprawl and reducing Fiber Channel Forwarder (FCF) table size).
- FCoE NPV provides a secure connect between FCoE hosts and the FCoE FCF.
- FCoE NPV does not have the management and troubleshooting issues that are inherent to managing hosts remotely at the FCF.
- FCoE NPV implements FIP snooping as an extension to the NPV function while retaining the traffic-engineering, VSAN-management, administration, and troubleshooting aspects of NPV.
- FCoE server connectivity with both FCoE NPV and FC NPV edge switches provides a smoother transition of servers from legacy FC networks to FCoE networks. Figure 23-64 illustrates the FCoE NPV topology.

23

FCoE - NPV

- **FCoE Pass—through device**
  - All FCoE Switching is performed at the upstream FCF.
  - Addressing is pass out by the upstream FCF.
- **Proxy's FIP functions between a CNA and an FCF**
  - FCoE VLAN configuration and assignment.
  - FCF Assignment.
- **FCoE-NPV load balance logins from the CNAs evenly across the available FCF uplink ports.**
  - FCoE-NPV will take VSAN into account when mapping or 'pinning' logins from a CNA to an FCF uplink.
- **Similar to NPV in a native Fibre Channel network.**

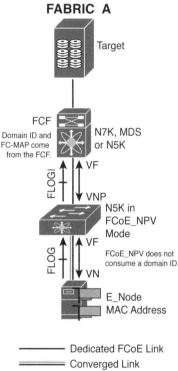

Figure 23-64 *FCoE NPV Topology*

Connectivity from an FCoE NPV bridge to the FCF is supported only over point-to-point links. These links can be individual Ethernet interfaces or port channel interfaces. For each FCF connected to an Ethernet interface, a vFC interface must be created and bound to it. These vFC interfaces must be configured as VNP ports. On the VNP port, the FCoE NPV bridge emulates an FCoE-capable host with multiple ENodes, each with a unique ENode MAC address. By default, the VNP port is enabled in trunk mode.

Multiple VSANs can be configured on the VNP port. The FCoE VLANs that correspond to the VNP port VSANs must be configured on the bound Ethernet interface. FCoE NPV feature can be enabled using the **feature fcoe-npv** command (shown in Figure 23-65).

Figure 23-65 illustrates FCoE NPV configuration and topology.

Figure 23-66 illustrates all configuration steps for multihop FCoE NPV topology between Nexus 7000 and Nexus 5000 Series switches.

FCoE - NPV Configuration Details

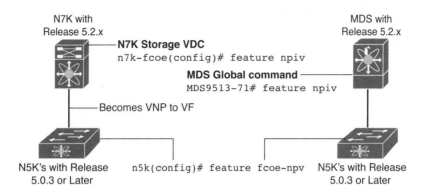

Figure 23-65 *FCoE-NPV Feature*

FCoE Multihop Configuration Example

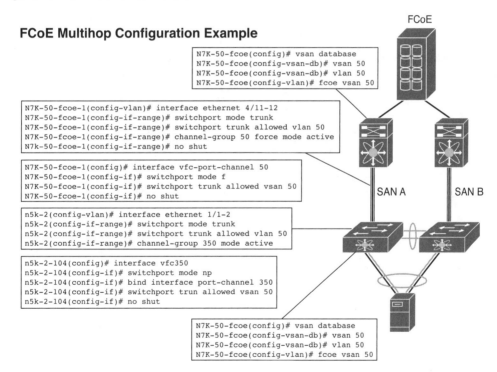

Figure 23-66 *FCoE Multihop Configuration Example*

Dynamic FCoE Using FabricPath

The FabricPath architecture provides an inherent multipath capability with redundancy to handle node failures. Fabric-level redundancy is provided through a double fabric model (SAN A and B). The separation of the two SANs is logically implemented as two different VSANs that map to two different VLANs (VLAN A and B). Fibre channel traffic in SAN

A becomes the FCoE traffic in VLAN A, the Fiber Channel traffic in SAN B becomes the FCoE traffic in VLAN B, and the LAN traffic is carried on one or more additional VLANs over the converged Ethernet infrastructure. In this logical environment, the VSAN A/B configuration protects against fabric-wide control plane failures.

The traditional method of hosts that connect to two separate SANs is still supported with the FCoE over FabricPath architecture. The host is connected to two different leaf nodes that host a disjointed set of VSANs. Beyond these leaf nodes, the fabric is converged on the same infrastructure, but the host continues to see two SAN fabrics.

In a dynamic FCoE environment, the topology, shown in Figure 23-67, is developed using the leaves as FCoE Forwarder (FCF) switches that are forwarded through transparent spines.

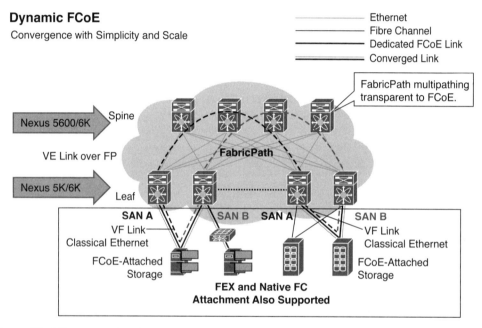

Figure 23-67 *Dynamic FCoE*

FCoE hosts and FCoE storage devices are connected to a FabricPath topology through the leaf switches. In this configuration, only the leaf switches perform FCoE forwarding (only the leaf switches behave as FCFs); the spine switches just forward MAC-in-MAC encapsulated Ethernet frames that are based on the outer destination MAC address.

Only the FCFs that are implemented by the leaf switches are part of this overlay topology. This topology is seen by Fabric Shortest Path First (FSPF), for each FCoE VLAN. FSPF computes over which virtual link to forward an FCoE frame based on its domain ID (D_ID). A virtual link is uniquely identified by the pair of MAC addresses associated with the two VE_Ports logically connected by it. Identifying the virtual link is equivalent to identifying which MAC addresses to use for the FCoE encapsulation on the transport network.

For dynamic FCoE, SAN A/B separation is realized in a logical manner across the backbone. As shown in Figure 23-67, physical SAN A/B separation is maintained from the FCF leafs to the end devices. Beyond the leafs, FCoE traffic for SANs A and B are carried by FabricPath Equal Cost Multipathing (ECMP) links across all spines, maintaining logical SAN A/B separation. The physical connectivity for the topology follows typical leaf/spine CLOS architectural best practices. Logically, SAN A and SAN B are isolated at the top-of-rack (ToR) switches physically. Once the traffic enters the FabricPath network, the storage traffic is logically separated across the network, where it is physically separated once more to the storage device edge.

Dynamic FCoE gains the additional redundancy that is inherent in the FabricPath network by using the increased spine connectivity. A larger network with a large number of spines means increased reliability and stability for the storage network. This is achieved while retaining the best practices requirements for storage environments. FabricPath provides redundant paths between a source and destination. Because FCoE traffic traverses the FabricPath network with one or more FCoE and non-FCoE nodes (spines, leafs), you must ensure in-order delivery through proper port channel hashing across the redundant paths. All FabricPath nodes have port channel hashing enabled that includes the exchange ID. Traffic from a single flow always traverses through only one set of nodes through the network to maintain in-order delivery.

Best Practices

Following are a few best practices that should be considered during the FCoE fabric design using Cisco Nexus Series switches:

- Configure a unique dedicated VLAN at every converged access switch to carry traffic for each Cisco virtual SAN (VSAN) in the SAN (for example, VLAN 1002 for VSAN 1, VLAN 1003 for VSAN 2, and so on).

- Configure the Unified Fabric links as trunk ports. Do not configure the FCoE VLAN as a native VLAN.

- Configure all FCoE VLANs as members of the Unified Fabric links to allow extensions for VF_Port trunking and VSAN management for the virtual Fibre Channel interfaces.

- Configure the Unified Fabric links as Spanning Tree edge ports.

- Do not configure the FCoE VLANs as members of Ethernet links that are not designated to carry FCoE traffic because you want to ensure that the scope of the shielded twisted pair (STP) for the FCoE VLANs is limited to Unified Fabric links only.

- If the converged access switches (in the same SAN fabric or in another) need to be connected to each other over Ethernet links for a LAN alternate path, then such links must explicitly be configured to exclude all FCoE VLANs from membership. This action helps ensure that the scope of the STP for the FCoE VLANs is limited to Unified Fabric links only.

- Use separate FCoE VLANs for FCoE in SAN A and SAN B.

- Make sure the QoS policies for the no-drop class are the same throughout the fabric.

23

Reference List

"Common RAID Disk Drive Format (DDF) Standard," SNIA.org, http://www.snia.org/tech_activities/standards/curr_standards/ddf/.

SNIA Dictionary, http://www.snia.org/education/dictionary.

SNIA Storage Virtualization Tutorial I and II, http://www.snia.org/education/storage_networking_primer/stor_virt.

Fred G. Moore, *Storage Virtualization for IT Flexibility*, Sun Microsystems, TechTarget 2006.

"N-Port Virtualization in the Data Center," http://www.cisco.com/c/en/us/products/collateral/storage-networking/mds-9000-nx-os-software-release-4-1/white_paper_c11-459263.html.

Gustavo A. A. Santana, *Data Center Virtualization Fundamentals*, Indianapolis: Cisco Press, 2013.

Marc Farley, *Storage Networking Fundamentals*, Indianapolis: Cisco Press, 2004.

Tom Clark. *Storage Virtualization—Technologies for Simplifying Data Storage and Management*, Indianapolis: Addison-Wesley Professional, 2005.

James Long, *Storage Networking Protocol Fundamentals*, *Volume 1 and 2*, Indianapolis: Cisco Press, 2006.

Cisco MDS 9700 Series Hardware Installation Guide, http://www.cisco.com/c/en/us/td/docs/switches/datacenter/mds9000/hw/9700/mds_9700_hig/overview.html.

Cisco MDS Install and Upgrade Guides, http://www.cisco.com/c/en/us/support/storage-networking/mds-9000-series-multilayer-switches/products-installation-guides-list.html.

Cisco MDS 9250i Multiservice Fabric Switch Hardware Installation Guide, http://www.cisco.com/en/US/docs/switches/datacenter/mds9000/hw/9250i/installation/guide/connect.html.

Cisco MDS 9148s Multilayer Switch Hardware Installation Guide, http://www.cisco.com/c/en/us/td/docs/switches/datacenter/mds9000/hw/9148S/install/guide/9148S_hig/connect.html.

Cisco MDS NX-OS Install and Upgrade Guides, http://www.cisco.com/c/en/us/support/storage-networking/mds-9000-nx-os-san-os-software/products-installation-guides-list.html.

Cisco MDS 9000 NX-OS Software Upgrade and Downgrade Guide, http://www.cisco.com/c/en/us/td/docs/switches/datacenter/mds9000/sw/6_2/upgrade/guides/nx-os/upgrade.html#pgfId-419386.

Cisco MDS 9000 NX-OS and SAN OS Software Configuration Guides, http://www.cisco.com/c/en/us/support/storage-networking/mds-9000-nx-os-san-os-software/products-installation-and-configuration-guides-list.html.

Cisco NX-OS FCoE Configuration Guide for Nexus 7000 Series and MDS 9000 Series, http://www.cisco.com/c/en/us/td/docs/switches/datacenter/mds9000/sw/7_3/configuration/fcoe/cisco_mds9000_fcoe_config_guide_7_x/configuring_fcoe.html.

Cisco Nexus 9000 Series NX-OS FCoE Configuration Guide, http://www.cisco.com/c/en/us/td/docs/switches/datacenter/nexus9000/sw/7-x/FCoE/configuration/guide/b_Cisco_Nexus_9000_Series_NX-OS_FCoE_Configuration_Guide_7x/b_Cisco_Nexus_9000_Series_NX-OS_FCoE_Configuration_Guide_7x_preface_00.html.

"Slow-Drain Device Detection, Troubleshooting, and Automatic Recovery," http://www.cisco.com/c/dam/en/us/products/collateral/storage-networking/mds-9700-series-multilayer-directors/whitepaper-c11-737315.pdf.

"Cisco Unified Fabric: Enable the Data Center Network," http://www.cisco.com/c/en/us/solutions/collateral/data-center-virtualization/unified-fabric/white_paper_c11-704054.html.

"IEEE Data Center Bridging," http://www.cisco.com/en/US/netsol/ns783/index.html.

"Priority Flow Control IEEE 802.1Qbb," http://www.ieee802.org/1/pages/802.1Qbb.html.

"Enhanced Transmission Selection IEEE 802.1Qaz," http://www.ieee802.org/1/pages/802.1Qaz.html.

"Congestion Notification IEEE 802.1Qau," http://www.ieee802.org/1/pages/802.1Qau.html.

"DCBX," http://www.ieee802.org/1/files/public/docs2008/az-wadekar-dcbcxp-overview-rev0.2.pdf.

23

Exam Preparation Tasks

Review All Key Topics

Review the most important topics in the chapter, noted with the key topics icon in the outer margin of the page. Table 23-18 lists a reference for these key topics and the page numbers on which each is found.

Table 23-18 Key Topics for Chapter 23

Key Topic Element	Description	Page
Figure 23-1	Storage Virtualization Mapping Heterogeneous Physical Storage to Virtual Storage	636
Figure 23-2	The SNIA Storage Virtualization Taxonomy Separates the Objects of Virtualization from Location and Means of Execution	637
Figure 23-3	Possible Alternatives on Where the Storage Virtualization May Occur	638
Table 23-2	Overview of Standard RAID Levels	640
Figure 23-4	RAID 0 Setup	640
Figure 23-5	RAID 1 Setup	641
Figure 23-6	RAID 2 Setup	641
Figure 23-7	RAID 3 Setup	642
Figure 23-8	RAID 4 Setup	642
Figure 23-9	RAID 5 Setup	643
Figure 23-10	RAID 6 Setup	643
Figure 23-11	RAID 1+0 Setup	644
Figure 23-12	RAID 0+1 Setup	644
List	Virtualizing Logical Unit Numbers (LUNs)	645
Figure 23-13	LUN Masking, LUN Mapping, and LUN Zoning on a Storage Area Network (SAN)	646
Section	Virtualizing Storage Area Networks	647
Figure 23-14	Independent Physical SAN Islands Virtualized onto a Common SAN Infrastructure	648
Figure 23-15	VSAN Enhanced Inter-Switch Link (EISL) Header	648
Section	N Port ID Virtualization (NPIV)	649
Figure 23-16	NPIV - Control and Monitor VMs in the SAN	649

23

Complete Tables and Lists from Memory

Print a copy of Appendix C, "Memory Tables," or at least the section for this chapter, and complete the tables and lists from memory. Appendix D, "Memory Tables Answer Key," includes completed tables and lists to check your work.

Define Key Terms

Define the following key terms from this chapter and check your answers in the Glossary:

virtual storage area network (VSAN), zoning, F port channel trunk, host bus adapter (HBA), Exchange Peer Parameter (EPP), Exchange Virtual Fabrics Protocol (EVFP), Power On Auto Provisioning (POAP), switch World Wide Name (sWWN), port World Wide Name (pWWN) slow drain, basic input/output system (BIOS), Port Trunking Protocol (PTP), Redundant Array of Inexpensive Disks (RAID), virtual LUN (vLUN), thin provisioning, Storage Networking Industry Association (SNIA), software-defined storage (SDS), metadata, in-band, out-of-band, virtual tape library (VTL), disk-to-disk-to-tape (D2D2T), N-Port virtualizer (NPV), N-Port ID virtualization (NPIV), virtual file system (VFS), asynchronous and synchronous mirroring, host-based virtualization, network-based virtualization, array-based virtualization, FCoE-NPV, FCoE-NPIV, dynamic FCoE, Inter-Switch Links (ISLs), Data Center Bridging, Priority-based Flow Control (PFC), IEEE 802.1Qbb, IEEE 802.1Qaz, Quantized Congestion Notification (QCN), IEEE 802.1Qau, Data Center Bridging Exchange (DCBX), IEEE 802.1AB, Link Layer Discovery Protocol (LLDP), type-length-value (TLV), Fibre Channel over Ethernet (FCoE), virtual network interface card (vNIC), converged network adapter (CNA), multihop FCoE, World Wide Node Name (WWNN)

23

Part V Review

Keep track of your part review progress with the checklist shown in Table P5-1. Details on each task follow the table.

Table P5-1 Part V Review Checklist

Activity	First Date Completed	Second Date Completed
Repeat All "Do I Know This Already?" Questions		
Answer "Part Review" questions		
Review Key Topics		

Repeat All "Do I Know This Already?" Questions: For this task, answer the "Do I Know This Already?" questions again for the chapters in this part of the book, using the PCPT software. Refer to the section in the Introduction titled "How to View Only 'Do I Know This Already?' Questions by Part" for help with how to make the PCPT software show you "Do I Know This Already?" questions for this part only.

Answer "Part Review" Questions: For this task, answer the "Part Review" questions for this part of the book, using the PCPT software. Refer to the section in the Introduction titled "How to View Only Part Review Questions by Part" for help with how to make the PCPT software show you "Part Review" questions for this part only.

Review Key Topics: Browse back through the chapters and look for the Key Topic icons. If you do not remember some details, take the time to reread those topics.

Part VI

Final Preparation

Final Review

Congratulations! You made it through the book, and now it's time to finish getting ready for the exam. This chapter helps you get ready to take and pass the exam in two ways.

This chapter begins by talking about the exam itself. You know the content and topics. Now you need to think about what happens during the exam and what you need to do in these last few weeks before taking it. At this point, everything you do should be focused on getting yourself ready to pass the exam so that you can finish up this hefty task.

The second section of this chapter gives you some exam review tasks as your final preparation for your DCICN exam.

Advice About the Exam Event

Now that you have finished the bulk of this book, you could just register for your Cisco DCICN exam, show up, and take the exam. However, if you spend a little time thinking about the exam event itself, learning more about the user interface of the real Cisco exams, and the environment at the Vue testing centers, you will be better prepared, particularly if this is your first Cisco exam. This first of two major sections in this chapter gives some advice about the Cisco exams and the exam event itself.

Learn the Question Types Using the Cisco Certification Exam Tutorial

In the weeks leading up to your exam, you should think more about the different types of exam questions and have a plan for how to approach those questions. One of the best ways to learn about the exam questions is to use the Cisco Certification Exam Tutorial.

To find the Cisco Certification Exam Tutorial, go to www.cisco.com and search for "exam tutorial." The tutorial sits inside a web page with a Flash presentation of the exam user interface. The tutorial even lets you take control as if you were taking the exam. When using the tutorial, make sure that you take control and try the following:

■ Try to click **Next** on the multiple-choice, single-answer question without clicking an answer, and see that the testing software tells you that you have too few answers.

■ On the multiple-choice, multiple-answer question, select too few answers and click **Next** to again see how the user interface responds.

■ In the drag-and-drop question, drag the answers to the obvious answer locations, but then drag them back to the original location. (You might do this on the real exam if you change your mind when answering the question.)

- On the simulation (sim) question, first just make sure that you can get to the command-line interface (CLI) on one of the routers. To do so, you have to click the PC icon for a PC connected to the router console; the console cable appears as a dashed line, and network cables are solid lines. (Note that the exam tutorial uses the IOS CLI, not NX-OS, but it is similar enough to get the idea.)

- Still on the sim question, make sure you look at the scroll areas at the top, at the side, and in the terminal emulator window.

- Still on the sim question, make sure you can toggle between the topology window and the terminal emulator window by clicking **Show Topology** and **Hide Topology**.

- On the testlet question, answer one multiple-choice question, move to the second and answer it, and then move back to the first question, confirming that inside a testlet you can move around between questions.

- Again on the testlet question, click the **Next** button to see the pop-up window that Cisco uses as a prompt to ask whether you want to move on. Testlets might actually allow you to give too few answers and still move on. After you click to move past the testlet, you cannot go back to change your answer for any of these questions.

Think About Your Time Budget Versus Numbers of Questions

On exam day, you need to keep an eye on your speed. Going too slowly hurts you because you might not have time to answer all the questions. Going too fast can hurt as well if your fast speed is because you are rushing and not taking the time to fully understand the questions. So, you need to be able to somehow know whether you are moving quickly enough to answer all the questions, while not rushing.

The exam user interface shows some useful time information—namely, a countdown timer and question counter. The question counter shows a question number for the question you are answering, and it shows the total number of questions on your exam.

Unfortunately, treating each question equally does not give you an accurate time estimate. For example, if your exam allows 90 minutes, and your exam has 45 questions, you would have 2 minutes per question. After answering 20 questions, if you had taken 40 minutes, you would be right on time. However, several factors make that kind of estimate difficult.

First, Cisco does not tell you beforehand the exact number of questions for each exam. For example, Cisco.com (at the time of this writing) listed DCICN as a 90-minute exam with 65 to 75 questions. So, you only know a range of questions. But you do not know how many questions are on your exam until it begins, when you go through the screens that lead up to the point where you click **Start Exam**.

Next, some questions (call them *time burners*) clearly take a lot more time to answer:

   Normal-time questions: Multiple-choice and drag-and-drop, approximately 1 minute each

   Time burners: Sims, simlets, and testlets, approximately 6 to 8 minutes each

Finally, the exam software counts each testlet and simlet question as one question in the question counter. For example, if a testlet question has four embedded multiple-choice questions, in the exam software's question counter that counts as one question.

NOTE While Cisco does not explain why you might get 65 questions and someone else taking the same exam might get 75 questions, it seems reasonable to think that the person with 65 questions might have a few more of the time burners, making the two exams equivalent.

You need a plan for how you will check your time—a plan that does not distract you from the exam. It might be worth taking a bit of a guess, to keep things simple, like this:

60 questions, 90 minutes, is exactly 1:30 per question. Then just guess a little based on how many time-burner questions you have seen so far.

No matter how you plan to check your time, think about it before exam day. You can even use the method listed under the next heading.

A Suggested Time-Check Method

You can use the following math to do your time check in a way that weights the time based on those time-burner questions. However, you do not have to use this method. The math uses only addition of whole numbers to keep it simple. It gives you a pretty close time estimate, in our opinion.

The concept is simple. Just do a simple calculation that estimates the time you should have used so far. Basically, this process gives you 1 minute per normal question and 7 minutes per time burner. Here's the math:

Number of Questions Answered So Far + 7 Per Time Burner

Then, you check the timer to figure out how much time you have spent:

■ **You have used exactly that much time, or a little more:** Your timing is perfect.

■ **You have used less time:** You are ahead of schedule.

■ **You have used noticeably more time:** You are behind schedule.

For example, if you have already finished 17 questions, two of which were time burners, then your time estimate is 17 + 7 + 7 = 31 minutes. If your actual time is also 31 minutes, or maybe 32 or 33 minutes, you are right on schedule. If you have spent less than 31 minutes, you are ahead of schedule.

So, the math is pretty easy: the number of questions answered, plus 7 per time burner, is the guesstimate of how long you should have taken so far if you are right on time.

NOTE This math is an estimate, with no guarantees that it will be an accurate predictor on every exam.

Miscellaneous Pre-Exam Suggestions

Here are just a few more suggestions for things to think about before your exam day arrives:

■ Get some earplugs. Testing centers often have some, but if you do not want to chance it, come prepared. The testing center is usually a room inside the space of a company that does something else as well, oftentimes a training center. So, there are people talking in nearby rooms and others office noises. Earplugs can help. (Headphones, as electronic devices, are not allowed.)

- Some people like to spend the first minute of the exam writing down some notes for reference. For example, maybe you want to write down the table of magic numbers for finding IPv4 subnet IDs. If you plan to do that, practice making those notes. Before each practice exam, transcribe those lists, just like you expect to do at the real exam.

- Plan your travel to the testing center with enough time so that you will not be rushing to make it just in time.

- If you tend to be nervous before exams, practice your favorite relaxation techniques for a few minutes before each practice exam, just to be ready to use them.

Exam-Day Advice

We hope the exam goes well for you. Certainly, the better prepared you are, the better chances you have on the exam. These small tips can help you do your best on exam day:

- Rest the night before the exam, rather than staying up late to study. Clarity of thought is more important than one extra fact, especially because the exam requires so much analysis and thinking rather than just remembering facts.

- If you did not bring earplugs, ask the testing center for some, even if you cannot imagine you would use them. You never know whether it might help.

- You can bring personal effects into the building and testing company's space, but not into the actual room in which you take the exam. So, take as little extra stuff with you as possible. If you have a safe place to leave briefcases, purses, electronics, and so on, leave them there. However, the testing center should have a place to store your things as well. Simply put, the less you bring, the less you have to worry about storing. (For example, I have even been asked to remove my analog wristwatch on more than one occasion.)

- The exam center will give you a laminated sheet and pen for taking notes. (Test center personnel usually do not let you bring paper and pen into the room, even if supplied by the testing center.)

- Leave for the testing center with extra time so that you do not have to rush.

- Plan on finding a restroom before going into the testing center. If you cannot find one, you can use one in the testing center, of course, and test personnel will direct you and give you time before your exam starts.

- Do not consume a 64-ounce drink on the trip to the testing center. After the exam starts, the exam timer will not stop while you go to the restroom.

- On exam day, use any relaxation techniques you have practiced to help get your mind focused while you wait for the exam.

Exam Review

This exam review completes the Study Plan materials as suggested by this book. At this point, you have read the other chapters of the book, and you have done the chapter review exam preparation tasks and part review tasks. Now you need to do the final study and review activities before taking the exam, as detailed in this section.

This section suggests some new activities and repeats some old ones. However, whether new or old, the activities all focus on filling in your knowledge gaps, finishing off your skills, and completing the study process. Although repeating some tasks you did at chapter review and part review can help, you need to be ready to take an exam, so this exam review asks you to spend a lot of time answering exam questions.

The exam review walks you through suggestions for several types of tasks and gives you some tracking tables for each activity. The main categories are as follows:

- Practicing for speed
- Taking practice exams
- Finding what you do not know well yet (knowledge gaps)
- Configuring and verifying functions from the command-line interface (CLI)
- Repeating the chapter and part review tasks

Practice Subnetting and Other Math-Related Skills

Like it or not, some of the questions on the DCICN exam require you to do some math. To pass, you have to be good at the math. You also need to know when to use each process.

The Cisco exams also have a timer. Some of the math crops up often enough so that if you go slow with the math, or if you have to write down all the details of how you compute the answers, you might well run out of time to answer all the questions. (The two biggest reasons we hear as to why people do not finish on time are slow speed with the math-related work and slow speed when doing simulator questions using the CLI.)

However, look at these math processes and the time crunch as a positive instead of a negative. Right now, before the exam, you know about the challenge. You know that if you keep practicing subnetting and other math, you will keep getting faster and better. As exam day approaches, if you have spare minutes, try more practice with anything to do with subnetting in particular. Look at it as a way to prepare now so that you do not have to worry about time pressure so much on the day of the exam.

Table 24-1 lists the topics in this chapter that require both math and speed. Table 24-2 lists items for which the math or process is important, but speed is probably less important. By this point in your study, you should already be confident at finding the right answer to these kinds of problems. Now is the time to perfect your skills at getting the right answers, plus getting faster so that you reduce your time pressure on the exams.

24

NOTE   The time goals in the table are goals chosen by the authors to give you an idea of a good time. If you happen to be a little slower on a few tasks, that does not mean you cannot do well on the test. But if you take several times as much time for almost every task, know that the math-related work can cause you some time-related problems.

Table 24-1   DCICN Math-Related Activities That Benefit from Speed Practice

Chapter	Activity	Book's Excellent Speed Goal (Seconds)	Self-Check: Date/Time	Self-Check: Date/Time
13	From a unicast IPv4 address, find key facts about its classful network.	10		
14	From one mask in any format, convert to the other two mask formats.	10		
14	Given an IPv4 address and mask, find the number of network, subnet, and host bits, plus the number of hosts/subnet and number of subnets.	15		
15	Given an IPv4 address and mask, find the resident subnet, subnet broadcast address, and range of usable addresses.	30		

Table 24-2   DCICN Math-Related Activities That Can Be Less Time Sensitive

Chapter	Activity	Self-Check: Date/Time	Self-Check: Date/Time
15	Find the best abbreviation for one IPv6 address.		
15	Find the IPv6 address of one router interface when using EUI-64.		
21	Build an ACL command to match a subnet's addresses.		
21	List the addresses matched by one existing ACL command.		

To practice the math listed in both Tables 24-1 and 24-2, look at the end of the respective chapters for some suggestions. For example, for many subnetting problems, you can make up your own problems and check your work with any subnet calculator.

Take Practice Exams

One day soon, you need to pass a real Cisco exam at a Vue testing center. So, it's time to practice the real event as much as possible.

A practice exam using the Pearson IT Certification Practice Test (PCPT) exam software lets you experience many of the same issues as when taking a real Cisco exam. The software gives you a number of questions, with a countdown timer shown in the window. After you answer a question, you cannot go back to it. (Yes, that's true on Cisco exams.) If you run out of time, the questions you did not answer count as incorrect.

The process of taking the timed practice exams helps you prepare in three key ways:

- To practice the exam event itself, including time pressure, the need to read carefully, and the need to concentrate for long periods

- To build your analysis and critical thinking skills when examining the network scenario built in to many questions

- To discover the gaps in your networking knowledge so that you can study those topics before the real exam

As much as possible, treat the practice exam events as if you were taking the real Cisco exam at a Vue testing center. The following list gives some advice on how to make your practice exam more meaningful, rather than as just one more thing to do before exam day rolls around:

- Set aside 2 hours for taking the 90-minute timed practice exam.

- Make a list of what you expect to do for the 10 minutes before the real exam event. Then visualize yourself doing those things. Before taking each practice exam, practice those final 10 minutes before your exam timer starts. (The earlier section "Exam-Day Advice" lists some suggestions about what to do in those last 10 minutes.)

- You cannot bring anything with you into the Vue exam room, so remove all notes and help materials from your work area before taking a practice exam. You can use blank paper, a pen, and your brain only. Do not use calculators, notes, web browsers, or any other app on your computer.

- Real life can get in the way, but if at all possible, ask anyone around you to leave you alone for the time you will practice. If you must do your practice exam in a distracting environment, wear headphones or earplugs to reduce distractions.

- Do not guess, hoping to improve your score. Answer only when you have confidence in the answer. Then, if you get the question wrong, you can go back and think more about the question in a later study session.

Practicing Taking the DCICN Exam

To take a DCICN practice exam, you need to select one or both of the DCICN exams from PCPT. If you followed the study plan in this book, you will not have seen any of the questions in these two exam databases before now. After you select one of these two exams, you simply need to choose the **Practice Exam** option in the upper right and start the exam.

You should plan to take between one and three DCICT practice exams with these exam databases. Even people who are already well prepared should do at least one practice exam, just to experience the time pressure and the need for prolonged concentration. For those who want more practice exams, these two exam databases have enough questions for more than two exams. As a result, if you take a fourth practice exam with these exam databases, you will have seen almost all the questions before, making the practice exam a little too easy. If you are interested in purchasing more practice exams, check out the *Cisco Data Center (DCICN) 200-150 Official Cert Guide Premium Edition eBook and Practice Test* product at www.ciscopress.com/title/9781587205965 and be sure to use the 70% off coupon included in the cardboard sleeve in the back of this book.

24

Table 24-3 gives you a checklist to record your different practice exam events. Recording both the date and the score is helpful for some other work you will do, so note both. Also, in the Time Notes column, if you finish on time, note how much extra time you had. If you run out of time, note how many questions you did not have time to answer.

Table 24-3   DCICN Practice Exam Checklist

Exam	Date	Score	Time Notes
DCICN			
DCICN			
DCICN			
DCICN			

Advice on How to Answer Exam Questions

Open a web browser. Yes, take a break and open a web browser on any device. Do a quick search on a fun topic. Then, before you click a link, get ready to think where your eyes go for the first 5 to 10 seconds after you click the link. Now, click a link and look at the page. Where did your eyes go?

Interestingly, web browsers, and the content on those web pages, have trained us all to scan. Web page designers actually design content with the expectation that people will scan with different patterns. Regardless of the pattern, when reading a web page, almost no one reads sequentially, and no one reads entire sentences. They scan for the interesting graphics and the big words, and then scan the space around those noticeable items.

Other parts of our electronic culture have also changed how the average person reads. For example, many of you grew up using texting and social media, sifting through hundreds or thousands of messages, but with each message barely filling an entire sentence. (In fact, that previous sentence would not fit in a tweet, being longer than 140 characters.)

Those everyday habits have changed how we all read and think in front of a screen. Unfortunately, those same habits often hurt our scores when taking computer-based exams.

If you scan exam questions like you read web pages, texts, and tweets, you will probably make some mistakes because you missed a key fact in the questions, answers, or exhibits. It helps to start at the beginning and read all the words—a process that is amazingly unnatural for many people today.

> **NOTE**   I have talked to many college professors, in multiple disciplines, as well as Cisco Networking Academy instructors, and they consistently tell me that the number-one test-taking issue today is that people do not read the question well enough to understand the details.

For when you are taking the practice exams, and answering individual questions, let me make two suggestions. First, before the practice exam, think about your own personal strategy for how you will read a question. Make your approach to multiple-choice questions in particular be a conscious decision on your part. Second, if you want some suggestions on how to read an exam question, use the following strategy:

Step 1.   Read the question itself thoroughly from start to finish.

Step 2.   Scan any exhibit (usually command output) or figure.

Step 3.   Scan the answers to look for the types of information. (Numeric? Terms? Single words? Phrases?)

Step 4.   Reread the question thoroughly from start to finish to make sure that you understand it.

Step 5.   Read each answer thoroughly while referring to the figure/exhibit as needed. After reading each answer, do the following before reading the next answer:

   A. If the answer is correct, select it as correct.

   B. If for sure the answer is incorrect, mentally rule it out.

   C. If you are unsure, mentally note it as a possible correct answer.

> **NOTE**   Cisco exams will tell you the number of correct answers. The exam software also helps you finish the question with the right number of answers noted. For example, the software prevents you from selecting too many answers. Also, if you try to move on to the next question but have too few answers noted, the exam software asks if you truly want to move on.

Use the practice exams as a place to practice your approach to reading. Every time you click to the next question, try to read the question following your approach. If you are feeling time pressure, that is the perfect time to keep practicing your approach, to reduce and eliminate questions you miss because of scanning the question instead of reading thoroughly.

Taking Other Practice Exams

Many people use other practice exams and questions other than the questions that come with this book. Frankly, using other practice exams in addition to the questions that come with this book can be a good idea, for many reasons. The other exam questions can use different terms in different ways, emphasize different topics, and show different scenarios that make you rethink some topics.

No matter where you get additional exam questions, if you use the exam questions for a timed practice exam, it helps to take a few notes about the results. Table 24-4 gives you a place to take those notes. Also, take a guess at the percentage of questions you have seen before when taking the exam, and note whether you think the questions are less, more, or the same challenge level as the questions that come with this book. And as usual, note whether you ran out of time or had extra time left over at the end.

24

Table 24-4   Checklist for Practice Exams from Other Sources

Exam Source	Other Exam Notes	% Questions Repeated (Estimate)	Challenging?	Date	Score	Time Notes

Note that the publisher does sell products that include additional test questions. The *Cisco Data Center (DCICN) 200-150 Official Cert Guide Premium Edition eBook and Practice Test* product is basically the publisher's eBook version of this book. It includes a soft copy of the book in formats you can read on your computer or on the most common book readers and tablets. The product includes all the content you would normally get with the print book, including all the question databases mentioned in this chapter. Additionally, this product includes two more DCICT exam databases for extra practice tests.

Find Knowledge Gaps Through Question Review

You just took a number of practice exams. You probably learned a lot, gained some exam-taking skills, and improved your networking knowledge and skills. But if you go back and look at all the questions you missed, you might be able to find a few small gaps in your knowledge.

One of the hardest things to find when doing your final exam preparation is to discover gaps in your knowledge and skills. In other words, what topics and skills do you need to know that you do not know? Or what topics do you think you know but you misunderstand some important fact about? Finding gaps in your knowledge at this late stage requires more than just your gut feel about your strengths and weaknesses.

This next task uses a feature of PCPT to help you find those gaps. The PCPT software tracks each practice exam you take, remembering your answer for every question and whether you got it wrong. You can view the results and move back and forth between seeing the question and seeing the results page. To find gaps in your knowledge, follow these steps:

Step 1.   Pick and review one of your practice exams.

Step 2.   Review each incorrect question until you are happy that you understand the question.

Step 3.   When finished with your review of a question, mark the question.

Step 4.   Review all incorrect questions from your exam until all are marked.

Step 5.   Move on to the next practice exam.

Figure 24-1 shows a sample Question Review page, in which all the questions were answered incorrectly. The results show a Correct column with no check marks, meaning that the answers were incorrect.

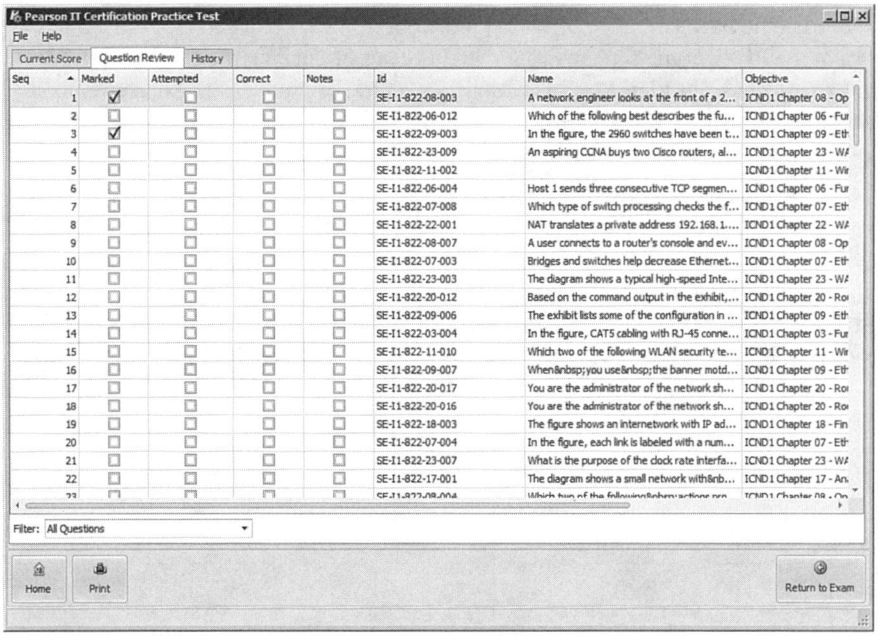

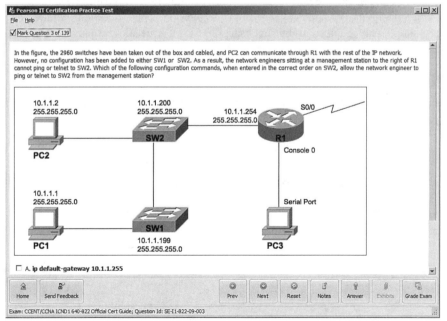

Figure 24-1 *PCPT Grading Results Page*

To perform the process of reviewing questions and marking them as complete, you can move between this Question Review page and the individual questions. Just double-click a question to move back to it. From the question, you can click **Grade Exam** to move back to the grading results and to the Question Review page shown in Figure 24-1. The question window also shows the place to mark the question, in the upper left, as shown in Figure 24-2.

Figure 24-2 *Reviewing a Question, with the Mark Feature in the Upper Left*

If you want to come back later to look through the questions you missed from an earlier exam, start at the PCPT home screen. From there, instead of clicking the **Start** button to start a new exam, click the **View Grade History** button to see your earlier exam attempts and work through any missed questions.

Track your progress through your gap review in Table 24-5. PCPT lists your previous practice exams by date and score, so it helps to note those values in the table for comparison to the PCPT menu.

Table 24-5 Tracking Checklist for Gap Review of Practice Exams

DCICN Exam	Original Practice Exam Date	Original Exam Score	Date Gap Review Was Completed

Practice Hands-on CLI Skills

To do well on sim and simlet questions, you need to be comfortable with many Cisco NX-OS commands and how to use them from the CLI. As described in the Introduction to this book, sim questions require you to decide what configuration commands need to be used to fix a problem or to complete a working configuration. Simlet questions require you to answer multiple-choice questions by first using the CLI to issue **show** commands to look at the status of routers and switches in a small network.

Other Study Tasks

If you get to this point and still feel the need to prepare some more, this last topic gives you three suggestions.

First, the chapter review "Exam Preparation Tasks" and "Part Review" sections give you some useful study tasks.

Second, take more exam questions from other sources. You can always get more questions in the Cisco Press *Premium Edition eBook and Practice Test* products, which include an eBook copy of this book, additional questions, and PCPT exam banks. However, you can search the Internet for questions from many sources, and review those questions as well.

> **NOTE**   Some vendors claim to sell practice exams that contain the literal questions from the exam. These exams, called brain dumps, are against the Cisco testing policies. Cisco strongly discourages using any such tools for study.

Finally, join in the discussions on the Cisco Learning Network. Try to answer questions asked by other learners; the process of answering a question makes you think much harder about the topic. When someone posts an answer with which you disagree, think about why and talk about it online. This is a great way to both learn more and build confidence.

Final Thoughts

You have studied quite a bit, worked hard, and sacrificed time and money to be ready for the exam. We hope your exam goes well and that you pass. What's more, we hope you pass because you really know your stuff and will do well in your IT and networking career.

We encourage you to celebrate when you pass, and ask advice if you do not. The Cisco Learning Network is a great place to make posts to celebrate and to ask advice for the next time around. We, the authors, would love to hear about your progress through Twitter (@chadh0517, @cobedien, @okarakok). We wish you well, and congratulations for working through the entire book!

24

Part VII

Appendices

Answers to the "Do I Know This Already?" Quizzes

Chapter 1

1. A, B, and E. The 9500 platform with the right line cards and the 9336 can be used in the ACI Spine Leaf topology as a spine.

2. False. Nexus N9K-X9736PQ is designed for use in a Cisco ACI spine switch role.

3. B. The Cisco QSFP BiDi transceiver has two 20-Gbps channels, each transmitted and received simultaneously over two wavelengths on a single MMF strand.

4. C. Up to six simultaneously active fabric modules work together, delivering up to 1.32 Tbps per slot.

5. False

6. C

7. True

8. A

9. True

10. B and C

11. B The Nexus 5672 has up to 48 10GE ports (of which 16 are UP) and 6 true 40GE QSFP ports.

12. E

13. A and B

14. B

15. D

Chapter 2

1. D and F. Of the remaining answers, Ethernet defines both physical and data link protocols, PPP is a data link protocol, IP is a network layer protocol, and SMTP and HTTP are application layer protocols.

2. A and G. Of the remaining answers, IP is a network layer protocol, TCP and UDP are transport layer protocols, and SMTP and HTTP are application layer protocols.

3. B. Adjacent-layer interaction occurs on one computer, with two adjacent layers in the model. The higher layer requests services from the next lower layer, and the lower layer provides the services to the next higher layer.

4. B. Same-layer interaction occurs on multiple computers. The functions defined by that layer typically need to be accomplished by multiple computers—for example, the sender setting a sequence number for a segment, and the receiver acknowledging receipt of that segment. A single layer defines that process, but the implementation of that layer on multiple devices is required to accomplish the function.

5. A. Encapsulation is defined as the process of adding a header in front of data supplied by a higher layer (and possibly adding a trailer as well).

6. D. By convention, the term *frame* refers to the part of a network message that includes the data link header and trailer, with encapsulated data. The term *packet* omits the data link header and trailer, leaving the network layer header with its encapsulated data. The term *segment* omits the network layer header, leaving the transport layer header and its encapsulated data.

7. C. The network layer concerns itself with delivery of data over the complete end-to-end path. That requires a way to identify each device, using addresses, and the addresses must be logical addresses that are therefore not tied to the physical details of the network.

8. A. The OSI physical layer includes all standards that specify the shape of connectors, wiring in cabling, electrical details, and encoding that the electrical signals use to encode bits over a cable.

9. C and E. The layer names, from top to bottom, are application, presentation, session, transport, network, data link, and physical.

Chapter 3

1. A. The IEEE defines Ethernet LAN standards, with standard names that begin with 802.3, all of which happen to use cabling. The IEEE also defines wireless LAN standards, with standard names that begin with 802.11, which are separate standards from Ethernet.

2. D. The number before the word "BASE" defines the speed, in megabits per second (Mbps). 1000 Mbps equals 1 gigabit per second (1 Gbps). The "T" in the suffix implies twisted-pair or UTP cabling, so 1000BASE-T is the UTP-based Gigabit Ethernet standard name.

3. B. Crossover cables cross the wire at one node's transmit pin pair to the different pins used as the receive pins on the other device. For 10- and 100-Mbps Ethernet, the specific crossover cable wiring connects the pair at pins 1 and 2 on each end of the cable to pins 3 and 6 on the other end of the cable, respectively.

4. B, D, and E. Routers, wireless access point Ethernet ports, and PC NICs all send using pins 1 and 2, whereas hubs and LAN switches transmit on pins 3 and 6. Straight-through cables connect devices that use opposite pin pairs for sending, because the cable does not need to cross the pairs.

5. B. NICs (and switch ports) use the carrier sense multiple access with collision detection (CSMA/CD) algorithm to implement half-duplex logic. While CSMA/CD attempts to avoid collisions, it also notices when collisions do occur, with rules about how the Ethernet nodes should stop sending, wait, and try again later.

6. C. The 4-byte Ethernet FCS field, found in the Ethernet trailer, allows the receiving node to see what the sending node computed with a math formula that is a key part of the error-detection process. Note that Ethernet defines the process of detecting errors (error detection), but not error recovery.

7. B, C, and E. The preassigned universal MAC address, given to each Ethernet port when manufactured, breaks the address into two 3-byte halves. The first half is called the organizationally unique identifier (OUI), which the IEEE assigns to the company that builds the product as a unique hex number only to be used by that company.

8. C and D. Ethernet supports unicast addresses, which identify a single Ethernet node, and group addresses, which can be used to send one frame to multiple Ethernet nodes. The two types of group addresses are the broadcast address and multicast addresses.

Chapter 4

1. A and D. The network layer defines logical addressing, in contrast to physical addressing. The logical address structure allows easy grouping of addresses, which makes routing more efficient. Path selection refers to the process of choosing the best routes to use in the network. Physical addressing and arbitration typically are data link layer functions, and error recovery typically is a transport layer function.

2. C and E. Because PC1 and PC2 are separated by routers, the PCs must rely on the routers to use routing logic. With routing, the router discards the data link header of an incoming frame, making a decision of where to forward the packet deencapsulated from the frame. As a result, the largest entity that passes from PC1 to PC2 is the IPv4 packet (or IPv6 packet), which goes by the more general name of L3PDU.

3. B. 224.1.1.1 is a Class D address. 223.223.223.255 is the network broadcast address for Class C network 223.223.223.0, so it cannot be assigned to a host.

4. D. The first octet of Class A addresses ranges from 1 to 126, inclusive; Class B, 128 to 191, inclusive; and Class C, 192 to 223 inclusive. 127 is technically in the Class A range, but it is a reserved address used as a loopback.

5. D and F. Without any subnetting in use, all addresses in the same network as 10.1.1.1—all addresses in Class A network 10.0.0.0—must be on the same LAN. Addresses separated from that network by some router cannot be in network 10.0.0.0. So, the two correct answers are the only two answers that list a valid unicast IP address that is not in network 10.0.0.0.

6. A. PC1 will send an Ethernet frame to Router1, with PC1's MAC address as the source address and Router1's MAC address as the destination address. Router1 will remove the encapsulated IP packet from that Ethernet frame, discarding the frame header and trailer. Router1 will forward the IP packet by first encapsulating it inside

A

an HDLC frame, but Router1 will not encapsulate the Ethernet frame in the HDLC frame, but rather the IP packet. Router2 will deencapsulate the IP packet from the HDLC frame and forward it onto the Ethernet LAN, adding a new Ethernet header and trailer, but this header will differ. It will list Router2's MAC address as the source address and PC2's MAC address as the destination address.

7.   C. Routers compare the packet's destination IP address to the router's IP routing table, making a match and using the forwarding instructions in the matched route to forward the IP packet.

8.   B and C. IPv4 hosts generally use basic two-branch logic. To send an IP packet to another host on the same IP network or subnet that is on the same LAN, the sender sends the IP packet directly to that host. Otherwise, the sender sends the packet to its default router (also called the default gateway).

9.   A and C. Routers do all the actions listed in all four answers. However, the routing protocol does the functions in the two listed answers. Independent of the routing protocol, a router learns routes for IP subnets and IP networks directly connected to its interfaces. Routers also forward (route) IP packets, but that process is called IP routing, or IP forwarding, and is an independent process as compared with the work of a routing protocol.

10.   C. Address Resolution Protocol (ARP) does allow PC1 to learn information, but the information is not stored on a server. The **ping** command does let the user at PC1 learn whether packets can flow in the network, but it again does not use a server. With the Domain Name System (DNS), PC1 acts as a DNS client, relying on a DNS server to respond with information about the IP addresses that match a given host name.

Chapter 5

1.   D. NX-OS enables you to execute EXEC command from any level of the command structure as long as your role has the privileges, too.

2.   B. Network-admin is the only role listed that enables you to reload the switch.

3.   B. SSH encrypts all passwords and data exchanges; telnet does not.

4.   A. Volatile random-access memory (VRAM) located on a supervisor module is used for temporary or pending changes.

5.   F. Nonvolatile random-access memory (NVRAM) located on a supervisor module is used for storing the startup-configuration file.

6.   A and B. In configuration mode, you are one mode above EXEC mode. Using **exit** will bring you down one mode level, and **end** will always return you to EXEC mode.

Chapter 6

1.   B. A VLAN is a set of devices in the same Layer 2 broadcast domain. A subnet often includes the exact same set of devices, but it is a Layer 3 concept. A collision domain refers to a set of Ethernet devices, but with different rules than VLAN rules for determining which devices are in the same collision domain.

2. D. Although a subnet and a VLAN are not equivalent concepts, the devices in one VLAN are typically in the same IP subnet and vice versa.

3. B. 802.1Q defines a 4-byte header, inserted after the original frame's destination and source MAC address fields. The insertion of this header does not change the original frame's source or destination address. The header itself holds a 12-bit VLAN ID field, which identifies the VLAN associated with the frame.

4. A. 802.1Q defines the native VLAN as one designated VLAN on a trunk for which the devices choose to not add an 802.1Q header for frames in that VLAN. The switches can set the native VLAN to any VLAN ID, but the switches should agree. The default native VLAN is VLAN 1. Note that only one such native VLAN is allowed on any one trunk; otherwise, that VLAN associated with untagged frames could not be discerned by the receiving switch.

5. B and C. Each VLAN, a Layer 2 concept, is its own broadcast domain. A Layer 2 switch purposefully keeps broadcast domains separate, purposefully choosing to not forward traffic that enters in a port in one broadcast domain (VLAN) into a second broadcast domain (VLAN). Bridges use the same forwarding logic as a Layer 2 switch. Devices that perform IP routing, like routers and switches configured as Layer 3 switches, can route IP packets between the devices in different VLANs.

6. B and C. Only VTP server and client modes allow a switch to learn new information with VTP. Transparent and off modes give switches a couple of ways to effectively not use VTP; switches using both these modes will not update their configuration based on receiving a VTP message.

7. D. Of the listed answers, VTP distributes only the VLAN ID and VLAN name. VTP does not distribute configuration that ties to specific ports on any one switch.

Chapter 7

1. B and C. **switchport access vlan 10** enables Ethernet 1/1 to participate in VLAN 10 and the interface must be in **no shutdown** mode for the interface to come up.

2. A and B. Issuing the **vlan 22** command, followed by the **name Evans-VLAN** command will configure VLAN 22 which will be shown in the output of the **show vlan brief** command as well as the **show running-config** command.

3. B and C. **show interface switchport** and **show interface trunk** are valid commands for identifying switch interfaces as being trunking interfaces. **show interface** does not show whether the interface is trunking, and **show trunks** is not a valid command.

4. A and C. **switchport mode trunk** and **no shutdown** are the valid responses here because switchport mode trunk or dot1q is the only supported protocol on Nexus for trunking, and the interface must be **no shutdown** for the interface to come up.

5. A and D. **feature vtp** and **vtp mode client** are the correct answers because the **feature vtp** command will enable VTP, and VTP mode client will set the mode of the VTP service to client.

A

Chapter 8

1. A and B. Listening and learning are transitory port states, used only when moving from the blocking to the forwarding state. Discarding is not an 802.1D STP port state.

2. C and D. Listening and learning are transitory port states, used only when moving from the blocking to the forwarding state. Discarding is not an 802.1D STP port state. Forwarding and blocking are stable states.

3. C. The smallest numeric bridge ID wins the election.

4. B. Nonroot switches forward Hellos received from the root; the root sends these Hellos based on the root's configured Hello timer.

5. D. The PortFast feature enables STP to move a port from blocking to forwarding, without going through the interim listening and learning states. STP allows this exception when the link is known to have no switch on the other end of the link, removing the risk of a switching loop. BPDU Guard is a common feature to use at the same time as PortFast, because it watches for incoming bridge protocol data units (BPDU), which should not happen on an access port, and prevents the loops from a rogue switch by disabling the port.

6. D. RSTP has several improvements over STP for faster convergence, including waiting on three times the hello timer when a wait is necessary. However, when the root port actually fails, both 802.1D and 802.1w can react without waiting (a fact that rules out two answers). Another RSTP optimization is that an alternate port (that is, a port that can be used as root port when the root port fails) can be used immediately and be placed into a forwarding state, without first spending MaxAge time in learning state.

7. D. RSTP refers to potential root ports to use when the current root port fails, an alternate port. The backup port role is used when one switch connects two or more ports to the same collision domain (for example, when connecting to a hub). Blocking (802.1D) and discarding (802.1w) are names of port states, not port roles.

Chapter 9

1. B and C. To change a switch's bridge ID value you can use the **root primary** or **secondary** command or hard code this value with the **priority** command.

2. A. You can tell by looking at the priority and sys-id-ext output. The sys-id-ext is always the VLAN number, which in this case is 1.

3. A and D. Hard code a cost of 2, or using the default cost would also be 2 because it is a 10 Gbps interface.

4. D. To add interfaces to a PortChannel you must use the **channel-group (x)** command under the interfaces to add them to the PortChannel.

5. B. The switch will choose the interface with the lowest root cost as its root port.

6. A and D. Both commands will provide output that lists a nonroot switch's root cost.

Chapter 10

1. C. The command **username Fred password Cisco123 role network-operator** is correct because the default user role of network-operator has read-only access to the switch.

2. D. None of these answers are correct because the username admin password mypassword role network-admin works for both Telnet and SSH.

3. C. The banner text that is displayed starts and stops with a delimiter character; in this case, we are using # as this character, so the text to be displayed will be between the # symbols.

4. A. On a Nexus switch is correct. The management interface mgmt0 is in the management VRF by default.

5. E. Interface configuration mode is correct because to configure the interface setting you must be in the interface configuration mode: (config-if)#.

Chapter 11

1. B and D. The general rule to determine whether two devices' interfaces should be in the same subnet is whether the two interfaces are separated from each other by a router. To provide a way for hosts in one VLAN to send data to hosts outside that VLAN, a local router must connect its LAN interface to the same VLAN as the hosts and have an address in the same subnet as the hosts. All the hosts in that same VLAN on the same switch would not be separated from each other by a router, so these hosts would also be in the same subnet. However, another PC, connected to the same switch but in a different VLAN, will require its packets to flow through a router to reach Host A, so Host A's IP address would need to be in a different subnet compared to this new host.

2. D. By definition, two address values in every IPv4 subnet cannot be used as host IPv4 addresses: the first (lowest) numeric value in the subnet for the subnet ID, and the last (highest) numeric value in the subnet for the subnet broadcast address.

3. B and C. At least 7 subnet bits are needed, because 26 = 64, so 6 subnet bits could not number 100 different subnets. Seven subnet bits could, because 27 = 128 => 100. Similarly, 6 host bits is not enough, because 26 – 2 = 62, but 7 host bits is enough, because 27 – 2 = 126 => 100.

   The number of network, subnet, and host bits must total 32 bits, making one of the answers incorrect. The answer with 8 network bits cannot be correct because the question states that a Class B network is used, so the number of network bits must always be 16. The two correct answers have 16 network bits (required because the question states the use of a Class B network), and at least 7 subnet and host bits each.

4. A and C. The private IPv4 networks, defined by RFC 1918, are Class A network 10.0.0.0, the 16 Class B networks from 172.16.0.0 to 172.31.0.0, and the 256 Class C networks that begin with 192.168.

5. A, D, and E. The private IPv4 networks, defined by RFC 1918, are Class A network 10.0.0.0, the 16 Class B networks from 172.16.0.0 to 172.31.0.0, and the 256 Class C networks that begin with 192.168. The three correct answers are from the public IP network range, and none are reserved values.

6. A and C. An unsubnetted Class A, B, or C network has two parts: the network and host parts.

7. B. An unsubnetted Class A, B, or C network has two parts: the network and host parts. To perform subnetting, the engineer creates a new subnet part by borrowing host bits, shrinking the number of host bits. The subnet part of the address structure exists only after the engineer chooses a nondefault mask. The network part remains a constant size.

8. C and D. Subnet ID (short for subnet identifier), subnet address, and subnet number are all synonyms and refer to the number that identifies the subnet. The actual value is a dotted-decimal number, so the term *subnet name* does not apply. The term *subnet broadcast*, a synonym for the subnet broadcast address, refers to the last (highest) numeric value in a subnet.

Chapter 12

1. B and C. Class A networks have a first octet in the range of 1–126, inclusive, and their network IDs have a 0 in the last three octets. 130.0.0.0 is actually a Class B network (first octet range 128–191, inclusive). All addresses that begin with 127 are reserved, so 127.0.0.0 is not a Class A network.

2. E. Class B networks all begin with values between 128 and 191, inclusive, in their first octets. The network ID has any value in the 128–191 range in the first octet, and any value from 0–255 inclusive in the second octet, with decimal 0s in the final two octets. Two of the answers show a 255 in the second octet, which is acceptable. Two of the answers show a 0 in the second octet, which is also acceptable.

3. B and D. The first octet (172) is in the range of values for Class B addresses (128–191). As a result, the network ID can be formed by copying the first two octets (172.16) and writing 0s for the last two octets (172.16.0.0). The default mask for all Class B networks is 255.255.0.0, and the number of host bits in all unsubnetted Class B networks is 16.

4. A and C. The first octet (192) is in the range of values for Class C addresses (192–223). As a result, the network ID can be formed by copying the first three octets (192.168.6) and writing 0 for the last octet (192.168.6.0). The default mask for all Class C networks is 255.255.255.0, and the number of host bits in all unsubnetted Class C networks is 8.

5. D. To find the network broadcast address, first determine the class, and then determine the number of host octets. At that point, convert the host octets to 255 to create the network broadcast address. In this case, 10.1.255.255 is in a Class A network, with the last three octets as host octets, for a network broadcast address of 10.255.255.255. For 192.168.255.1, it is a Class C address, with the last octet as the host part, for a network broadcast address of 192.168.255.255. Address 224.1.1.255

is a Class D address, so it is not in any unicast IP network, so the question does not apply. For 172.30.255.255, it is a Class B address, with the last two octets as host octets, so the network broadcast address is 172.30.255.255.

6. B. To find the network ID, first determine the class, and then determine the number of host octets. At that point, convert the host octets to 0 to create the network ID. In this case, 10.1.0.0 is in a Class A network, with the last three octets as host octets, for a network ID of 10.0.0.0. For 192.168.1.0, it is a Class C address, with the last octet as the host part, for a network ID of 192.168.1.0. Address 127.0.0.0 looks like a Class A network ID, but it begins with a reserved value (127), so it is not in any Class A, B, or C network. 172.20.0.1 is a Class B address, with the last two octets as host octets, so the network ID is 172.20.0.0.

Chapter 13

1. C. Thinking about the conversion one octet at a time, the first two octets each convert to 8 binary 1s. 254 converts to 8-bit binary 11111110, and decimal 0 converts to 8-bit binary 00000000. So, the total number of binary 1s (which defines the prefix length) is 8+8+7+0 = /23.

2. B. Thinking about the conversion one octet at a time, the first three octets each convert to 8 binary 1s. 240 converts to 8-bit binary 11110000, so the total number of binary 1s (which defines the prefix length) is 8+8+8+4 = /28.

3. C. /24 is the equivalent of the mask that in binary has 24 binary 1s. To convert that to DDN format, write down all the binary 1s (24 in this case), followed by binary 0s for the remainder of the 32-bit mask. Then take 8 bits at a time, and convert from binary to decimal (or memorize the nine possible DDN mask octet values and their binary equivalents). Using the /24 mask in this question, the binary mask is 11111111 11111111 11111111 00000000. Each of the first three octets is all binary 1, so each converts to 255. The last octet, all binary 0s, converts to decimal 0, for a DDN mask of 255.255.255.0. See Appendix I for a decimal/binary conversion table.

4. B. /30 is the equivalent of the mask that in binary has 30 binary 1s. To convert that to DDN format, write down all the binary 1s (30 in this case), followed by binary 0s for the remainder of the 32-bit mask. Then take 8 bits at a time, and convert from binary to decimal (or memorize the nine possible DDN mask octet values and their binary equivalents). Using the /30 mask in this question, the binary mask is 11111111 11111111 11111111 11111100. Each of the first three octets is all binary 1, so each converts to 255. The last octet, 11111100, converts to 252, for a DDN mask of 255.255.255.252. See Appendix I for a decimal/binary conversion table.

5. C. The size of the network part is always either 8, 16, or 24 bits, based on whether it is Class A, B, or C, respectively. As a Class A address, N=8. The mask 255.255.255.0, converted to prefix format, is /24. The number of subnet bits is the difference between the prefix length (24) and N, so S=16 in this case. The size of the host part is a number that, when added to the prefix length (24), gives you 32, so H=8 in this case.

6. A. The size of the network part is always either 8, 16, or 24 bits, based on whether it is Class A, B, or C, respectively. As a Class C address, N=24. The number of subnet

A

bits is the difference between the prefix length (27) and N, so S=3 in this case. The size of the host part is a number that, when added to the prefix length (27), gives you 32, so H=5 in this case.

7. B and D. Classless addressing rules define a two-part IP address structure: the prefix and the host part. The host part is defined the same way as with classful IP addressing rules. The classless address rules' prefix length is the length of the combined network and subnet parts when using classful IP addressing concepts. Mathematically, the prefix length is equal to the number of binary 1s in the mask. In this case, with a mask of 255.255.255.0, the prefix length is 24 bits. The host length is the number of bits added to 24 to total 32, for 8 host bits.

8. D. Classless addressing rules define a two-part IP address structure: the prefix and the host part. This logic ignores Class A, B, and C rules, and can be applied to the 32-bit IPv4 addresses from any address class. By ignoring Class A, B, and C rules, classless addressing ignores any distinction as to the network part of an IPv4 address.

9. A and B. The masks in binary define a number of binary 1s, and the number of binary 1s defines the length of the prefix (network + subnet) part. With a Class B network, the network part is 16 bits. To support 100 subnets, the subnet part must be at least 7 bits long. Six subnet bits would supply only 26 = 64 subnets, while 7 subnet bits supply 27 = 128 subnets. The /24 answer supplies 8 subnet bits, and the 255.255.255.252 answer supplies 14 subnet bits.

Chapter 14

1. D. When using classful IP addressing concepts as described in Chapter 13, "Analyzing Subnet Masks," addresses have three parts: network, subnet, and host. For addresses in a single classful network, the network parts must be identical for the numbers to be in the same network. For addresses in the same subnet, both the network and subnet parts must have identical values. The host part differs when comparing different addresses in the same subnet.

2. B and D. In any subnet, the subnet ID is the smallest number in the range, the subnet broadcast address is the largest number, and the usable IP addresses sit between those. All numbers in a subnet have identical binary values in the prefix part (classless view) and network + subnet part (classful view). To be the lowest number, the subnet ID must have the lowest possible binary value (all 0s) in the host part. To be the largest number, the broadcast address must have the highest possible binary value (all binary 1s) in the host part. The usable addresses do not include the subnet ID and subnet broadcast address, so the addresses in the range of usable IP addresses never have a value of all 0s or 1s in their host parts.

3. C. The mask converts to 255.255.255.0. To find the subnet ID, for each octet of the mask that is 255, you can copy the IP address's corresponding values. For mask octets of decimal 0, you can record a 0 in that octet of the subnet ID. As such, copy the 10.7.99 and write a 0 for the fourth octet, for a subnet ID of 10.7.99.0.

4. C. First, the resident subnet (the subnet ID of the subnet in which the address resides) must be numerically smaller than the IP address, which rules out one of the answers. The mask converts to 255.255.255.252. As such, you can copy the first three octets of the IP address because of their value of 255. For the fourth octet, the subnet ID value must be a multiple of 4, because 256 − 252 (mask) = 4. Those multiples include 96 and 100, and the right choice is the multiple closest to the IP address value in that octet (97) without going over. So, the correct subnet ID is 192.168.44.96.

5. C. The resident subnet ID in this case is 172.31.77.192. You can find the subnet broadcast address based on the subnet ID and mask using several methods. Following the decimal process in the book, the mask converts to 255.255.255.224, making the interesting octet 4, with magic number 256 − 224 = 32. For the three octets where the mask = 255, copy the subnet ID (172.31.77). For the interesting octet, take the subnet ID value (192), add magic (32), and subtract 1, for 223. That makes the subnet broadcast address 172.31.77.223.

6. C. To answer this question, you need to find the range of addresses in the subnet, which typically then means you need to calculate the subnet ID and subnet broadcast address. With subnet ID/mask of 10.1.4.0/23, the mask converts to 255.255.254.0. To find the subnet broadcast address, following the decimal process described in this chapter, you can copy the subnet ID's first two octets because the mask's value is 255 in each octet. You write a 255 in the fourth octet because the mask has a 0 on the fourth octet. In octet 3, the interesting octet, add the magic number (2) to the subnet ID's value (4), minus 1, for a value of 2 + 4 − 1 = 5. (The magic number in this case is calculated as 256 − 254 = 2.) That makes the broadcast address 10.1.5.255. The last usable address is 1 less: 10.1.5.254. The range that includes the last 100 addresses is 10.1.5.155–10.1.5.254.

7. B. To answer this question, you do not actually need to calculate the subnet broadcast address, because you only need to know the low end of the range of addresses in the subnet. The first IP address in the subnet is 1 more than the subnet ID, or 192.168.9.97. The first 20 addresses then include 192.168.9.97–192.168.9.116.

Chapter 15

1. D. The most compelling reason was the address-exhaustion problem. The rest of the motivations are true motivations and benefits of IPv6 as well.

2. D. If following the steps in the book, the first step removes up to three leading 0s in each quartet, leaving FE80:0:0:100:0:0:0:123. This leaves two strings of consecutive all-0 quartets; by changing the longest string of all 0s to ::, the address is FE80:0:0:100::123.

3. B. This question has many quartets that make it easy to make a common mistake: removing trailing 0s in a quartet of hex digits. To abbreviate IPv6 addresses, only leading 0s in a quartet should be removed. Many of the quartets have trailing 0s (0s on the right side of the quartet), so make sure to not remove those 0s.

A

4.   C. The /64 prefix length means that the last 64 bits, or last 16 digits, of the address should be changed to all 0s. That process leaves the unabbreviated prefix as 2000:000 0:0000:0005:0000:0000:0000:0000. The last four quartets are all 0s, making that string of all 0s the longest and best string of 0s to replace with ::. After you remove the leading 0s in other quartets, the answer is 2000:0:0:5::/64.

5.   A. Global unicast addresses can begin with many different initial values, but most commonly, they begin with either a hex 2 or 3.

6.   D. The global routing prefix is the address block, represented as a prefix value and prefix length, given to an organization by some numbering authority. All IPv6 addresses inside the company have the same value in these initial bits of their IPv6 addresses. Similarly, when a company uses a public IPv4 address block, all the addresses have the same value in the network part.

7.   B. Subnetting a global unicast address block, using a single prefix length for all subnets, breaks the addresses into three parts. The parts are the global routing prefix, subnet, and interface ID.

8.   B and D. With SLAAC, the host learns the prefix from a router using NDP RS/RA messages, and then the host builds the rest of the address (the interface ID). The host can use EUI-64 rules, or use a defined process to randomly generate the interface ID value. The host does not learn the interface ID from any other device, which helps make the process stateless, because no other device needs to assign the host its full address.

Chapter 16

1.   B. The PC will send packets to its default gateway when the device it is trying to communicate with is on a different network.

2.   A and C. The router will compare the subnet via the mask and subnet ID to determine which route is in the table it matches.

3.   A. To disable Layer 2 protocols on an individual interface you must use a routed interface on a Cisco Nexus switch.

4.   C. If you want to have Layer 2 and Layer 3 functionality simultaneously on a Cisco Nexus switch you would use a switched virtual interface (SVI).

5.   B. When dealing with link down detection for Layer 3 peering a routed interface is faster than an SVI because an SVI is a logical interface.

Chapter 17

1.   A. To disable Layer 2 functionality on a Cisco Nexus Switch you must use a routed interface, which is enabled by the **no switchport** command.

2.   B. To add an interface to a VLAN you use the command **switchport access vlan** *vlan number*.

3. B. To add an IP address to an SVI, you enter interface configuration mode using the **interface vlan** *vlan number* command. Then enter the **ip address** command with the address and mask.

4. C. You would see Interface VLAN in the routing table as a connected/direct route.

5. D. You do not need the next hop router's subnet mask to configure a static route to that router.

6. D. To configure a static route you must use the **ip route** statement followed by the route subnet and mask and either the outgoing interface or the next hop router's IP address.

Chapter 18

1. D. Split horizon causes a router to not advertise a route out of the same interface on which the router was learned. It also causes the router to not advertise about the connected route on an interface in updates sent out that interface. Route poisoning also helps prevent loops, although it does not affect how many routes a router advertises about on an interface. The other two answers are unrelated to loop prevention.

2. D. Route poisoning means advertising the failed route with an "infinite" metric, as opposed to simply ceasing to advertise the route. Of the incorrect answers, SPF defines how link-state protocols calculate and choose routes; hello refers to the messages some routing protocols use to discover and monitor neighboring routers; and split horizon limits what routes a router advertises to help avoid routing loops.

3. A and D. RIPv2 continues to use several features like RIPv1 in an effort to allow easier migration from RIPv1 to RIPv2. The features include using the same hop-count metric and using split horizon as one of the loop prevention mechanisms. The other two answers are true about RIPv2, but not RIPv1.

4. B. RIPv1 and RIPv2 both use hop-count as the metric, so the two answers referencing the bandwidth are incorrect. Both RIPv1 and RIPv2 consider a route with metric 16 to be a poisoned (bad) route, and the metric value 16 to be infinite, but a route with metric 15 is a usable route. So, R1 adds the route for 10.1.1.0/24 to its IP routing table.

5. A. EIGRP separates the function of monitoring neighbor state into the hello message process, relying on the receipt of a hello message. If a router does not receive an EIGRP hello within the configured EIGRP hold time, the local router believes the neighbor has failed.

6. A and B. EIGRP uses bandwidth and delay by default. Load and reliability can be added to the mix with configuration, but Cisco recommends against adding these to the metric calculation.

7. D. Both versions of RIP use distance vector logic, and EIGRP uses a different kind of logic, characterized either as advanced distance vector or a balanced hybrid.

A

8. B. Link-state protocols do not exchange data that lists routes. They do list metric information, but it is per-interface information, and it is not tied to a subnet. Link-state protocols do require the SPF algorithm to take the varied pieces of information and create routes based on that information.

Chapter 19

1. C. RIP is a distance vector routing protocol.

2. B. To show all of the RIP-specific configuration, the **show running-config rip** command should be used.

3. C. The default OSPF interface type for an Ethernet interface is broadcast.

4. A and C. Bandwidth and delay are the two default enabled K values for EIGRP.

5. C. To configure a router ID for EIGRP, the configuration command is **router-id** *address*.

Chapter 20

1. A. The primary function of the default gateway is to provide the capability to route between different subnets.

2. G. Cisco Nexus switches support HSRP and VRRP.

3. A. HSRPv1 leverages the well-known multicast address of 224.0.0.2.

4. A. Coup messages are sent by the standby router when the router wishes to become the active router.

5. A. peer-gateway was added to protect against third-party devices.

Chapter 21

1. A and C. An IP ACL can be configured to match the exact IP address by using the host keyword or using a /32 subnet mask for the source address. This can be done in one entry.

2. D. When creating an IOS ACL, you use the wildcard mask to match the ACL entry. The wildcard mask for 255.255.255.0 is 0.0.0.255.

3. E. When creating an IOS ACL, you use the wildcard mask to match the ACL entry. The wildcard mask for 255.255.240.0 is 0.0.15.255.

4. A. In an ACL the first match is used; in this case, 1.1.1.1 would match 1.0.0.0/8.

5. A. To permit only host 10.1.1.1 to host 192.168.1.3 on port 80 or the web, you must use the host keyword or a /32 subnet address. Using the host keyword will only allow a host to talk to a host on a particular port, in this case, port 80.

6. C. Following authentication, a user must gain authorization for doing certain tasks. After logging into a system, for instance, the user may try to issue commands. The authorization process determines whether the user has the authority to issue such commands.

Chapter 22

1. A, B, and D. Advantages of block-level storage systems are the following:

   - Block-level storage systems offer better performance and speed than file-level storage systems.

   - Each block/storage volume can be treated as an independent disk drive and is controlled by the external server OS.

   - Each block/storage volume can be formatted with the file system required by the application (NFS/NTFS/SMB).

   - Block-level storage systems are very popular with storage-area networks (SANs).

   - Block-level storage systems are more reliable, and their transport systems are very efficient.

   - Block-level storage can be used to store files and also provide the storage required for special applications such as databases, Virtual Machine File Systems (VMFS), and so on.

   - Block-level storage systems can support external boot of the systems connected to them.

2. A, B, and C. The advantages of SAN can be summarized in the following areas: consolidation, storage virtualization, automation, integrated storage, information lifecycle management, and business continuity.

3. A and D. CIFS and NFS are file-based protocols. SCSI, Fibre Channel, iSCSI, FCIP, and FCoE are block-based protocols.

4. A, B, and C. The characteristics of Tier 1 storage are the following: integrated large-scale disk array, centralized controller and cache system, capability to replicate between one or more devices, 10+K IOPS, and primarily structured data. Tier 1 use cases are transactional data: online retail, database, transaction processing, and mission-critical applications.

5. A, B, and C. Following are the key principals of the SAN design:

   - **Port density and topology requirements:** Number of ports required now and in the future

   - **Device performance and oversubscription ratios:** Determination of what is acceptable and what is unavoidable

   - **Traffic management:** Preferential routing or resource allocation

   - **Fault isolation:** Consolidation while maintaining isolation

   - **Control plane scalability:** Reduced routing complexity

A

6. A, B, and C. A dual-ported HBA has three WWNs: one nWWN, and one pWWN for each port. Every HBA, array controller, switch, gateway, and Fibre Channel disk drive has a single unique nWWN. The domain ID is an 8-bit field; only 239 domains are available to the fabric.

7. C. PRLI is the initiator to target a process login requesting an FC-4 session.

8. A. Expansion port (E port) is used to create an ISL.

9. A and C. An HBA or a storage device can belong to only a single VSAN—the VSAN associated with the Fx port. Membership is typically defined using the VSAN ID to Fx ports. On a Cisco MDS switch, up to 256 VSANs can be configured in a switch. Of these, one is a default VSAN (VSAN 1), and another is an isolated VSAN (VSAN 4094). User-specified VSAN IDs range from 2 to 4093.

10. B. iSCSI uses TCP (typically TCP ports 860 and 3260) for the protocols itself.

Chapter 23

1. C and D. Console port and MGMT interface are available on all MDS product family switches. COM1 port is available on all MDS product family switches except the MDS 9700 switch.

2. E. The initial setup script of MDS 9500 does not allow you to configure IPv6 addresses.

3. A. In the initial MDS NX-OS setup script there is the following question:

    Configure Advanced IP options (yes/no)? [n]: **yes**

    Continue with in-band (VSAN1) management configuration? (yes/no) [no]: **yes**

    Therefore, the user should answer **yes** to the first question to enter into the Advanced IP Options in the setup script.

4. B and C. Starting with NX-OS 6.2(9), the POAP capability is available on Cisco MDS 9148 and MDS 9148S Multilayer Fabric Switches (at the time of writing this book).

5. B. The Cisco MDS 9250i is available in a base configuration of 20 ports (upgradable to 40 through On-Demand Port Activation license) of 16Gbps Fibre Channel, two ports of 10 Gigabit Ethernet for FCIP and iSCSI storage services, and eight ports of 10 Gigabit Ethernet for FCoE connectivity.

    On the Cisco MDS 9148, the On-Demand Port Activation license allows the addition of eight 8Gbps ports. Customers have the option of purchasing preconfigured models of 16, 32, or 48 ports and upgrading the 16- and 32-port models onsite, all the way to 48 ports by adding these licenses.

    The Cisco MDS 9148S is a one rack-unit (1RU) switch that scales from 12 to 48 line-rate 16Gbps Fibre Channel ports. The base switch model comes with 12 ports enabled and can be upgraded as needed with the 12-port Cisco MDS 9148S On-Demand Port Activation license to support configurations of 24, 36, or 48 enabled ports.

6. B. Figure 23-4 explains the correct boot sequence. It is BIOS—Loader—Kickstart—System.

7. C. Table 23-6 has the correct in-band management configuration.

8. A, B, and D. The correct member for the specified zone is based on the type (pWWN, fabric pWWN, FC ID, FC alias, domain ID, IPv4 address, IPv6 address, or interface) and value specified.

9. A and D. The correct answer can be found in Table 23-15.

10. D. Unlike previous new protocols or architectures, storage virtualization has no standard measure defined by a reputable organization such as the INCITS (International Committee for Information Technology Standards) or the IETF (Internet Engineering Task Force). The closest vendor-neutral attempt to make storage virtualization concepts comprehensible has been the work of the Storage Networking Industry Association (SNIA).

11. A, B, C, and D. What is being virtualized may include disks, blocks, tape systems, file systems, and files or records.

12. D. RAID 1+0 creates a striped set from a series of mirrored drives. The array can sustain multiple drive losses as long as no mirror loses all its drives.

13. D. RAID 6 comprises block-level striping with double distributed parity.

14. B and C. LUN masking, a feature of enterprise storage arrays, provides basic LUN-level security by allowing LUNs to be seen only by selected servers that are identified by their port World Wide Name (pWWN). Each storage array vendor has its own management and proprietary techniques for LUN masking in the array. In a heterogeneous environment with arrays from different vendors, LUN management becomes more difficult.

15. A and D. The Logical Volume Manager performs virtualization tasks at the host operating systems. The LVM manipulates LUN representation to create virtualized storage to the file system or database manager. LVMs can be used to divide large physical disk arrays into more manageable virtual disks or to create large virtual disks from multiple physical disks. The logical volume manager treats any LUN as a vanilla resource for storage pooling; it will not differentiate the RAID levels. Therefore, the storage administrator must ensure that the appropriate classes of storage under LVM control are paired with individual application requirements.

16. B. Asynchronous mirroring follows this order of operation steps:

  1. The write operation is received by the primary storage array from the host.

  2. The primary storage array does not require a confirmation from the secondary storage array to acknowledge the write operation to the server.

  3. The primary storage array maintains new data queued to be copied to the secondary storage array at a later time. It initiates a write to the secondary storage array.

  4. An acknowledgement is sent to the primary storage array by the secondary storage array after the data is stored on the secondary storage array.

17. A, B, and E. The main advantages of host-based storage virtualization are that it is independent of the storage subsystem, it is close to the file system, it uses the operating system's built-in tools, there are no array controller cycles, it is independent of SAN transport, and it is a software solution.

18. A, B, and E.

- **Priority-based Flow Control (PFC):** IEEE 802.1Qbb provides a link-level flow-control mechanism that can be controlled independently for each frame priority. The goal of this mechanism is to ensure zero loss under congestion in DCB networks.

- **Enhanced Transmission Selection (ETS):** IEEE 802.1Qaz provides a common management framework for assignment of bandwidth-to-frame priorities.

- **Congestion Notification (QCN):** IEEE 802.1Qau provides end-to-end congestion management for protocols that are capable of transmission rate limiting to avoid frame loss. It is expected to benefit protocols such as TCP that do have native congestion management as it reacts to congestion in a timely manner.

- **Data Center Bridging Capabilities Exchange Protocol (DCBX):** A discovery and capability exchange protocol that is used for conveying capabilities and configuration of the preceding features between neighbors to ensure consistent configuration across the network. This protocol leverages functionality provided by IEEE 802.1AB (LLDP). It is actually included in the 802.1az standard.

19. B. A set of standards designed to transparently enhance Ethernet and IP traffic and provide special treatment and features for certain traffic types such as FCoE and HPC.

20. A. FCoE 0x8906, FIP 0x8914.

DCICN Exam Updates

Over time, reader feedback allows Cisco Press to gauge which topics give our readers the most problems when taking the exams. Additionally, Cisco might make small changes in the breadth of exam topics or in the emphasis of certain topics. To assist readers with those topics, the authors create new materials clarifying and expanding upon those troublesome exam topics.

DCICN has been updated with a few new topics. Therefore, we have updated in this book to cover those new exam topics. We have added chapters on the following topics to cover the changes in the exam topics provided by Cisco:

- Chapter 1: Introduction to Nexus Data Center Infrastructure and Architecture
- Chapter 20: Nexus First-Hop Redundancy Protocols and Configurations
- Part V: Data Center Storage Technologies
- Chapter 22: Introduction to Storage and Storage Networking
- Chapter 23: Advanced Data Center Storage

10BASE-2 An older 10-Mbps baseband Ethernet standard that uses a relatively thin coaxial cable that runs to each device, without the need for a networking device. Also known as thinnet.

10BASE-5 An older 10-Mbps baseband Ethernet standard that uses a relatively thick coaxial cable that runs to each device, without the need for a networking device. Also known as thicknet.

10BASE-T The 10-Mbps baseband Ethernet specification using two pairs of twistedpair cabling (Categories 3, 4, or 5): One pair transmits data and the other receives data. 10BASE-T, which is part of the IEEE 802.3 specification, has a distance limit of approximately 100 m (328 feet) per segment.

100BASE-T A name for the IEEE Fast Ethernet standard that uses two-pair copper cabling, a speed of 100 Mbps, and a maximum cable length of 100 meters.

1000BASE-T A name for the IEEE Gigabit Ethernet standard that uses four-pair copper cabling, a speed of 1000 Mbps (1 Gbps), and a maximum cable length of 100 meters.

802.2 The IEEE standard for the portion of the Data Link layer feature in common across LANs, known more commonly as Logical Link Control (LLC).

802.3 The IEEE standard for Ethernet.

802.4 The IEEE standard for Token Bus.

802.5 The IEEE standard for Token Ring.

802.1Q The IEEE standardized protocol for VLAN trunking.

802.11a The IEEE standard for wireless LANs using the U-NII spectrum, OFDM encoding, at speeds of up to 54 Mbps.

802.11b The IEEE standard for wireless LANs using the ISM spectrum, DSSS encoding, and speeds of up to 11 Mbps.

802.11g The IEEE standard for wireless LANs using the ISM spectrum, OFDM or DSSS encoding, and speeds of up to 54 Mbps.

802.11n The IEEE standard for wireless LANs using the ISM spectrum, OFDM encoding, and multiple antennas for singlestream speeds up to 150 Mbps.

802.11w The IEEE standard that defines the changes necessary to the operation of a MAC Bridge in order to provide rapid reconfiguration capability for STP.

802.1AB The IEEE standard for Link Layer Discovery Protocol, which is formally referred to as Station and Media Access Control Connectivity Discovery Protocol. It is a vendor-neutral link layer protocol in the Internet Protocol Suite used by network devices for advertising their identity, capabilities, and neighbors on an IEEE 802 local-area network, principally Ethernet.

802.1Qau   The IEEE standard for data center bridging (DCB) enhancements to Ethernet local-area networks for congestion notification. It provides end-to-end congestion management for protocols that are capable of transmission rate limiting to avoid frame loss. It is expected to benefit protocols such as TCP that have native congestion management, as it reacts to congestion in a timelier manner.

802.1Qaz   The IEEE standard for data center bridging (DCB) enhancements to Ethernet local-area networks for Enhanced Transmission Selection (ETS). It provides a common management framework for assignment of bandwidth to frame priorities.

802.1Qbb   The IEEE standard for data center bridging (DCB) enhancements to Ethernet local-area networks for Priority-based Flow Control (PFC). It provides a link level flow control mechanism that can be controlled independently for each frame priority. The goal of this mechanism is to ensure zero traffic loss under congestion in DCB networks.

A

AAA   Authentication, authorization, and accounting. Authentication confirms the identity of the user or device. Authorization determines what the user or device is allowed to do. Accounting records information about access attempts, including inappropriate requests.

access interface   A LAN network design term that refers to a switch interface connected to end-user devices, configured so that it does not use VLAN trunking.

access link   In Frame Relay, the physical serial link that connects a Frame Relay DTE device, usually a router, to a Frame Relay switch. The access link uses the same physical layer standards as do point-to-point leased lines.

access point   A wireless LAN device that provides a means for wireless clients to send data to each other and to the rest of a wired network, with the AP connecting to both the wireless LAN and the wired Ethernet LAN.

accounting   In security, the recording of access attempts. *See* AAA.

address block   In both IPv4 and IPv6, a set of consecutive addresses. This term is typically used for public addresses, assigned by some numbering authority (IANA/ICANN, an RIR, or an ISP).

adjacent-layer interaction   The general topic of how on one computer, two adjacent layers in a networking architectural model work together, with the lower layer providing services to the higher layer.

administrative distance   In Cisco routers, a means for one router to choose between multiple routes to reach the same subnet when those routes were learned by different routing protocols. The lower the administrative distance, the better the source of the routing information.

ADSL   Asymmetric digital subscriber line. One of many DSL technologies, ADSL is designed to deliver more bandwidth downstream (from the central office to the customer site) than upstream.

All-nodes multicast address   A specific IPv6 multicast address, FF02::1, with link-local scope, used to send packets to all devices on the link that support IPv6.

All-routers multicast address   A specific IPv6 multicast address, FF02::2, with link-local scope, used to send packets to all devices that act as IPv6 routers on the local link.

Alternate port   An RSTP port role in which a port sits in a discarding state, waiting to be used to replace the root port. That is, an alternate root port.

ANSI   American National Standards Institute. A private nonprofit organization that oversees the development of voluntary consensus standards for products, services, processes, systems, and personnel in the United States.

Area Border Router (ABR)   A router using OSPF in which the router has interfaces in multiple OSPF areas.

ARP   Address Resolution Protocol. An Internet protocol used to map an IP address to a MAC address. Defined in RFC 826.

ARP table   A list of IP addresses of neighbors on the same VLAN, along with their MAC addresses, as kept in memory by hosts and routers.

array-based virtualization   One "master" array will take over all IO for all other arrays. It must be fast enough to handle all aggregate storage traffic, and it must also interoperate with all existing disk arrays to realize the benefits. This method of virtualization provides the most benefits, including centralized management and seamless data migration.

ARPANET   The first packet-switched network, created around 1970, which served as the predecessor to the Internet.

asymmetric   A feature of many Internet access technologies, including DSL, cable, and modems, in which the downstream transmission rate is higher than the upstream transmission rate.

asynchronous   The lack of an imposed time ordering on a bit stream. Practically, both sides agree to the same speed, but there is no check or adjustment of the rates if they are slightly different. However, because only 1 byte per transfer is sent, slight differences in clock speed are not an issue.

asynchronous mirroring   It allows the local site to be updated immediately and the remote site to be updated as bandwidth allows. The information is cached and sent later, as network resources become available. Although this can greatly increase application response time, there is some risk of data loss.

authentication   In security, the verification of the identity of a person or a process. *See* AAA.

authorization   In security, the determination of the rights allowed for a particular user or device. *See* AAA.

autonegotiation   An IEEE standard mechanism (802.3u) with which two nodes can exchange messages for the purpose of choosing to use the same Ethernet standards on both ends of the link, ensuring that the link functions and functions well.

autonomous system   An internetwork in the administrative control of one organization, company, or governmental agency, inside which that organization typically runs an interior gateway protocol (IGP).

auxiliary port   A physical connector on a router that is designed to be used to allow a remote terminal, or PC with a terminal emulator, to access a router using an analog modem.

B

back-to-back link   A serial link between two routers, created without CSU/DSUs, by connecting a DTE cable to one router and a DCE cable to the other. Typically used in labs to build serial links without the expense of an actual leased line from the telco.

Backup port   An RSTP port role in which a port sits in a discarding state, waiting to be used to replace a particular designated port. That is, a backup designated port.

balanced hybrid   A term that, over the years, has been used to refer to the logic behind the EIGRP routing protocol. More commonly today, this logic is referred to as advanced distance vector logic.

bandwidth   A reference to the speed of a networking link. Its origins come from earlier communications technology in which the range, or width, of the frequency band dictated how fast communications could occur.

Big Data   An all-encompassing term for any collection of data sets so large and complex that it becomes difficult to process using traditional data processing applications.

BIOS   Basic Input Output System. In a computer system, it performs the Power on Self-Test procedure, searches, and loads to the Master Boot Record in the system booting process.

bitwise Boolean AND   A Boolean AND between two numbers of the same length in which the first bit in each number is ANDed, and then the second bit in each number, and then the third, and so on.

BNC connector   A round connector with a locking mechanism commonly used with 10BASE-2 Ethernet cabling.

Boolean AND   A math operation performed on a pair of one-digit binary numbers. The result is another one-digit binary number. 1 AND 1 yields 1; all other combinations yield a 0.

broadcast address   Generally, any address that represents all devices, and can be used to send one message to all devices. In Ethernet, the MAC address of all binary 1s, or FFFF.FFFF. FFFF in hex. For IPv4, see subnet broadcast address.

broadcast domain   A set of all devices that receive broadcast frames originating from any device within the set. Devices in the same VLAN are in the same broadcast domain.

broadcast frame   An Ethernet frame sent to destination address FFFF.FFFF.FFFF, meaning that the frame should be delivered to all hosts on that LAN.

broadcast subnet   When subnetting a Class A, B, or C network, the one subnet in each classful network for which all subnet bits have a value of binary 1. The subnet broadcast address in this subnet has the same numeric value as the classful network's network-wide broadcast address.

bus   A common physical signal path composed of wires or other media across which signals can be sent from one part of a computer to another.

C

cable Internet   An Internet access technology that uses a cable TV (CATV) cable, normally used for video, to send and receive data.

CDP   Cisco Discovery Protocol. A media and protocol-independent device-discovery protocol that runs on most Cisco-manufactured equipment, including routers, access servers, and switches. Using CDP, a device can advertise its existence to other devices and receive information about other devices on the same LAN or on the remote side of a WAN.

CDP neighbor   A device on the other end of some communications cable that is advertising CDP updates.

CIDR   Classless interdomain routing. An RFC-standard tool for global IP address range assignment. CIDR reduces the size of Internet routers' IP routing tables, helping deal with the rapid growth of the Internet. The term *classless* refers to the fact that the summarized groups of networks represent a group of addresses that do not conform to IPv4 classful (Class A, B, and C) grouping rules.

CIDR notation   *See* prefix notation.

circuit switching   A generic reference to network services, typically WAN services, in which the provider sets up a (Layer 1) circuit between two devices, and the provider makes no attempt to interpret the meaning of the bits. *See also* packet switching.

Cisco Express Forwarding (CEF)   A method of internal processing on Cisco routers, meant to make the routing process very efficient, doing so by caching IP routes in a table that can be searched very quickly, and by remembering data link headers rather than building them for every packet that is forwarded.

CFS   Cisco Fabric Services. Provides a common infrastructure for automatic configuration synchronization in the network. It provides the transport function and a set of common services to the features. CFS has the ability to discover CFS capable switches in the network and discover feature capabilities in all CFS capable switches.

CIFS   Common Internet File System. The standard way that computer users share files across corporate intranets and the Internet. An enhanced version of the Microsoft open, cross-platform Server Message Block (SMB) protocol, CIFS is a native file-sharing protocol in Windows 2000.

classful IP network   An IPv4 Class A, B, or C network; called a classful network because these networks are defined by the class rules for IPv4 addressing.

classful routing protocol   Does not transmit the mask information along with the subnet number, and therefore must consider Class A, B, and C network boundaries and perform auto-summarization at those boundaries. Does not support VLSM.

classless routing protocol   An inherent characteristic of a routing protocol, specifically that the routing protocol does send subnet masks in its routing updates, thereby removing any need to make assumptions about the addresses in a particular subnet or network, making it able to support VLSM and manual route summarization.

CLI   Command-line interface. An interface that enables the user to interact with the operating system by entering commands and optional arguments.

clock rate   The speed at which a serial link encodes bits on the transmission medium.

clock source   The device to which the other devices on the link adjust their speed when using synchronous links.

clocking   The process of supplying a signal over a cable, either on a separate pin on a serial cable or as part of the signal transitions in the transmitted signal, so that the receiving device can keep synchronization with the sending device.

CNA   Converged Network Adapter. A computer input/output device that combines the functionality of a host bus adapter (HBA) with a network interface controller (NIC). In other words, it "converges" access to a storage-area network and a general-purpose computer network.

collision domain   A set of network interface cards (NIC) for which a frame sent by one NIC could result in a collision with a frame sent by any other NIC in the same collision domain.

command-line interface   *See* CLI.

configuration mode   A part of the Cisco IOS Software CLI in which the user can type configuration commands that are then added to the device's currently used configuration file (running config).

connected   The single-item status code listed by a switch show interfaces status command, with this status referring to a working interface.

connected route   On a router, an IP route added to the routing table when the router interface is both up and has an IP address configured. The route is for the subnet that can be calculated based on the configured IP address and mask.

connection establishment   The process by which a connection-oriented protocol creates a connection. With TCP, a connection is established by a three-way transmission of TCP segments.

console port   A physical socket on a router or switch to which a cable can be connected between a computer and the router/switch, for the purpose of allowing the computer to use a terminal emulator and use the CLI to configure, verify, and troubleshoot the router/switch.

convergence   The time required for routing protocols to react to changes in the network, removing bad routes and adding new, better routes so that the current best routes are in all the routers' routing tables.

CPE   Customer premises equipment. Any equipment related to communications that is located at the customer site, as opposed to inside the telephone company's network.

crossover cable   An Ethernet cable that swaps the pair used for transmission on one device to a pair used for receiving on the device on the opposite end of the cable. In 10BASE-T and 100BASE-TX networks, this cable swaps the pair at pins 1,2 to pins 3,6 on the other end of the cable, and the pair at pins 3,6 to pins 1,2 as well.

CSMA/CD   Carrier sense multiple access with collision detection. A media-access mechanism in which devices ready to transmit data first check the channel for a carrier. If no carrier is sensed for a specific period of time, a device can transmit. If two devices transmit at once, a collision occurs and is detected by all colliding devices. This collision subsequently delays retransmissions from those devices for some random length of time.

CSU/DSU   Channel service unit/data service unit. A device that understands the Layer 1 details of serial links installed by a telco and how to use a serial cable to communicate with networking equipment such as routers.

cut-through switching   One of three options for internal processing on some models of Cisco LAN switches in which the frame is forwarded as soon as enough of the Ethernet header has been received for the switch to make a forwarding decision, including forwarding the first bits of the frame before the whole frame is received.

D

D2D2T   Disk-to-disk-to-tape. An approach to computer storage backup and archiving in which data is initially copied to backup storage on a disk and then later copied again to tape.

DCB   Data Center Bridging. A set of IEEE standards enhancing Ethernet networks to be able to accommodate convergence of network and storage traffic.

DCBX   Data Center Bridging Exchange. A discovery and capability exchange protocol to discover peers and exchange configuration information between DCB-compliant bridges. DCBX leverages functionality provided by IEEE 802.1AB (LLDP).

DCE   Data communications equipment. From a physical layer perspective, the device providing the clocking on a WAN link, typically a CSU/DSU, is the DCE. From a packet switching perspective, the service provider's switch, to which a router might connect, is considered the DCE.

deencapsulation   On a computer that receives data over a network, the process in which the device interprets the lower-layer headers and, when finished with each header, removes the header, revealing the next-higher layer PDU.

default gateway/default router   On an IP host, the IP address of some router to which the host sends packets when the packet's destination address is on a subnet other than the local subnet.

default mask   The mask used in a Class A, B, or C network that does not create any subnets; specifically, mask 255.0.0.0 for Class A networks, 255.255.0.0 for Class B networks, and 255.255.255.0 for Class C networks.

default route   On a router, the route that is considered to match all packets that are not otherwise matched by some more specific route.

demarc   The legal term for the demarcation or separation point between the telco's equipment and the customer's equipment.

denial of service (DoS)   A type of attack whose goal is to cause problems by preventing legitimate users from being able to access services, thereby preventing the normal operation of computers and networks.

DHCP   Dynamic Host Configuration Protocol. A protocol used by hosts to dynamically discover and lease an IP address, and learn the correct subnet mask, default gateway, and DNS server IP addresses.

DHCP Client   Any device that uses DHCP protocols to ask to lease an IP address from a DHCP server, or to learn any IP settings from that server.

DHCP Relay   The name of the router IOS feature that forwards DHCP messages from client to servers by changing the destination IP address from 255.255.255.255 to the IP address of the DHCP server.

DHCP Server   Software that waits for DHCP clients to request to lease IP addresses, with the server assigning a lease of an IP address as well as listing other important IP settings for the client.

direct route   A route that is available through a subnet that has been configured on a Cisco Nexus switch's interface.

directed broadcast address   *See* subnet broadcast address.

discarding state   The RSTP state that corresponds to the disabled, blocking, and listening operational states of the 802.1D STP.

distance vector   The logic behind the behavior of some interior routing protocols, such as RIP. Distance vector routing algorithms call for each router to send its entire routing table in each update, but only to its neighbors. Distance vector routing algorithms can be prone to routing loops but are computationally simpler than link-state routing algorithms.

DNS   Domain Name System. An application layer protocol used throughout the Internet for translating host names into their associated IP addresses.

dotted-decimal notation (DDN)   The format used for IP version 4 addresses, in which four decimal values are used, separated by periods (dots).

DPVM   Dynamic Port VSAN Membership. Dynamically assigns VSAN membership to ports by assigning VSANs based on the device WWN.

DS0   Digital signal level 0. A 64-kbps line, or channel of a faster line inside a telco, whose origins are to support a single voice call using the original voice (PCM) codecs.

DS1   Digital signal level 1. A 1.544-Mbps line from the telco, with 24 DS0 channels of 64 kbps each, plus an 8-kbps management and framing channel. Also called a T1.

DSL   Digital subscriber line. Public network technology that delivers high bandwidth over conventional telco local-loop copper wiring at limited distances. Typically used as an Internet access technology connecting a user to an ISP.

DSL modem   A device that connects to a telephone line, using DSL standards, to transmit and receive data to/from a telco using DSL.

DTE   Data terminal equipment. From a Layer 1 perspective, the DTE synchronizes its clock based on the clock sent by the DCE. From a packet-switching perspective, the DTE is the device outside the service provider's network, typically a router.

dual stack   A mode of operation in which a host or router runs both IPv4 and IPv6.

duplex mismatch   On opposite ends of any Ethernet link, the condition in which one of the two devices uses full-duplex logic and the other uses half-duplex logic, resulting in unnecessary frame discards and retransmissions on the link.

Duplicate Address Detection (DAD)   A term used in IPv6 to refer to how hosts first check whether another host is using a unicast address before the first host uses that address.

Dynamic FCoE   The ability to overlay FCoE traffic across Spine-Leaf data center switching architecture. In its first instantiation Dynamic FCoE allows running FCoE on top of Cisco FabricPath network in a converged fashion.

E

EIGRP   Enhanced Interior Gateway Routing Protocol. An advanced version of IGRP developed by Cisco. Provides superior convergence properties and operating efficiency and combines the advantages of link-state protocols with those of distance vector protocols.

EIGRP version 6   The version of the EIGRP routing protocol that supports IPv6, and not IPv4.

ELS   Extended Link Services. Link services provide a number of architected functions that are available to the users of the Fibre Channel port. There are basic link services, extended link services, and FC-4 link services (generic services). ELS are performed in a single exchange.

enable mode   A part of the Cisco IOS CLI in which the user can use the most powerful and potentially disruptive commands on a router or switch, including the ability to then reach configuration mode and reconfigure the router.

encapsulation   The placement of data from a higher-layer protocol behind the header (and in some cases, between a header and trailer) of the next-lower-layer protocol. For example, an IP packet could be encapsulated in an Ethernet header and trailer before being sent over an Ethernet.

encryption   Applying a specific algorithm to data to alter the appearance of the data, making it incomprehensible to those who are not authorized to see the information.

Enhanced Transmission Selection (ETS)   *See* 802.1Qaz.

EoR   End-of-Row. In the EOR network design, each server in individual racks is connected to a common EOR aggregation switch directly, without connecting to individual switches in each rack. Bigger cables are used to connect each server to chassis-based EOR/Aggregation Switches. There might be multiple such EOR switches in the same data center, one for each row or certain number of racks.

EPP   Exchange Peer Parameters. Fibre Channel port channel protocol uses EPP SW_ILS frames. SW_ILS frames are special Fibre Channel frames exchanged between storage switches on ISL links. There are many kinds of SW_ILS frames, and EPP is one of them.

error detection   The process of discovering whether a data link level frame was changed during transmission. This process typically uses a Frame Check Sequence (FCS) field in the data link trailer.

error disabled   An interface state on LAN switches that can be the result of one of many security violations.

error recovery   The process of noticing when some transmitted data was not successfully received and resending the data until it is successfully received.

Ethernet   A series of LAN standards defined by the IEEE, originally invented by Xerox Corporation and developed jointly by Xerox, Intel, and Digital Equipment Corporation.

Ethernet address   A 48-bit (6-byte) binary number, usually written as a 12-digit hexadecimal number, used to identify Ethernet nodes in an Ethernet network. Ethernet frame headers list a destination and source address field, used by the Ethernet devices to deliver Ethernet frames to the correct destination.

Ethernet frame   A term referring to an Ethernet data link header and trailer, plus the data encapsulated between the header and trailer.

Ethernet link   A generic term for any physical link between two Ethernet nodes, no matter what type of cabling is used.

Ethernet port   A generic term for the opening on the side of any Ethernet node, typically in an Ethernet NIC or LAN switch, into which an Ethernet cable can be connected.

EtherType   Jargon that shortens the term "Ethernet Type," which refers to the Type field in the Ethernet header. The Type field identifies the type of packet encapsulated inside an Ethernet frame.

EUI-64   Literally, a standard for an extended unique identifier that is 64 bits long. Specifically for IPv6, a set of rules for forming a 64-bit identifier, used as the interface ID in IPv6 addresses, by starting with a 48-bit MAC address, inserting FFFE (hex) in the middle, and inverting the seventh bit.

EVFP   Exchange Virtual Fabric Protocol. A single link can be established to connect an F port to an HBA to carry tagged frames using Exchange Virtual Fabrics Protocol (EVFP). The TF-TNP port link between a third-party NPV core and a Cisco NPV switch is established using the EVFP protocol.

Exec mode   Enables you to temporarily change terminal settings, perform basic tests, and display system information. Changes made in this mode are generally not saved across system resets.

extended access list   A list of IOS access list global configuration commands that can match multiple parts of an IP packet, including the source and destination IP address and TCP/UDP ports, for the purpose of deciding which packets to discard and which to allow through the router.

exterior gateway protocol (EGP)   A routing protocol that was designed to exchange routing information between different autonomous systems.

F

Fan-in ratio   The ratio of how many storage ports can be served from a single host channel.

Fan-out ratio   The relationship in quantity between a single port on a storage device and the number of servers that are attached to it.

Fast Ethernet   The common name for all the IEEE standards that send data at 100 megabits per second.

FC-GS   Fibre Channel Generic Services.

FCoE   Fibre Channel over Ethernet. A computer network technology that encapsulates Fibre Channel frames over Ethernet networks. This allows Fibre Channel to use 10 Gigabit Ethernet networks (or higher speeds) while preserving the Fibre Channel protocol characteristics. The specification is part of the International Committee for Information Technology Standards T11 FC-BB-5 standard published in 2009. FCoE maps Fibre Channel directly over Ethernet while being independent of the Ethernet forwarding scheme.

feasibility condition   In EIGRP, when a router has learned of multiple routes to reach one subnet, if the best route's metric is X, the feasibility condition is another route whose reported distance is < X.

feasible distance   In EIGRP, the metric of the best route to reach a subnet.

feasible successor   In EIGRP, a route that is not the best route (successor route) but that can be used immediately if the best route fails, without causing a loop. Such a route meets the feasibility condition.

feature interface-vlan   A command to enable the capability of a Cisco Nexus Switch to create a Switch Virtual Interface (SVI) on it.

Fiber Distributed Data Interchange (FDDI)   An old LAN technology that used a physical star topology, with a logic token passing ring, with fiber optic cabling, at speeds of 100 Mbps.

Fibre Channel (FC)   A high-speed network technology (commonly running at 2-, 4-, 8- and 16-gigabit per second rates) primarily used to connect computer data storage. Fibre Channel is standardized in the T11 Technical Committee of the International Committee for Information Technology Standards (INCITS), an American National Standards Institute (ANSI)-accredited standards committee.

Fibre Channel over Ethernet N-port Virtualization (FCoE-NPV)   Secure method to connect FCoE-capable hosts to an FCoE-capable FCoE forwarder (FCF) device. Switches operating in FCoE-NPV mode proxy all Fibre Channel processing and functions to the upstream switch operating in FCoE-NPIV mode.

Fibre Channel over Ethernet N-Port ID virtualization (FCoE-NPIV)   Fibre Channel mechanism to assign multiple Fibre Channel IDs on the same physical interface. FCoE-NPIV can work with FCoE-NPV to enable scaled-out SAN access layer.

FICON   Fibre Connection. The IBM proprietary name for the ANSI FC-SB-3 Single-Byte Command Code Sets-3 Mapping Protocol for Fibre Channel (FC) protocol. It is an FC Layer 4 protocol used to map both IBM's antecedent (either ESCON or parallel) channel-to-control-unit cabling infrastructure and protocol onto standard FC services and infrastructure. The topology is fabric utilizing FC switches or directors. Valid rates include 1, 2, 4, and 8 Gigabit per second data rates (at the time of writing this book) at distances up to 100 km. FICON has replaced ESCON in current deployments because of FICON's technical superiority (especially its higher performance) and lower cost.

filter   Generally, a process or a device that screens network traffic for certain characteristics, such as source address, destination address, or protocol, and determines whether to forward or discard that traffic based on the established criteria.

firewall   A device that forwards packets between the less secure and more secure parts of the network, applying rules that determine which packets are allowed to pass, and which are not.

flash   A type of read/write permanent memory that retains its contents even with no power applied to the memory, and uses no moving parts, making the memory less likely to fail over time.

FLOGI (F_Port Login)   Fabric Login command establishes a 24-bit address for the device logging in and establishes buffer-to-buffer credits and the class of service supported.

flooding   The result of the LAN switch forwarding process for broadcasts and unknown unicast frames. Switches forward these frames out all interfaces, except the interface in which the frame arrived. Switches also flood multicasts by default, although this behavior can be changed.

flow control   The process of regulating the amount of data sent by a sending computer toward a receiving computer. Several flow control mechanisms exist, including TCP flow control, which uses windowing.

forward   To send a frame received in one interface out another interface, toward its ultimate destination.

forward acknowledgment   A process used by protocols that do error recovery, in which the number that acknowledges data lists the next data that should be sent, not the last data that was successfully received.

four-wire circuit   A line from the telco with four wires, composed of two twisted-pair wires. Each pair is used to send in one direction, so a four-wire circuit allows full-duplex communication.

Fport-channel-trunk   Trunking F ports allows interconnected ports to transmit and receive tagged frames in more than one VSAN, over the same physical link.

fragment-free switching   One of three internal processing options on some Cisco LAN switches in which the first bits of the frame can be forwarded before the entire frame is received, but not until the first 64 bytes of the frame are received, in which case, in a well-designed LAN, collision fragments should not occur as a result of this forwarding logic.

frame   A term referring to a data link header and trailer, plus the data encapsulated between the header and trailer.

Frame Check Sequence   A field in many data link trailers used as part of the error detection process.

Frame Relay   An international standard data link protocol that defines the capabilities to create a frame-switched (packet-switched) service, allowing DTE devices (typically routers) to send data to many other devices using a single physical connection to the Frame Relay service.

full-duplex   Generically, any communication in which two communicating devices can concurrently send and receive data. In Ethernet LANs, the allowance for both devices to send and receive at the same time, allowed when both devices disable their CSMA/CD logic.

full mesh   A network topology in which more than two devices can physically communicate and, by choice, all pairs of devices are allowed to communicate directly.

G

Gigabit Ethernet   The common name for all the IEEE standards that send data at 1 gigabit per second.

Global Configuration Mode   Enables you to configure features that affect the system as a whole. Changes made in this mode are saved across system resets if you save your configuration.

global routing prefix   An IPv6 prefix that defines an IPv6 address block made up of global unicast addresses, assigned to one organization, so that the organization has a block of globally unique IPv6 addresses to use in its network.

global unicast address   A type of unicast IPv6 address that has been allocated from a range of public globally unique IP addresses, as registered through IANA/ICANN, its member agencies, and other registries or ISPs.

H

half-duplex   Generically, any communication in which only one device at a time can send data. In Ethernet LANs, the normal result of the CSMA/CD algorithm that enforces the rule that only one device should send at any point in time.

HBA   Host bus adapter. Host controller, host adapter, or host bus adapter (HBA) connects a host system (the computer) to other network and storage devices.

HDD   Hard disk drive. A disk drive that can read/write bits of information and is nonvolatile.

HDLC   High-Level Data Link Control. A bitoriented synchronous data link layer protocol developed by the International Organization for Standardization (ISO).

header   In computer networking, a set of bytes placed in front of some other data, encapsulating that data, as defined by a particular protocol.

host   Any device that uses an IP address.

host address   The IP address assigned to a network card on a computer.

host-based virtualization   It requires additional software running on the host, as a privileged task or process. In some cases volume management is built in to the operating system, and in other instances it is offered as a separate product. Volumes (LUNs) presented to the host system are handled by a traditional physical device driver. However, a software layer (the volume manager) resides above the disk device driver, intercepts the I/O requests, and provides the metadata lookup and I/O mapping.

host name   The alphameric name of an IP host.

host part   A term used to describe a part of an IPv4 address that is used to uniquely identify a host inside a subnet. The host part is identified by the bits of value 0 in the subnet mask.

host route   A route with a /32 mask, which by virtue of this mask represents a route to a single host IP address.

HTML Hypertext Markup Language. A simple document-formatting language that uses tags to indicate how a given part of a document should be interpreted by a viewing application, such as a web browser.

HTTP Hypertext Transfer Protocol. The protocol used by web browsers and web servers to transfer files, such as text and graphic files.

hub A LAN device that provides a centralized connection point for LAN cabling, repeating any received electrical signal out all other ports, thereby creating a logical bus. Hubs do not interpret the electrical signals as a frame of bits, so hubs are considered to be Layer 1 devices.

I

IANA The Internet Assigned Numbers Authority (IANA). An organization that owns the rights to assign many operating numbers and facts about how the global Internet works, including public IPv4 and IPv6 addresses. *See also* ICANN.

ICANN The Internet Corporation for Assigned Names and Numbers. An organization appointed by IANA to oversee the distributed process of assigning public IPv4 and IPv6 addresses across the globe.

ICMP Internet Control Message Protocol. A TCP/IP network layer protocol that reports errors and provides other information relevant to IP packet processing.

IEEE Institute of Electrical and Electronics Engineers. A professional organization that develops communications and network standards, among other activities.

IEEE 802.2 An IEEE LAN protocol that specifies an implementation of the LLC sublayer of the data link layer.

IEEE 802.3 A set of IEEE LAN protocols that specifies the many variations of what is known today as an Ethernet LAN.

IETF The Internet Engineering Task Force. The IETF serves as the primary organization that works directly to create new TCP/IP standards.

inactivity timer For switch MAC address tables, a timer associated with each entry that counts time upward from 0 and is reset to 0 each time a switch receives a frame with the same MAC address. The entries with the largest timers can be removed to make space for additional MAC address table entries.

In-band A storage virtualization method that places the virtualization engine directly in the data path, so that both block data and the control information that govern its virtual appearance transit the same link.

INCITS International Committee for Information Technology Standards. An ANSI-accredited forum of IT developers. It was formerly known as the X3 and NCITS.

initiator All SCSI devices are intelligent, but SCSI operates as a master/slave model. One SCSI device (the initiator) initiates communication with another SCSI device (the target) by issuing a command, to which a response is expected. Thus, the SCSI protocol is half-duplex by design and is considered a command/response protocol.

Inter-VLAN routing   The ability of a device to route between two or more VLANs.

Inter-VSAN routing (IVR)   Facilitates the communication between a target and initiator in different VSANs. IVR was a natural evolution of that same VSAN technology. By routing between VSANs, devices can maintain the level of separation in terms of fabric services and fabric-wide events required for the highest level of availability, yet take advantage of data sharing across thousands of devices.

interior gateway protocol (IGP)   *See* interior routing protocol.

interior routing protocol   A routing protocol designed for use within a single organization.

intrusion detection system (IDS)   A security function that examines more complex traffic patterns against a list of both known attack signatures and general characteristics of how attacks can be carried out, rating each perceived threat and reporting the threats.

intrusion prevention system (IPS)   A security function that examines more complex traffic patterns against a list of both known attack signatures and general characteristics of how attacks can be carried out, rating each perceived threat, and reacting to prevent the more significant threats.

IoE   Internet of Everything. Cisco defines the Internet of Everything (IoE) as bringing together people, process, data, and things to make networked connections more relevant and valuable than ever before—turning information into actions that create new capabilities, richer experiences, and unprecedented economic opportunity for businesses, individuals, and countries.

IOPS   Input/output Operations per Second, pronounced "eye-ops." A common performance measurement used to benchmark computer storage devices like hard disk drives (HDD), solid state drives (SSD), and storage-area networks (SAN).

IOS   Cisco Internetwork Operating System Software that provides the majority of a router's or switch's features, with the hardware providing the remaining features.

IOS image   A file that contains the IOS.

IP   Internet Protocol. The network layer protocol in the TCP/IP stack, providing routing and logical addressing standards and services.

IP address (IP version 4)   In IP version 4 (IPv4), a 32-bit address assigned to hosts using TCP/IP. Each address consists of a network number, an optional subnetwork number, and a host number. The network and subnetwork numbers together are used for routing, and the host number is used to address an individual host within the network or subnetwork.

IP address (IP version 6)   In IP version 6 (IPv6), a 128-bit address assigned to hosts using TCP/IP. Addresses use different formats, commonly using a routing prefix, subnet, and interface ID, corresponding to the IPv4 network, subnet, and host parts of an address.

IP network   *See* classful IP network.

IP packet   An IP header, followed by the data encapsulated after the IP header, but specifically not including any headers and trailers for layers below the network layer.

IP subnet   Subdivisions of a Class A, B, or C network, as configured by a network administrator. Subnets allow a single Class A, B, or C network to be used instead of multiple networks, and still allow for a large number of groups of IP addresses, as is required for efficient IP routing.

IP version 4   Literally, the version of the Internet Protocol defined in an old RFC 791, standardized in 1980, and used as the basis of TCP/IP networks and the Internet for more than 30 years.

IP version 6   A newer version of the Internet Protocol defined in RFC 2460, as well as many other RFCs, whose creation was motivated by the need to avoid the IPv4 address exhaustion problem.

IPv4 address exhaustion   The process by which the public IPv4 addresses, available to create the Internet, were consumed through the 1980s until today, with the expectation that eventually the world would run out of available IPv4 addresses.

IPv6 neighbor table   The IPv6 equivalent of the ARP table. A table that lists IPv6 addresses of other hosts on the same link, along with their matching MAC addresses, as typically learned using Neighbor Discovery Protocol (NDP).

iSCSI   Internet Small Computer Interface. An Internet Protocol (IP)-based storage networking standard for linking data storage facilities. By carrying SCSI commands over IP networks, iSCSI is used to facilitate data transfers over intranets and manage storage over long distances. iSCSI can be used to transmit data over local-area networks (LANs), wide-area networks (WANs), or the Internet and can enable location-independent data storage and retrieval. The protocol allows clients (called *initiators*) to send SCSI commands (*CDBs*) to SCSI storage devices (*targets*) on remote servers. It is a storage-area network (SAN) protocol, allowing organizations to consolidate storage into data center storage arrays while providing hosts (such as database and web servers) with the illusion of locally attached disks. iSCSI can be run over long distances using existing network infrastructure. iSCSI was pioneered by IBM and Cisco in 1998 and submitted as draft standard in March 2000.

ISL   Inter-Switch Link. A Cisco-proprietary protocol that maintains VLAN information as traffic flows between switches and routers.

ISO   International Organization for Standardization. An international organization that is responsible for a wide range of standards, including many standards relevant to networking. The ISO developed the OSI reference model, a popular networking reference model.

K

keepalive   A proprietary feature of Cisco routers in which the router sends messages on a periodic basis as a means of letting the neighboring router know that the first router is still alive and well.

L

L4PDU   Layer 4 protocol data unit. The data compiled by a Layer 4 protocol, including Layer 4 headers and encapsulated highlayer data, but not including lower-layer headers and trailers.

Layer 3 protocol   A protocol that has characteristics like OSI Layer 3, which defines logical addressing and routing. IPv4 and IPv6 are Layer 3 protocols.

Layer 3 switch   *See* multilayer switch.

learning   The process used by switches for discovering MAC addresses, and their relative location, by looking at the source MAC address of all frames received by a bridge or switch.

leased line   A serial communications circuit between two points, provided by some service provider, typically a telephone company (telco). Because the telco does not sell a physical cable between the two endpoints, instead charging a monthly fee for the ability to send bits between the two sites, the service is considered to be a leased service.

link-local address   A type of unicast IPv6 address that represents an interface on a single data link. Packets sent to a link-local address cross only that particular link and are never forwarded to other subnets by a router. Used for communications that do not need to leave the local link.

link-local scope   With IPv6 multicasts, a term that refers to the parts (scope) of the network to which a multicast packet can flow, with link-local referring to the fact that the packet stays on the subnet in which it originated.

link-state   A classification of the underlying algorithm used in some routing protocols. Link-state protocols build a detailed database that lists links (subnets) and their state (up, down), from which the best routes can then be calculated.

link-state advertisement (LSA)   In OSPF, the name of the data structure that resides inside the LSDB and describes in detail the various components in a network, including routers and links (subnets).

link-state database (LSDB)   In OSPF, the data structure in RAM of a router that holds the various LSAs, with the collective LSAs representing the entire topology of the network.

LLC   Logical Link Control. The higher of the two data link layer sublayers defined by the IEEE. Synonymous with IEEE 802.2.

LLDP   Link Layer Discovery Protocol. *See* 802.1AB.

local loop   A line from the premises of a telephone subscriber to the telephone company CO.

local route   A route that is locally connected to an interface (an IP address of the interface) on a Cisco Nexus Switch.

local subnet broadcast address   IPv4 address 255.255.255.255. A packet sent to this address is sent as a data link broadcast, but only flows to hosts in the subnet into which it was originally sent. Routers do not forward these packets.

local username   A username (with matching password), configured on a router or switch. It is considered local because it exists on the router or switch, and not on a remote server.

logical address   A generic reference to addresses as defined by Layer 3 protocols that do not have to be concerned with the physical details of the underlying physical media. Used mainly to contrast these addresses with data link addresses, which are generically considered to be physical addresses because they differ based on the type of physical medium.

Logical Bus Topology   A logical networking topology in which each electrical signal passes by each device, mimicking a bus stopping at bus stops on a route.

LOGO (Logout)   For FC devices, an N_Port logs out from the FC network by sending an FC LOGO message to the F_Port of an FC switch. The switch can also send a LOGO message to an N_Port to terminate its connection.

LUN   Logical unit number. In computer storage, a number used to identify a logical unit, which is a device addressed by the SCSI protocol or protocols that encapsulate SCSI, such as Fibre Channel or iSCSI. A LUN may be used with any device that supports read/write operations, such as a tape drive, but is most often used to refer to a logical disk as created on a SAN.

LUN mapping   This is the process by which the host operating system assigns a LUN value to a particular storage volume. LUN mapping is typically used in cases where the higher-level applications require specific LUN numbers for specific storage devices. When there are multiple paths between an SCSI initiator and SCSI target, multipathing software is used to properly map target volumes via both the paths.

LUN masking   LUN masking ensures that only one host can access a LUN; all other hosts are masked out. LUN masking is essentially a mapping table inside the front-end array controllers. LUN masking determines which LUNs are to be advertised through which storage array ports, and which host is allowed to own which LUNs.

M

MAC   Media Access Control. The lower of the two sublayers of the data link layer defined by the IEEE. Synonymous with IEEE 802.3 for Ethernet LANs.

MAC address   A standardized data link layer address that is required for every device that connects to a LAN. Ethernet MAC addresses are 6 bytes long and are controlled by the IEEE. Also known as a *hardware address*, a MAC *layer address*, and a *physical address*.

metadata   Data about data. The term is ambiguous because it is used for two fundamentally different concepts (types). Structural metadata is about the design and specification of data structures and is more properly called "data about the containers of data"; descriptive metadata, on the other hand, is about individual instances of application data, the data content. The main purpose of metadata is to facilitate in the discovery of relevant information, more often classified as resource discovery. Metadata also helps organize electronic resources, provides digital identification, and helps support archiving and preservation of the resource.

metric   A unit of measure used by routing protocol algorithms to determine the best route for traffic to use to reach a particular destination.

microsegmentation   The process in LAN design by which every switch port connects to a single device, with no hubs connected to the switch ports, creating a separate collision domain per interface. The term's origin relates to the fact that one definition for the word "segment" is "collision domain," with a switch separating each switch port into a separate collision domain or segment.

modem   Modulator-demodulator. A device that converts between digital and analog signals so that a computer can send data to another computer using analog telephone lines. At the source, a modem converts digital signals to a form suitable for transmission over analog communication facilities. At the destination, the analog signals are returned to their digital form.

multihop FCoE   Set of technologies and designs to extend convergence of network and storage traffic beyond the data center access layer.

multilayer switch   A LAN switch that can also perform Layer 3 routing functions. The name comes from the fact that this device makes forwarding decisions based on logic from multiple OSI layers (Layers 2 and 3).

multimode   A type of fiber-optic cabling with a larger core than single-mode cabling, allowing light to enter at multiple angles. Such cabling has lower bandwidth than single mode fiber but requires a typically cheaper light source, such as an LED rather than a laser.

multipathing   A technique that lets you use more than one physical path that transfers data between the host and an external storage device.

N

name server   A server connected to a network that resolves network names into network addresses.

named access list   An ACL that identifies the various statements in the ACL based on a name, rather than a number.

NAT   Network Address Translation. A mechanism for reducing the need for globally unique IP addresses. NAT allows an organization with addresses that are not globally unique to connect to the Internet, by translating those addresses into public addresses in the globally routable address space.

neighbor   In routing protocols, another router with which a router decides to exchange routing information.

Neighbor Advertisement (NA)   A message defined by the IPv6 Neighbor Discovery Protocol (NDP), used to declare to other neighbors a host's MAC address. Sometimes sent in response to a previously received NDP Neighbor Solicitation (NS) message.

Neighbor Discovery Protocol (NDP)   A protocol that is part of the IPv6 protocol suite, used to discover and exchange information about devices on the same subnet (neighbors). In particular, it replaces the IPv4 ARP protocol.

Neighbor Solicitation (NS)   A message defined by the IPv6 Neighbor Discovery Protocol (NDP), used to ask a neighbor to reply with a Neighbor Advertisement, which lists the neighbor's MAC address.

network   A collection of computers, printers, routers, switches, and other devices that can communicate with each other over some transmission medium.

network address   *See* network number.

network-based virtualization   In computing, network virtualization is the process of combining hardware and software network resources and network functionality into a single, software-based administrative entity, a virtual network. Network virtualization involves platform virtualization, often combined with resource virtualization.

network broadcast address   In IPv4, a special address in each classful network that can be used to broadcast a packet to all hosts in that same classful network. Numerically, the address has the same value as the network number in the network part of the address and all 255s in the host octets—for example, 10.255.255.255 is the network broadcast address for classful network 10.0.0.0.

Network File System   A distributed file system protocol originally developed by Sun Microsystems in 1984, allowing a user on a client computer to access files over a network much like local storage is accessed. NFS, like many other protocols, builds on the Open Network Computing Remote Procedure Call (ONC RPC) system. The Network File System is an open standard defined in RFCs, allowing anyone to implement the protocol.

network interface card (NIC)   A computer card, sometimes an expansion card and some-times integrated into the motherboard of the computer, that provides the electronics and other functions to connect to a computer network. Today, most NICs are specifically Ethernet NICs, and most have an RJ-45 port, the most common type of Ethernet port.

network number   A number that uses dotted-decimal notation like IP addresses, but the number itself represents all hosts in a single Class A, B, or C IP network.

network part   The portion of an IPv4 address that is either 1, 2, or 3 octets/bytes long, based on whether the address is in a Class A, B, or C network.

Network Time Protocol (NTP)   A protocol used to synchronize time-of-day clocks so that multiple devices use the same time of day, which allows log messages to be more easily matched based on their timestamps.

networking model   A generic term referring to any set of protocols and standards collected into a comprehensive grouping that, when followed by the devices in a network, allows all the devices to communicate. Examples include TCP/IP and OSI.

next-hop router   In an IP route in a routing table, part of a routing table entry that refers to the next IP router (by IP address) that should receive packets that match the route.

NIC   *See* network interface card.

NPIV   N_port ID virtualization. A technique that enables the sharing of a single Fibre Channel N_port between multiple N_ports. It is used in storage networking techniques that utilize Fibre Channel-based ports to send and receive data between virtual machines (VM) and virtual storage-area networks (SAN). NPIV is a component of the Fibre Channel Link Services (FC-LS) specification.

NPV   N-Port virtualization. A feature that has growing importance in the data center. In a tra-ditional SAN fabric, each switch gets assigned a Domain ID. The Domain ID is an 8-bit field in the FCID. There are officially 255 domain IDs. In reality, some of these IDs are reserved and can't be assigned to switches, leaving us with 239 switches. In large environments, that hard limit can become a serious issue as you try to scale the fabric. The solution to this problem is NPV. NPV allows SAN switches to essentially become N port proxies.

NVRAM   Nonvolatile RAM. A type of random-access memory (RAM) that retains its contents when a unit is powered off.

O

ordered data transfer A networking function, included in TCP, in which the protocol defines how the sending host should number the data transmitted, defines how the receiving device should attempt to reorder the data if it arrives out of order, and specifies to discard the data if it cannot be delivered in order.

OSI Open System Interconnection reference model. A network architectural model developed by the ISO. The model consists of seven layers, each of which specifies particular network functions, such as addressing, flow control, error control, encapsulation, and reliable message transfer.

OSPF Open Shortest Path First. A popular link-state IGP that uses a link-state database and the Shortest Path First (SPF) algorithm to calculate the best routes to reach each known subnet.

OSPF version 2 The version of the OSPF routing protocol that supports IPv4, and not IPv6, and has been commonly used for over 20 years.

OSPF version 3 The version of the OSPF routing protocol originally created to support IPv6.

outgoing interface In an IP route in a routing table, part of a routing table entry that refers to the local interface out which the local router should forward packets that match the route.

out-of-band A storage virtualization method that provides separate paths for data and control, presenting an image of virtual storage to the host by one link and allowing the host to directly retrieve data blocks from physical storage on another.

overlapping subnets An (incorrect) IP subnet design condition in which one subnet's range of addresses includes addresses in the range of another subnet.

P

packet A logical grouping of bytes that includes the network layer header and encapsulated data, but specifically does not include any headers and trailers below the network layer.

packet switching A generic reference to network services, typically WAN services, in which the service examines the contents of the transmitted data to make some type of forwarding decision. This term is mainly used to contrast with the WAN term *circuit switching*, in which the provider sets up a (Layer 1) circuit between two devices and the provider makes no attempt to interpret the meaning of the bits.

partial mesh A network topology in which more than two devices could physically communicate but, by choice, only a subset of the pairs of devices connected to the network is allowed to communicate directly.

partial update With IP routing protocols, the general concept that a routing protocol update lists a subset of all known routes. *See also* full update.

patch cable An Ethernet cable, usually short, that connects from a device's Ethernet port to a wall plate or switch. With wiring inside a building, electricians prewire from the wiring closet to each cubicle or other location, with a patch cable connecting the short distance from the wall plate to the user device.

PDU   Protocol data unit. An OSI term to refer generically to a grouping of information by a particular layer of the OSI model. More specifically, an LxPDU would imply the data and headers as defined by Layer x.

periodic update   With routing protocols, the concept that the routing protocol advertises routes in a routing update on a regular periodic basis. This is typical of distance vector routing protocols.

physical bus topology   A physical networking topology in which cables run near each device, mimicking a bus route. 10BASE-5 and 10BASE-2 are considered to use a physical bus topology.

physical star topology   A physical networking topology in which cables connect to a central networking device, mimicking what a child might draw to represent the sun.

physical topology   A description of a physical network based on its general shape or characteristics, useful when comparing different networking technology.

ping   An Internet Control Message Protocol (ICMP) echo message and its reply; ping often is used in IP networks to test the reachability of a network device.

pinout   The documentation and implementation of which wires inside a cable connect to each pin position in any connector.

PLOGI (N_Port Login)   Requests login to another N_port, before any data exchange between ports. This is done with port login (PLOGI) at the address 0xFFFFFC.

POAP   Power On Auto Provisioning. Automates the process of upgrading software images and installing configuration files on Cisco MDS and Nexus switches that are being deployed in the network.

port   In TCP and UDP, a number that is used to uniquely identify the application process that either sent (source port) or should receive (destination port) data. In LAN switching, another term for switch interface.

port number   A field in a TCP or UDP header that identifies the application that either sent (source port) or should receive (destination port) the data inside the data segment.

PPP   Point-to-Point Protocol. A protocol that provides router-to-router and host-to network connections over synchronous point-to-point and asynchronous point-to-point circuits.

prefix   In IPv6, this term refers to the number that identifies a group of IPv6 addresses. An IPv6 subnet identifier.

prefix length   In IPv6, the number of bits in an IPv6 prefix.

prefix notation (IP version 4)   A shorter way to write a subnet mask in which the number of binary 1s in the mask is simply written in decimal. For example, /24 denotes the subnet mask with 24 binary 1 bits in the subnet mask. The number of bits of value binary 1 in the mask is considered to be the prefix length.

Priority Flow Control (PFC)   *See* 802.1Qbb.

private addresses IP addresses in several Class A, B, and C networks that are set aside for use inside private organizations. These addresses, as defined in RFC 1918, are not routable through the Internet.

PRLI Process login. Establishes communication between two FC-4 layer processes (SCSI), between two different N_Ports.

PRLO Process logout. A process that logs out two FC-4 layer processes (SCSI) between two different N_Ports.

problem isolation The part of the troubleshooting process in which the engineer attempts to rule out possible causes of the problem until the root cause of the problem can be identified.

protocol data unit (PDU) A generic term referring to the header defined by some layer of a networking model, and the data encapsulated by the header (and possibly trailer) of that layer, but specifically not including any lower-layer headers and trailers.

Protocol Type field A field in a LAN header that identifies the type of header that follows the LAN header. Includes the DIX Ethernet Type field, the IEEE 802.2 DSAP field, and the SNAP protocol Type field.

PSTN Public switched telephone network. A general term referring to the variety of telephone networks and services in place worldwide. Sometimes called *POTS*, or *plain old telephone service.*

public IP address An IP address that is part of a registered network number, as assigned by an Internet Assigned Numbers Authority (IANA) member agency, so that only the organization to which the address is registered is allowed to use the address. Routers in the Internet should have routes allowing them to forward packets to all the publicly registered IP addresses.

pWWN *See* World Wide Port Name (WWPN).

Q

QCN Quantized congestion notifications. IEEE 802.1Qau standard defines Layer 2 traffic management system that pushes congestion to the edge of the network by instructing rate limiters to shape the traffic causing the congestion.

quartet A term used in this book, but not in other references, to refer to a set of four hex digits in an IPv6 address.

R

RAM Random-access memory. A type of volatile memory that can be read and written by a microprocessor.

RAID Redundant Array of Inexpensive Disks. Configured on disks allowing them to be presented as one logical unit with redundancy, availability, performance, and optimal usage of hard disk capacity.

Rapid Spanning-Tree Protocol (RSTP)   An enhancement to STP based on the IEEE 802.1w standard.

repeater   A networking device that operates with Layer 1 features to receive a signal, interpret the meaning, generate a new electrical signal to represent those same bits, and send those out another port.

revision number   With VTP, a number that identifies the version of the VLAN database believed to be the current VLAN database in that VTP domain.

RFC   Request For Comments. A document used as the primary means for communicating information about the TCP/IP protocols. Some RFCs are designated by the Internet Architecture Board (IAB) as Internet standards, and others are informational. RFCs are available online from numerous sources, including www.rfc-editor.org.

RIP   Routing Information Protocol. An interior gateway protocol (IGP) that uses distance vector logic and router hop count as the metric. RIP version 2 (RIP-2) replaced the older RIP version 1 (RIP-1), with RIP-2 providing more features, including support for VLSM.

RJ-45   A popular type of cabling connector used for Ethernet cabling. It is similar to the RJ-11 connector used for telephone wiring in homes in the United States. RJ-45 allows the connection of eight wires.

ROM   Read-only memory. A type of nonvolatile memory that can be read but not written to by the microprocessor.

root cause   A troubleshooting term that refers to the reason why a problem exists, specifically a reason for which, if changed, the problem would either be solved or changed to a different problem.

routed interface   An Ethernet interface on a multilayer switch that has been dedicated for Layer 3–only functionality. When enabled, the interface disables any Layer 2 functionality on this interface.

routed protocol   A protocol that defines packets that can be routed by a router. Examples of routed protocols include IPv4 and IPv6.

Router Advertisement (RA)   A message defined by the IPv6 Neighbor Discovery Protocol (NDP), used by routers to announce their willingness to act as an IPv6 router on a link. These can be sent in response to a previously received NDP Router Solicitation (RS) message.

router ID (RID)   In OSPF, a 32-bit number, written in dotted-decimal notation, that uniquely identifies each router.

Router Solicitation (RS)   A message defined by the IPv6 Neighbor Discovery Protocol (NDP), used to ask any routers on the link to reply, identifying the router, plus other configuration settings (prefixes and prefix lengths).

routing protocol   A set of messages and processes with which routers can exchange information about routes to reach subnets in a particular network. Examples of routing protocols include the Enhanced Interior Gateway Routing Protocol (EIGRP), the Open Shortest Path First (OSPF) protocol, and the Routing Information Protocol (RIP).

routing table   A list of routes in a router, with each route listing the destination subnet and mask, the router interface out which to forward packets destined to that subnet, and as needed, the next-hop router's IP address.

routing update   A generic reference to any routing protocol's messages in which it sends routing information to a neighbor.

RSCN   Registered State Change Notification. A Fibre Channel fabric's notification sent to all specified nodes in case of any major fabric changes. This allows nodes to immediately gain knowledge about the fabric and react accordingly.

running-config file   In Cisco IOS switches and routers, the name of the file that resides in RAM memory, holding the device's currently used configuration.

S

same-layer interaction   The communication between two networking devices for the purposes of the functions defined at a particular layer of a networking model, with that communication happening by using a header defined by that layer of the model. The two devices set values in the header, send the header and encapsulated data, with the receiving device(s) interpreting the header to decide what action to take.

SAN   Storage-Area Network. A dedicated network that provides access to consolidated, block-level data storage. SANs are primarily used to enhance storage devices, such as disk arrays, tape libraries, and optical jukeboxes, accessible to servers so that the devices appear like locally attached devices to the operating system. A SAN typically has its own network of storage devices that are generally not accessible through the local-area network (LAN) by other devices.

SAN-boot   The process of booting a computer operating system from a centralized online storage device, via a storage-area network, in contrast to having it boot from its local hard disk.

SCN   State change notification. Notifies other ports when login state changes at a designated N_Port.

SCR   State change registration. The Fibre Channel nodes register to the fabric controller 0xFFFFFD with a state change registration frame.

SCSI   Small Computer System Interface. A set of standards for physically connecting and transferring data between computers and peripheral devices. The SCSI standards define commands, protocols, and electrical and optical interfaces.

SDS   Software-defined storage. A term for computer data storage technologies that separate storage hardware from the software that manages the storage infrastructure. The software enabling a software-defined storage environment provides policy management for feature options such as deduplication, replication, thin provisioning, snapshots, and backup. By definition, SDS software is separate from hardware it is managing. That hardware may or may not have abstraction, pooling, or automation software embedded.

Secure Shell (SSH)   A TCP/IP application layer protocol that supports terminal emulation between a client and server, using dynamic key exchange and encryption to keep the communications private.

segment   In TCP, a term used to describe a TCP header and its encapsulated data (also called an *L4PDU*). Also in TCP, the process of accepting a large chunk of data from the application layer and breaking it into smaller pieces that fit into TCP segments. In Ethernet, a segment is either a single Ethernet cable or a single collision domain (no matter how many cables are used).

segmentation   The process of breaking a large piece of data from an application into pieces appropriate in size to be sent through the network.

serial cable   A type of cable with many different styles of connectors used to connect a router to an external CSU/DSU on a leased line installation.

serial interface   A type of interface on a router, used to connect to some types of WAN links, particularly leased lines and Frame Relay access links.

setup mode   An option on Cisco IOS switches and routers that prompts the user for basic configuration information, resulting in new running-config and startup-config files.

shared Ethernet   An Ethernet that uses a hub, or even the original coaxial cabling, that results in the devices having to take turns sending data, sharing the available bandwidth.

Shortest Path First (SPF) algorithm   The name of the algorithm used by link-state routing protocols to analyze the LSDB and find the least-cost routes from that router to each subnet.

show ip route   A command that will show the contents of a Cisco Nexus switch's current routing table.

single-mode   A type of fiber-optic cabling with a narrow core that allows light to enter only at a single angle. Such cabling has a higher bandwidth than multimode fiber but requires a light source with a narrow spectral width (such as a laser).

sliding windows   For protocols such as TCP that allow the receiving device to dictate the amount of data the sender can send before receiving an acknowledgment—a concept called a *window*—a reference to the fact that the mechanism to grant future windows is typically just a number that grows upward slowly after each acknowledgment, sliding upward.

slow drain   A device that does not accept frames at the rate generated by the source. In the presence of slow devices, Fibre Channel networks are likely to lack frame buffers, resulting in switch port credit starvation and potentially choking Inter-Switch Links (ISLs). Frames destined for slow devices need to be carefully isolated in separate queues and switched to egress ports without congesting the backplane. A decision then needs to be made about whether the frames are considered stuck and when to drop them.

SNIA   Storage Networking Industry Association. An association of producers and consumers of storage networking products; a registered 501 nonprofit trade association incorporated in December 1997. Its members are dedicated to "ensuring that storage networks become complete and trusted solutions across the IT community."

solicited-node multicast address   A type of IPv6 multicast address, with link-local scope, used to send packets to all hosts in the subnet that share the same value in the last six hex digits of their unicast IPv6 addresses. Begins with FF02::1:FF00:0/104.

Spanning Tree Protocol (STP)   A protocol that uses the Spanning Tree algorithm, allowing a switch to dynamically work around loops in a network topology by creating a spanning tree. Switches exchange bridge protocol data unit (BPDU) messages with other switches to detect loops and then remove the loops by blocking selected switch interfaces.

split horizon   A distant vector routing technique in which information about routes is prevented from exiting the router interface through which that information was received. Split-horizon updates are useful in preventing routing loops.

SSD   Solid-state drive. A data storage device using integrated circuit assemblies as memory to store data persistently. SSD technology uses electronic interfaces compatible with traditional block input/output (I/O) hard disk drives, thus permitting simple replacement in common applications.

standard access list   A list of IOS global configuration commands that can match only a packet's source IP address, for the purpose of deciding which packets to discard and which to allow through the router.

star   A network topology in which endpoints on a network are connected to a common central device by point-to-point links.

startup-config file   In Cisco IOS switches and routers, the name of the file that resides in NVRAM memory, holding the device's configuration that will be loaded into RAM as the running-config file when the device is next reloaded or powered on.

stateful DHCP   A term used in IPv6 to contrast with stateless DHCP. Stateful DHCP keeps track of which clients have been assigned which IPv6 addresses (state information).

Stateless Address Autoconfiguration (SLAAC)   A feature of IPv6 in which a host or router can be assigned an IPv6 unicast address without the need for a stateful DHCP server.

stateless DHCP   A term used in IPv6 to contrast with stateful DHCP. Stateless DHCP servers don't lease IPv6 addresses to clients. Instead, they supply other useful information, such as DNS server IP addresses, but with no need to track information about the clients (state information).

static route   An IP route on a router created by the user configuring the details of the route on the local router.

store-and-forward switching   One of three internal processing options on some Cisco LAN switches in which the Ethernet frame must be completely received before the switch can begin forwarding the first bit of the frame.

STP   Shielded twisted-pair. This type of cabling has a layer of shielded insulation to reduce electromagnetic interference (EMI).

straight-through cable   In Ethernet, a cable that connects the wire on pin 1 on one end of the cable to pin 1 on the other end of the cable, pin 2 on one end to pin 2 on the other end, and so on.

subnet   Subdivisions of a Class A, B, or C network, as configured by a network administrator. Subnets allow a single Class A, B, or C network to be used instead of multiple networks, and still allow for a large number of groups of IP addresses, as is required for efficient IP routing.

subnet address   *See* subnet number.

subnet broadcast address   A special address in each subnet, specifically the largest numeric address in the subnet, designed so that packets sent to this address should be delivered to all hosts in that subnet.

subnet ID (IPv4)   *See* subnet number.

subnet ID (IPv6)   The number that represents the IPv6 subnet. Also known as the IPv6 prefix, or more formally as the subnet router anycast address.

subnet mask   A 32-bit number that numerically describes the format of an IP address, by representing the combined network and subnet bits in the address with mask bit values of 1, and representing the host bits in the address with mask bit values of 0.

subnet number   In IPv4, a dotted-decimal number that represents all addresses in a single subnet. Numerically, the smallest value in the range of numbers in a subnet, reserved so that it cannot be used as a unicast IP address by a host.

subnet part   In a subnetted IPv4 address, interpreted with classful addressing rules, one of three parts of the structure of an IP address, with the subnet part uniquely identifying different subnets of a classful IP network.

subnetting   The process of subdividing a Class A, B, or C network into smaller groups called subnets.

SVI (Switched Virtual Interface)   A logical router that can be implemented on a multilayer switch that wants to support Layer 2 and Layer 3 functionality.

switch   A network device that filters, forwards, and floods Ethernet frames based on the destination address of each frame.

switched Ethernet   An Ethernet that uses a switch, and particularly not a hub, so that the devices connected to one switch port do not have to contend to use the bandwidth available on another port. This term contrasts with *shared Ethernet*, in which the devices must share bandwidth, whereas switched Ethernet provides much more capacity, as the devices do not have to share the available bandwidth.

sWWN   Switch WWN. The interface of a switch identified by the sWWN.

symmetric   A feature of many Internet access technologies in which the downstream transmission rate is the same as the upstream transmission rate.

synchronous   The imposition of time ordering on a bit stream. Practically, a device will try to use the same speed as another device on the other end of a serial link. However, by examining transitions between voltage states on the link, the device can notice slight variations in the speed on each end and can adjust its speed accordingly.

synchronous mirroring   Writes to both the local and remote sites at the same time, keeping your disaster recovery site up to date. Although having both sites up to date is definitely advantageous, the time that it takes to write to the remote physical volumes can have a large impact on application response time.

T

T11   Responsible for standards development in the areas of Intelligent Peripheral Interface (IPI), High-Performance Parallel Interface (HIPPI), and Fibre Channel (FC).

T-connector   A metal connector used with 10BASE-2 networks, roughly shaped like a capital letter T.

T1   A line from the telco that allows transmission of data at 1.544 Mbps, with the ability to treat the line as 24 different 64-kbps DS0 channels (plus 8 kbps of overhead).

TCP   Transmission Control Protocol. A connection- oriented transport layer TCP/IP protocol that provides reliable data transmission.

target   A typical name for SCSI storage devices.

TCP/IP   Transmission Control Protocol/Internet Protocol. A common name for the suite of protocols developed by the U.S. Department of Defense in the 1970s to support the construction of worldwide internetworks. TCP and IP are the two best-known protocols in the suite.

telco   A common abbreviation for telephone company.

Telnet   The standard terminal-emulation application layer protocol in the TCP/IP protocol stack. Telnet is used for remote terminal connection, enabling users to log in to remote systems and use resources as if they were connected to a local system. Telnet is defined in RFC 854.

thin provisioning   A LUN virtualization feature that helps reduce the waste of block storage resources. Using this technique, although a server can detect a vLUN with a "full" size, only blocks that are present in the vLUN are actually saved on the storage pool.

TLV   Type, length, value. Link Layer Discovery Protocol (LLDP) data units consist of an untagged Ethernet header and a sequence of short, variable-length information elements known as TLV. TLVs have Type, Length, and Value fields. Type identifies the kind of information being sent. Length indicates the length (in octets) of the information string. Value is the actual information being sent.

Token Ring   A LAN standard that originated with IBM, was standardized by the IEEE in the 802.5 series of standards, running at either 4 Mbps or 16 Mbps, and used a physical star topology with a logical token-passing ring topology to transmit frames around a loop (ring) without causing collisions.

ToR   Top-of-Rack. A small port count switch that sits on the very top or near the top of a Telco rack in data centers or co-location facilities. ToR solutions complement rack-at-a-time deployment by simplifying and shortening cable runs and facilitating the replication of rack configurations.

trace   Short for traceroute. A program available on many systems that traces the path that a packet takes to a destination. It is used mostly to troubleshoot routing problems between hosts.

trailer   In computer networking, a set of bytes placed behind some other data, encapsulating that data, as defined by a particular protocol. Typically, only data link layer protocols define trailers.

transparent bridge   The name of a networking device that was a precursor to modern LAN switches. Bridges forward frames between LAN segments based on the destination MAC address. Transparent bridging is so named because the presence of bridges is transparent to network end nodes.

trunk   In campus LANs, an Ethernet segment over which the devices add a VLAN header that identifies the VLAN in which the frame exists.

trunk interface   A switch interface configured so that it operates using VLAN trunking (either 802.1Q or ISL).

trunking   Also called VLAN trunking. A method (using either the Cisco ISL protocol or the IEEE 802.1Q protocol) to support multiple VLANs, allowing traffic from those VLANs to cross a single link.

trunking administrative mode   The configured trunking setting on a Cisco switch interface, as configured with the switchport mode command.

trunking operational mode   The current behavior of a Cisco switch interface for VLAN trunking.

twisted-pair   Transmission medium consisting of two insulated wires, with the wires twisted around each other in a spiral. An electrical circuit flows over the wire pair, with the current in opposite directions on each wire, which significantly reduces the interference between the two wires.

Type field   This term can refer in general to a class of networking header fields that identify the type of header that follows, or it can refer specifically to the 802.3 header's Type field used for that same purpose. A Type field lists a well-known standardized value that implies the protocol whose header should follow the header that holds the Type field.

U

UDP   User Datagram Protocol. Connectionless transport layer protocol in the TCP/IP protocol stack. UDP is a simple protocol that exchanges datagrams without acknowledgments or guaranteed delivery.

unicast address   Generally, any address in networking that represents a single device or interface, instead of a group of addresses (as would be represented by a multicast or broadcast address).

unicast IP address   An IP address that represents a single interface. In IPv4, these addresses come from the Class A, B, and C ranges.

unique local address   A type of IPv6 unicast address meant as a replacement for IPv4 private addresses.

unknown unicast frame   An Ethernet frame whose destination MAC address is not listed in a switch's MAC address table, so the switch must flood the frame.

up and up   Jargon referring to the two interface states on a Cisco IOS router or switch (line status and protocol status), with the first "up" referring to the line status and the second "up" referring to the protocol status. An interface in this state should be able to pass data link frames.

update timer   A timer used by a router to indicate when to send the next routing update.

URL   Uniform Resource Locator. A standard for how to refer to any piece of information retrievable via a TCP/IP network, most notably used to identify web pages. For example, http://www.certskills.com/blog is a URL that identifies the protocol (HTTP), host name (www. certskills.com), and web page (blog).

user mode   A mode of the user interface to a router or switch in which the user can type only nondisruptive EXEC commands, generally just to look at the current status, but not to change any operational settings.

UTP   Unshielded twisted-pair. A type of cabling, standardized by the Telecommunications Industry Association (TIA), that holds twisted pairs of copper wires (typically four pair) and does not contain any shielding from outside interference.

V

variable-length subnet mask (VLSM)   The capability to specify a different subnet mask for the same Class A, B, or C network number on different subnets. VLSM can help optimize available address space.

VFS   Virtual file system. An abstraction layer on top of a more concrete file system. It allows client applications using heterogeneous file-sharing network protocols to access a unified pool of storage resources.

vHBA   Virtual host bus adapter. The virtual representation of a typical host bus adapter used to connect to a Fibre Channel storage device or network.

virtual circuit (VC)   In packet-switched services like Frame Relay, VC refers to the ability of two DTE devices (typically routers) to send and receive data directly to each other, which supplies the same function as a physical leased line (leased circuit), but doing so without a physical circuit. This term is meant as a contrast with a leased line or leased circuit.

virtual LAN (VLAN)   A group of devices, connected to one or more switches, with the devices grouped into a single broadcast domain through switch configuration. VLANs allow switch administrators to separate the devices connected to the switches into separate VLANs without requiring separate physical switches, gaining design advantages of separating the traffic without the expense of buying additional hardware.

Virtual Private Network (VPN)   The process of securing communication between two devices whose packets pass over some public and unsecured network, typically the Internet. VPNs encrypt packets so that the communication is private, and authenticate the identity of the endpoints.

VLAN   *See* virtual LAN.

VLAN configuration database   The name of the collective configuration of VLAN IDs and names on a Cisco switch.

VLAN interface   A configuration concept inside Cisco switches, used as an interface between IOS running on the switch and a VLAN supported inside the switch, so that the switch can assign an IP address and send IP packets into that VLAN.

VLAN Trunking Protocol (VTP)   A Cisco proprietary messaging protocol used between Cisco switches to communicate configuration information about the existence of VLANs, including the VLAN ID and VLAN name.

vlan.dat   The default file used to store a Cisco switch's VLAN configuration database.

vLUN   Virtual Logical Unit Number. A LUN that is virtual for the real-time server and is exposed by the real-time target mode driver. A vLUN is treated as a normal LUN by an application host.

vNIC   Virtual network interface card. The virtual representation of a typical network interface card, used to connect to an Ethernet network.

VoIP   Voice over IP. The transport of voice traffic inside IP packets over an IP network.

VSAN   Virtual storage-area network. In computer networking, a virtual storage-area network (VSAN) is a collection of ports from a set of connected Fibre Channel switches that form a virtual fabric. Ports within a single switch can be partitioned into multiple VSANs, despite sharing hardware resources. Conversely, multiple switches can join a number of ports to form a single VSAN. VSANs were designed by Cisco modeled after the virtual local-area network (VLAN) concept in Ethernet networking, applied to a storage-area network. In October 2004, the Technical Committee T11 of the International Committee for Information Technology Standards approved VSAN technology to become a standard of the American National Standards Institute (ANSI).

VTL   Virtual tape library. A data storage virtualization technology used typically for backup and recovery purposes. A VTL presents a storage component (usually hard disk storage) as tape libraries or tape drives for use with existing backup software.

VTP   *See* VLAN Trunking Protocol.

VTP client mode   One of three VTP operational modes for a switch with which switches learn about VLAN numbers and names from other switches, but which does not allow the switch to be directly configured with VLAN information.

VTP Domain   A text name used by all the switches that cooperate to use VTP to exchange VLAN configuration information.

VTP server mode   One of three VTP operational modes. Switches in server mode can configure VLANs, tell other switches about the changes, and learn about VLAN changes from other switches.

VTP transparent mode   One of three VTP operational modes. Switches in transparent mode can configure VLANs, but they do not tell other switches about the changes, and they do not learn about VLAN changes from other switches.

W

web server   Software, running on a computer, that stores web pages and sends those web pages to web clients (web browsers) that request the web pages.

well-known port   A TCP or UDP port number reserved for use by a particular application. The use of well-known ports allows a client to send a TCP or UDP segment to a server, to the correct destination port for that application.

Wi-Fi Alliance   An organization formed by many companies in the wireless industry (an industry association) for the purpose of getting multivendor certified-compatible wireless products to market in a more timely fashion than would be possible by simply relying on standardization processes.

wide-area network (WAN)   A part of a larger network that implements mostly OSI Layer 1 and 2 technology, connects sites that typically sit far apart, and uses a business model in which a consumer (individual or business) must lease the WAN from a service provider (often a telco).

wildcard mask   The mask used in Cisco IOS ACL commands and OSPF and EIGRP network commands.

window   Represents the number of bytes that can be sent without receiving an acknowledgment.

wireless LAN   A local-area network (LAN) that physically transmits bits using radio waves. The name "wireless" compares these LANs to more traditional "wired" LANs, which are LANs that use cables (which often have copper wires inside).

WLAN client   A wireless device that wants to gain access to a wireless access point for the purpose of communicating with other wireless devices or other devices connected to the wired internetwork.

WWNN   World Wide Node Name. A name assigned to a node (an endpoint, a device) in a Fibre Channel fabric. It is valid for the same WWNN to be seen on many different ports (different addresses) on the network, identifying the ports as multiple network interfaces of a single network node.

WWPN   World Wide Port Name. A name assigned to a port in a Fibre Channel fabric. Used on storage-area networks, it performs a function equivalent to the MAC address in Ethernet protocol because it is supposed to be a unique identifier in the network.

Z

zero subnet   For every classful IPv4 network that is subnetted, the one subnet whose subnet number has all binary 0s in the subnet part of the number. In decimal, the zero subnet can be easily identified because it is the same number as the classful network number.

zoning   In storage networking, Fibre Channel zoning is the partitioning of a Fibre Channel fabric into smaller subsets to restrict interference, add security, and to simplify management. While a SAN makes available several devices and/or ports to a single device, each system connected to the SAN should be allowed access only to a controlled subset of these devices/ports. Zoning applies only to the switched fabric topology (FC-SW); it does not exist in simpler Fibre Channel topologies.

Index

C

I

J-K-L

M

O

P

Q-R

T

U